Python

ESSENTIAL REFERENCE

Fourth Edition

Developer's Library

ESSENTIAL REFERENCES FOR PROGRAMMING PROFESSIONALS

Developer's Library books are designed to provide practicing programmers with unique, high-quality references and tutorials on the programming languages and technologies they use in their daily work.

All books in the *Developer's Library* are written by expert technology practitioners who are especially skilled at organizing and presenting information in a way that's useful for other programmers.

Key titles include some of the best, most widely acclaimed books within their topic areas:

PHP and MySQL Web Development
Luke Welling & Laura Thomson
ISBN 978-0-672-32916-6

MySQL
Paul DuBois
ISBN-13: 978-0-672-32938-8

Linux Kernel Development
Robert Love
ISBN-13: 978-0-672-32946-3

Python Essential Reference
David Beazley
ISBN-13: 978-0-672-32862-6

Programming in Objective-C
Stephen G. Kochan
ISBN-13: 978-0-321-56615-7

PostgreSQL
Korry Douglas
ISBN-13: 978-0-672-33015-5

Developer's Library books are available at most retail and online bookstores, as well as by subscription from Safari Books Online at **safari.informit.com**

**Developer's
Library**
informit.com/devlibrary

Python

ESSENTIAL REFERENCE

Fourth Edition

David M. Beazley

✦✦Addison-Wesley

Upper Saddle River, NJ • Boston • Indianapolis • San Francisco
New York • Toronto • Montreal • London • Munich • Paris • Madrid
Cape Town • Sydney • Tokyo • Singapore • Mexico City

Python Essential Reference

Fourth Edition

Copyright © 2009 by Pearson Education, Inc.

ISBN-13: 978-0-672-32978-4
ISBN-10: 0-672-32978-6

Printed in the United States of America

Fourth Printing November 2010

Library of Congress Cataloging-in-Publication data is on file.

Trademarks

All terms mentioned in this book that are known to be trademarks or service marks have been appropriately capitalized. Addison-Wesley cannot attest to the accuracy of this information. Use of a term in this book should not be regarded as affecting the validity of any trademark or service mark.

Warning and Disclaimer

Every effort has been made to make this book as complete and as accurate as possible, but no warranty or fitness is implied. The information provided is on an "as is" basis. The author and the publisher shall have neither liability nor responsibility to any person or entity with respect to any loss or damages arising from the information contained in this book.

Bulk Sales

Addison-Wesley offers excellent discounts on this book when ordered in quantity for bulk purchases or special sales. For more information, please contact

U.S. Corporate and Government Sales

1-800-382-3419

corpsales@pearsontechgroup.com

For sales outside of the U.S., please contact

International Sales

international@pearson.com

To register this product and gain access to bonus content, go to www.informit.com/register to sign in and enter the ISBN. After you register the product, a link to the additional content will be listed on your Account page, under Registered Products.

Acquisitions Editor
Mark Taber

Development Editor
Michael Thurston

Managing Editor
Patrick Kanouse

Project Editor
Seth Kerney

Copy Editor
Lisa Thibault

Indexer
David Beazley

Proofreader
Megan Wade

Technical Editors
Noah Gift
Kurt Grandis

Publishing Coordinator
Vanessa Evans

Book Designer
Gary Adair

Compositor
Bronkella Publishing

❖

For Paula, Thomas., and his brother on the way.

❖

Contents at a Glance

Table of Contents

viii   Contents

About the Author

David M. Beazley is a long-time Python enthusiast, having been involved with the Python community since 1996. He is probably best known for his work on SWIG, a popular software package for integrating C/C++ programs with other programming languages, including Python, Perl, Ruby, Tcl, and Java. He has also written a number of other programming tools, including PLY, a Python implementation of lex and yacc. Dave spent seven years working in the Theoretical Physics Division at Los Alamos National Laboratory, where he helped pioneer the use of Python with massively parallel supercomputers. After that, Dave went off to work as an evil professor, where he enjoyed tormenting college students with a variety of insane programming projects. However, he has since seen the error of his ways and is now working as an independent software developer, consultant, Python trainer, and occasional jazz musician living in Chicago. He can be contacted at http://www.dabeaz.com.

About the Technical Editor

Noah Gift is the co-author of *Python For UNIX and Linux System Administration* (O'Reilly) and is also working on *Google App Engine In Action* (Manning). He is an author, speaker, consultant, and community leader, writing for publications such as *IBM developerWorks*, *Red Hat Magazine*, O'Reilly, and *MacTech*. His consulting company's website is http://www.giftcs.com, and much of his writing can be found at http://noahgift.com. You can also follow Noah on Twitter.

Noah has a master's degree in CIS from Cal State, Los Angeles, a B.S. in nutritional science from Cal Poly San Luis Obispo, is an Apple and LPI-certified SysAdmin, and has worked at companies such as Caltech, Disney Feature Animation, Sony Imageworks, and Turner Studios. He is currently working at Weta Digital in New Zealand. In his free time he enjoys spending time with his wife Leah and their son Liam, composing for the piano, running marathons, and exercising religiously.

Acknowledgments

This book would not be possible without the support of many people. First and foremost, I'd like to thank Noah Gift for jumping into the project and providing his amazing feedback on the fourth edition. Kurt Grandis also provided useful comments for many chapters. I'd also like to acknowledge past technical reviewers Timothy Boronczyk, Paul DuBois, Mats Wichmann, David Ascher, and Tim Bell for their valuable comments and advice that made earlier editions a success. Guido van Rossum, Jeremy Hylton, Fred Drake, Roger Masse, and Barry Warsaw also provided tremendous assistance with the first edition while hosting me for a few weeks back in the hot summer of 1999. Last, but not least, this book would not be possible without all of the feedback I received from readers. There are far too many people to list individually, but I have done my best to incorporate your suggestions for making the book even better. I'd also like to thank all the folks at Addison-Wesley and Pearson Education for their continued commitment to the project and assistance. Mark Taber, Michael Thurston, Seth Kerney, and Lisa Thibault all helped out to get this edition out the door in good shape. A special thanks is in order for Robin Drake, whose tremendous effort in editing previous editions made the third edition possible. Finally, I'd like to acknowledge my amazing wife and partner Paula Kamen for all of her encouragement, diabolical humor, and love.

We Want to Hear from You!

As the reader of this book, *you* are our most important critic and commentator. We value your opinion and want to know what we're doing right, what we could do better, what areas you'd like to see us publish in, and any other words of wisdom you're willing to pass our way.

You can email or write me directly to let me know what you did or didn't like about this book—as well as what we can do to make our books stronger.

Please note that I cannot help you with technical problems related to the topic of this book, and that due to the high volume of mail I receive, I might not be able to reply to every message.

When you write, please be sure to include this book's title and author as well as your name and phone or email address. I will carefully review your comments and share them with the author and editors who worked on the book.

Email: feedback@developers-library.info
Mail: Mark Taber
        Associate Publisher
        Pearson Education
        800 East 96th Street
        Indianapolis, IN 46240 USA

Reader Services

Visit our website and register this book at informit.com/register for convenient access to any updates, downloads, or errata that might be available for this book.

Introduction

This book is intended to be a concise reference to the Python programming language. Although an experienced programmer will probably be able to learn Python from this book, it's not intended to be an extended tutorial or a treatise on how to program. Rather, the goal is to present the core Python language, and the most essential parts of the Python library in a manner that's accurate and concise. This book assumes that the reader has prior programming experience with Python or another language such as C or Java. In addition, a general familiarity with systems programming topics (for example, basic operating system concepts and network programming) may be useful in understanding certain parts of the library reference.

Python is freely available for download at http://www.python.org. Versions are available for almost every operating system, including UNIX, Windows, and Macintosh. In addition, the Python website includes links to documentation, how-to guides, and a wide assortment of third-party software.

This edition of *Python Essential Reference* comes at a pivotal time in Python's evolution. Python 2.6 and Python 3.0 are being released almost simultaneously. Yet, Python 3 is a release that breaks backwards compatibility with prior Python versions. As an author and programmer, I'm faced with a dilemma: do I simply jump forward to Python 3.0 or do I build upon the Python 2.x releases that are more familiar to most programmers?

Years ago, as a C programmer I used to treat certain books as the ultimate authority on what programming language features should be used. For example, if you were using something that wasn't documented in the K&R book, it probably wasn't going to be portable and should be approached with caution. This approach served me very well as a programmer and it's the approach I have decided to take in this edition of the Essential Reference. Namely, I have chosen to omit features of Python 2 that have been removed from Python 3. Likewise, I don't focus on features of Python 3 that have not been back-ported (although such features are still covered in an appendix). As a result, I hope this book can be a useful companion for Python programmers, regardless of what Python version is being used.

The fourth edition of *Python Essential Reference* also includes some of the most exciting changes since its initial publication nearly ten years ago. Much of Python's development throughout the last few years has focused on new programming language features—especially related to functional and meta programming. As a result, the chapters on functions and object-oriented programming have been greatly expanded to cover topics such as generators, iterators, coroutines, decorators, and metaclasses. The library chapters have been updated to focus on more modern modules. Examples and code fragments have also been updated throughout the book. I think most programmers will be quite pleased with the expanded coverage.

Finally, it should be noted that Python already includes thousands of pages of useful documentation. The contents of this book are largely based on that documentation, but with a number of key differences. First, this reference presents information in a much more compact form, with different examples and alternative descriptions of many topics. Second, a significant number of topics in the library reference have been expanded to include outside reference material. This is especially true for low-level system and networking modules in which effective use of a module normally relies on a myriad of options listed in manuals and outside references. In addition, in order to produce a more concise reference, a number of deprecated and relatively obscure library modules have been omitted.

In writing this book, it has been my goal to produce a reference containing virtually everything I have needed to use Python and its large collection of modules. Although this is by no means a gentle introduction to the Python language, I hope that you find the contents of this book to be a useful addition to your programming reference library for many years to come. I welcome your comments.

David Beazley
Chicago, Illinois
June, 2009

The Python Language

A Tutorial Introduction

This chapter provides a quick introduction to Python. The goal is to illustrate most of Python's essential features without getting too bogged down in special rules or details. To do this, the chapter briefly covers basic concepts such as variables, expressions, control flow, functions, generators, classes, and input/output. This chapter is not intended to provide comprehensive coverage. However, experienced programmers should be able to extrapolate from the material in this chapter to create more advanced programs. Beginners are encouraged to try a few examples to get a feel for the language. If you are new to Python and using Python 3, you might want to follow this chapter using Python 2.6 instead. Virtually all the major concepts apply to both versions, but there are a small number of critical syntax changes in Python 3—mostly related to printing and I/O—that might break many of the examples shown in this section. Please refer to Appendix A, "Python 3," for further details.

Running Python

Python programs are executed by an interpreter. Usually, the interpreter is started by simply typing **python** into a command shell. However, there are many different implementations of the interpreter and Python development environments (for example, Jython, IronPython, IDLE, ActivePython, Wing IDE, pydev, etc.), so you should consult the documentation for startup details. When the interpreter starts, a prompt appears at which you can start typing programs into a simple read-evaluation loop. For example, in the following output, the interpreter displays its copyright message and presents the user with the >>> prompt, at which the user types the familiar "Hello World" command:

```
Python 2.6rc2 (r26rc2:66504, Sep 19 2008, 08:50:24)
[GCC 4.0.1 (Apple Inc. build 5465)] on darwin
Type "help", "copyright", "credits" or "license" for more information.
>>> print "Hello World"
Hello World
>>>
```

Note

If you try the preceding example and it fails with a `SyntaxError`, you are probably using Python 3. If this is the case, you can continue to follow along with this chapter, but be aware that the `print` statement turned into a function in Python 3. Simply add parentheses around the items to be printed in the examples that follow. For instance:

```
>>> print("Hello World")
Hello World
>>>
```

Putting parentheses around the item to be printed also works in Python 2 as long as you are printing just a single item. However, it's not a syntax that you commonly see in existing Python code. In later chapters, this syntax is sometimes used in examples in which the primary focus is a feature not directly related to printing, but where the example is supposed to work with both Python 2 and 3.

Python's interactive mode is one of its most useful features. In the interactive shell, you can type any valid statement or sequence of statements and immediately view the results. Many people, including the author, even use interactive Python as their desktop calculator. For example:

```
>>> 6000 + 4523.50 + 134.12
10657.620000000001
>>> _ + 8192.32
18849.940000000002
>>>
```

When you use Python interactively, the special variable _ holds the result of the last operation. This can be useful if you want to save or use the result of the last operation in subsequent statements. However, it's important to stress that this variable is only defined when working interactively.

If you want to create a program that you can run repeatedly, put statements in a file such as the following:

```
# helloworld.py
print "Hello World"
```

Python source files are ordinary text files and normally have a `.py` suffix. The # character denotes a comment that extends to the end of the line.

To execute the `helloworld.py` file, you provide the filename to the interpreter as follows:

```
% python helloworld.py
Hello World
%
```

On Windows, Python programs can be started by double-clicking a `.py` file or typing the name of the program into the Run command on the Windows Start menu. This launches the interpreter and runs the program in a console window. However, be aware that the console window will disappear immediately after the program completes its execution (often before you can read its output). For debugging, it is better to run the program within a Python development tool such as IDLE.

On UNIX, you can use #! on the first line of the program, like this:

```
#!/usr/bin/env python
print "Hello World"
```

The interpreter runs statements until it reaches the end of the input file. If it's running interactively, you can exit the interpreter by typing the EOF (end of file) character or by selecting Exit from pull-down menu of a Python IDE. On UNIX, EOF is Ctrl+D; on Windows, it's Ctrl+Z (or F6). A program can request to exit by raising the SystemExit exception.

```
>>> raise SystemExit
```

Variables and Arithmetic Expressions

The program in Listing 1.1 shows the use of variables and expressions by performing a simple compound-interest calculation.

Listing 1.1   **Simple Compound-Interest Calculation**

```
principal = 1000        # Initial amount
rate = 0.05             # Interest rate
numyears = 5            # Number of years
year = 1
while year <= numyears:
    principal = principal * (1 + rate)
    print year, principal    # Reminder: print(year, principal) in Python 3
    year += 1
```

The output of this program is the following table:

```
1 1050.0
2 1102.5
3 1157.625
4 1215.50625
5 1276.2815625
```

Python is a dynamically typed language where variable names are bound to different values, possibly of varying types, during program execution. The assignment operator simply creates an association between a name and a value. Although each value has an associated type such as an integer or string, variable names are untyped and can be made to refer to any type of data during execution. This is different from C, for example, in which a name represents a fixed type, size, and location in memory into which a value is stored. The dynamic behavior of Python can be seen in Listing 1.1 with the principal variable. Initially, it's assigned to an integer value. However, later in the program it's reassigned as follows:

```
principal = principal * (1 + rate)
```

This statement evaluates the expression and reassociates the name principal with the result. Although the original value of principal was an integer 1000, the new value is now a floating-point number (rate is defined as a float, so the value of the above expression is also a float). Thus, the apparent "type" of principal dynamically changes from an integer to a float in the middle of the program. However, to be precise, it's not the type of principal that has changed, but rather the value to which the principal name refers.

A newline terminates each statement. However, you can use a semicolon to separate statements on the same line, as shown here:

```
principal = 1000; rate = 0.05; numyears = 5;
```

The while statement tests the conditional expression that immediately follows. If the tested statement is true, the body of the while statement executes. The condition is then retested and the body executed again until the condition becomes false. Because the body of the loop is denoted by indentation, the three statements following while in Listing 1.1 execute on each iteration. Python doesn't specify the amount of required indentation, as long as it's consistent within a block. However, it is most common (and generally recommended) to use four spaces per indentation level.

One problem with the program in Listing 1.1 is that the output isn't very pretty. To make it better, you could right-align the columns and limit the precision of principal to two digits. There are several ways to achieve this formatting. The most widely used approach is to use the string formatting operator (%) like this:

```
print "%3d %0.2f" % (year, principal)
print ("%3d %0.2f" % (year, principal))    # Python 3
```

Now the output of the program looks like this:

```
1 1050.00
2 1102.50
3 1157.63
4 1215.51
5 1276.28
```

Format strings contain ordinary text and special formatting-character sequences such as "%d", "%s", and "%f". These sequences specify the formatting of a particular type of data such as an integer, string, or floating-point number, respectively. The special-character sequences can also contain modifiers that specify a width and precision. For example, "%3d" formats an integer right-aligned in a column of width 3, and "%0.2f" formats a floating-point number so that only two digits appear after the decimal point. The behavior of format strings is almost identical to the C printf() function and is described in detail in Chapter 4, "Operators and Expressions."

A more modern approach to string formatting is to format each part individually using the format() function. For example:

```
print format(year,"3d"),format(principal,"0.2f")
print (format(year,"3d"),format(principal,"0.2f")) # Python 3
```

format() uses format specifiers that are similar to those used with the traditional string formatting operator (%). For example, "3d" formats an integer right-aligned in a column of width 3, and "0.2f" formats a float-point number to have two digits of accuracy. Strings also have a format() method that can be used to format many values at once. For example:

```
print "{0:3d} {1:0.2f}".format(year,principal)
print ("{0:3d} {1:0.2f}".format(year,principal)) # Python 3
```

In this example, the number before the colon in "{0:3d}" and "{1:0.2f}" refers to the associated argument passed to the format() method and the part after the colon is the format specifier.

Conditionals

The `if` and `else` statements can perform simple tests. Here's an example:

```
if a < b:
    print "Computer says Yes"
else:
    print "Computer says No"
```

The bodies of the `if` and `else` clauses are denoted by indentation. The `else` clause is optional.

To create an empty clause, use the `pass` statement, as follows:

```
if a < b:
    pass        # Do nothing
else:
    print "Computer says No"
```

You can form Boolean expressions by using the `or`, `and`, and `not` keywords:

```
if product == "game" and type == "pirate memory" \
                        and not (age < 4 or age > 8):
    print "I'll take it!"
```

> **Note**
>
> Writing complex test cases commonly results in statements that involve an annoyingly long line of code. To improve readability, you can continue any statement to the next line by using a backslash (\) at the end of a line as shown. If you do this, the normal indentation rules don't apply to the next line, so you are free to format the continued lines as you wish. A backslash is never needed for code enclosed in (), [], or {}.

Python does not have a special `switch` or `case` statement for testing values. To handle multiple-test cases, use the `elif` statement, like this:

```
if suffix == ".htm":
    content = "text/html"
elif suffix == ".jpg":
    content = "image/jpeg"
elif suffix == ".png":
    content = "image/png"
else:
    raise RuntimeError("Unknown content type")
```

To denote truth values, use the Boolean values `True` and `False`. Here's an example:

```
if 'spam' in s:
    has_spam = True
else:
    has_spam = False
```

All relational operators such as `<` and `>` return `True` or `False` as results. The `in` operator used in this example is commonly used to check whether a value is contained inside of another object such as a string, list, or dictionary. It also returns `True` or `False`, so the preceding example could be shortened to this:

```
has_spam = 'spam' in s
```

File Input and Output

The following program opens a file and reads its contents line by line:

```
f = open("foo.txt")          # Returns a file object
line = f.readline()          # Invokes readline() method on file
while line:
    print line,              # trailing ',' omits newline character
    # print(line,end='')     # Use in Python 3
    line = f.readline()
f.close()
```

The open() function returns a new file object. By invoking methods on this object, you can perform various file operations. The readline() method reads a single line of input, including the terminating newline. The empty string is returned at the end of the file.

In the example, the program is simply looping over all the lines in the file foo.txt. Whenever a program loops over a collection of data like this (for instance input lines, numbers, strings, etc.), it is commonly known as *iteration*. Because iteration is such a common operation, Python provides a dedicated statement, for, that is used to iterate over items. For instance, the same program can be written much more succinctly as follows:

```
for line in open("foo.txt"):
    print line,
```

To make the output of a program go to a file, you can supply a file to the print statement using >>, as shown in the following example:

```
f = open("out","w")       # Open file for writing
while year <= numyears:
    principal = principal * (1 + rate)
    print >>f,"%3d %0.2f" % (year,principal)
    year += 1
f.close()
```

The >> syntax only works in Python 2. If you are using Python 3, change the print statement to the following:

```
print("%3d %0.2f" % (year,principal),file=f)
```

In addition, file objects support a write() method that can be used to write raw data. For example, the print statement in the previous example could have been written this way:

```
f.write("%3d %0.2f\n" % (year,principal))
```

Although these examples have worked with files, the same techniques apply to the standard output and input streams of the interpreter. For example, if you wanted to read user input interactively, you can read from the file sys.stdin. If you want to write data to the screen, you can write to sys.stdout, which is the same file used to output data produced by the print statement. For example:

```
import sys
sys.stdout.write("Enter your name :")
name = sys.stdin.readline()
```

In Python 2, this code can also be shortened to the following:

```
name = raw_input("Enter your name :")
```

In Python 3, the `raw_input()` function is called `input()`, but it works in exactly the same manner.

Strings

To create string literals, enclose them in single, double, or triple quotes as follows:

```
a = "Hello World"
b = 'Python is groovy'
c = """Computer says 'No'"""
```

The same type of quote used to start a string must be used to terminate it. Triple-quoted strings capture all the text that appears prior to the terminating triple quote, as opposed to single- and double-quoted strings, which must be specified on one logical line. Triple-quoted strings are useful when the contents of a string literal span multiple lines of text such as the following:

```
print '''Content-type: text/html

<h1> Hello World </h1>
Click <a href="http://www.python.org">here</a>.
'''
```

Strings are stored as sequences of characters indexed by integers, starting at zero. To extract a single character, use the indexing operator `s[i]` like this:

```
a = "Hello World"
b = a[4]                 # b = 'o'
```

To extract a substring, use the slicing operator `s[i:j]`. This extracts all characters from `s` whose index `k` is in the range `i <= k < j`. If either index is omitted, the beginning or end of the string is assumed, respectively:

```
c = a[:5]               # c = "Hello"
d = a[6:]               # d = "World"
e = a[3:8]              # e = "lo Wo"
```

Strings are concatenated with the plus (+) operator:

```
g = a + " This is a test"
```

Python never implicitly interprets the contents of a string as numerical data (i.e., as in other languages such as Perl or PHP). For example, + always concatenates strings:

```
x = "37"
y = "42"
z = x + y     # z = "3742" (String Concatenation)
```

To perform mathematical calculations, strings first have to be converted into a numeric value using a function such as `int()` or `float()`. For example:

```
z = int(x) + int(y)   # z = 79   (Integer +)
```

Non-string values can be converted into a string representation by using the `str()`, `repr()`, or `format()` function. Here's an example:

```
s = "The value of x is " + str(x)
s = "The value of x is " + repr(x)
s = "The value of x is " + format(x,"4d")
```

Although str() and repr() both create strings, their output is usually slightly different. str() produces the output that you get when you use the print statement,
whereas repr() creates a string that you type into a program to exactly represent the
value of an object. For example:

```
>>> x = 3.4
>>> str(x)
'3.4'
>>> repr(x)
'3.3999999999999999'
>>>
```

The inexact representation of 3.4 in the previous example is not a bug in Python. It is
an artifact of double-precision floating-point numbers, which by their design can not
exactly represent base-10 decimals on the underlying computer hardware.

The format() function is used to convert a value to a string with a specific formatting applied. For example:

```
>>> format(x,"0.5f")
'3.40000'
>>>
```

Lists

Lists are sequences of arbitrary objects. You create a list by enclosing values in square
brackets, as follows:

```
names = [ "Dave", "Mark", "Ann", "Phil" ]
```

Lists are indexed by integers, starting with zero. Use the indexing operator to access and
modify individual items of the list:

```
a = names[2]          # Returns the third item of the list, "Ann"
names[0] = "Jeff"     # Changes the first item to "Jeff"
```

To append new items to the end of a list, use the append() method:

```
names.append("Paula")
```

To insert an item into the middle of a list, use the insert() method:

```
names.insert(2, "Thomas")
```

You can extract or reassign a portion of a list by using the slicing operator:

```
b = names[0:2]                          # Returns [ "Jeff", "Mark" ]
c = names[2:]                           # Returns [ "Thomas", "Ann", "Phil", "Paula" ]
names[1] = 'Jeff'                       # Replace the 2nd item in names with 'Jeff'
names[0:2] = ['Dave','Mark','Jeff']     # Replace the first two items of
                                        # the list with the list on the right.
```

Use the plus (+) operator to concatenate lists:

```
a = [1,2,3] + [4,5]      # Result is [1,2,3,4,5]
```

An empty list is created in one of two ways:

```
names = []          # An empty list
names = list()      # An empty list
```

Lists can contain any kind of Python object, including other lists, as in the following example:

```
a = [1,"Dave",3.14, ["Mark", 7, 9, [100,101]], 10]
```

Items contained in nested lists are accessed by applying more than one indexing operation, as follows:

```
a[1]            # Returns "Dave"
a[3][2]         # Returns 9
a[3][3][1]      # Returns 101
```

The program in Listing 1.2 illustrates a few more advanced features of lists by reading a list of numbers from a file specified on the command line and outputting the minimum and maximum values.

Listing 1.2   **Advanced List Features**

```
import sys                          # Load the sys module
if len(sys.argv) != 2:             # Check number of command line arguments
    print "Please supply a filename"
    raise SystemExit(1)
f = open(sys.argv[1])              # Filename on the command line
lines = f.readlines()             # Read all lines into a list
f.close()

# Convert all of the input values from strings to floats
fvalues = [float(line) for line in lines]

# Print min and max values
print "The minimum value is ", min(fvalues)
print "The maximum value is ", max(fvalues)
```

The first line of this program uses the `import` statement to load the `sys` module from the Python library. This module is being loaded in order to obtain command-line arguments.

The `open()` function uses a filename that has been supplied as a command-line option and placed in the list `sys.argv`. The `readlines()` method reads all the input lines into a list of strings.

The expression `[float(line) for line in lines]` constructs a new list by looping over all the strings in the list `lines` and applying the function `float()` to each element. This particularly powerful method of constructing a list is known as a *list comprehension*. Because the lines in a file can also be read using a `for` loop, the program can be shortened by converting values using a single statement like this:

```
fvalues = [float(line) for line in open(sys.argv[1])]
```

After the input lines have been converted into a list of floating-point numbers, the built-in `min()` and `max()` functions compute the minimum and maximum values.

Tuples

To create simple data structures, you can pack a collection of values together into a single object using a *tuple*. You create a tuple by enclosing a group of values in parentheses like this:

```
stock = ('GOOG', 100, 490.10)
address = ('www.python.org', 80)
person = (first_name, last_name, phone)
```

Python often recognizes that a tuple is intended even if the parentheses are missing:

```
stock = 'GOOG', 100, 490.10
address = 'www.python.org',80
person = first_name, last_name, phone
```

For completeness, 0- and 1-element tuples can be defined, but have special syntax:

```
a = ()          # 0-tuple (empty tuple)
b = (item,)     # 1-tuple (note the trailing comma)
c = item,       # 1-tuple (note the trailing comma)
```

The values in a tuple can be extracted by numerical index just like a list. However, it is more common to unpack tuples into a set of variables like this:

```
name, shares, price = stock
host, port = address
first_name, last_name, phone = person
```

Although tuples support most of the same operations as lists (such as indexing, slicing, and concatenation), the contents of a tuple cannot be modified after creation (that is, you cannot replace, delete, or append new elements to an existing tuple). This reflects the fact that a tuple is best viewed as a single object consisting of several parts, not as a collection of distinct objects to which you might insert or remove items.

Because there is so much overlap between tuples and lists, some programmers are inclined to ignore tuples altogether and simply use lists because they seem to be more flexible. Although this works, it wastes memory if your program is going to create a large number of small lists (that is, each containing fewer than a dozen items). This is because lists slightly overallocate memory to optimize the performance of operations that add new items. Because tuples are immutable, they use a more compact representation where there is no extra space.

Tuples and lists are often used together to represent data. For example, this program shows how you might read a file consisting of different columns of data separated by commas:

```
# File containing lines of the form "name,shares,price"
filename = "portfolio.csv"
portfolio = []
for line in open(filename):
    fields = line.split(",")      # Split each line into a list
    name   = fields[0]            # Extract and convert individual fields
    shares = int(fields[1])
    price  = float(fields[2])
    stock  = (name,shares,price)  # Create a tuple (name, shares, price)
    portfolio.append(stock)       # Append to list of records
```

The split() method of strings splits a string into a list of fields separated by the given delimiter character. The resulting portfolio data structure created by this program looks like a two-dimension array of rows and columns. Each row is represented by a tuple and can be accessed as follows:

```
>>> portfolio[0]
('GOOG', 100, 490.10)
>>> portfolio[1]
('MSFT', 50, 54.23)
>>>
```

Individual items of data can be accessed like this:

```
>>> portfolio[1][1]
50
>>> portfolio[1][2]
54.23
>>>
```

Here's an easy way to loop over all of the records and expand fields into a set of variables:

```
total = 0.0
for name, shares, price in portfolio:
    total += shares * price
```

Sets

A *set* is used to contain an unordered collection of objects. To create a set, use the set() function and supply a sequence of items such as follows:

```
s = set([3,5,9,10])       # Create a set of numbers
t = set("Hello")          # Create a set of unique characters
```

Unlike lists and tuples, sets are unordered and cannot be indexed by numbers. Moreover, the elements of a set are never duplicated. For example, if you inspect the value of t from the preceding code, you get the following:

```
>>> t
set(['H', 'e', 'l', 'o'])
```

Notice that only one 'l' appears.

Sets support a standard collection of operations, including union, intersection, difference, and symmetric difference. Here's an example:

```
a = t | s       # Union of t and s
b = t & s       # Intersection of t and s
c = t - s       # Set difference (items in t, but not in s)
d = t ^ s       # Symmetric difference (items in t or s, but not both)
```

New items can be added to a set using add() or update():

```
t.add('x')              # Add a single item
s.update([10,37,42])    # Adds multiple items to s
```

An item can be removed using remove():

```
t.remove('H')
```

Dictionaries

A *dictionary* is an associative array or hash table that contains objects indexed by keys. You create a dictionary by enclosing the values in curly braces ({ }), like this:

```
stock = {
      "name"    : "GOOG",
      "shares"  : 100,
      "price"   : 490.10
   }
```

To access members of a dictionary, use the key-indexing operator as follows:

```
name  = stock["name"]
value = stock["shares"] * shares["price"]
```

Inserting or modifying objects works like this:

```
stock["shares"] = 75
stock["date"]   = "June 7, 2007"
```

Although strings are the most common type of key, you can use many other Python objects, including numbers and tuples. Some objects, including lists and dictionaries, cannot be used as keys because their contents can change.

A dictionary is a useful way to define an object that consists of named fields as shown previously. However, dictionaries are also used as a container for performing fast lookups on unordered data. For example, here's a dictionary of stock prices:

```
prices = {
    "GOOG" : 490.10,
    "AAPL" : 123.50,
    "IBM"  : 91.50,
    "MSFT" : 52.13
}
```

An empty dictionary is created in one of two ways:

```
prices = {}     # An empty dict
prices = dict() # An empty dict
```

Dictionary membership is tested with the in operator, as in the following example:

```
if "SCOX" in prices:
    p = prices["SCOX"]
else:
    p = 0.0
```

This particular sequence of steps can also be performed more compactly as follows:

```
p = prices.get("SCOX",0.0)
```

To obtain a list of dictionary keys, convert a dictionary to a list:

```
syms = list(prices)          # syms = ["AAPL", "MSFT", "IBM", "GOOG"]
```

Use the del statement to remove an element of a dictionary:

```
del prices["MSFT"]
```

Dictionaries are probably the most finely tuned data type in the Python interpreter. So, if you are merely trying to store and work with data in your program, you are almost always better off using a dictionary than trying to come up with some kind of custom data structure on your own.

Iteration and Looping

The most widely used looping construct is the `for` statement, which is used to iterate over a collection of items. Iteration is one of Python's richest features. However, the most common form of iteration is to simply loop over all the members of a sequence such as a string, list, or tuple. Here's an example:

```
for n in [1,2,3,4,5,6,7,8,9]:
    print "2 to the %d power is %d" % (n, 2**n)
```

In this example, the variable n will be assigned successive items from the list `[1,2,3,4,…,9]` on each iteration. Because looping over ranges of integers is quite common, the following shortcut is often used for that purpose:

```
for n in range(1,10):
    print "2 to the %d power is %d" % (n, 2**n)
```

The `range(i,j [,stride])` function creates an object that represents a range of integers with values `i` to `j-1`. If the starting value is omitted, it's taken to be zero. An optional stride can also be given as a third argument. Here's an example:

```
a = range(5)        # a = 0,1,2,3,4
b = range(1,8)      # b = 1,2,3,4,5,6,7
c = range(0,14,3)   # c = 0,3,6,9,12
d = range(8,1,-1)   # d = 8,7,6,5,4,3,2
```

One caution with `range()` is that in Python 2, the value it creates is a fully populated list with all of the integer values. For extremely large ranges, this can inadvertently consume all available memory. Therefore, in older Python code, you will see programmers using an alternative function `xrange()`. For example:

```
for i in xrange(100000000):     # i = 0,1,2,...,99999999
    statements
```

The object created by `xrange()` computes the values it represents on demand when lookups are requested. For this reason, it is the preferred way to represent extremely large ranges of integer values. In Python 3, the `xrange()` function has been renamed to `range()` and the functionality of the old `range()` function has been removed.

The `for` statement is not limited to sequences of integers and can be used to iterate over many kinds of objects including strings, lists, dictionaries, and files. Here's an example:

```
a = "Hello World"
# Print out the individual characters in a
for c in a:
    print c

b = ["Dave","Mark","Ann","Phil"]
# Print out the members of a list
for name in b:
    print name

c = { 'GOOG' : 490.10, 'IBM' : 91.50, 'AAPL' : 123.15 }
# Print out all of the members of a dictionary
for key in c:
    print key, c[key]

# Print all of the lines in a file
f = open("foo.txt")
```

```
for line in f:
    print line,
```

The for loop is one of Python's most powerful language features because you can create custom iterator objects and generator functions that supply it with sequences of values. More details about iterators and generators can be found later in this chapter and in Chapter 6, "Functions and Functional Programming."

Functions

You use the def statement to create a function, as shown in the following example:

```
def remainder(a,b):
    q = a // b        # // is truncating division.
    r = a - q*b
    return r
```

To invoke a function, simply use the name of the function followed by its arguments enclosed in parentheses, such as result = remainder(37,15). You can use a tuple to return multiple values from a function, as shown here:

```
def divide(a,b):
    q = a // b        # If a and b are integers, q is integer
    r = a - q*b
    return (q,r)
```

When returning multiple values in a tuple, you can easily unpack the result into separate variables like this:

```
quotient, remainder = divide(1456,33)
```

To assign a default value to a function parameter, use assignment:

```
def connect(hostname,port,timeout=300):
    # Function body
```

When default values are given in a function definition, they can be omitted from subsequent function calls. When omitted, the argument will simply take on the default value. Here's an example:

```
connect('www.python.org', 80)
```

You also can invoke functions by using keyword arguments and supplying the arguments in arbitrary order. However, this requires you to know the names of the arguments in the function definition. Here's an example:

```
connect(port=80,hostname="www.python.org")
```

When variables are created or assigned inside a function, their scope is local. That is, the variable is only defined inside the body of the function and is destroyed when the function returns. To modify the value of a global variable from inside a function, use the global statement as follows:

```
count = 0
...
def foo():
    global count
    count += 1              # Changes the global variable count
```

Generators

Instead of returning a single value, a function can generate an entire sequence of results if it uses the `yield` statement. For example:

```
def countdown(n):
    print "Counting down!"
    while n > 0:
        yield n          # Generate a value (n)
        n -= 1
```

Any function that uses `yield` is known as a *generator*. Calling a generator function creates an object that produces a sequence of results through successive calls to a `next()` method (or `__next__()` in Python 3). For example:

```
>>> c = countdown(5)
>>> c.next()
Counting down!
5
>>> c.next()
4
>>> c.next()
3
>>>
```

The `next()` call makes a generator function run until it reaches the next `yield` statement. At this point, the value passed to `yield` is returned by `next()`, and the function suspends execution. The function resumes execution on the statement following `yield` when `next()` is called again. This process continues until the function returns.

Normally you would not manually call `next()` as shown. Instead, you hook it up to a `for` loop like this:

```
>>> for i in countdown(5):
...     print i,
Counting down!
5 4 3 2 1
>>>
```

Generators are an extremely powerful way of writing programs based on processing pipelines, streams, or data flow. For example, the following generator function mimics the behavior of the UNIX `tail -f` command that's commonly used to monitor log files:

```
# tail a file (like tail -f)
import time
def tail(f):
    f.seek(0,2)        # Move to EOF
    while True:
        line = f.readline()    # Try reading a new line of text
        if not line:           # If nothing, sleep briefly and try again
            time.sleep(0.1)
            continue
        yield line
```

Here's a generator that looks for a specific substring in a sequence of lines:

```
def grep(lines, searchtext):
    for line in lines:
        if searchtext in line: yield line
```

Here's an example of hooking both of these generators together to create a simple processing pipeline:

```
# A python implementation of Unix "tail -f | grep python"
wwwlog  = tail(open("access-log"))
pylines = grep(wwwlog,"python")
for line in pylines:
    print line,
```

A subtle aspect of generators is that they are often mixed together with other iterable objects such as lists or files. Specifically, when you write a statement such as for *item* in *s*, *s* could represent a list of items, the lines of a file, the result of a generator function, or any number of other objects that support iteration. The fact that you can just plug different objects in for *s* can be a powerful tool for creating extensible programs.

Coroutines

Normally, functions operate on a single set of input arguments. However, a function can also be written to operate as a task that processes a sequence of inputs sent to it. This type of function is known as a *coroutine* and is created by using the yield statement as an expression (yield) as shown in this example:

```
def print_matches(matchtext):
    print "Looking for", matchtext
    while True:
        line = (yield)          # Get a line of text
        if matchtext in line:
            print line
```

To use this function, you first call it, advance it to the first (yield), and then start sending data to it using send(). For example:

```
>>> matcher = print_matches("python")
>>> matcher.next()      # Advance to the first (yield)
Looking for python
>>> matcher.send("Hello World")
>>> matcher.send("python is cool")
python is cool
>>> matcher.send("yow!")
>>> matcher.close()     # Done with the matcher function call
>>>
```

A coroutine is suspended until a value is sent to it using send(). When this happens, that value is returned by the (yield) expression inside the coroutine and is processed by the statements that follow. Processing continues until the next (yield) expression is encountered—at which point the function suspends. This continues until the coroutine function returns or close() is called on it as shown in the previous example.

Coroutines are useful when writing concurrent programs based on producer-consumer problems where one part of a program is producing data to be consumed by another part of the program. In this model, a coroutine represents a consumer of data. Here is an example of using generators and coroutines together:

```
# A set of matcher coroutines
matchers = [
    print_matches("python"),
    print_matches("guido"),
    print_matches("jython")
]
```

```
# Prep all of the matchers by calling next()
for m in matchers: m.next()

# Feed an active log file into all matchers.  Note for this to work,
# a web server must be actively writing data to the log.
wwwlog = tail(open("access-log"))
for line in wwwlog:
    for m in matchers:
        m.send(line)        # Send data into each matcher coroutine
```

Further details about coroutines can be found in Chapter 6.

Objects and Classes

All values used in a program are objects. An *object* consists of internal data and methods that perform various kinds of operations involving that data. You have already used objects and methods when working with the built-in types such as strings and lists. For example:

```
items = [37, 42]    # Create a list object
items.append(73)    # Call the append() method
```

The `dir()` function lists the methods available on an object and is a useful tool for interactive experimentation. For example:

```
>>> items = [37, 42]
>>> dir(items)
['__add__', '__class__', '__contains__', '__delattr__', '__delitem__',
...
 'append', 'count', 'extend', 'index', 'insert', 'pop',
 'remove', 'reverse', 'sort']
>>>
```

When inspecting objects, you will see familiar methods such as `append()` and `insert()` listed. However, you will also see special methods that always begin and end with a double underscore. These methods implement various language operations. For example, the `__add__()` method implements the + operator:

```
>>> items.__add__([73,101])
[37, 42, 73, 101]
>>>
```

The `class` statement is used to define new types of objects and for object-oriented programming. For example, the following class defines a simple stack with `push()`, `pop()`, and `length()` operations:

```
class Stack(object):
    def __init__(self):         # Initialize the stack
        self.stack = [ ]
    def push(self,object):
        self.stack.append(object)
    def pop(self):
        return self.stack.pop()
    def length(self):
        return len(self.stack)
```

In the first line of the class definition, the statement `class Stack(object)` declares `Stack` to be an `object`. The use of parentheses is how Python specifies inheritance—in this case, `Stack` inherits from `object`, which is the root of all Python types. Inside the class definition, methods are defined using the `def` statement. The first argument in each method always refers to the object itself. By convention, self is the name used for this argument. All operations involving the attributes of an object must explicitly refer to the self variable. Methods with leading and trailing double underscores are special methods. For example, __init__ is used to initialize an object after it's created.

To use a class, write code such as the following:

```
s = Stack()            # Create a stack
s.push("Dave")         # Push some things onto it
s.push(42)
s.push([3,4,5])
x = s.pop()            # x gets [3,4,5]
y = s.pop()            # y gets 42
del s                  # Destroy s
```

In this example, an entirely new object was created to implement the stack. However, a stack is almost identical to the built-in list object. Therefore, an alternative approach would be to inherit from list and add an extra method:

```
class Stack(list):
    # Add push() method for stack interface
    # Note: lists already provide a pop() method.
    def push(self,object):
        self.append(object)
```

Normally, all of the methods defined within a class apply only to instances of that class (that is, the objects that are created). However, different kinds of methods can be defined such as static methods familiar to C++ and Java programmers. For example:

```
class EventHandler(object):
    @staticmethod
    def dispatcherThread():
        while (1):
            # Wait for requests
            ...

EventHandler.dispatcherThread()          # Call method like a function
```

In this case, @staticmethod declares the method that follows to be a static method. @staticmethod is an example of using an a *decorator*, a topic that is discussed further in Chapter 6.

Exceptions

If an error occurs in your program, an exception is raised and a traceback message such as the following appears:

```
Traceback (most recent call last):
  File "foo.py", line 12, in <module>
IOError: [Errno 2] No such file or directory: 'file.txt'
```

The traceback message indicates the type of error that occurred, along with its location. Normally, errors cause a program to terminate. However, you can catch and handle exceptions using try and except statements, like this:

```
try:
    f = open("file.txt","r")
except IOError as e:
    print e
```

If an IOError occurs, details concerning the cause of the error are placed in e and control passes to the code in the except block. If some other kind of exception is raised, it's passed to the enclosing code block (if any). If no errors occur, the code in the except block is ignored. When an exception is handled, program execution resumes with the statement that immediately follows the last except block. The program does not return to the location where the exception occurred.

The raise statement is used to signal an exception. When raising an exception, you can use one of the built-in exceptions, like this:

```
raise RuntimeError("Computer says no")
```

Or you can create your own exceptions, as described in the section "Defining New Exceptions" in Chapter 5, " Program Structure and Control Flow."

Proper management of system resources such as locks, files, and network connections is often a tricky problem when combined with exception handling. To simplify such programming, you can use the with statement with certain kinds of objects. Here is an example of writing code that uses a mutex lock:

```
import threading
message_lock = threading.Lock()
...
with message_lock:
    messages.add(newmessage)
```

In this example, the message_lock object is automatically acquired when the with statement executes. When execution leaves the context of the with block, the lock is automatically released. This management takes place regardless of what happens inside the with block. For example, if an exception occurs, the lock is released when control leaves the context of the block.

The with statement is normally only compatible with objects related to system resources or the execution environment such as files, connections, and locks. However, user-defined objects can define their own custom processing. This is covered in more detail in the "Context Management Protocol" section of Chapter 3, "Types and Objects."

Modules

As your programs grow in size, you will want to break them into multiple files for easier maintenance. To do this, Python allows you to put definitions in a file and use them as a module that can be imported into other programs and scripts. To create a module, put the relevant statements and definitions into a file that has the same name as the module. (Note that the file must have a .py suffix.) Here's an example:

```
# file :  div.py
def divide(a,b):
    q = a/b        # If a and b are integers, q is an integer
    r = a - q*b
    return (q,r)
```

To use your module in other programs, you can use the import statement:

```
import div
a, b = div.divide(2305, 29)
```

The `import` statement creates a new namespace and executes all the statements in the associated `.py` file within that namespace. To access the contents of the namespace after import, simply use the name of the module as a prefix, as in `div.divide()` in the preceding example.

If you want to import a module using a different name, supply the `import` statement with an optional `as` qualifier, as follows:

```
import div as foo
a,b = foo.divide(2305,29)
```

To import specific definitions into the current namespace, use the `from` statement:

```
from div import divide
a,b = divide(2305,29)        # No longer need the div prefix
```

To load all of a module's contents into the current namespace, you can also use the following:

```
from div import *
```

As with objects, the `dir()` function lists the contents of a module and is a useful tool for interactive experimentation:

```
>>> import string
>>> dir(string)
['__builtins__', '__doc__', '__file__', '__name__', '_idmap',
 '_idmapL', '_lower', '_swapcase', '_upper', 'atof', 'atof_error',
 'atoi', 'atoi_error', 'atol', 'atol_error', 'capitalize',
 'capwords', 'center', 'count', 'digits', 'expandtabs', 'find',
 ...
>>>
```

Getting Help

When working with Python, you have several sources of quickly available information. First, when Python is running in interactive mode, you can use the `help()` command to get information about built-in modules and other aspects of Python. Simply type `help()` by itself for general information or `help('modulename')` for information about a specific module. The `help()` command can also be used to return information about specific functions if you supply a function name.

Most Python functions have documentation strings that describe their usage. To print the doc string, simply print the `__doc__` attribute. Here's an example:

```
>>> print issubclass.__doc__
issubclass(C, B) -> bool

Return whether class C is a subclass (i.e., a derived class) of class B.
When using a tuple as the second argument issubclass(X, (A, B, ...)),
is a shortcut for issubclass(X, A) or issubclass(X, B) or ... (etc.).
>>>
```

Last, but not least, most Python installations also include the command `pydoc`, which can be used to return documentation about Python modules. Simply type `pydoc topic` at a system command prompt.

2

Lexical Conventions and Syntax

This chapter describes the syntactic and lexical conventions of a Python program. Topics include line structure, grouping of statements, reserved words, literals, operators, tokens, and source code encoding.

Line Structure and Indentation

Each statement in a program is terminated with a newline. Long statements can span multiple lines by using the line-continuation character (\), as shown in the following example:

```
a = math.cos(3 * (x - n)) + \
    math.sin(3 * (y - n))
```

You don't need the line-continuation character when the definition of a triple-quoted string, list, tuple, or dictionary spans multiple lines. More generally, any part of a program enclosed in parentheses (...), brackets [...], braces { ... }, or triple quotes can span multiple lines without use of the line-continuation character because they clearly denote the start and end of a definition.

Indentation is used to denote different blocks of code, such as the bodies of functions, conditionals, loops, and classes. The amount of indentation used for the first statement of a block is arbitrary, but the indentation of the entire block must be consistent. Here's an example:

```
if a:
    statement1      # Consistent indentation
    statement2
else:
    statement3
      statement4    # Inconsistent indentation (error)
```

If the body of a function, conditional, loop, or class is short and contains only a single statement, it can be placed on the same line, like this:

```
if a:   statement1
else:   statement2
```

To denote an empty body or block, use the pass statement. Here's an example:

```
if a:
    pass
else:
    statements
```

Although tabs can be used for indentation, this practice is discouraged. The use of spaces is universally preferred (and encouraged) by the Python programming community. When tab characters are encountered, they're converted into the number of spaces required to move to the next column that's a multiple of 8 (for example, a tab appearing in column 11 inserts enough spaces to move to column 16). Running Python with the -t option prints warning messages when tabs and spaces are mixed inconsistently within the same program block. The -tt option turns these warning messages into TabError exceptions.

To place more than one statement on a line, separate the statements with a semicolon (;). A line containing a single statement can also be terminated by a semicolon, although this is unnecessary.

The # character denotes a comment that extends to the end of the line. A # appearing inside a quoted string doesn't start a comment, however.

Finally, the interpreter ignores all blank lines except when running in interactive mode. In this case, a blank line signals the end of input when typing a statement that spans multiple lines.

Identifiers and Reserved Words

An *identifier* is a name used to identify variables, functions, classes, modules, and other objects. Identifiers can include letters, numbers, and the underscore character (_) but must always start with a nonnumeric character. Letters are currently confined to the characters A–Z and a–z in the ISO–Latin character set. Because identifiers are case-sensitive, FOO is different from foo. Special symbols such as $, %, and @ are not allowed in identifiers. In addition, words such as if, else, and for are reserved and cannot be used as identifier names. The following list shows all the reserved words:

and	del	from	nonlocal	try
as	elif	global	not	while
assert	else	if	or	with
break	except	import	pass	yield
class	exec	in	print	
continue	finally	is	raise	
def	for	lambda	return	

Identifiers starting or ending with underscores often have special meanings. For example, identifiers starting with a single underscore such as _foo are not imported by the from module import * statement. Identifiers with leading and trailing double underscores such as __init__ are reserved for special methods, and identifiers with leading double underscores such as __bar are used to implement private class members, as described in Chapter 7, "Classes and Object-Oriented Programming." General-purpose use of similar identifiers should be avoided.

Numeric Literals

There are four types of built-in numeric literals:

- Booleans
- Integers

- Floating-point numbers
- Complex numbers

The identifiers `True` and `False` are interpreted as Boolean values with the integer values of 1 and 0, respectively. A number such as `1234` is interpreted as a decimal integer. To specify an integer using octal, hexadecimal, or binary notation, precede the value with `0o`, `0x`, or `0b`, respectively (for example, `0o644`, `0x100fea8`, or `0b11101010`).

Integers in Python can have an arbitrary number of digits, so if you want to specify a really large integer, just write out all of the digits, as in `12345678901234567890`. However, when inspecting values and looking at old Python code, you might see large numbers written with a trailing 1 (lowercase *L*) or L character, as in `12345678901234567890L`. This trailing L is related to the fact that Python internally represents integers as either a fixed-precision machine integer or an arbitrary precision long integer type depending on the magnitude of the value. In older versions of Python, you could explicitly choose to use either type and would add the trailing L to explicitly indicate the long type. Today, this distinction is unnecessary and is actively discouraged. So, if you want a large integer value, just write it without the L.

Numbers such as `123.34` and `1.2334e+02` are interpreted as floating-point numbers. An integer or floating-point number with a trailing j or J, such as `12.34J`, is an imaginary number. You can create complex numbers with real and imaginary parts by adding a real number and an imaginary number, as in `1.2 + 12.34J`.

String Literals

String literals are used to specify a sequence of characters and are defined by enclosing text in single (`'`), double (`"`), or triple (`'''` or `"""`) quotes. There is no semantic difference between quoting styles other than the requirement that you use the same type of quote to start and terminate a string. Single- and double-quoted strings must be defined on a single line, whereas triple-quoted strings can span multiple lines and include all of the enclosed formatting (that is, newlines, tabs, spaces, and so on). Adjacent strings (separated by white space, newline, or a line-continuation character) such as `"hello"` `'world'` are concatenated to form a single string `"helloworld"`.

Within string literals, the backslash (\) character is used to escape special characters such as newlines, the backslash itself, quotes, and nonprinting characters. Table 2.1 shows the accepted escape codes. Unrecognized escape sequences are left in the string unmodified and include the leading backslash.

Table 2.1   **Standard Character Escape Codes**

Character	Description
\	Newline continuation
\\	Backslash
\'	Single quote
\"	Double quote
\a	Bell
\b	Backspace
\e	Escape
\0	Null

Table 2.1   **Continued**

Character	Description
`\n`	Line feed
`\v`	Vertical tab
`\t`	Horizontal tab
`\r`	Carriage return
`\f`	Form feed
`\ooo`	Octal value (`\000` to `\377`)
`\uxxxx`	Unicode character (`\u0000` to `\uffff`)
`\Uxxxxxxxx`	Unicode character (`\U00000000` to `\Uffffffff`)
`\N{charname}`	Unicode character name
`\xhh`	Hexadecimal value (`\x00` to `\xff`)

The escape codes `\ooo` and `\x` are used to embed characters into a string literal that can't be easily typed (that is, control codes, nonprinting characters, symbols, international characters, and so on). For these escape codes, you have to specify an integer value corresponding to a character value. For example, if you wanted to write a string literal for the word "Jalapeño", you might write it as `"Jalape\xf1o"` where `\xf1` is the character code for ñ.

In Python 2 string literals correspond to 8-bit character or byte-oriented data. A serious limitation of these strings is that they do not fully support international character sets and Unicode. To address this limitation, Python 2 uses a separate string type for Unicode data. To write a Unicode string literal, you prefix the first quote with the letter "u". For example:

```
s = u"Jalape\u00f1o"
```

In Python 3, this prefix character is unnecessary (and is actually a syntax error) as all strings are already Unicode. Python 2 will emulate this behavior if you run the interpreter with the `-U` option (in which case all string literals will be treated as Unicode and the u prefix can be omitted).

Regardless of which Python version you are using, the escape codes of `\u`, `\U`, and `\N` in Table 2.1 are used to insert arbitrary characters into a Unicode literal. Every Unicode character has an assigned *code point*, which is typically denoted in Unicode charts as U+*XXXX* where *XXXX* is a sequence of four or more hexadecimal digits. (Note that this notation is not Python syntax but is often used by authors when describing Unicode characters.) For example, the character ñ has a code point of U+00F1. The `\u` escape code is used to insert Unicode characters with code points in the range U+0000 to U+FFFF (for example, `\u00f1`). The `\U` escape code is used to insert characters in the range U+10000 and above (for example, `\U00012345`). One subtle caution concerning the `\U` escape code is that Unicode characters with code points above U+10000 usually get decomposed into a pair of characters known as a *surrogate pair*. This has to do with the internal representation of Unicode strings and is covered in more detail in Chapter 3, "Types and Objects."

Unicode characters also have a descriptive name. If you know the name, you can use the `\N{character name}` escape sequence. For example:

```
s = u"Jalape\N{LATIN SMALL LETTER N WITH TILDE}o"
```

For an authoritative reference on code points and character names, consult http://www.unicode.org/charts.

Optionally, you can precede a string literal with an r or R, such as in r'\d'. These strings are known as *raw strings* because all their backslash characters are left intact—that is, the string literally contains the enclosed text, including the backslashes. The main use of raw strings is to specify literals where the backslash character has some significance. Examples might include the specification of regular expression patterns with the re module or specifying a filename on a Windows machine (for example, r'c:\newdata\tests').

Raw strings cannot end in a single backslash, such as r"\". Within raw strings, \uXXXX escape sequences are still interpreted as Unicode characters, provided that the number of preceding \ characters is odd. For instance, ur"\u1234" defines a raw Unicode string with the single character U+1234, whereas ur"\\u1234" defines a seven-character string in which the first two characters are slashes and the remaining five characters are the literal "u1234". Also, in Python 2.2, the r must appear after the u in raw Unicode strings as shown. In Python 3.0, the u prefix is unnecessary.

String literals should not be defined using a sequence of raw bytes that correspond to a data encoding such as UTF-8 or UTF-16. For example, directly writing a raw UTF-8 encoded string such as 'Jalape\xc3\xb1o' simply produces a nine-character string U+004A, U+0061, U+006C, U+0061, U+0070, U+0065, U+00C3, U+00B1, U+006F, which is probably not what you intended. This is because in UTF-8, the multi-byte sequence \xc3\xb1 is supposed to represent the single character U+00F1, not the two characters U+00C3 and U+00B1. To specify an encoded byte string as a literal, prefix the first quote with a "b" as in b"Jalape\xc3\xb1o". When defined, this literally creates a string of single bytes. From this representation, it is possible to create a normal string by decoding the value of the byte literal with its decode() method. More details about this are covered in Chapter 3 and Chapter 4, "Operators and Expressions."

The use of byte literals is quite rare in most programs because this syntax did not appear until Python 2.6, and in that version there is no difference between a byte literal and a normal string. In Python 3, however, byte literals are mapped to a new bytes datatype that behaves differently than a normal string (see Appendix A, "Python 3").

Containers

Values enclosed in square brackets [...], parentheses (...), and braces {...} denote a collection of objects contained in a list, tuple, and dictionary, respectively, as in the following example:

```
a = [ 1, 3.4, 'hello' ]        # A list
b = ( 10, 20, 30 )             # A tuple
c = { 'a': 3, 'b': 42 }        # A dictionary
```

List, tuple, and dictionary literals can span multiple lines without using the line-continuation character (\). In addition, a trailing comma is allowed on the last item. For example:

```
a = [ 1,
      3.4,
      'hello',
    ]
```

Operators, Delimiters, and Special Symbols

The following operators are recognized:

```
+     -     *     **     /     //     %     <<     >>     &     |
^     ~     <     >     <=     >=     ==     !=     <>     +=
-=    *=    /=    //=    %=    **=    &=     |=     ^=     >>=    <<=
```

The following tokens serve as delimiters for expressions, lists, dictionaries, and various parts of a statement:

```
(    )    [    ]    {    }    ,    :    .    `    =    ;
```

For example, the equal (=) character serves as a delimiter between the name and value of an assignment, whereas the comma (,) character is used to delimit arguments to a function, elements in lists and tuples, and so on. The period (.) is also used in floating-point numbers and in the ellipsis (. . .) used in extended slicing operations.

Finally, the following special symbols are also used:

```
'    "    #    \    @
```

The characters $ and ? have no meaning in Python and cannot appear in a program except inside a quoted string literal.

Documentation Strings

If the first statement of a module, class, or function definition is a string, that string becomes a documentation string for the associated object, as in the following example:

```
def fact(n):
    "This function computes a factorial"
    if (n <= 1): return 1
    else: return n * fact(n - 1)
```

Code-browsing and documentation-generation tools sometimes use documentation strings. The strings are accessible in the __doc__ attribute of an object, as shown here:

```
>>> print fact.__doc__
This function computes a factorial
>>>
```

The indentation of the documentation string must be consistent with all the other statements in a definition. In addition, a documentation string cannot be computed or assigned from a variable as an expression. The documentation string always has to be a string literal enclosed in quotes.

Decorators

Function, method, or class definitions may be preceded by a special symbol known as a *decorator*, the purpose of which is to modify the behavior of the definition that follows. Decorators are denoted with the @ symbol and must be placed on a separate line immediately before the corresponding function, method, or class. Here's an example:

```
class Foo(object):
    @staticmethod
    def bar():
        pass
```

More than one decorator can be used, but each one must be on a separate line. Here's an example:

```
@foo
@bar
def spam():
    pass
```

More information about decorators can be found in Chapter 6, "Functions and Functional Programming," and Chapter 7, "Classes and Object-Oriented Programming."

Source Code Encoding

Python source programs are normally written in standard 7-bit ASCII. However, users working in Unicode environments may find this awkward—especially if they must write a lot of string literals with international characters.

It is possible to write Python source code in a different encoding by including a special encoding comment in the first or second line of a Python program:

```
#!/usr/bin/env python
# -*- coding: UTF-8 -*-

s = "Jalapeño"   # String in quotes is directly encoded in UTF-8.
```

When the special coding: comment is supplied, string literals may be typed in directly using a Unicode-aware editor. However, other elements of Python, including identifier names and reserved words, should still be restricted to ASCII characters.

3

Types and Objects

All the data stored in a Python program is built around the concept of an *object*. Objects include fundamental data types such as numbers, strings, lists, and dictionaries. However, it's also possible to create user-defined objects in the form of classes. In addition, most objects related to program structure and the internal operation of the interpreter are also exposed. This chapter describes the inner workings of the Python object model and provides an overview of the built-in data types. Chapter 4, "Operators and Expressions," further describes operators and expressions. Chapter 7, "Classes and Object-Oriented Programming," describes how to create user-defined objects.

Terminology

Every piece of data stored in a program is an object. Each object has an identity, a type (which is also known as its class), and a value. For example, when you write a = 42, an integer object is created with the value of 42. You can view the *identity* of an object as a pointer to its location in memory. a is a name that refers to this specific location.

The *type* of an object, also known as the object's *class*, describes the internal representation of the object as well as the methods and operations that it supports. When an object of a particular type is created, that object is sometimes called an *instance* of that type. After an instance is created, its identity and type cannot be changed. If an object's value can be modified, the object is said to be *mutable*. If the value cannot be modified, the object is said to be *immutable*. An object that contains references to other objects is said to be a *container* or *collection*.

Most objects are characterized by a number of data attributes and methods. An *attribute* is a value associated with an object. A *method* is a function that performs some sort of operation on an object when the method is invoked as a function. Attributes and methods are accessed using the dot (.) operator, as shown in the following example:

```
a = 3 + 4j        # Create a complex number
r = a.real        # Get the real part (an attribute)

b = [1, 2, 3]     # Create a list
b.append(7)       # Add a new element using the append method
```

Object Identity and Type

The built-in function id() returns the identity of an object as an integer. This integer usually corresponds to the object's location in memory, although this is specific to the Python implementation and no such interpretation of the identity should be made. The is operator compares the identity of two objects. The built-in function `type()` returns the type of an object. Here's an example of different ways you might compare two objects:

```
# Compare two objects
def compare(a,b):
    if a is b:
        # a and b are the same object
        statements
    if a == b:
        # a and b have the same value
        statements
    if type(a) is type(b):
        # a and b have the same type
        statements
```

The type of an object is itself an object known as the object's class. This object is uniquely defined and is always the same for all instances of a given type. Therefore, the type can be compared using the `is` operator. All type objects are assigned names that can be used to perform type checking. Most of these names are built-ins, such as `list`, `dict`, and `file`. Here's an example:

```
if type(s) is list:
    s.append(item)

if type(d) is dict:
    d.update(t)
```

Because types can be specialized by defining classes, a better way to check types is to use the built-in `isinstance(object, type)` function. Here's an example:

```
if isinstance(s,list):
    s.append(item)

if isinstance(d,dict):
    d.update(t)
```

Because the `isinstance()` function is aware of inheritance, it is the preferred way to check the type of any Python object.

Although type checks can be added to a program, type checking is often not as useful as you might imagine. For one, excessive checking severely affects performance. Second, programs don't always define objects that neatly fit into an inheritance hierarchy. For instance, if the purpose of the preceding `isinstance(s,list)` statement is to test whether s is "list-like," it wouldn't work with objects that had the same programming interface as a list but didn't directly inherit from the built-in `list` type. Another option for adding type-checking to a program is to define abstract base classes. This is described in Chapter 7.

Reference Counting and Garbage Collection

All objects are reference-counted. An object's reference count is increased whenever it's assigned to a new name or placed in a container such as a list, tuple, or dictionary, as shown here:

```
a = 37       # Creates an object with value 37
b = a        # Increases reference count on 37
c = []
c.append(b)  # Increases reference count on 37
```

This example creates a single object containing the value 37. a is merely a name that refers to the newly created object. When b is assigned a, b becomes a new name for the same object and the object's reference count increases. Likewise, when you place b into a list, the object's reference count increases again. Throughout the example, only one object contains 37. All other operations are simply creating new references to the object.

An object's reference count is decreased by the del statement or whenever a reference goes out of scope (or is reassigned). Here's an example:

```
del a       # Decrease reference count of 37
b = 42      # Decrease reference count of 37
c[0] = 2.0  # Decrease reference count of 37
```

The current reference count of an object can be obtained using the sys.getrefcount() function. For example:

```
>>> a = 37
>>> import sys
>>> sys.getrefcount(a)
7
>>>
```

In many cases, the reference count is much higher than you might guess. For immutable data such as numbers and strings, the interpreter aggressively shares objects between different parts of the program in order to conserve memory.

When an object's reference count reaches zero, it is garbage-collected. However, in some cases a circular dependency may exist among a collection of objects that are no longer in use. Here's an example:

```
a = { }
b = { }
a['b'] = b       # a contains reference to b
b['a'] = a       # b contains reference to a
del a
del b
```

In this example, the del statements decrease the reference count of a and b and destroy the names used to refer to the underlying objects. However, because each object contains a reference to the other, the reference count doesn't drop to zero and the objects remain allocated (resulting in a memory leak). To address this problem, the interpreter periodically executes a cycle detector that searches for cycles of inaccessible objects and deletes them. The cycle-detection algorithm runs periodically as the interpreter allocates more and more memory during execution. The exact behavior can be fine-tuned and controlled using functions in the gc module (see Chapter 13, "Python Runtime Services").

References and Copies

When a program makes an assignment such as a = b, a new reference to b is created. For immutable objects such as numbers and strings, this assignment effectively creates a copy of b. However, the behavior is quite different for mutable objects such as lists and dictionaries. Here's an example:

```
>>> a = [1,2,3,4]
>>> b = a
>>> b is a               # b is a reference to a
True
```

```
>>> b[2] = -100          # Change an element in b
>>> a                    # Notice how a also changed
[1, 2, -100, 4]
>>>
```

Because a and b refer to the same object in this example, a change made to one of the variables is reflected in the other. To avoid this, you have to create a copy of an object rather than a new reference.

Two types of copy operations are applied to container objects such as lists and dictionaries: a shallow copy and a deep copy. A *shallow copy* creates a new object but populates it with references to the items contained in the original object. Here's an example:

```
>>> a = [ 1, 2, [3,4] ]
>>> b = list(a)          # Create a shallow copy of a.
>>> b is a
False
>>> b.append(100)        # Append element to b.
>>> b
[1, 2, [3, 4], 100]
>>> a                    # Notice that a is unchanged
[1, 2, [3, 4]]
>>> b[2][0] = -100       # Modify an element inside b
>>> b
[1, 2, [-100, 4], 100]
>>> a                    # Notice the change inside a
[1, 2, [-100, 4]]
>>>
```

In this case, a and b are separate list objects, but the elements they contain are shared. Therefore, a modification to one of the elements of a also modifies an element of b, as shown.

A *deep copy* creates a new object and recursively copies all the objects it contains. There is no built-in operation to create deep copies of objects. However, the copy.deepcopy() function in the standard library can be used, as shown in the following example:

```
>>> import copy
>>> a = [1, 2, [3, 4]]
>>> b = copy.deepcopy(a)
>>> b[2][0] = -100
>>> b
[1, 2, [-100, 4]]
>>> a                    # Notice that a is unchanged
[1, 2, [3, 4]]
>>>
```

First-Class Objects

All objects in Python are said to be "first class." This means that all objects that can be named by an identifier have equal status. It also means that all objects that can be named can be treated as data. For example, here is a simple dictionary containing two values:

```
items = {
    'number' : 42,
    'text' : 'Hello World'
}
```

The first-class nature of objects can be seen by adding some more unusual items to this dictionary. Here are some examples:

```
items["func"]   = abs            # Add the abs() function
import math
items["mod"]    = math           # Add a module
items["error"]  = ValueError     # Add an exception type
nums = [1,2,3,4]
items["append"] = nums.append    # Add a method of another object
```

In this example, the items dictionary contains a function, a module, an exception, and a method of another object. If you want, you can use dictionary lookups on items in place of the original names and the code will still work. For example:

```
>>> items["func"](-45)          # Executes abs(-45)
45
>>> items["mod"].sqrt(4)        # Executes math.sqrt(4)
2.0
>>> try:
...     x = int("a lot")
... except items["error"] as e:   # Same as except ValueError as e
...     print("Couldn't convert")
...
Couldn't convert
>>> items["append"](100)        # Executes nums.append(100)
>>> nums
[1, 2, 3, 4, 100]
>>>
```

The fact that everything in Python is first-class is often not fully appreciated by new programmers. However, it can be used to write very compact and flexible code. For example, suppose you had a line of text such as "GOOG,100,490.10" and you wanted to convert it into a list of fields with appropriate type-conversion. Here's a clever way that you might do it by creating a list of types (which are first-class objects) and executing a few simple list processing operations:

```
>>> line = "GOOG,100,490.10"
>>> field_types = [str, int, float]
>>> raw_fields = line.split(',')
>>> fields = [ty(val) for ty,val in zip(field_types,raw_fields)]
>>> fields
['GOOG', 100, 490.10000000000002]
>>>
```

Built-in Types for Representing Data

There are approximately a dozen built-in data types that are used to represent most of the data used in programs. These are grouped into a few major categories as shown in Table 3.1. The Type Name column in the table lists the name or expression that you can use to check for that type using isinstance() and other type-related functions. Certain types are only available in Python 2 and have been indicated as such (in Python 3, they have been deprecated or merged into one of the other types).

Table 3.1   **Built-In Types for Data Representation**

Type Category	Type Name	Description
None	type(None)	The null object None
Numbers	int	Integer
	long	Arbitrary-precision integer (Python 2 only)
	float	Floating point
	complex	Complex number
	bool	Boolean (True or False)
Sequences	str	Character string
	unicode	Unicode character string (Python 2 only)
	list	List
	tuple	Tuple
	xrange	A range of integers created by xrange() (In Python 3, it is called range.)
Mapping	dict	Dictionary
Sets	set	Mutable set
	frozenset	Immutable set

The None Type

The None type denotes a null object (an object with no value). Python provides exactly one null object, which is written as None in a program. This object is returned by functions that don't explicitly return a value. None is frequently used as the default value of optional arguments, so that the function can detect whether the caller has actually passed a value for that argument. None has no attributes and evaluates to False in Boolean expressions.

Numeric Types

Python uses five numeric types: Booleans, integers, long integers, floating-point numbers, and complex numbers. Except for Booleans, all numeric objects are signed. All numeric types are immutable.

Booleans are represented by two values: True and False. The names True and False are respectively mapped to the numerical values of 1 and 0.

Integers represent whole numbers in the range of −2147483648 to 2147483647 (the range may be larger on some machines). Long integers represent whole numbers of unlimited range (limited only by available memory). Although there are two integer types, Python tries to make the distinction seamless (in fact, in Python 3, the two types have been unified into a single integer type). Thus, although you will sometimes see references to long integers in existing Python code, this is mostly an implementation detail that can be ignored—just use the integer type for all integer operations. The one exception is in code that performs explicit type checking for integer values. In Python 2, the expression isinstance(x, int) will return False if x is an integer that has been promoted to a long.

Floating-point numbers are represented using the native double-precision (64-bit) representation of floating-point numbers on the machine. Normally this is IEEE 754, which provides approximately 17 digits of precision and an exponent in the range of

−308 to 308. This is the same as the `double` type in C. Python doesn't support 32-bit single-precision floating-point numbers. If precise control over the space and precision of numbers is an issue in your program, consider using the numpy extension (which can be found at http://numpy.sourceforge.net).

Complex numbers are represented as a pair of floating-point numbers. The real and imaginary parts of a complex number `z` are available in `z.real` and `z.imag`. The method `z.conjugate()` calculates the complex conjugate of `z` (the conjugate of `a+bj` is `a-bj`).

Numeric types have a number of properties and methods that are meant to simplify operations involving mixed arithmetic. For simplified compatibility with rational numbers (found in the `fractions` module), integers have the properties `x.numerator` and `x.denominator`. An integer or floating-point number `y` has the properties `y.real` and `y.imag` as well as the method `y.conjugate()` for compatibility with complex numbers. A floating-point number `y` can be converted into a pair of integers representing a fraction using `y.as_integer_ratio()`. The method `y.is_integer()` tests if a floating-point number `y` represents an integer value. Methods `y.hex()` and `y.fromhex()` can be used to work with floating-point numbers using their low-level binary representation.

Several additional numeric types are defined in library modules. The `decimal` module provides support for generalized base-10 decimal arithmetic. The `fractions` module adds a rational number type. These modules are covered in Chapter 14, "Mathematics."

Sequence Types

Sequences represent ordered sets of objects indexed by non-negative integers and include strings, lists, and tuples. Strings are sequences of characters, and lists and tuples are sequences of arbitrary Python objects. Strings and tuples are immutable; lists allow insertion, deletion, and substitution of elements. All sequences support iteration.

Operations Common to All Sequences

Table 3.2 shows the operators and methods that you can apply to all sequence types. Element `i` of sequence `s` is selected using the indexing operator `s[i]`, and subsequences are selected using the slicing operator `s[i:j]` or extended slicing operator `s[i:j:stride]` (these operations are described in Chapter 4). The length of any sequence is returned using the built-in `len(s)` function. You can find the minimum and maximum values of a sequence by using the built-in `min(s)` and `max(s)` functions. However, these functions only work for sequences in which the elements can be ordered (typically numbers and strings). `sum(s)` sums items in `s` but only works for numeric data.

Table 3.3 shows the additional operators that can be applied to mutable sequences such as lists.

Table 3.2   **Operations and Methods Applicable to All Sequences**

Item	Description
`s[i]`	Returns element `i` of a sequence
`s[i:j]`	Returns a slice
`s[i:j:stride]`	Returns an extended slice

Table 3.2   **Continued**

Item	Description
len(s)	Number of elements in s
min(s)	Minimum value in s
max(s)	Maximum value in s
sum(s [,initial])	Sum of items in s
all(s)	Checks whether all items in s are True.
any(s)	Checks whether any item in s is True.

Table 3.3   **Operations Applicable to Mutable Sequences**

Item	Description
s[i] = v	Item assignment
s[i:j] = t	Slice assignment
s[i:j:stride] = t	Extended slice assignment
del s[i]	Item deletion
del s[i:j]	Slice deletion
del s[i:j:stride]	Extended slice deletion

Lists

Lists support the methods shown in Table 3.4. The built-in function list(s) converts any iterable type to a list. If s is already a list, this function constructs a new list that's a shallow copy of s. The s.append(x) method appends a new element, x, to the end of the list. The s.index(x) method searches the list for the first occurrence of x. If no such element is found, a ValueError exception is raised. Similarly, the s.remove(x) method removes the first occurrence of x from the list or raises ValueError if no such item exists. The s.extend(t) method extends the list s by appending the elements in sequence t.

The s.sort() method sorts the elements of a list (all of which should be of a uniform type) and optionally accepts a key function and reverse flag, both of which must be specified as keyword arguments. The key function is a function that is applied to each element prior to comparison during sorting. If given, this function should take a single item as input and return the value that will be used to perform the comparison while sorting. Specifying a key function is useful if you want to perform special kinds of sorting operations such as sorting a list of strings, but with case insensitivity. The s.reverse() method reverses the order of the items in the list. Both the sort() and reverse() methods operate on the list elements in place and return None.

Table 3.4   **List Methods**

Method	Description
list(s)	Converts s to a list.
s.append(x)	Appends a new element, x, to the end of s.
s.extend(t)	Appends a new list, t, to the end of s.
s.count(x)	Counts occurrences of x in s.

Table 3.4   **Continued**

Method	Description
s.index(x [,start [,stop]])	Returns the smallest i where s[i]==x. start and stop optionally specify the starting and ending index for the search.
s.insert(i,x)	Inserts x at index i.
s.pop([i])	Returns the element i and removes it from the list. If i is omitted, the last element is returned.
s.remove(x)	Searches for x and removes it from s.
s.reverse()	Reverses items of s in place.
s.sort([key [, reverse]])	Sorts items of s in place. key is a key function. reverse is a flag that sorts the list in reverse order. key and reverse should always be specified as keyword arguments. The items in s should all be of a uniform type.

Strings

Python 2 provides two string object types. Byte strings are sequences of bytes containing 8-bit data. They may contain binary data and embedded NULL bytes. Unicode strings are sequences of unencoded Unicode characters, which are internally represented by 16-bit integers. This allows for 65,536 unique character values. Although the Unicode standard supports up to 1 million unique character values, these extra characters are not supported by Python by default. Instead, they are encoded as a special two-character (4-byte) sequence known as a *surrogate pair*—the interpretation of which is up to the application. As an optional feature, Python may be built to store Unicode characters using 32-bit integers. When enabled, this allows Python to represent the entire range of Unicode values from U+000000 to U+110000. All Unicode-related functions are adjusted accordingly.

Strings support the methods shown in Table 3.5. Although these methods operate on string instances, none of these methods actually modifies the underlying string data. Thus, methods such as s.capitalize(), s.center(), and s.expandtabs() always return a new string as opposed to modifying the string s. Character tests such as s.isalnum() and s.isupper() return True or False if all the characters in the string s satisfy the test. Furthermore, these tests always return False if the length of the string is zero.

The s.find(), s.index(), s.rfind(), and s.rindex() methods are used to search s for a substring. All these functions return an integer index to the substring in s. In addition, the find() method returns -1 if the substring isn't found, whereas the index() method raises a ValueError exception. The s.replace() method is used to replace a substring with replacement text. It is important to emphasize that all of these methods only work with simple substrings. Regular expression pattern matching and searching is handled by functions in the re library module.

The s.split() and s.rsplit() methods split a string into a list of fields separated by a delimiter. The s.partition() and s.rpartition() methods search for a separator substring and partition s into three parts corresponding to text before the separator, the separator itself, and text after the separator.

Many of the string methods accept optional *start* and *end* parameters, which are integer values specifying the starting and ending indices in s. In most cases, these values may be given negative values, in which case the index is taken from the end of the string.

The `s.translate()` method is used to perform advanced character substitutions such as quickly stripping all control characters out of a string. As an argument, it accepts a translation table containing a one-to-one mapping of characters in the original string to characters in the result. For 8-bit strings, the translation table is a 256-character string. For Unicode, the translation table can be any sequence object `s` where `s[n]` returns an integer character code or Unicode character corresponding to the Unicode character with integer value `n`.

The `s.encode()` and `s.decode()` methods are used to transform string data to and from a specified character encoding. As input, these accept an encoding name such as `'ascii'`, `'utf-8'`, or `'utf-16'`. These methods are most commonly used to convert Unicode strings into a data encoding suitable for I/O operations and are described further in Chapter 9, "Input and Output." Be aware that in Python 3, the `encode()` method is only available on strings, and the `decode()` method is only available on the bytes datatype.

The `s.format()` method is used to perform string formatting. As arguments, it accepts any combination of positional and keyword arguments. Placeholders in `s` denoted by `{item}` are replaced by the appropriate argument. Positional arguments can be referenced using placeholders such as `{0}` and `{1}`. Keyword arguments are referenced using a placeholder with a name such as `{name}`. Here is an example:

```
>>> a = "Your name is {0} and your age is {age}"
>>> a.format("Mike", age=40)
'Your name is Mike and your age is 40'
>>>
```

Within the special format strings, the `{item}` placeholders can also include simple index and attribute lookup. A placeholder of `{item[n]}` where `n` is a number performs a sequence lookup on `item`. A placeholder of `{item[key]}` where `key` is a non-numeric string performs a dictionary lookup of `item["key"]`. A placeholder of `{item.attr}` refers to attribute `attr` of `item`. Further details on the `format()` method can be found in the "String Formatting" section of Chapter 4.

Table 3.5 **String Methods**

Method	Description
`s.capitalize()`	Capitalizes the first character.
`s.center(width [, pad])`	Centers the string in a field of length `width`. `pad` is a padding character.
`s.count(sub [,start [,end]])`	Counts occurrences of the specified substring `sub`.
`s.decode([encoding [,errors]])`	Decodes a string and returns a Unicode string (byte strings only).
`s.encode([encoding [,errors]])`	Returns an encoded version of the string (unicode strings only).
`s.endswith(suffix [,start [,end]])`	Checks the end of the string for a suffix.
`s.expandtabs([tabsize])`	Replaces tabs with spaces.
`s.find(sub [, start [,end]])`	Finds the first occurrence of the specified substring `sub` or returns -1.

Table 3.5   **Continued**

Method	Description
`s.format(*args, **kwargs)`	Formats `s`.
`s.index(sub [, start [,end]])`	Finds the first occurrence of the specified substring `sub` or raises an error.
`s.isalnum()`	Checks whether all characters are alphanumeric.
`s.isalpha()`	Checks whether all characters are alphabetic.
`s.isdigit()`	Checks whether all characters are digits.
`s.islower()`	Checks whether all characters are lowercase.
`s.isspace()`	Checks whether all characters are whitespace.
`s.istitle()`	Checks whether the string is a title-cased string (first letter of each word capitalized).
`s.isupper()`	Checks whether all characters are uppercase.
`s.join(t)`	Joins the strings in sequence `t` with `s` as a separator.
`s.ljust(width [, fill])`	Left-aligns `s` in a string of size `width`.
`s.lower()`	Converts to lowercase.
`s.lstrip([chrs])`	Removes leading whitespace or characters supplied in `chrs`.
`s.partition(sep)`	Partitions a string based on a separator string `sep`. Returns a tuple `(head,sep,tail)` or `(s, "","")` if `sep` isn't found.
`s.replace(old, new [,maxreplace])`	Replaces a substring.
`s.rfind(sub [,start [,end]])`	Finds the last occurrence of a substring.
`s.rindex(sub [,start [,end]])`	Finds the last occurrence or raises an error.
`s.rjust(width [, fill])`	Right-aligns `s` in a string of length `width`.
`s.rpartition(sep)`	Partitions `s` based on a separator `sep`, but searches from the end of the string.
`s.rsplit([sep [,maxsplit]])`	Splits a string from the end of the string using `sep` as a delimiter. `maxsplit` is the maximum number of splits to perform. If `maxsplit` is omitted, the result is identical to the `split()` method.
`s.rstrip([chrs])`	Removes trailing whitespace or characters supplied in `chrs`.
`s.split([sep [,maxsplit]])`	Splits a string using `sep` as a delimiter. `maxsplit` is the maximum number of splits to perform.

Table 3.5 **Continued**

`s.splitlines([keepends])`	Splits a string into a list of lines. If `keepends` is 1, trailing newlines are preserved.
`s.startswith(prefix [,start [,end]])`	Checks whether a string starts with `prefix`.
`s.strip([chrs])`	Removes leading and trailing white-space or characters supplied in `chrs`.
`s.swapcase()`	Converts uppercase to lowercase, and vice versa.
`s.title()`	Returns a title-cased version of the string.
`s.translate(table [,deletechars])`	Translates a string using a character translation table `table`, removing characters in `deletechars`.
`s.upper()`	Converts a string to uppercase.
`s.zfill(width)`	Pads a string with the '0' digit character on the left up to the specified `width`.

xrange() **Objects**

The built-in function xrange([i,]j [,stride]) creates an object that represents a range of integers k such that $i <= k < j$. The first index, i, and the stride are optional and have default values of 0 and 1, respectively. An xrange object calculates its values whenever it's accessed and although an xrange object looks like a sequence, it is actually somewhat limited. For example, none of the standard slicing operations are supported. This limits the utility of xrange to only a few applications such as iterating in simple loops.

It should be noted that in Python 3, xrange() has been renamed to range(). However, it operates in exactly the same manner as described here.

Mapping Types

A *mapping object* represents an arbitrary collection of objects that are indexed by another collection of nearly arbitrary key values. Unlike a sequence, a mapping object is unordered and can be indexed by numbers, strings, and other objects. Mappings are mutable.

Dictionaries are the only built-in mapping type and are Python's version of a hash table or associative array. You can use any immutable object as a dictionary key value (strings, numbers, tuples, and so on). Lists, dictionaries, and tuples containing mutable objects cannot be used as keys (the dictionary type requires key values to remain constant).

To select an item in a mapping object, use the key index operator m[k], where k is a key value. If the key is not found, a KeyError exception is raised. The len(m) function returns the number of items contained in a mapping object. Table 3.6 lists the methods and operations.

Table 3.6 **Methods and Operations for Dictionaries**

Item	Description
`len(m)`	Returns the number of items in `m`.
`m[k]`	Returns the item of `m` with key `k`.
`m[k]=x`	Sets `m[k]` to `x`.
`del m[k]`	Removes `m[k]` from `m`.
`k in m`	Returns `True` if `k` is a key in `m`.
`m.clear()`	Removes all items from `m`.
`m.copy()`	Makes a copy of `m`.
`m.fromkeys(s [,value])`	Create a new dictionary with keys from sequence `s` and values all set to `value`.
`m.get(k [,v])`	Returns `m[k]` if found; otherwise, returns `v`.
`m.has_key(k)`	Returns `True` if `m` has key `k`; otherwise, returns `False`. (Deprecated, use the `in` operator instead. Python 2 only)
`m.items()`	Returns a sequence of all (`key`, `value`) pairs in `m`.
`m.keys()`	Returns a sequence of all key values in `m`.
`m.pop(k [,default])`	Returns `m[k]` if found and removes it from `m`; otherwise, returns `default` if supplied or raises `KeyError` if not.
`m.popitem()`	Removes a random (`key`, `value`) pair from `m` and returns it as a tuple.
`m.setdefault(k [, v])`	Returns `m[k]` if found; otherwise, returns `v` and sets `m[k] = v`.
`m.update(b)`	Adds all objects from `b` to `m`.
`m.values()`	Returns a sequence of all values in `m`.

Most of the methods in Table 3.6 are used to manipulate or retrieve the contents of a dictionary. The `m.clear()` method removes all items. The `m.update(b)` method updates the current mapping object by inserting all the (`key`, `value`) pairs found in the mapping object `b`. The `m.get(k [,v])` method retrieves an object but allows for an optional default value, `v`, that's returned if no such key exists. The `m.setdefault(k [,v])` method is similar to `m.get()`, except that in addition to returning `v` if no object exists, it sets `m[k] = v`. If `v` is omitted, it defaults to `None`. The `m.pop()` method returns an item from a dictionary and removes it at the same time. The `m.popitem()` method is used to iteratively destroy the contents of a dictionary.

The `m.copy()` method makes a shallow copy of the items contained in a mapping object and places them in a new mapping object. The `m.fromkeys(s [,value])` method creates a new mapping with keys all taken from a sequence `s`. The type of the resulting mapping will be the same as `m`. The value associated with all of these keys is set to `None` unless an alternative value is given with the optional `value` parameter. The `fromkeys()` method is defined as a class method, so an alternative way to invoke it would be to use the class name such as `dict.fromkeys()`.

The `m.items()` method returns a sequence containing (`key`, `value`) pairs. The `m.keys()` method returns a sequence with all the key values, and the `m.values()` method returns a sequence with all the values. For these methods, you should assume that the only safe operation that can be performed on the result is iteration. In Python 2 the result is a list, but in Python 3 the result is an iterator that iterates over the current contents of the mapping. If you write code that simply assumes it is an iterator, it will be generally compatible with both versions of Python. If you need to store the result of these methods as data, make a copy by storing it in a list. For example, items = list(m.items()). If you simply want a list of all keys, use keys = list(m).

Set Types

A *set* is an unordered collection of unique items. Unlike sequences, sets provide no indexing or slicing operations. They are also unlike dictionaries in that there are no key values associated with the objects. The items placed into a set must be immutable. Two different set types are available: set is a mutable set, and frozenset is an immutable set. Both kinds of sets are created using a pair of built-in functions:

```
s = set([1,5,10,15])
f = frozenset(['a',37,'hello'])
```

Both set() and frozenset() populate the set by iterating over the supplied argument. Both kinds of sets provide the methods outlined in Table 3.7.

Table 3.7   **Methods and Operations for Set Types**

Item	Description
len(s)	Returns the number of items in s.
s.copy()	Makes a copy of s.
s.difference(t)	Set difference. Returns all the items in s, but not in t.
s.intersection(t)	Intersection. Returns all the items that are both in s and in t.
s.isdisjoint(t)	Returns True if s and t have no items in common.
s.issubset(t)	Returns True if s is a subset of t.
s.issuperset(t)	Returns True if s is a superset of t.
s.symmetric_difference(t)	Symmetric difference. Returns all the items that are in s or t, but not in both sets.
s.union(t)	Union. Returns all items in s or t.

The s.difference(t), s.intersection(t), s.symmetric_difference(t), and s.union(t) methods provide the standard mathematical operations on sets. The returned value has the same type as s (set or frozenset). The parameter t can be any Python object that supports iteration. This includes sets, lists, tuples, and strings. These set operations are also available as mathematical operators, as described further in Chapter 4.

Mutable sets (set) additionally provide the methods outlined in Table 3.8.

Table 3.8   **Methods for Mutable Set Types**

Item	Description
s.add(item)	Adds item to s. Has no effect if item is already in s.
s.clear()	Removes all items from s.
s.difference_update(t)	Removes all the items from s that are also in t.

Table 3.8   **Continued**

Item	Description
s.discard(*item*)	Removes *item* from s. If *item* is not a member of s, nothing happens.
s.intersection_update(*t*)	Computes the intersection of s and t and leaves the result in s.
s.pop()	Returns an arbitrary set element and removes it from s.
s.remove(*item*)	Removes *item* from s. If *item* is not a member, KeyError is raised.
s.symmetric_difference_update(t)	Computes the symmetric difference of s and t and leaves the result in s.
s.update(*t*)	Adds all the items in t to s. t may be another set, a sequence, or any object that supports iteration.

All these operations modify the set s in place. The parameter t can be any object that supports iteration.

Built-in Types for Representing Program Structure

In Python, functions, classes, and modules are all objects that can be manipulated as data. Table 3.9 shows types that are used to represent various elements of a program itself.

Table 3.9   **Built-in Python Types for Program Structure**

Type Category	Type Name	Description
Callable	types.BuiltinFunctionType	Built-in function or method
	type	Type of built-in types and classes
	object	Ancestor of all types and classes
	types.FunctionType	User-defined function
	types.MethodType	Class method
Modules	types.ModuleType	Module
Classes	object	Ancestor of all types and classes
Types	type	Type of built-in types and classes

Note that object and type appear twice in Table 3.9 because classes and types are both callable as a function.

Callable Types

Callable types represent objects that support the function call operation. There are several flavors of objects with this property, including user-defined functions, built-in functions, instance methods, and classes.

User-Defined Functions

User-defined functions are callable objects created at the module level by using the `def` statement or with the `lambda` operator. Here's an example:

```
def foo(x,y):
    return x + y

bar = lambda x,y: x + y
```

A user-defined function `f` has the following attributes:

Attribute(s)	Description
`f.__doc__`	Documentation string
`f.__name__`	Function name
`f.__dict__`	Dictionary containing function attributes
`f.__code__`	Byte-compiled code
`f.__defaults__`	Tuple containing the default arguments
`f.__globals__`	Dictionary defining the global namespace
`f.__closure__`	Tuple containing data related to nested scopes

In older versions of Python 2, many of the preceding attributes had names such as `func_code`, `func_defaults`, and so on. The attribute names listed are compatible with Python 2.6 and Python 3.

Methods

Methods are functions that are defined inside a class definition. There are three common types of methods—instance methods, class methods, and static methods:

```
class Foo(object):
    def instance_method(self,arg):
        statements
    @classmethod
    def class_method(cls,arg):
        statements
    @staticmethod
    def static_method(arg):
        statements
```

An *instance method* is a method that operates on an instance belonging to a given class. The instance is passed to the method as the first argument, which is called `self` by convention. A *class method* operates on the class itself as an object. The class object is passed to a class method in the first argument, `cls`. A *static method* is a just a function that happens to be packaged inside a class. It does not receive an instance or a class object as a first argument.

Both instance and class methods are represented by a special object of type `types.MethodType`. However, understanding this special type requires a careful understanding of how object attribute lookup (.) works. The process of looking something up on an object (.) is always a separate operation from that of making a function call. When you invoke a method, both operations occur, but as distinct steps. This example illustrates the process of invoking `f.instance_method(arg)` on an instance of `Foo` in the preceding listing:

```
f = Foo()                       # Create an instance
meth = f.instance_method        # Lookup the method and notice the lack of ()
meth(37)                        # Now call the method
```

In this example, meth is known as a *bound method*. A bound method is a callable object that wraps both a function (the method) and an associated instance. When you call a bound method, the instance is passed to the method as the first parameter (self). Thus, meth in the example can be viewed as a method call that is primed and ready to go but which has not been invoked using the function call operator ().

Method lookup can also occur on the class itself. For example:

```
umeth = Foo.instance_method    # Lookup instance_method on Foo
umeth(f,37)                    # Call it, but explicitly supply self
```

In this example, umeth is known as an *unbound method*. An unbound method is a callable object that wraps the method function, but which expects an instance of the proper type to be passed as the first argument. In the example, we have passed f, an instance of Foo, as the first argument. If you pass the wrong kind of object, you get a TypeError. For example:

```
>>> umeth("hello",5)
Traceback (most recent call last):
  File "<stdin>", line 1, in <module>
TypeError: descriptor 'instance_method' requires a 'Foo' object but received a
'str'
>>>
```

For user-defined classes, bound and unbound methods are both represented as an object of type types.MethodType, which is nothing more than a thin wrapper around an ordinary function object. The following attributes are defined for method objects:

Attribute	Description
m.__doc__	Documentation string
m.__name__	Method name
m.__class__	Class in which this method was defined
m.__func__	Function object implementing the method
m.__self__	Instance associated with the method (None if unbound)

One subtle feature of Python 3 is that unbound methods are no longer wrapped by a types.MethodType object. If you access Foo.instance_method as shown in earlier examples, you simply obtain the raw function object that implements the method. Moreover, you'll find that there is no longer any type checking on the self parameter.

Built-in Functions and Methods

The object types.BuiltinFunctionType is used to represent functions and methods implemented in C and C++. The following attributes are available for built-in methods:

Attribute	Description
b.__doc__	Documentation string
b.__name__	Function/method name
b.__self__	Instance associated with the method (if bound)

For built-in functions such as len(), __self__ is set to None, indicating that the function isn't bound to any specific object. For built-in methods such as x.append, where x is a list object, __self__ is set to x.

Classes and Instances as Callables

Class objects and instances also operate as callable objects. A class object is created by the class statement and is called as a function in order to create new instances. In this case, the arguments to the function are passed to the __init__() method of the class in order to initialize the newly created instance. An instance can emulate a function if it defines a special method, __call__(). If this method is defined for an instance, x, then x(args) invokes the method x.__call__(args).

Classes, Types, and Instances

When you define a class, the class definition normally produces an object of type type. Here's an example:

```
>>> class Foo(object):
...     pass
...
>>> type(Foo)
<type 'type'>
```

The following table shows commonly used attributes of a type object t:

Attribute	Description
t.__doc__	Documentation string
t.__name__	Class name
t.__bases__	Tuple of base classes
t.__dict__	Dictionary holding class methods and variables
t.__module__	Module name in which the class is defined
t.__abstractmethods__	Set of abstract method names (may be undefined if there aren't any)

When an object instance is created, the type of the instance is the class that defined it. Here's an example:

```
>>> f = Foo()
>>> type(f)
<class '__main__.Foo'>
```

The following table shows special attributes of an instance i:

Attribute	Description
i.__class__	Class to which the instance belongs
i.__dict__	Dictionary holding instance data

The __dict__ attribute is normally where all of the data associated with an instance is stored. When you make assignments such as i.attr = value, the value is stored here. However, if a user-defined class uses __slots__, a more efficient internal representation is used and instances will not have a __dict__ attribute. More details on objects and the organization of the Python object system can be found in Chapter 7.

Modules

The *module* type is a container that holds objects loaded with the import statement. When the statement import foo appears in a program, for example, the name foo is assigned to the corresponding module object. Modules define a namespace that's implemented using a dictionary accessible in the attribute `__dict__`. Whenever an attribute of a module is referenced (using the dot operator), it's translated into a dictionary lookup. For example, $m.x$ is equivalent to `m.__dict__["x"]`. Likewise, assignment to an attribute such as $m.x = y$ is equivalent to `m.__dict__["x"] = y`. The following attributes are available:

Attribute	Description
`m.__dict__`	Dictionary associated with the module
`m.__doc__`	Module documentation string
`m.__name__`	Name of the module
`m.__file__`	File from which the module was loaded
`m.__path__`	Fully qualified package name, only defined when the module object refers to a package

Built-in Types for Interpreter Internals

A number of objects used by the internals of the interpreter are exposed to the user. These include traceback objects, code objects, frame objects, generator objects, slice objects, and the `Ellipsis` as shown in Table 3.10. It is relatively rare for programs to manipulate these objects directly, but they may be of practical use to tool-builders and framework designers.

Table 3.10   **Built-in Python Types for Interpreter Internals**

Type Name	Description
`types.CodeType`	Byte-compiled code
`types.FrameType`	Execution frame
`types.GeneratorType`	Generator object
`types.TracebackType`	Stack traceback of an exception
`slice`	Generated by extended slices
`Ellipsis`	Used in extended slices

Code Objects

Code objects represent raw byte-compiled executable code, or *bytecode*, and are typically returned by the built-in `compile()` function. Code objects are similar to functions except that they don't contain any context related to the namespace in which the code was defined, nor do code objects store information about default argument values. A code object, c, has the following read-only attributes:

Attribute	Description
`c.co_name`	Function name.
`c.co_argcount`	Number of positional arguments (including default values).
`c.co_nlocals`	Number of local variables used by the function.
`c.co_varnames`	Tuple containing names of local variables.

Attribute	Description
c.co_cellvars	Tuple containing names of variables referenced by nested functions.
c.co_freevars	Tuple containing names of free variables used by nested functions.
c.co_code	String representing raw bytecode.
c.co_consts	Tuple containing the literals used by the bytecode.
c.co_names	Tuple containing names used by the bytecode.
c.co_filename	Name of the file in which the code was compiled.
c.co_firstlineno	First line number of the function.
c.co_lnotab	String encoding bytecode offsets to line numbers.
c.co_stacksize	Required stack size (including local variables).
c.co_flags	Integer containing interpreter flags. Bit 2 is set if the function uses a variable number of positional arguments using "*args". Bit 3 is set if the function allows arbitrary keyword arguments using "**kwargs". All other bits are reserved.

Frame Objects

Frame objects are used to represent execution frames and most frequently occur in traceback objects (described next). A frame object, f, has the following read-only attributes:

Attribute	Description
f.f_back	Previous stack frame (toward the caller).
f.f_code	Code object being executed.
f.f_locals	Dictionary used for local variables.
f.f_globals	Dictionary used for global variables.
f.f_builtins	Dictionary used for built-in names.
f.f_lineno	Line number.
f.f_lasti	Current instruction. This is an index into the bytecode string of f_code.

The following attributes can be modified (and are used by debuggers and other tools):

Attribute	Description
f.f_trace	Function called at the start of each source code line
f.f_exc_type	Most recent exception type (Python 2 only)
f.f_exc_value	Most recent exception value (Python 2 only)
f.f_exc_traceback	Most recent exception traceback (Python 2 only)

Traceback Objects

Traceback objects are created when an exception occurs and contain stack trace information. When an exception handler is entered, the stack trace can be retrieved using the `sys.exc_info()` function. The following read-only attributes are available in traceback objects:

Attribute	Description
`t.tb_next`	Next level in the stack trace (toward the execution frame where the exception occurred)
`t.tb_frame`	Execution frame object of the current level
`t.tb_lineno`	Line number where the exception occurred
`t.tb_lasti`	Instruction being executed in the current level

Generator Objects

Generator objects are created when a generator function is invoked (see Chapter 6, "Functions and Functional Programming"). A generator function is defined whenever a function makes use of the special `yield` keyword. The generator object serves as both an iterator and a container for information about the generator function itself. The following attributes and methods are available:

Attribute	Description
`g.gi_code`	Code object for the generator function.
`g.gi_frame`	Execution frame of the generator function.
`g.gi_running`	Integer indicating whether or not the generator function is currently running.
`g.next()`	Execute the function until the next yield statement and return the value (this method is called `__next__` in Python 3).
`g.send(value)`	Sends a value to a generator. The passed value is returned by the `yield` expression in the generator that executes until the next `yield` expression is encountered. `send()` returns the value passed to `yield` in this expression.
`g.close()`	Closes a generator by raising a `GeneratorExit` exception in the generator function. This method executes automatically when a generator object is garbage-collected.
`g.throw(exc [,exc_value [,exc_tb ]])`	Raises an exception in a generator at the point of the current `yield` statement. `exc` is the exception type, `exc_value` is the exception value, and `exc_tb` is an optional traceback. If the resulting exception is caught and handled, returns the value passed to the next `yield` statement.

Slice Objects

Slice objects are used to represent slices given in extended slice syntax, such as `a[i:j:stride]`, `a[i:j, n:m]`, or `a[..., i:j]`. Slice objects are also created using the built-in `slice([i,] j [,stride])` function. The following read-only attributes are available:

Attribute	Description
s.start	Lower bound of the slice; None if omitted
s.stop	Upper bound of the slice; None if omitted
s.step	Stride of the slice; None if omitted

Slice objects also provide a single method, s.indices(length). This function takes a length and returns a tuple (start, stop, stride) that indicates how the slice would be applied to a sequence of that length. Here's an example:

```
s = slice(10,20)    # Slice object represents [10:20]
s.indices(100)      # Returns (10,20,1) -> [10:20]
s.indices(15)       # Returns (10,15,1) -> [10:15]
```

Ellipsis Object

The Ellipsis object is used to indicate the presence of an ellipsis (...) in an index lookup []. There is a single object of this type, accessed through the built-in name Ellipsis. It has no attributes and evaluates as True. None of Python's built-in types make use of Ellipsis, but it may be useful if you are trying to build advanced functionality into the indexing operator [] on your own objects. The following code shows how an Ellipsis gets created and passed into the indexing operator:

```
class Example(object):
    def __getitem__(self,index):
        print(index)
e = Example()
e[3, ..., 4]        # Calls e.__getitem__((3, Ellipsis, 4))
```

Object Behavior and Special Methods

Objects in Python are generally classified according to their behaviors and the features that they implement. For example, all of the sequence types such as strings, lists, and tuples are grouped together merely because they all happen to support a common set of sequence operations such as s[n], len(s), etc. All basic interpreter operations are implemented through special object methods. The names of special methods are always preceded and followed by double underscores (_). These methods are automatically triggered by the interpreter as a program executes. For example, the operation x + y is mapped to an internal method, x.__add__(y), and an indexing operation, x[k], is mapped to x.__getitem__(k). The behavior of each data type depends entirely on the set of special methods that it implements.

User-defined classes can define new objects that behave like the built-in types simply by supplying an appropriate subset of the special methods described in this section. In addition, built-in types such as lists and dictionaries can be specialized (via inheritance) by redefining some of the special methods.

The next few sections describe the special methods associated with different categories of interpreter features.

Object Creation and Destruction

The methods in Table 3.11 create, initialize, and destroy instances. __new__() is a class method that is called to create an instance. The __init__() method initializes the attributes of an object and is called immediately after an object has been newly created. The __del__() method is invoked when an object is about to be destroyed. This method is invoked only when an object is no longer in use. It's important to note that the statement del x only decrements an object's reference count and doesn't necessarily result in a call to this function. Further details about these methods can be found in Chapter 7.

Table 3.11   **Special Methods for Object Creation and Destruction**

Method	Description
__new__(cls [,*args [,**kwargs]])	A class method called to create a new instance
__init__(self [,*args [,**kwargs]])	Called to initialize a new instance
__del__(self)	Called when an instance is being destroyed

The __new__() and __init__() methods are used together to create and initialize new instances. When an object is created by calling A(args), it is translated into the following steps:

```
x = A.__new__(A,args)
if isinstance(x,A): x.__init__(args)
```

In user-defined objects, it is rare to define __new__() or __del__(). __new__() is usually only defined in metaclasses or in user-defined objects that happen to inherit from one of the immutable types (integers, strings, tuples, and so on). __del__() is only defined in situations in which there is some kind of critical resource management issue, such as releasing a lock or shutting down a connection.

Object String Representation

The methods in Table 3.12 are used to create various string representations of an object.

Table 3.12   **Special Methods for Object Representation**

Method	Description
__format__(self, format_spec)	Creates a formatted representation
__repr__(self)	Creates a string representation of an object
__str__(self)	Creates a simple string representation

The __repr__() and __str__() methods create simple string representations of an object. The __repr__() method normally returns an expression string that can be evaluated to re-create the object. This is also the method responsible for creating the output of values you see when inspecting variables in the interactive interpreter. This method is invoked by the built-in repr() function. Here's an example of using repr() and eval() together:

```
a = [2,3,4,5]      # Create a list
s = repr(a)        # s = '[2, 3, 4, 5]'
b = eval(s)        # Turns s back into a list
```

If a string expression cannot be created, the convention is for __repr__() to return a string of the form <...message...>, as shown here:

```
f = open("foo")
a = repr(f)          # a = "<open file 'foo', mode 'r' at dc030>"
```

The __str__() method is called by the built-in str() function and by functions related to printing. It differs from __repr__() in that the string it returns can be more concise and informative to the user. If this method is undefined, the __repr__() method is invoked.

The __format__() method is called by the format() function or the format() method of strings. The format_spec argument is a string containing the format specification. This string is the same as the format_spec argument to format(). For example:

```
format(x,"spec")         # Calls x.__format__("spec")
"x is {0:spec}".format(x)  # Calls x.__format__("spec")
```

The syntax of the format specification is arbitrary and can be customized on an object-by-object basis. However, a standard syntax is described in Chapter 4.

Object Comparison and Ordering

Table 3.13 shows methods that can be used to perform simple tests on an object. The __bool__() method is used for truth-value testing and should return True or False. If undefined, the __len__() method is a fallback that is invoked to determine truth. The __hash__() method is defined on objects that want to work as keys in a dictionary. The value returned is an integer that should be identical for two objects that compare as equal. Furthermore, mutable objects should not define this method; any changes to an object will alter the hash value and make it impossible to locate an object on subsequent dictionary lookups.

Table 3.13   Special Methods for Object Testing and Hashing

Method	Description
__bool__(self)	Returns False or True for truth-value testing
__hash__(self)	Computes an integer hash index

Objects can implement one or more of the relational operators (<, >, <=, >=, ==, !=). Each of these methods takes two arguments and is allowed to return any kind of object, including a Boolean value, a list, or any other Python type. For instance, a numerical package might use this to perform an element-wise comparison of two matrices, returning a matrix with the results. If a comparison can't be made, these functions may also raise an exception. Table 3.14 shows the special methods for comparison operators.

Table 3.14   Methods for Comparisons

Method	Result
__lt__(self,other)	self < other
__le__(self,other)	self <= other
__gt__(self,other)	self > other
__ge__(self,other)	self >= other

Table 3.14   **Continued**

Method	Result
`__eq__(self,other)`	`self == other`
`__ne__(self,other)`	`self != other`

It is not necessary for an object to implement all of the operations in Table 3.14. However, if you want to be able to compare objects using == or use an object as a dictionary key, the `__eq__()` method should be defined. If you want to be able to sort objects or use functions such as `min()` or `max()`, then `__lt__()` must be minimally defined.

Type Checking

The methods in Table 3.15 can be used to redefine the behavior of the type checking functions `isinstance()` and `issubclass()`. The most common application of these methods is in defining abstract base classes and interfaces, as described in Chapter 7.

Table 3.15   **Methods for Type Checking**

Method	Result
`__instancecheck__(cls,object)`	`isinstance(object, cls)`
`__subclasscheck__(cls, sub)`	`issubclass(sub, cls)`

Attribute Access

The methods in Table 3.16 read, write, and delete the attributes of an object using the dot (.) operator and the `del` operator, respectively.

Table 3.16   **Special Methods for Attribute Access**

Method	Description
`__getattribute__(self,name)`	Returns the attribute `self.name`.
`__getattr__(self, name)`	Returns the attribute `self.name` if not found through normal attribute lookup or raise `AttributeError`.
`__setattr__(self, name, value)`	Sets the attribute `self.name = value`. Overrides the default mechanism.
`__delattr__(self, name)`	Deletes the attribute `self.name`.

Whenever an attribute is accessed, the `__getattribute__()` method is always invoked. If the attribute is located, it is returned. Otherwise, the `__getattr__()` method is invoked. The default behavior of `__getattr__()` is to raise an `AttributeError` exception. The `__setattr__()` method is always invoked when setting an attribute, and the `__delattr__()` method is always invoked when deleting an attribute.

Attribute Wrapping and Descriptors

A subtle aspect of attribute manipulation is that sometimes the attributes of an object are wrapped with an extra layer of logic that interact with the get, set, and delete operations described in the previous section. This kind of wrapping is accomplished by creating a *descriptor* object that implements one or more of the methods in Table 3.17. Keep in mind that descriptors are optional and are rarely defined directly.

Table 3.17   **Special Methods for Descriptor Object**

Method	Description
__get__(self, instance, cls)	Returns the value of an attribute on `instance`. If `instance` is None, `self` should be returned.
__set__(self, instance, value)	Sets the attribute to `value`
__delete__(self, instance)	Deletes the attribute

The __get__(), __set__(), and __delete__() methods of a descriptor are meant to interact with the default implementation of __getattribute__(), __setattr__(), and __delattr__() methods on classes and types. This interaction occurs if you place an instance of a descriptor object in the body of a user-defined class. In this case, all access to the descriptor attribute will implicitly invoke the appropriate method on the descriptor object itself. Typically, descriptors are used to implement the low-level functionality of the object system including bound and unbound methods, class methods, static methods, and properties. Further examples appear in Chapter 7.

Sequence and Mapping Methods

The methods in Table 3.18 are used by objects that want to emulate sequence and mapping objects.

Table 3.18   **Methods for Sequences and Mappings**

Method	Description
__len__(self)	Returns the length of `self`
__getitem__(self, key)	Returns `self[key]`
__setitem__(self, key, value)	Sets `self[key] = value`
__delitem__(self, key)	Deletes `self[key]`
__contains__(self, obj)	Returns `True` if `obj` is in `self`; otherwise, returns `False`

Here's an example:

```
a = [1,2,3,4,5,6]
len(a)              # a.__len__()
x = a[2]            # x = a.__getitem__(2)
a[1] = 7            # a.__setitem__(1,7)
del a[2]            # a.__delitem__(2)
5 in a              # a.__contains__(5)
```

The __len__ method is called by the built-in len() function to return a nonnegative length. This function also determines truth values unless the __bool__() method has also been defined.

For manipulating individual items, the __getitem__() method can return an item by key value. The key can be any Python object but is typically an integer for sequences. The __setitem__() method assigns a value to an element. The __delitem__() method is invoked whenever the del operation is applied to a single element. The __contains__() method is used to implement the in operator.

The slicing operations such as x = s[i:j] are also implemented using __getitem__(), __setitem__(), and __delitem__(). However, for slices, a special slice object is passed as the key. This object has attributes that describe the range of the slice being requested. For example:

```
a = [1,2,3,4,5,6]
x = a[1:5]              # x = a.__getitem__(slice(1,5,None))
a[1:3] = [10,11,12]     # a.__setitem__(slice(1,3,None), [10,11,12])
del a[1:4]              # a.__delitem__(slice(1,4,None))
```

The slicing features of Python are actually more powerful than many programmers realize. For example, the following variations of extended slicing are all supported by Python's syntax and are sometimes used to manipulate multidimensional data structures, such as matrices and arrays in third-party extensions, such as NumPy:

```
a = m[0:100:10]            # Strided slice (stride=10)
b = m[1:10, 3:20]          # Multidimensional slice
c = m[0:100:10, 50:75:5]   # Multiple dimensions with strides
m[0:5, 5:10] = n           # extended slice assignment
del m[:10, 15:]            # extended slice deletion
```

The general format for each dimension of an extended slice is i:j[:stride], where stride is optional. As with ordinary slices, you can omit the starting or ending values for each part of a slice. In addition, the ellipsis (written as . . .) is available to denote any number of trailing or leading dimensions in an extended slice:

```
a = m[..., 10:20]     # extended slice access with Ellipsis
m[10:20, ...] = n
```

When using extended slices, the __getitem__(), __setitem__(), and __delitem__() methods implement access, modification, and deletion, respectively. However, instead of an integer, the value passed to these methods is a tuple containing a combination of slice or Ellipsis objects. For example,

```
a = m[0:10, 0:100:5, ...]
```

invokes __getitem__() as follows:

```
a = m.__getitem__((slice(0,10,None), slice(0,100,5), Ellipsis))
```

Python strings, tuples, and lists currently provide some support for extended slices, which is described in Chapter 4. Special-purpose extensions to Python, especially those with a scientific flavor, may provide new types and objects with advanced support for extended slicing operations.

Iteration

If an object, obj, supports iteration, it must provide a method, obj.__iter__(), that returns an iterator object. The iterator object iter, in turn, must implement a single method, iter.next() (or iter.__next__() in Python 3), that returns the next object or raises StopIteration to signal the end of iteration. Both of these methods are used by the implementation of the for statement as well as other operations that implicitly perform iteration. For example, the statement for x in s is carried out by performing steps equivalent to the following:

```
_iter = s.__iter__()
while 1:
    try:
        x = _iter.next() #_iter.__next__() in Python 3
    except StopIteration:
        break
    # Do statements in body of for loop
    ...
```

Mathematical Operations

Table 3.19 lists special methods that objects must implement to emulate numbers. Mathematical operations are always evaluated from left to right according the precedence rules described in Chapter 4; when an expression such as $x + y$ appears, the interpreter tries to invoke the method x.__add__(y). The special methods beginning with r support operations with reversed operands. These are invoked only if the left operand doesn't implement the specified operation. For example, if x in $x + y$ doesn't support the __add__() method, the interpreter tries to invoke the method y.__radd__(x).

Table 3.19   **Methods for Mathematical Operations**

Method	Result
__add__(self,other)	self + other
__sub__(self,other)	self - other
__mul__(self,other)	self * other
__div__(self,other)	self / other (Python 2 only)
__truediv__(self,other)	self / other (Python 3)
__floordiv__(self,other)	self // other
__mod__(self,other)	self % other
__divmod__(self,other)	divmod(self,other)
__pow__(self,other [,modulo])	self ** other, pow(self, other, modulo)
__lshift__(self,other)	self << other
__rshift__(self,other)	self >> other
__and__(self,other)	self & other
__or__(self,other)	self | other
__xor__(self,other)	self ^ other
__radd__(self,other)	other + self
__rsub__(self,other)	other - self
__rmul__(self,other)	other * self
__rdiv__(self,other)	other / self (Python 2 only)
__rtruediv__(self,other)	other / self (Python 3)
__rfloordiv__(self,other)	other // self
__rmod__(self,other)	other % self
__rdivmod__(self,other)	divmod(other,self)

Table 3.19   **Continued**

Method	Result
__rpow__(*self*,*other*)	*other* ** *self*
__rlshift__(*self*,*other*)	*other* << *self*
__rrshift__(*self*,*other*)	*other* >> *self*
__rand__(*self*,*other*)	*other* & *self*
__ror__(*self*,*other*)	*other* | *self*
__rxor__(*self*,*other*)	*other* ^ *self*
__iadd__(*self*,*other*)	*self* += *other*
__isub__(*self*,*other*)	*self* -= *other*
__imul__(*self*,*other*)	*self* *= *other*
__idiv__(*self*,*other*)	*self* /= *other* (Python 2 only)
__itruediv__(*self*,*other*)	*self* /= *other* (Python 3)
__ifloordiv__(*self*,*other*)	*self* //= *other*
__imod__(*self*,*other*)	*self* %= *other*
__ipow__(*self*,*other*)	*self* **= *other*
__iand__(*self*,*other*)	*self* &= *other*
__ior__(*self*,*other*)	*self* |= *other*
__ixor__(*self*,*other*)	*self* ^= *other*
__ilshift__(*self*,*other*)	*self* <<= *other*
__irshift__(*self*,*other*)	*self* >>= *other*
__neg__(*self*)	-*self*
__pos__(*self*)	+*self*
__abs__(*self*)	abs(*self*)
__invert__(*self*)	~*self*
__int__(*self*)	int(*self*)
__long__(*self*)	long(*self*) (Python 2 only)
__float__(*self*)	float(*self*)
__complex__(*self*)	complex(*self*)

The methods __iadd__(), __isub__(), and so forth are used to support in-place arithmetic operators such as a+=b and a-=b (also known as *augmented assignment*). A distinction is made between these operators and the standard arithmetic methods because the implementation of the in-place operators might be able to provide certain customizations such as performance optimizations. For instance, if the *self* parameter is not shared, the value of an object could be modified in place without having to allocate a newly created object for the result.

The three flavors of division operators—__div__(), __truediv__(), and __floordiv__()—are used to implement true division (/) and truncating division (//) operations. The reasons why there are three operations deal with a change in the semantics of integer division that started in Python 2.2 but became the default behavior in Python 3. In Python 2, the default behavior of Python is to map the / operator to __div__(). For integers, this operation truncates the result to an integer. In Python 3, division is mapped to __truediv__() and for integers, a float is returned. This latter

behavior can be enabled in Python 2 as an optional feature by including the statement
`from __future__ import division` in a program.

The conversion methods `__int__()`, `__long__()`, `__float__()`, and
`__complex__()` convert an object into one of the four built-in numerical types. These
methods are invoked by explicit type conversions such as `int()` and `float()`.
However, these methods are not used to implicitly coerce types in mathematical operations. For example, the expression `3 + x` produces a `TypeError` even if `x` is a user-
defined object that defines `__int__()` for integer conversion.

Callable Interface

An object can emulate a function by providing the `__call__(self [,*args [,`
`**kwargs]])` method. If an object, `x`, provides this method, it can be invoked like a
function. That is, `x(arg1, arg2, ...)` invokes `x.__call__(self, arg1, arg2,`
`...)`. Objects that emulate functions can be useful for creating functors or proxies.
Here is a simple example:

```
class DistanceFrom(object):
    def __init__(self,origin):
        self.origin = origin
    def __call__(self, x):
        return abs(x - self.origin)

nums = [1, 37, 42, 101, 13, 9, -20]
nums.sort(key=DistanceFrom(10))          # Sort by distance from 10
```

In this example, the `DistanceFrom` class creates instances that emulate a single-
argument function. These can be used in place of a normal function—for instance, in
the call to `sort()` in the example.

Context Management Protocol

The `with` statement allows a sequence of statements to execute under the control of
another object known as a *context manager*. The general syntax is as follows:

```
with context [ as var]:
    statements
```

The *context* object shown here is expected to implement the methods shown in Table
3.20. The `__enter__()` method is invoked when the `with` statement executes. The
value returned by this method is placed into the variable specified with the optional as
var specifier. The `__exit__()` method is called as soon as control-flow leaves from the
block of statements associated with the `with` statement. As arguments, `__exit__()`
receives the current exception type, value, and traceback if an exception has been raised.
If no errors are being handled, all three values are set to `None`.

Table 3.20   **Special Methods for Context Managers**

Method	Description
`__enter__(self)`	Called when entering a new context. The return value is placed in the variable listed with the as specifier to the with state-ment.

Table 3.20   **Continued**

Method	Description
`__exit__(self, type, value, tb)`	Called when leaving a context. If an exception occurred, `type`, `value`, and `tb` have the exception type, value, and traceback information. The primary use of the context management interface is to allow for simplified resource control on objects involving system state such as open files, network connections, and locks. By implementing this interface, an object can safely clean up resources when execution leaves a context in which an object is being used. Further details are found in Chapter 5, "Program Structure and Control Flow."

Object Inspection and `dir()`

The `dir()` function is commonly used to inspect objects. An object can supply the list of names returned by `dir()` by implementing `__dir__(self)`. Defining this makes it easier to hide the internal details of objects that you don't want a user to directly access. However, keep in mind that a user can still inspect the underlying `__dict__` attribute of instances and classes to see everything that is defined.

4

Operators and Expressions

This chapter describes Python's built-in operators, expressions, and evaluation rules. Although much of this chapter describes Python's built-in types, user-defined objects can easily redefine any of the operators to provide their own behavior.

Operations on Numbers

The following operations can be applied to all numeric types:

Operation	Description
x + y	Addition
x - y	Subtraction
x * y	Multiplication
x / y	Division
x // y	Truncating division
x ** y	Power (x^y)
x % y	Modulo (x mod y)
-x	Unary minus
+x	Unary plus

The truncating division operator (//, also known as *floor division*) truncates the result to an integer and works with both integers and floating-point numbers. In Python 2, the true division operator (/) also truncates the result to an integer if the operands are integers. Therefore, 7/4 is 1, not 1.75. However, this behavior changes in Python 3, where division produces a floating-point result. The modulo operator returns the remainder of the division x // y. For example, 7 % 4 is 3. For floating-point numbers, the modulo operator returns the floating-point remainder of x // y, which is x - (x // y) * y. For complex numbers, the modulo (%) and truncating division operators (//) are invalid.

The following shifting and bitwise logical operators can be applied only to integers:

Operation	Description
x << y	Left shift
x >> y	Right shift
x & y	Bitwise and
x | y	Bitwise or
x ^ y	Bitwise xor (exclusive or)
~x	Bitwise negation

The bitwise operators assume that integers are represented in a 2's complement binary representation and that the sign bit is infinitely extended to the left. Some care is required if you are working with raw bit-patterns that are intended to map to native integers on the hardware. This is because Python does not truncate the bits or allow values to overflow—instead, the result will grow arbitrarily large in magnitude.

In addition, you can apply the following built-in functions to all the numerical types:

Function	Description
abs(x)	Absolute value
divmod(x,y)	Returns (x // y, x % y)
pow(x,y [,modulo])	Returns (x ** y) % modulo
round(x, [n])	Rounds to the nearest multiple of 10^{-n} (floating-point numbers only)

The abs() function returns the absolute value of a number. The divmod() function returns the quotient and remainder of a division operation and is only valid on non-complex numbers. The pow() function can be used in place of the ** operator but also supports the ternary power-modulo function (often used in cryptographic algorithms). The round() function rounds a floating-point number, x, to the nearest multiple of 10 to the power minus n. If n is omitted, it's set to 0. If x is equally close to two multiples, Python 2 rounds to the nearest multiple away from zero (for example, 0.5 is rounded to 1.0 and -0.5 is rounded to -1.0). One caution here is that Python 3 rounds equally close values to the nearest even multiple (for example, 0.5 is rounded to 0.0, and 1.5 is rounded to 2.0). This is a subtle portability issue for mathematical programs being ported to Python 3.

The following comparison operators have the standard mathematical interpretation and return a Boolean value of True for true, False for false:

Operation	Description
x < y	Less than
x > y	Greater than
x == y	Equal to
x != y	Not equal to
x >= y	Greater than or equal to
x <= y	Less than or equal to

Comparisons can be chained together, such as in w < x < y < z. Such expressions are evaluated as w < x and x < y and y < z. Expressions such as x < y > z are legal but are likely to confuse anyone reading the code (it's important to note that no comparison is made between x and z in such an expression). Comparisons involving complex numbers are undefined and result in a TypeError.

Operations involving numbers are valid only if the operands are of the same type. For built-in numbers, a coercion operation is performed to convert one of the types to the other, as follows:

1. If either operand is a complex number, the other operand is converted to a complex number.

2. If either operand is a floating-point number, the other is converted to a float.

3. Otherwise, both numbers must be integers and no conversion is performed.

For user-defined objects, the behavior of expressions involving mixed operands depends on the implementation of the object. As a general rule, the interpreter does not try to perform any kind of implicit type conversion.

Operations on Sequences

The following operators can be applied to sequence types, including strings, lists, and tuples:

Operation	Description
s + r	Concatenation
s * n, n * s	Makes n copies of s, where n is an integer
v1, v2,…, vn = s	Variable unpacking
s[i]	Indexing
s[i:j]	Slicing
s[i:j:stride]	Extended slicing
x in s, x not in s	Membership
for x in s:	Iteration
all(s)	Returns True if all items in s are true.
any(s)	Returns True if any item in s is true.
len(s)	Length
min(s)	Minimum item in s
max(s)	Maximum item in s
sum(s [, initial])	Sum of items with an optional initial value

The + operator concatenates two sequences of the same type. The s * n operator makes n copies of a sequence. However, these are shallow copies that replicate elements by reference only. For example, consider the following code:

```
>>> a = [3,4,5]
>>> b = [a]
>>> c = 4*b
>>> c
[[3, 4, 5], [3, 4, 5], [3, 4, 5], [3, 4, 5]]
>>> a[0] = -7
>>> c
[[-7, 4, 5], [-7, 4, 5], [-7, 4, 5], [-7, 4, 5]]
>>>
```

Notice how the change to a modified every element of the list c. In this case, a reference to the list a was placed in the list b. When b was replicated, four additional references to a were created. Finally, when a was modified, this change was propagated to all the other "copies" of a. This behavior of sequence multiplication is often unexpected and not the intent of the programmer. One way to work around the problem is to manually construct the replicated sequence by duplicating the contents of a. Here's an example:

```
a = [ 3, 4, 5 ]
c = [list(a) for j in range(4)]   # list() makes a copy of a list
```

The copy module in the standard library can also be used to make copies of objects.

All sequences can be unpacked into a sequence of variable names. For example:

```
items = [ 3, 4, 5 ]
x,y,z = items          # x = 3, y = 4, z = 5

letters = "abc"
x,y,z = letters        # x = 'a', y = 'b', z = 'c'

datetime = ((5, 19, 2008), (10, 30, "am"))
(month,day,year),(hour,minute,am_pm) = datetime
```

When unpacking values into variables, the number of variables must exactly match the number of items in the sequence. In addition, the structure of the variables must match that of the sequence. For example, the last line of the example unpacks values into six variables, organized into two 3-tuples, which is the structure of the sequence on the right. Unpacking sequences into variables works with any kind of sequence, including those created by iterators and generators.

The indexing operator $s[n]$ returns the nth object from a sequence in which $s[0]$ is the first object. Negative indices can be used to fetch characters from the end of a sequence. For example, $s[-1]$ returns the last item. Otherwise, attempts to access elements that are out of range result in an IndexError exception.

The slicing operator $s[i:j]$ extracts a subsequence from s consisting of the elements with index k, where i <= k < j. Both i and j must be integers or long integers. If the starting or ending index is omitted, the beginning or end of the sequence is assumed, respectively. Negative indices are allowed and assumed to be relative to the end of the sequence. If i or j is out of range, they're assumed to refer to the beginning or end of a sequence, depending on whether their value refers to an element before the first item or after the last item, respectively.

The slicing operator may be given an optional stride, $s[i:j:stride]$, that causes the slice to skip elements. However, the behavior is somewhat more subtle. If a stride is supplied, i is the starting index; j is the ending index; and the produced subsequence is the elements $s[i]$, $s[i+stride]$, $s[i+2*stride]$, and so forth until index j is reached (which is not included). The stride may also be negative. If the starting index i is omitted, it is set to the beginning of the sequence if stride is positive or the end of the sequence if stride is negative. If the ending index j is omitted, it is set to the end of the sequence if stride is positive or the beginning of the sequence if stride is negative. Here are some examples:

```
a = [0, 1, 2, 3, 4, 5, 6, 7, 8, 9]

b = a[::2]        # b = [0, 2, 4, 6, 8 ]
c = a[::-2]       # c = [9, 7, 5, 3, 1 ]
d = a[0:5:2]      # d = [0,2,4]
e = a[5:0:-2]     # e = [5,3,1]
f = a[:5:1]       # f = [0,1,2,3,4]
g = a[:5:-1]      # g = [9,8,7,6]
h = a[5::1]       # h = [5,6,7,8,9]
i = a[5::-1]      # i = [5,4,3,2,1,0]
j = a[5:0:-1]     # j = [5,4,3,2,1]
```

The x in s operator tests to see whether the object x is in the sequence s and returns True or False. Similarly, the x not in s operator tests whether x is not in the sequence s. For strings, the in and not in operators accept subtrings. For example,

'hello' in 'hello world' produces True. It is important to note that the in operator does not support wildcards or any kind of pattern matching. For this, you need to
use a library module such as the re module for regular expression patterns.

The for x in s operator iterates over all the elements of a sequence and is
described further in Chapter 5, "Program Structure and Control Flow." len(s) returns
the number of elements in a sequence. min(s) and max(s) return the minimum and
maximum values of a sequence, respectively, although the result may only make sense if
the elements can be ordered with respect to the < operator (for example, it would make
little sense to find the maximum value of a list of file objects). sum(s) sums all of the
items in s but usually works only if the items represent numbers. An optional initial
value can be given to sum(). The type of this value usually determines the result. For
example, if you used sum(items, decimal.Decimal(0)), the result would be a
Decimal object (see more about the decimal module in Chapter 14, "Mathematics").

Strings and tuples are immutable and cannot be modified after creation. Lists can be
modified with the following operators:

Operation	Description
s[i] = x	Index assignment
s[i:j] = r	Slice assignment
s[i:j:stride] = r	Extended slice assignment
del s[i]	Deletes an element
del s[i:j]	Deletes a slice
del s[i:j:stride]	Deletes an extended slice

The s[i] = x operator changes element i of a list to refer to object x, increasing the
reference count of x. Negative indices are relative to the end of the list, and attempts to
assign a value to an out-of-range index result in an IndexError exception. The slicing
assignment operator s[i:j] = r replaces element k, where i <= k < j, with elements from sequence r. Indices may have the same values as for slicing and are adjusted
to the beginning or end of the list if they're out of range. If necessary, the sequence s is
expanded or reduced to accommodate all the elements in r. Here's an example:

```
a = [1,2,3,4,5]
a[1] = 6          # a = [1,6,3,4,5]
a[2:4] = [10,11]  # a = [1,6,10,11,5]
a[3:4] = [-1,-2,-3] # a = [1,6,10,-1,-2,-3,5]
a[:] = [7,8]      # a = [7,8]. id(a) remains the same
```

Slicing assignment may be supplied with an optional stride argument. However, the
behavior is somewhat more restricted in that the argument on the right side must have
exactly the same number of elements as the slice that's being replaced. Here's an
example:

```
a = [1,2,3,4,5]
a[1::2] = [10,11]   # a = [1,10,3,11,5]
a[1::2] = [30,40,50]  # ValueError. Only two elements in slice on left
```

The del s[i] operator removes element i from a list and decrements its reference
count. del s[i:j] removes all the elements in a slice. A stride may also be supplied, as
in del s[i:j:stride].

Sequences are compared using the operators <, >, <=, >=, ==, and !=. When comparing two sequences, the first elements of each sequence are compared. If they differ, this determines the result. If they're the same, the comparison moves to the second element of each sequence. This process continues until two different elements are found or no more elements exist in either of the sequences. If the end of both sequences is reached, the sequences are considered equal. If a is a subsequence of b, then a < b.

Strings are compared using lexicographical ordering. Each character is assigned a unique numerical index determined by the character set (such as ASCII or Unicode). A character is less than another character if its index is less. One caution concerning character ordering is that the preceding simple comparison operators are not related to the character ordering rules associated with locale or language settings. Thus, you would not use these operations to order strings according to the standard conventions of a foreign language (see the unicodedata and locale modules for more information).

Another caution, this time involving strings. Python has two types of string data: byte strings and Unicode strings. Byte strings differ from their Unicode counterpart in that they are usually assumed to be encoded, whereas Unicode strings represent raw unencoded character values. Because of this, you should never mix byte strings and Unicode together in expressions or comparisons (such as using + to concatenate a byte string and Unicode string or using == to compare mixed strings). In Python 3, mixing string types results in a TypeError exception, but Python 2 attempts to perform an implicit promotion of byte strings to Unicode. This aspect of Python 2 is widely considered to be a design mistake and is often a source of unanticipated exceptions and inexplicable program behavior. So, to keep your head from exploding, don't mix string types in sequence operations.

String Formatting

The modulo operator (s % d) produces a formatted string, given a format string, s, and a collection of objects in a tuple or mapping object (dictionary) d. The behavior of this operator is similar to the C sprintf() function. The format string contains two types of objects: ordinary characters (which are left unmodified) and conversion specifiers, each of which is replaced with a formatted string representing an element of the associated tuple or mapping. If d is a tuple, the number of conversion specifiers must exactly match the number of objects in d. If d is a mapping, each conversion specifier must be associated with a valid key name in the mapping (using parentheses, as described shortly). Each conversion specifier starts with the % character and ends with one of the conversion characters shown in Table 4.1.

Table 4.1   **String Formatting Conversions**

Character	Output Format
d, i	Decimal integer or long integer.
u	Unsigned integer or long integer.
o	Octal integer or long integer.
x	Hexadecimal integer or long integer.
X	Hexadecimal integer (uppercase letters).
f	Floating point as [-] m.dddddd.
e	Floating point as [-] m.dddddde±xx.

Table 4.1   **Continued**

Character	Output Format
E	Floating point as $[-]m.ddddddE{\pm}xx$.
g,G	Use %e or %E for exponents less than −4 or greater than the precision; otherwise, use %f.
s	String or any object. The formatting code uses str() to generate strings.
r	Produces the same string as produced by repr().
c	Single character.
%	Literal %.

Between the % character and the conversion character, the following modifiers may appear, in this order:

1. A key name in parentheses, which selects a specific item out of the mapping object. If no such element exists, a KeyError exception is raised.
2. One or more of the following:
   - − sign, indicating left alignment. By default, values are right-aligned.
   - + sign, indicating that the numeric sign should be included (even if positive).
   - 0, indicating a zero fill.
3. A number specifying the minimum field width. The converted value will be printed in a field at least this wide and padded on the left (or right if the − flag is given) to make up the field width.
4. A period separating the field width from a precision.
5. A number specifying the maximum number of characters to be printed from a string, the number of digits following the decimal point in a floating-point number, or the minimum number of digits for an integer.

In addition, the asterisk (*) character may be used in place of a number in any width field. If present, the width will be read from the next item in the tuple.

The following code illustrates a few examples:

```
a = 42
b = 13.142783
c = "hello"
d = {'x':13, 'y':1.54321, 'z':'world'}
e = 5628398123741234

r = "a is %d" % a            # r = "a is 42"
r = "%10d %f" % (a,b)        # r = "        42 13.142783"
r = "%+010d %E" % (a,b)      # r = "+000000042 1.314278E+01"
r = "%(x)-10d %(y)0.3g" % d  # r = "13          1.54"
r = "%0.4s %s" % (c, d['z']) # r = "hell world"
r = "%*.*f" % (5,3,b)        # r = "13.143"
r = "e = %d" % e             # r = "e = 5628398123741234"
```

When used with a dictionary, the string formatting operator % is often used to mimic the string interpolation feature often found in scripting languages (e.g., expansion of

$var symbols in strings). For example, if you have a dictionary of values, you can expand those values into fields within a formatted string as follows:

```
stock = {
    'name' : 'GOOG',
    'shares' : 100,
    'price' : 490.10 }

r = "%(shares)d of %(name)s at %(price)0.2f" % stock
# r = "100 shares of GOOG at 490.10"
```

The following code shows how to expand the values of currently defined variables within a string. The vars() function returns a dictionary containing all of the variables defined at the point at which vars() is called.

```
name = "Elwood"
age  = 41
r = "%(name)s is %(age)d years old" % vars()
```

Advanced String Formatting

A more advanced form of string formatting is available using the s.format(*args, **kwargs) method on strings. This method collects an arbitrary collection of positional and keyword arguments and substitutes their values into placeholders embedded in s. A placeholder of the form '{n}', where n is a number, gets replaced by positional argument n supplied to format(). A placeholder of the form '{name}' gets replaced by keyword argument name supplied to format. Use '{{' to output a single '{' and '}}' to output a single '}'. For example:

```
r = "{0} {1} {2}".format('GOOG',100,490.10)
r = "{name} {shares} {price}".format(name='GOOG',shares=100,price=490.10)
r = "Hello {0}, your age is {age}".format("Elwood",age=47)
r = "Use {{ and }} to output single curly braces".format()
```

With each placeholder, you can additionally perform both indexing and attribute lookups. For example, in '{name[n]}' where n is an integer, a sequence lookup is performed and in '{name[key]}' where key is a non-numeric string, a dictionary lookup of the form name['key'] is performed. In '{name.attr}', an attribute lookup is performed. Here are some examples:

```
stock = { 'name' : 'GOOG',
    'shares' : 100,
    'price' : 490.10 }
r = "{0[name]} {0[shares]} {0[price]}".format(stock)

x = 3 + 4j
r = "{0.real} {0.imag}".format(x)
```

In these expansions, you are only allowed to use names. Arbitrary expressions, method calls, and other operations are not supported.

You can optionally specify a format specifier that gives more precise control over the output. This is supplied by adding an optional format specifier to each placeholder using a colon (:), as in '{place:format_spec}'. By using this specifier, you can specify column widths, decimal places, and alignment. Here is an example:

```
r = "{name:8} {shares:8d} {price:8.2f}".format
(name="GOOG",shares=100,price=490.10)
```

The general format of a specifier is `[[fill[align]] [sign] [0] [width]`
`[.precision] [type]` where each part enclosed in `[]` is optional. The `width` specifier
specifies the minimum field width to use, and the `align` specifier is one of `'<'`, `'>'`, or
`'^'` for left, right, and centered alignment within the field. An optional fill character
`fill` is used to pad the space. For example:

```
name = "Elwood"
r = "{0:<10}".format(name)      # r = 'Elwood    '
r = "{0:>10}".format(name)      # r = '    Elwood'
r = "{0:^10}".format(name)      # r = '  Elwood  '
r = "{0:=^10}".format(name)     # r = '==Elwood=='
```

The `type` specifier indicates the type of data. Table 4.2 lists the supported format codes.
If not supplied, the default format code is `'s'` for strings, `'d'` for integers, and `'f'` for
floats.

Table 4.2 **Advanced String Formatting Type Specifier Codes**

Character	Output Format
d	Decimal integer or long integer.
b	Binary integer or long integer.
o	Octal integer or long integer.
x	Hexadecimal integer or long integer.
X	Hexadecimal integer (uppercase letters).
f, F	Floating point as $[-]m.dddddd$.
e	Floating point as $[-]m.dddddde\pm xx$.
E	Floating point as $[-]m.ddddddE\pm xx$.
g, G	Use e or E for exponents less than −4 or greater than the precision; otherwise, use f.
n	Same as g except that the current locale setting determines the decimal point character.
%	Multiplies a number by 100 and displays it using f format followed by a % sign.
s	String or any object. The formatting code uses str() to generate strings.
c	Single character.

The `sign` part of a format specifier is one of `'+'`, `'-'`, or `' '`. A `'+'` indicates that a
leading sign should be used on all numbers. `'-'` is the default and only adds a sign
character for negative numbers. A `' '` adds a leading space to positive numbers. The
`precision` part of the specifier supplies the number of digits of accuracy to use for
decimals. If a leading `'0'` is added to the field width for numbers, numeric values are
padded with leading 0s to fill the space. Here are some examples of formatting different
kinds of numbers:

```
x = 42
r = '{0:10d}'.format(x)      # r = '        42'
r = '{0:10x}'.format(x)      # r = '        2a'
r = '{0:10b}'.format(x)      # r = '    101010'
r = '{0:010b}'.format(x)     # r = '0000101010'

y = 3.1415926
r = '{0:10.2f}'.format(y)    # r = '      3.14'
```

```
r = '{0:10.2e}'.format(y)        # r = '   3.14e+00'
r = '{0:+10.2f}'.format(y)       # r = '     +3.14'
r = '{0:+010.2f}'.format(y)      # r = '+000003.14'
r = '{0:+10.2%}'.format(y)       # r = '   +314.16%'
```

Parts of a format specifier can optionally be supplied by other fields supplied to the format function. They are accessed using the same syntax as normal fields in a format string. For example:

```
y = 3.1415926
r = '{0:{width}.{precision}f}'.format(y,width=10,precision=3)
r = '{0:{1}.{2}f}'.format(y,10,3)
```

This nesting of fields can only be one level deep and can only occur in the format specifier portion. In addition, the nested values cannot have any additional format specifiers of their own.

One caution on format specifiers is that objects can define their own custom set of specifiers. Underneath the covers, advanced string formatting invokes the special method __format__(self, format_spec) on each field value. Thus, the capabilities of the format() operation are open-ended and depend on the objects to which it is applied. For example, dates, times, and other kinds of objects may define their own format codes.

In certain cases, you may want to simply format the str() or repr() representation of an object, bypassing the functionality implemented by its __format__() method. To do this, you can add the '!s' or '!r' modifier before the format specifier. For example:

```
name = "Guido"
r = '{0!r:^20}'.format(name)     # r = "       'Guido'       "
```

Operations on Dictionaries

Dictionaries provide a mapping between names and objects. You can apply the following operations to dictionaries:

Operation	Description
x = d[k]	Indexing by key
d[k] = x	Assignment by key
del d[k]	Deletes an item by key
k in d	Tests for the existence of a key
len(d)	Number of items in the dictionary

Key values can be any immutable object, such as strings, numbers, and tuples. In addition, dictionary keys can be specified as a comma-separated list of values, like this:

```
d = { }
d[1,2,3] = "foo"
d[1,0,3] = "bar"
```

In this case, the key values represent a tuple, making the preceding assignments identical to the following:

```
d[(1,2,3)] = "foo"
d[(1,0,3)] = "bar"
```

Operations on Sets

The set and frozenset type support a number of common set operations:

Operation	Description
s | t	Union of s and t
s & t	Intersection of s and t
s - t	Set difference
s ^ t	Symmetric difference
len(s)	Number of items in the set
max(s)	Maximum value
min(s)	Minimum value

The result of union, intersection, and difference operations will have the same type as the left-most operand. For example, if s is a frozenset, the result will be a frozenset even if t is a set.

Augmented Assignment

Python provides the following set of augmented assignment operators:

Operation	Description
x += y	x = x + y
x -= y	x = x - y
x *= y	x = x * y
x /= y	x = x / y
x //= y	x = x // y
x **= y	x = x ** y
x %= y	x = x % y
x &= y	x = x & y
x |= y	x = x | y
x ^= y	x = x ^ y
x >>= y	x = x >> y
x <<= y	x = x << y

These operators can be used anywhere that ordinary assignment is used. Here's an example:

```
a = 3
b = [1,2]
c = "Hello %s %s"
a += 1                      # a = 4
b[1] += 10                  # b = [1, 12]
c %= ("Monty", "Python")    # c = "Hello Monty Python"
```

Augmented assignment may or may not perform in-place modification of an object depending on its implementation. Therefore, writing x += y might modify x in-place or create an entirely new object with the value x + y. User-defined classes can redefine the augmented assignment operators using the special methods described in Chapter 3, "Types and Objects."

The Attribute (.) Operator

The dot (.) operator is used to access the attributes of an object. Here's an example:

```
foo.x = 3
print foo.y
a = foo.bar(3,4,5)
```

More than one dot operator can appear in a single expression, such as in `foo.y.a.b`. The dot operator can also be applied to the intermediate results of functions, as in `a = foo.bar(3,4,5).spam`.

User-defined classes can redefine or customize the behavior of (.). More details are found in Chapter 3 and Chapter 7, "Classes and Object-Oriented Programming."

The Function Call () Operator

The `f(args)` operator is used to make a function call on `f`. Each argument to a function is an expression. Prior to calling the function, all of the argument expressions are fully evaluated from left to right. This is sometimes known as *applicative order evaluation*.

It is possible to partially evaluate function arguments using the `partial()` function in the `functools` module. For example:

```
def foo(x,y,z):
    return x + y + z

from functools import partial
f = partial(foo,1,2)   # Supply values to x and y arguments of foo
result = f(3)          # Calls foo(1,2,3), result is 6
```

The `partial()` function evaluates some of the arguments to a function and returns an object that you can call to supply the remaining arguments at a later point. In the previous example, the variable `f` represents a partially evaluated function where the first two arguments have already been calculated. You merely need to supply the last remaining argument value for the function to execute. Partial evaluation of function arguments is closely related to a process known as *currying*, a mechanism by which a function taking multiple arguments such as `f(x,y)` is decomposed into a series of functions each taking only one argument (for example, you partially evaluate `f` by fixing `x` to get a new function to which you give values of `y` to produce a result).

Conversion Functions

Sometimes it's necessary to perform conversions between the built-in types. To convert between types, you simply use the type name as a function. In addition, several built-in functions are supplied to perform special kinds of conversions. All of these functions return a new object representing the converted value.

Function	Description
int(x [,base])	Converts x to an integer. base specifies the base if x is a string.
float(x)	Converts x to a floating-point number.
complex(real [,imag])	Creates a complex number.
str(x)	Converts object x to a string representation.

Function	Description
repr(x)	Converts object x to an expression string.
format(x [,format_spec])	Converts object x to a formatted string.
eval(str)	Evaluates a string and returns an object.
tuple(s)	Converts s to a tuple.
list(s)	Converts s to a list.
set(s)	Converts s to a set.
dict(d)	Creates a dictionary. d must be a sequence of (key,value) tuples.
frozenset(s)	Converts s to a frozen set.
chr(x)	Converts an integer to a character.
unichr(x)	Converts an integer to a Unicode character (Python 2 only).
ord(x)	Converts a single character to its integer value.
hex(x)	Converts an integer to a hexadecimal string.
bin(x)	Converts an integer to a binary string.
oct(x)	Converts an integer to an octal string.

Note that the str() and repr() functions may return different results. repr() typically creates an expression string that can be evaluated with eval() to re-create the object. On the other hand, str() produces a concise or nicely formatted representation of the object (and is used by the print statement). The format(x, [format_spec]) function produces the same output as that produced by the advanced string formatting operations but applied to a single object x. As input, it accepts an optional format_spec, which is a string containing the formatting code. The ord() function returns the integer ordinal value of a character. For Unicode, this value will be the integer code point. The chr() and unichr() functions convert integers back into characters.

To convert strings back into numbers, use the int(), float(), and complex() functions. The eval() function can also convert a string containing a valid expression to an object. Here's an example:

```
a = int("34")          # a = 34
b = long("0xfe76214", 16)  # b = 266822164L (0xfe76214L)
b = float("3.1415926")  # b = 3.1415926
c = eval("3, 5, 6")    # c = (3,5,6)
```

In functions that create containers (list(), tuple(), set(), and so on), the argument may be any object that supports iteration used to generate all the items used to populate the object that's being created.

Boolean Expressions and Truth Values

The and, or, and not keywords can form Boolean expressions. The behavior of these operators is as follows:

Operator	Description
x or y	If x is false, return y; otherwise, return x.
x and y	If x is false, return x; otherwise, return y.
not x	If x is false, return 1; otherwise, return 0.

When you use an expression to determine a true or false value, True, any nonzero number, nonempty string, list, tuple, or dictionary is taken to be true. False; zero; None; and empty lists, tuples, and dictionaries evaluate as false. Boolean expressions are evaluated from left to right and consume the right operand only if it's needed to determine the final value. For example, a and b evaluates b only if a is true. This is sometimes known as *"short-circuit" evaluation.*

Object Equality and Identity

The equality operator (x == y) tests the values of x and y for equality. In the case of lists and tuples, all the elements are compared and evaluated as true if they're of equal value. For dictionaries, a true value is returned only if x and y have the same set of keys and all the objects with the same key have equal values. Two sets are equal if they have the same elements, which are compared using equality (==).

The identity operators (x is y and x is not y) test two objects to see whether they refer to the same object in memory. In general, it may be the case that x == y, but x is not y.

Comparison between objects of noncompatible types, such as a file and a floating-point number, may be allowed, but the outcome is arbitrary and may not make any sense. It may also result in an exception depending on the type.

Order of Evaluation

Table 4.3 lists the order of operation (precedence rules) for Python operators. All operators except the power (**) operator are evaluated from left to right and are listed in the table from highest to lowest precedence. That is, operators listed first in the table are evaluated before operators listed later. (Note that operators included together within subsections, such as x * y, x / y, x / y, and x % y, have equal precedence.)

Table 4.3   **Order of Evaluation (Highest to Lowest)**

Operator	Name
(...), [...], {...}	Tuple, list, and dictionary creation
s[i], s[i:j]	Indexing and slicing
s.attr	Attributes
f(...)	Function calls
+x, -x, ~x	Unary operators
x ** y	Power (right associative)
x * y, x / y, x // y, x % y	Multiplication, division, floor division, modulo
x + y, x - y	Addition, subtraction
x << y, x >> y	Bit-shifting
x & y	Bitwise and
x ^ y	Bitwise exclusive or
x | y	Bitwise or
x < y, x <= y,	Value comparison, object identity, and
x > y, x >= y,	sequence membership tests
x == y, x != y,	

Table 4.3   **Continued**

Operator	Name
x is y, x is not y,	
x in s, x not in s	
not x	Logical negation
x and y	Logical and
x or y	Logical or
lambda args: expr	Anonymous function

The order of evaluation is not determined by the types of x and y in Table 4.3. So, even though user-defined objects can redefine individual operators, it is not possible to customize the underlying evaluation order, precedence, and associativity rules.

Conditional Expressions

A common programming pattern is that of conditionally assigning a value based on the result of an expression. For example:

```
if a <= b:
    minvalue = a
else:
    minvalue = b
```

This code can be shortened using a *conditional expression*. For example:

```
minvalue = a if a <= b else b
```

In such expressions, the condition in the middle is evaluated first. The expression to the left of the if is then evaluated if the result is True. Otherwise, the expression after the else is evaluated.

Conditional expressions should probably be used sparingly because they can lead to confusion (especially if they are nested or mixed with other complicated expressions). However, one particularly useful application is in list comprehensions and generator expressions. For example:

```
values = [1, 100, 45, 23, 73, 37, 69 ]
clamped = [x if x < 50 else 50 for x in values]
print(clamped)      # [1, 50, 45, 23, 50, 37, 50]
```

Program Structure and Control Flow

This chapter covers the details of program structure and control flow. Topics include conditionals, iteration, exceptions, and context managers.

Program Structure and Execution

Python programs are structured as a sequence of statements. All language features, including variable assignment, function definitions, classes, and module imports, are statements that have equal status with all other statements. In fact, there are no "special" statements, and every statement can be placed anywhere in a program. For example, this code defines two different versions of a function:

```
if debug:
    def square(x):
        if not isinstance(x,float):
            raise TypeError("Expected a float")
        return x * x
else:
    def square(x):
        return x * x
```

When loading source files, the interpreter always executes every statement in order until there are no more statements to execute. This execution model applies both to files you simply run as the main program and to library files that are loaded via import.

Conditional Execution

The if, else, and elif statements control conditional code execution. The general format of a conditional statement is as follows:

```
if expression:
    statements
elif expression:
    statements
elif expression:
    statements
...
else:
    statements
```

If no action is to be taken, you can omit both the `else` and `elif` clauses of a conditional. Use the `pass` statement if no statements exist for a particular clause:

```
if expression:
    pass            # Do nothing
else:
    statements
```

Loops and Iteration

You implement loops using the `for` and `while` statements. Here's an example:

```
while expression:
    statements

for i in s:
    statements
```

The `while` statement executes statements until the associated expression evaluates to false. The `for` statement iterates over all the elements of s until no more elements are available. The `for` statement works with any object that supports iteration. This obviously includes the built-in sequence types such as lists, tuples, and strings, but also any object that implements the iterator protocol.

An object, s, supports iteration if it can be used with the following code, which mirrors the implementation of the `for` statement:

```
it = s.__iter__()            # Get an iterator for s
while 1:
    try:
        i = it.next()        # Get next item (Use __next__ in Python 3)
    except StopIteration:    # No more items
        break
        # Perform operations on i
    ...
```

In the statement for *i* in *s*, the variable *i* is known as the *iteration variable*. On each iteration of the loop, it receives a new value from *s*. The scope of the iteration variable is not private to the `for` statement. If a previously defined variable has the same name, that value will be overwritten. Moreover, the iteration variable retains the last value after the loop has completed.

If the elements used in iteration are sequences of identical size, you can unpack their values into individual iteration variables using a statement such as the following:

```
for x,y,z in s:
    statements
```

In this example, *s* must contain or produce sequences, each with three elements. On each iteration, the contents of the variables *x*, *y*, and *z* are assigned the items of the corresponding sequence. Although it is most common to see this used when *s* is a sequence of tuples, unpacking works if the items in *s* are any kind of sequence including lists, generators, and strings.

When looping, it is sometimes useful to keep track of a numerical index in addition to the data values. Here's an example:

```
i = 0
for x in s:
```

```
    statements
    i += 1
```

Python provides a built-in function, `enumerate()`, that can be used to simplify this code:

```
for i,x in enumerate(s):
    statements
```

`enumerate(s)` creates an iterator that simply returns a sequence of tuples `(0, s[0])`, `(1, s[1])`, `(2, s[2])`, and so on.

Another common looping problem concerns iterating in parallel over two or more sequences—for example, writing a loop where you want to take items from different sequences on each iteration as follows:

```
# s and t are two sequences
i = 0
while i < len(s) and i < len(t):
    x = s[i]      # Take an item from s
    y = t[i]      # Take an item from t
    statements
    i += 1
```

This code can be simplified using the `zip()` function. For example:

```
# s and t are two sequences
for x,y in zip(s,t):
    statements
```

`zip(s,t)` combines sequences `s` and `t` into a sequence of tuples `(s[0],t[0])`, `(s[1],t[1])`, `(s[2], t[2])`, and so forth, stopping with the shortest of the sequences `s` and `t` should they be of unequal length. One caution with `zip()` is that in Python 2, it fully consumes both `s` and `t`, creating a list of tuples. For generators and sequences containing a large amount of data, this may not be what you want. The function `itertools.izip()` achieves the same effect as `zip()` but generates the zipped values one at a time rather than creating a large list of tuples. In Python 3, the `zip()` function also generates values in this manner.

To break out of a loop, use the `break` statement. For example, this code reads lines of text from a file until an empty line of text is encountered:

```
for line in open("foo.txt"):
    stripped = line.strip()
    if not stripped:
        break          # A blank line, stop reading
    # process the stripped line
    ...
```

To jump to the next iteration of a loop (skipping the remainder of the loop body), use the `continue` statement. This statement tends to be used less often but is sometimes useful when the process of reversing a test and indenting another level would make the program too deeply nested or unnecessarily complicated. As an example, the following loop skips all of the blank lines in a file:

```
for line in open("foo.txt"):
    stripped = line.strip()
    if not stripped:
        continue       # Skip the blank line
    # process the stripped line
    ...
```

The break and continue statements apply only to the innermost loop being executed. If it's necessary to break out of a deeply nested loop structure, you can use an exception. Python doesn't provide a "goto" statement.

You can also attach the else statement to loop constructs, as in the following example:

```
# for-else
for line in open("foo.txt"):
    stripped = line.strip()
    if not stripped:
        break
    # process the stripped line
    ...
else:
    raise RuntimeError("Missing section separator")
```

The else clause of a loop executes only if the loop runs to completion. This either occurs immediately (if the loop wouldn't execute at all) or after the last iteration. On the other hand, if the loop is terminated early using the break statement, the else clause is skipped.

The primary use case for the looping else clause is in code that iterates over data but which needs to set or check some kind of flag or condition if the loop breaks prematurely. For example, if you didn't use else, the previous code might have to be rewritten with a flag variable as follows:

```
found_separator = False
for line in open("foo.txt"):
    stripped = line.strip()
    if not stripped:
        found_separator = True
        break
    # process the stripped line
    ...
if not found_separator:
    raise RuntimeError("Missing section separator")
```

Exceptions

Exceptions indicate errors and break out of the normal control flow of a program. An exception is raised using the raise statement. The general format of the raise statement is raise *Exception*([*value*]), where *Exception* is the exception type and *value* is an optional value giving specific details about the exception. Here's an example:

```
raise RuntimeError("Unrecoverable Error")
```

If the raise statement is used by itself, the last exception generated is raised again (although this works only while handling a previously raised exception).

To catch an exception, use the try and except statements, as shown here:

```
try:
    f = open('foo')
except IOError as e:
    statements
```

When an exception occurs, the interpreter stops executing statements in the try block and looks for an except clause that matches the exception that has occurred. If one is found, control is passed to the first statement in the except clause. After the except clause is executed, control continues with the first statement that appears after the try-except block. Otherwise, the exception is propagated up to the block of code in which the try statement appeared. This code may itself be enclosed in a try-except that can handle the exception. If an exception works its way up to the top level of a program without being caught, the interpreter aborts with an error message. If desired, uncaught exceptions can also be passed to a user-defined function, sys.excepthook(), as described in Chapter 13, "Python Runtime Services."

The optional as *var* modifier to the except statement supplies the name of a variable in which an instance of the exception type supplied to the raise statement is placed if an exception occurs. Exception handlers can examine this value to find out more about the cause of the exception. For example, you can use isinstance() to check the exception type. One caution on the syntax: In previous versions of Python, the except statement was written as except *ExcType, var* where the exception type and variable were separated by a comma (,). In Python 2.6, this syntax still works, but it is deprecated. In new code, use the as *var* syntax because it is required in Python 3.

Multiple exception-handling blocks are specified using multiple except clauses, as in the following example:

```
try:
    do something
except IOError as e:
    # Handle I/O error
    ...
except TypeError as e:
    # Handle Type error
    ...
except NameError as e:
    # Handle Name error
    ...
```

A single handler can catch multiple exception types like this:

```
try:
    do something
except (IOError, TypeError, NameError) as e:
    # Handle I/O, Type, or Name errors
    ...
```

To ignore an exception, use the pass statement as follows:

```
try:
    do something
except IOError:
    pass                # Do nothing (oh well).
```

To catch all exceptions except those related to program exit, use Exception like this:

```
try:
    do something
except Exception as e:
    # error_log is previously opened file-like object
    error_log.write('An error occurred : %s\n' % e)
```

When catching all exceptions, you should take care to report accurate error information to the user. For example, in the previous code, an error message and the associated exception value is being logged. If you don't include any information about the exception value, it can make it very difficult to debug code that is failing for reasons that you don't expect.

All exceptions can be caught using except with no exception type as follows:

```
try:
    do something
except:
    error_log.write('An error occurred\n')
```

Correct use of this form of except is a lot trickier than it looks and should probably be avoided. For instance, this code would also catch keyboard interrupts and requests for program exit—things that you may not want to catch.

The try statement also supports an else clause, which must follow the last except clause. This code is executed if the code in the try block doesn't raise an exception. Here's an example:

```
try:
    f = open('foo', 'r')
except IOError as e:
    error_log.write('Unable to open foo : %s\n' % e)
else:
    data = f.read()
    f.close()
```

The finally statement defines a cleanup action for code contained in a try block. Here's an example:

```
f = open('foo','r')
try:
    # Do some stuff
    ...
finally:
    f.close()
    # File closed regardless of what happened
```

The finally clause isn't used to catch errors. Rather, it's used to provide code that must always be executed, regardless of whether an error occurs. If no exception is raised, the code in the finally clause is executed immediately after the code in the try block. If an exception occurs, control is first passed to the first statement of the finally clause. After this code has executed, the exception is re-raised to be caught by another exception handler.

Built-in Exceptions

Python defines the built-in exceptions listed in Table 5.1.

Table 5.1   **Built-in Exceptions**

Exception	Description
BaseException	The root of all exceptions.
GeneratorExit	Raised by `.close()` method on a generator.
KeyboardInterrupt	Generated by the interrupt key (usually Ctrl+C).
SystemExit	Program exit/termination.
Exception	Base class for all non-exiting exceptions.
StopIteration	Raised to stop iteration.
StandardError	Base for all built-in exceptions (Python 2 only). In Python 3, all exceptions below are grouped under `Exception`.
ArithmeticError	Base for arithmetic exceptions.
FloatingPointError	Failure of a floating-point operation.
OverflowError	Integer value too large.
ZeroDivisionError	Division or modulus operation with 0.
AssertionError	Raised by the `assert` statement.
AttributeError	Raised when an attribute name is invalid.
EnvironmentError	Errors that occur externally to Python.
IOError	I/O or file-related error.
OSError	Operating system error.
WindowsError	Windows-specific error
EOFError	Raised when the end of the file is reached.
ImportError	Failure of the `import` statement.
LookupError	Indexing and key errors.
IndexError	Out-of-range sequence index.
KeyError	Nonexistent dictionary key.
MemoryError	Out of memory.
NameError	Failure to find a local or global name.
UnboundLocalError	Unbound local variable.
ReferenceError	Weak reference used after referent destroyed.
RuntimeError	A generic catchall error.
NotImplementedError	Unimplemented feature.
SyntaxError	Parsing error.
IndentationError	Indentation error.
TabError	Inconsistent tab usage (generated with -tt option).
SystemError	Nonfatal system error in the interpreter.
TypeError	Passing an inappropriate type to an operation.
ValueError	Invalid type.
UnicodeError	Unicode error.
UnicodeDecodeError	Unicode decoding error.
UnicodeEncodeError	Unicode encoding error.
UnicodeTranslateError	Unicode translation error.

Exceptions are organized into a hierarchy as shown in the table. All the exceptions in a particular group can be caught by specifying the group name in an except clause. Here's an example:

```
try:
     statements
except LookupError:     # Catch IndexError or KeyError
     statements
```

or

```
try:
     statements
except Exception:    # Catch any program-related exception
     statements
```

At the top of the exception hierarchy, the exceptions are grouped according to whether or not the exceptions are related to program exit. For example, the SystemExit and KeyboardInterrupt exceptions are not grouped under Exception because programs that want to catch all program-related errors usually don't want to also capture program termination by accident.

Defining New Exceptions

All the built-in exceptions are defined in terms of classes. To create a new exception, create a new class definition that inherits from Exception, such as the following:

```
class NetworkError(Exception): pass
```

To use your new exception, use it with the raise statement as follows:

```
raise NetworkError("Cannot find host.")
```

When raising an exception, the optional values supplied with the raise statement are used as the arguments to the exception's class constructor. Most of the time, this is simply a string indicating some kind of error message. However, user-defined exceptions can be written to take one or more exception values as shown in this example:

```
class DeviceError(Exception):
    def __init__(self,errno,msg):
        self.args = (errno, msg)
        self.errno = errno
        self.errmsg = msg

# Raises an exception (multiple arguments)
raise DeviceError(1, 'Not Responding')
```

When you create a custom exception class that redefines __init__(), it is important to assign a tuple containing the arguments to __init__() to the attribute self.args as shown. This attribute is used when printing exception traceback messages. If you leave it undefined, users won't be able to see any useful information about the exception when an error occurs.

Exceptions can be organized into a hierarchy using inheritance. For instance, the NetworkError exception defined earlier could serve as a base class for a variety of more specific errors. Here's an example:

```
class HostnameError(NetworkError): pass
class TimeoutError(NetworkError): pass
```

```
def error1():
    raise HostnameError("Unknown host")

def error2():
    raise TimeoutError("Timed out")

try:
    error1()
except NetworkError as e:
    if type(e) is HostnameError:
        # Perform special actions for this kind of error
        ...
```

In this case, the except `NetworkError` statement catches any exception derived from `NetworkError`. To find the specific type of error that was raised, examine the type of the execution value with `type()`. Alternatively, the `sys.exc_info()` function can be used to retrieve information about the last raised exception.

Context Managers and the `with` Statement

Proper management of system resources such as files, locks, and connections is often a tricky problem when combined with exceptions. For example, a raised exception can cause control flow to bypass statements responsible for releasing critical resources such as a lock.

The `with` statement allows a series of statements to execute inside a runtime context that is controlled by an object that serves as a context manager. Here is an example:

```
with open("debuglog","a") as f:
    f.write("Debugging\n")
    statements
    f.write("Done\n")

import threading
lock = threading.Lock()
with lock:
    # Critical section
    statements
    # End critical section
```

In the first example, the `with` statement automatically causes the opened file to be closed when control-flow leaves the block of statements that follows. In the second example, the `with` statement automatically acquires and releases a lock when control enters and leaves the block of statements that follows.

The `with` *obj* statement allows the object *obj* to manage what happens when control-flow enters and exits the associated block of statements that follows. When the `with` *obj* statement executes, it executes the method *obj*.`__enter__`() to signal that a new context is being entered. When control flow leaves the context, the method *obj*.`__exit__`(*type*, *value*, *traceback*) executes. If no exception has been raised, the three arguments to `__exit__`() are all set to `None`. Otherwise, they contain the type, value, and traceback associated with the exception that has caused control-flow to leave the context. The `__exit__`() method returns `True` or `False` to indicate whether the raised exception was handled or not (if `False` is returned, any exceptions raised are propagated out of the context).

The with *obj* statement accepts an optional as *var* specifier. If given, the value returned by *obj*.__enter__() is placed into *var*. It is important to emphasize that *obj* is not necessarily the value assigned to *var*.

The with statement only works with objects that support the context management protocol (the __enter__() and __exit__() methods). User-defined classes can implement these methods to define their own customized context-management. Here is a simple example:

```
class ListTransaction(object):
    def __init__(self,thelist):
        self.thelist = thelist
    def __enter__(self):
        self.workingcopy = list(self.thelist)
        return self.workingcopy
    def __exit__(self,exctype,value,tb):
        if exctype is None:
            self.thelist[:] = self.workingcopy
        return False
```

This class allows one to make a sequence of modifications to an existing list. However, the modifications only take effect if no exceptions occur. Otherwise, the original list is left unmodified. For example:

```
items = [1,2,3]
with ListTransaction(items) as working:
    working.append(4)
    working.append(5)
print(items)        # Produces [1,2,3,4,5]

try:
    with ListTransaction(items) as working:
        working.append(6)
        working.append(7)
        raise RuntimeError("We're hosed!")
except RuntimeError:
    pass
print(items)    # Produces [1,2,3,4,5]
```

The contextlib module allows custom context managers to be more easily implemented by placing a wrapper around a generator function. Here is an example:

```
from contextlib import contextmanager
@contextmanager
def ListTransaction(thelist):
    workingcopy = list(thelist)
    yield workingcopy
    # Modify the original list only if no errors
    thelist[:] = workingcopy
```

In this example, the value passed to yield is used as the return value from __enter__(). When the __exit__() method gets invoked, execution resumes after the yield. If an exception gets raised in the context, it shows up as an exception in the generator function. If desired, an exception could be caught, but in this case, exceptions will simply propagate out of the generator to be handled elsewhere.

Assertions and __debug__

The `assert` statement can introduce debugging code into a program. The general form of `assert` is

```
assert test [, msg]
```

where `test` is an expression that should evaluate to `True` or `False`. If `test` evaluates to `False`, `assert` raises an `AssertionError` exception with the optional message `msg` supplied to the `assert` statement. Here's an example:

```
def write_data(file,data):
    assert file, "write_data: file not defined!"
    ...
```

The `assert` statement should not be used for code that must be executed to make the program correct because it won't be executed if Python is run in optimized mode (specified with the `-O` option to the interpreter). In particular, it's an error to use `assert` to check user input. Instead, `assert` statements are used to check things that should always be true; if one is violated, it represents a bug in the program, not an error by the user.

For example, if the function `write_data()`, shown previously, were intended for use by an end user, the `assert` statement should be replaced by a conventional `if` statement and the desired error-handling.

In addition to `assert`, Python provides the built-in read-only variable `__debug__`, which is set to `True` unless the interpreter is running in optimized mode (specified with the `-O` option). Programs can examine this variable as needed—possibly running extra error-checking procedures if set. The underlying implementation of the `__debug__` variable is optimized in the interpreter so that the extra control-flow logic of the `if` statement itself is not actually included. If Python is running in its normal mode, the statements under the `if __debug__` statement are just inlined into the program without the `if` statement itself. In optimized mode, the `if __debug__` statement and all associated statements are completely removed from the program.

The use of `assert` and `__debug__` allow for efficient dual-mode development of a program. For example, in debug mode, you can liberally instrument your code with assertions and debug checks to verify correct operation. In optimized mode, all of these extra checks get stripped, resulting in no extra performance penalty.

6

Functions and Functional Programming

Substantial programs are broken up into functions for better modularity and ease of maintenance. Python makes it easy to define functions but also incorporates a surprising number of features from functional programming languages. This chapter describes functions, scoping rules, closures, decorators, generators, coroutines, and other functional programming features. In addition, list comprehensions and generator expressions are described—both of which are powerful tools for declarative-style programming and data processing.

Functions

Functions are defined with the `def` statement:

```
def add(x,y):
    return x + y
```

The body of a function is simply a sequence of statements that execute when the function is called. You invoke a function by writing the function name followed by a tuple of function arguments, such as `a = add(3,4)`. The order and number of arguments must match those given in the function definition. If a mismatch exists, a `TypeError` exception is raised.

You can attach default arguments to function parameters by assigning values in the function definition. For example:

```
def split(line,delimiter=','):
    statements
```

When a function defines a parameter with a default value, that parameter and all the parameters that follow are optional. If values are not assigned to all the optional parameters in the function definition, a `SyntaxError` exception is raised.

Default parameter values are always set to the objects that were supplied as values when the function was defined. Here's an example:

```
a = 10
def foo(x=a):
    return x

a = 5              # Reassign 'a'.
foo()              # returns 10 (default value not changed)
```

In addition, the use of mutable objects as default values may lead to unintended behavior:

```
def foo(x, items=[]):
    items.append(x)
    return items
foo(1)          # returns [1]
foo(2)          # returns [1, 2]
foo(3)          # returns [1, 2, 3]
```

Notice how the default argument retains modifications made from previous invocations. To prevent this, it is better to use None and add a check as follows:

```
def foo(x, items=None):
    if items is None:
        items = []
    items.append(x)
    return items
```

A function can accept a variable number of parameters if an asterisk (*) is added to the last parameter name:

```
def fprintf(file, fmt, *args):
    file.write(fmt % args)

# Use fprintf. args gets (42,"hello world", 3.45)
fprintf(out,"%d %s %f", 42, "hello world", 3.45)
```

In this case, all the remaining arguments are placed into the *args* variable as a tuple. To pass a tuple *args* to a function as if they were parameters, the *args syntax can be used in a function call as follows:

```
def printf(fmt, *args):
        # Call another function and pass along args
        fprintf(sys.stdout, fmt, *args)
```

Function arguments can also be supplied by explicitly naming each parameter and specifying a value. These are known as *keyword arguments*. Here is an example:

```
def foo(w,x,y,z):
    statements

# Keyword argument invocation
foo(x=3, y=22, w='hello', z=[1,2])
```

With keyword arguments, the order of the parameters doesn't matter. However, unless there are default values, you must explicitly name all of the required function parameters. If you omit any of the required parameters or if the name of a keyword doesn't match any of the parameter names in the function definition, a TypeError exception is raised. Also, since any Python function can be called using the keyword calling style, it is generally a good idea to define functions with descriptive argument names.

Positional arguments and keyword arguments can appear in the same function call, provided that all the positional arguments appear first, values are provided for all non-optional arguments, and no argument value is defined more than once. Here's an example:

```
foo('hello', 3, z=[1,2], y=22)
foo(3, 22, w='hello', z=[1,2])    # TypeError. Multiple values for w
```

If the last argument of a function definition begins with **, all the additional keyword arguments (those that don't match any of the other parameter names) are placed in a dictionary and passed to the function. This can be a useful way to write functions that accept a large number of potentially open-ended configuration options that would be too unwieldy to list as parameters. Here's an example:

```
def make_table(data, **parms):
    # Get configuration parameters from parms (a dict)
    fgcolor = parms.pop("fgcolor","black")
    bgcolor = parms.pop("bgcolor","white")
    width = parms.pop("width",None)
    ...
    # No more options
    if parms:
        raise TypeError("Unsupported configuration options %s" % list(parms))

make_table(items, fgcolor="black", bgcolor="white", border=1,
                  borderstyle="grooved", cellpadding=10,
                  width=400)
```

You can combine extra keyword arguments with variable-length argument lists, as long as the ** parameter appears last:

```
# Accept variable number of positional or keyword arguments
def spam(*args, **kwargs):
    # args is a tuple of positional args
    # kwargs is dictionary of keyword args
    ...
```

Keyword arguments can also be passed to another function using the **kwargs syntax:

```
def callfunc(*args, **kwargs):
    func(*args,**kwargs)
```

This use of *args and **kwargs is commonly used to write wrappers and proxies for other functions. For example, the callfunc() accepts any combination of arguments and simply passes them through to func().

Parameter Passing and Return Values

When a function is invoked, the function parameters are simply names that refer to the passed input objects. The underlying semantics of parameter passing doesn't neatly fit into any single style, such as "pass by value" or "pass by reference," that you might know about from other programming languages. For example, if you pass an immutable value, the argument effectively looks like it was passed by value. However, if a mutable object (such as a list or dictionary) is passed to a function where it's then modified, those changes will be reflected in the original object. Here's an example:

```
a = [1, 2, 3, 4, 5]
def square(items):
    for i,x in enumerate(items):
        items[i] = x * x      # Modify items in-place

square(a)      # Changes a to [1, 4, 9, 16, 25]
```

Functions that mutate their input values or change the state of other parts of the program behind the scenes like this are said to have *side effects*. As a general rule, this is a

programming style that is best avoided because such functions can become a source of
subtle programming errors as programs grow in size and complexity (for example, it's
not obvious from reading a function call if a function has side effects). Such functions
interact poorly with programs involving threads and concurrency because side effects
typically need to be protected by locks.

The `return` statement returns a value from a function. If no value is specified or
you omit the `return` statement, the `None` object is returned. To return multiple values,
place them in a tuple:

```
def factor(a):
    d = 2
    while (d <= (a / 2)):
        if ((a / d) * d == a):
            return ((a / d), d)
        d = d + 1
    return (a, 1)
```

Multiple return values returned in a tuple can be assigned to individual variables:

```
x, y = factor(1243)    # Return values placed in x and y.
```

or   .

```
(x, y) = factor(1243)  # Alternate version. Same behavior.
```

Scoping Rules

Each time a function executes, a new local namespace is created. This namespace represents a local environment that contains the names of the function parameters, as well as
the names of variables that are assigned inside the function body. When resolving names,
the interpreter first searches the local namespace. If no match exists, it searches the global namespace. The global namespace for a function is always the module in which the
function was defined. If the interpreter finds no match in the global namespace, it
makes a final check in the built-in namespace. If this fails, a `NameError` exception is
raised.

One peculiarity of namespaces is the manipulation of global variables within a function. For example, consider the following code:

```
a = 42
def foo():
    a = 13
foo()
# a is still 42
```

When this code executes, a returns its value of 42, despite the appearance that we
might be modifying the variable a inside the function foo. When variables are assigned
inside a function, they're always bound to the function's local namespace; as a result, the
variable a in the function body refers to an entirely new object containing the value
13, not the outer variable. To alter this behavior, use the `global` statement. `global` simply declares names as belonging to the global namespace, and it's necessary only when
global variables will be modified. It can be placed anywhere in a function body and
used repeatedly. Here's an example:

```
a = 42
b = 37
def foo():
    global a        # 'a' is in global namespace
    a = 13
    b = 0
foo()
# a is now 13. b is still 37.
```

Python supports nested function definitions. Here's an example:

```
def countdown(start):
    n = start
    def display():              # Nested function definition
        print('T-minus %d' % n)
    while n > 0:
        display()
        n -= 1
```

Variables in nested functions are bound using *lexical scoping*. That is, names are resolved by first checking the local scope and then all enclosing scopes of outer function definitions from the innermost scope to the outermost scope. If no match is found, the global and built-in namespaces are checked as before. Although names in enclosing scopes are accessible, Python 2 only allows variables to be reassigned in the innermost scope (local variables) and the global namespace (using `global`). Therefore, an inner function can't reassign the value of a local variable defined in an outer function. For example, this code does not work:

```
def countdown(start):
    n = start
    def display():
        print('T-minus %d' % n)
    def decrement():
        n -= 1                  # Fails in Python 2
    while n > 0:
        display()
        decrement()
```

In Python 2, you can work around this by placing values you want to change in a list or dictionary. In Python 3, you can declare n as `nonlocal` as follows:

```
def countdown(start):
    n = start
    def display():
        print('T-minus %d' % n)
    def decrement():
        nonlocal n     # Bind to outer n (Python 3 only)
        n -= 1
    while n > 0:
        display()
        decrement()
```

The `nonlocal` declaration does not bind a name to local variables defined inside arbitrary functions further down on the current call-stack (that is, *dynamic scope*). So, if you're coming to Python from Perl, `nonlocal` is not the same as declaring a Perl `local` variable.

If a local variable is used before it's assigned a value, an `UnboundLocalError` exception is raised. Here's an example that illustrates one scenario of how this might occur:

```
i = 0
def foo():
    i = i + 1      # Results in UnboundLocalError exception
    print(i)
```

In this function, the variable `i` is defined as a local variable (because it is being assigned inside the function and there is no `global` statement). However, the assignment `i = i + 1` tries to read the value of `i` before its local value has been first assigned. Even though there is a global variable `i` in this example, it is not used to supply a value here. Variables are determined to be either local or global at the time of function definition and cannot suddenly change scope in the middle of a function. For example, in the preceding code, it is not the case that the `i` in the expression `i + 1` refers to the global variable `i`, whereas the `i` in `print(i)` refers to the local variable `i` created in the previous statement.

Functions as Objects and Closures

Functions are first-class objects in Python. This means that they can be passed as arguments to other functions, placed in data structures, and returned by a function as a result. Here is an example of a function that accepts another function as input and calls it:

```
# foo.py
def callf(func):
    return func()
```

Here is an example of using the above function:

```
>>> import foo
>>> def helloworld():
...      return 'Hello World'
...
>>> foo.callf(helloworld)      # Pass a function as an argument
'Hello World'
>>>
```

When a function is handled as data, it implicitly carries information related to the surrounding environment where the function was defined. This affects how free variables in the function are bound. As an example, consider this modified version `foo.py` that now contains a variable definition:

```
# foo.py
x = 42
def callf(func):
    return func()
```

Now, observe the behavior of this example:

```
>>> import foo
>>> x = 37
>>> def helloworld():
...      return "Hello World. x is %d" % x
...
>>> foo.callf(helloworld)      # Pass a function as an argument
'Hello World. x is 37'
>>>
```

In this example, notice how the function helloworld() uses the value of x that's defined in the same environment as where helloworld() was defined. Thus, even though there is also an x defined in foo.py and that's where helloworld() is actually being called, that value of x is not the one that's used when helloworld() executes.

When the statements that make up a function are packaged together with the environment in which they execute, the resulting object is known as a *closure*. The behavior of the previous example is explained by the fact that all functions have a __globals__ attribute that points to the global namespace in which the function was defined. This always corresponds to the enclosing module in which a function was defined. For the previous example, you get the following:

```
>>> helloworld.__globals__
{'__builtins__': <module '__builtin__' (built-in)>,
 'helloworld': <function helloworld at 0x7bb30>,
 'x': 37, '__name__': '__main__', '__doc__': None
 'foo': <module 'foo' from 'foo.py'>}
>>>
```

When nested functions are used, closures capture the entire environment needed for the inner function to execute. Here is an example:

```
import foo
def bar():
    x = 13
    def helloworld():
        return "Hello World. x is %d" % x
    foo.callf(helloworld)          # returns 'Hello World, x is 13'
```

Closures and nested functions are especially useful if you want to write code based on the concept of lazy or delayed evaluation. Here is another example:

```
from urllib import urlopen
# from urllib.request import urlopen (Python 3)
def page(url):
    def get():
        return urlopen(url).read()
    return get
```

In this example, the page() function doesn't actually carry out any interesting computation. Instead, it merely creates and returns a function get() that will fetch the contents of a web page when it is called. Thus, the computation carried out in get() is actually delayed until some later point in a program when get() is evaluated. For example:

```
>>> python = page("http://www.python.org")
>>> jython = page("http://www.jython.org")
>>> python
<function get at 0x95d5f0>
>>> jython
<function get at 0x9735f0>
>>> pydata = python()          # Fetches http://www.python.org
>>> jydata = jython()          # Fetches http://www.jython.org
>>>
```

In this example, the two variables python and jython are actually two different versions of the get() function. Even though the page() function that created these values is no longer executing, both get() functions implicitly carry the values of the outer variables that were defined when the get() function was created. Thus, when get()

executes, it calls `urlopen(url)` with the value of `url` that was originally supplied to `page()`. With a little inspection, you can view the contents of variables that are carried along in a closure. For example:

```
>>> python.__closure__
(<cell at 0x67f50: str object at 0x69230>,)
>>> python.__closure__[0].cell_contents
'http://www.python.org'
>>> jython.__closure__[0].cell_contents
'http://www.jython.org'
>>>
```

A closure can be a highly efficient way to preserve state across a series of function calls. For example, consider this code that runs a simple counter:

```
def countdown(n):
    def next():
        nonlocal n
        r = n
        n -= 1
        return r
    return next

# Example use
next = countdown(10)
while True:
    v = next()          # Get the next value
    if not v: break
```

In this code, a closure is being used to store the internal counter value n. The inner function `next()` updates and returns the previous value of this counter variable each time it is called. Programmers not familiar with closures might be inclined to implement similar functionality using a class such as this:

```
class Countdown(object):
    def __init__(self,n):
        self.n = n
    def next(self):
        r = self.n
        self.n -= 1
        return r

# Example use
c = Countdown(10)
while True:
    v = c.next()          # Get the next value
    if not v: break
```

However, if you increase the starting value of the countdown and perform a simple timing benchmark, you will find that that the version using closures runs much faster (almost a 50% speedup when tested on the author's machine).

The fact that closures capture the environment of inner functions also make them useful for applications where you want to wrap existing functions in order to add extra capabilities. This is described next.

Decorators

A *decorator* is a function whose primary purpose is to wrap another function or class. The primary purpose of this wrapping is to transparently alter or enhance the behavior of the object being wrapped. Syntactically, decorators are denoted using the special @ symbol as follows:

```
@trace
def square(x):
    return x*x
```

The preceding code is shorthand for the following:

```
def square(x):
    return x*x
square = trace(square)
```

In the example, a function `square()` is defined. However, immediately after its definition, the function object itself is passed to the function `trace()`, which returns an object that replaces the original `square`. Now, let's consider an implementation of `trace` that will clarify how this might be useful:

```
enable_tracing = True
if enable_tracing:
    debug_log = open("debug.log","w")

def trace(func):
    if enable_tracing:
        def callf(*args,**kwargs):
            debug_log.write("Calling %s: %s, %s\n" %
                              (func.__name__, args, kwargs))
            r = func(*args,**kwargs)
            debug_log.write("%s returned %s\n" % (func.__name__, r))
            return r
        return callf
    else:
        return func
```

In this code, `trace()` creates a wrapper function that writes some debugging output and then calls the original function object. Thus, if you call `square()`, you will see the output of the `write()` methods in the wrapper. The function `callf` that is returned from `trace()` is a closure that serves as a replacement for the original function. A final interesting aspect of the implementation is that the tracing feature itself is only enabled through the use of a global variable `enable_tracing` as shown. If set to `False`, the `trace()` decorator simply returns the original function unmodified. Thus, when tracing is disabled, there is no added performance penalty associated with using the decorator.

When decorators are used, they must appear on their own line immediately prior to a function or class definition. More than one decorator can also be applied. Here's an example:

```
@foo
@bar
@spam
def grok(x):
    pass
```

In this case, the decorators are applied in the order listed. The result is the same as this:

```
def grok(x):
    pass
grok = foo(bar(spam(grok)))
```

A decorator can also accept arguments. Here's an example:

```
@eventhandler('BUTTON')
def handle_button(msg):
    ...

@eventhandler('RESET')
def handle_reset(msg):
    ...
```

If arguments are supplied, the semantics of the decorator are as follows:

```
def handle_button(msg):
    ...
temp = eventhandler('BUTTON')         # Call decorator with supplied arguments
handle_button = temp(handle_button)   # Call the function returned by the decorator
```

In this case, the decorator function only accepts the arguments supplied with the @ specifier. It then returns a function that is called with the function as an argument. Here's an example:

```
# Event handler decorator
event_handlers = { }
def eventhandler(event):
    def register_function(f):
        event_handlers[event] = f
        return f
    return register_function
```

Decorators can also be applied to class definitions. For example:

```
@foo
class Bar(object):
    def __init__(self,x):
        self.x = x
    def spam(self):
        statements
```

For class decorators, you should always have the decorator function return a class object as a result. Code that expects to work with the original class definition may want to reference members of the class directly such as Bar.spam. This won't work correctly if the decorator function foo() returns a function.

Decorators can interact strangely with other aspects of functions such as recursion, documentation strings, and function attributes. These issues are described later in this chapter.

Generators and yield

If a function uses the yield keyword, it defines an object known as a *generator*. A generator is a function that produces a sequence of values for use in iteration. Here's an example:

```
def countdown(n):
    print("Counting down from %d" % n)
    while n > 0:
        yield n
        n -= 1
    return    # Note: generators can only return None
```

If you call this function, you will find that none of its code starts executing. For example:

```
>>> c = countdown(10)
>>>
```

Instead, a generator object is returned. The generator object, in turn, executes the function whenever next() is called (or __next__() in Python 3). Here's an example:

```
>>> c.next()            # Use c.__next__() in Python 3
Counting down from 10
10
>>> c.next()
9
```

When next() is invoked, the generator function executes statements until it reaches a yield statement. The yield statement produces a result at which point execution of the function stops until next() is invoked again. Execution then resumes with the statement following yield.

You normally don't call next() directly on a generator but use it with the for statement, sum(), or some other operation that consumes a sequence. For example:

```
for n in countdown(10):
    statements
a = sum(countdown(10))
```

A generator function signals completion by returning or raising StopIteration, at which point iteration stops. It is never legal for a generator to return a value other than None upon completion.

A subtle problem with generators concerns the case where a generator function is only partially consumed. For example, consider this code:

```
for n in countdown(10):
    if n == 2: break
    statements
```

In this example, the for loop aborts by calling break, and the associated generator never runs to full completion. To handle this case, generator objects have a method close() that is used to signal a shutdown. When a generator is no longer used or deleted, close() is called. Normally it is not necessary to call close(), but you can also call it manually as shown here:

```
>>> c = countdown(10)
>>> c.next()
Counting down from 10
10
>>> c.next()
9
>>> c.close()
>>> c.next()
Traceback (most recent call last):
  File "<stdin>", line 1, in <module>
StopIteration
>>>
```

Inside the generator function, close() is signaled by a GeneratorExit exception occurring on the yield statement. You can optionally catch this exception to perform cleanup actions.

```
def countdown(n):
    print("Counting down from %d" % n)
    try:
        while n > 0:
            yield n
            n = n - 1
    except GeneratorExit:
        print("Only made it to %d" % n)
```

Although it is possible to catch GeneratorExit, it is illegal for a generator function to handle the exception and produce another output value using yield. Moreover, if a program is currently iterating on a generator, you should not call close() asynchronously on that generator from a separate thread of execution or from a signal handler.

Coroutines and yield Expressions

Inside a function, the yield statement can also be used as an expression that appears on the right side of an assignment operator. For example:

```
def receiver():
    print("Ready to receive")
    while True:
        n = (yield)
        print("Got %s" % n)
```

A function that uses yield in this manner is known as a *coroutine*, and it executes in response to values being sent to it. Its behavior is also very similar to a generator. For example:

```
>>> r = receiver()
>>> r.next()   # Advance to first yield (r.__next__() in Python 3)
Ready to receive
>>> r.send(1)
Got 1
>>> r.send(2)
Got 2
>>> r.send("Hello")
Got Hello
>>>
```

In this example, the initial call to next() is necessary so that the coroutine executes statements leading to the first yield expression. At this point, the coroutine suspends, waiting for a value to be sent to it using the send() method of the associated generator object r. The value passed to send() is returned by the (yield) expression in the coroutine. Upon receiving a value, a coroutine executes statements until the next yield statement is encountered.

The requirement of first calling next() on a coroutine is easily overlooked and a common source of errors. Therefore, it is recommended that coroutines be wrapped with a decorator that automatically takes care of this step.

```
def coroutine(func):
    def start(*args,**kwargs):
        g = func(*args,**kwargs)
        g.next()
        return g
    return start
```

Using this decorator, you would write and use coroutines using:

```
@coroutine
def receiver():
    print("Ready to receive")
    while True:
        n = (yield)
        print("Got %s" % n)
# Example use
r = receiver()
r.send("Hello World")          # Note : No initial .next() needed
```

A coroutine will typically run indefinitely unless it is explicitly shut down or it exits on its own. To close the stream of input values, use the `close()` method like this:

```
>>> r.close()
>>> r.send(4)
Traceback (most recent call last):
  File "<stdin>", line 1, in <module>
StopIteration
```

Once closed, a `StopIteration` exception will be raised if further values are sent to a coroutine. The `close()` operation raises `GeneratorExit` inside the coroutine as described in the previous section on generators. For example:

```
def receiver():
    print("Ready to receive")
    try:
        while True:
            n = (yield)
            print("Got %s" % n)
    except GeneratorExit:
        print("Receiver done")
```

Exceptions can be raised inside a coroutine using the `throw(exctype [, value [, tb]])` method where *exctype* is an exception type, *value* is the exception value, and *tb* is a traceback object. For example:

```
>>> r.throw(RuntimeError,"You're hosed!")
Traceback (most recent call last):
  File "<stdin>", line 1, in <module>
  File "<stdin>", line 4, in receiver
RuntimeError: You're hosed!
```

Exceptions raised in this manner will originate at the currently executing `yield` statement in the coroutine. A coroutine can elect to catch exceptions and handle them as appropriate. It is not safe to use `throw()` as an asynchronous signal to a coroutine—it should never be invoked from a separate execution thread or in a signal handler.

A coroutine may simultaneously receive and emit return values using `yield` if values are supplied in the `yield` expression. Here is an example that illustrates this:

```
def line_splitter(delimiter=None):
    print("Ready to split")
    result = None
    while True:
        line = (yield result)
        result = line.split(delimiter)
```

In this case, we use the coroutine in the same way as before. However, now calls to send() also produce a result. For example:

```
>>> s = line_splitter(",")
>>> s.next()
Ready to split
>>> s.send("A,B,C")
['A', 'B', 'C' ]
>>> s.send("100,200,300")
['100', '200', '300']
>>>
```

Understanding the sequencing of this example is critical. The first next() call advances the coroutine to (yield result), which returns None, the initial value of result. On subsequent send() calls, the received value is placed in line and split into result. The value returned by send() is the value passed to the next yield statement encountered. In other words, the value returned by send() comes from the next yield expression, not the one responsible for receiving the value passed by send().

If a coroutine returns values, some care is required if exceptions raised with throw() are being handled. If you raise an exception in a coroutine using throw(), the value passed to the next yield in the coroutine will be returned as the result of throw(). If you need this value and forget to save it, it will be lost.

Using Generators and Coroutines

At first glance, it might not be obvious how to use generators and coroutines for practical problems. However, generators and coroutines can be particularly effective when applied to certain kinds of programming problems in systems, networking, and distributed computation. For example, generator functions are useful if you want to set up a processing pipeline, similar in nature to using a pipe in the UNIX shell. One example of this appeared in the Introduction. Here is another example involving a set of generator functions related to finding, opening, reading, and processing files:

```
import os
import fnmatch

def find_files(topdir, pattern):
    for path, dirname, filelist in os.walk(topdir):
        for name in filelist:
            if fnmatch.fnmatch(name, pattern):
                yield os.path.join(path,name)

import gzip, bz2
def opener(filenames):
    for name in filenames:
        if name.endswith(".gz"):  f = gzip.open(name)
        elif name.endswith(".bz2"): f = bz2.BZ2File(name)
        else: f = open(name)
        yield f

def cat(filelist):
    for f in filelist:
        for line in f:
            yield line

def grep(pattern, lines):
    for line in lines:
        if pattern in line:
            yield line
```

Here is an example of using these functions to set up a processing pipeline:

```
wwwlogs = find_files("www","access-log*")
files   = opener(wwwlogs)
lines   = cat(files)
pylines = grep("python", lines)
for line in pylines:
    sys.stdout.write(line)
```

In this example, the program is processing all lines in all "access-log*" files found within all subdirectories of a top-level directory "www". Each "access-log" is tested for file compression and opened using an appropriate file opener. Lines are concatenated together and processed through a filter that is looking for a substring "python". The entire program is being driven by the for statement at the end. Each iteration of this loop pulls a new value through the pipeline and consumes it. Moreover, the implementation is highly memory-efficient because no temporary lists or other large data structures are ever created.

Coroutines can be used to write programs based on data-flow processing. Programs organized in this way look like inverted pipelines. Instead of pulling values through a sequence of generator functions using a for loop, you send values into a collection of linked coroutines. Here is an example of coroutine functions written to mimic the generator functions shown previously:

```
import os
import fnmatch

@coroutine
def find_files(target):
    while True:
        topdir, pattern = (yield)
        for path, dirname, filelist in os.walk(topdir):
            for name in filelist:
                if fnmatch.fnmatch(name,pattern):
                    target.send(os.path.join(path,name))

import gzip, bz2
@coroutine
def opener(target):
    while True:
        name = (yield)
        if name.endswith(".gz"):  f = gzip.open(name)
        elif name.endswith(".bz2"): f = bz2.BZ2File(name)
        else: f = open(name)
        target.send(f)

@coroutine
def cat(target):
    while True:
        f = (yield)
        for line in f:
            target.send(line)
```

```
@coroutine
def grep(pattern, target):
    while True:
        line = (yield)
        if pattern in line:
            target.send(line)

@coroutine
def printer():
    while True:
        line = (yield)
        sys.stdout.write(line)
```

Here is how you would link these coroutines to create a dataflow processing pipeline:

```
finder = find_files(opener(cat(grep("python",printer()))))

# Now, send a value
finder.send(("www","access-log*"))
finder.send(("otherwww","access-log*"))
```

In this example, each coroutine sends data to another coroutine specified in the `target` argument to each coroutine. Unlike the generator example, execution is entirely driven by pushing data into the first coroutine `find_files()`. This coroutine, in turn, pushes data to the next stage. A critical aspect of this example is that the coroutine pipeline remains active indefinitely or until `close()` is explicitly called on it. Because of this, a program can continue to feed data into a coroutine for as long as necessary—for example, the two repeated calls to `send()` shown in the example.

Coroutines can be used to implement a form of concurrency. For example, a centralized task manager or event loop can schedule and send data into a large collection of hundreds or even thousands of coroutines that carry out various processing tasks. The fact that input data is "sent" to a coroutine also means that coroutines can often be easily mixed with programs that use message queues and message passing to communicate between program components. Further information on this can be found in Chapter 20, "Threads."

List Comprehensions

A common operation involving functions is that of applying a function to all of the items of a list, creating a new list with the results. For example:

```
nums = [1, 2, 3, 4, 5]
squares = []
for n in nums:
    squares.append(n * n)
```

Because this type of operation is so common, it is has been turned into an operator known as a *list comprehension*. Here is a simple example:

```
nums = [1, 2, 3, 4, 5]
squares = [n * n for n in nums]
```

The general syntax for a list comprehension is as follows:

```
[expression for item1 in iterable1 if condition1
            for item2 in iterable2 if condition2
            ...
            for itemN in iterableN if conditionN ]
```

This syntax is roughly equivalent to the following code:

```
s = []
for item1 in iterable1:
    if condition1:
        for item2 in iterable2:
            if condition2:
                ...
                    for itemN in iterableN:
                        if conditionN: s.append(expression)
```

To illustrate, here are some more examples:

```
a = [-3,5,2,-10,7,8]
b = 'abc'

c = [2*s for s in a]         # c = [-6,10,4,-20,14,16]
d = [s for s in a if s >= 0] # d = [5,2,7,8]
e = [(x,y) for x in a        # e = [(5,'a'),(5,'b'),(5,'c'),
           for y in b        #      (2,'a'),(2,'b'),(2,'c'),
           if x > 0 ]        #      (7,'a'),(7,'b'),(7,'c'),
                             #      (8,'a'),(8,'b'),(8,'c')]

f = [(1,2), (3,4), (5,6)]
g = [math.sqrt(x*x+y*y)      # g = [2.23606, 5.0, 7.81024]
     for x,y in f]
```

The sequences supplied to a list comprehension don't have to be the same length because they're iterated over their contents using a nested set of for loops, as previously shown. The resulting list contains successive values of expressions. The if clause is optional; however, if it's used, *expression* is evaluated and added to the result only if *condition* is true.

If a list comprehension is used to construct a list of tuples, the tuple values must be enclosed in parentheses. For example, [(x,y) for x in a for y in b] is legal syntax, whereas [x,y for x in a for y in b] is not.

Finally, it is important to note that in Python 2, the iteration variables defined within a list comprehension are evaluated within the current scope and remain defined after the list comprehension has executed. For example, in [x for x in a], the iteration variable x overwrites any previously defined value of x and is set to the value of the last item in a after the resulting list is created. Fortunately, this is not the case in Python 3 where the iteration variable remains private.

Generator Expressions

A *generator expression* is an object that carries out the same computation as a list comprehension, but which iteratively produces the result. The syntax is the same as for list comprehensions except that you use parentheses instead of square brackets. Here's an example:

```
(expression for item1 in iterable1 if condition1
            for item2 in iterable2 if condition2
            ...
            for itemN in iterableN if conditionN)
```

Unlike a list comprehension, a generator expression does not actually create a list or immediately evaluate the expression inside the parentheses. Instead, it creates a generator object that produces the values on demand via iteration. Here's an example:

```
>>> a = [1, 2, 3, 4]
>>> b = (10*i for i in a)
>>> b
<generator object at 0x590a8>
>>> b.next()
10
>>> b.next()
20
...
```

The difference between list and generator expressions is important, but subtle. With a list comprehension, Python actually creates a list that contains the resulting data. With a generator expression, Python creates a generator that merely knows how to produce data on demand. In certain applications, this can greatly improve performance and memory use. Here's an example:

```
# Read a file
f = open("data.txt")                       # Open a file
lines = (t.strip() for t in f)             # Read lines, strip
                                           # trailing/leading whitespace
comments = (t for t in lines if t[0] == '#') # All comments
for c in comments:
    print(c)
```

In this example, the generator expression that extracts lines and strips whitespace does not actually read the entire file into memory. The same is true of the expression that extracts comments. Instead, the lines of the file are actually read when the program starts iterating in the for loop that follows. During this iteration, the lines of the file are produced upon demand and filtered accordingly. In fact, at no time will the entire file be loaded into memory during this process. Therefore, this would be a highly efficient way to extract comments from a gigabyte-sized Python source file.

Unlike a list comprehension, a generator expression does not create an object that works like a sequence. It can't be indexed, and none of the usual list operations will work (for example, append()). However, a generator expression can be converted into a list using the built-in list() function:

```
clist = list(comments)
```

Declarative Programming

List comprehensions and generator expressions are strongly tied to operations found in declarative languages. In fact, the origin of these features is loosely derived from ideas in mathematical set theory. For example, when you write a statement such as [x*x for x in a if x > 0], it's somewhat similar to specifying a set such as $\{ x^2 \mid x \in a, x > 0 \}$.

Instead of writing programs that manually iterate over data, you can use these declarative features to structure programs as a series of computations that simply operate on all of the data all at once. For example, suppose you had a file "portfolio.txt" containing stock portfolio data like this:

```
AA 100 32.20
IBM 50 91.10
CAT 150 83.44
MSFT 200 51.23
GE 95 40.37
MSFT 50 65.10
IBM 100 70.44
```

Here is a declarative-style program that calculates the total cost by summing up the second column multiplied by the third column:

```
lines  = open("portfolio.txt")
fields = (line.split() for line in lines)
print(sum(float(f[1]) * float(f[2]) for f in fields))
```

In this program, we really aren't concerned with the mechanics of looping line-by-line over the file. Instead, we just declare a sequence of calculations to perform on all of the data. Not only does this approach result in highly compact code, but it also tends to run faster than this more traditional version:

```
total = 0
for line in open("portfolio.txt"):
    fields = line.split()
    total += float(fields[1]) * float(fields[2])
print(total)
```

The declarative programming style is somewhat tied to the kinds of operations a programmer might perform in a UNIX shell. For instance, the preceding example using generator expressions is similar to the following one-line awk command:

```
% awk '{ total += $2 * $3} END { print total }' portfolio.txt
44671.2
%
```

The declarative style of list comprehensions and generator expressions can also be used to mimic the behavior of SQL select statements, commonly used when processing databases. For example, consider these examples that work on data that has been read in a list of dictionaries:

```
fields = (line.split() for line in open("portfolio.txt"))
portfolio = [ {'name'   : f[0],
               'shares' : int(f[1]),
               'price'  : float(f[2]) }
              for f in fields]

# Some queries
msft = [s for s in portfolio if s['name'] == 'MSFT']
large_holdings = [s for s in portfolio
                        if s['shares']*s['price'] >= 10000]
```

In fact, if you are using a module related to database access (see Chapter 17), you can often use list comprehensions and database queries together all at once. For example:

```
sum(shares*cost for shares,cost in
        cursor.execute("select shares, cost from portfolio")
            if shares*cost >= 10000)
```

The `lambda` Operator

Anonymous functions in the form of an expression can be created using the `lambda` statement:

```
lambda args : expression
```

args is a comma-separated list of arguments, and *expression* is an expression involving those arguments. Here's an example:

```
a = lambda x,y : x+y
r = a(2,3)              # r gets 5
```

The code defined with `lambda` must be a valid expression. Multiple statements and other non-expression statements, such as `for` and `while`, cannot appear in a `lambda` statement. `lambda` expressions follow the same scoping rules as functions.

The primary use of `lambda` is in specifying short callback functions. For example, if you wanted to sort a list of names with case-insensitivity, you might write this:

```
names.sort(key=lambda n: n.lower())
```

Recursion

Recursive functions are easily defined. For example:

```
def factorial(n):
    if n <= 1: return 1
    else: return n * factorial(n - 1)
```

However, be aware that there is a limit on the depth of recursive function calls. The function `sys.getrecursionlimit()` returns the current maximum recursion depth, and the function `sys.setrecursionlimit()` can be used to change the value. The default value is `1000`. Although it is possible to increase the value, programs are still limited by the stack size limits enforced by the host operating system. When the recursion depth is exceeded, a `RuntimeError` exception is raised. Python does not perform tail-recursion optimization that you often find in functional languages such as Scheme.

Recursion does not work as you might expect in generator functions and coroutines. For example, this code prints all items in a nested collection of lists:

```
def flatten(lists):
    for s in lists:
        if isinstance(s,list):
            flatten(s)
        else:
            print(s)

items = [[1,2,3],[4,5,[5,6]],[7,8,9]]
flatten(items)      # Prints 1 2 3 4 5 6 7 8 9
```

However, if you change the `print` operation to a `yield`, it no longer works. This is because the recursive call to `flatten()` merely creates a new generator object without actually iterating over it. Here's a recursive generator version that works:

```
def genflatten(lists):
    for s in lists:
        if isinstance(s,list):
            for item in genflatten(s):
                yield item
        else:
            yield item
```

Care should also be taken when mixing recursive functions and decorators. If a decorator is applied to a recursive function, all inner recursive calls now get routed through the decorated version. For example:

```
@locked
def factorial(n):
    if n <= 1: return 1
    else: return n * factorial(n - 1)  # Calls the wrapped version of factorial
```

If the purpose of the decorator was related to some kind of system management such as synchronization or locking, recursion is something probably best avoided.

Documentation Strings

It is common practice for the first statement of a function to be a documentation string describing its usage. For example:

```
def factorial(n):
    """Computes n factorial. For example:

    >>> factorial(6)
    120
    >>>
    """
    if n <= 1: return 1
    else: return n*factorial(n-1)
```

The documentation string is stored in the __doc__ attribute of the function that is commonly used by IDEs to provide interactive help.

If you are using decorators, be aware that wrapping a function with a decorator can break the help features associated with documentation strings. For example, consider this code:

```
def wrap(func):
    call(*args,**kwargs):
        return func(*args,**kwargs)
    return call
@wrap
def factorial(n):
    """Computes n factorial."""
    ...
```

If a user requests help on this version of `factorial()`, he will get a rather cryptic explanation:

```
>>> help(factorial)
Help on function call in module __main__:

call(*args, **kwargs)
(END)
>>>
```

To fix this, write decorator functions so that they propagate the function name and documentation string. For example:

```
def wrap(func):
    call(*args,**kwargs):
        return func(*args,**kwargs)
    call.__doc__ = func.__doc__
    call.__name__ = func.__name__
    return call
```

Because this is a common problem, the functools module provides a function wraps that can automatically copy these attributes. Not surprisingly, it is also a decorator:

```
from functools import wraps
def wrap(func):
    @wraps(func)
    call(*args,**kwargs):
        return func(*args,**kwargs)
    return call
```

The @wraps(func) decorator, defined in functools, propagates attributes from func to the wrapper function that is being defined.

Function Attributes

Functions can have arbitrary attributes attached to them. Here's an example:

```
def foo():
    statements

foo.secure = 1
foo.private = 1
```

Function attributes are stored in a dictionary that is available as the __dict__ attribute of a function.

The primary use of function attributes is in highly specialized applications such as parser generators and application frameworks that would like to attach additional information to function objects.

As with documentation strings, care should be given if mixing function attributes with decorators. If a function is wrapped by a decorator, access to the attributes will actually take place on the decorator function, not the original implementation. This may or may not be what you want depending on the application. To propagate already defined function attributes to a decorator function, use the following template or the functools.wraps() decorator as shown in the previous section:

```
def wrap(func):
    call(*args,**kwargs):
        return func(*args,**kwargs)
    call.__doc__ = func.__doc__
    call.__name__ = func.__name__
    call.__dict__.update(func.__dict__)
    return call
```

eval(), exec(), **and** compile()

The eval(*str* [,*globals* [,*locals*]]) function executes an expression string and returns the result. Here's an example:

```
a = eval('3*math.sin(3.5+x) + 7.2')
```

Similarly, the exec(*str* [, *globals* [, *locals*]]) function executes a string containing arbitrary Python code. The code supplied to exec() is executed as if the code actually appeared in place of the exec operation. Here's an example:

```
a = [3, 5, 10, 13]
exec("for i in a: print(i)")
```

One caution with exec is that in Python 2, exec is actually defined as a statement. Thus, in legacy code, you might see statements invoking exec without the surrounding parentheses, such as exec "for i in a: print i". Although this still works in Python 2.6, it breaks in Python 3. Modern programs should use exec() as a function.

Both of these functions execute within the namespace of the caller (which is used to resolve any symbols that appear within a string or file). Optionally, eval() and exec() can accept one or two mapping objects that serve as the global and local namespaces for the code to be executed, respectively. Here's an example:

```
globals = {'x': 7,
           'y': 10,
           'birds': ['Parrot', 'Swallow', 'Albatross']
          }
locals = { }

# Execute using the above dictionaries as the global and local namespace
a = eval("3 * x + 4 * y", globals, locals)
exec("for b in birds: print(b)", globals, locals)
```

If you omit one or both namespaces, the current values of the global and local namespaces are used. Also, due to issues related to nested scopes, the use of exec() inside of a function body may result in a SyntaxError exception if that function also contains nested function definitions or uses the lambda operator.

When a string is passed to exec() or eval() the parser first compiles it into bytecode. Because this process is expensive, it may be better to precompile the code and reuse the bytecode on subsequent calls if the code will be executed multiple times.

The compile(*str*, *filename*, *kind*) function compiles a string into bytecode in which *str* is a string containing the code to be compiled and *filename* is the file in which the string is defined (for use in traceback generation). The *kind* argument specifies the type of code being compiled—'single' for a single statement, 'exec' for a set of statements, or 'eval' for an expression. The code object returned by the compile() function can also be passed to the eval() function and exec() statement. Here's an example:

```
s = "for i in range(0,10): print(i)"
c = compile(s,'','exec')       # Compile into a code object
exec(c)                        # Execute it

s2 = "3 * x + 4 * y"
c2 = compile(s2, '', 'eval')   # Compile into an expression
result = eval(c2)              # Evaluate it
```

Classes and Object-Oriented Programming

Classes are the mechanism used to create new kinds of objects. This chapter covers the details of classes, but is not intended to be an in-depth reference on object-oriented programming and design. It's assumed that the reader has some prior experience with data structures and object-oriented programming in other languages such as C or Java. (Chapter 3, "Types and Objects," contains additional information about the terminology and internal implementation of objects.)

The `class` Statement

A *class* defines a set of attributes that are associated with, and shared by, a collection of objects known as *instances*. A class is most commonly a collection of functions (known as *methods*), variables (which are known as *class variables*), and computed attributes (which are known as *properties*).

A class is defined using the `class` statement. The body of a class contains a series of statements that execute during class definition. Here's an example:

```
class Account(object):
    num_accounts = 0
    def __init__(self,name,balance):
        self.name = name
        self.balance = balance
        Account.num_accounts += 1
    def __del__(self):
        Account.num_accounts -= 1
    def deposit(self,amt):
        self.balance = self.balance + amt
    def withdraw(self,amt):
        self.balance = self.balance - amt
    def inquiry(self):
        return self.balance
```

The values created during the execution of the class body are placed into a class object that serves as a namespace much like a module. For example, the members of the `Account` class are accessed as follows:

```
Account.num_accounts
Account.__init__
Account.__del__
Account.deposit
Account.withdraw
Account.inquiry
```

It's important to note that a class statement by itself doesn't create any instances of the class (for example, no accounts are actually created in the preceding example). Rather, a class merely sets up the attributes that will be common to all the instances that will be created later. In this sense, you might think of it as a blueprint.

The functions defined inside a class are known as *instance methods*. An instance method is a function that operates on an instance of the class, which is passed as the first argument. By convention, this argument is called self, although any legal identifier name can be used. In the preceding example, deposit(), withdraw(), and inquiry() are examples of instance methods.

Class variables such as num_accounts are values that are shared among all instances of a class (that is, they're not individually assigned to each instance). In this case, it's a variable that's keeping track of how many Account instances are in existence.

Class Instances

Instances of a class are created by calling a class object as a function. This creates a new instance that is then passed to the __init__() method of the class. The arguments to __init__() consist of the newly created instance self along with the arguments supplied when calling the class object. For example:

```
# Create a few accounts
a = Account("Guido", 1000.00)   # Invokes Account.__init__(a,"Guido",1000.00)
b = Account("Bill", 10.00)
```

Inside __init__(), attributes are saved in the instance by assigning to self. For example, self.name = name is saving a name attribute in the instance. Once the newly created instance has been returned to the user, these attributes as well as attributes of the class are accessed using the dot (.) operator as follows:

```
a.deposit(100.00)      # Calls Account.deposit(a,100.00)
b.withdraw(50.00)      # Calls Account.withdraw(b,50.00)
name = a.name          # Get account name
```

The dot (.) operator is responsible for attribute binding. When you access an attribute, the resulting value may come from several different places. For example, a.name in the previous example returns the name attribute of the instance a. However, a.deposit returns the deposit attribute (a method) of the Account class. When you access an attribute, the instance is checked first and if nothing is known, the search moves to the instance's class instead. This is the underlying mechanism by which a class shares its attributes with all of its instances.

Scoping Rules

Although classes define a namespace, classes do not create a scope for names used inside the bodies of methods. Therefore, when you're implementing a class, references to attributes and methods must be fully qualified. For example, in methods you always reference attributes of the instance through self. Thus, in the example you use self.balance, not balance. This also applies if you want to call a method from another method, as shown in the following example:

```
class Foo(object):
    def bar(self):
        print("bar!")
    def spam(self):
        bar(self)      # Incorrect! 'bar' generates a NameError
        self.bar()     # This works
        Foo.bar(self)  # This also works
```

The lack of scoping in classes is one area where Python differs from C++ or Java. If you have used those languages, the self parameter in Python is the same as the this pointer. The explicit use of self is required because Python does not provide a means to explicitly declare variables (that is, a declaration such as int x or float y in C). Without this, there is no way to know whether an assignment to a variable in a method is supposed to be a local variable or if it's supposed to be saved as an instance attribute. The explicit use of self fixes this—all values stored on self are part of the instance and all other assignments are just local variables.

Inheritance

Inheritance is a mechanism for creating a new class that specializes or modifies the behavior of an existing class. The original class is called a *base class* or a *superclass*. The new class is called a *derived class* or a *subclass*. When a class is created via inheritance, it "inherits" the attributes defined by its base classes. However, a derived class may redefine any of these attributes and add new attributes of its own.

Inheritance is specified with a comma-separated list of base-class names in the class statement. If there is no logical base class, a class inherits from object, as has been shown in prior examples. object is a class which is the root of all Python objects and which provides the default implementation of some common methods such as __str__(), which creates a string for use in printing.

Inheritance is often used to redefine the behavior of existing methods. As an example, here's a specialized version of Account that redefines the inquiry() method to periodically overstate the current balance with the hope that someone not paying close attention will overdraw his account and incur a big penalty when making a payment on their subprime mortgage:

```
import random
class EvilAccount(Account):
    def inquiry(self):
        if random.randint(0,4) == 1:
            return self.balance * 1.10    # Note: Patent pending idea
        else:
            return self.balance

c = EvilAccount("George", 1000.00)
c.deposit(10.0)              # Calls Account.deposit(c,10.0)
available = c.inquiry()      # Calls EvilAccount.inquiry(c)
```

In this example, instances of EvilAccount are identical to instances of Account except for the redefined inquiry() method.

Inheritance is implemented with only a slight enhancement of the dot (.) operator. Specifically, if the search for an attribute doesn't find a match in the instance or the instance's class, the search moves on to the base class. This process continues until there are no more base classes to search. In the previous example, this explains why c.deposit() calls the implementation of deposit() defined in the Account class.

A subclass can add new attributes to the instances by defining its own version of
`__init__()`. For example, this version of `EvilAccount` adds a new attribute
`evilfactor`:

```
class EvilAccount(Account):
    def __init__(self,name,balance,evilfactor):
        Account.__init__(self,name,balance)    # Initialize Account
        self.evilfactor = evilfactor
    def inquiry(self):
        if random.randint(0,4) == 1:
            return self.balance * self.evilfactor
        else:
            return self.balance
```

When a derived class defines `__init__()`, the `__init__()` methods of base classes are
not automatically invoked. Therefore, it's up to a derived class to perform the proper
initialization of the base classes by calling their `__init__()` methods. In the previous
example, this is shown in the statement that calls `Account.__init__()`. If a base class
does not define `__init__()`, this step can be omitted. If you don't know whether the
base class defines `__init__()`, it is always safe to call it without any arguments because
there is always a default implementation that simply does nothing.

Occasionally, a derived class will reimplement a method but also want to call the
original implementation. To do this, a method can explicitly call the original method in
the base class, passing the instance `self` as the first parameter as shown here:

```
class MoreEvilAccount(EvilAccount):
    def deposit(self,amount):
        self.withdraw(5.00)                    # Subtract the "convenience" fee
        EvilAccount.deposit(self,amount)  # Now, make deposit
```

A subtlety in this example is that the class `EvilAccount` doesn't actually implement the
`deposit()` method. Instead, it is implemented in the `Account` class. Although this code
works, it might be confusing to someone reading the code (e.g., was `EvilAccount` supposed to implement `deposit()`?). Therefore, an alternative solution is to use the
`super()` function as follows:

```
class MoreEvilAccount(EvilAccount):
    def deposit(self,amount):
        self.withdraw(5.00)                               # Subtract convenience fee
        super(MoreEvilAccount,self).deposit(amount)  # Now, make deposit
```

`super(cls, instance)` returns a special object that lets you perform attribute
lookups on the base classes. If you use this, Python will search for an attribute using the
normal search rules that would have been used on the base classes. This frees you from
hard-coding the exact location of a method and more clearly states your intentions (that
is, you want to call the previous implementation without regard for which base class
defines it). Unfortunately, the syntax of `super()` leaves much to be desired. If you are
using Python 3, you can use the simplified statement `super().deposit(amount)` to
carry out the calculation shown in the example. In Python 2, however, you have to use
the more verbose version.

Python supports multiple inheritance. This is specified by having a class list multiple
base classes. For example, here are a collection of classes:

```
class DepositCharge(object):
    fee = 5.00
    def deposit_fee(self):
        self.withdraw(self.fee)

class WithdrawCharge(object):
    fee = 2.50
    def withdraw_fee(self):
        self.withdraw(self.fee)

# Class using multiple inheritance
class MostEvilAccount(EvilAccount, DepositCharge, WithdrawCharge):
    def deposit(self,amt):
        self.deposit_fee()
        super(MostEvilAccount,self).deposit(amt)
    def withdraw(self,amt):
        self.withdraw_fee()
        super(MostEvilAccount,self).withdraw(amt)
```

When multiple inheritance is used, attribute resolution becomes considerably more complicated because there are many possible search paths that could be used to bind attributes. To illustrate the possible complexity, consider the following statements:

```
d = MostEvilAccount("Dave",500.00,1.10)
d.deposit_fee()    # Calls DepositCharge.deposit_fee().  Fee is 5.00
d.withdraw_fee()   # Calls WithdrawCharge.withdraw_fee(). Fee is 5.00 ??
```

In this example, methods such as deposit_fee() and withdraw_fee() are uniquely named and found in their respective base classes. However, the withdraw_fee() function doesn't seem to work right because it doesn't actually use the value of fee that was initialized in its own class. What has happened is that the attribute fee is a class variable defined in two different base classes. One of those values is used, but which one? (Hint: it's DepositCharge.fee.)

To find attributes with multiple inheritance, all base classes are ordered in a list from the "most specialized" class to the "least specialized" class. Then, when searching for an attribute, this list is searched in order until the first definition of the attribute is found. In the example, the class EvilAccount is more specialized than Account because it inherits from Account. Similarly, within MostEvilAccount, DepositCharge is considered to be more specialized than WithdrawCharge because it is listed first in the list of base classes. For any given class, the ordering of base classes can be viewed by printing its __mro__ attribute. Here's an example:

```
>>> MostEvilAccount.__mro__
(<class '__main__.MostEvilAccount'>,
 <class '__main__.EvilAccount'>,
 <class '__main__.Account'>,
 <class '__main__.DepositCharge'>,
 <class '__main__.WithdrawCharge'>,
 <type 'object'>)
>>>
```

In most cases, this list is based on rules that "make sense." That is, a derived class is always checked before its base classes and if a class has more than one parent, the parents are always checked in the same order as listed in the class definition. However, the precise ordering of base classes is actually quite complex and not based on any sort of "simple" algorithm such as depth-first or breadth-first search. Instead, the ordering is determined according to the C3 linearization algorithm, which is described in the paper "A Monotonic Superclass Linearization for Dylan" (K. Barrett, et al, presented at

OOPSLA'96). A subtle aspect of this algorithm is that certain class hierarchies will be rejected by Python with a `TypeError`. Here's an example:

```
class X(object): pass
class Y(X): pass
class Z(X,Y): pass  # TypeError.
                    # Can't create consistent method resolution order
```

In this case, the method resolution algorithm rejects class `Z` because it can't determine an ordering of the base classes that makes sense. For example, the class `X` appears before class `Y` in the inheritance list, so it must be checked first. However, class `Y` is more specialized because it inherits from `X`. Therefore, if `X` is checked first, it would not be possible to resolve specialized methods in `Y`. In practice, these issues should rarely arise—and if they do, it usually indicates a more serious design problem with a program.

As a general rule, multiple inheritance is something best avoided in most programs. However, it is sometimes used to define what are known as *mixin* classes. A mixin class typically defines a set of methods that are meant to be "mixed in" to other classes in order to add extra functionality (almost like a macro). Typically, the methods in a mixin will assume that other methods are present and will build upon them. The `DepositCharge` and `WithdrawCharge` classes in the earlier example illustrate this. These classes add new methods such as `deposit_fee()` to classes that include them as one of the base classes. However, you would never instantiate `DepositCharge` by itself. In fact, if you did, it wouldn't create an instance that could be used for anything useful (that is, the one defined method wouldn't even execute correctly).

Just as a final note, if you wanted to fix the problematic references to `fee` in this example, the implementation of `deposit_fee()` and `withdraw_fee()` should be changed to refer to the attribute directly using the class name instead of `self` (for example, `DepositChange.fee`).

Polymorphism Dynamic Binding and Duck Typing

Dynamic binding (also sometimes referred to as *polymorphism* when used in the context of inheritance) is the capability to use an instance without regard for its type. It is handled entirely through the attribute lookup process described for inheritance in the preceding section. Whenever an attribute is accessed as `obj.attr`, `attr` is located by searching within the instance itself, the instance's class definition, and then base classes, in that order. The first match found is returned.

A critical aspect of this binding process is that it is independent of what kind of object `obj` is. Thus, if you make a lookup such as `obj.name`, it will work on any `obj` that happens to have a name attribute. This behavior is sometimes referred to as *duck typing* in reference to the adage "if it looks like, quacks like, and walks like a duck, then it's a duck."

Python programmers often write programs that rely on this behavior. For example, if you want to make a customized version of an existing object, you can either inherit from it or you can simply create a completely new object that looks and acts like it but is otherwise unrelated. This latter approach is often used to maintain a loose coupling of program components. For example, code may be written to work with any kind of object whatsoever as long as it has a certain set of methods. One of the most common examples is with various "file-like" objects defined in the standard library. Although these objects work like files, they don't inherit from the built-in file object.

Static Methods and Class Methods

In a class definition, all functions are assumed to operate on an instance, which is always passed as the first parameter `self`. However, there are two other common kinds of methods that can be defined.

A *static method* is an ordinary function that just happens to live in the namespace defined by a class. It does not operate on any kind of instance. To define a static method, use the `@staticmethod` decorator as shown here:

```
class Foo(object):
    @staticmethod
    def add(x,y):
        return x + y
```

To call a static method, you just prefix it by the class name. You do not pass it any additional information. For example:

```
x = Foo.add(3,4)        # x = 7
```

A common use of static methods is in writing classes where you might have many different ways to create new instances. Because there can only be one `__init__()` function, alternative creation functions are often defined as shown here:

```
import time
class Date(object):
    def __init__(self,year,month,day):
        self.year = year
        self.month = month
        self.day = day
    @staticmethod
    def now():
        t = time.localtime()
        return Date(t.tm_year, t.tm_mon, t.tm_day)
    @staticmethod
    def tomorrow():
        t = time.localtime(time.time()+86400)
        return Date(t.tm_year, t.tm_mon, t.tm_day)

# Example of creating some dates
a = Date(1967, 4, 9)
b = Date.now()          # Calls static method now()
c = Date.tomorrow()     # Calls static method tomorrow()
```

Class methods are methods that operate on the class itself as an object. Defined using the `@classmethod` decorator, a class method is different than an instance method in that the class is passed as the first argument which is named `cls` by convention. For example:

```
class Times(object):
    factor = 1
    @classmethod
    def mul(cls,x):
        return cls.factor*x

class TwoTimes(Times):
    factor = 2

x = TwoTimes.mul(4)         # Calls Times.mul(TwoTimes, 4) -> 8
```

In this example, notice how the class TwoTimes is passed to mul() as an object. Although this example is esoteric, there are practical, but subtle, uses of class methods. As an example, suppose that you defined a class that inherited from the Date class shown previously and customized it slightly:

```
class EuroDate(Date):
    # Modify string conversion to use European dates
    def __str__(self):
        return "%02d/%02d/%4d" % (self.day, self.month, self.year)
```

Because the class inherits from Date, it has all of the same features. However, the now() and tomorrow() methods are slightly broken. For example, if someone calls EuroDate.now(), a Date object is returned instead of a EuroDate object. A class method can fix this:

```
class Date(object):
    ...
    @classmethod
    def now(cls):
        t = time.localtime()
        # Create an object of the appropriate type
        return cls(t.tm_year, t.tm_mon, t.tm_day)

class EuroDate(Date):
    ...
```

```
a = Date.now()       # Calls Date.now(Date) and returns a Date
b = EuroDate.now()   # Calls Date.now(EuroDate) and returns a EuroDate
```

One caution about static and class methods is that Python does not manage these methods in a separate namespace than the instance methods. As a result, they can be invoked on an instance. For example:

```
a = Date(1967,4,9)
b = d.now()          # Calls Date.now(Date)
```

This is potentially quite confusing because a call to d.now() doesn't really have anything to do with the instance d. This behavior is one area where the Python object system differs from that found in other OO languages such as Smalltalk and Ruby. In those languages, class methods are strictly separate from instance methods.

Properties

Normally, when you access an attribute of an instance or a class, the associated value that is stored is returned. A *property* is a special kind of attribute that computes its value when accessed. Here is a simple example:

```
class Circle(object):
    def __init__(self,radius):
        self.radius = radius
    # Some additional properties of Circles
    @property
    def area(self):
        return math.pi*self.radius**2
    @property
    def perimeter(self):
        return 2*math.pi*self.radius
```

The resulting `Circle` object behaves as follows:

```
>>> c = Circle(4.0)
>>> c.radius
4.0
>>> c.area
50.26548245743669
>>> c.perimeter
25.132741228718345
>>> c.area = 2
Traceback (most recent call last):
  File "<stdin>", line 1, in <module>
AttributeError: can't set attribute
>>>
```

In this example, `Circle` instances have an instance variable `c.radius` that is stored. `c.area` and `c.perimeter` are simply computed from that value. The `@property` decorator makes it possible for the method that follows to be accessed as a simple attribute, without the extra `()` that you would normally have to add to call the method. To the user of the object, there is no obvious indication that an attribute is being computed other than the fact that an error message is generated if an attempt is made to redefine the attribute (as shown in the `AttributeError` exception above).

Using properties in this way is related to something known as the *Uniform Access Principle*. Essentially, if you're defining a class, it is always a good idea to make the programming interface to it as uniform as possible. Without properties, certain attributes of an object would be accessed as a simple attribute such as `c.radius` whereas other attributes would be accessed as methods such as `c.area()`. Keeping track of when to add the extra `()` adds unnecessary confusion. A property can fix this.

Python programmers don't often realize that methods themselves are implicitly handled as a kind of property. Consider this class:

```
class Foo(object):
    def __init__(self,name):
        self.name = name
    def spam(self,x):
        print("%s, %s" % (self.name, x))
```

When a user creates an instance such as `f = Foo("Guido")` and then accesses `f.spam`, the original function object `spam` is not returned. Instead, you get something known as a *bound method*, which is an object that represents the method call that will execute when the `()` operator is invoked on it. A bound method is like a partially evaluated function where the `self` parameter has already been filled in, but the additional arguments still need to be supplied by you when you call it using `()`. The creation of this bound method object is silently handled through a property function that executes behind the scenes. When you define static and class methods using `@staticmethod` and `@classmethod`, you are actually specifying the use of a different property function that will handle the access to those methods in a different way. For example, `@staticmethod` simply returns the method function back "as is" without any special wrapping or processing.

Properties can also intercept operations to set and delete an attribute. This is done by attaching additional setter and deleter methods to a property. Here is an example:

```
class Foo(object):
    def __init__(self,name):
        self.__name = name
    @property
    def name(self):
        return self.__name
    @name.setter
    def name(self,value):
        if not isinstance(value,str):
            raise TypeError("Must be a string!")
        self.__name = value
    @name.deleter
    def name(self):
        raise TypeError("Can't delete name")

f = Foo("Guido")
n = f.name           # calls f.name() - get function
f.name = "Monty"     # calls setter name(f,"Monty")
f.name = 45          # calls setter name(f,45) -> TypeError
del f.name           # Calls deleter name(f) -> TypeError
```

In this example, the attribute name is first defined as a read-only property using the
@property decorator and associated method. The @name.setter and @name.deleter
decorators that follow are associating additional methods with the set and deletion
operations on the name attribute. The names of these methods must exactly match the
name of the original property. In these methods, notice that the actual value of the
name is stored in an attribute __name. The name of the stored attribute does not have
to follow any convention, but it has to be different than the property in order to distin-
guish it from the name of the property itself.

In older code, you will often see properties defined using the property(getf=None,
setf=None, delf=None, doc=None) function with a set of uniquely named methods
for carrying out each operation. For example:

```
class Foo(object):
    def getname(self):
        return self.__name
    def setname(self,value):
        if not isinstance(value,str):
            raise TypeError("Must be a string!")
        self.__name = value
    def delname(self):
        raise TypeError("Can't delete name")
    name = property(getname,setname,delname)
```

This older approach is still supported, but the decorator version tends to lead to classes
that are a little more polished. For example, if you use decorators, the get, set, and
delete functions aren't also visible as methods.

Descriptors

With properties, access to an attribute is controlled by a series of user-defined get, set,
and delete functions. This sort of attribute control can be further generalized through
the use of a *descriptor object*. A descriptor is simply an object that represents the value of
an attribute. By implementing one or more of the special methods __get__(),
__set__(), and __delete__(), it can hook into the attribute access mechanism and
can customize those operations. Here is an example:

```
class TypedProperty(object):
    def __init__(self,name,type,default=None):
        self.name = "_" + name
        self.type = type
        self.default = type() if default is None else default
    def __get__(self,instance,cls):
        return getattr(instance,self.name,self.default) if instance else self
    def __set__(self,instance,value):
        if not isinstance(value,self.type):
            raise TypeError("Must be a %s" % self.type)
        setattr(instance,self.name,value)
    def __delete__(self,instance):
        raise AttributeError("Can't delete attribute")

class Foo(object):
    name = TypedProperty("name",str)
    num  = TypedProperty("num",int,42)
```

In this example, the class `TypedProperty` defines a descriptor where type checking is performed when the attribute is assigned and an error is produced if an attempt is made to delete the attribute. For example:

```
f = Foo()
a = f.name             # Implicitly calls Foo.name.__get__(f,Foo)
f.name = "Guido"       # Calls Foo.name.__set__(f,"Guido")
del f.name             # Calls Foo.name.__delete__(f)
```

Descriptors can only be instantiated at the class level. It is not legal to create descriptors on a per-instance basis by creating descriptor objects inside `__init__()` and other methods. Also, the attribute name used by the class to hold a descriptor takes precedence over attributes stored on instances. In the previous example, this is why the descriptor object takes a name parameter and why the name is changed slightly by inserting a leading underscore. In order for the descriptor to store a value on the instance, it has to pick a name that is different than that being used by the descriptor itself.

Data Encapsulation and Private Attributes

By default, all attributes and methods of a class are "public." This means that they are all accessible without any restrictions. It also implies that everything defined in a base class is inherited and accessible within a derived class. This behavior is often undesirable in object-oriented applications because it exposes the internal implementation of an object and can lead to namespace conflicts between objects defined in a derived class and those defined in a base class.

To fix this problem, all names in a class that start with a double underscore, such as `__Foo`, are automatically mangled to form a new name of the form `_Classname__Foo`. This effectively provides a way for a class to have private attributes and methods because private names used in a derived class won't collide with the same private names used in a base class. Here's an example:

```
class A(object):
    def __init__(self):
        self.__X = 3          # Mangled to self._A__X
    def __spam(self):         # Mangled to _A__spam()
        pass
    def bar(self):
        self.__spam()         # Only calls A.__spam()
```

```
class B(A):
    def __init__(self):
        A.__init__(self)
        self.__X = 37         # Mangled to self._B__X
    def __spam(self):         # Mangled to _B__spam()
        pass
```

Although this scheme provides the illusion of data hiding, there's no strict mechanism in place to actually prevent access to the "private" attributes of a class. In particular, if the name of the class and corresponding private attribute are known, they can be accessed using the mangled name. A class can make these attributes less visible by redefining the __dir__() method, which supplies the list of names returned by the dir() function that's used to inspect objects.

Although this name mangling might look like an extra processing step, the mangling process actually only occurs once at the time a class is defined. It does not occur during execution of the methods, nor does it add extra overhead to program execution. Also, be aware that name mangling does not occur in functions such as getattr(), hasattr(), setattr(), or delattr() where the attribute name is specified as a string. For these functions, you need to explicitly use the mangled name such as _Classname__name to access the attribute.

It is recommended that private attributes be used when defining mutable attributes via properties. By doing so, you will encourage users to use the property name rather than accessing the underlying instance data directly (which is probably not what you intended if you wrapped it with a property to begin with). An example of this appeared in the previous section.

Giving a method a private name is a technique that a superclass can use to prevent a derived class from redefining and changing the implementation of a method. For example, the A.bar() method in the example only calls A.__spam(), regardless of the type of self or the presence of a different __spam() method in a derived class.

Finally, don't confuse the naming of private class attributes with the naming of "private" definitions in a module. A common mistake is to define a class where a single leading underscore is used on attribute names in an effort to hide their values (e.g., _name). In modules, this naming convention prevents names from being exported by the from module import * statement. However, in classes, this naming convention does not hide the attribute nor does it prevent name clashes that arise if someone inherits from the class and defines a new attribute or method with the same name.

Object Memory Management

When a class is defined, the resulting class is a factory for creating new instances. For example:

```
class Circle(object):
    def __init__(self,radius):
        self.radius = radius

# Create some Circle instances
c = Circle(4.0)
d = Circle(5.0)
```

The creation of an instance is carried out in two steps using the special method __new__(), which creates a new instance, and __init__(), which initializes it. For example, the operation c = Circle(4.0) performs these steps:

```
c = Circle.__new__(Circle, 4.0)
if isinstance(c,Circle):
    Circle.__init__(c,4.0)
```

The __new__() method of a class is something that is rarely defined by user code. If it is defined, it is typically written with the prototype __new__(cls, *args, **kwargs) where args and kwargs are the same arguments that will be passed to __init__(). __new__() is always a class method that receives the class object as the first parameter. Although __new__() creates an instance, it does not automatically call __init__().

If you see __new__() defined in a class, it usually means the class is doing one of two things. First, the class might be inheriting from a base class whose instances are immutable. This is common if defining objects that inherit from an immutable built-in type such as an integer, string, or tuple because __new__() is the only method that executes prior to the instance being created and is the only place where the value could be modified (in __init__(), it would be too late). For example:

```
class Upperstr(str):
    def __new__(cls,value=""):
        return str.__new__(cls, value.upper())

u = Upperstr("hello")     # value is "HELLO"
```

The other major use of __new__() is when defining metaclasses. This is described at the end of this chapter.

Once created, instances are managed by reference counting. If the reference count reaches zero, the instance is immediately destroyed. When the instance is about to be destroyed, the interpreter first looks for a __del__() method associated with the object and calls it. In practice, it's rarely necessary for a class to define a __del__() method. The only exception is when the destruction of an object requires a cleanup action such as closing a file, shutting down a network connection, or releasing other system resources. Even in these cases, it's dangerous to rely on __del__() for a clean shutdown because there's no guarantee that this method will be called when the interpreter exits. A better approach may be to define a method such as close() that a program can use to explicitly perform a shutdown.

Occasionally, a program will use the del statement to delete a reference to an object. If this causes the reference count of the object to reach zero, the __del__() method is called. However, in general, the del statement doesn't directly call __del__().

A subtle danger involving object destruction is that instances for which __del__() is defined cannot be collected by Python's cyclic garbage collector (which is a strong reason not to define __del__ unless you need to). Programmers coming from languages without automatic garbage collection (e.g., C++) should take care not to adopt a programming style where __del__() is unnecessarily defined. Although it is rare to break the garbage collector by defining __del__(), there are certain types of programming patterns, especially those involving parent-child relationships or graphs, where this can be a problem. For example, suppose you had an object that was implementing a variant of the "Observer Pattern."

```python
class Account(object):
    def __init__(self,name,balance):
        self.name = name
        self.balance = balance
        self.observers = set()
    def __del__(self):
        for ob in self.observers:
            ob.close()
        del self.observers
    def register(self,observer):
        self.observers.add(observer)
    def unregister(self,observer):
        self.observers.remove(observer)
    def notify(self):
        for ob in self.observers:
            ob.update()
    def withdraw(self,amt):
        self.balance -= amt
        self.notify()

class AccountObserver(object):
    def __init__(self, theaccount):
        self.theaccount = theaccount
        theaccount.register(self)
    def __del__(self):
        self.theaccount.unregister(self)
        del self.theaccount
    def update(self):
        print("Balance is %0.2f" % self.theaccount.balance)
    def close(self):
        print("Account no longer in use")

# Example setup
a = Account('Dave',1000.00)
a_ob = AccountObserver(a)
```

In this code, the `Account` class allows a set of `AccountObserver` objects to monitor an `Account` instance by receiving an update whenever the balance changes. To do this, each `Account` keeps a set of the observers and each `AccountObserver` keeps a reference back to the account. Each class has defined `__del__()` in an attempt to provide some sort of cleanup (such as unregistering and so on). However, it just doesn't work. Instead, the classes have created a reference cycle in which the reference count never drops to 0 and there is no cleanup. Not only that, the garbage collector (the `gc` module) won't even clean it up, resulting in a permanent memory leak.

One way to fix the problem shown in this example is for one of the classes to create a weak reference to the other using the `weakref` module. A *weak reference* is a way of creating a reference to an object without increasing its reference count. To work with a weak reference, you have to add an extra bit of functionality to check whether the object being referred to still exists. Here is an example of a modified observer class:

```python
import weakref
class AccountObserver(object):
    def __init__(self, theaccount):
        self.accountref = weakref.ref(theaccount)   # Create a weakref
        theaccount.register(self)
```

```
    def __del__(self):
        acc = self.accountref()          # Get account
        if acc:                          # Unregister if still exists
            acc.unregister(self)
    def update(self):
        print("Balance is %0.2f" % self.accountref().balance)
    def close(self):
        print("Account no longer in use")

# Example setup
a = Account('Dave',1000.00)
a_ob = AccountObserver(a)
```

In this example, a weak reference accountref is created. To access the underlying Account, you call it like a function. This either returns the Account or None if it's no longer around. With this modification, there is no longer a reference cycle. If the Account object is destroyed, its __del__ method runs and observers receive notification. The gc module also works properly. More information about the weakref module can be found in Chapter 13, "Python Runtime Services."

Object Representation and Attribute Binding

Internally, instances are implemented using a dictionary that's accessible as the instance's __dict__ attribute. This dictionary contains the data that's unique to each instance. Here's an example:

```
>>> a = Account('Guido', 1100.0)
>>> a.__dict__
{'balance': 1100.0, 'name': 'Guido'}
```

New attributes can be added to an instance at any time, like this:

```
a.number = 123456    # Add attribute 'number' to a.__dict__
```

Modifications to an instance are always reflected in the local __dict__ attribute. Likewise, if you make modifications to __dict__ directly, those modifications are reflected in the attributes.

Instances are linked back to their class by a special attribute __class__. The class itself is also just a thin layer over a dictionary which can be found in its own __dict__ attribute. The class dictionary is where you find the methods. For example:

```
>>> a.__class__
<class '__main__.Account'>
>>> Account.__dict__.keys()
['__dict__', '__module__', 'inquiry', 'deposit', 'withdraw',
'__del__', 'num_accounts', '__weakref__', '__doc__', '__init__']
>>>
```

Finally, classes are linked to their base classes in a special attribute __bases__, which is a tuple of the base classes. This underlying structure is the basis for all of the operations that get, set, and delete the attributes of objects.

Whenever an attribute is set using obj.name = value, the special method obj.__setattr__("name", value) is invoked. If an attribute is deleted using del obj.name, the special method obj.__delattr__("name") is invoked. The default behavior of these methods is to modify or remove values from the local __dict__ of obj unless the requested attribute happens to correspond to a property or descriptor. In that case, the set and delete operation will be carried out by the set and delete functions associated with the property.

For attribute lookup such as obj.*name*, the special method obj.__getattribute__("*name*") is invoked. This method carries out the search process for finding the attribute, which normally includes checking for properties, looking in the local __dict__ attribute, checking the class dictionary, and searching the base classes. If this search process fails, a final attempt to find the attribute is made by trying to invoke the __getattr__() method of the class (if defined). If this fails, an AttributeError exception is raised.

User-defined classes can implement their own versions of the attribute access functions, if desired. For example:

```
class Circle(object):
    def __init__(self,radius):
        self.radius = radius
    def __getattr__(self,name):
        if name == 'area':
            return math.pi*self.radius**2
        elif name == 'perimeter':
            return 2*math.pi*self.radius
        else:
            return object.__getattr__(self,name)
    def __setattr__(self,name,value):
        if name in ['area','perimeter']:
            raise TypeError("%s is readonly" % name)
        object.__setattr__(self,name,value)
```

A class that reimplements these methods should probably rely upon the default implementation in object to carry out the actual work. This is because the default implementation takes care of the more advanced features of classes such as descriptors and properties.

As a general rule, it is relatively uncommon for classes to redefine the attribute access operators. However, one application where they are often used is in writing general-purpose wrappers and proxies to existing objects. By redefining __getattr__(), __setattr__(), and __delattr__(), a proxy can capture attribute access and transparently forward those operations on to another object.

__slots__

A class can restrict the set of legal instance attribute names by defining a special variable called __slots__. Here's an example:

```
class Account(object):
    __slots__ = ('name','balance')
    ...
```

When __slots__ is defined, the attribute names that can be assigned on instances are restricted to the names specified. Otherwise, an AttributeError exception is raised. This restriction prevents someone from adding new attributes to existing instances and solves the problem that arises if someone assigns a value to an attribute that they can't spell correctly.

In reality, __slots__ was never implemented to be a safety feature. Instead, it is actually a performance optimization for both memory and execution speed. Instances of a class that uses __slots__ no longer use a dictionary for storing instance data. Instead, a much more compact data structure based on an array is used. In programs that create a large number of objects, using `__slots__` can result in a substantial reduction in memory use and execution time.

Be aware that the use of `__slots__` has a tricky interaction with inheritance. If a class inherits from a base class that uses `__slots__`, it also needs to define `__slots__` for storing its own attributes (even if it doesn't add any) to take advantage of the benefits `__slots__` provides. If you forget this, the derived class will run slower and use even more memory than what would have been used if `__slots__` had not been used on *any* of the classes!

The use of `__slots__` can also break code that expects instances to have an underlying `__dict__` attribute. Although this often does not apply to user code, utility libraries and other tools for supporting objects may be programmed to look at `__dict__` for debugging, serializing objects, and other operations.

Finally, the presence of `__slots__` has no effect on the invocation of methods such as `__getattribute__()`, `__getattr__()`, and `__setattr__()` should they be redefined in a class. However, the default behavior of these methods will take `__slots__` into account. In addition, it should be stressed that it is not necessary to add method or property names to `__slots__`, as they are stored in the class, not on a per-instance basis.

Operator Overloading

User-defined objects can be made to work with all of Python's built-in operators by adding implementations of the special methods described in Chapter 3 to a class. For example, if you wanted to add a new kind of number to Python, you could define a class in which special methods such as `__add__()` were defined to make instances work with the standard mathematical operators.

The following example shows how this works by defining a class that implements the complex numbers with some of the standard mathematical operators.

> **Note**
>
> Because Python already provides a complex number type, this class is only provided for the purpose of illustration.

```
class Complex(object):
    def __init__(self,real,imag=0):
        self.real = float(real)
        self.imag = float(imag)
    def __repr__(self):
        return "Complex(%s,%s)" % (self.real, self.imag)
    def __str__(self):
        return "(%g+%gj)" % (self.real, self.imag)
    # self + other
    def __add__(self,other):
        return Complex(self.real + other.real, self.imag + other.imag)
    # self - other
    def __sub__(self,other):
        return Complex(self.real - other.real, self.imag - other.imag)
```

In the example, the `__repr__()` method creates a string that can be evaluated to re-create the object (that is, `"Complex(real,imag)"`). This convention should be followed for all user-defined objects as applicable. On the other hand, the `__str__()` method creates a string that's intended for nice output formatting (this is the string that would be produced by the print statement).

The other operators, such as __add__() and __sub__(), implement mathematical operations. A delicate matter with these operators concerns the order of operands and type coercion. As implemented in the previous example, the __add__() and __sub__() operators are applied *only* if a complex number appears on the left side of the operator. They do not work if they appear on the right side of the operator and the left-most operand is not a Complex. For example:

```
>>> c = Complex(2,3)
>>> c + 4.0
Complex(6.0,3.0)
>>> 4.0 + c
Traceback (most recent call last):
  File "<stdin>", line 1, in <module>
TypeError: unsupported operand type(s) for +: 'int' and 'Complex'
>>>
```

The operation c + 4.0 works partly by accident. All of Python's built-in numbers already have .real and .imag attributes, so they were used in the calculation. If the other object did not have these attributes, the implementation would break. If you want your implementation of Complex to work with objects missing these attributes, you have to add extra conversion code to extract the needed information (which might depend on the type of the other object).

The operation 4.0 + c does not work at all because the built-in floating point type doesn't know anything about the Complex class. To fix this, you can add reversed-operand methods to Complex:

```
class Complex(object):
    ...
    def __radd__(self,other):
        return Complex(other.real + self.real, other.imag + self.imag)
    def __rsub__(self,other):
        return Complex(other.real - self.real, other.imag - self.img)
    ...
```

These methods serve as a fallback. If the operation 4.0 + c fails, Python tries to execute c.__radd__(4.0) first before issuing a TypeError.

Older versions of Python have tried various approaches to coerce types in mixed-type operations. For example, you might encounter legacy Python classes that implement a __coerce__() method. This is no longer used by Python 2.6 or Python 3. Also, don't be fooled by special methods such as __int__(), __float__(), or __complex__(). Although these methods are called by explicit conversions such as int(x) or float(x), they are never called implicitly to perform type conversion in mixed-type arithmetic. So, if you are writing classes where operators must work with mixed types, you have to explicitly handle the type conversion in the implementation of each operator.

Types and Class Membership Tests

When you create an instance of a class, the type of that instance is the class itself. To test for membership in a class, use the built-in function isinstance(obj, cname). This function returns True if an object, *obj*, belongs to the class *cname* or any class derived from *cname*. Here's an example:

```
class A(object): pass
class B(A): pass
class C(object): pass

a = A()            # Instance of 'A'
b = B()            # Instance of 'B'
c = C()            # Instance of 'C'

type(a)            # Returns the class object A
isinstance(a,A)    # Returns True
isinstance(b,A)    # Returns True, B derives from A
isinstance(b,C)    # Returns False, C not derived from A
```

Similarly, the built-in function issubclass(*A*, *B*) returns True if the class *A* is a subclass of class *B*. Here's an example:

```
issubclass(B,A)    # Returns True
issubclass(C,A)    # Returns False
```

A subtle problem with type-checking of objects is that programmers often bypass inheritance and simply create objects that mimic the behavior of another object. As an example, consider these two classes:

```
class Foo(object):
    def spam(self,a,b):
        pass

class FooProxy(object):
    def __init__(self,f):
        self.f = f
    def spam(self,a,b):
        return self.f.spam(a,b)
```

In this example, FooProxy is functionally identical to Foo. It implements the same methods, and it even uses Foo underneath the covers. Yet, in the type system, FooProxy is different than Foo. For example:

```
f = Foo()              # Create a Foo
g = FooProxy(f)        # Create a FooProxy
isinstance(g, Foo)     # Returns False
```

If a program has been written to explicitly check for a Foo using isinstance(), then it certainly won't work with a FooProxy object. However, this degree of strictness is often not exactly what you want. Instead, it might make more sense to assert that an object can simply be used as Foo because it has the same interface. To do this, it is possible to define an object that redefines the behavior of isinstance() and issubclass() for the purpose of grouping objects together and type-checking. Here is an example:

```
class IClass(object):
    def __init__(self):
        self.implementors = set()
    def register(self,C):
        self.implementors.add(C)
    def __instancecheck__(self,x):
        return self.__subclasscheck__(type(x))
```

```
    def __subclasscheck__(self,sub):
        return any(c in self.implementors for c in sub.mro())

# Now, use the above object
IFoo = IClass()
IFoo.register(Foo)
IFoo.register(FooProxy)
```

In this example, the class IClass creates an object that merely groups a collection of other classes together in a set. The register() method adds a new class to the set. The special method __instancecheck__() is called if anyone performs the operation isinstance(x, IClass). The special method __subclasscheck__() is called if the operation issubclass(C,IClass) is called.

By using the IFoo object and registered implementers, one can now perform type checks such as the following:

```
f = Foo()           # Create a Foo
g = FooProxy(f)     # Create a FooProxy
isinstance(f, IFoo)         # Returns True
isinstance(g, IFoo)         # Returns True
issubclass(FooProxy, IFoo) # Returns True
```

In this example, it's important to emphasize that no strong type-checking is occurring. The IFoo object has overloaded the instance checking operations in a way that allows you to assert that a class belongs to a group. It doesn't assert any information on the actual programming interface, and no other verification actually occurs. In fact, you can simply register any collection of objects you want to group together without regard to how those classes are related to each other. Typically, the grouping of classes is based on some criteria such as all classes implementing the same programming interface. However, no such meaning should be inferred when overloading __instancecheck__() or __subclasscheck__(). The actual interpretation is left up to the application.

Python provides a more formal mechanism for grouping objects, defining interfaces, and type-checking. This is done by defining an abstract base class, which is defined in the next section.

Abstract Base Classes

In the last section, it was shown that the isinstance() and issubclass() operations can be overloaded. This can be used to create objects that group similar classes together and to perform various forms of type-checking. *Abstract base classes* build upon this concept and provide a means for organizing objects into a hierarchy, making assertions about required methods, and so forth.

To define an abstract base class, you use the abc module. This module defines a metaclass (ABCMeta) and a set of decorators (@abstractmethod and @abstractproperty) that are used as follows:

```
from abc import ABCMeta, abstractmethod, abstractproperty
class Foo:                    # In Python 3, you use the syntax
    __metaclass__ = ABCMeta   # class Foo(metaclass=ABCMeta)
    @abstractmethod
    def spam(self,a,b):
        pass
    @abstractproperty
```

```
    def name(self):
        pass
```

The definition of an abstract class needs to set its metaclass to `ABCMeta` as shown (also, be aware that the syntax differs between Python 2 and 3). This is required because the implementation of abstract classes relies on a metaclass (described in the next section). Within the abstract class, the `@abstractmethod` and `@abstractproperty` decorators specify that a method or property must be implemented by subclasses of `Foo`.

An abstract class is not meant to be instantiated directly. If you try to create a `Foo` for the previous class, you will get the following error:

```
>>> f = Foo()
Traceback (most recent call last):
  File "<stdin>", line 1, in <module>
TypeError: Can't instantiate abstract class Foo with abstract methods spam
>>>
```

This restriction carries over to derived classes as well. For instance, if you have a class `Bar` that inherits from `Foo` but it doesn't implement one or more of the abstract methods, attempts to create a `Bar` will fail with a similar error. Because of this added checking, abstract classes are useful to programmers who want to make assertions on the methods and properties that must be implemented on subclasses.

Although an abstract class enforces rules about methods and properties that must be implemented, it does not perform conformance checking on arguments or return values. Thus, an abstract class will not check a subclass to see whether a method has used the same arguments as an abstract method. Likewise, an abstract class that requires the definition of a property does not check to see whether the property in a subclass supports the same set of operations (`get`, `set`, and `delete`) of the property specified in a base.

Although an abstract class cannot be instantiated, it can define methods and properties for use in subclasses. Moreover, an abstract method in the base can still be called from a subclass. For example, calling `Foo.spam(a,b)` from the subclass is allowed.

Abstract base classes allow preexisting classes to be registered as belonging to that base. This is done using the `register()` method as follows:

```
class Grok(object):
    def spam(self,a,b):
        print("Grok.spam")

Foo.register(Grok)        # Register with Foo abstract base class
```

When a class is registered with an abstract base, type-checking operations involving the abstract base (such as `isinstance()` and `issubclass()`) will return `True` for instances of the registered class. When a class is registered with an abstract class, no checks are made to see whether the class actually implements any of the abstract methods or properties. This registration process only affects type-checking. It does not add extra error checking to the class that is registered.

Unlike many other object-oriented languages, Python's built-in types are organized into a relatively flat hierarchy. For example, if you look at the built-in types such as `int` or `float`, they directly inherit from `object`, the root of all objects, instead of an intermediate base class representing numbers. This makes it clumsy to write programs that want to inspect and manipulate objects based on a generic category such as simply being an instance of a number.

The abstract class mechanism addresses this issue by allowing preexisting objects to be organized into user-definable type hierarchies. Moreover, some library modules aim to organize the built-in types according to different capabilities that they possess. The `collections` module contains abstract base classes for various kinds of operations involving sequences, sets, and dictionaries. The `numbers` module contains abstract base classes related to organizing a hierarchy of numbers. Further details can be found in Chapter 14, "Mathematics," and Chapter 15, "Data Structures, Algorithms, and Utilities."

Metaclasses

When you define a class in Python, the class definition itself becomes an object. Here's an example:

```
class Foo(object): pass
isinstance(Foo,object)        # Returns True
```

If you think about this long enough, you will realize that something had to create the Foo object. This creation of the class object is controlled by a special kind of object called a *metaclass*. Simply stated, a metaclass is an object that knows how to create and manage classes.

In the preceding example, the metaclass that is controlling the creation of Foo is a class called `type`. In fact, if you display the type of Foo, you will find out that it *is* a type:

```
>>> type(Foo)
<type 'type'>
```

When a new class is defined with the `class` statement, a number of things happen. First, the body of the class is executed as a series of statements within its own private dictionary. The execution of statements is exactly the same as in normal code with the addition of the name mangling that occurs on private members (names that start with `__`). Finally, the name of the class, the list of base classes, and the dictionary are passed to the constructor of a metaclass to create the corresponding class object. Here is an example of how it works:

```
class_name = "Foo"              # Name of class
class_parents = (object,)       # Base classes
class_body = """
def __init__(self,x):
    self.x = x
def blah(self):
    print("Hello World")
"""
class_dict = { }
# Execute the body in the local dictionary class_dict
exec(class_body,globals(),class_dict)

# Create the class object Foo
Foo = type(class_name,class_parents,class_dict)
```

The final step of class creation where the metaclass `type()` is invoked can be customized. The choice of what happens in the final step of class definition is controlled in

a number of ways. First, the class can explicitly specify its metaclass by either setting a
`__metaclass__` class variable (Python 2), or supplying the `metaclass` keyword argument in the tuple of base classes (Python 3).

```
class Foo:                  # In Python 3, use the syntax
    __metaclass__ = type    # class Foo(metaclass=type)
    ...
```

If no metaclass is explicitly specified, the `class` statement examines the first entry in
the tuple of base classes (if any). In this case, the metaclass is the same as the type of the
first base class. Therefore, when you write

```
class Foo(object): pass
```

`Foo` will be the same type of class as `object`.

If no base classes are specified, the `class` statement checks for the existence of a
global variable called `__metaclass__`. If this variable is found, it will be used to create
classes. If you set this variable, it will control how classes are created when a simple class
statement is used. Here's an example:

```
__metaclass__ = type
class Foo:
    pass
```

Finally, if no `__metaclass__` value can be found anywhere, Python uses the default
metaclass. In Python 2, this defaults to `types.ClassType`, which is known as an *old-
style class*. This kind of class, deprecated since Python 2.2, corresponds to the original
implementation of classes in Python. Although these classes are still supported, they
should be avoided in new code and are not covered further here. In Python 3, the
default metaclass is simply `type()`.

The primary use of metaclasses is in frameworks that want to assert more control
over the definition of user-defined objects. When a custom metaclass is defined, it typically inherits from `type()` and reimplements methods such as `__init__()` or
`__new__()`. Here is an example of a metaclass that forces all methods to have a
documentation string:

```
class DocMeta(type):
    def __init__(self,name,bases,attrs):
        for key, value in attrs.items():
            # Skip special and private methods
            if key.startswith("__"): continue
            # Skip anything not callable
            if not hasattr(value,"__call__"): continue
            # Check for a doc-string
            if not getattr(value,"__doc__"):
                raise TypeError("%s must have a docstring" % key)
        type.__init__(self,name,bases,attrs)
```

In this metaclass, the `__init__()` method has been written to inspect the contents of
the class dictionary. It scans the dictionary looking for methods and checking to see
whether they all have documentation strings. If not, a `TypeError` exception is generated. Otherwise, the default implementation of `type.__init__()` is called to initialize
the class.

To use this metaclass, a class needs to explicitly select it. The most common technique for doing this is to first define a base class such as the following:

```
class Documented:                # In Python 3, use the syntax
    __metaclass__ = DocMeta      # class Documented(metaclass=DocMeta)
```

This base class is then used as the parent for all objects that are to be documented. For example:

```
class Foo(Documented):
    spam(self,a,b):
        "spam does something"
        pass
```

This example illustrates one of the major uses of metaclasses, which is that of inspecting and gathering information about class definitions. The metaclass isn't changing anything about the class that actually gets created but is merely adding some additional checks.

In more advanced metaclass applications, a metaclass can both inspect and alter the contents of a class definition prior to the creation of the class. If alterations are going to be made, you should redefine the __new__() method that runs prior to the creation of the class itself. This technique is commonly combined with techniques that wrap attributes with descriptors or properties because it is one way to capture the names being used in the class. As an example, here is a modified version of the TypedProperty descriptor that was used in the "Descriptors" section:

```
class TypedProperty(object):
    def __init__(self,type,default=None):
        self.name = None
        self.type = type
        if default: self.default = default
        else:       self.default = type()
    def __get__(self,instance,cls):
        return getattr(instance,self.name,self.default)
    def __set__(self,instance,value):
        if not isinstance(value,self.type):
            raise TypeError("Must be a %s" % self.type)
        setattr(instance,self.name,value)
    def __delete__(self,instance):
        raise AttributeError("Can't delete attribute")
```

In this example, the name attribute of the descriptor is simply set to None. To fill this in, we'll rely on a meta class. For example:

```
class TypedMeta(type):
    def __new__(cls,name,bases,attrs):
        slots = []
        for key,value in attrs.items():
            if isinstance(value,TypedProperty):
                value.name = "_" + key
                slots.append(value.name)
        dict['__slots__'] = slots
        return type.__new__(cls,name,bases,attrs)

# Base class for user-defined objects to use
class Typed:                      # In Python 3, use the syntax
    __metaclass__ = TypedMeta     # class Typed(metaclass=TypedMeta)
```

In this example, the metaclass scans the class dictionary and looks for instances of TypedProperty. If found, it sets the name attribute and builds a list of names in slots. After this is done, a __slots__ attribute is added to the class dictionary, and the class is constructed by calling the __new__() method of the type() metaclass. Here is an example of using this new metaclass:

```
class Foo(Typed):
    name = TypedProperty(str)
    num  = TypedProperty(int,42)
```

Although metaclasses make it possible to drastically alter the behavior and semantics of user-defined classes, you should probably resist the urge to use metaclasses in a way that makes classes work wildly different from what is described in the standard Python documentation. Users will be confused if the classes they must write don't adhere to any of the normal coding rules expected for classes.

Class Decorators

In the previous section, it was shown how the process of creating a class can be customized by defining a metaclass. However, sometimes all you want to do is perform some kind of extra processing after a class is defined, such as adding a class to a registry or database. An alternative approach for such problems is to use a class decorator. A *class decorator* is a function that takes a class as input and returns a class as output. For example:

```
registry = { }
def register(cls):
    registry[cls.__clsid__] = cls
    return cls
```

In this example, the register function looks inside a class for a __clsid__ attribute. If found, it's used to add the class to a dictionary mapping class identifiers to class objects. To use this function, you can use it as a decorator right before the class definition. For example:

```
@register
class Foo(object):
    __clsid__ = "123-456"
    def bar(self):
        pass
```

Here, the use of the decorator syntax is mainly one of convenience. An alternative way to accomplish the same thing would have been this:

```
class Foo(object):
    __clsid__ = "123-456"
    def bar(self):
        pass
register(Foo)        # Register the class
```

Although it's possible to think of endless diabolical things one might do to a class in a class decorator function, it's probably best to avoid excessive magic such as putting a wrapper around the class or rewriting the class contents.

8

Modules, Packages, and Distribution

Large Python programs are organized into modules and packages. In addition, a large number of modules are included in the Python standard library. This chapter describes the module and package system in more detail. In addition, it provides information on how to install third-party modules and distribute source code.

Modules and the `import` Statement

Any Python source file can be used as a module. For example, consider the following code:

```
# spam.py
a = 37
def foo():
    print("I'm foo and a is %s" % a)
def bar():
    print("I'm bar and I'm calling foo")
    foo()
class Spam(object):
    def grok(self):
        print("I'm Spam.grok")
```

To load this code as a module, use the statement `import spam`. The first time `import` is used to load a module, it does three things:

1. It creates a new namespace that serves as a container for all the objects defined in the corresponding source file. This is the namespace accessed when functions and methods defined within the module use the `global` statement.

2. It executes the code contained in the module within the newly created namespace.

3. It creates a name within the caller that refers to the module namespace. This name matches the name of the module and is used as follows:

```
import spam          # Loads and executes the module 'spam'
x = spam.a           # Accesses a member of module 'spam'
spam.foo()           # Call a function in module 'spam'
s = spam.Spam()      # Create an instance of spam.Spam()
s.grok()
...
```

It is important to emphasize that import executes all of the statements in the loaded source file. If a module carries out a computation or produces output in addition to defining variables, functions, and classes, you will see the result. Also, a common confusion with modules concerns the access to classes. Keep in mind that if a file spam.py defines a class Spam, you must use the name spam.Spam to refer to the class.

To import multiple modules, you can supply import with a comma-separated list of module names, like this:

```
import socket, os, re
```

The name used to refer to a module can be changed using the as qualifier. Here's an example:

```
import spam as sp
import socket as net
sp.foo()
sp.bar()
net.gethostname()
```

When a module is loaded using a different name like this, the new name only applies to the source file or context where the import statement appeared. Other program modules can still load the module using its original name.

Changing the name of the imported module can be a useful tool for writing extensible code. For example, suppose you have two modules, xmlreader.py and csvreader.py, that both define a function read_data(filename) for reading some data from a file, but in different input formats. You can write code that selectively picks the reader module like this:

```
if format == 'xml':
    import xmlreader as reader
elif format == 'csv':
    import csvreader as reader
data = reader.read_data(filename)
```

Modules are first class objects in Python. This means that they can be assigned to variables, placed in data structures such as a list, and passed around in a program as a data. For instance, the reader variable in the previous example simply refers to the corresponding module object. Underneath the covers, a module object is a layer over a dictionary that is used to hold the contents of the module namespace. This dictionary is available as the __dict__ of a module, and whenever you look up or change a value in a module, you're working with this dictionary.

The import statement can appear at any point in a program. However, the code in each module is loaded and executed only once, regardless of how often you use the import statement. Subsequent import statements simply bind the module name to the module object already created by the previous import. You can find a dictionary containing all currently loaded modules in the variable sys.modules. This dictionary maps module names to module objects. The contents of this dictionary are used to determine whether import loads a fresh copy of a module.

Importing Selected Symbols from a Module

The from statement is used to load specific definitions within a module into the current namespace. The from statement is identical to import except that instead of creating a name referring to the newly created module namespace, it places references to one or more of the objects defined in the module into the current namespace:

```
from spam import foo   # Imports spam and puts 'foo' in current namespace
foo()                  # Calls spam.foo()
spam.foo()             # NameError: spam
```

The from statement also accepts a comma-separated list of object names. For example:

```
from spam import foo, bar
```

If you have a very long list of names to import, the names can be enclosed in parentheses. This makes it easier to break the import statement across multiple lines. Here's an example:

```
from spam import (foo,
                  bar,
                  Spam)
```

In addition, the as qualifier can be used to rename specific objects imported with from. Here's an example:

```
from spam import Spam as Sp
s = Sp()
```

The asterisk (*) wildcard character can also be used to load all the definitions in a module, except those that start with an underscore. Here's an example:

```
from spam import *   # Load all definitions into current namespace
```

The from *module* import * statement may only be used at the top level of a module. In particular, it is illegal to use this form of import inside function bodies due to the way in which it interacts with function scoping rules (e.g., when functions are compiled into internal bytecode, all of the symbols used within the function need to be fully specified).

Modules can more precisely control the set of names imported by from *module* import * by defining the list __all__. Here's an example:

```
# module: spam.py
__all__ = [ 'bar', 'Spam' ]  # Names I will export with from spam import *
```

Importing definitions with the from form of import does not change their scoping rules. For example, consider this code:

```
from spam import foo
a = 42
foo()     # Prints "I'm foo and a is 37"
```

In this example, the definition of foo() in spam.py refers to a global variable a. When a reference to foo is placed into a different namespace, it doesn't change the binding rules for variables within that function. Thus, the global namespace for a function is always the module in which the function was defined, not the namespace into which a function is imported and called. This also applies to function calls. For example, in the following code, the call to `bar()` results in a call to `spam.foo()`, not the redefined `foo()` that appears in the previous code example:

```
from spam import bar
def foo():
    print("I'm a different foo")
bar()       # When bar calls foo(), it calls spam.foo(), not
            # the definition of foo() above
```

Another common confusion with the `from` form of import concerns the behavior of global variables. For example, consider this code:

```
from spam import a, foo    # Import a global variable
a = 42                     # Modify the variable
foo()                      # Prints "I'm foo and a is 37"
print(a)                   # Prints "42"
```

Here, it is important to understand that variable assignment in Python is not a storage operation. That is, the assignment to a in the earlier example is not storing a new value in a, overwriting the previous value. Instead, a new object containing the value 42 is created and the name a is made to refer to it. At this point, a is no longer bound to the value in the imported module but to some other object. Because of this behavior, it is not possible to use the `from` statement in a way that makes variables behave similarly as global variables or common blocks in languages such as C or Fortran. If you want to have mutable global program parameters in your program, put them in a module and use the module name explicitly using the `import` statement (that is, use `spam.a` explicitly).

Execution as the Main Program

There are two ways in which a Python source file can execute. The `import` statement executes code in its own namespace as a library module. However, code might also execute as the main program or script. This occurs when you supply the program as the script name to the interpreter:

```
% python spam.py
```

Each module defines a variable, `__name__`, that contains the module name. Programs can examine this variable to determine the module in which they're executing. The top-level module of the interpreter is named `__main__`. Programs specified on the command line or entered interactively run inside the `__main__` module. Sometimes a program may alter its behavior, depending on whether it has been imported as a module or is running in `__main__`. For example, a module may include some testing code that is executed if the module is used as the main program but which is not executed if the module is simply imported by another module. This can be done as follows:

```
# Check if running as a program
if __name__ == '__main__':
    # Yes
    statements
else:
    # No, I must have been imported as a module
    statements
```

It is common practice for source files intended for use as libraries to use this technique for including optional testing or example code. For example, if you're developing a module, you can put code for testing the features of your library inside an `if` statement as shown and simply run Python on your module as the main program to run it. That code won't run for users who import your library.

The Module Search Path

When loading modules, the interpreter searches the list of directories in `sys.path`. The first entry in `sys.path` is typically an empty string `' '`, which refers to the current working directory. Other entries in `sys.path` may consist of directory names, `.zip` archive files, and `.egg` files. The order in which entries are listed in `sys.path` determines the search order used when modules are loaded. To add new entries to the search path, simply add them to this list.

Although the path usually contains directory names, zip archive files containing Python modules can also be added to the search path. This can be a convenient way to package a collection of modules as a single file. For example, suppose you created two modules, `foo.py` and `bar.py`, and placed them in a zip file called `mymodules.zip`. The file could be added to the Python search path as follows:

```
import sys
sys.path.append("mymodules.zip")
import foo, bar
```

Specific locations within the directory structure of a zip file can also be used. In addition, zip files can be mixed with regular pathname components. Here's an example:

```
sys.path.append("/tmp/modules.zip/lib/python")
```

In addition to `.zip` files, you can also add `.egg` files to the search path. `.egg` files are packages created by the `setuptools` library. This is a common format encountered when installing third-party Python libraries and extensions. An `.egg` file is actually just a `.zip` file with some extra metadata (e.g., version number, dependencies, etc.) added to it. Thus, you can examine and extract data from an `.egg` file using standard tools for working with `.zip` files.

Despite support for zip file imports, there are some restrictions to be aware of. First, the only file types that can be imported from an archive are `.py`, `.pyc`, `.pyo`, and `.pyw`. Shared libraries and extension modules written in C cannot be loaded directly from archives, although packaging systems such as `setuptools` are sometimes able to provide a workaround (typically by extracting C extensions to a temporary directory and loading modules from it). Moreover, Python will not create `.pyc` and `.pyo` files when `.py` files are loaded from an archive (described next). Thus, it is important to make sure these files are created in advance and placed in the archive in order to avoid poor performance when loading modules.

Module Loading and Compilation

So far, this chapter has presented modules as files containing pure Python code. However, modules loaded with `import` really fall into four general categories:

- Code written in Python (`.py` files)
- C or C++ extensions that have been compiled into shared libraries or DLLs

- Packages containing a collection of modules
- Built-in modules written in C and linked into the Python interpreter

When looking for a module (for example, foo), the interpreter searches each of the directories in sys.path for the following files (listed in search order):

1. A directory, foo, defining a package

2. foo.pyd, foo.so, foomodule.so, or foomodule.dll (compiled extensions)

3. foo.pyo (only if the -O or -OO option has been used)

4. foo.pyc

5. foo.py (on Windows, Python also checks for .pyw files.)

Packages are described shortly; compiled extensions are described in Chapter 26, "Extending and Embedding Python." For .py files, when a module is first imported, it's compiled into bytecode and written back to disk as a .pyc file. On subsequent imports, the interpreter loads this precompiled bytecode unless the modification date of the .py file is more recent (in which case, the .pyc file is regenerated). .pyo files are used in conjunction with the interpreter's -O option. These files contain bytecode stripped of line numbers, assertions, and other debugging information. As a result, they're somewhat smaller and allow the interpreter to run slightly faster. If the -OO option is specified instead of -O, documentation strings are also stripped from the file. This removal of documentation strings occurs only when .pyo files are created—not when they're loaded. If none of these files exists in any of the directories in sys.path, the interpreter checks whether the name corresponds to a built-in module name. If no match exists, an ImportError exception is raised.

The automatic compilation of files into .pyc and .pyo files occurs only in conjunction with the import statement. Programs specified on the command line or standard input don't produce such files. In addition, these files aren't created if the directory containing a module's .py file doesn't allow writing (e.g., either due to insufficient permission or if it's part of a zip archive). The -B option to the interpreter also disables the generation of these files.

If .pyc and .pyo files are available, it is not necessary for a corresponding .py file to exist. Thus, if you are packaging code and don't wish to include source, you can merely bundle a set of .pyc files together. However, be aware that Python has extensive support for introspection and disassembly. Knowledgeable users will still be able to inspect and find out a lot of details about your program even if the source hasn't been provided. Also, be aware that .pyc files tend to be version-specific. Thus, a .pyc file generated for one version of Python might not work in a future release.

When import searches for files, it matches filenames in a case-sensitive manner—even on machines where the underlying file system is case-insensitive, such as on Windows and OS X (such systems are case-preserving, however). Therefore, import foo will only import the file foo.py and not the file FOO.PY. However, as a general rule, you should avoid the use of module names that differ in case only.

Module Reloading and Unloading

Python provides no real support for reloading or unloading of previously imported modules. Although you can remove a module from `sys.modules`, this does not generally unload a module from memory. This is because references to the module object may still exist in other program components that used `import` to load that module. Moreover, if there are instances of classes defined in the module, those instances contain references back to their class object, which in turn holds references to the module in which it was defined.

The fact that module references exist in many places makes it generally impractical to reload a module after making changes to its implementation. For example, if you remove a module from `sys.modules` and use `import` to reload it, this will not retroactively change all of the previous references to the module used in a program. Instead, you'll have one reference to the new module created by the most recent `import` statement and a set of references to the old module created by imports in other parts of the code. This is rarely what you want and never safe to use in any kind of sane production code unless you are able to carefully control the entire execution environment.

Older versions of Python provided a `reload()` function for reloading a module. However, use of this function was never really safe (for all of the aforementioned reasons), and its use was actively discouraged except as a possible debugging aid. Python 3 removes this feature entirely. So, it's best not to rely upon it.

Finally, it should be noted that C/C++ extensions to Python cannot be safely unloaded or reloaded in any way. No support is provided for this, and the underlying operating system may prohibit it anyways. Thus, your only recourse is to restart the Python interpreter process.

Packages

Packages allow a collection of modules to be grouped under a common package name. This technique helps resolve namespace conflicts between module names used in different applications. A package is defined by creating a directory with the same name as the package and creating the file `__init__.py` in that directory. You can then place additional source files, compiled extensions, and subpackages in this directory, as needed. For example, a package might be organized as follows:

```
Graphics/
        __init__.py
        Primitive/
            __init__.py
            lines.py
            fill.py
            text.py
            ...
        Graph2d/
            __init__.py
            plot2d.py
            ...
        Graph3d/
            __init__.py
            plot3d.py
            ...
        Formats/
            __init__.py
            gif.py
```

```
png.py
tiff.py
jpeg.py
```

The import statement is used to load modules from a package in a number of ways:

- `import Graphics.Primitive.fill`

  This loads the submodule `Graphics.Primitive.fill`. The contents of this module have to be explicitly named, such as `Graphics.Primitive.fill.floodfill(img,x,y,color)`.

- `from Graphics.Primitive import fill`

  This loads the submodule `fill` but makes it available without the package prefix; for example, `fill.floodfill(img,x,y,color)`.

- `from Graphics.Primitive.fill import floodfill`

  This loads the submodule `fill` but makes the `floodfill` function directly accessible; for example, `floodfill(img,x,y,color)`.

Whenever any part of a package is first imported, the code in the file `__init__.py` is executed. Minimally, this file may be empty, but it can also contain code to perform package-specific initializations. All the `__init__.py` files encountered during an import are executed. Therefore, the statement `import Graphics.Primitive.fill`, shown earlier, would first execute the `__init__.py` file in the `Graphics` directory and then the `__init__.py` file in the `Primitive` directory.

One peculiar problem with packages is the handling of this statement:

```
from Graphics.Primitive import *
```

A programmer who uses this statement usually wants to import all the submodules associated with a package into the current namespace. However, because filename conventions vary from system to system (especially with regard to case sensitivity), Python cannot accurately determine what modules those might be. As a result, this statement just imports all the names that are defined in the `__init__.py` file in the `Primitive` directory. This behavior can be modified by defining a list, `__all__`, that contains all the module names associated with the package. This list should be defined in the package `__init__.py` file, like this:

```
# Graphics/Primitive/__init__.py
__all__ = ["lines","text","fill"]
```

Now when the user issues a `from Graphics.Primitive import *` statement, all the listed submodules are loaded as expected.

Another subtle problem with packages concerns submodules that want to import other submodules within the same package. For example, suppose the `Graphics.Primitive.fill` module wants to import the `Graphics.Primitive.lines` module. To do this, you can simply use the fully specified name (e.g., `from Graphics.Primitives import lines`) or use a package relative import like this:

```
# fill.py
from . import lines
```

In this example, the `.` used in the statement `from . import lines` refers to the same directory of the calling module. Thus, this statement looks for a module `lines` in the same directory as the file `fill.py`. Great care should be taken to avoid using a statement such as `import module` to import a package submodule. In older versions of Python, it was unclear whether the `import module` statement was referring to a standard library module or a submodule of a package. Older versions of Python would first try to load the module from the same package directory as the submodule where the `import` statement appeared and then move on to standard library modules if no match was found. However, in Python 3, `import` assumes an absolute path and will simply try to load `module` from the standard library. A relative import more clearly states your intentions.

Relative imports can also be used to load submodules contained in different directories of the same package. For example, if the module `Graphics.Graph2D.plot2d` wanted to import `Graphics.Primitives.lines`, it could use a statement like this:

```
# plot2d.py
from ..Primitives import lines
```

Here, the `..` moves out one directory level and `Primitives` drops down into a different package directory.

Relative imports can only be specified using the `from module import symbol` form of the import statement. Thus, statements such as `import ..Primitives.lines` or `import .lines` are a syntax error. Also, `symbol` has to be a valid identifier. So, a statement such as `from .. import Primitives.lines` is also illegal. Finally, relative imports can only be used within a package; it is illegal to use a relative import to refer to modules that are simply located in a different directory on the filesystem.

Importing a package name alone doesn't import all the submodules contained in the package. For example, the following code doesn't work:

```
import Graphics
Graphics.Primitive.fill.floodfill(img,x,y,color)   # Fails!
```

However, because the `import Graphics` statement executes the `__init__.py` file in the `Graphics` directory, relative imports can be used to load all the submodules automatically, as follows:

```
# Graphics/__init__.py
from . import Primitive, Graph2d, Graph3d
```

```
# Graphics/Primitive/__init__.py
from . import lines, fill, text, ...
```

Now the `import Graphics` statement imports all the submodules and makes them available using their fully qualified names. Again, it is important to stress that a package relative import should be used as shown. If you use a simple statement such as `import module`, standard library modules may be loaded instead.

Finally, when Python imports a package, it defines a special variable, `__path__`, which contains a list of directories that are searched when looking for package submodules (`__path__` is a package-specific version of the `sys.path` variable). `__path__` is accessible to the code contained in `__init__.py` files and initially contains a single item with the directory name of the package. If necessary, a package can supply additional directories to the `__path__` list to alter the search path used for finding submodules. This might be useful if the organization of a package on the file system is complicated and doesn't neatly match up with the package hierarchy.

Distributing Python Programs and Libraries

To distribute Python programs to others, you should use the `distutils` module. As preparation, you should first cleanly organize your work into a directory that has a `README` file, supporting documentation, and your source code. Typically, this directory will contain a mix of library modules, packages, and scripts. Modules and packages refer to source files that will be loaded with `import` statements. Scripts are programs that will run as the main program to the interpreter (e.g., running as `python scriptname`). Here is an example of a directory containing Python code:

```
spam/
    README.txt
    Documentation.txt
    libspam.py          # A single library module
    spampkg/            # A package of support modules
        __init__.py
        foo.py
        bar.py
    runspam.py          # A script to run as: python runspam.py
```

You should organize your code so that it works normally when running the Python interpreter in the top-level directory. For example, if you start Python in the `spam` directory, you should be able to import modules, import package components, and run scripts without having to alter any of Python's settings such as the module search path.

After you have organized your code, create a file `setup.py` in the top most directory (spam in the previous examples). In this file, put the following code:

```
# setup.py
from distutils.core import setup

setup(name = "spam",
      version = "1.0",
      py_modules = ['libspam'],
      packages = ['spampkg'],
      scripts = ['runspam.py'],
      )
```

In the `setup()` call, the `py_modules` argument is a list of all of the single-file Python modules, `packages` is a list of all package directories, and `scripts` is a list of script files. Any of these arguments may be omitted if your software does not have any matching components (i.e., there are no scripts). `name` is the name of your package, and `version` is the version number as a string.

The call to `setup()` supports a variety of other parameters that supply various metadata about your package. Table 8.1 shows the most common parameters that can be specified. All values are strings except for the `classifiers` parameter, which is a list of strings such as `['Development Status :: 4 - Beta', 'Programming Language :: Python']` (a full list can be found at http://pypi.python.org).

Table 8.1   **Parameters to** `setup()`

Parameter	Description
`name`	Name of the package (required)
`version`	Version number (required)
`author`	Author's name
`author_email`	Author's email address

Table 8.1   **Continued**

Parameter	Description
maintainer	Maintainer's name
maintainer_email	Maintainer's email
url	Home page for the package
description	Short description of the package
long_description	Long description of the package
download_url	Location where package can be downloaded
classifiers	List of string classifiers

Creating a setup.py file is enough to create a source distribution of your software. Type the following shell command to make a source distribution:

```
% python setup.py sdist
...
%
```

This creates an archive file such as spam-1.0.tar.gz or spam-1.0.zip in the directory spam/dist. This is the file you would give to others to install your software. To install, a user simply unpacks the archive and performs these steps:

```
% unzip spam-1.0.zip
...
% cd spam-1.0
% python setup.py install
...
%
```

This installs the software into the local Python distribution and makes it available for general use. Modules and packages are normally installed into a directory called "site-packages" in the Python library. To find the exact location of this directory, inspect the value of sys.path. Scripts are normally installed into the same directory as the Python interpreter on UNIX-based systems or into a "Scripts" directory on Windows (found in "C:\Python26\Scripts" in a typical installation).

On UNIX, if the first line of a script starts with #! and contains the text "python", the installer will rewrite the line to point to the local installation of Python. Thus, if you have written scripts that have been hard-coded to a specific Python location such as /usr/local/bin/python, they should still work when installed on other systems where Python is in a different location.

The setup.py file has a number of other commands concerning the distribution of software. If you type 'python setup.py bdist', a binary distribution is created in which all of the .py files have already been precompiled into .pyc files and placed into a directory structure that mimics that of the local platform. This kind of distribution is needed only if parts of your application have platform dependencies (for example, if you also have C extensions that need to be compiled). If you run 'python setup.py bdist_wininst' on a Windows machine, an .exe file will be created. When opened, a Windows installer dialog will start, prompting the user for information about where the software should be installed. This kind of distribution also adds entries to the registry, making it easy to uninstall your package at a later date.

The distutils module assumes that users already have a Python installation on their machine (downloaded separately). Although it is possible to create software packages where the Python runtime and your software are bundled together into a single binary executable, that is beyond the scope of what can be covered here (look at a third-party module such as py2exe or py2app for further details). If all you are doing is distributing libraries or simple scripts to people, it is usually unnecessary to package your code with the Python interpreter and runtime as well.

Finally, it should be noted that there are many more options to distutils than those covered here. Chapter 26 describes how distutils can be used to compile C and C++ extensions.

Although not part of the standard Python distribution, Python software is often distributed in the form of an .egg file. This format is created by the popular setuptools extension (http://pypi.python.org/pypi/setuptools). To support setuptools, you can simply change the first part of your setup.py file as follows:

```
# setup.py
try:
    from setuptools import setup
except ImportError:
    from distutils.core import setup

setup(name = "spam",
    ...
)
```

Installing Third-Party Libraries

The definitive resource for locating third-party libraries and extensions to Python is the *Python Package Index (PyPI)*, which is located at http://pypi.python.org. Installing third-party modules is usually straightforward but can become quite involved for very large packages that also depend on other third-party modules. For the more major extensions, you will often find a platform-native installer that simply steps you through the process using a series of dialog screens. For other modules, you typically unpack the download, look for the setup.py file, and type **python setup.py install** to install the software.

By default, third-party modules are installed in the site-packages directory of the Python standard library. Access to this directory typically requires root or administrator access. If this is not the case, you can type **python setup.py install --user** to have the module installed in a per-user library directory. This installs the package in a per-user directory such as "/Users/beazley/.local/lib/python2.6/site-packages" on UNIX.

If you want to install the software somewhere else entirely, use the --prefix option to setup.py. For example, typing python setup.py install --prefix=/home/beazley/pypackages installs a module under the directory /home/beazley/pypackages. When installing in a nonstandard location, you will probably have to adjust the setting of sys.path in order for Python to locate your newly installed modules.

Be aware that many extensions to Python involve C or C++ code. If you have downloaded a source distribution, your system will have to have a C++ compiler installed in order to run the installer. On UNIX, Linux, and OS X, this is usually not an issue. On Windows, it has traditionally been necessary to have a version of Microsoft Visual Studio installed. If you're working on that platform, you're probably better off looking for a precompiled version of your extension.

If you have installed `setuptools`, a script `easy_install` is available to install packages. Simply type **`easy_install` *`pkgname`*** to install a specific package. If configured correctly, this will download the appropriate software from PyPI along with any dependencies and install it for you. Of course, your mileage might vary.

If you would like to add your own software to PyPI, simply type `python` **`setup.py register`**. This will upload metadata about the latest version of your software to the index (note that you will have to register a username and password first).

Input and Output

This chapter describes the basics of Python input and output (I/O), including command-line options, environment variables, file I/O, Unicode, and how to serialize objects using the `pickle` module.

Reading Command-Line Options

When Python starts, command-line options are placed in the list `sys.argv`. The first element is the name of the program. Subsequent items are the options presented on the command line *after* the program name. The following program shows a minimal prototype of manually processing simple command-line arguments:

```
import sys
if len(sys.argv) != 3:
    sys.stderr.write("Usage : python %s inputfile outputfile\n" % sys.argv[0])
    raise SystemExit(1)
inputfile  = sys.argv[1]
outputfile = sys.argv[2]
```

In this program, `sys.argv[0]` contains the name of the script being executed. Writing an error message to `sys.stderr` and raising `SystemExit` with a non-zero exit code as shown is standard practice for reporting usage errors in command-line tools.

Although you can manually process command options for simple scripts, use the `optparse` module for more complicated command-line handling. Here is a simple example:

```
import optparse
p = optparse.OptionParser()

# An option taking an argument
p.add_option("-o",action="store",dest="outfile")
p.add_option("--output",action="store",dest="outfile")

# An option that sets a boolean flag
p.add_option("-d",action="store_true",dest="debug")
p.add_option("--debug",action="store_true",dest="debug")

# Set default values for selected options
p.set_defaults(debug=False)

# Parse the command line
opts, args = p.parse_args()

# Retrieve the option settings
outfile   = opts.outfile
debugmode = opts.debug
```

In this example, two types of options are added. The first option, -o or --output, has a required argument. This behavior is selected by specifying action='store' in the call to p.add_option(). The second option, -d or --debug, is merely setting a Boolean flag. This is enabled by specifying action='store_true' in p.add_option(). The dest argument to p.add_option() selects an attribute name where the argument value will be stored after parsing. The p.set_defaults() method sets default values for one or more of the options. The argument names used with this method should match the destination names selected for each option. If no default value is selected, the default value is set to None.

The previous program recognizes all of the following command-line styles:

```
% python prog.py -o outfile -d infile1 ... infileN
% python prog.py --output=outfile --debug infile1 ... infileN
% python prog.py -h
% python prog.py --help
```

Parsing is performed using the p.parse_args() method. This method returns a 2-tuple (opts, args) where opts is an object containing the parsed option values and args is a list of items on the command line not parsed as options. Option values are retrieved using opts.*dest* where *dest* is the destination name used when adding an option. For example, the argument to the -o or --output argument is placed in opts.outfile, whereas args is a list of the remaining arguments such as ['infile1', ..., 'infileN']. The optparse module automatically provides a -h or --help option that lists the available options if requested by the user. Bad options also result in an error message.

This example only shows the simplest use of the optparse module. Further details on some of the more advanced options can be found in Chapter 19, "Operating System Services."

Environment Variables

Environment variables are accessed in the dictionary os.environ. Here's an example:

```
import os
path   = os.environ["PATH"]
user   = os.environ["USER"]
editor = os.environ["EDITOR"]
... etc ...
```

To modify the environment variables, set the os.environ variable. For example:

```
os.environ["FOO"] = "BAR"
```

Modifications to os.environ affect both the running program and subprocesses created by Python.

Files and File Objects

The built-in function open(*name* [,*mode* [,*bufsize*]]) opens and creates a file object, as shown here:

```
f = open("foo")        # Opens "foo" for reading
f = open("foo",'r')    # Opens "foo" for reading (same as above)
f = open("foo",'w')    # Open for writing
```

The file mode is 'r' for read, 'w' for write, or 'a' for append. These file modes assume text-mode and may implicitly perform translation of the newline character '\n'. For example, on Windows, writing the character '\n' actually outputs the two-character sequence '\r\n' (and when reading the file back, '\r\n' is translated back into a single '\n' character). If you are working with binary data, append a 'b' to the file mode such as 'rb' or 'wb'. This disables newline translation and should be included if you are concerned about portability of code that processes binary data (on UNIX, it is a common mistake to omit the 'b' because there is no distinction between text and binary files). Also, because of the distinction in modes, you might see text-mode specified as 'rt', 'wt', or 'at', which more clearly expresses your intent.

A file can be opened for in-place updates by supplying a plus (+) character, such as 'r+' or 'w+'. When a file is opened for update, you can perform both input and output, as long as all output operations flush their data before any subsequent input operations. If a file is opened using 'w+' mode, its length is first truncated to zero.

If a file is opened with mode 'U' or 'rU', it provides universal newline support for reading. This feature simplifies cross-platform work by translating different newline encodings (such as '\n', '\r', and '\r\n') to a standard '\n' character in the strings returned by various file I/O functions. This can be useful if, for example, you are writing scripts on UNIX systems that must process text files generated by programs on Windows.

The optional *bufsize* parameter controls the buffering behavior of the file, where 0 is unbuffered, 1 is line buffered, and a negative number requests the system default. Any other positive number indicates the approximate buffer size in bytes that will be used.

Python 3 adds four additional parameters to the open() function, which is called as open(*name* [,*mode* [,*bufsize* [, *encoding* [, *errors* [, *newline* [, *closefd*]]]]]]). *encoding* is an encoding name such as 'utf-8' or 'ascii'. *errors* is the error-handling policy to use for encoding errors (see the later sections in this chapter on Unicode for more information). *newline* controls the behavior of universal newline mode and is set to None, '', '\n', '\r', or '\r\n'. If set to None, any line ending of the form '\n', '\r', or '\r\n' is translated into '\n'. If set to '' (the empty string), any of these line endings are recognized as newlines, but left untranslated in the input text. If *newline* has any other legal value, that value is what is used to terminate lines. *closefd* controls whether the underlying file descriptor is actually closed when the close() method is invoked. By default, this is set to True.

Table 9.1 shows the methods supported by file objects.

Table 9.1   File Methods

Method	Description
f.read([*n*])	Reads at most *n* bytes.
f.readline([*n*])	Reads a single line of input up to *n* characters. If *n* is omitted, this method reads the entire line.
f.readlines([size])	Reads all the lines and returns a list. *size* optionally specifies the approximate number of characters to read on the file before stopping.
f.write(*s*)	Writes string *s*.
f.writelines(*lines*)	Writes all strings in sequence *lines*.
f.close()	Closes the file.

Table 9.1   **Continued**

Method	Description
`f.tell()`	Returns the current file pointer.
`f.seek(offset [, whence])`	Seeks to a new file position.
`f.isatty()`	Returns 1 if `f` is an interactive terminal.
`f.flush()`	Flushes the output buffers.
`f.truncate([size])`	Truncates the file to at most `size` bytes.
`f.fileno()`	Returns the integer file descriptor or raises `valueError` if closed.
`f.next()`	Returns the next line or raises `StopIteration`. In Python 3, it is called `f.__next__()`.

The `read()` method returns the entire file as a string unless an optional *length* parameter is given specifying the maximum number of characters. The `readline()` method returns the next line of input, including the terminating newline; the `readlines()` method returns all the input lines as a list of strings. The `readline()` method optionally accepts a maximum line length, *n*. If a line longer than *n* characters is read, the first *n* characters are returned. The remaining line data is not discarded and will be returned on subsequent read operations. The `readlines()` method accepts a size parameter that specifies the approximate number of characters to read before stopping. The actual number of characters read may be larger than this depending on how much data has been buffered.

Both the `readline()` and `readlines()` methods are platform-aware and handle different representations of newlines properly (for example, `'\n'` versus `'\r\n'`). If the file is opened in universal newline mode (`'U'` or `'rU'`), newlines are converted to `'\n'`.

`read()` and `readline()` indicate end-of-file (EOF) by returning an empty string. Thus, the following code shows how you can detect an EOF condition:

```
while True:
    line = f.readline()
    if not line:        # EOF
        break
```

A convenient way to read all lines in a file is to use iteration with a `for` loop. For example:

```
for line in f:          # Iterate over all lines in the file
    # Do something with line
    ...
```

Be aware that in Python 2, the various read operations always return 8-bit strings, regardless of the file mode that was specified (text or binary). In Python 3, these operations return Unicode strings if a file has been opened in text mode and byte strings if the file is opened in binary mode.

The `write()` method writes a string to the file, and the `writelines()` method writes a list of strings to the file. `write()` and `writelines()` do not add newline characters to the output, so all output that you produce should already include all necessary formatting. These methods can write raw-byte strings to a file, but only if the file has been opened in binary mode.

Internally, each file object keeps a file pointer that stores the byte offset at which the next read or write operation will occur. The `tell()` method returns the current value of the file pointer as a long integer. The `seek()` method is used to randomly access parts of a file given an *offset* and a placement rule in *whence*. If *whence* is 0 (the default), `seek()` assumes that *offset* is relative to the start of the file; if *whence* is 1, the position is moved relative to the current position; and if *whence* is 2, the offset is taken from the end of the file. `seek()` returns the new value of the file pointer as an integer. It should be noted that the file pointer is associated with the file object returned by `open()` and not the file itself. The same file can be opened more than once in the same program (or in different programs). Each instance of the open file has its own file pointer that can be manipulated independently.

The `fileno()` method returns the integer file descriptor for a file and is sometimes used in low-level I/O operations in certain library modules. For example, the `fcntl` module uses the file descriptor to provide low-level file control operations on UNIX systems.

File objects also have the read-only data attributes shown in Table 9.2.

Table 9.2   **File Object Attributes**

Attribute	Description
`f.closed`	Boolean value indicates the file state: `False` if the file is open, `True` if closed.
`f.mode`	The I/O mode for the file.
`f.name`	Name of the file if created using `open()`. Otherwise, it will be a string indicating the source of the file.
`f.softspace`	Boolean value indicating whether a space character needs to be printed before another value when using the `print` statement. Classes that emulate files must provide a writable attribute of this name that's initially initialized to zero (Python 2 only).
`f.newlines`	When a file is opened in universal newline mode, this attribute contains the newline representation actually found in the file. The value is `None` if no newlines have been encountered, a string containing `'\n'`, `'\r'`, or `'\r\n'`, or a tuple containing all the different newline encodings seen.
`f.encoding`	A string that indicates file encoding, if any (for example, `'latin-1'` or `'utf-8'`). The value is `None` if no encoding is being used.

Standard Input, Output, and Error

The interpreter provides three standard file objects, known as *standard input*, *standard output*, and *standard error*, which are available in the `sys` module as `sys.stdin`, `sys.stdout`, and `sys.stderr`, respectively. `stdin` is a file object corresponding to the stream of input characters supplied to the interpreter. `stdout` is the file object that receives output produced by `print`. `stderr` is a file that receives error messages. More often than not, `stdin` is mapped to the user's keyboard, whereas `stdout` and `stderr` produce text onscreen.

The methods described in the preceding section can be used to perform raw I/O with the user. For example, the following code writes to standard output and reads a line of input from standard input:

```
import sys
sys.stdout.write("Enter your name : ")
name = sys.stdin.readline()
```

Alternatively, the built-in function `raw_input(prompt)` can read a line of text from `stdin` and optionally print a prompt:

```
name = raw_input("Enter your name : ")
```

Lines read by `raw_input()` do not include the trailing newline. This is different than reading directly from `sys.stdin` where newlines are included in the input text. In Python 3, `raw_input()` has been renamed to `input()`.

Keyboard interrupts (typically generated by Ctrl+C) result in a `KeyboardInterrupt` exception that can be caught using an exception handler.

If necessary, the values of `sys.stdout`, `sys.stdin`, and `sys.stderr` can be replaced with other file objects, in which case the `print` statement and input functions use the new values. Should it ever be necessary to restore the original value of `sys.stdout`, it should be saved first. The original values of `sys.stdout`, `sys.stdin`, and `sys.stderr` at interpreter startup are also available in `sys.__stdout__`, `sys.__stdin__`, and `sys.__stderr__`, respectively.

Note that in some cases `sys.stdin`, `sys.stdout`, and `sys.stderr` may be altered by the use of an integrated development environment (IDE). For example, when Python is run under IDLE, `sys.stdin` is replaced with an object that behaves like a file but is really an object in the development environment. In this case, certain low-level methods, such as `read()` and `seek()`, may be unavailable.

The `print` Statement

Python 2 uses a special `print` statement to produce output on the file contained in `sys.stdout`. `print` accepts a comma-separated list of objects such as the following:

```
print "The values are", x, y, z
```

For each object, the `str()` function is invoked to produce an output string. These output strings are then joined and separated by a single space to produce the final output string. The output is terminated by a newline unless a trailing comma is supplied to the `print` statement. In this case, the next `print` statement will insert a space before printing more items. The output of this space is controlled by the `softspace` attribute of the file being used for output.

```
print "The values are ", x, y, z, w
# Print the same text, using two print statements
print "The values are ", x, y,    # Omits trailing newline
print z, w                        # A space is printed before z
```

To produce formatted output, use the string-formatting operator (`%`) or the `.format()` method as described in Chapter 4, "Operators and Expressions." Here's an example:

```
print "The values are %d %7.5f %s" % (x,y,z) # Formatted I/O
print "The values are {0:d} {1:7.5f} {2}".format(x,y,z)
```

You can change the destination of the `print` statement by adding the special `>>file` modifier followed by a comma, where `file` is a file object that allows writes. Here's an example:

```
f = open("output","w")
print >>f, "hello world"
...
f.close()
```

The `print()` Function

One of the most significant changes in Python 3 is that `print` is turned into a function. In Python 2.6, it is also possible to use `print` as a function if you include the statement `from __future__ import print_function` in each module where used. The `print()` function works almost exactly the same as the `print` statement described in the previous section.

To print a series of values separated by spaces, just supply them all to `print()` like this:

```
print("The values are", x, y, z)
```

To suppress or change the line ending, use the `end=ending` keyword argument (Note: if you specify something other than a newline, you may have to flush `sys.stdout` to see the output.). For example:

```
print("The values are", x, y, z, end='')   # Suppress the newline
```

To redirect the output to a file, use the `file=outfile` keyword argument. For example:

```
print("The values are", x, y, z, file=f)   # Redirect to file object f
```

To change the separator character between items, use the `sep=sepchr` keyword argument. For example:

```
print("The values are", x, y, z, sep=',')   # Put commas between the values
```

Variable Interpolation in Text Output

A common problem when generating output is that of producing large text fragments containing embedded variable substitutions. Many scripting languages such as Perl and PHP allow variables to be inserted into strings using dollar-variable substitutions (that is, $name, $address, and so on). Python provides no direct equivalent of this feature, but it can be emulated using formatted I/O combined with triple-quoted strings. For example, you could write a short form letter, filling in a name, an `item` name, and an amount, as shown in the following example:

```
# Note: trailing slash right after """ prevents
# a blank line from appearing as the first line
form = """\
Dear  %(name)s,
```

```
Please send back my %(item)s or pay me $%(amount)0.2f.
                                 Sincerely yours,

                               Joe Python User
"""
print form % { 'name': 'Mr. Bush',
               'item': 'blender',
               'amount': 50.00 }
```

This produces the following output:

```
Dear Mr. Bush,

Please send back my blender or pay me $50.00.

                             Sincerely yours,

                             Joe Python User
```

The format() method is a more modern alternative that cleans up some of the previous code. For example:

```
form = """\
Dear {name},
Please send back my {item} or pay me {amount:0.2f}.
                               Sincerely yours,

                             Joe Python User
"""
print form.format(name='Mr. Bush', item='blender', amount=50.0)
```

For certain kinds of forms, you can also use Template strings, as follows:

```
import string
form = string.Template("""\
Dear  $name,
Please send back my $item or pay me $amount.
                             Sincerely yours,

                             Joe Python User
""")
print form.substitute({'name': 'Mr. Bush',
                        'item': 'blender',
                        'amount': "%0.2f" % 50.0})
```

In this case, special $ variables in the string indicate substitutions. The form.substitute() method takes a dictionary of replacements and returns a new string. Although the previous approaches are simple, they aren't always the most powerful solutions to text generation. Web frameworks and other large application frameworks tend to provide their own template string engines that support embedded control-flow, variable substitutions, file inclusion, and other advanced features.

Generating Output

Working directly with files is the I/O model most familiar to programmers. However, generator functions can also be used to emit an I/O stream as a sequence of data fragments. To do this, simply use the yield statement like you would use a write() or print statement. Here is an example:

```
def countdown(n):
```

```
    while n > 0:
        yield "T-minus %d\n" % n
        n -= 1
    yield "Kaboom!\n"
```

Producing an output stream in this manner provides great flexibility because the production of the output stream is decoupled from the code that actually directs the stream to its intended destination. For example, if you wanted to route the above output to a file f, you could do this:

```
count = countdown(5)
f.writelines(count)
```

If, instead, you wanted to redirect the output across a socket s, you could do this:

```
for chunk in count:
    s.sendall(chunk)
```

Or, if you simply wanted to capture all of the output in a string, you could do this:

```
out = "".join(count)
```

More advanced applications can use this approach to implement their own I/O buffering. For example, a generator could be emitting small text fragments, but another function could be collecting the fragments into large buffers to create a larger, more efficient I/O operation:

```
chunks = []
buffered_size = 0
for chunk in count:
    chunks.append(chunk)
    buffered_size += len(chunk)
    if buffered_size >= MAXBUFFERSIZE:
        outf.write("".join(chunks))
        chunks.clear()
        buffered_size = 0
outf.write("".join(chunks))
```

For programs that are routing output to files or network connections, a generator approach can also result in a significant reduction in memory use because the entire output stream can often be generated and processed in small fragments as opposed to being first collected into one large output string or list of strings. This approach to output is sometimes seen when writing programs that interact with the Python Web Services Gateway Interface (WSGI) that's used to communicate between components in certain web frameworks.

Unicode String Handling

A common problem associated with I/O handling is that of dealing with international characters represented as Unicode. If you have a string s of raw bytes containing an encoded representation of a Unicode string, use the s.decode([encoding [, errors]]) method to convert it into a proper Unicode string. To convert a Unicode string, u, to an encoded byte string, use the string method u.encode([encoding [, errors]]). Both of these conversion operators require the use of a special encoding name that specifies how Unicode character values are mapped to a sequence of 8-bit characters in byte strings, and vice versa. The encoding parameter is specified as a string and is one of more than a hundred different character encodings. The following values, and is one of more than a hundred different character encodings. The following values, however, are most common:

Value	Description
`'ascii'`	7-bit ASCII
`'latin-1'` or `'iso-8859-1'`	ISO 8859-1 Latin-1
`'cp1252'`	Windows 1252 encoding
`'utf-8'`	8-bit variable-length encoding
`'utf-16'`	16-bit variable-length encoding (may be little or big endian)
`'utf-16-le'`	UTF-16, little endian encoding
`'utf-16-be'`	UTF-16, big endian encoding
`'unicode-escape'`	Same format as Unicode literals u"string"
`'raw-unicode-escape'`	Same format as raw Unicode literals ur"string"

The default encoding is set in the `site` module and can be queried using `sys.getdefaultencoding()`. In many cases, the default encoding is `'ascii'`, which means that ASCII characters with values in the range `[0x00, 0x7f]` are directly mapped to Unicode characters in the range `[U+0000, U+007F]`. However, `'utf-8'` is also a very common setting. Technical details concerning common encodings appears in a later section.

When using the `s.decode()` method, it is always assumed that `s` is a string of bytes. In Python 2, this means that `s` is a standard string, but in Python 3, `s` must be a special bytes type. Similarly, the result of `t.encode()` is always a byte sequence. One caution if you care about portability is that these methods are a little muddled in Python 2. For instance, Python 2 strings have both `decode()` and `encode()` methods, whereas in Python 3, strings only have an `encode()` method and the bytes type only has a `decode()` method. To simplify code in Python 2, make sure you only use `encode()` on Unicode strings and `decode()` on byte strings.

When string values are being converted, a `UnicodeError` exception might be raised if a character that can't be converted is encountered. For instance, if you are trying to encode a string into `'ascii'` and it contains a Unicode character such as U+1F28, you will get an encoding error because this character value is too large to be represented in the ASCII character set. The `errors` parameter of the `encode()` and `decode()` methods determines how encoding errors are handled. It's a string with one of the following values:

Value	Description
`'strict'`	Raises a `UnicodeError` exception for encoding and decoding errors.
`'ignore'`	Ignores invalid characters.
`'replace'`	Replaces invalid characters with a replacement character (U+FFFD in Unicode, `'?'` in standard strings).
`'backslashreplace'`	Replaces invalid characters with a Python character escape sequence. For example, the character U+1234 is replaced by `'\u1234'`.
`'xmlcharrefreplace'`	Replaces invalid characters with an XML character reference. For example, the character U+1234 is replaced by `'&#4660;'`.

The default error handling is `'strict'`.

The `'xmlcharrefreplace'` error handling policy is often a useful way to embed international characters into ASCII-encoded text on web pages. For example, if you output the Unicode string `'Jalape\u00f1o'` by encoding it to ASCII with `'xmlcharrefreplace'` handling, browsers will almost always correctly render the output text as "Jalapeño" and not some garbled alternative.

To keep your brain from exploding, encoded byte strings and unencoded strings should never be mixed together in expressions (for example, using + to concatenate). Python 3 prohibits this altogether, but Python 2 will silently go ahead with such operations by automatically promoting byte strings to Unicode according to the default encoding setting. This behavior is often a source of surprising results or inexplicable error messages. Thus, you should carefully try to maintain a strict separation between encoded and unencoded character data in your program.

Unicode I/O

When working with Unicode strings, it is never possible to directly write raw Unicode data to a file. This is due to the fact that Unicode characters are internally represented as multibyte integers and that writing such integers directly to an output stream causes problems related to byte ordering. For example, you would have to arbitrarily decide if the Unicode character U+HHLL is to be written in "little endian" format as the byte sequence LL HH or in "big endian" format as the byte sequence HH LL. Moreover, other tools that process Unicode would have to know which encoding you used.

Because of this problem, the external representation of Unicode strings is always done according to a specific encoding rule that precisely defines how Unicode characters are to be represented as a byte sequence. Thus, to support Unicode I/O, the encoding and decoding concepts described in the previous section are extended to files. The built-in `codecs` module contains a collection of functions for converting byte-oriented data to and from Unicode strings according to a variety of different data-encoding schemes.

Perhaps the most straightforward way to handle Unicode files is to use the `codecs.open(filename [, mode [, encoding [, errors]]])` function, as follows:

```
f = codecs.open('foo.txt','r','utf-8','strict')    # Reading
g = codecs.open('bar.txt','w','utf-8')             # Writing
```

This creates a file object that reads or writes Unicode strings. The encoding parameter specifies the underlying character encoding that will be used to translate data as it is read or written to the file. The *errors* parameter determines how errors are handled and is one of `'strict'`, `'ignore'`, `'replace'`, `'backslashreplace'`, or `'xmlcharrefreplace'` as described in the previous section.

If you already have a file object, the `codecs.EncodedFile(file, inputenc [, outputenc [, errors]])` function can be used to place an encoding wrapper around it. Here's an example:

```
f = open("foo.txt","rb")
...
fenc = codecs.EncodedFile(f,'utf-8')
```

In this case, data read from the file will be interpreted according to the encoding supplied in *inputenc*. Data written to the file will be interpreted according to the encoding in *inputenc* and written according to the encoding in *outputenc*. If *outputenc* is omitted, it defaults to the same as *inputenc*. *errors* has the same meaning as described earlier. When putting an EncodedFile wrapper around an existing file, make sure that file is in binary mode. Otherwise, newline translation might break the encoding.

When you're working with Unicode files, the data encoding is often embedded in the file itself. For example, XML parsers may look at the first few bytes of the string '<?xml ...>' to determine the document encoding. If the first four values are 3C 3F 78 6D ('<?xm'), the encoding is assumed to be UTF-8. If the first four values are 00 3C 00 3F or 3C 00 3F 00, the encoding is assumed to be UTF-16 big endian or UTF-16 little endian, respectively. Alternatively, a document encoding may appear in MIME headers or as an attribute of other document elements. Here's an example:

```
<?xml ... encoding="ISO-8859-1" ... ?>
```

Similarly, Unicode files may also include special byte-order markers (BOM) that indicate properties of the character encoding. The Unicode character U+FEFF is reserved for this purpose. Typically, the marker is written as the first character in the file. Programs then read this character and look at the arrangement of the bytes to determine encoding (for example, '\xff\xfe' for UTF-16-LE or '\xfe\xff' UTF-16-BE). Once the encoding is determined, the BOM character is discarded and the remainder of the file is processed. Unfortunately, all of this extra handling of the BOM is not something that happens behind the scenes. You often have to take care of this yourself if your application warrants it.

When the encoding is read from a document, code similar to the following can be used to turn the input file into an encoded stream:

```
f = open("somefile","rb")
# Determine encoding of the file
...
# Put an appropriate encoding wrapper on the file.
# Assumes that the BOM (if any) has already been discarded
# by earlier statements.
fenc = codecs.EncodedFile(f,encoding)
data = fenc.read()
```

Unicode Data Encodings

Table 9.3 lists some of the most commonly used encoders in the codecs module.

Table 9.3   **Encoders in the** codecs **Module**

Encoder	Description
'ascii'	ASCII encoding
'latin-1', 'iso-8859-1'	Latin-1 or ISO-8859-1 encoding
'cp437'	CP437 encoding
'cp1252'	CP1252 encoding
'utf-8'	8-bit variable-length encoding
'utf-16'	16-bit variable-length encoding

Table 9.3   **Continued**

Encoder	Description
`'utf-16-le'`	UTF-16, but with explicit little endian encoding
`'utf-16-be'`	UTF-16, but with explicit big endian encoding
`'unicode-escape'`	Same format as u"*string*"
`'raw-unicode-escape'`	Same format as ur"*string*"

The following sections describe each of the encoders in more detail.

`'ascii'` Encoding

In `'ascii'` encoding, character values are confined to the ranges [0x00,0x7f] and [U+0000, U+007F]. Any character outside this range is invalid.

`'iso-8859-1'`, `'latin-1'` Encoding

Characters can be any 8-bit value in the ranges [0x00,0xff] and [U+0000, U+00FF]. Values in the range [0x00,0x7f] correspond to characters from the ASCII character set. Values in the range [0x80,0xff] correspond to characters from the ISO-8859-1 or extended ASCII character set. Any characters with values outside the range [0x00,0xff] result in an error.

`'cp437'` Encoding

This encoding is similar to `'iso-8859-1'` but is the default encoding used by Python when it runs as a console application on Windows. Certain characters in the range [x80,0xff] correspond to special symbols used for rendering menus, windows, and frames in legacy DOS applications.

`'cp1252'` Encoding

This is an encoding that is very similar to `'iso-8859-1'` used on Windows. However, this encoding defines characters in the range [0x80-0x9f] that are undefined in `'iso-8859-1'` and which have different code points in Unicode.

`'utf-8'` Encoding

UTF-8 is a variable-length encoding that allows all Unicode characters to be represented. A single byte is used to represent ASCII characters in the range 0–127. All other characters are represented by multibyte sequences of 2 or 3 bytes. The encoding of these bytes is shown here:

Unicode Characters	Byte 0	Byte 1	Byte 2
U+0000 - U+007F	0*nnnnnnn*		
U+007F - U+07FF	110*nnnnn*	10*nnnnnn*	
U+0800 - U+FFFF	1110*nnnn*	10*nnnnnn*	10*nnnnnn*

For 2-byte sequences, the first byte always starts with the bit sequence 110. For 3-byte sequences, the first byte starts with the bit sequence 1110. All subsequent data bytes in multibyte sequences start with the bit sequence 10.

In full generality, the UTF-8 format allows for multibyte sequences of up to 6 bytes. In Python, 4-byte UTF-8 sequences are used to encode a pair of Unicode characters known as a *surrogate pair*. Both characters have values in the range [U+D800, U+DFFF] and are combined to encode a 20-bit character value. The surrogate encoding is as follows: The 4-byte sequence 11110*nnn* 10*nnnnnn* 10*nmmmm* 10*mmmmmm* is encoded as the pair U+D800 + N, U+DC00 + M, where N is the upper 10 bits and M is the lower 10 bits of the 20-bit character encoded in the 4-byte UTF-8 sequence. Five- and 6-byte UTF-8 sequences (denoted by starting bit sequences of 111110 and 1111110, respectively) are used to encode character values up to 32 bits in length. These values are not supported by Python and currently result in a UnicodeError exception if they appear in an encoded data stream.

UTF-8 encoding has a number of useful properties that allow it to be used by older software. First, the standard ASCII characters are represented in their standard encoding. This means that a UTF-8–encoded ASCII string is indistinguishable from a traditional ASCII string. Second, UTF-8 doesn't introduce embedded NULL bytes for multibyte character sequences. Therefore, existing software based on the C library and programs that expect NULL-terminated 8-bit strings will work with UTF-8 strings. Finally, UTF-8 encoding preserves the lexicographic ordering of strings. That is, if a and b are Unicode strings and a < b, then a < b also holds when a and b are converted to UTF-8. Therefore, sorting algorithms and other ordering algorithms written for 8-bit strings will also work for UTF-8.

'utf-16', 'utf-16-be', and 'utf-16-le' Encoding

UTF-16 is a variable-length 16-bit encoding in which Unicode characters are written as 16-bit values. Unless a byte ordering is specified, big endian encoding is assumed. In addition, a byte-order marker of U+FEFF can be used to explicitly specify the byte ordering in a UTF-16 data stream. In big endian encoding, U+FEFF is the Unicode character for a zero-width nonbreaking space, whereas the reversed value U+FFFE is an illegal Unicode character. Thus, the encoder can use the byte sequence FE FF or FF FE to determine the byte ordering of a data stream. When reading Unicode data, Python removes the byte-order markers from the final Unicode string.

'utf-16-be' encoding explicitly selects UTF-16 big endian encoding. 'utf-16-le' encoding explicitly selects UTF-16 little ending encoding.

Although there are extensions to UTF-16 to support character values greater than 16 bits, none of these extensions are currently supported.

'unicode-escape' and 'raw-unicode-escape' Encoding

These encoding methods are used to convert Unicode strings to the same format as used in Python Unicode string literals and Unicode raw string literals. Here's an example:

```
s = u'\u14a8\u0345\u2a34'
t = s.encode('unicode-escape')    #t = '\u14a8\u0345\u2a34'
```

Unicode Character Properties

In addition to performing I/O, programs that use Unicode may need to test Unicode characters for various properties such as capitalization, numbers, and whitespace. The unicodedata module provides access to a database of character properties. General character properties can be obtained with the unicodedata.category(c) function. For example, unicodedata.category(u"A") returns 'Lu', signifying that the character is an uppercase letter.

Another tricky problem with Unicode strings is that there might be multiple representations of the same Unicode string. For example, the character U+00F1 (ñ), might be fully composed as a single character U+00F1 or decomposed into a multicharacter sequence U+006e U+0303 (n, ˜). If consistent processing of Unicode strings is an issue, use the unicodedata.normalize() function to ensure a consistent character representation. For example, unicodedata.normalize('NFC', *s*) will make sure that all characters in *s* are fully composed and not represented as a sequence of combining characters.

Further details about the Unicode character database and the unicodedata module can be found in Chapter 16, "Strings and Text Handling."

Object Persistence and the `pickle` Module

Finally, it's often necessary to save and restore the contents of an object to a file. One approach to this problem is to write a pair of functions that simply read and write data from a file in a special format. An alternative approach is to use the pickle and shelve modules.

The pickle module serializes an object into a stream of bytes that can be written to a file and later restored. The interface to pickle is simple, consisting of a dump() and load() operation. For example, the following code writes an object to a file:

```
import pickle
obj = SomeObject()
f = open(filename,'wb')
pickle.dump(obj, f)        # Save object on f
f.close()
```

To restore the object, you can use the following code:

```
import pickle
f = open(filename,'rb')
obj = pickle.load(f)   # Restore the object
f.close()
```

A sequence of objects can be saved by issuing a series of dump() operations one after the other. To restore these objects, simply use a similar sequence of load() operations.

The shelve module is similar to pickle but saves objects in a dictionary-like database:

```
import shelve
obj = SomeObject()
db = shelve.open("filename")       # Open a shelve
db['key'] = obj                    # Save object in the shelve
...
obj = db['key']                    # Retrieve it
db.close()                         # Close the shelve
```

Although the object created by shelve looks like a dictionary, it also has restrictions. First, the keys must be strings. Second, the values stored in a shelf must be compatible with pickle. Most Python objects will work, but special-purpose objects such as files and network connections maintain an internal state that cannot be saved and restored in this manner.

The data format used by pickle is specific to Python. However, the format has evolved several times over Python versions. The choice of protocol can be selected using an optional protocol parameter to the pickle dump(*obj*, *file*, *protocol*) operation.

By default, protocol 0 is used. This is the oldest pickle data format that stores objects in a format understood by virtually all Python versions. However, this format is also incompatible with many of Python's more modern features of user-defined classes such as slots. Protocol 1 and 2 use a more efficient binary data representation. To use these alternative protocols, you would perform operations such as the following:

```
import pickle
obj = SomeObject()
f = open(filename,'wb')
pickle.dump(obj,f,2)                       # Save using protocol 2
pickle.dump(obj,f,pickle.HIGHEST_PROTOCOL)  # Use the most modern protocol
f.close()
```

It is not necessary to specify the protocol when restoring an object using load(). The underlying protocol is encoded into the file itself.

Similarly, a shelve can be opened to save Python objects using an alternative pickle protocol like this:

```
import shelve
db = shelve.open(filename,protocol=2)
...
```

It is not normally necessary for user-defined objects to do anything extra to work with pickle or shelve. However, the special methods __getstate__() and __setstate__() can be used to assist the pickling process. The __getstate__() method, if defined, will be called to create a value representing the state of an object. The value returned by __getstate__() should typically be a string, tuple, list, or dictionary. The __setstate__() method receives this value during unpickling and should restore the state of an object from it. Here is an example that shows how these methods could be used with an object involving an underlying network connection. Although the actual connection can't be pickled, the object saves enough information to reestablish it when it's unpickled later:

```
import socket
class Client(object):
    def __init__(self,addr):
        self.server_addr = addr
        self.sock = socket.socket(socket.AF_INET,socket.SOCK_STREAM)
        self.sock.connect(addr)
    def __getstate__(self):
        return self.server_addr
    def __setstate__(self,value):
        self.server_addr = value
        self.sock = socket.socket(socket.AF_INET,socket.SOCK_STREAM)
        self.sock.connect(self.server_addr)
```

Because the data format used by pickle is Python-specific, you would not use this feature as a means for exchanging data between applications written in different programming languages. Moreover, due to security concerns, programs should not process pickled data from untrusted sources (a knowledgeable attacker can manipulate the pickle data format to execute arbitrary system commands during unpickling).

The pickle and shelve modules have many more customization features and advanced usage options. For more details, consult Chapter 13, "Python Runtime Services."

10

Execution Environment

This chapter describes the environment in which Python programs are executed. The goal is to describe the runtime behavior of the interpreter, including program startup, configuration, and program termination.

Interpreter Options and Environment

The interpreter has a number of options that control its runtime behavior and environment. Options are given to the interpreter on the command line as follows:

```
python [options] [-c cmd | filename | - ] [args]
```

Here's a list of the most common command-line options:

Table 10.1 **Interpreter Command-Line Arguments**

Option	Description
-3	Enables warnings about features that are being removed or changed in Python 3.
-B	Prevents the creation of .pyc or .pyo files on import.
-E	Ignores environment variables.
-h	Prints a list of all available command-line options.
-i	Enters interactive mode after program execution.
-m module	Runs library module module as a script.
-O	Optimized mode.
-OO	Optimized mode plus removal of documentation strings when creating .pyo files.
-Q arg	Specifies the behavior of the division operator in Python 2. One of -Qold (the default), -Qnew, -Qwarn, or -Qwarnall.
-s	Prevents the addition of the user site directory to sys.path.
-S	Prevents inclusion of the site initialization module.
-t	Reports warnings about inconsistent tab usage.
-tt	Inconsistent tab usage results in a TabError exception.
-u	Unbuffered binary stdout and stdin.
-U	Unicode literals. All string literals are handled as Unicode (Python 2 only).
-v	Verbose mode. Traces import statements.
-V	Prints the version number and exits.
-x	Skips the first line of the source program.
-c cmd	Executes cmd as a string.

The -i option starts an interactive session immediately after a program has finished execution and is useful for debugging. The -m option runs a library module as a script which executes inside the __main__ module prior to the execution of the main script. The -O and -OO options apply some optimization to byte-compiled files and are described in Chapter 8, "Modules, Packages, and Distribution." The -S option omits the site initialization module described in the later section "Site Configuration Files." The -t, -tt, and -v options report additional warnings and debugging information. -x ignores the first line of a program in the event that it's not a valid Python statement (for example, when the first line starts the Python interpreter in a script).

The program name appears after all the interpreter options. If no name is given, or the hyphen (-) character is used as a filename, the interpreter reads the program from standard input. If standard input is an interactive terminal, a banner and prompt are presented. Otherwise, the interpreter opens the specified file and executes its statements until an end-of-file marker is reached. The -c cmd option can be used to execute short programs in the form of a command-line option—for example, python -c "print('hello world')".

Command-line options appearing after the program name or hyphen (-) are passed to the program in sys.argv, as described in the section "Reading Options and Environment Variables" in Chapter 9, "Input and Output."

Additionally, the interpreter reads the following environment variables:

Table 10.2   **Interpreter Environment Variables**

Environment Variable	Description
PYTHONPATH	Colon-separated module search path.
PYTHONSTARTUP	File executed on interactive startup.
PYTHONHOME	Location of the Python installation.
PYTHONINSPECT	Implies the -i option.
PYTHONUNBUFFERED	Implies the -u option.
PYTHONIOENCODING	Encoding and error handling for stdin, stdout, and stderr. This is a string of the form "encoding[:errors]" such as "utf-8" or "utf-8:ignore".
PYTHONDONTWRITEBYTECODE	Implies the -B option
PYTHONOPTIMIZE	Implies the -O option.
PYTHONNOUSERSITE	Implies the -s option.
PYTHONVERBOSE	Implies the -v option.
PYTHONUSERBASE	Root directory for per-user site packages.
PYTHONCASEOK	Indicates to use case-insensitive matching for module names used by import.

PYTHONPATH specifies a module search path that is inserted into the beginning of sys.path, which is described in Chapter 9. PYTHONSTARTUP specifies a file to execute when the interpreter runs in interactive mode. The PYTHONHOME variable is used to set the location of the Python installation but is rarely needed because Python knows how to find its own libraries and the site-packages directory where extensions are normally installed. If a single directory such as /usr/local is given, the interpreter expects to find all files in that location. If two directories are given, such as /usr/local:/usr/local/sparc-solaris-2.6, the interpreter searches for platform-independent files in the first directory and platform-dependent files in the second. PYTHONHOME has no effect if no valid Python installation exists at the specified location.

The PYTHONIOENCODING environment setting might be of interest to users of Python 3 because it sets both the encoding and error handling of the standard I/O streams. This might be important because Python 3 directly outputs Unicode while running the interactive interpreter prompt. This, in turn, can cause unexpected exceptions merely while inspecting data. For example:

```
>>> a = 'Jalape\xf1o'
>>> a
Traceback (most recent call last):
  File "<stdin>", line 1, in <module>
  File "/tmp/lib/python3.0/io.py", line 1486, in write
    b = encoder.encode(s)
  File "/tmp/lib/python3.0/encodings/ascii.py", line 22, in encode
    return codecs.ascii_encode(input, self.errors)[0]
UnicodeEncodeError: 'ascii' codec can't encode character '\xf1' in position 7:
ordinal not in range(128)
>>>
```

To fix this, you can set the environment variable PYTHONIOENCODING to something such as 'ascii:backslashreplace' or 'utf-8'. Now, you will get this:

```
>>> a = 'Jalape\xf1o'
>>> a
'Jalape\xf1o'
>>>
```

On Windows, some of the environment variables such as PYTHONPATH are additionally read from registry entries found in HKEY_LOCAL_MACHINE/Software/Python.

Interactive Sessions

If no program name is given and the standard input to the interpreter is an interactive terminal, Python starts in interactive mode. In this mode, a banner message is printed and the user is presented with a prompt. In addition, the interpreter evaluates the script contained in the PYTHONSTARTUP environment variable (if set). This script is evaluated as if it's part of the input program (that is, it isn't loaded using an import statement). One application of this script might be to read a user configuration file such as .pythonrc.

When interactive input is being accepted, two user prompts appear. The >>> prompt appears at the beginning of a new statement; the ... prompt indicates a statement continuation. Here's an example:

```
>>> for i in range(0,4):
...     print i,
...
0 1 2 3
>>>
```

In customized applications, you can change the prompts by modifying the values of sys.ps1 and sys.ps2.

On some systems, Python may be compiled to use the GNU readline library. If enabled, this library provides command histories, completion, and other additions to Python's interactive mode.

By default, the output of commands issued in interactive mode is generated by printing the output of the built-in repr() function on the result. This can be changed by setting the variable sys.displayhook to a function responsible for displaying results. Here's an example that truncates long results:

```
>>> def my_display(x):
...     r = repr(x)
...     if len(r) > 40: print(r[:40]+"..."+r[-1])
...     else: print(r)
>>> sys.displayhook = my_display
>>> 3+4
7
>>> range(100000)
[0, 1, 2, 3, 4, 5, 6, 7, 8, 9, 10, 11, 1...]
>>>
```

Finally, in interactive mode, it is useful to know that the result of the last operation is stored in a special variable (_). This variable can be used to retrieve the result should you need to use it in subsequent operations. Here's an example:

```
>>> 7 + 3
10
>>> _ + 2
12
>>>
```

The setting of the _ variable occurs in the displayhook() function shown previously. If you redefine displayhook(), your replacement function should also set _ if you want to retain that functionality.

Launching Python Applications

In most cases, you'll want programs to start the interpreter automatically, rather than first having to start the interpreter manually. On UNIX, this is done by giving the program execute permission and setting the first line of a program to something like this:

```
#!/usr/bin/env python
# Python code from this point on...
print "Hello world"
...
```

On Windows, double-clicking a .py, .pyw, .wpy, .pyc, or .pyo file automatically launches the interpreter. Normally, programs run in a console window unless they're renamed with a .pyw suffix (in which case the program runs silently). If it's necessary to supply options to the interpreter, Python can also be started from a .bat file. For example, this .bat file simply runs Python on a script and passes any options supplied on the command prompt along to the interpreter:

```
:: foo.bat
:: Runs foo.py script and passes supplied command line options along (if any)
c:\python26\python.exe c:\pythonscripts\foo.py %*
```

Site Configuration Files

A typical Python installation may include a number of third-party modules and packages. To configure these packages, the interpreter first imports the module `site`. The role of `site` is to search for package files and to add additional directories to the module search path `sys.path`. In addition, the `site` module sets the default encoding for Unicode string conversions.

The `site` module works by first creating a list of directory names constructed from the values of `sys.prefix` and `sys.exec_prefix` as follows:

```
[ sys.prefix,                   # Windows only
  sys.exec_prefix,              # Windows only
  sys.prefix + 'lib/pythonvers/site-packages',
  sys.prefix + 'lib/site-python',
  sys.exec_prefix + 'lib/pythonvers/site-packages',
  sys.exec_prefix + 'lib/site-python' ]
```

In addition, if enabled, a user-specific site packages directory may be added to this list (described in the next section).

For each directory in the list, a check is made to see whether the directory exists. If so, it's added to the `sys.path` variable. Next, a check is made to see whether it contains any path configuration files (files with a `.pth` suffix). A path configuration file contains a list of directories, zip files, or `.egg` files relative to the location of the path file that should be added to `sys.path`. For example:

```
# foo package configuration file 'foo.pth'
foo
bar
```

Each directory in the path configuration file must be listed on a separate line. Comments and blank lines are ignored. When the `site` module loads the file, it checks to see whether each directory exists. If so, the directory is added to `sys.path`. Duplicated items are added to the path only once.

After all paths have been added to `sys.path`, an attempt is made to import a module named `sitecustomize`. The purpose of this module is to perform any additional (and arbitrary) site customization. If the import of `sitecustomize` fails with an `ImportError`, the error is silently ignored. The import of `sitecustomize` occurs prior to adding any user directories to `sys.path`. Thus, placing this file in your own directory has no effect.

The `site` module is also responsible for setting the default Unicode encoding. By default, the encoding is set to `'ascii'`. However, the encoding can be changed by placing code in `sitecustomize.py` that calls `sys.setdefaultencoding()` with a new encoding such as `'utf-8'`. If you're willing to experiment, the source code of `site` can also be modified to automatically set the encoding based on the machine's locale settings.

Per-user Site Packages

Normally, third-party modules are installed in a way that makes them accessible to all users. However, individual users can install modules and packages in a per-user site directory. On UNIX and Macintosh systems, this directory is found under `~/.local` and is named something such as `~/.local/lib/python2.6/site-packages`. On Windows systems, this directory is determined by the `%APPDATA%` environment variable, which is usually something similar to C:\Documents and Settings\David Beazley\Application Data. Within that folder, you will find a "Python\Python26\site-packages" directory.

If you are writing your own Python modules and packages that you want to use in a library, they can be placed in the per-user site directory. If you are installing third-party modules, you can manually install them in this directory by supplying the --user option to setup.py. For example: python setup.py install --user.

Enabling Future Features

New language features that affect compatibility with older versions of Python are often disabled when they first appear in a release. To enable these features, the statement from __future__ import *feature* can be used. Here's an example:

```
# Enable new division semantics
from __future__ import division
```

When used, this statement should appear as the first statement of a module or program. Moreover, the scope of a __future__ import is restricted only to the module in which it is used. Thus, importing a future feature does not affect the behavior of Python's library modules or older code that requires the previous behavior of the interpreter to operate correctly.

Currently, the following features have been defined:

Table 10.3   **Feature Names in the __future__ Module**

Feature Name	Description
nested_scopes	Support for nested scopes in functions. First introduced in Python 2.1 and made the default behavior in Python 2.2.
generators	Support for generators. First introduced in Python 2.2 and made the default behavior in Python 2.3.
division	Modified division semantics where integer division returns a fractional result. For example, 1/4 yields 0.25 instead of 0. First introduced in Python 2.2 and is still an optional feature as of Python 2.6. This is the default behavior in Python 3.0.
absolute_import	Modified behavior of package-relative imports. Currently, when a submodule of a package makes an import statement such as import string, it first looks in the current directory of the package and then directories in sys.path. However, this makes it impossible to load modules in the standard library if a package happens to use conflicting names. When this feature is enabled, the statement import module is an absolute import. Thus, a statement such as import string will always load the string module from the standard library. First introduced in Python 2.5 and still disabled in Python 2.6. It is enabled in Python 3.0.
with_statement	Support for context managers and the with statement. First introduced in Python 2.5 and enabled by default in Python 2.6.
print_function	Use Python 3.0 print() function instead of the print statement. First introduced in Python 2.6 and enabled by default in Python 3.0.

It should be noted that no feature name is ever deleted from `__future__`. Thus, even if a feature is turned on by default in a later Python version, no existing code that uses that feature name will break.

Program Termination

A program terminates when no more statements exist to execute in the input program, when an uncaught SystemExit exception is raised (as generated by sys.exit()), or when the interpreter receives a SIGTERM or SIGHUP signal (on UNIX). On exit, the interpreter decrements the reference count of all objects in all the currently known namespaces (and destroys each namespace as well). If the reference count of an object reaches zero, the object is destroyed and its `__del__()` method is invoked.

It's important to note that in some cases the `__del__()` method might not be invoked at program termination. This can occur if circular references exist between objects (in which case objects may be allocated but accessible from no known namespace). Although Python's garbage collector can reclaim unused circular references during execution, it isn't normally invoked on program termination.

Because there's no guarantee that `__del__()` will be invoked at termination, it may be a good idea to explicitly clean up certain objects, such as open files and network connections. To accomplish this, add specialized cleanup methods (for example, close()) to user-defined objects. Another possibility is to write a termination function and register it with the atexit module, as follows:

```
import atexit
connection = open_connection("deaddot.com")

def cleanup():
    print "Going away..."
    close_connection(connection)

atexit.register(cleanup)
```

The garbage collector can also be invoked in this manner:

```
import atexit, gc
atexit.register(gc.collect)
```

One final peculiarity about program termination is that the `__del__` method for some objects may try to access global data or methods defined in other modules. Because these objects may already have been destroyed, a NameError exception occurs in `__del__`, and you may get an error such as the following:

```
Exception exceptions.NameError: 'c' in <method Bar.__del__
of Bar instance at c0310> ignored
```

If this occurs, it means that `__del__` has aborted prematurely. It also implies that it may have failed in an attempt to perform an important operation (such as cleanly shutting down a server connection). If this is a concern, it's probably a good idea to perform an explicit shutdown step in your code, rather than rely on the interpreter to destroy objects cleanly at program termination. The peculiar NameError exception can also be

eliminated by declaring default arguments in the declaration of the __del__()
method:

```
import foo
class Bar(object):
    def __del__(self, foo=foo):
        foo.bar()          # Use something in module foo
```

In some cases, it may be useful to terminate program execution without performing any
cleanup actions. This can be accomplished by calling os._exit(*status*). This function
provides an interface to the low-level exit() system call responsible for killing the
Python interpreter process. When it's invoked, the program immediately terminates
without any further processing or cleanup.

## 11

Testing, Debugging, Profiling, and Tuning

Unlike programs in languages such as C or Java, Python programs are not processed by a compiler that produces an executable program. In those languages, the compiler is the first line of defense against programming errors—catching mistakes such as calling functions with the wrong number of arguments or assigning improper values to variables (that is, type checking). In Python, however, these kinds of checks do not occur until a program runs. Because of this, you will never really know if your program is correct until you run and test it. Not only that, unless you are able to run your program in a way that executes every possible branch of its internal control-flow, there is always some chance of a hidden error just waiting to strike (fortunately, this usually only happens a few days *after* shipping, however).

To address these kinds of problems, this chapter covers techniques and library modules used to test, debug, and profile Python code. At the end, some strategies for optimizing Python code are discussed.

Documentation Strings and the `doctest` Module

If the first line of a function, class, or module is a string, that string is known as a *documentation string*. The inclusion of documentation strings is considered good style because these strings are used to supply information to Python software development tools. For example, the `help()` command inspects documentation strings, and Python IDEs look at the strings as well. Because programmers tend to view documentation strings while experimenting in the interactive shell, it is common for the strings to include short interactive examples. For example:

```
# splitter.py
def split(line, types=None, delimiter=None):
    """Splits a line of text and optionally performs type conversion.
    For example:

        >>> split('GOOG 100 490.50')
        ['GOOG', '100', '490.50']
        >>> split('GOOG 100 490.50',[str, int, float])
        ['GOOG', 100, 490.5]
        >>>
```

By default, splitting is performed on whitespace, but a different
delimiter can be selected with the delimiter keyword argument:

```
>>> split('GOOG,100,490.50',delimiter=',')
['GOOG', '100', '490.50']
>>>
"""
fields = line.split(delimiter)
if types:
    fields = [ ty(val) for ty,val in zip(types,fields) ]
return fields
```

A common problem with writing documentation is keeping the documentation synchronized with the actual implementation of a function. For example, a programmer
might modify a function but forget to update the documentation.

To address this problem, use the doctest module. doctest collects documentation
strings, scans them for interactive sessions, and executes them as a series of tests. To use
doctest, you typically create a separate module for testing. For example, if the previous
function is in a file splitter.py, you would create a file testsplitter.py for testing, as follows:

```
# testsplitter.py
import splitter
import doctest

nfail, ntests = doctest.testmod(splitter)
```

In this code, the call to doctest.testmod(*module*) runs tests on the specified module
and returns the number of failures and total number of tests executed. No output is
produced if all of the tests pass. Otherwise, you will get a failure report that shows the
difference between the expected and received output. If you want to see verbose output
of the tests, you can use testmod(*module*, verbose=True).

As an alternative to creating a separate testing file, library modules can test themselves by including code such as this at the end of the file:

```
...
if __name__ == '__main__':
    # test myself
    import doctest
    doctest.testmod()
```

With this code, documentation tests will run if the file is run as the main program to
the interpreter. Otherwise, the tests are ignored if the file is loaded with import.

doctest expects the output of functions to literally match the exact output you get
in the interactive interpreter. As a result, it is quite sensitive to issues of white space and
numerical precision. For example, consider this function:

```
def half(x):
    """Halves x.  For example:

    >>> half(6.8)
    3.4
    >>>
    """
    return x/2
```

If you run doctest on this function, you will get a failure report such as this:

```
***********************************************************************
File "half.py", line 4, in __main__.half
Failed example:
    half(6.8)
Expected:
    3.4
Got:
    3.3999999999999999
***********************************************************************
```

To fix this, you either need to make the documentation exactly match the output or need to pick a better example in the documentation.

Because using doctest is almost trivial, there is almost no excuse for not using it with your own programs. However, keep in mind that doctest is not a module you would typically use for exhaustive program testing. Doing so tends to result in excessively long and complicated documentation strings—which defeats the point of producing useful documentation (e.g., a user will probably be annoyed if he asks for help and the documentation lists 50 examples covering all sorts of tricky corner cases). For this kind of testing, you want to use the unittest module.

Last, the doctest module has a large number of configuration options that concerns various aspects of how testing is performed and how results are reported. Because these options are not required for the most common use of the module, they are not covered here. Consult http://docs.python.org/library/doctest.html for more details.

Unit Testing and the `unittest` Module

For more exhaustive program testing, use the unittest module. With unit testing, a developer writes a collection of isolated test cases for each element that makes up a program (for example, individual functions, methods, classes, and modules). These tests are then run to verify correct behavior of the basic building blocks that make up larger programs. As programs grow in size, unit tests for various components can be combined to create large testing frameworks and testing tools. This can greatly simplify the task of verifying correct behavior as well as isolating and fixing problems when they do occur. Use of this module can be illustrated by the code listing in the previous section:

```python
# splitter.py
def split(line, types=None, delimiter=None):
    """Splits a line of text and optionally performs type conversion.
    ...
    """
    fields = line.split(delimiter)
    if types:
        fields = [ ty(val) for ty,val in zip(types,fields) ]
    return fields
```

If you wanted to write unit tests for testing various aspects of the split() function, you would create a separate module testsplitter.py, like this:

```
# testsplitter.py
import splitter
import unittest

# Unit tests
class TestSplitFunction(unittest.TestCase):
    def setUp(self):
        # Perform set up actions (if any)
        pass
    def tearDown(self):
        # Perform clean-up actions (if any)
        pass
    def testsimplestring(self):
        r = splitter.split('GOOG 100 490.50')
        self.assertEqual(r,['GOOG','100','490.50'])
    def testtypeconvert(self):
        r = splitter.split('GOOG 100 490.50',[str, int, float])
        self.assertEqual(r,['GOOG', 100, 490.5])
    def testdelimiter(self):
        r = splitter.split('GOOG,100,490.50',delimiter=',')
        self.assertEqual(r,['GOOG','100','490.50'])

# Run the unittests
if __name__ == '__main__':
    unittest.main()
```

To run tests, simply run Python on the file testsplitter.py. Here's an example:

```
% python testsplitter.py
...
-----------------------------------------------------------------------
Ran 3 tests in 0.014s

OK
```

Basic use of unittest involves defining a class that inherits from unittest.TestCase. Within this class, individual tests are defined by methods starting with the name 'test'—for example, 'testsimplestring', 'testtypeconvert', and so on. (It is important to emphasize that the names are entirely up to you as long as they start with 'test'.) Within each test, various assertions are used to check for different conditions.

An instance, t, of unittest.TestCase has the following methods that are used when writing tests and for controlling the testing process:

t.setUp()

Called to perform set-up steps prior to running any of the testing methods.

t.tearDown()

Called to perform clean-up actions after running the tests.

```
t.assert_(expr [, msg])
t.failUnless(expr [, msg])
```

Signals a test failure if *expr* evaluates as `False`. *msg* is a message string giving an explanation for the failure (if any).

```
t.assertEqual(x, y [,msg])
t.failUnlessEqual(x, y [, msg])
```

Signals a test failure if *x* and *y* are not equal to each other. *msg* is a message explaining the failure (if any).

```
t.assertNotEqual(x, y [, msg])
t.failIfEqual(x, y, [, msg])
```

Signals a test failure if *x* and *y* are equal to each other. *msg* is a message explaining the failure (if any).

```
t.assertAlmostEqual(x, y [, places [, msg]])
t.failUnlessAlmostEqual(x, y, [, places [, msg]])
```

Signals a test failure if numbers *x* and *y* are not within *places* decimal places of each other. This is checked by computing the difference of *x and* y and rounding the result to the given number of places. If the result is zero, *x* and *y* are almost equal. *msg* is a message explaining the failure (if any).

```
t.assertNotAlmostEqual(x, y, [, places [, msg]])
t.failIfAlmostEqual(x, y [, places [, msg]])
```

Signals a test failure if *x* and *y* are not at least *places* decimal places apart. *msg* is a message explaining the failure (if any).

```
t.assertRaises(exc, callable, ...)
t.failUnlessRaises(exc, callable, ...)
```

Signals a test failure if the callable object `callable` does not raise the exception `exc`. Remaining arguments are passed as arguments to `callable`. Multiple exceptions can be checked by using a tuple of exceptions as `exc`.

```
t.failIf(expr [, msg])
```

Signals a test failure if *expr* evaluates as `True`. *msg* is a message explaining the failure (if any).

```
t.fail([msg])
```

Signals a test failure. *msg* is a message explaining the failure (if any).

```
t.failureException
```

This attribute is set to the last exception value caught in a test. This may be useful if you not only want to check that an exception was raised, but that the exception raises an appropriate value—for example, if you wanted to check the error message generated as part of raising an exception.

It should be noted that the unittest module contains a large number of advanced customization options for grouping tests, creating test suites, and controlling the environment in which tests run. These features are not directly related to the process of writing tests for your code (you tend to write testing classes as shown independently of how tests actually get executed). Consult the documentation at http://docs.python.org/library/unittest.html for more information on how to organize tests for larger programs.

The Python Debugger and the pdb Module

Python includes a simple command-based debugger which is found in the pdb module. The pdb module supports post-mortem debugging, inspection of stack frames, breakpoints, single-stepping of source lines, and code evaluation.

There are several functions for invoking the debugger from a program or from the interactive Python shell.

`run(statement [, globals [, locals]])`

Executes the string *statement* under debugger control. The debugger prompt will appear immediately before any code executes. Typing 'continue' will force it to run. *globals* and *locals* define the global and local namespaces, respectively, in which the code runs.

`runeval(expression [, globals [, locals]])`

Evaluates the *expression* string under debugger control. The debugger prompt will appear before any code executes, so you will need to type 'continue' to force it to execute as with run(). On success, the value of the expression is returned.

`runcall(function [, argument, ...])`

Calls a function within the debugger. *function* is a callable object. Additional arguments are supplied as the arguments to *function*. The debugger prompt will appear before any code executes. The return value of the function is returned upon completion.

`set_trace()`

Starts the debugger at the point at which this function is called. This can be used to hard-code a debugger breakpoint into a specific code location.

`post_mortem(traceback)`

Starts post-mortem debugging of a traceback object. *traceback* is typically obtained using a function such as sys.exc_info().

`pm()`

Enters post-mortem debugging using the traceback of the last exception.

Of all of the functions for launching the debugger, the set_trace() function may be the easiest to use in practice. If you are working on a complicated application but you have detected a problem in one part of it, you can insert a set_trace() call into the code and simply run the application. When encountered, this will suspend the program and go directly to the debugger where you can inspect the execution environment. Execution resumes after you leave the debugger.

Debugger Commands

When the debugger starts, it presents a (Pdb) prompt such as the following:

```
>>> import pdb
>>> import buggymodule
>>> pdb.run('buggymodule.start()')
> <string>(0)?()
(Pdb)
```

(Pdb) is the debugger prompt at which the following commands are recognized. Note that some commands have a short and a long form. In this case, parentheses are used to indicate both forms. For example, h(elp) means that either h or help is acceptable.

[!] *statement*

Executes the (one-line) *statement* in the context of the current stack frame. The exclamation point may be omitted, but it must be used to avoid ambiguity if the first word of the statement resembles a debugger command. To set a global variable, you can prefix the assignment command with a "global" command on the same line:

```
(Pdb) global list_options; list_options = ['-1']
(Pdb)
```

a(rgs)

Prints the argument list of the current function.

alias *[name [command]]*

Creates an alias called *name* that executes *command*. Within the *command* string, the substrings '%1', '%2', and so forth are replaced by parameters when the alias is typed. '%*' is replaced by all parameters. If no command is given, the current alias list is shown. Aliases can be nested and can contain anything that can be legally typed at the Pdb prompt. Here's an example:

```
# Print instance variables (usage "pi classInst")
alias pi for k in %1.__dict__.keys(): print "%1.",k,"=",%1.__dict__[k]
# Print instance variables in self
alias ps pi self
```

b(reak) *[loc [, condition]]*

Sets a breakpoint at location *loc*. *loc* either specifies a specific filename and line number or is the name of a function within a module. The following syntax is used:

Setting	Description
n	A line number in the current file
filename:n	A line number in another file
function	A function name in the current module
module.function	A function name in a module

If *loc* is omitted, all the current breakpoints are printed. *condition* is an expression that must evaluate to true before the breakpoint is honored. All breakpoints are assigned numbers that are printed as output upon the completion of this command. These numbers are used in several other debugger commands that follow.

`cl(ear) [bpnumber [bpnumber ...]]`

Clears a list of breakpoint numbers. If breakpoints are specified, all breaks are cleared.

`commands [bpnumber]`

Sets a series of debugger commands to execute automatically when the breakpoint *bpnumber* is encountered. When listing the commands to execute, simply type them on the subsequent lines and use end to mark the end of the command sequence. If you include the `continue` command, the execution of the program will resume automatically when the breakpoint is encountered. If *bpnumber* is omitted, the last breakpoint set is used.

`condition bpnumber [condition]`

Places a condition on a breakpoint. *condition* is an expression that must evaluate to true before the breakpoint is recognized. Omitting the condition clears any previous condition.

`c(ont(inue))`

Continues execution until the next breakpoint is encountered.

`disable [bpnumber [bpnumber ...]]`

Disables the set of specified breakpoints. Unlike with `clear`, they can be reenabled later.

`d(own)`

Moves the current frame one level down in the stack trace.

`enable [bpnumber [bpnumber ...]]`

Enables a specified set of breakpoints.

`h(elp) [command]`

Shows the list of available commands. Specifying a command returns help for that command.

`ignore bpnumber [count]`

Ignores a breakpoint for *count* executions.

`j(ump) lineno`

Sets the next line to execute. This can only be used to move between statements in the same execution frame. Moreover, you can't jump into certain statements, such as statements in the middle of a loop.

`l(ist) [first [, last]]`

Lists source code. Without arguments, this command lists 11 lines around the current line (5 lines before and 5 lines after). With one argument, it lists 11 lines around that line. With two arguments, it lists lines in a given range. If *last* is less than *first*, it's interpreted as a count.

`n(ext)`

Executes until the next line of the current function. Skips the code contained in function calls.

`p expression`

Evaluates the expression in the current context and prints its value.

`pp expression`

The same as the p command, but the result is formatted using the pretty-printing module (pprint).

`q(uit)`

Quits from the debugger.

`r(eturn)`

Runs until the current function returns.

`run [args]`

Restarts the program and uses the command-line arguments in args as the new setting of sys.argv. All breakpoints and other debugger settings are preserved.

`s(tep)`

Executes a single source line and stops inside called functions.

`tbreak [loc [, condition]]`

Sets a temporary breakpoint that's removed after its first hit.

`u(p)`

Moves the current frame one level up in the stack trace.

`unalias name`

Deletes the specified alias.

`until`

Resumes execution until control leaves the current execution frame or until a line number greater than the current line number is reached. For example, if the debugger was stopped at the last line in a loop body, typing **until** will execute all of the statements in the loop until the loop is finished.

`w(here)`

Prints a stack trace.

Debugging from the Command Line

An alternative method for running the debugger is to invoke it on the command line. Here's an example:

```
% python -m pdb someprogram.py
```

In this case, the debugger is launched automatically at the beginning of program startup where you are free to set breakpoints and make other configuration changes. To make the program run, simply use the continue command. For example, if you wanted to debug the split() function from within a program that used it, you might do this:

```
% python -m pdb someprogram.py
> /Users/beazley/Code/someprogram.py(1)<module>()
-> import splitter
(Pdb) b splitter.split
Breakpoint 1 at /Users/beazley/Code/splitter.py:1
(Pdb) c
> /Users/beazley/Code/splitter.py(18)split()
-> fields = line.split(delimiter)
(Pdb)
```

Configuring the Debugger

If a .pdbrc file exists in the user's home directory or in the current directory, it's read in and executed as if it had been typed at the debugger prompt. This can be useful for specifying debugging commands that you want to execute each time the debugger is started (as opposed to having to interactively type the commands each time).

Program Profiling

The profile and cProfile modules are used to collect profiling information. Both modules work in the same way, but cProfile is implemented as a C extension, is significantly faster, and is more modern. Either module is used to collect both coverage information (that is, what functions get executed) as well as performance statistics. The easiest way to profile a program is to execute it from the command line as follows:

```
% python -m cProfile someprogram.py
```

Alternatively, the following function in the profile module can be used:

```
run(command [, filename])
```

Executes the contents of command using the exec statement under the profiler. filename is the name of a file in which raw profiling data is saved. If it's omitted, a report is printed to standard output.

The result of running the profiler is a report such as the following:

```
126 function calls (6 primitive calls) in 5.130 CPU seconds
Ordered by: standard name
ncalls  tottime  percall  cumtime  percall filename:lineno(function)
     1    0.030    0.030    5.070    5.070 <string>:1(?)
 121/1    5.020    0.041    5.020    5.020 book.py:11(process)
     1    0.020    0.020    5.040    5.040 book.py:5(?)
     2    0.000    0.000    0.000    0.000 exceptions.py:101(__init__)
     1    0.060    0.060    5.130    5.130 profile:0(execfile('book.py'))
     0    0.000             0.000          profile:0(profiler)
```

Different parts of the report generated by run() are interpreted as follows:

Section	Description
primitive calls	Number of nonrecursive function calls
ncalls	Total number of calls (including self-recursion)
tottime	Time spent in this function (not counting subfunctions)
percall	tottime/ncalls
cumtime	Total time spent in the function
percall	cumtime/(primitive calls)
filename:lineno(function)	Location and name of each function

When there are two numbers in the first column (for example, "121/1"), the latter is the number of primitive calls and the former is the actual number of calls.

Simply inspecting the generated report of the profiler is often enough for most applications of this module—for example, if you simply want to see how your program is spending its time. However, if you want to save the data and analyze it further, the pstats module can be used. Consult http://docs.python.org/library/profile.html for more details about saving and analyzing the profile data.

Tuning and Optimization

This section covers some general rules of thumb that can be used to make Python programs run faster and use less memory. The techniques described here are by no means exhaustive but should give programmers some ideas when looking at their own code.

Making Timing Measurements

If you simply want to time a long-running Python program, the easiest way to do it is often just to run it under the control of something like the UNIX time command. Alternatively, if you have a block of long-running statements you want to time, you can insert calls to time.clock() to get a current reading of the elapsed CPU time or calls to time.time() to read the current wall-clock time. For example:

```
start_cpu = time.clock()
start_real= time.time()
statements
statements
end_cpu = time.clock()
end_real = time.time()
print("%f Real Seconds" % (end_real - start_real))
print("%f CPU seconds" % (end_cpu - start_cpu))
```

Keep in the mind that this technique really works only if the code to be timed runs for a reasonable period of time. If you have a fine-grained statement you want to benchmark, you can use the timeit(code [, setup]) function in the timeit module. For example:

```
>>> from timeit import timeit
>>> timeit('math.sqrt(2.0)','import math')
0.20388007164001465
>>> timeit('sqrt(2.0)','from math import sqrt')
0.14494490623474121
```

In this example, the first argument to `timeit()` is the code you want to benchmark. The second argument is a statement that gets executed once in order to set up the execution environment. The `timeit()` function runs the supplied statement one million times and reports the execution time. The number of repetitions can be changed by supplying a `number=count` keyword argument to `timeit()`.

The `timeit` module also has a function `repeat()` that can be used to make measurements. This function works the same way as `timeit()` except that it repeats the timing measurement three times and returns a list of the results. For example:

```
>>> from timeit import repeat
>>> repeat('math.sqrt(2.0)','import math')
[0.20306601524353027, 0.19715800285339355, 0.20907392501831055]
>>>
```

When making performance measurement, it is common to refer to the associated *speedup*, which usually refers to the original execution time divided by the new execution time. For example, in the previous timing measurements, using `sqrt(2.0)` instead of `math.sqrt(2.0)` represents a speedup of 0.20388/0.14494 or about 1.41. Sometimes this gets reported as a percentage by saying the speedup is about 41 percent.

Making Memory Measurements

The `sys` module has a function `getsizeof()` that can be used to investigate the memory footprint (in bytes) of individual Python objects. For example:

```
>>> import sys
>>> sys.getsizeof(1)
14
>>> sys.getsizeof("Hello World")
52
>>> sys.getsizeof([1,2,3,4])
52
>>> sum(sys.getsizeof(x) for x in [1,2,3,4])
56
```

For containers such as lists, tuples, and dictionaries, the size that gets reported is just for the container object itself, not the cumulative size of all objects contained inside of it. For instance, in the previous example, the reported size of the list `[1,2,3,4]` is actually smaller than the space required for four integers (which are 14 bytes each). This is because the contents of the list are not included in the total. You can use `sum()` as shown here to calculate the total size of the list contents.

Be aware that the `getsizeof()` function is only going to give you a rough idea of overall memory use for various objects. Internally, the interpreter aggressively shares objects via reference counting so the actual memory consumed by an object might be far less than you first imagine. Also, given that C extensions to Python can allocate memory outside of the interpreter, it may be difficult to precisely get a measurement of overall memory use. Thus, a secondary technique for measuring the actual memory footprint is to inspect your running program from an operating system process viewer or task manager.

Frankly, a better way to get a handle on memory use may be to sit down and be analytical about it. If you know your program is going to allocate various kinds of data structures and you know what kinds of data will be stored in those structures (that is, ints, floats, strings, and so on), you can use the results of the `getsizeof()` function to obtain figures for calculating an upper bound on your program's memory footprint—or at the very least, you can get enough information to carry out a "back of the envelope" estimate.

Disassembly

The dis module can be used to disassemble Python functions, methods, and classes into low-level interpreter instructions. The module defines a function dis() that can be used like this:

```
>>> from dis import dis
>>> dis(split)
  2           0 LOAD_FAST            0 (line)
              3 LOAD_ATTR            0 (split)
              6 LOAD_FAST            1 (delimiter)
              9 CALL_FUNCTION        1
             12 STORE_FAST           2 (fields)

  3          15 LOAD_GLOBAL          1 (types)
             18 JUMP_IF_FALSE       58 (to 79)
             21 POP_TOP

  4          22 BUILD_LIST           0
             25 DUP_TOP
             26 STORE_FAST           3 (_[1])
             29 LOAD_GLOBAL          2 (zip)
             32 LOAD_GLOBAL          1 (types)
             35 LOAD_FAST            2 (fields)
             38 CALL_FUNCTION        2
             41 GET_ITER
        >>   42 FOR_ITER            25 (to 70)
             45 UNPACK_SEQUENCE      2
             48 STORE_FAST           4 (ty)
             51 STORE_FAST           5 (val)
             54 LOAD_FAST            3 (_[1])
             57 LOAD_FAST            4 (ty)
             60 LOAD_FAST            5 (val)
             63 CALL_FUNCTION        1
             66 LIST_APPEND
             67 JUMP_ABSOLUTE       42
        >>   70 DELETE_FAST          3 (_[1])
             73 STORE_FAST           2 (fields)
             76 JUMP_FORWARD         1 (to 80)
        >>   79 POP_TOP

  5     >>   80 LOAD_FAST            2 (fields)
             83 RETURN_VALUE
>>>
```

Expert programmers can use this information in two ways. First, a disassembly will show you exactly what operations are involved in executing a function. With careful study, you might spot opportunities for making speedups. Second, if you are programming with threads, each line printed in the disassembly represents a single interpreter operation—each of which has atomic execution. Thus, if you are trying to track down a tricky race condition, this information might be useful.

Tuning Strategies

The following sections outline a few optimization strategies that, in the opinion of the author, have proven to be useful with Python code.

Understand Your Program

Before you optimize anything, know that speedup obtained by optimizing part of a program is directly related to that part's total contribution to the execution time. For example, if you optimize a function by making it run 10 times as fast but that function only contributes to 10 percent of the program's total execution time, you're only going to get an overall speedup of about 9%–10%. Depending on the effort involved in making the optimization, this may or may not be worth it.

It is always a good idea to first use the profiling module on code you intend to optimize. You really only want to focus on functions and methods where your program spends most of its time, not obscure operations that are called only occasionally.

Understand Algorithms

A poorly implemented O(n log n) algorithm will outperform the most finely tuned O(n³) algorithm. Don't optimize inefficient algorithms—look for a better algorithm first.

Use the Built-In Types

Python's built-in tuple, list, set, and dictionary types are implemented entirely in C and are the most finely tuned data structures in the interpreter. You should actively use these types to store and manipulate data in your program and resist the urge to build your own custom data structures that mimic their functionality (that is, binary search trees, linked lists, and so on).

Having said that, you should still look more closely at types in the standard library. Some library modules provide new types that outperform the built-ins at certain tasks. For instance, the `collection.deque` type provides similar functionality to a list but has been highly optimized for the insertion of new items at both ends. A list, in contrast, is only efficient when appending items at the end. If you insert items at the front, all of the other elements need to be shifted in order to make room. The time required to do this grows as the list gets larger and larger. Just to give you an idea of the difference, here is a timing measurement of inserting one million items at the front of a list and a deque:

```
>>> from timeit import timeit
>>> timeit('s.appendleft(37)',
...         'import collections; s = collections.deque()',
...         number=1000000)
0.24434304237365723
>>> timeit('s.insert(0,37)', 's = []', number=1000000)
612.95199513435364
```

Don't Add Layers

Any time you add an extra layer of abstraction or convenience to an object or a function, you will slow down your program. However, there is also a trade-off between usability and performance. For instance, the whole point of adding an extra layer is often to simplify coding, which is also a good thing.

To illustrate with a simple example, consider a program that makes use of the `dict()` function to create dictionaries with string keys like this:

```
s = dict(name='GOOG',shares=100,price=490.10)
# s = {'name':'GOOG', 'shares':100, 'price':490.10 }
```

A programmer might create dictionaries in this way to save typing (you don't have to put quotes around the key names). However, this alternative way of creating a dictionary also runs much more slowly because it adds an extra function call.

```
>>> timeit("s = {'name':'GOOG','shares':100,'price':490.10}")
0.38917303085327148
>>> timeit("s = dict(name='GOOG',shares=100,price=490.10)")
0.94420003890991211
```

If your program creates millions of dictionaries as it runs, then you should know that the first approach is faster. With few exceptions, any feature that adds an enhancement or changes the way in which an existing Python object works will run more slowly.

Know How Classes and Instances Build Upon Dictionaries

User-defined classes and instances are built using dictionaries. Because of this, operations that look up, set, or delete instance data are almost always going to run more slowly than directly performing these operations on a dictionary. If all you are doing is building a simple data structure for storing data, a dictionary may be a more efficient choice than defining a class.

Just to illustrate the difference, here is a simple class that represents a holding of stock:

```
class Stock(object):
    def __init__(self,name,shares,price):
        self.name = name
        self.shares = shares
        self.price = price
```

If you compare the performance of using this class against a dictionary, the results are interesting. First, let's compare the performance of simply creating instances:

```
>>> from timeit import timeit
>>> timeit("s = Stock('GOOG',100,490.10)","from stock import Stock")
1.3166780471801758
>>> timeit("s = {'name' : 'GOOG', 'shares' : 100, 'price' : 490.10 }")
0.37812089920043945
>>>
```

Here, the speedup of creating new objects is about 3.5. Next, let's look at the performance of performing a simple calculation:

```
>>> timeit("s.shares*s.price",
...         "from stock import Stock; s = Stock('GOOG',100,490.10)")
0.29100513458251953
>>> timeit("s['shares']*s['price']",
...         "s = {'name' : 'GOOG', 'shares' : 100, 'price' : 490.10 }")
0.23622798919677734
>>>
```

Here, the speedup is about 1.2. The lesson here is that just because you can define a new object using a `class`, it's not the only way to work with data. Tuples and dictionaries are often good enough. Using them will make your program run more quickly and use less memory.

Use __slots__

If your program creates a large number of instances of user-defined classes, you might consider using the __slots__ attribute in a class definition. For example:

```
class Stock(object):
    __slots__ = ['name','shares','price']
    def __init__(self,name,shares,price):
        self.name = name
        self.shares = shares
        self.price = price
```

__slots__ is sometimes viewed as a safety feature because it restricts the set of attribute names. However, it is really more of a performance optimization. Classes that use __slots__ don't use a dictionary for storing instance data (instead, a more efficient internal data structure is used). So, not only will instances use far less memory, but access to instance data is also more efficient. In some cases, simply adding __slots__ will make a program run noticeably faster without making any other changes.

There is one caution with using __slots__, however. Adding this feature to a class may cause other code to break mysteriously. For example, it is generally well-known that instances store their data in a dictionary that can be accessed as the __dict__ attribute. When slots are defined, this attribute doesn't exist so any code that relies on __dict__ will fail.

Avoid the (.) Operator

Whenever you use the (.) to look up an attribute on an object, it always involves a name lookup. For example, when you say x.name, there is a lookup for the variable name "x" in the environment and then a lookup for the attribute "name" on x. For user-defined objects, attribute lookup may involve looking in the instance dictionary, the class dictionary, and the dictionaries of base-classes.

For calculations involving heavy use of methods or module lookups, it is almost always better to eliminate the attribute lookup by putting the operation you want to perform into a local variable first. For example, if you were performing a lot of square root operations, it is faster to use 'from math import sqrt' and 'sqrt(x)' rather than typing 'math.sqrt(x)'. In the first part of this section, we saw that this approach resulted in speedup of about 1.4.

Obviously you should not try to eliminate attribute lookups everywhere in your program because it will make your code very difficult to read. However, for performance-critical sections, this is a useful technique.

Use Exceptions to Handle Uncommon Cases

To avoid errors, you might be inclined to add extra checks to a program. For example:

```
def parse_header(line):
    fields = line.split(":")
    if len(fields) != 2:
        raise RuntimeError("Malformed header")
    header, value = fields
    return header.lower(), value.strip()
```

However, an alternative way to handle errors is to simply let the program generate an exception and to catch it. For example:

```
def parse_header(line):
    fields = line.split(":")
    try:
        header, value = fields
        return header.lower(), value.strip()
    except ValueError:
        raise RuntimeError("Malformed header")
```

If you benchmark both versions on a properly formatted line, the second version of code runs about 10 percent faster. Setting up a `try` block for code that normally doesn't raise an exceptions runs more quickly than executing an `if` statement.

Avoid Exceptions for Common Cases

Don't write code that uses exception handling for the common case. For example, suppose you had a program that performed a lot of dictionary lookups, but most of these lookups were for keys that didn't exist. Now, consider two approaches to performing a lookup:

```
# Approach 1 : Perform a lookup and catch an exception
try:
    value = items[key]
except KeyError:
    value = None

# Approach 2: Check if the key exists and perform a lookup
if key in items:
    value = items[key]
else:
    value = None
```

In a simple performance measurement where the key is not found, the second approach runs more than 17 times faster! In case you were wondering, this latter approach also runs almost twice as fast as using `items.get(key)` because the in operator is faster to execute than a method call.

Embrace Functional Programming and Iteration

List comprehensions, generator expressions, generators, coroutines, and closures are much more efficient than most Python programmers realize. For data processing especially, list comprehensions and generator expressions run significantly more quickly than code that manually iterates over data and carries out similar operations. These operations also run much more quickly than legacy Python code that uses functions such as `map()` and `filter()`. Generators can be used to write code that not only runs fast, but which makes efficient use of memory.

Use Decorators and Metaclasses

Decorators and metaclasses are features that are used to modify functions and classes. However, because they operate at the time of function or class definition, they can be used in ways that lead to improved performance—especially if a program has many optional features that might be turned on or off. Chapter 6, "Functions and Functional Programming," has an example of using a decorator to enable logging of functions, but in a way that does not impact performance when logging is disabled.

II

The Python Library

12

Built-In Functions and Exceptions

This chapter describes Python's built-in functions and exceptions. Much of this material is covered less formally in earlier chapters of this book. This chapter merely consolidates all this information into one section and expands upon some of the more subtle features of certain functions. Also, Python 2 includes a number of built-in functions that are considered to be obsolete and which have been removed from Python 3. Those functions are not documented here—instead the focus is on modern functionality.

Built-in Functions and Types

Certain types, functions, and variables are always available to the interpreter and can be used in any source module. Although you don't need to perform any extra imports to access these functions, they are contained in a module `__builtin__` in Python 2 and in a module `builtins` in Python 3. Within other modules that you import, the variable `__builtins__` is also bound to this module.

`abs(x)`

Returns the absolute value of x.

`all(s)`

Returns `True` if all of the values in the iterable s evaluate as `True`.

`any(s)`

Returns `True` if any of the values in the iterable s evaluate as `True`.

`ascii(x)`

Creates a printable representation of the object x just like the `repr()`, but only uses ASCII characters in the result. Non-ASCII characters are turned into appropriate escape sequences. This can be used to view Unicode strings in a terminal or shell that doesn't support Unicode. Python 3 only.

basestring

This is an abstract data type that is the superclass of all strings in Python 2 (str and unicode). It is only used for type testing of strings. For example, isinstance(s,basestring) returns True if s is either kind of string. Python 2 only.

bin(x)

Returns a string containing the binary representation of the integer x.

bool([x])

Type representing Boolean values True and False. If used to convert x, it returns True if x evaluates to true using the usual truth-testing semantics (that is, nonzero number, non-empty list, and so on). Otherwise, False is returned. False is also the default value returned if bool() is called without any arguments. The bool class inherits from int so the Boolean values True and False can be used as integers with values 1 and 0 in mathematical calculations.

bytearray([x])

A type representing a mutable array of bytes. When creating an instance, x may be an iterable sequence of integers in the range 0 to 255, an 8-bit string or bytes literal, or an integer that specifies the size of the byte array (in which case every entry will be initialized to 0). A bytearray object a looks like an array of integers. If you perform a lookup such as a[i], you will get an integer value representing the byte value at index i. Assignments such as a[i] = v also require v to be an integer byte value. However, a bytearray also provides all of the operations normally associated with strings (that is, slicing, find(), split(), replace(), and so on). When using these string operations, you should be careful to preface all string literals with b in order to indicate that you're working with bytes. For example, if you wanted to split a byte array a into fields using a comma character separator, you would use a.split(b',') not a.split(',').The result of these operations is always new bytearray objects, not strings. To turn a bytearray a into a string, use the a.decode(encoding) method. An encoding of 'latin-1' will directly turn a bytearray of 8-bit characters into a string without any modification of the underlying character values.

bytearray(s ,encoding)

An alternative calling convention for creating a bytearray instance from characters in a string s where encoding specifies the character encoding to use in the conversion.

bytes([x])

A type representing an immutable array of bytes. In Python 2, this is an alias for str() which creates a standard 8-bit string of characters. In Python 3, bytes is a completely separate type that is an immutable version of the bytearray type described earlier. In that case, the argument x has the same interpretation and can be used in the same manner. One portability caution is that even though bytes is defined in Python 2, the resulting object does not behave consistently with Python 3. For example, if a is an instance created by bytes(), then a[i] returns a character string in Python 2, but returns an integer in Python 3.

bytes(*s*, *encoding*)

An alternative calling convention for creating a bytes instance from characters in a string *s* where *encoding* specifies the character encoding to use. Python 3 only.

chr(*x*)

Converts an integer value, *x*, into a one-character string. In Python 2, *x* must be in the range 0 <= *x* <= 255, and in Python 3, *x* must represent a valid Unicode code point. If *x* is out of range, a ValueError exception is raised.

classmethod(*func*)

This function creates a class method for the function *func*. It is typically only used inside class definitions where it is implicitly invoked by the @classmethod decorator. Unlike a normal method, a class method receives the class as the first argument, not an instance. For example, if you had an object, f, that is an instance of class Foo, invoking a class method on f will pass the class Foo as the first argument to the method, not the instance f.

cmp(*x*, *y*)

Compares *x* and *y* and returns a negative number if *x* < *y*, a positive number if *x* > *y*, or 0 if *x* == *y*. Any two objects can be compared, although the result may be meaningless if the two objects have no meaningful comparison method defined (for example, comparing a number with a file object). In certain circumstances, such comparisons may also raise an exception (Python 3 only).

compile(*string*, *filename*, *kind* [, *flags* [, *dont_inherit*]])

Compiles *string* into a code object for use with exec() or eval(). *string* is a string containing valid Python code. If this code spans multiple lines, the lines must be terminated by a single newline ('\n') and not platform-specific variants (for example, '\r\n' on Windows). *filename* is a string containing the name of the file in which the string was defined. *kind* is 'exec' for a sequence of statements, 'eval' for a single expression, or 'single' for a single executable statement. The *flags* parameter determines which optional features (associated with the __future__ module) are enabled. Features are specified using the bitwise OR of flags defined in the __future__ module. For example, if you wanted to enable new division semantics, you would set *flags* to __future__.division.compiler_flag. If *flags* is omitted or set to 0, the code is compiled with whatever features are currently in effect. If *flags* is supplied, the features specified are added to those features already in effect. If dont_inherit is set, only those features specified in *flags* are enabled—features currently enabled are ignored.

complex([*real* [, *imag*]])

Type representing a complex number with real and imaginary components, *real* and *imag*, which can be supplied as any numeric type. If *imag* is omitted, the imaginary component is set to zero. If *real* is passed as a string, the string is parsed and converted to a complex number. In this case, *imag* should be omitted. If no arguments are given, 0j is returned.

delattr(*object*, *attr*)

Deletes an attribute of an object. *attr* is a string. Same as del *object*.*attr*.

`dict([m])` or `dict(key1 = value1, key2 = value2, ...)`

Type representing a dictionary. If no argument is given, an empty dictionary is returned. If `m` is a mapping object (such as a dictionary), a new dictionary having the same keys and same values as `m` is returned. For example, if `m` is a dictionary, `dict(m)` simply makes a shallow copy of it. If `m` is not a mapping, it must support iteration in which a sequence of `(key, value)` pairs is produced. These pairs are used to populate the dictionary. `dict()` can also be called with keyword arguments. For example, `dict(foo=3, bar=7)` creates the dictionary `{ 'foo' : 3, 'bar' : 7 }`.

`dir([object])`

Returns a sorted list of attribute names. If `object` is a module, it contains the list of symbols defined in that module. If `object` is a type or class object, it returns a list of attribute names. The names are typically obtained from the object's `__dict__` attribute if defined, but other sources may be used. If no argument is given, the names in the current local symbol table are returned. It should be noted that this function is primarily used for informational purposes (for example, used interactively at the command line). It should not be used for formal program analysis because the information obtained may be incomplete. Also, user-defined classes can define a special method `__dir__()` that alters the result of this function.

`divmod(a, b)`

Returns the quotient and remainder of long division as a tuple. For integers, the value `(a // b, a % b)` is returned. For floats, `(math.floor(a / b), a % b)` is returned. This function may not be called with complex numbers.

`enumerate(iter[, initial_value])`

Given an iterable object, `iter`, returns a new iterator (of type enumerate) that produces tuples containing a count and the value produced from `iter`. For example, if `iter` produces `a, b, c`, then `enumerate(iter)` produces `(0,a), (1,b), (2,c)`.

`eval(expr [, globals [, locals]])`

Evaluates an expression. `expr` is a string or a code object created by `compile()`. `globals` and `locals` are mapping objects that define the global and local namespaces, respectively, for the operation. If omitted, the expression is evaluated in the namespace of the caller. It is most common for `globals` and `locals` to be specified as dictionaries, but advanced applications can supply custom mapping objects.

`exec(code [, global [, locals]])`

Executes Python statements. `code` is a string, a file, or a code object created by `compile()`. `globals` and `locals` define the global and local namespaces, respectively, for the operation. If omitted, the code is executed in the namespace of the caller. If no global or local dictionaries are given, the behavior of this function is a little muddled between Python versions. In Python 2, exec is actually implemented as a special language statement, whereas Python 3 implements it as a standard library function. A subtle side effect of this implementation difference is that in Python 2, code evaluated by exec can freely mutate local variables in the caller's namespace. In Python 3, you can execute code that makes such changes, but they don't seem to have any lasting effect beyond the `exec()` call itself. This is because Python 3 uses `locals()` to obtain the local namespace if one isn't supplied. As you will note in the documentation for `locals()`, the returned dictionary is only safe to inspect, not modify.

`filter(function, iterable)`

In Python 2, this creates a list consisting of the objects from *iterable* for which *function* evaluates to true. In Python 3, the result is an iterator that produces this result. If *function* is None, the identity function is used and all the elements of *iterable* that are false are removed. *iterable* can be any object that supports iteration. As a general rule, it is significantly faster to use a generator expression or list comprehension to filter data (refer to Chapter 6).

`float([x])`

Type representing a floating-point number. If *x* is a number, it is converted to a float. If *x* is a string, it is parsed into a float. If no argument is supplied, 0.0 is returned.

`format(value [, format_spec])`

Converts *value* to a formatted string according to the format specification string in *format_spec*. This operation invokes *value*.__format__(), which is free to interpret the format specification as it sees fit. For simple types of data, the format specifier typically includes an alignment character of '<', '>', or '^'; a number (which indicates the field width); and a character code of 'd', 'f', or 's' for integer, floating point, or string values, respectively. For example, a format specification of 'd' formats an integer, a specification of '8d' right aligns an integer in an 8-character field and '<8d' left aligns an integer in an 8-character field. More details on format() and format specifiers can be found in Chapter 3, "Types and Objects," and Chapter 4, "Operators and Expressions."

`frozenset([items])`

Type representing an immutable set object populated with values taken from *items* that must be an iterable. The values must also be immutable. If no argument is given, an empty set is returned.

`getattr(object, name [,default])`

Returns the value of a named attribute of an object. *name* is a string containing the attribute name. *default* is an optional value to return if no such attribute exists. Otherwise, AttributeError is raised. Same as *object.name*.

`globals()`

Returns the dictionary of the current module that represents the global namespace. When called inside another function or method, it returns the global namespace of the module in which the function or method was defined.

`hasattr(object, name)`

Returns True if *name* is the name of an attribute of *object*. False is returned otherwise. *name* is a string.

`hash(object)`

Returns an integer hash value for an object (if possible). The hash value is primarily used in the implementation of dictionaries, sets, and other mapping objects. The hash value is the same for any two objects that compare as equals. Mutable objects don't define a hash value, although user-defined classes can define a method __hash__() to support this operation.

`help([object])`

Calls the built-in help system during interactive sessions. `object` may be a string representing the name of a module, class, function, method, keyword, or documentation topic. If it is any other kind of object, a help screen related to that object will be produced. If no argument is supplied, an interactive help tool will start and provide more information.

`hex(x)`

Creates a hexadecimal string from an integer `x`.

`id(object)`

Returns the unique integer identity of `object`. You should not interpret the return value in any way (that is, as a memory location).

`input([prompt])`

In Python 2, this prints a prompt, reads a line of input, and processes it through `eval()` (that is, it's the same as `eval(raw_input(prompt))`. In Python 3, a prompt is printed to standard output and a single line of input is read without any kind of evaluation or modification. The returned line does not include a trailing newline character.

`int(x [,base])`

Type representing an integer. If `x` is a number, it is converted to an integer by truncating toward 0. If it is a string, it is parsed into an integer value. `base` optionally specifies a base when converting from a string. In Python 2, a long integer is created if the value exceeds the 32-bit range of the `int` type.

`isinstance(object, classobj)`

Returns `True` if `object` is an instance of `classobj`, is a subclass of `classobj`, or belongs to an abstract base class `classobj`. The `classobj` parameter can also be a tuple of possible types or classes. For example, `isinstance(s, (list,tuple))` returns `True` if `s` is a tuple or a list.

`issubclass(class1, class2)`

Returns `True` if `class1` is a subclass of (derived from) `class2` or if `class1` is registered with an abstract base class `class2`. `class2` can also be a tuple of possible classes, in which case each class will be checked. Note that `issubclass(A, A)` is true.

`iter(object [,sentinel])`

Returns an iterator for producing items in `object`. If the `sentinel` parameter is omitted, the object must either provide the method `__iter__()`, which creates an iterator, or implement `__getitem__()`, which accepts integer arguments starting at 0. If `sentinel` is specified, `object` is interpreted differently. Instead, `object` should be a callable object that takes no parameters. The returned iterator object will call this function repeatedly until the returned value is equal to `sentinel`, at which point iteration will stop. A `TypeError` will be generated if `object` does not support iteration.

`len(s)`

Returns the number of items contained in `s`. `s` should be a list, tuple, string, set, or dictionary. A `TypeError` is generated if `s` is an iterable such as a generator.

`list([items])`

Type representing a list. *items* may be any iterable object, the values of which are used to populate the list. If *items* is already a list, a copy is made. If no argument is given, an empty list is returned.

`locals()`

Returns a dictionary corresponding to the local namespace of the caller. This dictionary should only be used to inspect the execution environment—it is not safe to modify the contents of this dictionary.

`long([x [, base]])`

Type representing long integers in Python 2. If x is a number, it is converted to an integer by truncating toward 0. If x is a string, it is parsed into a long value. If no argument is given, this function returns 0L. For portability, you should avoid direct use of long. Using int(x) will create a long as necessary. For type checking, use isinstance(x, numbers.Integral) to check if x is any integer type.

`map(function, items, ...)`

In Python 2, this applies *function* to every item of *items* and returns a list of results. In Python 3, an iterator producing the same results is created. If multiple input sequences are supplied, *function* is assumed to take that many arguments, with each argument taken from a different sequence. The behavior when processing multiple input sequences differs between Python 2 and Python 3. In Python 2, the result is the same length as the longest input sequence with None used as a padding value when the shorter input sequences are exhausted. In Python 3, the result is only as long as the shortest sequence. The functionality provided by map() is almost always better expressed using a generator expression or list comprehension (both of which provide better performance). For example, map(*function*, s) can usually be replaced by [*function*(x) for x in s].

`max(s [, args, ...])`

For a single argument, s, this function returns the maximum value of the items in s, which may be any iterable object. For multiple arguments, it returns the largest of the arguments.

`min(s [, args, ...])`

For a single argument, s, this function returns the minimum value of the items in s, which may be any iterable object. For multiple arguments, it returns the smallest of the arguments.

`next(s [, default])`

Returns the next item from the iterator s. If the iterator has no more items, a StopIteration exception is raised unless a value is supplied to the *default* argument. In that case, *default* is returned instead. For portability, you should always use this function instead of calling s.next() directly on an iterator s. In Python 3, the name of the underlying iterator method changed to s.__next__(). If you write your code to use the next() function, you won't have to worry about this difference.

`object()`

The base class for all objects in Python. You can call it to create an instance, but the result isn't especially interesting.

`oct(x)`

Converts an integer, x, to an octal string.

`open(filename [, mode [, bufsize]])`

In Python 2, opens the file `filename` and returns a new file object (refer to Chapter 9, "Input and Output"). *mode* is a string that indicates how the file should be opened: `'r'` for reading, `'w'` for writing, and `'a'` for appending. A second character `'t'` or `'b'` is used to indicate text-mode (the default) or binary mode. For example, `'r'` or `'rt'` opens a file in text mode, whereas `'rb'` opens a file in binary mode. An optional `'+'` can be added to the mode to open the file for updating (which allows both reading and writing). A mode of `'w+'` truncates the file to zero length if it already exists. A mode of `'r+'` or `'a+'` opens the file for both reading and writing but leaves the original contents intact when the file is opened. If a mode of `'U'` or `'rU'` is specified, the file is opened in universal newline mode. In this mode, all variants of a newline (`'\n'`, `'\r'`, `'\r\n'`) are converted to the standard `'\n'` character. If the mode is omitted, a mode of `'rt'` is assumed. The `bufsize` argument specifies the buffering behavior, where 0 is unbuffered, 1 is line buffered, and any other positive number indicates an approximate buffer size in bytes. A negative number indicates that the system default buffering should be used (this is the default behavior).

`open(filename [, mode [, bufsize [, encoding [, errors [, newline [, closefd]]]]]])`

In Python 3, this opens the file `filename` and returns a file object. The first three arguments have the same meaning as for the Python 2 version of `open()` described earlier. *encoding* is an encoding name such as `'utf-8'`. *errors* is the error handling policy and is one of `'strict'`, `'ignore'`, `'replace'`, `'backslashreplace'`, or `'xmlcharrefreplace'`. *newline* controls the behavior of universal newline mode and is set to None, `''`, `'\n'`, `'\r'`, or `'\r\n'`. *closefd* is a Boolean flag that specifies whether the underlying file descriptor is closed when the `close()` method executes. Unlike Python 2, different kinds of objects are returned depending on the selected I/O mode. For example, if you open a file in binary mode, you get an object where I/O operations such as `read()` and `write()` operate on byte arrays instead of strings. File I/O is one area where there are significant differences between Python 2 and 3. Consult Appendix A, "Python 3," for more details.

`ord(c)`

Returns the integer ordinal value of a single character, c. For ordinary characters, a value in the range [0,255] is returned. For single Unicode characters, a value in the range [0,65535] is usually returned. In Python 3, c may also be a Unicode surrogate pair, in which case it is converted into the appropriate Unicode code point.

`pow(x, y [, z])`

Returns x ** y. If z is supplied, this function returns (x ** y) % z. If all three arguments are given, they must be integers and y must be nonnegative.

`print(value, ... [, sep=separator, end=ending, file=outfile])`

Python 3 function for printing a series of values. As input, you can supply any number of values, all of which are printed on the same line. The `sep` keyword argument is used to specify a different separator character (a space by default). The end keyword argument specifies a different line ending (`'\n'` by default). The `file` keyword argument redirects the output to a file object. This function can be used in Python 2 if you add the statement `from __future__ import print_function` to your code.

`property([fget [,fset [,fdel [,doc]]]])`

Creates a property attribute for classes. `fget` is a function that returns the attribute value, `fset` sets the attribute value, and `fdel` deletes an attribute. `doc` provides a documentation string. These parameters may be supplied using keyword arguments—for example, `property(fget=getX, doc="some text")`.

`range([start,] stop [, step])`

In Python 2, this creates a fully populated list of integers from `start` to `stop`. `step` indicates a stride and is set to `1` if omitted. If `start` is omitted (when `range()` is called with one argument), it defaults to `0`. A negative `step` creates a list of numbers in descending order. In Python 3, `range()` creates a special `range` object that computes its values on demand (like `xrange()` in previous Python versions).

`raw_input([prompt])`

Python 2 function that reads a line of input from standard input (`sys.stdin`) and returns it as a string. If `prompt` is supplied, it's first printed to standard output (`sys.stdout`). Trailing newlines are stripped, and an `EOFError` exception is raised if an EOF is read. If the `readline` module is loaded, this function will use it to provide advanced line-editing and command-completion features. Use `input()` to read input in Python 3.

`repr(object)`

Returns a string representation of `object`. In most cases, the returned string is an expression that can be passed to `eval()` to re-create the object. Be aware that in Python 3, the result of this function may be a Unicode string that can't be displayed in the terminal or shell window (resulting in an exception). Use the `ascii()` function to create an ASCII representation of `object`.

`reversed(s)`

Creates a reverse iterator for sequence `s`. This function only works if `s` implements the sequence methods `__len__()` and `__getitem__()`. In addition, `s` must index items starting at 0. It does not work with generators or iterators.

`round(x [, n])`

Rounds the result of rounding the floating-point number `x` to the closest multiple of 10 to the power minus `n`. If `n` is omitted, it defaults to `0`. If two multiples are equally close, Python 2 rounds away from `0` (for example, `0.5` is rounded to `1.0` and `-0.5` is rounded to `-1.0`). Python 3 rounds toward `0` if the previous digit is even and away from `0` otherwise (for example, `0.5` is rounded to `0.0` and `1.5` is rounded to `2`).

`set([items])`

Creates a set populated with items taken from the iterable object `items`. The items must be immutable. If `items` contains other sets, those sets must be of type `frozenset`. If `items` is omitted, an empty set is returned.

`setattr(object, name, value)`

Sets an attribute of an object. `name` is a string. Same as `object.name = value`.

`slice([start,] stop [, step])`

Returns a slice object representing integers in the specified range. Slice objects are also generated by the extended slice syntax `a[i:j:k]`. Refer to the section "Sequence and Mapping Methods" in Chapter 3 for details.

`sorted(iterable [, key=keyfunc [, reverse=reverseflag]])`

Creates a sorted list from items in `iterable`. The keyword argument `key` is a single-argument function that transforms values before they are passed to the compare function. The keyword argument `reverse` is a Boolean flag that specifies whether or not the resulting list is sorted in reverse order. The `key` and `reverse` arguments must be specified using keywords—for example, `sorted(a,key=get_name)`.

`staticmethod(func)`

Creates a static method for use in classes. This function is implicitly invoked by the `@staticmethod` decorator.

`str([object])`

Type representing a string. In Python 2, a string contains 8-bit characters, whereas in Python 3 strings are Unicode. If `object` is supplied, a string representation of its value is created by calling its `__str__()` method. This is the same string that you see when you print the object. If no argument is given, an empty string is created.

`sum(items [,initial])`

Computes the sum of a sequence of items taken from the iterable object `items`. `initial` provides the starting value and defaults to 0. This function only works with numbers.

`super(type [, object])`

Returns an object that represents the superclasses of `type`. The primary purpose of this object is to invoke methods in base classes. Here's an example:

```
class B(A):
    def foo(self):
        super(B,self).foo()
```

If `object` is an object, then `isinstance(object, type)` must be true. If `object` is a type, then it must be a subclass of `type`. Refer to Chapter 7, "Classes and Object-Oriented Programming," for more details. In Python 3, you can use `super()` in a method with no arguments. In this case, `type` is set to the class in which the method is defined and `object` is set to the first argument of the method. Although this cleans up the syntax, it's not backwards-compatible with Python 2 so it should be avoided if you're concerned about portability.

`tuple([items])`

Type representing a tuple. If supplied, *items* is an iterable object that is used to populate the tuple. However, if *items* is already a tuple, it's simply returned unmodified. If no argument is given, an empty tuple is returned.

`type(object)`

The base class of all types in Python. When called as a function, returns the type of *object*. This type is the same as the object's class. For common types such as integers, floats, and lists, the type will refer to one of the other built-in classes such as `int`, `float`, `list`, and so forth. For user-defined objects, the type is the associated class. For objects related to Python's internals, you will typically get a reference to one of the classes defined in the `types` module.

`type(name,bases,dict)`

Creates a new *type* object (which is the same as defining a new class). *name* is the name of the type, *bases* is a tuple of base classes, and *dict* is a dictionary containing definitions corresponding to a class body. This function is most commonly used when working with metaclasses. This is described further in Chapter 7.

`unichr(x)`

Converts the integer or long integer *x*, where $0 <= x <= 65535$, to a single Unicode character. Python 2 only. In Python 3, just use `chr(x)`.

`unicode(string [,encoding [,errors]])`

In Python 2, this converts *string* to a Unicode string. *encoding* specifies the data encoding of *string*. If omitted, the default encoding as returned by `sys.getdefaultencoding()` is used. *errors* specifies how encoding errors are handled and is one of `'strict'`, `'ignore'`, `'replace'`, `'backslashreplace'`, or `'xmlcharrefreplace'`. Refer to Chapter 9 and Chapter 3 for details. Not available in Python 3.

`vars([object])`

Returns the symbol table of *object* (usually found in its `__dict__` attribute). If no argument is given, a dictionary corresponding to the local namespace is returned. The dictionary returned by this function should be assumed to be read-only. It's not safe to modify its contents.

`xrange([start,] stop [, step])`

A type representing a range of integer values from *start* to *stop* that is not included. *step* provides an optional stride. The values are not actually stored but are computed on demand when accessed. In Python 2, `xrange()` is the preferred function to use when you want to write loops over ranges of integer values. In Python 3, `xrange()` has been renamed to `range()` and `xrange()` is unavailable. *start*, *stop*, and *step* are limited to the set of values supported by machine integers (typically 32 bits).

`zip([s1 [, s2 [,..]]])`

In Python 2, returns a list of tuples where the *n*th tuple is `(s1[n], s2[n], ...)`. The resulting list is truncated to the length of the shortest argument sequence. If no arguments are given, an empty list is returned. In Python 3, the behavior is similar, but the result is an iterator that produces a sequence of tuples. In Python 2, be aware that using `zip()` with long input sequences is something that can unintentionally consume large amounts of memory. Consider using `itertools.izip()` instead.

Built-In Exceptions

Built-in exceptions are contained in the `exceptions` module, which is always loaded prior to the execution of any program. Exceptions are defined as classes.

Exception Base Classes

The following exceptions serve as base classes for all the other exceptions:

`BaseException`

The root class for all exceptions. All built-in exceptions are derived from this class.

`Exception`

The base class for all program-related exceptions that includes all built-in exceptions except for `SystemExit`, `GeneratorExit`, and `KeyboardInterrupt`. User-defined exceptions should be defined by inheriting from `Exception`.

`ArithmeticError`

The base class for arithmetic exceptions, including `OverflowError`, `ZeroDivisionError`, and `FloatingPointError`.

`LookupError`

The base class for indexing and key errors, including `IndexError` and `KeyError`.

`EnvironmentError`

The base class for errors that occur outside Python, including `IOError` and `OSError`.

The preceding exceptions are never raised explicitly. However, they can be used to catch certain classes of errors. For instance, the following code would catch any sort of numerical error:

```python
try:
    # Some operation
    ...
except ArithmeticError as e:
    # Math error
```

Exception Instances

When an exception is raised, an instance of an exception class is created. This instance is placed in the optional variable supplied to the `except` statement. Here's an example:

```python
except IOError as e:
    # Handle error
    # 'e' has an instance of IOError
```

Instances of an exception `e` have a few standard attributes that can be useful to inspect and/or manipulate in certain applications.

`e.args`

The tuple of arguments supplied when raising the exception. In most cases, this is a one-item tuple with a string describing the error. For `EnvironmentError` exceptions, the value is a 2-tuple or 3-tuple containing an integer error number, a string error message, and an optional filename. The contents of this tuple might be useful if you need to re-create the exception in a different context; for example, to raise an exception in a different Python interpreter process.

`e.message`

A string representing the error message that gets printed when the exception is displayed (Python 2 only).

`e.__cause__`

Previous exception when using explicit chained exceptions (Python 3 only). See Appendix A.

`e.__context__`

Previous exception for implicitly chained exceptions (Python 3 only). See Appendix A.

`e.__traceback__`

Traceback object associated with the exception (Python 3 only). See Appendix A.

Predefined Exception Classes

The following exceptions are raised by programs:

`AssertionError`

Failed `assert` statement.

`AttributeError`

Failed attribute reference or assignment.

`EOFError`

End of file. Generated by the built-in functions `input()` and `raw_input()`. It should be noted that most other I/O operations such as the `read()` and `readline()` methods of files return an empty string to signal EOF instead of raising an exception.

`FloatingPointError`

Failed floating-point operation. It should be noted that floating-point exception-handling is a tricky problem and that this exception only gets raised if Python has been configured and built in a way that enables it. It is more common for floating-point errors to silently produce results such as `float('nan')` or `float('inf')`. A subclass of `ArithmeticError`.

`GeneratorExit`

Raised inside a generator function to signal termination. This happens when a generator is destroyed prematurely (before all generator values are consumed) or the `close()` method of a generator is called. If a generator ignores this exception, the generator is terminated and the exception is silently ignored.

IOError

Failed I/O operation. The value is an `IOError` instance with the attributes `errno`, `strerror`, and `filename`. `errno` is an integer error number, `strerror` is a string error message, and `filename` is an optional filename. A subclass of `EnvironmentError`.

ImportError

Raised when an `import` statement can't find a module or when `from` can't find a name in a module.

IndentationError

Indentation error. A subclass of `SyntaxError`.

IndexError

Sequence subscript out of range. A subclass of `LookupError`.

KeyError

Key not found in a mapping. A subclass of `LookupError`.

KeyboardInterrupt

Raised when the user hits the interrupt key (usually Ctrl+C).

MemoryError

Recoverable out-of-memory error.

NameError

Name not found in local or global namespaces.

NotImplementedError

Unimplemented feature. Can be raised by base classes that require derived classes to implement certain methods. A subclass of `RuntimeError`.

OSError

Operating system error. Primarily raised by functions in the `os` module. The value is the same as for `IOError`. A subclass of `EnvironmentError`.

OverflowError

Result of an integer value being too large to be represented. This exception usually only arises if large integer values are passed to objects that internally rely upon fixed-precision machine integers in their implementation. For example, this error can arise with `range` or `xrange` objects if you specify starting or ending values that exceed 32 bits in size. A subclass of `ArithmeticError`.

ReferenceError

Result of accessing a weak reference after the underlying object has been destroyed. See the `weakref` module.

RuntimeError

A generic error not covered by any of the other categories.

`StopIteration`

Raised to signal the end of iteration. This normally happens in the `next()` method of an object or in a generator function.

`SyntaxError`

Parser syntax error. Instances have the attributes `filename`, `lineno`, `offset`, and `text`, which can be used to gather more information.

`SystemError`

Internal error in the interpreter. The value is a string indicating the problem.

`SystemExit`

Raised by the `sys.exit()` function. The value is an integer indicating the return code. If it's necessary to exit immediately, `os._exit()` can be used.

`TabError`

Inconsistent tab usage. Generated when Python is run with the `-tt` option. A subclass of `SyntaxError`.

`TypeError`

Occurs when an operation or a function is applied to an object of an inappropriate type.

`UnboundLocalError`

Unbound local variable referenced. This error occurs if a variable is referenced before it's defined in a function. A subclass of `NameError`.

`UnicodeError`

Unicode encoding or decoding error. A subclass of `ValueError`.

`UnicodeEncodeError`

Unicode encoding error. A subclass of `UnicodeError`.

`UnicodeDecodeError`

Unicode decoding error. A subclass of `UnicodeError`.

`UnicodeTranslateError`

Unicode error occurred during translation. A subclass of `UnicodeError`.

`ValueError`

Generated when the argument to a function or an operation is the right type but an inappropriate value.

`WindowsError`

Generated by failed system calls on Windows. A subclass of `OSError`.

`ZeroDivisionError`

Dividing by zero. A subclass of `ArithmeticError`.

Built-In Warnings

Python has a `warnings` module that is typically used to notify programmers about deprecated features. Warnings are issued by including code such as the following:

```
import warnings
warnings.warn("The MONDO flag is no longer supported", DeprecationWarning)
```

Although warnings are issued by a library module, the names of the various warnings are built-in. Warnings are somewhat similar to exceptions. There is a hierarchy of built-in warnings that all inherit from `Exception`.

Warning

The base class of all warnings. A subclass of `Exception`.

UserWarning

A generic user-defined warning. A subclass of `Warning`.

DeprecationWarning

A warning for deprecated features. A subclass of `Warning`.

SyntaxWarning

A warning for deprecated Python syntax. A subclass of `Warning`.

RuntimeWarning

A warning for potential runtime problems. A subclass of `Warning`.

FutureWarning

A warning that the behavior of a feature will change in the future. A subclass of `Warning`.

Warnings are different than exceptions in that the issuing of a warning with the `warn()` function may or may not cause a program to stop. For example, a warning may just print something to the output or it may raise an exception. The actual behavior can be configured with the `warnings` module or with the `-W` option to the interpreter. If you are using someone else's code that generates a warning, but you would like to proceed anyways, you can catch warnings that have been turned into exceptions using `try` and `except`. For example:

```
try:
    import md5
except DeprecationWarning:
    pass
```

It should be emphasized that code such as this is rare. Although it will catch a warning that has been turned into an exception, it doesn't suppress warning messages (you have to use the `warnings` module to control that). Plus, ignoring warnings is a good way to write code that doesn't work correctly when new versions of Python are released.

future_builtins

The `future_builtins` module, only available in Python 2, provides implementations of the built-in functions whose behavior is changed in Python 3. The following functions are defined:

ascii(`object`)

Produces the same output as `repr()`. Refer to the description in the "Built-In Functions" section of this chapter.

filter(`function, iterable`)

Creates an iterator instead of a list. The same as `itertools.ifilter()`.

hex(`object`)

Creates a hexadecimal string, but uses the `__index__()` special method to get an integer value instead of calling `__hex__()`.

map(`function, iterable, ...`)

Creates an iterator instead of a list. The same as `itertools.imap()`.

oct(`object`)

Creates an octal string, but uses the `__index__()` special method to get an integer value instead of calling `__oct__()`.

zip(`iterable, iterable, ...`)

Creates an iterator instead of a list. The same as `itertools.izip()`.

Be aware that the functions listed in this module are not a complete list of changes to the built-in module. For instance, Python 3 also renames `raw_input()` to `input()` and `xrange()` to `range()`.

## 13

Python Runtime Services

This chapter describes modules that are related to the Python interpreter runtime. Topics include garbage collection, basic management of objects (copying, marshalling, and so on), weak references, and interpreter environment.

atexit

The atexit module is used to register functions to execute when the Python interpreter exits. A single function is provided:

register(func [,args [,kwargs]])

Adds function *func* to a list of functions that will execute when the interpreter exits. *args* is a tuple of arguments to pass to the function. *kwargs* is a dictionary of keyword arguments. The function is invoked as *func(*args,**kwargs)*. Upon exit, functions are invoked in reverse order of registration (the most recently added exit function is invoked first). If an error occurs, an exception message will be printed to standard error but will otherwise be ignored.

copy

The copy module provides functions for making shallow and deep copies of compound objects, including lists, tuples, dictionaries, and instances of user-defined objects.

copy(x)

Makes a shallow copy of *x* by creating a new compound object and duplicating the members of *x* by reference. For built-in types, it is somewhat uncommon to use this function. Instead, you use calls such as list(x), dict(x), set(x), and so forth to create a shallow copy of *x* (it should be noted that using the type name directly like this is also significantly faster than using copy()).

deepcopy(x [, visit])

Makes a deep copy of *x* by creating a new compound object and recursively duplicating all the members of *x*. *visit* is an optional dictionary that's used to keep track of visited objects in order to detect and avoid cycles in recursively defined data structures. This argument is typically only supplied if deepcopy() is being called recursively as described later in this chapter.

Although it is not usually necessary, a class can implement customized copy methods by implementing the methods `__copy__(self)` and `__deepcopy__(self, visit)`, which implement the shallow and deep copy operations respectively. The `__deepcopy__()` method must accept a dictionary, `visit`, which is used to keep track of previously encountered objects during the copy process. It's not necessary for `__deepcopy__()` to do anything with `visit` other than pass it to other `deepcopy()` operations carried out in the implementation (if any).

If a class implements the methods `__getstate__()` and `__setstate__()` that are used by the `pickle` module, they will be used by the `copy` module to create copies.

Notes

- This module can be used with simple types such as integers and strings, but there's little need to do so.
- The copy functions don't work with modules, class objects, functions, methods, tracebacks, stack frames, files, sockets, and other similar types. When an object can't be copied, the `copy.error` exception is raised.

gc

The `gc` module provides an interface for controlling the garbage collector used to collect cycles in objects such as lists, tuples, dictionaries, and instances. As various types of container objects are created, they're placed on a list that's internal to the interpreter. Whenever container objects are deallocated, they're removed from this list. If the number of allocations exceeds the number of deallocations by a user-definable threshold value, the garbage collector is invoked. The garbage collector works by scanning this list and identifying collections of objects that are no longer being used but haven't been deallocated due to circular dependencies. In addition, the garbage collector uses a three-level generational scheme in which objects that survive the initial garbage-collection step are placed onto lists of objects that are checked less frequently. This provides better performance for programs that have a large number of long-lived objects.

`collect([generation])`

Runs a full garbage collection. This function checks all generations and returns the number of unreachable objects found. `generation` is an optional integer in the range 0 - 2 that specifies the generation to collect.

`disable()`

Disables garbage collection.

`enable()`

Enables garbage collection.

`garbage`

A variable containing a read-only list of user-defined instances that are no longer in use, but which cannot be garbage collected because they are involved in a reference cycle and they define a `__del__()` method. Such objects cannot be garbage-collected because in order to break the reference cycle, the interpreter must arbitrarily destroy one of the objects first. However, there is no way to know if the __del__() method of the remaining objects in the cycle needs to perform critical operations on the object that was just destroyed.

get_count()

Returns a tuple (*count0*, *count1*, *count2*) containing the number of objects currently in each generation.

get_debug()

Returns the debugging flags currently set.

get_objects()

Returns a list of all objects being tracked by the garbage collector. Does not include the returned list.

get_referrers(*obj1*, *obj2*, ...)

Returns a list of all objects that directly refer to the objects *obj1*, *obj2*, and so on. The returned list may include objects that have not yet been garbage-collected as well as partially constructed objects.

get_referents(*obj1*, *obj2*, ...)

Returns a list of objects that the objects *obj1*, *obj2*, and so on refer to. For example, if *obj1* is a container, this would return a list of the objects in the container.

get_threshold()

Returns the current collection threshold as a tuple.

isenabled()

Returns True if garbage collection is enabled.

set_debug(*flags*)

Sets the garbage-collection debugging flags, which can be used to debug the behavior of the garbage collector. *flags* is the bitwise OR of the constants DEBUG_STATS, DEBUG_COLLECTABLE, DEBUG_UNCOLLECTABLE, DEBUG_INSTANCES, DEBUG_OBJECTS, DEBUG_SAVEALL, and DEBUG_LEAK. The DEBUG_LEAK flag is probably the most useful because it will have the collector print information useful for debugging programs with memory leaks.

set_threshold(*threshold0* [, *threshold1*[, *threshold2*]])

Sets the collection frequency of garbage collection. Objects are classified into three generations, where generation 0 contains the youngest objects and generation 2 contains the oldest objects. Objects that survive a garbage-collection step are moved to the next-oldest generation. Once an object reaches generation 2, it stays in that generation. *threshold0* is the difference between the number of allocations and deallocations that must be reached before garbage collection occurs in generation 0. *threshold1* is the number of collections of generation 0 that must occur before generation 1 is scanned. *threshold2* is the number of collections that must occur in generation 1 before generation 2 is collected. The default threshold is currently set to (700,10,10). Setting *threshold0* to 0 disables garbage collection.

Notes

- Circular references involving objects with a __del__() method are not garbage-collected and are placed on the list gc.garbage (uncollectable objects). These objects are not collected due to difficulties related to object finalization.

- The functions get_referrers() and get_referents() only apply to objects that support garbage collection. In addition, these functions are only intended for debugging. They should not be used for other purposes.

inspect

The inspect module is used to gather information about live Python objects such as attributes, documentation strings, source code, stack frames, and so on.

cleandoc(doc)

Cleans up a documentation string doc by changing all tabs into whitespace and removing indentation that might have been inserted to make the docstring line up with other statements inside a function or method.

currentframe()

Returns the frame object corresponding to the caller's stack frame.

formatargspec(args [, varags [, varkw [, defaults]]])

Produces a nicely formatted string representing the values returned by getargspec().

formatargvalues(args [, varargs [, varkw [, locals]]])

Produces a nicely formatted string representing the values returned by getargvalues().

getargspec(func)

Given a function, func, returns a named tuple ArgSpec(args, varargs, varkw, defaults). args is a list of argument names, and varargs is the name of the * argument (if any). varkw is the name of the ** argument (if any), and defaults is a tuple of default argument values or None if there are no default argument values. If there are default argument values, the defaults tuple represents the values of the last n arguments in args, where n is the len(defaults).

getargvalues(frame)

Returns the values of arguments supplied to a function with execution frame frame. Returns a tuple ArgInfo(args, varargs, varkw, locals). args is a list of argument names, varargs is the name of the * argument (if any), and varkw is the name of the ** argument (if any). locals is the local dictionary of the frame.

getclasstree(classes [, unique])

Given a list of related classes, classes, this function organizes the classes into a hierarchy based on inheritance. The hierarchy is represented as a collection of nested lists, where each entry in the list is a list of classes that inherit from the class that immediately precedes the list. Each entry in the list is a 2-tuple (cls, bases), where cls is the class object and *bases* is a tuple of base classes. If *unique* is True, each class only appears once in the returned list. Otherwise, a class may appear multiple times if multiple inheritance is being used.

getcomments(*object*)

Returns a string consisting of comments that immediately precede the definition of *object* in Python source code. If *object* is a module, comments defined at the top of the module are returned. Returns None if no comments are found.

getdoc(*object*)

Returns the documentation string for *object*. The documentation string is first processed using the cleandoc() function before being returned.

getfile(*object*)

Returns the name of the file in which *object* was defined. May return TypeError if this information is not applicable or available (for example, for built-in functions).

getframeinfo(*frame* [, *context*])

Returns a named tuple Traceback(*filename*, *lineno*, *function*, *code_context*, *index*) containing information about the frame object *frame*. *filename* and *line* specify a source code location. The *context* parameter specifies the number of lines of context from the source code to retrieve. The *contextlist* field in the returned tuple contains a list of source lines corresponding to this context. The *index* field is a numerical index within this list for the line corresponding to *frame*.

getinnerframes(*traceback* [, *context*])

Returns a list of frame records for the frame of a traceback and all inner frames. Each frame-record is a 6-tuple consisting of (*frame*, *filename*, *line*, *funcname*, *contextlist*, *index*). *filename*, *line*, *context*, *contextlist*, and *index* have the same meaning as with getframeinfo().

getmembers(*object* [, *predicate*])

Returns all of the members of *object*. Typically, the members are obtained by looking in the __dict__ attribute of an object, but this function may return attributes of *object* stored elsewhere (for example, docstrings in __doc__, objects' names in __name__, and so on). The members are returned a list of (*name*, *value*) pairs. *predicate* is an optional function that accepts a member object as an argument and returns True or False. Only members for which *predicate* returns True are returned. Functions such as isfunction() and isclass() can be used as predicate functions.

getmodule(*object*)

Returns the module in which *object* was defined (if possible).

getmoduleinfo(*path*)

Returns information about how Python would interpret the file *path*. If *path* is not a Python module, None is returned. Otherwise, a named tuple ModuleInfo(*name*, *suffix*, *mode*, *module_type*) is returned where *name* is the name of the module, *suffix* is the filename suffix, *mode* is the file mode that would be used to open the module, and *module_type* is an integer code specifying the module type. Module type codes are defined in the imp module as follows:

Module Type	Description
imp.PY_SOURCE	Python source file
imp.PY_COMPILED	Python compiled object file (.pyc)
imp.C_EXTENSION	Dynamically loadable C extension
imp.PKG_DIRECTORY	Package directory
imp.C_BUILTIN	Built-in module
imp.PY_FROZEN	Frozen module

getmodulename(*path*)

Returns the name of the module that would be used for the file *path*. If *path* does not look like a Python module, None is returned.

getmro(*cls*)

Returns a tuple of classes that represent the method-resolution ordering used to resolve methods in class *cls*. Refer to Chapter 7, "Classes and Object-Oriented Programming," for further details.

getouterframes(*frame* [, *context*])

Returns a list of frame records for *frame* and all outer frames. This list represents the calling sequence where the first entry contains information for *frame*. Each frame record is a 6-tuple (*frame, filename, line, funcname, contextlist, index*) where the fields have the same meaning as for getinnerframes() The *context* argument has the same meaning as for getframeinfo().

getsourcefile(*object*)

Returns the name of the Python source file in which *object* was defined.

getsourcelines(*object*)

Returns a tuple (*sourcelines, firstline*) corresponding to the definition of *object*. *sourcelines* is a list of source code lines, and *firstline* is the line number of the first source code line. Raises IOError if source code can't be found.

getsource(*object*)

Returns source code of *object* as a single string. Raises IOError if the source code can't be found.

isabstract(*object*)

Returns True if *object* is an abstract base class.

isbuiltin(*object*)

Returns True if *object* is a built-in function.

isclass(*object*)

Returns True if *object* is a class.

`iscode(object)`

Returns True if *object* is a code object.

`isdatadescriptor(object)`

Returns True if *object* is a data descriptor object. This is the case if *object* defines both a __get__() and __set__() method.

`isframe(object)`

Returns True if *object* is a frame object.

`isfunction(object)`

Returns True if *object* is a function object.

`isgenerator(object)`

Returns True if *object* is a generator object.

`isgeneratorfunction(object)`

Returns True if *object* is a generator function. This is different than isgenerator() in that it tests if *object* is a function that creates a generator when called. It is not used to check if *object* is an actively running generator.

`ismethod(object)`

Returns True if *object* is a method.

`ismethoddescriptor(object)`

Returns True if *object* is a method descriptor object. This is the case if *object* is not a method, class, or function and it defines a __get__() method but does not define __set__().

`ismodule(object)`

Returns True if *object* is a module object.

`isroutine(object)`

Returns True if *object* is a user-defined or built-in function or method.

`istraceback(object)`

Returns True if *object* is a traceback object.

`stack([context])`

Returns a list of frame records corresponding to the stack of the caller. Each frame record is a 6-tuple (*frame, filename, line, funcname, contextlist, index*), which contains the same information as returned by getinnerframes(). *context* specifies the number of lines of source context to return in each frame record.

`trace([context])`

Returns a list of frame records for the stack between the current frame and the frame in which the current exception was raised. The first frame record is the caller, and the last frame record is the frame where the exception occurred. *context* specifies the number of lines of source context to return in each frame record.

marshal

The `marshal` module is used to serialize Python objects in an "undocumented" Python-specific data format. `marshal` is similar to the `pickle` and `shelve` modules, but it is less powerful and intended for use only with simple objects. It shouldn't be used to implement persistent objects in general (use `pickle` instead). However, for simple built-in types, the `marshal` module is a very fast approach for saving and loading data.

dump(*value, file* [, *version*])

Writes the object value to the open file object *file*. If *value* is an unsupported type, a `ValueError` exception is raised. *version* is an integer that specifies the data format to use. The default output format is found in `marshal.version` and is currently set to 2. Version 0 is an older format used by earlier versions of Python.

dumps(*value* [,*version*])

Returns the byte string written by the `dump()` function. If *value* is an unsupported type, a `ValueError` exception is raised. *version* is the same as described previously.

load(*file*)

Reads and returns the next value from the open file object *file*. If no valid value is read, an `EOFError`, `ValueError`, or `TypeError` exception will be raised. The format of the input data is automatically detected.

loads(*bytes*)

Reads and returns the next value from the byte string *bytes*.

Notes

- Data is stored in a binary architecture-independent format.
- Only `None`, integers, long integers, floats, complex numbers, strings, Unicode strings, tuples, lists, dictionaries, and code objects are supported. Lists, tuples, and dictionaries can only contain supported objects. Class instances and recursive references in lists, tuples, and dictionaries are not supported.
- Integers may be promoted to long integers if the built-in integer type doesn't have enough precision—for example, if the marshalled data contains a 64-bit integer, but the data is being read on a 32-bit machine.
- `marshal` is not intended to be secure against erroneous or maliciously constructed data and should not be used to unmarshal data from untrusted sources.
- `marshal` is significantly faster than `pickle`, but it isn't as flexible.

pickle

The `pickle` module is used to serialize Python objects into a stream of bytes suitable for storing in a file, transferring across a network, or placing in a database. This process is variously called *pickling*, *serializing*, *marshalling*, or *flattening*. The resulting byte stream can also be converted back into a series of Python objects using an unpickling process.

The following functions are used to turn an object into a byte-stream.

dump(*object, file* [, *protocol*])

Dumps a pickled representation of *object* to the file object *file*. *protocol* specifies the output format of the data. Protocol 0 (the default) is a text-based format that is backwards-compatible with earlier versions of Python. Protocol 1 is a binary protocol that is also compatible with most earlier Python versions. Protocol 2 is a newer protocol that provides more efficient pickling of classes and instances. Protocol 3 is used by Python 3 and is not backwards-compatible. If *protocol* is negative, the most modern protocol will be selected. The variable `pickle.HIGHEST_PROTOCOL` contains the highest protocol available. If *object* doesn't support pickling, a `pickle.PicklingError` exception is raised.

dumps(*object* [, *protocol*])

Same as dump(), but returns a byte string containing the pickled data.

The following example shows how you use these functions to save objects to a file:

```
f = open('myfile', 'wb')
pickle.dump(x, f)
pickle.dump(y, f)
... dump more objects ...
f.close()
```

The following functions are used to restore a pickled object.

load(*file*)

Loads and returns a pickled representation of an object from the file object *file*. It is not necessary to specify the input protocol as it is automatically detected. A `pickle.UnpicklingError` exception is raised if the file contains corrupted data that can't be decoded. If an end-of-file is detected, an EOFError exception is raised.

loads(*bytes*)

Same as load(), but reads the pickled representation of an object from a byte string.

The following example shows how you use these functions to load data:

```
f = open('myfile', 'rb')
x = pickle.load(f)
y = pickle.load(f)
... load more objects ...
f.close()
```

When loading, it is not necessary to specify the protocol or any information about the type of object being loaded. That information is saved as part of the pickle data format itself.

If you are pickling more than one Python object, you can simply make repeated calls to dump() and load() as shown in the previous examples. When making multiple calls, you simply have to make sure the sequence of load() calls matches the sequence of dump() calls that were used to write the file.

When working with complicated data structures involving cycles or shared references, using dump() and load() can be problematic because they don't maintain any internal state about objects that have already been pickled or restored. This can result in output files that are excessively large and that don't properly restore the relationship between objects when loaded. An alternative approach is to use `Pickler` and `Unpickler` objects.

`Pickler(file [, protocol ])`

Creates a pickling object that writes data to the file object `file` with the specified pickle `protocol`. An instance p of `Pickler` has a method p.dump(x) that dumps an object x to `file`. Once x has been dumped, its identity is remembered. If a subsequent p.dump() operation is used to write the same object, a reference to the previously dumped object is saved instead of writing a new copy. The method p.clear_memo() clears the internal dictionary used to track previously dumped objects. You would use this if you wanted to write a fresh copy of a previously dumped object (that is, if its value changed since the last dump() operation).'

`Unpickler(file)`

Creates an unpickling object that reads data from the file object `file`. An instance u of `Unpickler` has a method u.load() that loads and returns a new object from `file`. An `Unpickler` keeps track of objects it has returned because the input source might contain an object reference created by the `Pickler` object. In this case, u.load() returns a reference to the previously loaded object.

The `pickle` module works with most kinds of normal Python objects. This includes:

- `None`
- Numbers and strings
- Tuples, lists, and dictionaries containing only pickleable objects
- Instances of user-defined classes defined at the top level of a module

When instances of a user-defined class are pickled, the instance data is the only part that gets pickled. The corresponding class definition is not saved—instead, the pickled data merely contains the *name* of the associated class and module. When instances are unpickled, the module in which the class is defined is automatically imported in order to access the class definition when re-creating instances. It should also be noted that when restoring an instance, the _ _init_ _() method of a class is not invoked. Instead, the instance is re-created through other means and the instance data restored.

One restriction on instances is that the corresponding class definition must appear at the top level of a module (that is, no nested classes). In addition, if the instance's class definition was originally defined in _ _main_ _, that class definition must be manually reloaded prior to unpickling a saved object (because there's no way for the interpreter to know how to automatically load the necessary class definitions back into _ _main_ _ when unpickling).

It is not normally necessary to do anything to make a user-defined class work with pickle. However, a class can define customized methods for saving and restoring its state by implementing the special methods _ _getstate_ _() and _ _setstate_ _(). The _ _getstate_ _() method must return a pickleable object (such as a string or tuple) representing the state of the object. The _ _setstate_ _() method accepts the pickled object and restores its state. If these methods are undefined, the default behavior is to pickle an instance's underlying _ _dict_ _ attribute. It should be noted that if these methods are defined, they will also be used by the copy module to implement the shallow and deep copy operations.

Notes

- In Python 2, a module called cPickle contains a C implementation of functions in the pickle module. It is significantly faster than pickle, but is restricted in that it doesn't allow subclassing of the Pickler and Unpickler objects. Python 3 has a support module that also contains C implementation, but it is used more transparently (pickle takes advantage of it automatically as appropriate).
- The data format used by pickle is Python-specific and shouldn't be assumed to be compatible with any external standards such as XML.
- Whenever possible, the pickle module should be used instead of the marshal module because pickle is more flexible, the data encoding is documented, and additional error-checking is performed.
- Due to security concerns, programs should not unpickle data received from untrusted sources.
- Use of the pickle module with types defined in extension modules is much more involved than what is described here. Implementers of extension types should consult the online documentation for details concerning the low-level protocol required to make these objects work with pickle—in particular, details on how to implement the _ _reduce_ _() and _ _reduce_ex_ _() special methods that pickle uses to create the serialized byte sequences.

sys

The sys module contains variables and functions that pertain to the operation of the interpreter and its environment.

Variables

The following variables are defined.

api_version

An integer representing the C API version of the Python interpreter. Used when working with extension modules.

argv

List of command-line options passed to a program. argv[0] is the name of the program.

builtin_module_names

Tuple containing names of modules built into the Python executable.

byteorder

Native byte-ordering of the machine—'little' for little-endian or 'big' for big-endian.

copyright

String containing copyright message.

__displayhook__

Original value of the displayhook() function.

dont_write_bytecode

Boolean flag that determines whether or not Python writes bytecode (.pyc or .pyo files) when importing modules. The initial value is True unless the -B option to the interpreter is given. The setting can be changed as needed in your own program.

dllhandle

Integer handle for the Python DLL (Windows).

__excepthook__

Original value of the excepthook() function.

exec_prefix

Directory where platform-dependent Python files are installed.

executable

String containing the name of the interpreter executable.

flags

An object representing the settings of different command-line options supplied to the Python interpreter itself. The following table lists the attributes of flags along with the corresponding command-line option that turns the flag on. These attributes are read-only.

Attribute	Command-Line Option
flags.debug	-d
flags.py3k_warning	-3
flags.division_warning	-Q
flags.division_new	-Qnew
flags.inspect	-i
flags.interactive	-i
flags.optimize	-O or -OO
flags.dont_write_bytecode	-B
flags.no_site	-S
flags.ignore_environment	-E
flags.tabcheck	-t or -tt
flags.verbose	-v
flags.unicode	-U

`float_info`

An object that holds information about internal representation of floating-point numbers. The values of these attributes are taken from the `float.h` C header file.

Attribute	Description
`float_info.epsilon`	Difference between 1.0 and the next largest float.
`float_info.dig`	Number of decimal digits that can be represented without any changes after rounding.
`float_info.mant_dig`	Number of digits that can be represented using the numeric base specified in `float_info.radix`.
`float_info.max`	Maximum floating-point number.
`float_info.max_exp`	Maximum exponent in the numeric base specified in `float_info.radix`.
`float_info.max_10_exp`	Maximum exponent in base 10.
`float_info.min`	Minimum positive floating-point value.
`float_info.min_exp`	Minimum exponent in the numeric base specified in `float_info.radix`.
`float_info.min_10_exp`	Minimum exponent in base 10.
`float_info.radix`	Numeric base used for exponents.
`float_info.rounds`	Rounding behavior (-1 undetermined, 0 towards zero, 1 nearest, 2 towards positive infinity, 3 towards negative infinity).

`hexversion`

Integer whose hexadecimal representation encodes the version information contained in `sys.version_info`. The value of this integer is always guaranteed to increase with newer versions of the interpreter.

`last_type, last_value, last_traceback`

These variables are set when an unhandled exception is encountered and the interpreter prints an error message. `last_type` is the last exception type, `last_value` is the last exception value, and `last_traceback` is a stack trace. Note that the use of these variables is not thread-safe. `sys.exc_info()` should be used instead.

`maxint`

Largest integer supported by the integer type (Python 2 only).

`maxsize`

Largest integer value supported by the C `size_t` datatype on the system. This value determines the largest possible length for strings, lists, dicts, and other built-in types.

`maxunicode`

Integer that indicates the largest Unicode code point that can be represented. The default value is 65535 for the 16-bit UCS-2 encoding. A larger value will be found if Python has been configured to use UCS-4.

`modules`

Dictionary that maps module names to module objects.

path

List of strings specifying the search path for modules. The first entry is always set to the directory in which the script used to start Python is located (if available). Refer to Chapter 8, "Iterators and Generators."

platform

Platform identifier string, such as `'linux-i386'`.

prefix

Directory where platform-independent Python files are installed.

ps1, ps2

Strings containing the text for the primary and secondary prompts of the interpreter. Initially, ps1 is set to `'>>> '` and ps2 is set to `'... '`. The `str()` method of whatever object is assigned to these values is evaluated to generate the prompt text.

py3kwarning

Flag set to `True` in Python 2 when the interpreter is run with the `-3` option.

stdin, stdout, stderr

File objects corresponding to standard input, standard output, and standard error. stdin is used for the raw_input() and input() functions. stdout is used for print and the prompts of raw_input() and input(). stderr is used for the interpreter's prompts and error messages. These variables can be assigned to any object that supports a write() method operating on a single string argument.

_ _stdin_ _, _ _stdout_ _, _ _stderr_ _

File objects containing the values of stdin, stdout, and stderr at the start of the interpreter.

tracebacklimit

Maximum number of levels of traceback information printed when an unhandled exception occurs. The default value is 1000. A value of 0 suppresses all traceback information and causes only the exception type and value to be printed.

version

Version string.

version_info

Version information represented as a tuple (*major, minor, micro, releaselevel, serial*). All values are integers except *releaselevel*, which is the string `'alpha'`, `'beta'`, `'candidate'`, or `'final'`.

warnoptions

List of warning options supplied to the interpreter with the -W command-line option.

winver

The version number used to form registry keys on Windows.

Functions

The following functions are available:

`_clear_type_cache()`

Clears the internal type cache. To optimize method lookups, a small 1024-entry cache of recently used methods is maintained inside the interpreter. This cache speeds up repeated method lookups—especially in code that has deep inheritance hierarchies. Normally, you don't need to clear this cache, but you might do so if you are trying to track down a really tricky memory reference counting issue. For example, if a method in the cache was holding a reference to an object that you were expecting to be destroyed.

`_current_frames()`

Returns a dictionary mapping thread identifiers to the topmost stack frame of the executing thread at the time of call. This information can be useful in writing tools related to thread debugging (that is, tracking down deadlock). Keep in mind that the values returned by this function only represent a snapshot of the interpreter at the time of call. Threads may be executing elsewhere by the time you look at the returned data.

`displayhook([value])`

This function is called to print the result of an expression when the interpreter is running in interactive mode. By default, the value of `repr(value)` is printed to standard output and `value` is saved in the variable `__builtins__._`. The `displayhook` function can be redefined to provide different behavior if desired.

`excepthook(type, value, traceback)`

This function is called when an uncaught exception occurs. `type` is the exception class, `value` is the value supplied by the `raise` statement, and `traceback` is a traceback object. The default behavior is to print the exception and traceback to standard error. However, this function can be redefined to provide alternative handling of uncaught exceptions (which may be useful in specialized applications such as debuggers or CGI scripts).

`exc_clear()`

Clears all information related to the last exception that occurred. It only clears information specific to the calling thread.

`exc_info()`

Returns a tuple (`type, value, traceback`) containing information about the exception that's currently being handled. `type` is the exception type, `value` is the exception parameter passed to raise, and `traceback` is a traceback object containing the call stack at the point where the exception occurred. Returns `None` if no exception is currently being handled.

`exit([n])`

Exits Python by raising the `SystemExit` exception. `n` is an integer exit code indicating a status code. A value of 0 is considered normal (the default); nonzero values are considered abnormal. If a noninteger value is given to `n`, it's printed to `sys.stderr` and an exit code of 1 is used.

getcheckinterval()

Returns the value of the check interval, which specifies how often the interpreter checks for signals, thread switches, and other periodic events.

getdefaultencoding()

Gets the default string encoding in Unicode conversions. Returns a value such as 'ascii' or 'utf-8'. The default encoding is set by the site module.

getdlopenflags()

Returns the flags parameter that is supplied to the C function dlopen() when loading extension modules on UNIX. See dl module.

getfilesystemencoding()

Returns the character encoding used to map Unicode filenames to filenames used by the underlying operating system. Returns 'mbcs' on Windows or 'utf-8' on Macintosh OS X. On UNIX systems, the encoding depends on locale settings and will return the value of the locale CODESET parameter. May return None, in which case the system default encoding is used.

_getframe([depth])

Returns a frame object from the call stack. If depth is omitted or zero, the topmost frame is returned. Otherwise, the frame for that many calls below the current frame is returned. For example, _getframe(1) returns the caller's frame. Raises ValueError if depth is invalid.

getprofile()

Returns the profile function set by the setprofile() function.

getrecursionlimit()

Returns the recursion limit for functions.

getrefcount(object)

Returns the reference count of object.

getsizeof(object [, default])

Returns the size of object in bytes. This calculation is made by calling the __sizeof__() special method of object. If undefined, a TypeError will be generated unless a default value has been specified with the default argument. Because objects are free to define __sizeof__() however they wish, there is no guarantee that the result of this function is a true measure of memory use. However, for built-in types such as lists or string, it is correct.

gettrace()

Returns the trace function set by the settrace() function.

getwindowsversion()

Returns a tuple (major, minor, build, platform, text) that describes the version of Windows being used. major is the major version number. For example, a value of 4 indicates Windows NT 4.0, and a value of 5 indicates Windows 2000 and Windows XP variants. *minor* is the minor version number. For example, 0 indicates Windows 2000, whereas 1 indicates Windows XP. *build* is the Windows build number. *platform* identifies the platform and is an integer with one of the following common values: 0 (Win32s on Windows 3.1), 1 (Windows 95,98, or Me), 2 (Windows NT, 2000, XP), or 3 (Windows CE). *text* is a string containing additional information such as "Service Pack 3".

setcheckinterval(n)

Sets the number of Python virtual machine instructions that must be executed by the interpreter before it checks for periodic events such as signals and thread context switches. The default value is 10.

setdefaultencoding(enc)

Sets the default encoding. *enc* is a string such as 'ascii' or 'utf-8'. This function is only defined inside the site module. It can be called from user-definable sitecustomize modules.

setdlopenflags(flags)

Sets the flags passed to the C dlopen() function, which is used to load extension modules on UNIX. This will affect the way in which symbols are resolved between libraries and other extension modules. *flags* is the bitwise OR of values that can be found in the dl module (see Chapter 19, "Network Programming")—for example, sys.setdlopenflags(dl.RTLD_NOW | dl.RTLD_GLOBAL).

setprofile(pfunc)

Sets the system profile function that can be used to implement a source code profiler.

setrecursionlimit(n)

Changes the recursion limit for functions. The default value is 1000. Note that the operating system may impose a hard limit on the stack size, so setting this too high may cause the Python interpreter process to crash with a Segmentation Fault or Access Violation.

settrace(tfunc)

Sets the system trace function, which can be used to implement a debugger. Refer to Chapter 11 for information about the Python debugger.

traceback

The traceback module is used to gather and print stack traces of a program after an exception has occurred. The functions in this module operate on traceback objects such as the third item returned by the sys.exc_info() function. The main use of this module is in code that needs to report errors in a non-standard way—for example, if you were running Python programs deeply embedded within a network server and you wanted to redirect tracebacks to a log file.

print_tb(traceback [, limit [, file]])

Prints up to *limit* stack trace entries from *traceback* to the file *file*. If *limit* is omitted, all the entries are printed. If *file* is omitted, the output is sent to sys.stderr.

print_exception(*type, value, traceback* [, *limit* [, *file*]]**)**

Prints exception information and a stack trace to *file*. *type* is the exception type, and *value* is the exception value. *limit* and *file* are the same as in print_tb().

print_exc([*limit* [, *file*]]**)**

Same as print_exception() applied to the information returned by the sys.exc_info() function.

format_exc([*limit* [, *file*]]**)**

Returns a string containing the same information printed by print_exc().

print_last([*limit* [, *file*]]**)**

Same as print_exception (sys.last_type, sys.last_value, sys.last_traceback, *limit*, *file*).

print_stack([*frame* [, *limit* [, *file*]]]**)**

Prints a stack trace from the point at which it's invoked. *frame* specifies an optional stack frame from which to start. *limit* and *file* have the same meaning as for print_tb().

extract_tb(*traceback* [, *limit*]**)**

Extracts the stack trace information used by print_tb(). The return value is a list of tuples of the form (*filename, line, funcname, text*) containing the same information that normally appears in a stack trace. *limit* is the number of entries to return.

extract_stack([*frame* [, *limit*]]**)**

Extracts the same stack trace information used by print_stack(), but obtained from the stack frame *frame*. If *frame* is omitted, the current stack frame of the caller is used and *limit* is the number of entries to return.

format_list(*list*)**

Formats stack trace information for printing. *list* is a list of tuples as returned by extract_tb() or extract_stack().

format_exception_only(*type, value*)**

Formats exception information for printing.

format_exception(*type, value, traceback* [, *limit*]**)**

Formats an exception and stack trace for printing.

format_tb(*traceback* [, *limit*]**)**

Same as format_list(extract_tb(*traceback, limit*)).

format_stack([*frame* [, *limit*]]**)**

Same as format_list(extract_stack(*frame, limit*)).

tb_lineno(*traceback*)**

Returns the line number set in a traceback object.

types

The **types** module defines names for the built-in types that correspond to functions, modules, generators, stack frames, and other program elements. The contents of this module are often used in conjunction with the built-in `isinstance()` function and other type-related operations.

Variable	Description
BuiltinFunctionType	Type of built-in functions
CodeType	Type of code objects
FrameType	Type of execution frame object
FunctionType	Type of user-defined functions and lambdas
GeneratorType	Type of generator-iterator objects
GetSetDescriptorType	Type of getset descriptor objects
LambdaType	Alternative name for FunctionType
MemberDescriptorType	Type of member descriptor objects
MethodType	Type of user-defined class methods
ModuleType	Type of modules
TracebackType	Type of traceback objects

Most of the preceding type objects serve as constructors that can be used to create an object of that type. The following descriptions provide the parameters used to create functions, modules, code objects, and methods. Chapter 3 contains detailed information about the attributes of the objects created and the arguments that need to be supplied to the functions described next.

`FunctionType(code, globals [, name [, defarags [, closure]]])`

Creates a new function object.

`CodeType(argcount, nlocals, stacksize, flags, codestring, constants, names, varnames, filename, name, firstlineno, lnotab [, freevars [, cellvars ]])`

Creates a new code object.

`MethodType(function, instance, class)`

Creates a new bound instance method.

`ModuleType(name [, doc])`

Creates a new module object.

Notes

- The **types** module should not be used to refer to the type of built-in objects such as integers, lists, or dictionaries. In Python 2, **types** contains other names such as `IntType` and `DictType`. However, these names are just aliases for the built-in type names of `int` and `dict`. In modern code, you should just use the built-in type names because the **types** module only contains the names listed previously in Python 3.

warnings

The `warnings` module provides functions to issue and filter warning messages. Unlike exceptions, warnings are intended to alert the user to potential problems, but without generating an exception or causing execution to stop. One of the primary uses of the warnings module is to inform users about deprecated language features that may not be supported in future versions of Python. For example:

```
>>> import regex
__main__:1: DeprecationWarning: the regex module is deprecated;  use the re
module
>>>
```

Like exceptions, warnings are organized into a class hierarchy that describes general categories of warnings. The following lists the currently supported categories:

Warning Object	Description
Warning	Base class of all warning types
UserWarning	User-defined warning
DeprecationWarning	Warning for use of a deprecated feature
SyntaxWarning	Potential syntax problem
RuntimeWarning	Potential runtime problem
FutureWarning	Warning that the semantics of a particular feature will change in a future release

Each of these classes is available in the `__builtin__` module as well as the `exceptions` module. In addition, they are also instances of `Exception`. This makes it possible to easily convert warnings into errors.

Warnings are issued using the `warn()` function. For example:

```
warnings.warn("feature X is deprecated.")
warnings.warn("feature Y might be broken.", RuntimeWarning)
```

If desired, warnings can be filtered. The filtering process can be used to alter the output behavior of warning messages, to ignore warnings, or to turn warnings into exceptions. The `filterwarnings()` function is used to add a filter for a specific type of warning. For example:

```
warnings.filterwarnings(action="ignore",
                message=".*regex.*",
                category=DeprecationWarning)
import regex     # Warning message disappears
```

Limited forms of filtering can also be specified using the `-W` option to the interpreter. For example:

```
% python -Wignore:the\ regex:DeprecationWarning
```

The following functions are defined in the `warnings` module:

`warn(`*`message`*`[, `*`category`*`[, `*`stacklevel`*`]])`

Issues a warning. *message* is a string containing the warning message, *category* is the warning class (such as DeprecationWarning), and *stacklevel* is an integer that specifies the stack frame from which the warning message should originate. By default, *category* is UserWarning and *stacklevel* is 1.

`warn_explicit(`*`message, category, filename, lineno`*`[, `*`module`*`[, `*`registry`*`]])`

This is a low-level version of the warn() function. *message* and *category* have the same meaning as for warn(). *filename*, *lineno*, and *module* explicitly specify the location of the warning. *registry* is an object representing all the currently active filters. If *registry* is omitted, the warning message is not suppressed.

`showwarning(`*`message, category, filename, lineno`*`[, `*`file`*`])`

Writes a warning to a file. If *file* is omitted, the warning is printed to sys.stderr.

`formatwarning(`*`message, category, filename, lineno`*`)`

Creates the formatted string that is printed when a warning is issued.

`filterwarnings(`*`action`*`[, `*`message`*`[, `*`category`*`[, `*`module`*`[, `*`lineno`*`[, `*`append`*`]]]]])`

Adds an entry to the list of warning filters. *action* is one of 'error', 'ignore', 'always', 'default', 'once', or 'module'. The following list provides an explanation of each:

Action	Description
'error'	Convert the warning into an exception
'ignore'	Ignore the warning
'always'	Always print a warning message
'default'	Print the warning once for each location where the warning occurs
'module'	Print the warning once for each module in which the warning occurs
'once'	Print the warning once regardless of where it occurs

message is a regular expression string that is used to match against the warning message. *category* is a warning class such as DeprecationError. *module* is a regular expression string that is matched against the module name. *lineno* is a specific line number or 0 to match against all lines. *append* specifies that the filter should be appended to the list of all filters (checked last). By default, new filters are added to the beginning of the filter list. If any argument is omitted, it defaults to a value that matches all warnings.

`resetwarnings()`

Resets all the warning filters. This discards all previous calls to filterwarnings() as well as options specified with -W.

Notes

- The list of currently active filters is found in the warnings.filters variable.
- When warnings are converted to exceptions, the warning category becomes the exception type. For instance, an error on DeprecationWarning will raise a DeprecationWarning exception.

- The -W option can be used to specify a warning filter on the command line. The general format of this option is

      -Waction:message:category:module:lineno

  where each part has the same meaning as for the `filterwarning()` function. However, in this case, the *message* and *module* fields specify substrings (instead of regular expressions) for the first part of the warning message and module name to be filtered, respectively.

weakref

The `weakref` module is used to provide support for weak references. Normally, a reference to an object causes its reference count to increase—effectively keeping the object alive until the reference goes away. A weak reference, on the other hand, provides a way of referring to an object without increasing its reference count. This can be useful in certain kinds of applications that must manage objects in unusual ways. For example, in an object-oriented program, where you might implement a relationship such as the Observer pattern, a weak reference can be used to avoid the creation of reference cycles. An example of this is shown in the "Object Memory Management" section of Chapter 7.

A weak reference is created using the `weakref.ref()` function as follows:

```
>>> class A: pass
>>> a = A()
>>> ar = weakref.ref(a)          # Create a weak reference to a
>>> print ar
<weakref at 0x135a24; to 'instance' at 0x12ce0c>
```

Once a weak reference is created, the original object can be obtained from the weak reference by simply calling it as a function with no arguments. If the underlying object still exists, it will be returned. Otherwise, None is returned to indicate that the original object no longer exists. For example:

```
>>> print ar()                   # Print original object
<__main__.A instance at 12ce0c>
>>> del a                        # Delete the original object
>>> print ar()                   # a is gone, so this now returns None
None
>>>
```

The following functions are defined by the `weakref` module:

ref(*object*[, *callback*])

Creates a weak reference to *object*. *callback* is an optional function that will be called when *object* is about to be destroyed. If supplied, this function should accept a single argument, which is the corresponding weak reference object. More than one weak reference may refer to the same object. In this case, the `callback` functions will be called in order from the most recently applied reference to the oldest reference. *object* can be obtained from a weak reference by calling the returned weak reference object as a function with no arguments. If the original object no longer exists, None will be returned. `ref()` actually defines a type, `ReferenceType`, that can be used for type-checking and subclasses.

proxy(*object*[, *callback*])

Creates a proxy using a weak reference to *object*. The returned proxy object is really a wrapper around the original object that provides access to its attributes and methods. As long as the original object exists, manipulation of the proxy object will transparently mimic the behavior of the underlying object. On the other hand, if the original object has been destroyed, operations on the proxy will raise a `weakref.ReferenceError` to indicate that the object no longer exists. *callback* is a callback function with the same meaning as for the `ref()` function. The type of a proxy object is either `ProxyType` or `CallableProxyType`, depending on whether or not the original object is callable.

getweakrefcount(*object*)

Returns the number of weak references and proxies that refer to *object*.

getweakrefs(*object*)

Returns a list of all weak reference and proxy objects that refer to *object*.

WeakKeyDictionary([*dict*])

Creates a dictionary in which the keys are referenced weakly. When there are no more strong references to a key, the corresponding entry in the dictionary is automatically removed. If supplied, the items in *dict* are initially added to the returned `WeakKeyDictionary` object. Because only certain types of objects can be weakly referenced, there are numerous restrictions on acceptable key values. In particular, built-in strings cannot be used as weak keys. However, instances of user-defined classes that define a `__hash__()` method can be used as keys. An instance of `WeakKeyDictionary` has two methods, `iterkeyrefs()` and `keyrefs()`, that return the weak key references.

WeakValueDictionary([*dict*])

Creates a dictionary in which the values are referenced weakly. When there are no more strong references to a value, corresponding entries in the dictionary will be discarded. If supplied, the entries in *dict* are added to the returned `WeakValueDictionary`. An instance of `WeakValueDictionary` has two methods, `itervaluerefs()` and `valuerefs()`, that return the weak value references.

ProxyTypes

This is a tuple (`ProxyType`, `CallableProxyType`) that can be used for testing if an object is one of the two kinds of proxy objects created by the `proxy()` function—for example, `isinstance(*object*, ProxyTypes)`.

Example

One application of weak references is to create caches of recently computed results. For instance, if a function takes a long time to compute a result, it might make sense to cache these results and to reuse them as long as they are still in use someplace in the application. For example:

```
_resultcache = { }
def foocache(x):
    if x in resultcache:
        r = _resultcache[x]()        # Get weak ref and dereference it
        if r is not None: return r
    r = foo(x)
    _resultcache[x] = weakref.ref(r)
    return r
```

Notes

- Only class instances, functions, methods, sets, frozen sets, files, generators, type objects, and certain object types defined in library modules (for example, sockets, arrays, and regular expression patterns) support weak references. Built-in functions and most built-in types such as lists, dictionaries, strings, and numbers cannot be used.

- If iteration is ever used on a `WeakKeyDictionary` or `WeakValueDictionary`, great care should be taken to ensure that the dictionary does not change size because this may produce bizarre side effects such as items mysteriously disappearing from the dictionary for no apparent reason.

- If an exception occurs during the execution of a callback registered with `ref()` or `proxy()`, the exception is printed to standard error and ignored.

- Weak references are hashable as long as the original object is hashable. Moreover, the weak reference will maintain its hash value after the original object has been deleted, provided that the original hash value is computed while the object still exists.

- Weak references can be tested for equality but not for ordering. If the objects are still alive, references are equal if the underlying objects have the same value. Otherwise, references are equal if they are the same reference.

14

Mathematics

This chapter describes modules for performing various kinds of mathematical operations. In addition, the `decimal` module, which provides generalized support for decimal floating-point numbers, is described.

decimal

The Python `float` data type is represented using a double-precision binary floating-point encoding (usually as defined by the IEEE 754 standard). A subtle consequence of this encoding is that decimal values such as 0.1 can't be represented exactly. Instead, the closest value is 0.10000000000000001. This inexactness carries over to calculations involving floating-point numbers and can sometimes lead to unexpected results (for example, 3*0.1 == 0.3 evaluates as `False`).

The `decimal` module provides an implementation of the IBM General Decimal Arithmetic Standard, which allows for the exact representation of decimals. It also gives precise control over mathematical precision, significant digits, and rounding behavior. These features can be useful if interacting with external systems that precisely define properties of decimal numbers. For example, if writing Python programs that must interact with business applications.

The `decimal` module defines two basic data types: a `Decimal` type that represents a decimal number and a `Context` type that represents various parameters concerning computation such as precision and round-off error-handling. Here are a few simple examples that illustrate the basics of how the module works:

```
import decimal
x = decimal.Decimal('3.4')       # Create some decimal numbers
y = decimal.Decimal('4.5')

# Perform some math calculations using the default context
a = x * y        # a = decimal.Decimal('15.30')
b = x / y        # b = decimal.Decimal('0.7555555555555555555555555556')

# Change the precision and perform calculations
decimal.getcontext().prec = 3
c = x * y        # c = decimal.Decimal('15.3')
d = x / y        # d = decimal.Decimal('0.756')

# Change the precision for just a single block of statements
with decimal.localcontext(decimal.Context(prec=10)):
    e = x * y    # e = decimal.Decimal('15.30')
    f = x / y    # f = decimal.Decimal('0.7555555556')
```

Decimal **Objects**

Decimal numbers are represented by the following class:

`Decimal([value [, context]])`

value is the value of the number specified as either an integer, a string containing a decimal value such as `'4.5'`, or a tuple (*sign, digits, exponent*). If a tuple is supplied, *sign* is 0 for positive, 1 for negative; *digits* is a tuple of digits specified as integers; and *exponent* is an integer exponent. The special strings `'Infinity'`, `'-Infinity'`, `'NaN'`, and `'sNaN'` may be used to specify positive and negative infinity as well as Not a Number (NaN). `'sNaN'` is a variant of NaN that results in an exception if it is ever subsequently used in a calculation. An ordinary `float` object may *not* be used as the initial value because that value may not be exact (which defeats the purpose of using `decimal` in the first place). The *context* parameter is a `Context` object, which is described later. If supplied, *context* determines what happens if the initial value is not a valid number—raising an exception or returning a decimal with the value NaN.

The following examples show how to create various decimal numbers:

```
a = decimal.Decimal(42)              # Creates Decimal("42")
b = decimal.Decimal("37.45")         # Creates Decimal("37.45")
c = decimal.Decimal((1,(2,3,4,5),-2)) # Creates Decimal("-23.45")
d = decimal.Decimal("Infinity")
e = decimal.Decimal("NaN")
```

Decimal objects are immutable and have all the usual numeric properties of the built-in `int` and `float` types. They can also be used as dictionary keys, placed in sets, sorted, and so forth. For the most part, you manipulate `Decimal` objects using the standard Python math operators. However, the methods in the following list can be used to carry out several common mathematical operations. All operations take an optional *context* parameter that controls the behavior of precision, rounding, and other aspects of the calculation. If omitted, the current context is used.

Method	Description
`x.exp([context])`	Natural exponent e**d
`x.fma(y, z [, context])`	$x*y + z$ with no rounding of $x*y$ component
`x.ln([context])`	Natural logarithm (base e) of x
`x.log10([context])`	Base-10 logarithm of x
`x.sqrt([context])`	Square root of x

Context **Objects**

Various properties of decimal numbers, such as rounding and precision, are controlled through the use of a `Context` object:

```
Context(prec=None, rounding=None, traps=None, flags=None,
Emin=None, Emax=None, capitals=1)
```

This creates a new decimal context. The parameters should be specified using keyword arguments with the names shown. *prec* is an integer that sets the number of digits of precision for arithmetic operations, *rounding* determines the rounding behavior, and *traps* is a list of signals that produce a Python exception when certain events occur during computation (such as division by zero). *flags* is a list of signals that indicate the initial state of the context (such as overflow). Normally, *flags* is not specified. *Emin* and *Emax* are integers representing the minimum and maximum range for exponents, respectively. *capitals* is a boolean flag that indicates whether to use 'E' or 'e' for exponents. The default is 1 ('E').

Normally, new Context objects aren't created directly. Instead, the function getcontext() or localcontext() is used to return the currently active Context object. That object is then modified as needed. Examples of this appear later in this section. However, in order to better understand those examples, it is necessary to explain these context parameters in further detail.

Rounding behavior is determined by setting the *rounding* parameter to one of the following values:

Constant	Description
ROUND_CEILING	Rounds toward positive infinity. For example, 2.52 rounds up to 2.6 and -2.58 rounds up to -2.5.
ROUND_DOWN	Rounds toward zero. For example, 2.58 rounds down to 2.5 and -2.58 rounds up to -2.5.
ROUND_FLOOR	Rounds toward negative infinity. For example, 2.58 rounds down to 2.5 and -2.52 rounds down to -2.6.
ROUND_HALF_DOWN	Rounds away from zero if the fractional part is greater than half; otherwise, rounds toward zero. For example, 2.58 rounds up to 2.6, 2.55 rounds down to 2.5 -2.55 rounds up to -2.5, and -2.58 rounds down to -2.6.
ROUND_HALF_EVEN	The same as ROUND_HALF_DOWN except that if the fractional part is exactly half, the result is rounded down if the preceding digit is even and rounded up if the preceding digit is odd. For example, 2.65 is rounded down to 2.6 and 2.55 is rounded up to 2.6.
ROUND_HALF_UP	The same as ROUND_HALF_DOWN except that if the fractional part is exactly half, it is rounded away from zero. For example 2.55 rounds up to 2.6, and -2.55 rounds down to -2.6.
ROUND_UP	Rounds away from zero. For example, 2.52 rounds up to 2.6 and -2.52 rounds down to -2.6.
ROUND_05UP	Rounds away from zero if the last digit after toward zero would have been 0 or 5. Otherwise, rounds toward zero. For example, 2.54 rounds to 2.6 and 2.64 rounds to 2.6.

The *traps* and *flags* parameters of Context() are lists of signals. A signal represents a type of arithmetic exception that may occur during computation. Unless listed in *traps*, signals are ignored. Otherwise, an exception is raised. The following signals are defined:

Signal	Description
Clamped	Exponent adjusted to fit the allowed range.
DivisionByZero	Division of non-infinite number by 0.
Inexact	Rounding error occurred.
InvalidOperation	Invalid operation performed.
Overflow	Exponent exceeds $Emax$ after rounding. Also generates Inexact and Rounded.
Rounded	Rounding occurred. May occur even if no information was lost (for example, "1.00 " rounded to "1.0").
Subnormal	Exponent is less than $Emin$ prior to rounding.
Underflow	Numerical underflow. Result rounded to 0. Also generates Inexact and Subnormal.

These signal names correspond to Python exceptions that can be used for error checking. Here's an example:

```
try:
    x = a/b
except decimal.DivisionByZero:
    print "Division by zero"
```

Like exceptions, the signals are organized into a hierarchy:

```
ArithmeticError (built-in exception)
        DecimalException
                Clamped
                DivisionByZero
        Inexact
                Overflow
                Underflow
        InvalidOperation
        Rounded
                Overflow
                Underflow
        Subnormal
                Underflow
```

The Overflow and Underflow signals appear more than once in the table because those signals also result in the parent signal (for example, an Underflow also signals Subnormal). The decimal.DivisionByZero signal also derives from the built-in DivisionByZero exception.

In many cases, arithmetic signals are silently ignored. For instance, a computation may produce a round-off error but generate no exception. In this case, the signal names can be used to check a set of sticky flags that indicate computation state. Here's an example:

```
ctxt = decimal.getcontext()        # Get current context
x = a + b
if ctxt.flags[Rounded]:
    print "Result was rounded!"
```

When flags get set, they stay set until they are cleared using the `clear_flags()` method. Thus, one could perform an entire sequence of calculations and only check for errors at the end.

The settings on an existing `Context` object *c* can be changed through the following attributes and methods:

c.`capitals`

Flag set to 1 or 0 that determines whether to use *E* or *e* as the exponent character.

c.`Emax`

Integer specifying maximum exponent.

c.`Emin`

Integer specifying minimum exponent.

c.`prec`

Integer specifying digits of precision.

c.`flags`

Dictionary containing current flag values corresponding to signals. For example, *c*.`flags[Rounded]` returns the current flag value for the `Rounded` signal.

c.`rounding`

Rounding rule in effect. An example is `ROUND_HALF_EVEN`.

c.`traps`

Dictionary containing `True`/`False` settings for the signals that result in Python exceptions. For example, *c*.`traps[DivisionByZero]` is usually `True`, whereas *c*.`traps[Rounded]` is `False`.

c.`clear_flags()`

Resets all sticky flags (clears *c*.`flags`).

c.`copy()`

Returns a copy of context *c*.

c.`create_decimal(value)`

Creates a new `Decimal` object using *c* as the context. This may be useful in generating numbers whose precision and rounding behavior override that of the default context.

Functions and Constants

The following functions and constants are defined by the `decimal` module.

`getcontext()`

Returns the current decimal context. Each thread has its own decimal context so this returns the context of the calling thread.

`localcontext([c])`

Creates a context manager that sets the current decimal context to a copy of *c* for statements defined inside the body of a `with` statement. If *c* is omitted, a copy of the current context is created. Here is an example of using this function that temporarily sets the precision to five decimal places for a series of statements:

```
with localcontext() as c:
    c.prec = 5
    statements
```

`setcontext(c)`

Sets the decimal context of the calling thread to *c*.

`BasicContext`

A premade context with nine digits of precision. Rounding is `ROUND_HALF_UP`; Emin is
-999999999; Emax is 999999999; and all traps are enabled except for `Inexact`,
`Rounded`, and `Subnormal`.

`DefaultContext`

The default context used when creating new contexts (the values stored here are used as default values for the new context). Defines 28 digits of precision; `ROUND_HALF_EVEN` rounding; and traps for `Overflow`, `InvalidOperation`, and `DivisionByZero`.

`ExtendedContext`

A premade context with nine digits of precision. Rounding is `ROUND_HALF_EVEN`, Emin is -999999999, Emax is 999999999, and all traps are disabled. Never raises exceptions. Instead, results may be set to `NaN` or `Infinity`.

`Inf`

The same as `Decimal("Infinity")`.

`negInf`

The same as `Decimal("-Infinity")`.

`NaN`

The same as `Decimal("NaN")`.

Examples

Here are some more examples showing basic usage of decimal numbers:

```
>>> a = Decimal("42.5")
>>> b = Decimal("37.1")
>>> a + b
Decimal("79.6")
>>> a / b
Decimal("1.145552560646900269541778976")
>>> divmod(a,b)
(Decimal("1"), Decimal("5.4"))
>>> max(a,b)
Decimal("42.5")
>>> c = [Decimal("4.5"), Decimal("3"), Decimal("1.23e3")]
>>> sum(c)
Decimal("1237.5")
```

```
>>> [10*x for x in c]
[Decimal("45.0"), Decimal("30"), Decimal("1.230e4")]
>>> float(a)
42.5
>>> str(a)
'42.5'
```

Here's an example of changing parameters in the context:

```
>>> getcontext().prec = 4
>>> a = Decimal("3.4562384105")
>>> a
Decimal("3.4562384105")
>>> b = Decimal("5.6273833")
>>> getcontext().flags[Rounded]
0
>>> a + b
9.084
>>> getcontext().flags[Rounded]
1
>>> a / Decimal("0")
Traceback (most recent call last):
  File "<stdin>", line 1, in ?
decimal.DivisionByZero: x / 0
>>> getcontext().traps[DivisionByZero] = False
>>> a / Decimal("0")
Decimal("Infinity")
```

Notes

- The Decimal and Context objects have a large number of methods related to low-level details concerning the representation and behavior of decimal operations. These have not been documented here because they are not essential for the basic use of this module. However, you should consult the online documentation at http://docs.python.org/library/decimal.html for more information.

- The decimal context is unique to each thread. Changes to the context only affect that thread and not others.

- A special number, Decimal("sNaN"), may be used as a signaled-NaN. This number is never generated by any of the built-in functions. However, if it appears in a computation, an error is always signaled. You can use this to indicate invalid computations that must result in an error and must not be silently ignored. For example, a function could return sNaN as a result.

- The value of 0 may be positive or negative (that is, Decimal(0) and Decimal("-0")). The distinct zeros still compare as equals.

- This module is probably unsuitable for high-performance scientific computing due to the significant amount of overhead involved in calculations. Also, there is often little practical benefit in using decimal floating point over binary floating point in such applications.

- A full mathematical discussion of floating-point representation and error analysis is beyond the scope of this book. Readers should consult a book on numerical analysis for further details. The article "What Every Computer Scientist Should

Know About Floating-Point Arithmetic" by David Goldberg, in *Computing Surveys*, Association for Computing Machinery, March 1991 is also a worthy read (this article is easy to find on the Internet if you simply search for the title).

- The IBM General Decimal Arithmetic Specification contains more information and can be easily located online through search engines.

fractions

The `fractions` module defines a class `Fraction` that represents a rational number. Instances can be created in three different ways using the class constructor:

`Fraction([numerator [,denominator]])`

Creates a new rational number. `numerator` and `denominator` have integral values and default to 0 and 1, respectively.

`Fraction(fraction)`

If `fraction` is an instance of `numbers.Rational`, creates a new rational number with the same value as `fraction`.

`Fraction(s)`

If `s` is a string containing a fraction such as `"3/7"` or `"-4/7"`, a fraction with the same value is created. If `s` is a decimal number such as `"1.25"`, a fraction with that value is created (e.g., `Fraction(5,4)`).

The following class methods can create `Fraction` instances from other types of objects:

`Fraction.from_float(f)`

Creates a fraction representing the exact value of the floating-point number `f`.

`Fraction.from_decimal(d)`

Creates a fraction representing the exact value of the `Decimal` number `d`.

Here are some examples of using these functions:

```
>>> f = fractions.Fraction(3,4)
>>> g = fractions.Fraction("1.75")
>>> g
Fraction(7, 4)
>>> h = fractions.Fraction.from_float(3.1415926)
Fraction(3537118815677477, 1125899906842624)
>>>
```

An instance `f` of `Fraction` supports all of the usual mathematical operations. The numerator and denominator are stored in the `f.numerator` and `f.denominator` attributes, respectively. In addition, the following method is defined:

`f.limit_denominator([max_denominator])`

Returns the fraction that has the closest value to `f`. `max_denominator` specifies the largest denominator to use and defaults to 1000000.

Here are some examples of using Fraction instances (using the values created in the earlier example):

```
>>> f + g
Fraction(5, 2)
>>> f * g
Fraction(21, 16)
>>> h.limit_denominator(10)
Fraction(22, 7)
>>>
```

The fractions module also defines a single function:

gcd(a, b)

Computes the greatest common divisor of integers a and b. The result has the same sign as b if b is nonzero; otherwise, it's the same sign as a.

math

The math module defines the following standard mathematical functions. These functions operate on integers and floats but don't work with complex numbers (a separate module cmath can be used to perform similar operations on complex numbers). The return value of all functions is a float. All trigonometric functions assume the use of radians.

Function	Description
acos(x)	Returns the arc cosine of x.
acosh(x)	Returns the hyperbolic arc cosine of x.
asin(x)	Returns the arc sine of x.
asinh(x)	Returns the hyperbolic arc sine of x.
atan(x)	Returns the arc tangent of x.
atan2(y, x)	Returns atan(y / x).
atanh(x)	Returns the hyperbolic arc tangent of x.
ceil(x)	Returns the ceiling of x.
copysign(x, y)	Returns x with the same sign as y.
cos(x)	Returns the cosine of x.
cosh(x)	Returns the hyperbolic cosine of x.
degrees(x)	Converts x from radians to degrees.
radians(x)	Converts x from degrees to radians.
exp(x)	Returns e ** x.
fabs(x)	Returns the absolute value of x.
factorial(x)	Returns x factorial.
floor(x)	Returns the floor of x.
fmod(x, y)	Returns x % y as computed by the C fmod() function.
frexp(x)	Returns the positive mantissa and exponent of x as a tuple.
fsum(s)	Returns the full precision sum of floating-point values in the iterable sequence s. See the following note for a description.
hypot(x, y)	Returns the Euclidean distance, sqrt(x * x + y * y).

continues

Function	Description
isinf(x)	Return True if x is infinity.
isnan(x)	Returns True if x is NaN.
ldexp(x, i)	Returns x * (2 ** i).
log(x [, base])	Returns the logarithm of x to the given base. If base is omitted, this function computes the natural logarithm.
log10(x)	Returns the base 10 logarithm of x.
log1p(x)	Returns the natural logarithm of 1+x.
modf(x)	Returns the fractional and integer parts of x as a tuple. Both have the same sign as x.
pow(x, y)	Returns x ** y.
sin(x)	Returns the sine of x.
sinh(x)	Returns the hyperbolic sine of x.
sqrt(x)	Returns the square root of x.
tan(x)	Returns the tangent of x.
tanh(x)	Returns the hyperbolic tangent of x.
trunc(x)	Truncates x to the nearest integer towards 0.

The following constants are defined:

Constant	Description
pi	Mathematical constant pi
e	Mathematical constant e

Notes

- The floating-point values +inf, -inf, and nan can be created by passing strings into the float() function—for example, float("inf"), float("-inf"), or float("nan").

- The math.fsum() function is more accurate than the built-in sum() function because it uses a different algorithm that tries to avoid floating-point errors introduced by cancellation effects. For example, consider the sequence s = [1, 1e100, -1e100]. If you use sum(s), you will get a result of 0.0 (because the value of 1 is lost when added to the large value 1e100). However, using math.sum(s) produces the correct result of 1.0. The algorithm used by math.sum() is described in "Adaptive Precision Floating-Point Arithmetic and Fast Robust Geometric Predicates" by Jonathan Richard Shewchuk, Carnegie Mellon University School of Computer Science Technical Report CMU-CS-96-140, 1996.

numbers

The numbers module defines a series of abstract base classes that serve to organize various kinds of numbers. The numeric classes are organized into a hierarchy in which each level progressively adds more capabilities.

Number

A class that serves as the top of the numeric hierarchy.

Complex

A class that represents the complex numbers. Numbers of this type have `real` and `imag` attributes. This class inherits from `Number`.

Real

A class that represents the real numbers. Inherits from `Complex`.

Rational

A class that represents fractions. Numbers of this type have `numerator` and `denominator` attributes. Inherits from `Real`.

Integral

A class that represents the integers. Inherits from `Rational`.

The classes in this module are not meant to be instantiated. Instead, they can be used to perform various kinds of type checks on values. For example:

```
if isinstance(x, numbers.Number)    # x is any kind of number
    statements

if isinstance(x, numbers.Integral)    # x is an integral value
    statements
```

If one of these type checks returns `True`, it means that x is compatible with all of the usual mathematical operations associated with that type and that a conversion to one of the built-in types such as `complex()`, `float()`, or `int()` will work.

The abstract base classes can also be used as a base class for user-defined classes that are meant to emulate numbers. Doing this is not only just a good idea for type checking, but it adds extra safety checks that make sure you implement all of the required methods. For example:

```
>>> class Foo(numbers.Real): pass
...
>>> f = Foo()
Traceback (most recent call last):
  File "<stdin>", line 1, in <module>
TypeError: Can't instantiate abstract class Foo with abstract methods
  __abs__, __add__, __div__, __eq__, __float__, __floordiv__, __le__, __lt__,
  __mod__, __mul__, __neg__, __pos__, __pow__, __radd__, __rdiv__,
➡ __rfloordiv__,
  __rmod__, __rmul__, __rpow__, __rtruediv__, __truediv__, __trunc__
>>>
```

Notes

- Refer to Chapter 7 ("Classes and Object-Oriented Programming") for more information on abstract base classes.

- PEP 3141 (http://www.python.org/dev/peps/pep-3141) has more information about the type hierarchy and intended use of this module.

random

The `random` module provides a variety of functions for generating pseudo-random numbers as well as functions for randomly generating values according to various distributions on the real numbers. Most of the functions in this module depend on the function `random()`, which generates uniformly distributed numbers in the range [0.0, 1.0) using the Mersenne Twister generator.

Seeding and Initialization

The following functions are used to control the state of the underlying random number generator:

`seed([x])`

Initializes the random number generator. If x is omitted or `None`, the system time is used to seed the generator. Otherwise, if x is an integer or long integer, its value is used. If x is not an integer, it must be a hashable object and the value of `hash(x)` is used as a seed.

`getstate()`

Returns an object representing the current state of the generator. This object can later be passed to `setstate()` to restore the state.

`setstate(state)`

Restores the state of the random number generator from an object returned by `getstate()`.

`jumpahead(n)`

Quickly changes the state of the generator to what it would be if `random()` were called n times in a row. n must be a nonnegative integer.

Random Integers

The following functions are used to manipulate random integers.

`getrandbits(k)`

Creates a long integer containing k random bits.

`randint(a,b)`

Returns a random integer, x, in the range $a <= x <= b$.

`randrange(start,stop [,step])`

Returns a random integer in `range(start,stop,step)`. Does not include the endpoint.

Random Sequences

The following functions are used to randomize sequence data.

`choice(seq)`

Returns a random element from the nonempty sequence `seq`.

`sample(s, len)`

Returns a sequence length, `len`, containing elements chosen randomly from the sequence `s`. The elements in the resulting sequence are placed in the order in which they were selected.

`shuffle(x [,random])`

Randomly shuffles the items in the list *x* in place. `random` is an optional argument that specifies a random generation function. If supplied, it must be a function that takes no arguments and returns a floating-point number in the range [0.0, 1.0).

Real-Valued Random Distributions

The following functions generate random numbers on real numbers. Distribution and parameter names correspond to the standard names used in probability and statistics. You will need to consult an appropriate text to find out more details.

`random()`

Returns a random number in the range [`0.0, 1.0`).

`uniform(a,b)`

Returns a uniformly distributed random number in the range [a, b).

`betavariate(alpha, beta)`

Returns a value between `0` and `1` from the Beta distribution. `alpha > -1` and `beta > -1`.

`cunifvariate(mean, arc)`

Circular uniform distribution. `mean` is the mean angle, and `arc` is the range of the distribution, centered around the mean angle. Both of these values must be specified in radians in the range between `0` and `pi`. Returned values are in the range (`mean - arc/2, mean + arc/2`).

`expovariate(lambd)`

Exponential distribution. `lambd` is `1.0` divided by the desired mean. Returns values in the range [`0, +Infinity`).

`gammavariate(alpha, beta)`

Gamma distribution. `alpha > -1, beta > 0`.

`gauss(mu, sigma)`

Gaussian distribution with mean `mu` and standard deviation `sigma`. Slightly faster than `normalvariate()`.

`lognormvariate(mu, sigma)`

Log normal distribution. Taking the natural logarithm of this distribution results in a normal distribution with mean `mu` and standard deviation `sigma`.

`normalvariate(mu, sigma)`

Normal distribution with mean `mu` and standard deviation `sigma`.

`paretovariate(alpha)`

Pareto distribution with shape parameter `alpha`.

`triangular([low [, high [, mode]]])`

Triangular distribution. A random number n in the range `low <= n < high` with mode `mode`. By default, `low` is 0, `high` is 1.0, and `mode` is set to the midpoint of `low` and `high`.

`vonmisesvariate(mu, kappa)`

von Mises distribution, where `mu` is the mean angle in radians between 0 and 2 * pi and `kappa` is a nonnegative concentration factor. If `kappa` is zero, the distribution reduces to a uniform random angle over the range 0 to 2 * pi.

`weibullvariate(alpha, beta)`

Weibull distribution with scale parameter `alpha` and shape parameter `beta`.

Notes

- The functions in this module are not thread-safe. If you are generating random numbers in different threads, you should use locking to prevent concurrent access.
- The period of the random number generator (before numbers start repeating) is 2**19937−1.
- The random numbers generated by this module are deterministic and should not be used for cryptography.
- New types of random number generators can be created by subclassing `random.Random` and implementing the `random()`, `seed()`, `getstate()`, `getstate()`, and `jumpahead()` methods. All the other functions in this module are actually internally implemented as methods of `Random`. Thus, they could be accessed as methods of an instance of the new random number generator.
- The module provides two alternative random number generators classes— `WichmannHill` and `SystemRandom`—that are used by instantiating the appropriate class and calling the preceding functions as methods. The `WichmannHill` class implements the Wichmann-Hill generator that was used in earlier Python releases. The `SystemRandom` class generates random numbers using the system random number generator `os.urandom()`.

15

Data Structures, Algorithms, and Code Simplification

The modules in this chapter are used to address common programming problems related to data structures; algorithms; and the simplification of code involving iteration, function programming, context managers, and classes. These modules should be viewed as a extension of Python's built-in types and functions. In many cases, the underlying implementation is highly efficient and may be better suited to certain kinds of problems than what is available with the built-ins.

abc

The abc module defines a metaclass and a pair of decorators for defining new abstract base classes.

ABCMeta

A metaclass that represents an abstract base class. To define an abstract class, you define a class that uses ABCMeta as a metaclass. For example:

```
import abc
class Stackable:                       # In Python 3, use the syntax
    __metaclass__ = abc.ABCMeta    # class Stackable(metaclass=abc.ABCMETA)
    ...
```

A class created in this manner differs from an ordinary class in a few critical ways:

- First, if the abstract class defines methods or properties that are decorated with the abstractmethod and abstractproperty decorators described later, then instances of derived classes can't be created unless those classes provide a non-abstract implementation of those methods and properties.

- Second, an abstract class has a class method register(subclass) that can be used to register additional types as a logical subclass. For any type subclass registered with this function, the operation isinstance(x, AbstractClass) will return True if x is an instance of subclass.

- A final feature of abstract classes is that they can optionally define a special class method __subclasshook__(cls, subclass). This method should return True if the type subclass is considered to be a subclass, return False if subclass is not a subclass, or raise a NotImplemented exception if nothing is known.

abstractmethod(*method*)

A decorator that declares *method* to be abstract. When used in an abstract base class, derived classes defined directly via inheritance can only be instantiated if they define a nonabstract implementation of the method. This decorator has no effect on subclasses registered using the `register()` method of an abstract base.

abstractproperty(*fget* [, *fset* [, *fdel* [, *doc*]]])

Creates an abstract property. The parameters are the same as the normal `property()` function. When used in an abstract base, derived classes defined directly via inheritance can only be instantiated if they define a nonabstract implementation of the property.

The following code provides an example of defining a simple abstract class:

```
from abc import ABCMeta, abstractmethod, abstractproperty
class Stackable:                        # In Python 3, use the syntax
    __metaclass__ = ABCMeta             # class Stackable(metaclass=ABCMeta)
    @abstractmethod
    def push(self,item):
        pass
    @abstractmethod
    def pop(self):
        pass
    @abstractproperty
    def size(self):
        pass
```

Here is an example of a class that derives from `Stackable`:

```
class Stack(Stackable):
    def __init__(self):
        self.items = []
    def push(self,item):
        self.items.append(item)
    def pop(self):
        return self.items.pop()
```

Here is the error message that you get if you try to create a `Stack`:

```
>>> s = Stack()
Traceback (most recent call last):
  File "<stdin>", line 1, in <module>
TypeError: Can't instantiate abstract class Stack with abstract methods size
>>>
```

This error can be fixed by adding a `size()` property to `Stack`. You can either do this by modifying the definition of `Stack` itself or inheriting from it and adding the required method or property:

```
class CompleteStack(Stack):
    @property
    def size(self):
        return len(self.items)
```

Here is an example of using the complete stack object:

```
>>> s = CompleteStack()
>>> s.push("foo")
>>> s.size
1
>>>
```

See Also:

Chapter 7, "Classes and Object-Oriented Programming," numbers (**p. 252**), collections (**p. 262**).

array

The array module defines a new object type, array, that works almost exactly like a list, except that its contents are constrained to a single type. The type of an array is determined at the time of creation, using one of the type codes shown in Table 15.1.

Table 15.1 **Type Codes**

Type Code	Description	C Type	Minimum Size (in Bytes)
'b'	8-bit integer	signed char	1
'B'	8-bit unsigned integer	unsigned char	1
'u'	Unicode character	PY_UNICODE	2 or 4
'h'	16-bit integer	short	2
'H'	16-bit unsigned integer	unsigned short	2
'i'	Integer	int	4 or 8
'I'	Unsigned integer	unsigned int	4 or 8
'l'	Long integer	long	4 or 8
'L'	Unsigned long integer	unsigned long	4 or 8
'f'	Single-precision float	float	4
'd'	Double-precision float	double	8

The representation of integers and long integers is determined by the machine architecture (they may be 32 or 64 bits). When values stored as 'L' or 'I' are returned, they're returned as long integers in Python 2.

The module defines the following type:

array(typecode [, initializer])

Creates an array of type typecode. initializer is a string or list of values used to initialize values in the array. The following attributes and methods apply to an array object, a:

Item	Description
a.typecode	Type code character used to create the array.
a.itemsize	Size of items stored in the array (in bytes).
a.append(x)	Appends x to the end of the array.
a.buffer_info()	Returns (address, length), giving the memory location and length of the buffer used to store the array.
a.byteswap()	Swaps the byte ordering of all items in the array from big-endian to little-endian, or vice versa. This is only supported for integer values.

continues

Item	Description
a.count(x)	Returns the number of occurrences of x in a.
a.extend(b)	Appends b to the end of array a. b can be an array or an iterable object whose elements are the same type as in a.
a.fromfile(f, n)	Reads n items (in binary format) from the file object f and appends to the end of the array. f must be a file object. Raises EOFError if fewer than n items can be read.
a.fromlist(list)	Appends items from list to the end of the array. list can be any iterable object.
a.fromstring(s)	Appends items from string s, where s is interpreted as a string of binary values—same as would have been read using fromfile().
a.index(x)	Returns the index of the first occurrence of x in a. Raises ValueError if not found.
a.insert(i, x)	Inserts x before position i.
a.pop([i])	Removes item i from the array and returns it. If i is omitted, the last element is removed.
a.remove(x)	Removes the first occurrence of x from the array. Raises ValueError if not found.
a.reverse()	Reverses the order of the array.
a.tofile(f)	Writes all items to file f. Data is saved in native binary format.
a.tolist()	Converts the array to an ordinary list of values.
a.tostring()	Converts to a string of binary data—the same data as would be written using tofile().
a.tounicode()	Converts the array to a Unicode string. Raises ValueError if the array is not of type 'u'.

When items are inserted into an array, a TypeError exception is generated if the type of the item doesn't match the type used to create the array.

The array module is useful if you need to have space-efficient storage for lists of data and you know that all items in the list are going to be the same type. For example, storing 10 million integers in a list requires about 160MB of memory whereas an array of 10 million integers requires only 40MB. Despite this space savings, none of the basic operations on an array tend to be faster than their list counterparts—in fact, they may be slower.

In performing calculations with arrays, you will want to be careful with operations that create lists. For example, using a list comprehension on an array will convert the entire array into a list, defeating any space-saving benefit. A better way to handle this is to create new arrays using generator expressions. For example:

```
a = array.array("i", [1,2,3,4,5])
b = array.array(a.typecode, (2*x for x in a))    # Create a new array from a
```

Because the point of using an array is to save space, it may be more desirable to perform "in-place" operations. An efficient way to do this is with code that uses enumerate(), like this:

```
a = array.array("i", [1,2,3,4,5])
for i, x in enumerate(a):
    a[i] = 2*x
```

For large arrays, this in-place modification runs about 15 percent faster than the code that creates a new array with a generator expression.

Notes

- The arrays created by this module are not suitable for numeric work such as matrix or vector math. For example, the addition operator doesn't add the corresponding elements of the arrays; instead, it appends one array to the other. To create storage and calculation efficient arrays, use the numpy extension available at http://numpy.sourceforge.net/. Note that the numpy API is completely different.
- The += operator can be used to append the contents of another array. The *= operator can be used to repeat an array.

See Also:

struct (**p. 290**)

bisect

The bisect module provides support for keeping lists in sorted order. It uses a bisection algorithm to do most of its work.

bisect(`list`, `item` [, `low` [, `high`]])

Returns the index of the insertion point for *item* to be placed in *list* in order to maintain *list* in sorted order. *low* and *high* are indices specifying a subset of the list to examine. If *items* is already in the list, the insertion point will always be to the right of existing entries in the list.

bisect_left(`list`, `item` [, `low` [, `high`]])

Returns the index of the insertion point for *item* to be placed in *list* in order to maintain *list* in sorted order. *low* and *high* are indices specifying a subset of the list to examine. If *items* is already in the list, the insertion point will always be to the left of existing entries in the list.

bisect_right(`list`, `item` [, `low` [, `high`]])

The same as bisect().

insort(`list`, `item` [, `low` [, `high`]])

Inserts *item* into *list* in sorted order. If *item* is already in the list, the new entry is inserted to the right of any existing entries.

insort_left(`list`, `item` [, `low` [, `high`]])

Inserts *item* into *list* in sorted order. If *item* is already in the list, the new entry is inserted to the left of any existing entries.

insort_right(`list`, `item` [, `low` [, `high`]])

The same as insort().

collections

The collections module contains high-performance implementations of a few useful container types, abstract base classes for various kinds of containers, and a utility function for creating name-tuple objects. Each is described in the sections that follow.

deque **and** defaultdict

Two new containers are defined in the collections module: deque and defaultdict.

deque([iterable [, maxlen]])

Type representing a double-ended queue (deque, pronounced "deck") object. *iterable* is an iterable object used to populate the deque. A *deque* allows items to be inserted or removed from either end of the queue. The implementation has been optimized so that the performance of these operations is approximately the same as (O(1)). This is slightly different from a list where operations at the front of the list may require shifting of all the elements that follow. If the optional *maxlen* argument is supplied, the resulting deque object becomes a circular buffer of that size. That is, if new items are added, but there is no more space, items are deleted from the opposite end to make room.

An instance, d, of deque has the following methods:

d.append(x)

Adds x to the right side of d.

d.appendleft(x)

Adds x to the left side of d.

d.clear()

Removes all items from d.

d.extend(iterable)

Extends d by adding all the items in *iterable* on the right.

d.extendleft(iterable)

Extends d by adding all the items in *iterable* on the left. Due to the sequence of left appends that occur, items in *iterable* will appear in reverse order in d.

d.pop()

Returns and removes an item from the right side of d. Raises IndexError if d is empty.

d.popleft()

Returns and removes an item from the left side of d. Raises IndexError if d is empty.

d.remove(item)

Removes the first occurrence of *item*. Raises ValueError if no match is found.

`d.rotate(n)`

Rotates all the items *n* steps to the right. If *n* is negative, items are rotated to the left.

Deques are often overlooked by many Python programmers. However, this type offers many advantages. First, the implementation is highly efficient—even to a level of using internal data structures that provide good processor cache behavior. Appending items at the end is only slightly slower than the built-in `list` type, whereas inserting items at the front is significantly faster. Operations that add new items to a deque are also thread-safe, making this type appropriate for implementing queues. `deques` can also be serialized using the `pickle` module.

`defaultdict([default_factory], ...)`

A type that is exactly the same as a dictionary except for the handling of missing keys. When a lookup occurs on a key that does not yet exist, the function supplied as `default_factory` is called to provide a default value which is then saved as the value of the associated key. The remaining arguments to `defaultdict` are exactly the same as the built-in `dict()` function. An instance *d* of `defaultdictionary` has the same operations as a built-in dictionary. The attribute `d.default_factory` contains the function passed as the first argument and can be modified as necessary.

A `defaultdict` object is useful if you are trying to use a dictionary as a container for tracking data. For example, suppose you wanted to keep track of the position of each word in a string *s*. Here is how you could use a `defaultdict` to do this easily:

```
>>> from collections import defaultdict
>>> s = "yeah but no but yeah but no but yeah"
>>> words = s.split()
>>> wordlocations = defaultdict(list)
>>> for n, w in enumerate(words):
...         wordlocations[w].append(n)
...
>>> wordlocations
defaultdict(<type 'list'>, {'yeah': [0, 4, 8], 'but': [1, 3, 5, 7], 'no': [2, 6]})
>>>
```

In this example, the lookup `wordlocations[w]` will "fail" the first time a word is encountered. However, instead of raising a `KeyError`, the function `list` supplied as `default_factory` is called to create a new value. Built-in dictionaries have a method `setdefault()` that can be used to achieve a similar result, but it often makes code confusing to read and run slower. For example, the statement that appends a new item shown previously could be replaced by `wordlocations.setdefault(w, []).append(n)`. This is not nearly as clear and in a simple timing test, it runs nearly twice as slow as using a `defaultdict` object.

Named Tuples

Tuples are frequently used to represent simple data structures. For example, a network address might be represented as a tuple `addr = (hostname, port)`. A common complaint with tuples is that the individual items have to be accessed by numerical index—for example, `addr[0]` or `addr[1]`. This leads to code that is confusing to read and hard to maintain unless you can remember what all of the index values mean (and the problem gets worse the larger the tuple gets).

The collections module contains a function namedtuple() that is used to create subclasses of tuple in which attribute names can be used to access tuple elements.

namedtuple(*typename, fieldnames* [, *verbose*])

Creates a subclass of tuple with name *typename*. *fieldnames* is a list of attribute names specified as strings. The names in this list must be valid Python identifiers, must not start with an underscore, and are specified in the same order as the items appearing in the tuple—for example, ['hostname', 'port']. Alternatively, *fieldnames* can be specified as a string such as 'hostname port' or 'hostname, port'. The value returned by this function is a *class* whose name has been set to the value supplied in *typename*. You use this class to create instances of named tuples. The *verbose* flag, if set to True, prints the resulting class definition to standard output.

Here is an example of using this function:

```
>>> from collections import namedtuple
>>> NetworkAddress = namedtuple('NetworkAddress',['hostname','port'])
>>> a = NetworkAddress('www.python.org',80)
>>> a.hostname
'www.python.org'
>>> a.port
80
>>> host, port = a
>>> len(a)
2
>>> type(a)
<class '__main__.NetworkAddress'>
>>> isinstance(a, tuple)
True
>>>
```

In this example, the named tuple NetworkAddress is, in every way, indistinguished from a normal tuple except for the added support of being able to use attribute lookup such as a.hostname or a.port to access tuple components. The underlying implementation is efficient—the class that is created does not use an instance dictionary or add any additional memory overhead in a built-in tuple. All of the normal tuple operations still work.

A named tuple can be useful if defining objects that really only serve as a data structures. For example, instead of a defining a class, like this:

```
class Stock(object):
    def __init__(self,name,shares,price):
        self.name = name
        self.shares = shares
        self.price = price
```

you could define a named tuple instead:

```
import collections
Stock = collections.namedtuple('Stock','name shares price')
```

Both versions are going to work in a nearly identical manner. For example, in either case, you would access fields by writing s.name, s.shares, and so on. However, the benefit of the named tuple is that it is more memory-efficient and supports various tuple operations such as unpacking (for example, if you had a list of named tuples, you could unpack values in a for-loop with a statement such as for name, shares, `price in stockList)`. The downside to a named tuple is that attribute access is not as efficient as with a class. For example, accessing `s.shares` is more than twice as slow if `s` is an instance of a named tuple instead of an ordinary class.

Named tuples are frequently used in other parts of the Python standard library. Here, their use is partly historical—in many library modules, tuples were originally used as the return value of various functions that would return information about files, stack frames, or other low-level details. Code that used these tuples wasn't always so elegant. Thus, the switch to a named tuple was made to clean up their usage without breaking backwards compatibility. Another subtle problem with tuples is that once you start using a tuple, the expected number of fields is locked forever (e.g., if you suddenly add a new field, old code will break). Variants of named tuples have been used in the library to add new fields to the data returned by certain functions. For example, an object might support a legacy tuple interface, but then provide additional values that are only available as named attributes.

Abstract Base Classes

The `collections` module defines a series of abstract base classes. The purpose of these classes is to describe programming interfaces on various kinds of containers such as lists, sets, and dictionaries. There are two primary uses of these classes. First, they can be used as a base class for user-defined objects that want to emulate the functionality of built-in container types. Second, they can be used for type checking. For example, if you wanted to check that `s` worked like a sequence, you could use `isinstance(s, collections.Sequence)`.

Container

Base class for all containers. Defines a single abstract method `__contains__()`, which implements the `in` operator.

Hashable

Base class for objects that can be used as a hash table key. Defines a single abstract method `__hash__()`.

Iterable

Base class for objects that support the iteration protocol. Defines a single abstract method `__iter__()`.

Iterator

Base class for iterator objects. Defines the abstract method `next()` but also inherits from `Iterable` and provides a default implementation of `__iter__()` that simply does nothing.

Sized

Base class for containers whose size can be determined. Defines the abstract method `__len__()`.

Callable

Base class for objects that support function call. Defines the abstract method `__call__()`.

Sequence

Base class for objects that look like sequences. Inherits from Container, Iterable, and Sized and defines the abstract methods `__getitem__()` and `__len__()`. Also provides a default implementation of `__contains__()`, `__iter__()`, `__reversed__()`, `index()`, and `count()` that are implemented using nothing but the `__getitem__()` and `__len__()` methods.

MutableSequence

Base class for mutable sequences. Inherits from Sequence and adds the abstract methods `__setitem__()` and `__delitem__()`. Also provides a default implementation of `append()`, `reverse()`, `extend()`, `pop()`, `remove()`, and `__iadd__()`.

Set

Base class for objects that work like sets. Inherits from Container, Iterable, and Sized and defines the abstract methods `__len__()`, `__iter__()`, and `__contains__()`. Also provides a default implementation of the set operators `__le__()`, `__lt__()`, `__eq__()`, `__ne__()`, `__gt__()`, `__ge__()`, `__and__()`, `__or__()`, `__xor__()`, `__sub__()`, and `isdisjoint()`.

MutableSet

Base class for mutable sets. Inherits from Set and adds the abstract methods `add()` and `discard()`. Also provides a default implementation of `clear()`, `pop()`, `remove()`, `__ior__()`, `__iand__()`, `__ixor__()`, and `__isub__()`.

Mapping

Base class for objects that support mapping (dictionary) lookup. Inherits from Sized, Iterable, and Container and defines the abstract methods `__getitem__()`, `__len__()`, and `__iter__()`. A default implementation of `__contains__()`, `keys()`, `items()`, `values()`, `get()`, `__eq__()`, and `__ne__()` is also provided.

MutableMapping

Base class for mutable mapping objects. Inherits from Mapping and adds the abstract methods `__setitem__()` and `__delitem__()`. An implementation of `pop()`, `popitem()`, `clear()`, `update()`, and `setdefault()` is also added.

MappingView

Base class for mapping views. A *mapping view* is an object that is used for accessing the internals of a mapping object as a set. For example, a key view is a set-like object that shows the keys in a mapping. See Appendix A, "Python 3" for more details.

KeysView

Base class for a key view of a mapping. Inherits from MappingView and Set.

ItemsView

Base class for item view of a mapping. Inherits from MappingView and Set.

ValuesView

Base class for a (*key*, *item*) view of a mapping. Inherits from MappingView and Set.

Python's built-in types are already registered with all of these base classes as appropriate. Also, by using these base classes, it is possible to write programs that are more precise in their type checking. Here are some examples:

```
# Pull off the last item of a sequence
if isinstance(x, collections.Sequence):
    last = x[-1]

# Only iterate over an object if its size is known
if isinstance(x, collections.Iterable) and isinstance(x, collections.Sized):
    for item in x:
        statements

# Add a new item to a set
if isinstance(x, collections.MutableSet):
    x.add(item)
```

See Also:

Chapter 7, "Classes and Object-Oriented Programming."

contextlib

The `contextlib` module provides a decorator and utility functions for creating context managers used in conjunction with the `with` statement.

contextmanager(*func*)

A decorator that creates a context manager from a generator function *func*. The way in which you use this decorator is as follows:

```
@contextmanager
def foo(args):
    statements
    try:
        yield value
    except Exception as e:
        error handling (if any)
    statements
```

When the statement `with foo(args) as value` appears, the generator function is executed with the supplied arguments until the first `yield` statement is reached. The value returned by `yield` is placed into the variable *value*. At this point, the body of the `with` statement executes. Upon completion, the generator function resumes. If any kind of exception is raised inside the with-body, that exception is raised inside the generator function where it can be handled as appropriate. If the error is to be propagated, the generator should use raise to re-raise the exception. An example of using this decorator can be found in the "Context Managers" section of Chapter 5.

nested(*mgr1*, *mgr2*, ..., *mgrN*)

A function that invokes more than one context manager *mgr1*, *mgr2*, and so on as a single operation. Returns a tuple containing the different return values of the with statements. The statement `with nested(m1,m2) as (x,y): statements` is the same as saying `with m1 as x: with m2 as y: `*statements*. Be aware that if an inner context manager traps and suppresses an exception, no exception information is passed along to the outer managers.

closing(*object*)

Creates a context manager that automatically executes *object*.`close()` when execution leaves the body of the `with` statement. The value returned by the `with` statement is the same as *object*.

functools

The `functools` module contains functions and decorators that are useful for creating higher-order functions, functional programming, and decorators.

partial(*function* [, *args [, **kwargs]])

Creates a function-like object, `partial`, that when called, calls *function* with positional arguments *args*, keyword arguments *kwargs*, and any additional positional or keyword arguments that are supplied. Additional positional arguments are added to the end of *args*, and additional keyword arguments are merged into *kwargs*, overwriting any previously defined values (if any). A typical use of `partial()` is when making a large number of function calls where many of the arguments are held fixed. For example:

```
from functools import partial
mybutton = partial(Button, root, fg="black",bg="white",font="times",size="12")
b1 = mybutton(text="Ok")        # Calls Button() with text="Ok" and all of the
b2 = mybutton(text="Cancel")    # additional arguments supplied to partial() above
b3 = mybutton(text="Restart")
```

An instance *p* of the object created by *partial* has the following attributes:

Item	Description
p.func	Function that is called when *p* is called.
p.args	Tuple containing the leftmost positional arguments supplied to *p*.func when called. Additional positional arguments are concatenated to the end of this value.
p.keywords	Dictionary containing the keyword arguments supplied to *p*.func when called. Additional keyword arguments are merged into this dictionary.

Use caution when using a `partial` object as a stand-in for a regular function. The result is not exactly the same as a normal function. For instance, if you use `partial()` inside a class definition, it behaves like a static method, not an instance method.

reduce(*function, items* [, *initial*])

Applies a function, *function*, cumulatively to the items in the iterable *items* and returns a single value. *function* must take two arguments and is first applied to the first two items of *items*. This result and subsequent elements of *items* are then combined one at a time in a similar manner, until all elements of *items* have been consumed. *initial* is an optional starting value used in the first computation and when *items* is empty. This function is the same as the reduce() function that was a built-in in Python 2. For future compatibility, use this version instead.

update_wrapper(*wrapper, wrapped* [, *assigned* [, *updated*]])

This is a utility function that is useful when writing decorators. Copies attributes from a function *wrapped* to a wrapper function *wrapper* in order to make the wrapped function look like the original function. *assigned* is a tuple of attribute names to copy and is set to ('__name__','__module__','__doc__') by default. *updated* is a tuple containing the names of function attributes that are dictionaries and which you want values merged in the wrapper. By default, it is a tuple ('__dict__',).

wraps(*function* [, *assigned* [, *updated*]])

A decorator carries out the same task as update_wrapper() on the function to which it is applied. *assigned* and *updated* have the same meaning. A typical use of this decorator is when writing other decorators. For example:

```
from functools import wraps
def debug(func):
    @wraps(func)
    def wrapped(*args,**kwargs):
        print("Calling %s" % func.__name__)
        r = func(*args,**kwargs)
        print("Done calling %s" % func.__name__)
    return wrapped

@debug
def add(x,y):
    return x+y
```

> **See Also:**
>
> Chapter 6, "Functions and Functional Programming."

heapq

The heapq module implements a priority queue using a heap. *Heaps* are simply lists of ordered items in which the heap condition has been imposed. Specifically, heap[n] <= heap[2*n+1] and heap[n] <= heap[2*n+2] for all n, starting with n = 0. heap[0] always contains the smallest item.

heapify(*x*)

Converts a list, *x*, into a heap, in place.

heappop(*heap*)

Returns and removes the smallest item from *heap*, preserving the heap condition. Raises IndexError if *heap* is empty.

heappush(*heap, item*)

Adds *item* to the heap, preserving the heap condition.

heappushpop(*heap*, *item*)

Adds *item* to the heap and removes the smallest item from *heap* in a single operation. This is more efficient than calling heappush() and heappop() separately.

heapreplace(*heap*, *item*)

Returns and removes the smallest *item* from the heap. At the same time, a new *item* is added. The heap condition is preserved in the process. This function is more efficient than calling heappop() and heappush() in sequence. In addition, the returned value is obtained prior to adding the new item. Therefore, the return value could be larger than *item*. Raises IndexError if *heap* is empty.

merge(*s1*, *s2*, ...)

Creates an iterator that merges the sorted iterables *s1*, *s2*, and so on into a single sorted sequence. This function does not consume the inputs but returns an iterator that incrementally processes the data.

nlargest(*n*, *iterable* [, *key*])

Creates a list consisting of the *n* largest items in *iterable*. The largest item appears first in the returned list. *key* is an optional function that takes a single input parameter and computes the comparison key for each item in *iterable*.

nsmallest(*n*, *iterable* [, *key*])

Creates a list consisting of the *n* smallest items in *iterable*. The smallest item appears first in the returned list. *key* is an optional key function.

> **Note**
>
> The theory and implementation of heap queues can be found in most books on algorithms.

itertools

The itertools module contains functions for creating efficient iterators, useful for looping over data in various ways. All the functions in this module return iterators that can be used with the for statement and other functions involving iterators such as generators and generator expressions.

chain(*iter1*, *iter2*, ..., *iterN*)

Given a group of iterators (*iter1*, ... , *iterN*), this function creates a new iterator that chains all the iterators together. The returned iterator produces items from *iter1* until it is exhausted. Then items from *iter2* are produced. This continues until all the items in *iterN* are exhausted.

chain.from_iterable(*iterables*)

An alternative constructor for a chain where the *iterables* is an iterable that produces a sequence of iterable objects. The result of this operation is the same as what would be produced by the following fragment of generator code:

```
for it in iterables:
    for x in it:
        yield x
```

combinations(*iterable, r*)

Creates an iterator that returns all *r*-length subsequences of items taken from *iterable*. The items in the returned subsequences are ordered in the same way in which they were ordered in the input *iterable*. For example, if *iterable* is the list [1,2,3,4], the sequence produced by combinations([1,2,3,4], 2) is [1,2], [1,3], [1,4], [2,3], [3,4].

count([n])

Creates an iterator that produces consecutive integers starting with *n*. If *n* is omitted, counting starts at 0. (Note that this iterator does not support long integers. If sys.maxint is exceeded, the counter overflows and continues to count starting with -sys.maxint - 1.)

cycle(*iterable*)

Creates an iterator that cycles over the elements in *iterable* over and over again. Internally, a copy of the elements in *iterable* is made. This copy is used to return the repeated items in the cycle.

dropwhile(*predicate, iterable*)

Creates an iterator that discards items from *iterable* as long as the function *predicate(item)* is True. Once *predicate* returns False, that item and all subsequent items in *iterable* are produced.

groupby(*iterable* [, *key*])

Creates an iterator that groups consecutive items produced by *iterable*. The grouping process works by looking for duplicate items. For instance, if *iterable* produces the same item on several consecutive iterations, that defines a group. If this is applied to a sorted list, the groups would define all the unique items in the list. *key*, if supplied, is a function that is applied to each item. If present, the return value of this function is used to compare successive items instead of the items themselves. The iterator returned by this function produces tuples *(key, group)*, where *key* is the key value for the group and *group* is an iterator that yields all the items that made up the group.

ifilter(*predicate, iterable*)

Creates an iterator that only produces items from *iterable* for which *predicate(item)* is True. If *predicate* is None, all the items in *iterable* that evaluate as True are returned.

ifilterfalse(*predicate, iterable*)

Creates an iterator that only produces items from *iterable* for which *predicate(item)* is False. If *predicate* is None, all the items in *iterable* that evaluate as False are returned.

`imap(`*`function,`* `iter1, iter2,` `...,` `iterN)`

Creates an iterator that produces items *function*(*i1,i2,* `..` *iN*), where *i1, i2, ...,*
iN are items taken from the iterators *iter1, iter2, ..., iterN*, respectively. If *function*
is None, the tuples of the form (*i1,* *i2,* `...,` *iN*) are returned. Iteration stops
whenever one of the supplied iterators no longer produces any values.

`islice(`*`iterable,`* `[start,]` *`stop`* `[,` *`step`*`])`

Creates an iterator that produces items in a manner similar to what would be returned
by a slice, *iterable*[*start*:*stop*:*step*]. The first *start* items are skipped and iteration stops at the position specified in *stop*. *step* specifies a stride that's used to skip
items. Unlike slices, negative values may not be used for any of *start*, *stop*, or *step*.
If *start* is omitted, iteration starts at 0. If *step* is omitted, a step of 1 is used.

`izip(`*`iter1, iter2,`* `...` *`iterN`*`)`

Creates an iterator that produces tuples (*i1,* *i2,* `...,` *iN*), where *i1, i2, ..., iN* are
taken from the iterators *iter1, iter2, ..., iterN*, respectively. Iteration stops whenever
one of the supplied iterators no longer produces any values. This function produces the
same values as the built-in `zip()` function.

`izip_longest(`*`iter1, iter2,`* `...,` *`iterN`* `[,fillvalue=None])`

The same as `izip()` except that iteration continues until all of the input iterables
iter1, iter2, and so on are exhausted. None is used to fill in values for the iterables
that are already consumed unless a different value is specified with the `fillvalue` keyword argument.

`permutations(`*`iterable`* `[,` *`r`*`])`

Creates an iterator that returns all *r*-length permutations of items from *iterable*. If *r*
is omitted, then permutations have the same length as the number of items in
iterable.

`product(`*`iter1, iter2,`* `...` *`iterN,`* `[repeat=1])`

Creates an iterator that produces tuples representing the Cartesian product of items in
item1, item2, and so on. *repeat* is a keyword argument that specifies the number of
times to repeat the produced sequence.

`repeat(`*`object`* `[,` *`times`*`])`

Creates an iterator that repeatedly produces *object*. *times*, if supplied, specifies a
repeat count. Otherwise, the object is returned indefinitely.

`starmap(`*`func`* `[,` *`iterable`*`])`

Creates an iterator that produces the values *func*(`*`*item*), where *item* is taken from
iterable. This only works if *iterable* produces items suitable for calling a function
in this manner.

`takewhile(`*`predicate`* `[,` *`iterable`*`])`

Creates an iterator that produces items from *iterable* as long as *predicate*(*item*) is
True. Iteration stops immediately once *predicate* evaluates as False.

```
tee(iterable [, n])
```

Creates *n* independent iterators from `iterable`. The created iterators are returned as an n-tuple. The default value of *n* is 2. This function works with any iterable object. However, in order to clone the original iterator, the items produced are cached and used in all the newly created iterators. Great care should be taken not to use the original iterator `iterable` after `tee()` has been called. Otherwise, the caching mechanism may not work correctly.

Examples

The following examples illustrate how some of the functions in the `itertools` module operate:

```
from itertools import *
# Iterate over the numbers 0,1,...,10,9,8,...,1 in an endless cycle
for i in cycle(chain(range(10),range(10,0,-1))):
    print i

# Create a list of unique items in a
a = [1,4,5,4,9,1,2,3,4,5,1]
a.sort()
b = [k for k,g in groupby(a)]    # b = [1,2,3,4,5,9]

# Iterate over all possible combinations of pairs of values from x and y
x = [1,2,3,4,5]
y = [10,11,12]
for r in product(x,y):
    print(r)
# Produces output (1,10),(1,11),(1,12), ... (5,10),(5,11),(5,12)
```

operator

The `operator` module provides functions that access the built-in operators and special methods of the interpreter described in Chapter 3, "Types and Objects." For example, `add(3, 4)` is the same as `3 + 4`. For operations that also have an in-place version, you can use a function such as `iadd(x,y)` which is the same as `x += y`. The following list shows functions defined in the `operator` module and how they are mapped onto various operators:

Function	Description
add(*a*, *b*)	Returns *a* + *b* for numbers
sub(*a*, *b*)	Returns *a* - *b*
mul(*a*, *b*)	Returns *a* * *b* for numbers
div(*a*, *b*)	Returns *a* / *b* (old division)
floordiv(*a*, *b*)	Returns *a* // *b*
truediv(*a*, *b*)	Returns *a* / *b* (new division)
mod(*a*, *b*)	Returns *a* % *b*
neg(*a*)	Returns -*a*
pos(*a*)	Returns +*a*
abs(*a*)	Returns the absolute value of *a*
inv(*a*), invert(*a*)	Returns the inverse of *a*

continues

Function	Description
lshift(a, b)	Returns a << b
rshift(a, b)	Returns a >> b
and_(a, b)	Returns a & b (bitwise AND)
or_(a, b)	Returns a | b (bitwise OR)
xor(a, b)	Returns a ^ b (bitwise XOR)
not_(a)	Returns not a
lt(a, b)	Returns a < b
le(a, b)	Returns a <= b
eq(a, b)	Returns a == b
ne(a, b)	Returns a != b
gt(a, b)	Returns a > b
ge(a, b)	Returns a >= b
truth(a)	Returns True if a is true, False otherwise
concat(a, b)	Returns a + b for sequences
repeat(a, b)	Returns a * b for sequence a and integer b
contains(a, b)	Returns the result of b in a
countOf(a, b)	Returns the number of occurrences of b in a
indexOf(a, b)	Returns the index of the first occurrence of b in a
getitem(a, b)	Returns a [b]
setitem(a, b, c)	a [b] = c
delitem(a, b)	del a [b]
getslice(a, b, c)	Returns a[b:c]
setslice(a, b, c, v)	Sets a[b:c] = v
delslice(a, b, c)	del a[b:c]
is_(a, b)	a is b
is_not(a, b)	a is not b

At first glance, it might not be obvious why anyone would want to use these functions because the operations they perform can easily be accomplished by simply typing the normal syntax. Where these functions are useful is when working with code uses call-back functions and where you might otherwise be defining an anonymous function with lambda. For example, consider the following timing benchmark that uses the functools.reduce() function:

```
>>> from timeit import timeit
>>> timeit("reduce(operator.add,a)","import operator; a = range(100)")
12.055853843688965
>>> timeit("reduce(lambda x,y: x+y,a)","import operator; a = range(100)")
25.012306928634644
>>>
```

In the example, notice how using operator.add as the callback runs more than twice as fast as the version that uses lambda x,y: x+y.

The operator module also defines the following functions that create wrappers around attribute access, item lookup, and method calls.

attrgetter(*name* [, *name2* [, ... [, *nameN*]]])

Creates a callable object, f, where a call to f(*obj*) returns *obj*.*name*. If more than one argument is given, a tuple of results is returned. For example, attrgetter('name','shares') returns (*obj*.name, *obj*.shares) when called. *name* can also include additional dot lookups. For example, if *name* is "address.hostname", then f(*obj*) returns *obj*.address.hostname.

itemgetter(*item* [, *item2* [, ... [, *itemN*]]])

Creates a callable object, f, where a call to f(*obj*) returns *obj*[*item*]. If more than one item is given as arguments, a call to f(*obj*) returns a tuple containing (*obj*[*item*], *obj*[*item2*], ..., *obj*[*itemN*]).

methodcaller(*name* [, **args* [, ***kwargs*]])

Creates a callable object, f, where a call to f(*obj*) returns *obj*.name(**args*, ***kwargs*).

These functions are also useful for optimizing the performance of operations involving callback function, especially those involving common data processing operations such as sorting. For example, if you wanted to sort a list of tuples *rows* on column 2, you could either use sorted(*rows*, key=lambda r: r[2]) or use sorted(*rows*, key=itemgetter(2)). The second version runs much faster because it avoids the overhead associated with lambda.

## 16

String and Text Handling

This chapter describes the most commonly used Python modules related to basic string and text processing. The focus of this chapter is on the most common string operations such as processing text, regular expression pattern matching, and text formatting.

codecs

The codecs module is used to handle different character encodings used with Unicode text I/O. The module is used both to define new character encodings and to process character data using a wide range of existing encodings such as UTF-8, UTF-16, etc. It is far more common for programmers to simply use one of the existing encodings, so that is what is discussed here. If you want to create new encodings, consult the online documentation for further details.

Low-Level codecs Interface

Each character encoding is assigned a common name such as 'utf-8' or 'big5'. The following function is used to perform a lookup.

`lookup(encoding)`

Looks up a codec in the codec registry. encoding is a string such as 'utf-8'. If nothing is known about the requested encoding, LookupError is raised. Otherwise, an instance c of CodecInfo is returned.

A CodecInfo instance c has the following methods:

`c.encode(s [, errors])`

A stateless encoding function that encodes the Unicode string s and returns a tuple (bytes, length_consumed). bytes is an 8-bit string or byte-array containing the encoded data. length_consumed is the number of characters in s that were encoded. errors is the error handling policy and is set to 'strict' by default.

`c.decode(bytes [, errors])`

A stateless encoding function that decodes a byte string bytes and returns a tuple (s, length_consumed). s is a Unicode string, and length_consumed is the number of bytes in bytes that were consumed during decoding. errors is the error-handling policy and is set to 'strict' by default.

c.streamreader(*bytestream* [, *errors*])

Returns a StreamReader instance that is used to read encoded data. *bytestream* is a file-like object that has been opened in binary mode. *errors* is the error-handling policy and is 'strict' by default. An instance *r* of StreamReader supports the following low-level I/O operations:

Method	Description
r.read([*size* [, *chars* [, *firstline*]]])	Returns at most *chars* characters of decoded text. *size* is the maximum number of bytes to read from low-level byte-stream and is used to control internal buffering. *firstline* is a flag that, if set, returns the first line even if a decoding error occurs later in the file.
r.readline([*size* [, *keepends*]])	Returns a single line of decoded text. *keepends* is a flag that controls whether or not the line endings are preserved (true by default).
r.readlines([*size* [, *keepends*]])	Reads all of the lines into a list.
r.reset()	Resets the internal buffers and state.

c.streamwriter(*bytestream* [, *errors*])

Returns a StreamWriter instance that is used to write encoded data. *bytestream* is a file-like object that has been opened in byte-mode. *errors* is the error handling policy and is 'strict' by default. An instance *w* of StreamWriter supports the following low-level I/O operations:

Method	Description
w.write(s)	Writes an encoded representation of string *s*
w.writelines(*lines*)	Writes a list of strings in *lines* to the file
w.reset()	Resets the internal buffers and state

c.incrementalencoder([*errors*])

Returns an IncrementalEncoder instance that can be used to encode strings in multiple steps. *errors* is 'strict' by default. An instance *e* of IncrementalEncoder has these methods:

Method	Description
e.encode(s [,*final*])	Returns an encoded representation of string *s* as a byte string. *final* is a flag that should be set to True on the final call to encode().
e.reset()	Resets the internal buffers and state.

`c.incrementaldecoder([errors])`

Returns an `IncrementalDecoder` instance that can be used to decode byte strings in multiple steps. *errors* is `'strict'` by default. An instance *d* of `IncrementalDecoder` has these methods:

Method	Description
`d.decode(bytes [,final])`	Returns a decoded string from the encoded bytes in *bytes*. *final* is a flag that should be set to `True` on the final call to `decode()`.
`d.reset()`	Resets the internal buffers and state.

I/O-Related Functions

The `codecs` module provides a collection of high-level functions that are used to simplify I/O involving encoded text. Most programmers will use one of these functions instead of the low-level codecs interface described in the first section.

`open(filename, mode[, encoding[, errors[, buffering]]])`

Opens *filename* in the given *mode* and provides transparent data encoding/decoding according to the encoding specified in *encoding*. *errors* is one of `'strict'`, `'ignore'`, `'replace'`, `'backslashreplace'`, or `'xmlcharrefreplace'`. The default is `'strict'`. *buffering* has the same meaning as for the built-in `open()` function. Regardless of the mode specified in *mode*, the underlying file is always opened in binary mode. In Python 3, you can use the built-in `open()` function instead of `codecs.open()`.

`EncodedFile(file, inputenc[, outputenc [, errors]])`

A class that provides an encoding wrapper around an existing file object, *file*. Data written to the file is first interpreted according to the input encoding *inputenc* and then written to the file using the output encoding *outputenc*. Data read from the file is decoded according to *inputenc*. If *outputenc* is omitted, it defaults to *inputenc*. *errors* has the same meaning as for `open()` and defaults to `'strict'`.

`iterencode(iterable, encoding [, errors])`

A generator function that incrementally encodes all of the strings in *iterable* to the specified *encoding*. *errors* is `'strict'` by default.

`iterdecode(iterable, encoding [, errors])`

A generator function that incrementally decodes all of the byte strings in *iterable* according to the specified *encoding*. *errors* is `'strict'` by default.

Useful Constants

`codecs` defines the following byte-order marker constants that can be used to help interpret files when you don't know anything about the underlying encoding. These byte-order markers are sometimes written at the beginning of a file to indicate its character encoding and can be used to pick an appropriate codec to use.

Constant	Description
BOM	Native byte-order marker for the machine (BOM_BE or BOM_LE)
BOM_BE	Big-endian byte-order marker ('\xfe\xff')
BOM_LE	Little-endian byte-order marker ('\xff\xfe')
BOM_UTF8	UTF-8 marker ('\xef\xbb\xbf')
BOM_UTF16_BE	16-bit UTF-16 big-endian marker ('\xfe\xff')
BOM_UTF16_LE	16-bit UTF-16 little-endian marker ('\xff\xfe')
BOM_UTF32_BE	32-bit UTF-32 big-endian marker ('\x00\x00\xfe\xff')
BOM_UTF32_LE	32-bit UTF-32 little-endian marker ('\xff\xfe\x00\x00')

Standard Encodings

The following is a list of some of the most commonly used character encodings. The encoding name is what you would pass to functions such as open() or lookup() when specifying an encoding. A full list of encodings can be found by consulting the online documentation for the codecs module (http://docs.python.org/library/codecs).

Codec Name	Description
ascii	7-bit ASCII characters
cp437	Extended ASCII character set from MS-DOS
cp1252	Extended ASCII character set from Windows
latin-1, iso-8859-1	ASCII extended with Latin characters
utf-16	UTF-16
utf-16-be	UTF-16 big-endian
utf-16-le	UTF-16 little-endian
utf-32	UTF-32
utf-32-be	UTF-32 big-endian
utf-32-le	UTF-32 little-endian
utf-8	UTF-8

Notes

- Further use of the codecs module is described in Chapter 9, "Input and Output."
- Consult the online documentation for information on how to create new kinds of character encodings.
- Great care needs to be taken with the inputs to encode() and decode() operations. All encode() operations should be given Unicode strings, and all decode() operations should be given byte strings. Python 2 is not entirely consistent in this regard, whereas Python 3 strictly enforces the distinction between strings. For example, Python 2 has some codecs that map byte-strings to byte-strings (e.g., the "bz2" codec). These are unavailable in Python 3 and should not be used if you care about compatibility.

re

The re module is used to perform regular-expression pattern matching and replacement in strings. Both unicode and byte-strings are supported. Regular-expression patterns are specified as strings containing a mix of text and special-character sequences. Because patterns often make extensive use of special characters and the backslash, they're usually written as "raw" strings, such as r'(?P<int>\d+)\.(\d*)'. For the remainder of this section, all regular-expression patterns are denoted using the raw string syntax.

Pattern Syntax

The following special-character sequences are recognized in regular expression patterns:

Character(s)	Description
text	Matches the literal string text.
.	Matches any character except newline.
^	Matches the start of a string.
$	Matches the end of a string.
*	Matches zero or more repetitions of the preceding expression, matching as many repetitions as possible.
+	Matches one or more repetitions of the preceding expression, matching as many repetitions as possible.
?	Matches zero repetitions or one repetition of the preceding expression.
*?	Matches zero or more repetitions of the preceding expression, matching as few repetitions as possible.
+?	Matches one or more repetitions of the preceding expression, matching as few repetitions as possible.
??	Matches zero or one repetitions of the preceding expression, matching as few repetitions as possible.
{m}	Matches exactly m repetitions of the preceding expression.
{m, n}	Matches from m to n repetitions of the preceding expression, matching as many repetitions as possible. If m is omitted, it defaults to 0. If n is omitted, it defaults to infinity.
{m, n}?	Matches from m to n repetitions of the preceding expression, matching as few repetitions as possible.
[...]	Matches a set of characters such as r'[abcdef]' or r'[a-zA-z]'. Special characters such as * are not active inside a set.
[^...]	Matches the characters not in the set, such as r'[^0-9]'.
A|B	Matches either A or B, where A and B are both regular expressions.
(...)	Matches the regular expression inside the parentheses as a group and saves the matched substring. The contents of a group can be obtained using the group() method of MatchObject objects obtained while matching.

continues

Character(s)	Description
`(?aiLmsux)`	Interprets the letters `"a"`, `"i"`, `"L"`, `"m"`, `"s"`, `"u"`, and `"x"` as flag settings corresponding to the `re.A`, `re.I`, `re.L`, `re.M`, `re.S`, `re.U`, `re.X` flag settings given to `re.compile()`. `"a"` only available in Python 3.
`(?:...)`	Matches the regular expression inside the parentheses but discards the matched substring.
`(?P<name>...)`	Matches the regular expression in the parentheses and creates a named group. The group name must be a valid Python identifier.
`(?P=name)`	Matches the same text that was matched by an earlier named group.
`(?#...)`	A comment. The contents of the parentheses are ignored.
`(?=...)`	Matches the preceding expression only if followed by the pattern in the parentheses. For example, `r'Hello (?=World)'` matches `'Hello '` only if followed by `'World'`.
`(?!...)`	Matches the preceding expression only if it's *not* followed by the pattern in parentheses. For example, `r'Hello (?!World)'` matches `'Hello '` only if it's not followed by `'World'`.
`(?<=...)`	Matches the following expression if it's preceded by a match of the pattern in parentheses. For example, `r'(?<=abc)def'` matches `'def'` only if it's preceded by `'abc'`.
`(?<!...)`	Matches the following expression only if it's *not* preceded by a match of the pattern in parentheses. For example, `r'(?<!abc)def'` matches `'def'` only if it's not preceded by `'abc'`.
`(?(id|name)ypat|npat)`	Checks to see whether the regular expression group identified by `id` or `name` exists. If so, the regular expression `ypat` is matched. If not, the optional expression `npat` is matched. For example, the pattern `r'(Hello)?(?(1) World|Howdy)'` matches the string `'Hello World'` or the string `'Howdy'`.

Standard character escape sequences such as `'\n'` and `'\t'` are recognized as standard characters in a regular expression (for example, `r'\n+'` would match one or more newline characters). In addition, literal symbols that normally have special meaning in a regular expression can be specified by preceding them with a backslash. For example, `r'\*'` matches the character `*`. In addition, a number of backslash sequences correspond to special sets of characters:

Character(s)	Description
`\number`	Matches the text that was matched by a previous group number. Groups are numbered from 1 to 99, starting from the left.
`\A`	Matches only at the start of the string.
`\b`	Matches the empty string at the beginning or end of a word. A *word* is a sequence of alphanumeric characters terminated by whitespace or any other nonalphanumeric character.

Character(s)	Description
\B	Matches the empty string not at the beginning or end of a word.
\d	Matches any decimal digit. Same as `r'[0-9]'`.
\D	Matches any nondigit character. Same as `r'[^0-9]'`.
\s	Matches any whitespace character. Same as `r'[\t\n\r\f\v]'`.
\S	Matches any nonwhitespace character. Same as `r'[^ \t\n\r\f\v]'`.
\w	Matches any alphanumeric character.
\W	Matches any character not contained in the set defined by \w.
\Z	Matches only at the end of the string.
\\	Matches a literal backslash.

The \d, \D, \s, \S, \w, and \W special characters are interpreted differently if matching Unicode strings. In this case, they match all Unicode characters that match the described property. For example, \d matches any Unicode character that is classified as a digit such as European, Arabic, and Indic digits which each occupy a different range of Unicode characters.

Functions

The following functions are used to perform pattern matching and replacement:

`compile(pattern [, flags])`

Compiles a regular-expression pattern string into a regular-expression object. This object can be passed as the pattern argument to all the functions that follow. The object also provides a number of methods that are described shortly. `flags` is the bitwise OR of the following:

Flag	Description
A or ASCII	Perform 8-bit ASCII-only matching (Python 3 only).
I or IGNORECASE	Performs non–case-sensitive matching.
L or LOCALE	Uses locale settings for \w, \W, \b, and \B.
M or MULTILINE	Makes ^ and $ apply to each line in addition to the beginning and end of the entire string. (Normally ^ and $ apply only to the beginning and end of an entire string.)
S or DOTALL	Makes the dot (.) character match all characters, including the newline.
U or UNICODE	Uses information from the Unicode character properties database for \w, \W, \b, and \B. (Python 2 only. Python 3 uses Unicode by default.)
X or VERBOSE	Ignores unescaped whitespace and comments in the pattern string.

`escape(string)`

Returns a string with all nonalphanumerics backslashed.

`findall(pattern, string [,flags])`

Returns a list of all nonoverlapping matches of `pattern` in `string`, including empty matches. If the pattern has groups, a list of the text matched by the groups is returned.

If more than one group is used, each item in the list is a tuple containing the text for each group. *flags* has the same meaning as for `compile()`.

finditer(*pattern*, *string*, [, *flags*])

The same as `findall()`, but returns an iterator object instead. The iterator returns items of type `MatchObject`.

match(*pattern*, *string* [, *flags*])

Checks whether zero or more characters at the beginning of *string* match *pattern*. Returns a `MatchObject` on success or `None` otherwise. *flags* has the same meaning as for `compile()`.

search(*pattern*, *string* [, *flags*])

Searches *string* for the first match of *pattern*. *flags* has the same meaning as for `compile()`. Returns a `MatchObject` on success or `None` if no match was found.

split(*pattern*, *string* [, *maxsplit* = 0])

Splits *string* by the occurrences of *pattern*. Returns a list of strings including the text matched by any groups in the pattern. *maxsplit* is the maximum number of splits to perform. By default, all possible splits are performed.

sub(*pattern*, *repl*, *string* [, *count* = 0])

Replaces the leftmost nonoverlapping occurrences of *pattern* in *string* by using the replacement *repl*. *repl* can be a string or a function. If it's a function, it's called with a `MatchObject` and should return the replacement string. If *repl* is a string, back-references such as `'\6'` are used to refer to groups in the pattern. The sequence `'\g<name>'` is used to refer to a named group. *count* is the maximum number of substitutions to perform. By default, all occurrences are replaced. Although these functions don't accept a *flags* parameter like `compile()`, the same effect can be achieved by using the `(?iLmsux)` notation described earlier in this section.

subn(*pattern*, *repl*, *string* [, *count* = 0])

Same as `sub()`, but returns a tuple containing the new string and the number of substitutions.

Regular Expression Objects

A compiled regular-expression object, *r*, created by the `compile()` function has the following methods and attributes:

r.flags

The *flags* argument used when the regular expression object was compiled, or 0 if no flags were specified.

r.groupindex

A dictionary mapping symbolic group names defined by `r'(?P<id>)'` to group numbers.

r.pattern

The pattern string from which the regular expression object was compiled.

`r.findall(`*`string`* `[, `*`pos`* `[, `*`endpos`*`]])`

Identical to the `findall()` function. *pos* and *endpos* specify the starting and ending positions for the search.

`r.finditer(`*`string`* `[, `*`pos`* `[, `*`endpos`*`]])`

Identical to the `finditer()` function. *pos* and *endpos* specify the starting and ending positions for the search.

`r.match(`*`string`* `[, `*`pos`*`] [, `*`endpos`*`])`

Checks whether zero or more characters at the beginning of *string* match. *pos* and *endpos* specify the range of *string* to be searched. Returns a `MatchObject` for a match and returns `None` otherwise.

`r.search(`*`string`* `[, `*`pos`*`] [, `*`endpos`*`])`

Searches *string* for a match. *pos* and *endpos* specify the starting and ending positions for the search. Returns a `MatchObject` for a match and returns `None` otherwise.

`r.split(`*`string`* `[, `*`maxsplit`* `= 0])`

Identical to the `split()` function.

`r.sub(`*`repl`*`, `*`string`* `[, `*`count`* `= 0])`

Identical to the `sub()` function.

`r.subn(`*`repl`*`, `*`string`* `[, `*`count`* `= 0])`

Identical to the `subn()` function.

Match Objects

The `MatchObject` instances returned by `search()` and `match()` contain information about the contents of groups as well as positional data about where matches occurred. A `MatchObject` instance, *m*, has the following methods and attributes:

`m.expand(`*`template`*`)`

Returns a string that would be obtained by doing regular-expression backslash substitution on the string *template*. Numeric back-references such as `"\1"` and `"\2"` and named references such as `"\g<n>"` and `"\g<name>"` are replaced by the contents of the corresponding group. Note that these sequences should be specified using raw strings or with a literal backslash character such as `r'\1'` or `'\\1'`.

`m.group(`*`[group1, group2, ...]`*`)`

Returns one or more subgroups of the match. The arguments specify group numbers or group names. If no group name is given, the entire match is returned. If only one group is given, a string containing the text matched by the group is returned. Otherwise, a tuple containing the text matched by each of the requested groups is returned. An `IndexError` is raised if an invalid group number or name is given.

`m.groups(`*`[default]`*`)`

Returns a tuple containing the text matched by all groups in a pattern. *default* is the value returned for groups that didn't participate in the match (the default is `None`).

m.groupdict([default])

Returns a dictionary containing all the named subgroups of the match. *default* is the value returned for groups that didn't participate in the match (the default is None).

m.start([group])
m.end([group])

These two methods return the indices of the start and end of the substring matched by a group. If *group* is omitted, the entire matched substring is used. Returns None if the group exists but didn't participate in the match.

m.span([group])

Returns a 2-tuple (m.start(group), m.end(group)). If *group* didn't contribute to the match, this returns (None, None). If *group* is omitted, the entire matched substring is used.

m.pos

The value of *pos* passed to the search() or match() function.

m.endpos

The value of *endpos* passed to the search() or match() function.

m.lastindex

The numerical index of the last group that was matched. It's None if no groups were matched.

m.lastgroup

The name of the last named group that was matched. It's None if no named groups were matched or present in the pattern.

m.re

The regular-expression object whose match() or search() method produced this MatchObject instance.

m.string

The string passed to match() or search().

Example

The following example shows how to use the re module to search for, extract data from, and replace a text pattern in a string.

```
import re
text = "Guido will be out of the office from 12/15/2012 - 1/3/2013."

# A regex pattern for a date.
datepat = re.compile('(\d+)/(\d+)/(\d+)')

# Find and print all dates
for m in datepat.finditer(text):
    print(m.group())
```

```
# Find all dates, but print in a different format
monthnames = [None,'Jan','Feb','Mar','Apr','May','Jun',
              'Jul','Aug','Sep','Oct','Nov','Dec']
for m in datepat.finditer(text):
    print ("%s %s, %s" % (monthnames[int(m.group(1)], m.group(2), m.group(3)))

# Replace all dates with fields in the European format (day/month/year)
def fix_date(m):
    return "%s/%s/%s" % (m.group(2),m.group(1),m.group(3))
newtext = datepat.sub(fix_date, text)

# An alternative replacement
newtext = datepat.sub(r'\2/\1/\3', text)
```

Notes

- Detailed information about the theory and implementation of regular expressions
  can be found in textbooks on compiler construction. The book *Mastering Regular
  Expressions* by Jeffrey Friedl (O'Reilly & Associates, 1997) may also be useful.
- The most difficult part of using the re module is writing the regular expression
  patterns. For writing patterns, consider using a tool such as Kodos
  (http://kodos.sourceforget.net).

string

The string module contains a number of useful constants and functions for manipulating strings. It also contains classes for implementing new string formatters.

Constants

The following constants define various sets of characters that may be useful in various string processing operations.

Constant	Description
ascii_letters	A string containing all lowercase and uppercase ASCII letters.
ascii_lowercase	The string `'abcdefghijklmnopqrstuvwxyz'`.
ascii_uppercase	The string `'ABCDEFGHIJKLMNOPQRSTUVWXYZ'`.
digits	The string `'0123456789'`.
hexdigits	The string `'0123456789abcdefABCDEF'`.
letters	Concatenation of `lowercase` and `uppercase`.
lowercase	String containing all lowercase letters specific to the current locale setting.
octdigits	The string `'01234567'`.
punctuation	String of ASCII punctuation characters.
printable	String of printable characters—a combination of `letters`, `digits`, `punctuation`, and `whitespace`.
uppercase	String containing all uppercase letters specific to the current locale setting.
whitespace	String containing all whitespace characters. This usually includes space, tab, linefeed, return, formfeed, and vertical tab.

Note that some of these constants (for example, `letters` and `uppercase`) will vary depending on the locale settings of the system.

Formatter **Objects**

The `str.format()` method of strings is used to perform advanced string formatting operations. As seen in Chapter 3, "Types and Objects," and Chapter 4, "Operators and Expressions," this method can access items of sequences or mappings, attributes of objects, and other kinds of related operations. The `string` module defines a class `Formatter` that can be used to implement your own customized formatting operation. This class exposes the pieces that implement the string formatting operation and allow you to customize them.

`Formatter()`

Creates a new `Formatter` instance. An instance `f` of `Formatter` supports the following operations.

`f.format(format_string, *args, **kwargs)`

Formats the string `format_string`. By default, the output is the same as calling `format_string.format(*args, **kwargs)`. For example, `f.format("{name} is {0:d} years old", 39,name="Dave")` creates the string `"Dave is 39 years old"`.

`f.vformat(format_string, args, kwargs)`

A method that actually carries out the work of `f.format()`. `args` is a tuple of positional arguments, and `kwargs` is a dictionary of keyword arguments. This is a faster method to use if you have already captured argument information in a tuple and dictionary.

`f.parse(format_string)`

A function that creates an iterator for parsing the contents of the format string `format_string`. The iterator sweeps over the format string and produces tuples of the format (`literal_text, field_name, format_spec, conversion`). `literal_text` is any literal text that precedes the next format specifier enclosed in braces { ... }. It may be an empty string if there is no leading text. `field_name` is a string that specifies the field name in the format specifier. For example, if the specifier is `'{0:d}'`, then the field name is `'0'`. `format_spec` is the format specifier that appears after the colon—for example, `'d'` in the previous example. It will be an empty string if it wasn't specified. `conversion` is a string containing the conversion specifier (if any). In the previous example, it is `None`, but if the specifier was `'{0!s:d}'`, it would be set to `'s'`. `field_name`, `format_spec`, and `conversion` will all be `None` for the last fragment of the format string.

`f.get_field(fieldname, args, kwargs)`

Extracts the value associated with a given `fieldname` from `args` and `kwargs`. `fieldname` is a string such as `"0"` or `"name"` as returned by the `parse()` method shown previously. Returns a tuple (`value, key`) where `value` is the field value and `key` is used to locate the value in `args` or `kwargs`. If `key` is an integer, it is an index in `args`. If it is a string, it is the key used in `kwargs`. The fieldname may include additional indexing and attribute lookup such as `'0.name'` or `'0[name]'`. In this case, the method carries out the extra lookup and returns the appropriate value. However, the value of *key* in the returned tuple is just set to '0'.

f.get_value(*key*, *args*, *kwargs*)

Extracts the object from *args* or *kwargs* corresponding to *key*. If *key* is an integer, the object is taken from *args*. If it is a string, it is taken from *kwargs*.

f.check_unused_args(*used_args*, *args*, *kwargs*)

Checks for unused arguments in the format() operation. *used_args* is a set of all of the used argument keys (see get_field()) that were found in the format string. *args* and *kwargs* are the positional and keyword arguments passed to format(). The default behavior is to raise a TypeError for unused arguments.

f.format_value(*value*, *format_spec*)

Formats a single value according to the given format specification. By default, this simply executes the built-in function format(*value*, *format_spec*).

f.convert_field(*value*, *conversion*)

Converts a *value* returned by get_field() according to the specified conversion code. If *conversion* is None, *value* is returned unmodified. If conversion is 's' or 'r', *value* is converted to a string using str() or repr(), respectively.

If you want to create your own customized string formatting, you can create a Formatter object and simply use the default methods to carry out the formatting as you wish. It is also possible to define a new class that inherits from Formatter and reimplements any of the methods shown earlier.

For details on the syntax of format specifiers and advanced string formatting, refer to Chapter 3 and Chapter 4.

Template **Strings**

The string module defines a new string type, Template, that simplifies certain string substitutions. An example can be found in Chapter 9.

The following creates a new template string object:

Template(*s*)

Here, *s* is a string and Template is defined as a class.

A Template object, *t*, supports the following methods:

t.substitute(*m* [, **kwargs*])

This method takes a mapping object, *m* (for example, a dictionary), or a list of keyword arguments and performs a keyword substitution on the string *t*. This substitution replaces the string '$$' with a single '$' and the strings '$*key*' or '${*key*}' with *m*['*key*'] or *kwargs*['*key*'] if keyword arguments were supplied. *key* must spell a valid Python identifier. If the final string contains any unresolved '$*key*' patterns, a KeyError exception is raised.

t.safe_substitute(*m* [, **kwargs*])

The same as substitute() except that no exceptions or errors will be generated. Instead, unresolved $*key* references will be left in the string unmodified.

t.template

Contains the original strings passed to `Template()`.

The behavior of the `Template` class can be modified by subclassing it and redefining the attributes `delimiter` and `idpattern`. For example, this code changes the escape character $ to @ and restricts key names to letters only:

```
class MyTemplate(string.Template):
    delimiter = '@'          # Literal character for escape sequence
    idpattern = '[A-Z]*'    # Identifier regular expression pattern
```

Utility Functions

The `string` module also defines a couple of functions for manipulating strings that aren't defined as a method on string objects.

capwords(*s*)

Capitalizes the first letter of each word in *s*, replaces repeated whitespace characters with a single space, and removes leading and trailing whitespace.

maketrans(*from, to*)

Creates a translation table that maps each character in *from* to the character in the same position in *to*. *from* and *to* must be the same length. This function is used to create arguments suitable for use with the `translate()` method of strings.

struct

The `struct` module is used to convert data between Python and binary data structures (represented as Python byte strings). These data structures are often used when interacting with functions written in C, binary file formats, network protocols, or binary communication over serial ports.

Packing and Unpacking Functions

The following module-level functions are used to pack and unpack data in byte strings. If your program is repeatedly performing these operations, consider the use of a `Struct` object described in the next section.

pack(*fmt, v1, v2, ...*)

Packs the values *v1*, *v2*, and so on into a byte string according to the format string in *fmt*.

pack_into(*fmt, buffer, offset, v1, v2 ...*)

Packs the values *v1*, *v2*, and so forth into a writable buffer object *buffer* starting at byte offset *offset*. This only works with objects that support the buffer interface. Examples include `array.array` and `bytearray` objects.

unpack(*fmt, string*)

Unpacks the contents of a byte *string* according to the format string in *fmt*. Returns a tuple of the unpacked values. The length of *string* must exactly match the size of the format as determined by the `calcsize()` function.

unpack_from(fmt, *buffer*, *offset*)

Unpacks the contents of a *buffer* object according to the format string in *fmt* starting at offset *offset*. Returns a tuple of the unpacked values.

calcsize(*fmt*)

Calculates the size in bytes of the structure corresponding to a format string *fmt*.

Struct **Objects**

The struct module defines a class Struct that provides an alternative interface for packing and unpacking. Using this class is more efficient because the format string is only interpreted once.

Struct(*fmt*)

Creates a Struct instance representing data packed according to the given format code. An instance s of Struct has the following methods that work exactly the same as their functional counterparts described in the previous section:

Method	Description
s.pack(*v1*, *v2*, ...)	Packs values into a byte string
s.pack_into(*buffer*, *offset*, *v1*, *v2*, ...)	Packs values into a buffer object
s.unpack(*bytes*)	Unpacks values from a byte string
s.unpack_from(*buffer*, *offset*)	Unpacks values from a buffer object
s.format	The format code being used
s.size	The size in bytes of the format

Format Codes

The format strings used in the struct module are a sequence of characters with the following interpretations:

Format	C Type	Python Type
'x'	pad byte	No value
'c'	char	String of length 1
'b'	signed char	Integer
'B'	unsigned char	Integer
'?'	_Bool (C99)	Boolean
'h'	short	Integer
'H'	unsigned short	Integer
'i'	int	Integer
'I'	unsigned int	Integer
'l'	long	Integer
'L'	unsigned long	Integer
'q'	long long	Long
'Q'	unsigned long long	Long

continues

Format	C Type	Python Type
'f'	float	Float
'd'	double	Float
's'	char[]	String
'p'	char[]	String with length encoded in the first byte
'P'	void *	Integer

Each format character can be preceded by an integer to indicate a repeat count (for example, '4i' is the same as 'iiii'). For the 's' format, the count represents the maximum length of the string, so '10s' represents a 10-byte string. A format of '0s' indicates a string of zero length. The 'p' format is used to encode a string in which the length appears in the first byte, followed by the string data. This is useful when dealing with Pascal code, as is sometimes necessary on the Macintosh. Note that the length of the string in this case is limited to 255 characters.

When the 'I' and 'L' formats are used to unpack a value, the return value is a Python long integer. In addition, the 'P' format may return an integer or long integer, depending on the word size of the machine.

The first character of each format string can also specify a byte ordering and alignment of the packed data, as shown here:

Format	Byte Order	Size and Alignment
'@'	Native	Native
'='	Native	Standard
'<'	Little-endian	Standard
'>'	Big-endian	Standard
'!'	Network (big-endian)	Standard

Native byte ordering may be little-endian or big-endian, depending on the machine architecture. The native sizes and alignment correspond to the values used by the C compiler and are implementation-specific. The standard alignment assumes that no alignment is needed for any type. The standard size assumes that short is 2 bytes, int is 4 bytes, long is 4 bytes, float is 32 bits, and double is 64 bits. The 'P' format can only use native byte ordering.

Notes

- Sometimes it's necessary to align the end of a structure to the alignment requirements of a particular type. To do this, end the structure-format string with the code for that type with a repeat count of zero. For example, the format '11h0l' specifies a structure that ends on a 4-byte boundary (assuming that longs are aligned on 4-byte boundaries). In this case, two pad bytes would be inserted after the short value specified by the 'h' code. This only works when native size and alignment are being used—standard size and alignment don't enforce alignment rules.

- The 'q' and 'Q' formats are only available in "native" mode if the C compiler used to build Python supports the long long data type.

See Also:
array (**p. 259**), ctypes (**p. 612**)

unicodedata

The unicodedata module provides access to the Unicode character database, which contains character properties for all Unicode characters.

bidirectional(*unichr*)

Returns the bidirectional category assigned to *unichr* as a string or an empty string if no such value is defined. Returns one of the following:

Value	Description
L	Left-to-Right
LRE	Left-to-Right embedding
LRO	Left-to-Right override
R	Right-to-Left
AL	Right-to-Left Arabic
RLE	Right-to-Left embedding
RLO	Right-to-Left override
PDF	Pop directional format
EN	European number
ES	European number separator
ET	European number terminator
AN	Arabic number
CS	Common number separator
NSM	Nonspacing mark
BN	Boundary neutral
B	Paragraph separator
S	Segment separator
WS	Whitespace
ON	Other neutrals

category(*unichr*)

Returns a string describing the general category of *unichr*. The returned string is one of the following values:

Value	Description
Lu	Letter, uppercase
Ll	Letter, lowercase
Lt	Letter, title case
Mn	Mark, nonspacing
Mc	Mark, spacing combining
Me	Mark, enclosing

continues

Value	Description
Nd	Number, decimal digit
Nl	Number, letter
No	Number, other
Zs	Separator, space
Zl	Separator, line
Zp	Separator, paragraph
Cc	Other, control
Cf	Other, format
Cs	Other, surrogate
Co	Other, private use
Cn	Other, not assigned
Lm	Letter, modifier
Lo	Letter, other
Pc	Punctuation, connector
Pd	Punctuation, dash
Ps	Punctuation, open
Pe	Punctuation, close
Pi	Punctuation, initial quote
Pf	Punctuation, final quote
Po	Punctuation, other
Sm	Symbol, math
Sc	Symbol, currency
Sk	Symbol, modifier
So	Symbol, other

`combining(unichr)`

Returns an integer describing the combining class for `unichr` or 0 if no combining class is defined. One of the following values is returned:

Value	Description
0	Spacing, split, enclosing, reordrant, and Tibetan subjoined
1	Overlays and interior
7	Nuktas
8	Hiragana/Katakana voicing marks
9	Viramas
10-199	Fixed-position classes
200	Below left attached
202	Below attached
204	Below right attached
208	Left attached
210	Right attached
212	Above left attached
214	Above attached
216	Above right attached

Value	Description
218	Below left
220	Below
222	Below right
224	Left
226	Right
228	Above left
230	Above
232	Above right
233	Double below
234	Double above
240	Below (iota subscript)

decimal(*unichr***[, ***default***])**

Returns the decimal integer value assigned to the character *unichr*. If *unichr* is not a decimal digit, *default* is returned or ValueError is raised.

decomposition(*unichr***)**

Returns a string containing the decomposition mapping of *unichr* or the empty string if no such mapping is defined. Typically, characters containing accent marks can be decomposed into multicharacter sequences. For example, decomposition(u"\u00fc") ("ü") returns the string "0075 0308" corresponding to the letter *u* and the umlaut (¨) accent mark. The string returned by this function may also include the following strings:

Value	Description
<font>	A font variant (for example, a blackletter form)
<noBreak>	A nonbreaking version of a space or hyphen
<initial>	An initial presentation form (Arabic)
<medial>	A medial presentation form (Arabic)
<final>	A final presentation form (Arabic)
<isolated>	An isolated presentation form (Arabic)
<circle>	An encircled form
<super>	A superscript form
<sub>	A subscript form
<vertical>	A vertical layout presentation form
<wide>	A wide (or zenkaku) compatibility character
<narrow>	A narrow (or hankaku) compatibility character
<small>	A small variant form (CNS compatibility)
<square>	A CJK squared-font variant
<fraction>	A vulgar fraction form
<compat>	Otherwise unspecified compatibility character

digit(*unichr***[, ***default***])**

Returns the integer digit value assigned to the character *unichr*. If *unichr* is not a digit, *default* is returned or ValueError is raised. This function differs from decimal() in that it works with characters that may represent digits but that are not decimal digits.

east_asian_width(unichr)

Returns the east Asian width assigned to unichr.

lookup(name)

Looks up a character by name. For example, lookup('COPYRIGHT SIGN') returns the corresponding Unicode character. Common names can be found at http://www.unicode.org/charts.

mirrored(unichr)

Returns 1 if unichr is a "mirrored" character in bidirectional text and returns 0 otherwise. A mirrored character is one whose appearance might be changed to appear properly if text is rendered in reverse order. For example, the character '(' is mirrored because it might make sense to flip it to ')' in cases where text is printed from right to left.

name(unichr [, default])

Returns the name of a Unicode character, unichr. Raises ValueError if no name is defined or returns default if provided. For example, name(u'\xfc') returns 'LATIN SMALL LETTER U WITH DIAERESIS'.

normalize(form, unistr)

Normalizes the Unicode string unistr according to normal form form. form is one of 'NFC', 'NFKC', 'NFD', or 'NFKD'. The normalization of a string partly pertains to the composition and decomposition of certain characters. For example, the Unicode string for the word "resumé" could be represented as u'resum\u00e9' or as the string u'resume\u0301'. In the first string, the accented character é is represented as a single character. In the second string, the accented character is represented by the letter e followed by a combining accent mark ('). 'NFC' normalization converts the string unistr so that all of the characters are fully composed (for example, é is a single character). 'NFD' normalization converts unistr so that characters are decomposed (for example, é is the letter e followed by an accent). 'NFKC' and 'NFKD' perform the same function as 'NFC' and 'NFD' except that they additionally transform certain characters that may be represented by more than one Unicode character value into a single standard value. For example, Roman numerals have their own Unicode character values but are also just represented by the Latin letters I, V, M, and so on. 'NFKC' and 'NFKD' would convert the special Roman numeral characters into their Latin equivalents.

numeric(unichr[, default])

Returns the value assigned to the Unicode character unichr as a floating-point number. If no numeric value is defined, default is returned or ValueError is raised. For example, the numeric value of U+2155 (the character for the fraction "1/5") is 0.2.

unidata_version

A string containing the Unicode database version used (for example, '5.1.0').

> **Note**
> For further details about the Unicode character database, see http://www.unicode.org.

17

Python Database Access

This chapter describes the programming interfaces that Python uses to interface with relational and hash table style databases. Unlike other chapters that describe specific library modules, the material in this chapter partly applies to third-party extensions. For example, if you want Python to interface with a MySQL or Oracle database, you would first have to download a third-party extension module. That module, in turn, would then follow the basic conventions described here.

Relational Database API Specification

For accessing relational databases, the Python community has developed a standard known as the *Python Database API Specification V2.0*, or PEP 249 for short (the formal description can be found at http://www.python.org/dev/peps/pep-249/). Specific database modules (e.g., MySQL, Oracle, and so on) follow this specification, but may add even more features. This section covers the essential elements needed to use it for most applications.

At a high level, the database API defines a set of functions and objects for connecting to a database server, executing SQL queries, and obtaining results. Two primary objects are used for this: a `Connection` object that manages the connection to the database and a `Cursor` object that is used to perform queries.

Connections

To connect to a database, every database module provides a module-level function `connect(parameters)`. The exact parameters depend on the database but typically include information such as the data source name, user name, password, host name, and database name. Typically these are provided with keyword arguments `dsn`, `user`, `password`, `host`, and `database`, respectively. So, a call to `connect()` might look like this:

```
connect(dsn="hostname:DBNAME",user="michael",password="peekaboo")
```

If successful, a `Connection` object is returned. An instance `c` of `Connection` has the following methods:

```
c.close()
```

Closes the connection to the server.

`c.commit()`

Commits all pending transactions to the database. If the database supports transactions, this must be called for any changes to take effect. If the underlying database does not support transactions, this method does nothing.

`c.rollback()`

Rolls back the database to the start of any pending transactions. This method is sometimes used in databases that do not support transactions in order to undo any changes made to the database. For example, if an exception occurred in code that was in the middle of updating a database, you might use this to undo changes made before the exception.

`c.cursor()`

Creates a new `Cursor` object that uses the connection. A cursor is an object that you will use to execute SQL queries and obtain results. This is described in the next section.

Cursors

In order to perform any operations on the database, you first create a connection `c` and then you call `c.cursor()` method to create a `Cursor` object. An instance `cur` of a `Cursor` has a number of standard methods and attributes that are used to execute queries:

`cur.callproc(procname [, parameters])`

Calls a stored procedure with name `procname`. `parameters`, which is a sequence of values that are used as the arguments to the procedure. The result of this function is a sequence with the same number of items as `parameters`. This sequence is a copy of `parameters` where the values of any output arguments have been replaced with their modified values after execution. If a procedure also produces an output set, it can be read using the `fetch*()` methods described next.

`cur.close()`

Closes the cursor, preventing any further operations on it.

`cur.execute(query [, parameters])`

Executes a query or command `query` on the database. `query` is a string containing the command (usually SQL), and `parameters` is either a sequence or mapping that is used to supply values to variables in the query string (this is described in the next section).

`cur.executemany(query [, parametersequence])`

Repeatedly executes a query or command. `query` is a query string, and `parametersquence` is a sequence of parameters. Each item in this sequence is a sequence or mapping object that you would have used with the `execute()` method shown earlier.

`cur.fetchone()`

Returns the next row of the result set produced by `execute()` or `executemany()`. The result is typically a list or tuple containing values for the different columns of the result. None is returned if there are no more rows available. An exception is raised if there is no pending result or if the previously executed operation didn't create a result set.

`cur.fetchmany([size])`

Returns a sequence of result rows (e.g., a list of tuples). `size` is the number of rows to return. If omitted, the value of `cur.arraysize` is used as a default. The actual number of rows returned may be less than requested. An empty sequence is returned if no more rows are available.

`cur.fetchall()`

Returns a sequence of all remaining result rows (e.g., a list of tuples).

`cur.nextset()`

Discards all remaining rows in the current result set and skips to the next result set (if any). Returns `None` if there are no more result sets; otherwise, a `True` value is returned and subsequent `fetch*()` operations return data from the new set.

`cur.setinputsize(sizes)`

Gives the cursor a hint about the parameters to be passed on subsequent `execute*()` methods. `sizes` is a sequence of type objects (described shortly) or integers which give the maximum expected string length for each parameter. Internally, this is used to pre-define memory buffers for creating the queries and commands sent to the database. Using this can speed up subsequent `execute*()` operations.

`cur.setoutputsize(size [, column])`

Sets the buffer size for a specific column in result sets. `column` is an integer index into the result row, and `size` is the number of bytes. A typical use of this method is to set limits on large database columns such as strings, BLOBs, and LONGs prior to making any `execute*()` calls. If `column` is omitted, it sets a limit for all columns in the result.

Cursors have a number of attributes that describe the current result set and give information about the cursor itself.

`cur.arraysize`

An integer that gives the default value used for the `fetchmany()` operation. This value may vary between database modules and may be initially set to a value that the module considers to be "optimal."

`cur.description`

A sequence of tuples that give information about each column in the current result set. Each tuple has the form (`name, type_code, display_size, internal_size, precision, scale, null_ok`). The first field is always defined and corresponds to the column name. The `type_code` can be used in comparisons involving the type objects described in the "Type Objects" section. The other fields may be set to `None` if they don't apply to the column.

`cur.rowcount`

The number of rows in the last result produced by one of the `execute*()` methods. If set to –1, it means that there is either no result set or that the row count can't be determined.

Although not required by the specification, the `Cursor` object in most database modules also implements the iteration protocol. In this case, a statement such as `for row in cur:` will iterate over the rows the result set created by the last `execute*()` method.

Here is a simple example showing how some of these operations are used with the `sqlite3` database module, which is a built-in library:

```python
import sqlite3
conn = sqlite3.connect("dbfile")
cur = conn.cursor()

# Example of a simple query
cur.execute("select name, shares, price from portfolio where account=12345")

# Looping over the results
while True:
    row = cur.fetchone()
        if not row: break
        # Process the row
        name, shares, price = row
        ...

# An alternative approach (using iteration)
cur.execute("select name, shares, price from portfolio where account=12345")
for name, shares, price in cur:
    # Process the row
    ...
```

Forming Queries

A critical part of using the database API involves forming SQL query strings to pass into the `execute*()` methods of cursor objects. Part of the problem here is that you need to fill in parts of the query string with parameters supplied by the user. For example, you might be inclined to write code like this:

```python
symbol = "AIG"
account = 12345

cur.execute("select shares from portfolio where name='%s' and account=%d" %
            (symbol, account))
```

Although this "works," you should never manually form queries using Python string operations like this. If you do, it opens up your code to a potential SQL injection attack—a vulnerability that someone can use to execute arbitrary statements on the database server. For example, in the previous code, someone might supply a value for `symbol` that looks like `"EVIL LAUGH'; drop table portfolio;--"` which probably does something other than what you anticipated.

All database modules provide their own mechanism for value substitution. For example, instead of forming the entire query as shown, you might do this instead:

```python
symbol  = "AIG"
account = 12345

cur.execute("select shares from portfolio where name=? and account=?",
            (symbol, account))
```

Here, the `'?'` placeholders are successively replaced with values from the tuple `(symbol, account)`. `'?'` can only be used for values, not other parts of the query, such as the command or table name.

Sadly, there is no standard convention for placeholders across database module implementations. However, each module defines a variable `paramstyle` that indicates the formatting of value substitutions to be used in queries. Possible values of this variable are as follows:

Parameter Style	Description
`'qmark'`	Question mark style where each `?` in the query is replaced by successive items in a sequence. For example, `cur.execute("... where name=? and account=?", (symbol, account))`. The parameters are specified as a tuple.
`'numeric'`	Numeric style where `:n` is filled in with the parameter value at index n. For example, `cur.execute("... where name=:0 and account=:1", (symbol, account))`.
`'named'`	Named style where `:name` is filled in with a named value. For this style, the parameters must be given as a mapping. For example, `cur.execute("... where name=:symbol and account=:account", {'symbol':symbol, 'account': account})`.
`'format'`	Printf-style format codes such as `%s`, `%d`, etc. For example, `cur.execute("... where name=%s and account=%d", (symbol, account))`.
`'pyformat'`	Python extended format codes such as `%(name)s`. Similar to the `'named'` style. Parameters must be specified as a mapping instead of a tuple.

Type Objects

When working with database data, built-in types such as integers and strings are usually mapped to an equivalent type in the database. However, for dates, binary data, and other special types, data management is more tricky. To assist with this mapping, database modules implement a set of constructor functions for creating objects of various types.

`Date(year, month, day)`

Creates an object representing a date.

`Time(hour, minute, second)`

Creates an object representing a time.

`Timestamp(year, month, day, hour, minute, second)`

Creates an object representing a timestamp.

`DateFromTicks(ticks)`

Creates a date object from a value of the system time. `ticks` is the number of seconds as returned by a function such as `time.time()`.

`TimeFromTicks(ticks)`

Creates a time object from a value of the system time.

`TimestampFromTicks(ticks)`

Creates a timestamp object from a value of the system time.

`Binary(s)`

Creates a binary object from a byte-string `s`.

In addition to these constructor functions, the following type objects might be defined. The purpose of these codes is to perform type checking against the `type_code` field of `cur.description`, which describes the contents of the current result set.

Type Object	Description
STRING	Character or text data
BINARY	Binary data such as BLOBs
NUMBER	Numeric data
DATETIME	Date and time data
ROWID	Row ID data

Error Handling

Database modules define a top-level exception `Error` that is a base class for all other errors. The following exceptions are for more specific kinds of database errors:

Exception	Description
InterfaceError	Errors related to the database interface, but not the database itself.
DatabaseError	Errors related to the database itself.
DataError	Errors related to the processed data. For example, bad type conversions, division by zero, etc.
OperationalError	Errors related to the operation of the database itself. For example, a lost connection.
IntegrityError	Error when relational integrity of the database is broken.
InternalError	Internal error in the database. For example, if a stale cursor.
ProgrammingError	Errors in SQL queries.
NotSupportedError	Error for methods in the database API that aren't supported by the underlying database.

Modules may also define a `Warning` exception that is used by the database module to warn about things such as data truncation during updates.

Multithreading

If you are mixing database access with multithreading, the underlying database module may or may not be thread-safe. The following variable is defined in each module to provide more information.

`threadsafety`

An integer that indicates the thread safety of the module. Possible values are:

0	No thread safety. Threads may not share any part of the module.
1	The module is thread-safe, but connections may not be shared.
2	The module and connections are thread-safe, but cursors may not be shared.
3	The module, connections, and cursors are all thread-safe.

Mapping Results into Dictionaries

A common issue concerning database results is the mapping of tuples or lists into a dictionary of named fields. For example, if the result set of a query contains a large number of columns, it may be easier to work with this data using descriptive field names instead of hard-coding the numeric index of specific fields within a tuple.

There are many ways to handle this, but one of the most elegant ways to process result data is through the use of generator functions. For example:

```
def generate_dicts(cur):
    import itertools
    fieldnames = [d[0].lower() for d in cur.description ]
    while True:
        rows = cur.fetchmany()
        if not row: return
        for row in rows:
            yield dict(itertools.izip(fieldnames,row))

# Sample use
cur.execute("select name, shares, price from portfolio")
for r in generate_dicts(cur):
    print r['name'],r['shares'],r['price']
```

Be aware that the naming of columns is not entirely consistent between databases—especially with respect to things such as case sensitivity. So, you'll need to be a little careful if you try to apply this technique to code that's meant to work with a variety of different database modules.

Database API Extensions

Finally, many extensions and advanced features can be added to specific database modules—for example, support for two-phase commits and extended error handling. PEP-249 has additional information about the recommended interface for these features and should be consulted by advanced users. Third-party library modules also may simplify the use of relational database interfaces.

sqlite3 Module

The sqlite3 module provides a Python interface to the SQLite database library (http://www.sqlite.org). SQLite is a C library that implements a self-contained relational database entirely within a file or in memory. Although it is simple, this library is attractive for various reasons. For one, it does not rely upon a separate database server nor does it require any kind of special configuration—you can start to use it right away in your programs by simply connecting to a database file (and if it doesn't exist, a new file is created). The database also supports transactions for improved reliability (even across system crashes) as well as locking to allow the same database file to be simultaneously accessed from multiple processes.

The programming interface to the library follows the conventions described in the previous section on the Database API, so much of that detail is not repeated here. Instead, this section focuses on the technical details of using this module as well as features that are specific to the sqlite3 module.

Module-Level Functions

The following functions are defined by the `sqlite3` module:

`connect(database [, timeout [, isolation_level [, detect_types]]])`

Creates a connection to a SQLite database. `database` is a string that specifies the name of the database file. It can also be a string `":memory:"`, in which case an in-memory database is used (note that this kind of database only persists as long as the Python process remains running and would be lost on program exit). The `timeout` parameter specifies the amount of time to wait for an internal reader-writer lock to be released when other connections are updating the database. By default, `timeout` is 5 seconds. When SQL statements such as `INSERT` or `UPDATE` are used, a new transaction is automatically started if one wasn't already in effect. The `isolation_level` parameter is a string that provides an optional modifier to the underlying SQL `BEGIN` statement that is used to start this transaction. Possible values are `""` (the default), `"DEFERRED"`, `"EXCLUSIVE"`, or `"IMMEDIATE"`. The meaning of these settings is related to the underlying database lock and is as follows:

Isolation Level	Description
`""` (empty string)	Use the default setting (`DEFERRED`).
`"DEFERRED"`	Starts a new transaction, but does not acquire the lock until the first database operation is actually performed.
`"EXCLUSIVE"`	Starts a new transaction and guarantees that no other connections can read or write the database until changes are committed.
`"IMMEDIATE"`	Starts a new transaction and guarantees that no other connection can make database modifications until changes are committed. Other connections can still read from the database, however.

The `detect_types` parameter enables some extra type detection (implemented by extra parsing of SQL queries) when returning results. By default it is 0 (meaning no extra detection). It can be set to the bitwise-or of `PARSE_DECLTYPES` and `PARSE_COLNAMES`. If `PARSE_DECLTYPES` is enabled, queries are examined for SQL type-names such as `"integer"` or `"number(8)"` in order to determine the type of result columns. If `PARSE_COLNAMES` is enabled, special strings of the form `"colname [typename]"` (including the double quotes) can be embedded into queries where `colname` is the column name and `typename` is the name of a type registered with the `register_converter()` function described next. These strings are simply transformed into `colname` when passed to the SQLite engine, but the extra type specifier is used when converting values in the results of a query. For example, a query such as `'select price as "price [decimal]" from portfolio'` is interpreted as `'select price as price from portfolio'`, and the results will be converted according to the "decimal" conversion rule.

`register_converter(typename, func)`

Registers a new type name for use with the `detect_types` option to `connect()`. `typename` is a string containing the type name as it will be used in queries, and `func` is a function that takes a single bytestring as input and returns a Python datatype as a result.

For example, if you call `sqlite3.register_converter('decimal', decimal.Decimal)`, then you can have values in queries converted to `Decimal` objects by writing queries such as `'select price as "price [decimal]" from stocks'`.

register_adapter(*type*, *func*)

Registers an adapter function for a Python type *type* that is used when storing values of that type in the datatype. *func* is a function that accepts an instance of type *type* as input and returns a `int`, `float`, UTF-8–encoded byte string, Unicode string, or buffer as a result. For example, if you wanted to store `Decimal` objects, you might use `sqlite3.register_adapter(decimal.Decimal,float)`.

complete_statement(*s*)

Returns `True` if the string *s* represents one or more complete SQL statements separated by semicolons. This might be useful if writing an interactive program that reads queries from the user.

enable_callback_tracebacks(*flag*)

Determines the handling of exceptions in user-defined callback functions such as converters and adapters. By default, exceptions are ignored. If *flag* is set to `True`, traceback messages will be printed on `sys.stderr`.

Connection Objects

The `Connection` object *c* returned by the `connect()` function supports the standard operations described in the Database API. In addition, the following methods specific to the `sqlite3` module are provided.

c.create_function(*name*, *num_params*, *func*)

Creates a user-defined function that can be used in SQL statements. *name* is a string containing the name of the function, *num_params* is an integer giving the number of parameters, and *func* is a Python function that provides the implementation. Here is a simple example:

```
def toupper(s):
    return s.upper()
c.create_function("toupper",1,toupper)
# Sample use in a query
c.execute("select toupper(name),foo,bar from sometable")
```

Although a Python function is being defined, the parameters and inputs of this function should only be `int`, `float`, `str`, `unicode`, `buffer`, or `None`.

c.create_aggregate(*name*, *num_params*, *aggregate_class*)

Creates a user-defined aggregation function for use in SQL statements. *name* is a string containing the name of the function, and *num_params* is an integer giving the number of input parameters. *aggregate_class* is a class that implements the aggregation operation. This class must support initialization with no arguments and implements a `step(params)` method that accepts the same number of parameters as given in *num_params* and a `finalize()` method that returns the final result. Here is a simple example:

```
class Averager(object):
    def __init__(self):
        self.total = 0.0
        self.count = 0
```

```
    def step(self,value):
        self.total += value
        self.count += 1
    def finalize(self):
        return self.total / self.count

c.create_aggregate("myavg",1,Averager)
# Sample use in a query

c.execute("select myavg(num) from sometable")
```

Aggregation works by making repeated calls to the step() method with input values and then calling finalize() to obtain the final value.

c.create_collation(*name, func*)

Registers a user-defined collation function for use in SQL statements. *name* is a string containing the name of the collation function, and *func* is a function that accepts two inputs and returns -1, 0, 1 depending on whether or not the first input is below, equal to, or above the second input. You use the user-defined function using a SQL expression such as "select * from *table* order by *colname* collate *name*".

c.execute(*sql* [, *params*])

A shortcut method that creates a cursor object using c.cursor() and executes the cursor's execute() method with SQL statements in *sql* with the parameters in *params*.

c.executemany(*sql* [, *params*])

A shortcut method that creates a cursor object using c.cursor() and executes the cursor's executemany() method with SQL statements in *sql* with the parameters in *params*.

c.executescript(*sql*)

A shortcut method that creates a cursor object using c.cursor() and executes the cursor's executescript() method with SQL statements in *sql*.

c.interrupt()

Aborts any currently executing queries on the connection. This is meant to be called from a separate thread.

c.iterdump()

Returns an iterator that dumps the entire database contents to a series of SQL statements that could be executed to recreate the database. This could be useful if exporting the database elsewhere or if you need to dump the contents of an in-memory database to a file for later restoration.

c.set_authorizer(*auth_callback*)

Registers an authorization callback function that gets executed on every access to a column of data in the database. The callback function must take five arguments as *auth_callback(code, arg1, arg2, dbname, innername)*. The value returned by this callback is one of SQLITE_OK if access is allowed, SQLITE_DENY if the SQL statement should fail with an error, or SQLITE_IGNORE if the column should be ignored by treating it as a Null value. The first argument *code* is an integer action code. *arg1* and arg2 are parameters whose values depend on the value of code. dbname is a string containing the name of the database (usually "main"), and innername is the name of the innermost view or trigger that is attempting access or None if no view or trigger is active. The following table lists the values for code and meaning of the arg1 and arg2 parameters:

Code	Arg1	Arg2
SQLITE_CREATE_INDEX	Index name	Table name
SQLITE_CREATE_TABLE	Table name	None
SQLITE_CREATE_TEMP_INDEX	Index name	Table name
SQLITE_CREATE_TEMP_TABLE	Table name	None
SQLITE_CREATE_TEMP_TRIGGER	Trigger name	Table name
SQLITE_CREATE_TEMP_VIEW	View name	None
SQLITE_CREATE_TRIGGER	Trigger name	Table name
SQLITE_CREATE_VIEW	View name	None
SQLITE_DELETE	Table name	None
SQLITE_DROP_INDEX	Index name	Table name
SQLITE_DROP_TABLE	Table name	None
SQLITE_DROP_TEMP_INDEX	Index name	Table name
SQLITE_DROP_TEMP_TABLE	Table name	None
SQLITE_DROP_TEMP_TRIGGER	Trigger name	Table name
SQLITE_DROP_TEMP_VIEW	View name	None
SQLITE_DROP_TRIGGER	Trigger name	Table name
SQLITE_DROP_VIEW	View name	None
SQLITE_INSERT	Table name	None
SQLITE_PRAGMA	Pragma name	None
SQLITE_READ	Table name	Column name
SQLITE_SELECT	None	None
SQLITE_TRANSACTION	None	None
SQLITE_UPDATE	Table name	Column name
SQLITE_ATTACH	Filename	None
SQLITE_DETACH	Database name	None
SQLITE_ALTER_TABLE	Database name	Table name
SQLITE_REINDEX	Index name	None
SQLITE_ANALYZE	Table name	None
SQLITE_CREATE_VTABLE	Table name	Module name
SQLITE_DROP_VTABLE	Table name	Module name
SQLITE_FUNCTION	Function name	None

c.set_progress_handler(handler, n)

Registers a callback function that gets executed every n instructions of the SQLite virtual machine. handler is a function that takes no arguments.

The following attributes are also defined on connection objects.

`c.row_factory`

A function that gets called to create the object representing the contents of each result row. This function takes two arguments: the cursor object used to obtain the result and a tuple with the raw result row.

`c.text_factory`

A function that is called to create the objects representing text values in the database. The function must take a single argument that is a UTF-8–encoded byte string. The return value should be some kind of string. By default, a Unicode string is returned.

`c.total_changes`

An integer representing the number of rows that have been modified since the database connection was opened.

A final feature of connection objects is that they can be used with the context-manager protocol to automatically handle transactions. For example:

```
conn = sqlite.connect("somedb")
with conn:
    conn.execute("insert into sometable values (?,?)", ("foo","bar")))
```

In this example, a `commit()` operation is automatically performed after all statements in the `with` block have executed and no errors have occurred. If any kind of exception is raised, a `rollback()` operation is performed and the exception is reraised.

Cursors and Basic Operations

To perform basic operations on a `sqlite3` database, you first have to create a cursor object using the `cursor()` method of a connection. You then use the `execute()`, `executemany()`, or `executescript()` methods of the cursor to execute SQL statements. See the Database API section for further details about the general operation of these methods. Instead of repeating that information here, a set of common database use cases are presented along with sample code. The goal is to show both the operation of cursor objects and some common SQL operations for those programmers who might need a brief refresher on the syntax.

Creating New Database Tables

The following code shows how to open a database and create a new table:

```
import sqlite3
conn = sqlite3.connect("mydb")
cur = conn.cursor()
cur.execute("create table stocks (symbol text, shares integer, price real)")
conn.commit()
```

When defining tables, a few primitive SQLite datatypes should be used: `text`, `integer`, `real`, and `blob`. The `blob` type is a bytestring, whereas the `text` type is assumed to be UTF-8–encoded Unicode.

Inserting New Values into a Table

The following code shows how to insert new items into a table:

```
import sqlite3
conn = sqlite3.connect("mydb")
cur = conn.cursor()
cur.execute("insert into stocks values (?,?,?)",('IBM',50,91.10))
cur.execute("insert into stocks values (?,?,?)",('AAPL',100,123.45))
conn.commit()
```

When inserting values, you should always use the ? substitutions as shown. Each ? is replaced by a value from a tuple of values supplied as parameters.

If you have a sequence of data to insert, you can use the executemany() method of a cursor like this:

```
stocks = [ ('GOOG',75,380.13),
           ('AA',60,14.20),
           ('AIG',125, 0.99) ]
cur.executemany("insert into stocks values (?,?,?)",stocks)
```

Updating an Existing Row

The following code shows how you might update columns for an existing row:

```
cur.execute("update stocks set shares=? where symbol=?",(50,'IBM'))
```

Again, when you need to insert values into the SQL statement, make sure you use the ? placeholders and supply a tuple of values as parameters.

Deleting Rows

The following code shows how to delete rows:

```
cur.execute("delete from stocks where symbol=?",('SCOX',))
```

Performing Basic Queries

The following code shows how you can perform basic queries and obtain the results:

```
# Select all columns from a table
for row in cur.execute("select * from stocks"):
    statements

# Select a few columns
for shares, price in cur.execute("select shares,price from stocks"):
    statements

# Select matching rows
for row in cur.execute("select * from stocks where symbol=?",('IBM',))
    statements

# Select matching rows with ordering
for row in cur.execute("select * from stocks order by shares"):
    statements

# Select matching rows with ordering in reverse
for row in cur.execute("select * from stocks order by shares desc"):
    statements

# Joining tables on a common column name (symbol)
for row in cur.execute("""select s.symbol, s.shares, p.price
                           from stocks as s, prices as p using(symbol)"""):
    statements
```

DBM-Style Database Modules

Python includes a number of library modules for supporting UNIX DBM-style database files. Several standard types of these databases are supported. The dbm module is used to read standard UNIX-dbm database files. The gdbm module is used to read GNU dbm database files (http://www.gnu.org/software/gdbm). The dbhash module is used to read database files created by the Berkeley DB library (http://www.oracle.com/database/berkeley-db/index.html). The dumbdbm module is a pure-Python module that implements a simple DBM-style database on its own.

All of these modules provide an object that implements a persistent string-based dictionary. That is, it works like a Python dictionary except that all keys and values are restricted to strings. A database file is typically opened using a variation of the open() function.

```
open(filename [, flag [, mode]])
```

This function opens the database file *filename* and returns a database object. *flag* is 'r' for read-only access, 'w' for read-write access, 'c' to create the database if it doesn't exist, or 'n' to force the creation of a new database. *mode* is the integer file-access mode used when creating the database (the default is 0666 on UNIX).

The object returned by the open() function minimally supports the following dictionary-like operations:

Operation	Description
d[key] = value	Inserts value into the database
value = d[key]	Gets data from the database
del d[key]	Removes a database entry
d.close()	Closes the database
key in d	Tests for a key
d.sync()	Writes all changes out to the database

Specific implementations may also add additional features (consult the appropriate module reference for details).

One issue with the various DBM-style database modules is that not every module is installed on every platform. For example, if you use Python on Windows, the dbm and gdbm modules are typically unavailable. However, a program may still want to create a DBM-style database for its own use. To address this issue, Python provides a module anydbm that can be used to open and create a DBM-style database file. This module provides an open() function as described previously, but it is guaranteed to work on all platforms. It does this by looking at the set of available DBM modules and picking the most advanced library that is available (typically dbhash if it's installed). As a fallback, it uses the dumbdbm module which is always available.

Another module is whichdb, which has a function whichdb(filename) that can be used to probe a file in order to determine what kind of DBM-database created it.

As a general rule, it is probably best not to rely upon these low-level modules for any application where portability is important. For example, if you create a DBM database on one machine and then transfer the database file to another machine, there is a chance that Python won't be able to read it if the underlying DBM module isn't installed. A high degree of caution is also in order if you are using these database modules to store large amounts of data, have a situation where multiple Python programs might be opening the same database file concurrently, or need high reliability and transactions (the `sqlite3` module might be a safer choice for that).

shelve **Module**

The `shelve` module provides support for persistent objects using a special "shelf" object. This object behaves like a dictionary except that all the objects it contains are stored on disk using a hash-table based database such as `dbhash`, `dbm` or `gdbm`. Unlike those modules, however, the values stored in a shelf are not restricted to strings. Instead, any object that is compatible with the `pickle` module may be stored. A shelf is created using the `shelve.open()` function.

`open(filename [,flag='c' [, protocol [, writeback]]])`

Opens a shelf file. If the file doesn't exist, it's created. `filename` should be the database filename and should not include a suffix. `flag` has the same meaning as described in the previous section and is one of `'r'`, `'w'`, `'c'`, or `'n'`. If the database file doesn't exist, it is created. `protocol` specifies the protocol used to pickle objects stored in the database. It has the same meaning as described in the `pickle` module. `writeback` controls the caching behavior of the database object. If `True`, all accessed entries are cached in memory and only written back when the shelf is closed. The default value is `False`. Returns a shelf object.

Once a shelf is opened, the following dictionary operations can be performed on it:

Operation	Description
`d[key] = data`	Stores data at `key`. Overwrites existing data.
`data = d[key]`	Retrieves data at `key`.
`del d[key]`	Deletes data at `key`.
`key in d`	Tests for the existence of `key`.
`d.keys()`	Returns all keys.
`d.close()`	Closes the shelf.
`d.sync()`	Writes unsaved data to disk.

The key values for a shelf must be strings. The objects stored in a shelf must be serializable using the `pickle` module.

`Shelf(dict [, protocol [, writeback]])`

A mixin class that implements the functionality of a shelf on top of a dictionary object, `dict`. When this is used, objects stored in the returned shelf object will be pickled and stored in the underlying dictionary `dict`. Both `protocol` and `writeback` have the same meaning as for `shelve.open()`.

The `shelve` module uses the `anydbm` module to select an appropriate DBM module for use. In most standard Python installations, it is likely to be the `dbhash`, which relies upon the Berkeley DB library.

18

File and Directory Handling

This chapter describes Python modules for high-level file and directory handling. Topics include modules for processing various kinds of basic file encodings such as gzip and bzip2 files, modules for extracting file archives such as zip and tar files, and modules for manipulating the file system itself (e.g., directory listings, moving, renaming, copying, and so on). Low-level operating system calls related to files are covered in Chapter 19, "Operating System Services." Modules for parsing the contents of files such as XML and HTML are mostly covered in Chapter 24, "Internet Data Handling and Encoding."

bz2

The `bz2` module is used to read and write data compressed according to the bzip2 compression algorithm.

BZ2File(`filename` [, `mode` [, `buffering` [, `compresslevel`]]])

Opens a `.bz2` file, `filename`, and returns a file-like object. `mode` is `'r'` for reading or `'w'` for writing. Universal newline support is also available by specifying a mode of `'rU'`. `buffering` specifies the buffer size in bytes with a default value of 0 (no buffering). `compresslevel` is a number between 1 and 9. A value of 9 (the default) provides the highest level of compression but consumes the most processing time. The returned object supports all the common file operations, including `close()`, `read()`, `readline()`, `readlines()`, `seek()`, `tell()`, `write()`, and `writelines()`.

BZ2Compressor([`compresslevel`])

Creates a compressor object that can be used to sequentially compress a sequence of data blocks. `compresslevel` specifies the compression level as a number between 1 and 9 (the default).

An instance, `c`, of `BZ2Compressor` has the following two methods:

`c.compress(data)`

Feeds new byte string data to the compressor object, `c`. Returns a byte string of compressed data if possible. Because compression involves chunks of data, the returned byte string may not include all the data and may include compressed data from previous calls to `compress()`. The `flush()` method should be used to return any remaining data stored in the compressor after all input data has been supplied.

c.flush()

Flushes the internal buffers and returns a byte string containing the compressed version of all remaining data. After this operation, no further compress() calls should be made on the object.

BZ2Decompressor()

Creates a decompressor object.

An instance, *d*, of BZ2Decompressor supports just one method:

d.decompress(*data*)

Given a chunk of compressed data in the byte string *data*, this method returns uncompressed data. Because data is processed in chunks, the returned byte string may or may not include a decompressed version of everything supplied in *data*. Repeated calls to this method will continue to decompress data blocks until an end-of-stream marker is found in the input. If subsequent attempts are made to decompress data after that, an EOFError exception will be raised.

compress(*data* [, *compresslevel*])

Returns a compressed version of the data supplied in the byte string *data*. *compresslevel* is a number between 1 and 9 (the default).

decompress(*data*)

Returns a byte string containing the decompressed data in the byte string *data*.

filecmp

The filecmp module provides the following functions, which can be used to compare files and directories:

cmp(*file1*, *file2* [, *shallow*])

Compares the files *file1* and *file2* and returns True if they're equal, False if not. By default, files that have identical attributes as returned by os.stat() are considered to be equal. If the *shallow* parameter is specified and is False, the contents of the two files are compared to determine equality.

cmpfiles(*dir1*, *dir2*, *common* [, *shallow*])

Compares the contents of the files contained in the list *common* in the two directories *dir1* and *dir2*. Returns a tuple containing three lists of filenames (*match*, *mismatch*, *errors*). *match* lists the files that are the same in both directories, *mismatch* lists the files that don't match, and *errors* lists the files that could not be compared for some reason. The *shallow* parameter has the same meaning as for cmp().

dircmp(*dir1*, *dir2* [, *ignore*[, *hide*]])

Creates a directory comparison object that can be used to perform various comparison operations on the directories *dir1* and *dir2*. *ignore* is a list of filenames to ignore and has a default value of ['RCS','CVS','tags']. *hide* is a list of filenames to hide and defaults to the list [os.curdir, os.pardir] (['.', '..'] on UNIX).

A directory object, *d*, returned by dircmp() has the following methods and attributes:

d.report()

Compares directories *dir1* and *dir2* and prints a report to sys.stdout.

d.report_partial_closure()

Compares *dir1* and *dir2* and common immediate subdirectories. Results are printed to sys.stdout.

d.report_full_closure()

Compares *dir1* and *dir2* and all subdirectories recursively. Results are printed to sys.stdout.

d.left_list

Lists the files and subdirectories in *dir1*. The contents are filtered by *hide* and *ignore*.

d.right_list

Lists the files and subdirectories in *dir2*. The contents are filtered by *hide* and *ignore*.

d.common

Lists the files and subdirectories found in both *dir1* and *dir2*.

d.left_only

Lists the files and subdirectories found only in *dir1*.

d.right_only

Lists the files and subdirectories found only in *dir2*.

d.common_dirs

Lists the subdirectories that are common to *dir1* and *dir2*.

d.common_files

Lists the files that are common to *dir1* and *dir2*.

d.common_funny

Lists the files in *dir1* and *dir2* with different types or for which no information can be obtained from os.stat().

d.same_files

Lists the files with identical contents in *dir1* and *dir2*.

d.diff_files

Lists the files with different contents in *dir1* and *dir2*.

d.funny_files

Lists the files that are in both *dir1* and *dir2* but that could not be compared for some reason (for example, insufficient permission to access).

d.subdirs

A dictionary that maps names in d.common_dirs to additional dircmp objects.

> **Note**
> The attributes of a `dircmp` object are evaluated lazily and not determined at the time the `dircmp` object is first created. Thus, if you're interested in only some of the attributes, there's no added performance penalty related to the other unused attributes.

fnmatch

The `fnmatch` module provides support for matching filenames using UNIX shell-style wildcard characters. This module only performs filename matching, whereas the `glob` module can be used to actually obtain file listings. The pattern syntax is as follows:

Character(s)	Description
*	Matches everything
?	Matches any single character
[*seq*]	Matches any character in *seq*
[!*seq*]	Matches any character not in *seq*

The following functions can be used to test for a wildcard match:

`fnmatch(filename, pattern)`

Returns `True` or `False` depending on whether *filename* matches *pattern*. Case sensitivity depends on the operating system (and may be non–case-sensitive on certain platforms such as Windows).

`fnmatchcase(filename, pattern)`

Performs a case-sensitive comparison of *filename* against *pattern*.

`filter(names, pattern)`

Applies the `fnmatch()` function to all of the names in the sequence *names* and returns a list of all names that match *pattern*.

Examples

```
fnmatch('foo.gif', '*.gif')              # Returns True
fnmatch('part37.html', 'part3[0-5].html') # Returns False

# Example of finding files in an entire directory tree
# using os.walk(), fnmatch, and generators
def findall(topdir, pattern):
    for path, files, dirs in os.walk(topdir):
        for name in files:
            if fnmatch.fnmatch(name,pattern):
                yield os.path.join(path,name)
# Find all .py files
for pyfile in findall(".","*.py"):
    print (pyfile)
```

glob

The glob module returns all filenames in a directory that match a pattern specified using the rules of the UNIX shell (as described in the fnmatch module).

glob(*pattern*)

Returns a list of pathnames that match *pattern*.

iglob(*pattern*)

Returns the same results as glob() but using an iterator.

Example

```
htmlfile = glob('*.html')
imgfiles = glob('image[0-5]*.gif')
```

> **Note**
>
> Tilde (~) and shell variable expansion are not performed. Use os.path.expanduser() and os.path.expandvars(), respectively, to perform these expansions prior to calling glob().

gzip

The gzip module provides a class, GzipFile, that can be used to read and write files compatible with the GNU gzip program. GzipFile objects work like ordinary files except that data is automatically compressed or decompressed.

GzipFile([*filename* [, *mode* [, *compresslevel* [, *fileobj*]]]])

Opens a GzipFile. *filename* is the name of a file, and *mode* is one of 'r', 'rb', 'a', 'ab', 'w', or 'wb'. The default is 'rb'. *compresslevel* is an integer from 1 to 9 that controls the level of compression. 1 is the fastest and produces the least compression; 9 is the slowest and produces the most compression (the default). *fileobj* is an existing file object that should be used. If supplied, it's used instead of the file named by *filename*.

open(*filename* [, *mode* [, *compresslevel*]])

Same as GzipFile(*filename*, *mode*, *compresslevel*). The default mode is 'rb'. The default *compresslevel* is 9.

Notes

- Calling the close() method of a GzipFile object doesn't close files passed in *fileobj*. This allows additional information to be written to a file after the compressed data.
- Files produced by the UNIX compress program are not supported.
- This module requires the zlib module.

shutil

The shutil module is used to perform high-level file operations such as copying, removing, and renaming. The functions in this module should only be used for proper files and directories. In particular, they do not work for special kinds of files on the file system such as named pipes, block devices, etc. Also, be aware that these functions don't always correctly deal with advanced kinds of file metadata (e.g., resource forks, creator codes, etc.).

copy(src,dst)

Copies the file *src* to the file or directory *dst*, retaining file permissions. *src* and *dst* are strings.

copy2(src, dst)

Like copy() but also copies the last access and modification times.

copyfile(src, dst)

Copies the contents of *src* to *dst*. *src* and *dst* are strings.

copyfileobj(f1, f2 [, length])

Copies all data from open file object *f1* to open file object *f2*. *length* specifies a maximum buffer size to use. A negative length will attempt to copy the data entirely with one operation (that is, all data will be read as a single chunk and then written).

copymode(src, dst)

Copies the permission bits from *src* to *dst*.

copystat(src, dst)

Copies the permission bits, last access time, and last modification time from *src* to *dst*. The contents, owner, and group of *dst* are unchanged.

copytree(src, dst, symlinks [,ignore])

Recursively copies an entire directory tree rooted at *src*. The destination directory *dst* will be created (and should not already exist). Individual files are copied using copy2(). If *symlinks* is true, symbolic links in the source tree are represented as symbolic links in the new tree. If *symlinks* is false or omitted, the contents of linked files are copied to the new directory tree. *ignore* is an optional function that can be used to filter out specific files. As input, this function should accept a directory name and a list of directory contents. As a return value, it should return a list of filenames to be ignored. If errors occur during the copy process, they are collected and the Error exception is raised at the end of processing. The exception argument is a list of tuples containing (*srcname, dstname, exception*) for all errors that occurred.

ignore_pattern(pattern1, pattern2, ...)

Creates a function that can be used for ignoring all of the glob-style patterns given in *pattern1, pattern2*, etc. The returned function accepts as input two arguments, the first of which is a directory name and the second of which is a list of directory contents. As a result, a list of filenames to be ignored is returned. The primary use of the returned function is as the *ignore* parameter to the copytree() function shown earlier. However, the resulting function might also be used for operations involving the os.walk() function.

move(*src*, *dst*)

Moves a file or directory *src* to *dst*. Will recursively copy *src* if it is being moved to a different file system.

rmtree(*path* [, *ignore_errors* [, *onerror*]])

Deletes an entire directory tree. If *ignore_errors* is true, errors will be ignored. Otherwise, errors are handled by the *onerror* function (if supplied). This function must accept three parameters (*func*, *path*, and *excinfo*), where *func* is the function that caused the error (os.remove() or os.rmdir()), *path* is the pathname passed to the function, and *excinfo* is the exception information returned by sys.exc_info(). If an error occurs and *onerror* is omitted, an exception is raised.

tarfile

The tarfile module is used to manipulate tar archive files. Using this module, it is possible to read and write tar files, with or without compression.

is_tarfile(*name*)

Returns True if *name* appears to be a valid tar file that can be read by this module.

open([*name* [, *mode* [, *fileobj* [, *bufsize*]]]])

Creates a new TarFile object with the pathname *name*. *mode* is a string that specifies how the tar file is to be opened. The *mode* string is a combination of a file mode and a compression scheme specified as '*filemode*[:*compression*]'. Valid combinations include the following:

Mode	Description
'r'	Open for reading. If the file is compressed, it is decompressed transparently. This is the default mode.
'r:'	Open for reading without compression.
'r:gz'	Open for reading with gzip compression.
'r:bz2'	Open for reading with bzip2 compression.
'a', 'a:'	Open for appending with no compression.
'w', 'w:'	Open for writing with no compression.
'w:gz'	Open for writing with gzip compression.
'w:bz2'	Open for writing with bzip2 compression.

The following modes are used when creating a TarFile object that only allows sequential I/O access (no random seeks):

Mode	Description
'r|'	Open a stream of uncompressed blocks for reading
'r|gz'	Open a gzip compressed stream for reading
'r|bz2'	Open a bzip2 compressed stream for reading
'w|'	Open an uncompressed stream for writing
'w|gz'	Open a gzip compressed stream for writing
'w|bz2'	Open a bzip2 compressed stream for writing

If the parameter *fileobj* is specified, it must be an open file object. In this case, the file overrides any filename specified with *name*. *bufsize* specifies the block size used in a tar file. The default is 20*512 bytes.

A TarFile instance, *t*, returned by open() supports the following methods and attributes:

t.add(*name* [, *arcname* [, *recursive*]])

Adds a new file to the tar archive. *name* is the name of any kind of file (directory, symbolic link, and so on). *arcname* specifies an alternative name to use for the file inside the archive. *recursive* is a Boolean flag that indicates whether or not to recursively add the contents of directories. By default, it is set to True.

t.addfile(*tarinfo* [, *fileobj*])

Adds a new object to the tar archive. *tarinfo* is a TarInfo structure that contains information about the archive member. *fileobj* is an open file object from which data will be read and saved in the archive. The amount of data to read is determined by the size attribute of *tarinfo*.

t.close()

Closes the tar archive, writing two zero blocks to the end if the archive was opened for writing.

t.debug

Controls the amount of debugging information produced, with 0 producing no output and 3 producing all debugging messages. Messages are written to sys.stderr.

t.dereference

If this attribute is set to True, symbolic and hard links are dereferenced and the entire contents of the referenced file are added to the archive. If it's set to False, just the link is added.

t.errorlevel

Determines how errors are handled when an archive member is being extracted. If this attribute is set to 0, errors are ignored. If it's set to 1, errors result in OSError or IOError exceptions. If it's set to 2, nonfatal errors additionally result in TarError exceptions.

t.extract(*member* [, *path*])

Extracts a member from the archive, saving it to the current directory. *member* is either an archive member name or a TarInfo instance. *path* is used to specify a different destination directory.

t.extractfile(*member*)

Extracts a member from the archive, returning a read-only file-like object that can be used to read its contents using read(), readline(), readlines(), seek(), and tell() operations. *member* is either an archive member name or a TarInfo object. If *member* refers to a link, an attempt will be made to open the target of the link.

t.getmember(*name*)

Looks up archive member *name* and returns a TarInfo object containing information about it. Raises KeyError if no such archive member exists. If member *name* appears more than once in the archive, information for the last entry is returned (which is assumed to be the more recent).

`t.getmembers()`

Returns a list of `TarInfo` objects for all members of the archive.

`t.getnames()`

Returns a list of all archive member names.

`t.gettarinfo([name [, arcname [, fileobj]]])`

Returns a `TarInfo` object corresponding to a file, *name*, on the file system or an open file object, *fileobj*. *arcname* is an alternative name for the object in the archive. The primary use of this function is to create an appropriate `TarInfo` object for use in methods such as `add()`.

`t.ignore_zeros`

If this attribute is set to `True`, empty blocks are skipped when reading an archive. If it's set to `False` (the default), an empty block signals the end of the archive. Setting this method to `True` may be useful for reading a damaged archive.

`t.list([verbose])`

Lists the contents of the archive to `sys.stdout`. *verbose* determines the level of detail. If this method is set to `False`, only the archive names are printed. Otherwise, full details are printed (the default).

`t.next()`

A method used for iterating over the members of an archive. Returns the `TarInfo` structure for the next archive member or `None`.

`t.posix`

If this attribute is set to `True`, the tar file is created according to the POSIX 1003.1–1990 standard. This places restrictions on filename lengths and file size (filenames must be less than 256 characters and files must be less than 8GB in size). If this attribute is set to `False`, the archive is created using GNU extensions that lift these restrictions. The default value is `False`.

Many of the previous methods manipulate `TarInfo` instances. The following table shows the methods and attributes of a `TarInfo` instance *ti*.

Attribute	Description
`ti.gid`	Group ID
`ti.gname`	Group name
`ti.isblk()`	Returns `True` if the object is a block device
`ti.ischr()`	Returns `True` if the object is a character device
`ti.isdev()`	Returns `True` if the object is a device (character, block, or FIFO)
`ti.isdir()`	Returns `True` if the object is a directory
`ti.isfifo()`	Returns `True` if the object is a FIFO
`ti.isfile()`	Returns `True` if the object is a regular file
`ti.islnk()`	Returns `True` if the object is a hard link
`ti.isreg()`	Same as `isfile()`

Attribute	Description
`ti.issym()`	Returns `True` if the object is a symbolic link
`ti.linkname`	Target filename of a hard or symbolic link
`ti.mode`	Permission bits
`ti.mtime`	Last modification time
`ti.name`	Archive member name
`ti.size`	Size in bytes
`ti.type`	File type that is one of the constants `REGTYPE`, `AREGTYPE`, `LNKTYPE`, `SYMTYPE`, `DIRTYPE`, `FIFOTYPE`, `CONTTYPE`, `CHRTYPE`, `BLKTYPE`, or `GNUTYPE_SPARSE`
`ti.uid`	User ID
`ti.uname`	Username

Exceptions

The following exceptions are defined by the `tarfile` module:

TarError

Base class for all other exceptions.

ReadError

Raised when an error occurs while opening a tar file (for example, when opening an invalid file).

CompressionError

Raised when data can't be decompressed.

StreamError

Raised when an unsupported operation is performed on a stream-like `TarFile` object (for instance, an operation that requires random access).

ExtractError

Raised for nonfatal errors during extraction (only if `errorlevel` is set to 2).

Example

```
# Open a tar file and put some files into it
t = tarfile.open("foo.tar","w")
t.add("README")
import glob
for pyfile in glob.glob("*.py"):
    t.add(pyfile)
t.close()

# Open a tar file and iterate over all of its members
t = tarfile.open("foo.tar")
for f in t:
    print("%s %d" % (f.name, f.size))

# Scan a tar file and print the contents of "README" files
t = tarfile.open("foo.tar")
```

```
for f in t:
    if os.path.basename(f.name) == "README":
        data = t.extractfile(f).read()
        print("**** %s ****" % f.name)
```

tempfile

The `tempfile` module is used to generate temporary filenames and files.

mkdtemp([suffix [,prefix [, dir]]])

Creates a temporary directory accessible only by the owner of the calling process and returns its absolute pathname. *suffix* is an optional suffix that will be appended to the directory name, *prefix* is an optional prefix that will be inserted at the beginning of the directory name, and *dir* is a directory where the temporary directory should be created.

mkstemp([suffix [,prefix [, dir [,text]]]])

Creates a temporary file and returns a tuple (*fd, pathname*), where *fd* is an integer file descriptor returned by `os.open()` and *pathname* is absolute pathname of the file. *suffix* is an optional suffix appended to the filename, *prefix* is an optional prefix inserted at the beginning of the filename, *dir* is the directory in which the file should be created, and *text* is a boolean flag that indicates whether to open the file in text mode or binary mode (the default). The creation of the file is guaranteed to be atomic (and secure) provided that the system supports the O_EXCL flag for `os.open()`.

mktemp([suffix [, prefix [,dir]]])

Returns a unique temporary filename. *suffix* is an optional file suffix to append to the filename, *prefix* is an optional prefix inserted at the beginning of the filename, and *dir* is the directory in which the file is created. This function only generates a unique filename and doesn't actually create or open a temporary file. Because this function generates a name before the file is actually opened, it introduces a potential security problem. To address this, consider using `mkstemp()` instead.

gettempdir()

Returns the directory in which temporary files are created.

gettempprefix()

Returns the prefix used to generate temporary files. Does not include the directory in which the file would reside.

TemporaryFile([mode [, bufsize [, suffix [,prefix [, dir]]]]])

Creates a temporary file using `mkstemp()` and returns a file-like object that supports the same methods as an ordinary file object. *mode* is the file mode and defaults to `'w+b'`. *bufsize* specifies the buffering behavior and has the same meaning as for the `open()` function. *suffix, prefix,* and *dir* have the same meaning as for `mkstemp()`. The object returned by this function is only a wrapper around a built-in file object that's accessible in the file attribute. The file created by this function is automatically destroyed when the temporary file object is destroyed.

`NamedTemporaryFile([mode [, bufsize [, suffix [,prefix [, dir [, delete ]]]]]])`

Creates a temporary file just like `TemporaryFile()` but makes sure the filename is visible on the file system. The filename can be obtained by accessing the name attribute of the returned file object. Note that certain systems may prevent the file from being reopened using this name until the temporary file has been closed. The `delete` parameter, if set to `True` (the default), forces the temporary file to be deleted as soon as it is closed.

`SpooledTemporaryFile([max_size [, mode [, bufsize [, suffix [, prefix [, dir]]]]]])`

Creates a temporary file such as `TemporaryFile` except that the file contents are entirely held in memory until they exceed the size given in `max_size`. This internal spooling is implemented by first holding the file contents in a `StringIO` object until it is necessary to actually go to the file system. If any kind of low-level file I/O operation is performed involving the `fileno()` method, the memory contents are immediately written to a proper temporary file as defined by the `TemporaryFile` object. The file object returned by `SpooledTemporaryFile` also has a method `rollover()` that can be used to force the contents to be written to the file system.

Two global variables are used to construct temporary names. They can be assigned to new values if desired. Their default values are system-dependent.

Variable	Description
tempdir	The directory in which filenames returned by `mktemp()` reside.
template	The prefix of filenames generated by `mktemp()`. A string of decimal digits is added to `template` to generate unique filenames.

> **Note**
>
> By default, the `tempfile` module creates files by checking a few standard locations. For example, on UNIX, files are created in one of `/tmp`, `/var/tmp`, or `/usr/tmp`. On Windows, files are created in one of `C:\TEMP`, `C:\TMP`, `\TEMP`, or `\TMP`. These directories can be overridden by setting one or more of the `TMPDIR`, `TEMP`, and `TMP` environment variables. If, for whatever reason, temporary files can't be created in any of the usual locations, they will be created in the current working directory.

zipfile

The `zipfile` module is used to manipulate files encoded in the popular zip format (originally known as PKZIP, although now supported by a wide variety of programs). Zip files are widely used by Python, mainly for the purpose of packaging. For example, if zip files containing Python source code are added to `sys.path`, then files contained within the zip file can be loaded via `import` (the `zipimport` library module implements this functionality, although it's never necessary to use that library directly). Packages distributed as `.egg` files (created by the setuptools extension) are also just zip files in disguise (an `.egg` file is actually just a zip file with some extra metadata added to it).

The following functions and classes are defined by the `zipfile` module:

`is_zipfile(filename)`

Tests `filename` to see if it's a valid zip file. Returns `True` if `filename` is a zip file; returns `False` otherwise.

`ZipFile(filename [, mode [, compression [,allowZip64]]])`

Opens a zip file, `filename`, and returns a `ZipFile` instance. `mode` is `'r'` to read from an existing file, `'w'` to truncate the file and write a new file, or `'a'` to append to an existing file. For `'a'` mode, if `filename` is an existing zip file, new files are added to it. If `filename` is not a zip file, the archive is simply appended to the end of the file. `compression` is the zip compression method used when writing to the archive and is either `ZIP_STORED` or `ZIP_DEFLATED`. The default is `ZIP_STORED`. The `allowZip64` argument enables the use of ZIP64 extensions, which can be used to create zip files that exceed 2GB in size. By default, this is set to `False`.

`PyZipFile(filename [, mode[, compression [,allowZip64]]])`

Opens a zip file like `ZipFile()` but returns a special `PyZipFile` instance with one extra method, `writepy()`, used to add Python source files to the archive.

`ZipInfo([filename [, date_time]])`

Manually creates a new `ZipInfo` instance, used to contain information about an archive member. Normally, it's not necessary to call this function except when using the `z.writestr()` method of a `ZipFile` instance (described later). The `filename` and `date_time` arguments supply values for the `filename` and `date_time` attributes described below.

An instance, `z`, of `ZipFile` or `PyZipFile` supports the following methods and attributes:

`z.close()`

Closes the archive file. This must be called in order to flush records to the zip file before program termination.

`z.debug`

Debugging level in the range of 0 (no output) to 3 (most output).

`z.extract(name [, path [, pwd ]])`

Extracts a file from the archive and places it in the current working directory. `name` is either a string that fully specifies the archive member or a `ZipInfo` instance. `path` specifies a different directory in which the file will extracted, and `pwd` is the password to use for encrypted archives.

`z.extractall([path [members [, pwd]]])`

Extracts all members of an archive into the current working directory. `path` specifies a different directory, and `pwd` is a password for encrypted archives. `members` is a list of members to extract, which must be a proper subset of the list returned by the `namelist()` method (described next).

`z.getinfo(name)`

Returns information about the archive member name as a `ZipInfo` instance (described shortly).

`z.infolist()`

Returns a list of `ZipInfo` objects for all the members of the archive.

`z.namelist()`

Returns a list of the archive member names.

`z.open(name [, mode [, pwd]])`

Opens an archive member named *name* and returns a file-like object for reading the contents. *name* can either be a string or a `ZipInfo` instance describing one of the archive members. *mode* is the file mode and must be one of the read-only file modes such as `'r'`, `'rU'`, or `'U'`. *pwd* is the password to use for encrypted archive members. The file object that is returned supports the `read()`, `readline()`, and `readlines()` methods as well as iteration with the `for` statement.

`z.printdir()`

Prints the archive directory to `sys.stdout`.

`z.read(name [,pwd])`

Reads archive contents for member *name* and returns the data as a string. *name* is either a string or a `ZipInfo` instance describing the archive member. *pwd* is the password to use for encrypted archive members.

`z.setpassword(pwd)`

Sets the default password used to extract encrypted files from the archive.

`z.testzip()`

Reads all the files in the archive and verifies their CRC checksums. Returns the name of the first corrupted file or `None` if all files are intact.

`z.write(filename[, arcname[, compress_type]])`

Writes *filename* to the archive with the archive name *arcname*. *compress_type* is the compression parameter and is either `ZIP_STORED` or `ZIP_DEFLATED`. By default, the compression parameter given to the `ZipFile()` or `PyZipFile()` function is used. The archive must be opened in `'w'` or `'a'` mode for writes to work.

`z.writepy(pathname)`

This method, available only with `PyZipFile` instances, is used to write Python source files (`*.py` files) to a zip archive and can be used to easily package Python applications for distribution. If *pathname* is a file, it must end with `.py`. In this case, one of the corresponding `.pyo`, `.pyc`, or `.py` files will be added (in that order). If *pathname* is a directory and the directory is not a Python package directory, all the corresponding `.pyo`, `.pyc`, or `.py` files are added at the top level. If the directory is a package, the files are added under the package name as a file path. If any subdirectories are also package directories, they are added recursively.

z.writestr(arcinfo, s)

Writes the string *s* into the zip file. *arcinfo* is either a filename within the archive in which the data will be stored or a `ZipInfo` instance containing a filename, date, and time.

ZipInfo instances *i* returned by the `ZipInfo()`, `z.getinfo()`, and `z.infolist()` functions have the following attributes:

Attribute	Description
i.filename	Archive member name.
i.date_time	Tuple (*year*, *month*, *day*, *hours*, *minutes*, *seconds*) containing the last modification time. *month* and *day* are numbers in the range 1–12 and 1–31, respectively. All other values start at 0.
i.compress_type	Compression type for the archive member. Only ZIP_STORED and ZIP_DEFLATED are currently supported by this module.
i.comment	Archive member comment.
i.extra	Expansion field data, used to contain additional file attributes. The data stored here depends on the system that created the file.
i.create_system	Integer code describing the system that created the archive. Common values are 0 (MS-DOS FAT), 3 (UNIX), 7 (Macintosh), and 10 (Windows NTFS).
i.create_version	PKZIP version code that created the zip archive.
i.extract_version	Minimum version needed to extract the archive.
i.reserved	Reserved field. Currently set to 0.
i.flag_bits	Zip flag bits that describe the data encoding including encryption and compression.
i.volume	Volume number of the file header.
i.internal_attr	Describes the internal structure of the archive contents. If the low-order bit is 1, the data is ASCII text. Otherwise, binary data is assumed.
i.external_attr	External file attributes which are operating system dependent.
i.header_offset	Byte offset to the file header.
i.file_offset	Byte offset to the start of the file data.
i.CRC	CRC checksum of the uncompressed file.
i.compress_size	Size of the compressed file data.
i.file_size	Size of the uncompressed file.

Note

Detailed documentation about the internal structure of zip files can be found as a PKZIP Application Note at http://www.pkware.com/appnote.html.

zlib

The `zlib` module supports data compression by providing access to the zlib library.

adler32(*string* [, *value*])

Computes the Adler-32 checksum of *string*. *value* is used as the starting value (which can be used to compute a checksum over the concatenation of several strings). Otherwise, a fixed default value is used.

compress(*string* [, *level*])

Compresses the data in *string*, where *level* is an integer from 1 to 9 controlling the level of compression. 1 is the least (fastest) compression, and 9 is the best (slowest) compression. The default value is 6. Returns a string containing the compressed data or raises `error` if an error occurs.

compressobj([*level*])

Returns a compression object. *level* has the same meaning as in the `compress()` function.

crc32(*string* [, *value*])

Computes a CRC checksum of *string*. If *value* is present, it's used as the starting value of the checksum. Otherwise, a fixed value is used.

decompress(*string* [, *wbits* [, *buffsize*]])

Decompresses the data in *string*. *wbits* controls the size of the window buffer, and *buffsize* is the initial size of the output buffer. Raises `error` if an error occurs.

decompressobj([*wbits*])

Returns a compression object. The *wbits* parameter controls the size of the window buffer.

A compression object, *c*, has the following methods:

c.compress(*string*)

Compresses *string*. Returns a string containing compressed data for at least part of the data in *string*. This data should be concatenated to the output produced by earlier calls to `c.compress()` to create the output stream. Some input data may be stored in internal buffers for later processing.

c.flush([*mode*])

Compresses all pending input and returns a string containing the remaining compressed output. *mode* is `Z_SYNC_FLUSH`, `Z_FULL_FLUSH`, or `Z_FINISH` (the default). `Z_SYNC_FLUSH` and `Z_FULL_FLUSH` allow further compression and are used to allow partial error recovery on decompression. `Z_FINISH` terminates the compression stream.

A decompression object, *d*, has the following methods and attributes:

d.decompress(*string* [,*max_length*])

Decompresses *string* and returns a string containing uncompressed data for at least part of the data in *string*. This data should be concatenated with data produced by earlier calls to `decompress()` to form the output stream. Some input data may be stored in internal buffers for later processing. *max_length* specifies the maximum size of returned data. If exceeded, unprocessed data will be placed in the *d*.unconsumed_tail attribute.

d.flush()

All pending input is processed, and a string containing the remaining uncompressed output is returned. The decompression object cannot be used again after this call.

d.unconsumed_tail

String containing data not yet processed by the last decompress() call. This would contain data if decompression needs to be performed in stages due to buffer size limitations. In this case, this variable would be passed to subsequent decompress() calls.

d.unused_data

String containing extra bytes that remain past the end of the compressed data.

> **Note**
> The zlib library is available at http://www.zlib.net.

19

Operating System Services

The modules in this chapter provide access to a wide variety of operating system services with an emphasis on low-level I/O, process management, and the operating environment. Modules that are commonly used in conjunction with writing systems programs are also included—for example, modules to read configuration files, write log files, and so forth. Chapter 18, "File and Directory Handling," covers high-level modules related to file and filesystem manipulation—the material presented here tends be at a lower level than that.

Most of Python's operating system modules are based on POSIX interfaces. POSIX is a standard that defines a core set of operating system interfaces. Most UNIX systems support POSIX, and other platforms such as Windows support large portions of the interface. Throughout this chapter, functions and modules that only apply to a specific platform are noted as such. UNIX systems include both Linux and Mac OS X. Windows systems include all versions of Windows unless otherwise noted.

Readers may want to supplement the material presented here with additional references. *The C Programming Language,* Second Edition by Brian W. Kernighan and Dennis M. Ritchie (Prentice Hall, 1989) provides a good overview of files, file descriptors, and the low-level interfaces on which many of the modules in this section are based. More advanced readers may want to consult a book such as *Advanced Programming in the UNIX Environment,* 2nd Edition by W. Richard Stevens and Stephen Rago (Addison Wesley, 2005). For an overview of general concepts, you may want to locate a college textbook on operating systems. However, given the high cost and limited day-to-day practical utility of these books, you're probably better off asking a nearby computer science student to loan you their copy for a weekend.

commands

The commands module is used to execute simple system commands specified as a string and return their output as a string. It only works on UNIX systems. The functionality provided by this module is somewhat similar to using backquotes (`) in a UNIX shell script. For example, typing `x = commands.getoutput('ls -l')` is similar to saying `x=`ls -l``.

getoutput(*cmd*)

Executes *cmd* in a shell and returns a string containing both the standard output and standard error streams of the command.

getstatusoutput(*cmd*)

Like getoutput(), except that a 2-tuple (*status, output*) is returned, where *status* is the exit code, as returned by the os.wait() function, and *output* is the string returned by getoutput().

Notes

- This module is only available in Python 2. In Python 3, both of the previous functions are found in the subprocess module.

- Although this module can be used for simple shell operations, you are almost always better off using the subprocess module for launching subprocesses and collecting their output.

See Also:

subprocess **(p. 402)**

ConfigParser, configparser

The ConfigParser module (called configparser in Python 3) is used to read .ini format configuration files based on the Windows INI format. These files consist of named sections, each with its own variable assignments such as the following:

```
# A comment
; A comment
[section1]
name1 = value1
name2 = value2

[section2]
; Alternative syntax for assigning values
name1: value1
name2: value2
...
```

The ConfigParser Class

The following class is used to manage configuration variables:

ConfigParser([*defaults* [, *dict_type*]])

Creates a new ConfigParser instance. *defaults* is an optional dictionary of values that can be referenced in configuration variables by including string format specifiers such as '%(*key*)s' where *key* is a key of *defaults*. *dict_type* specifies the type of dictionary that is used internally for storing configuration variables. By default, it is dict (the built-in dictionary).

An instance *c* of ConfigParser has the following operations:

c.add_section(*section*)

Adds a new section to the stored configuration parameters. *section* is a string with the section name.

`c.defaults()`

Returns the dictionary of default values.

`c.get(section, option [, raw [, vars]])`

Returns the value of option *option* from section *section* as a string. By default, the returned string is processed through an interpolation step where format strings such as `'%(option)s'` are expanded. In this case, *option* may the name of another configuration option in the same section or one of the default values supplied in the *defaults* parameter to `ConfigParser`. *raw* is a Boolean flag that disables this interpolation feature, returning the option unmodified. *vars* is an optional dictionary containing more values for use in `'%'` expansions.

`c.getboolean(section, option)`

Returns the value of *option* from section *section* converted to Boolean value. Values such as `"0"`, `"true"`, `"yes"`, `"no"`, `"on"`, and `"off"` are all understood and checked in a case-insensitive manner. Variable interpolation is always performed by this method (see `c.get()`).

`c.getfloat(section, option)`

Returns the value of *option* from section *section* converted to a float with variable interpolation.

`c.getint(section, option)`

Returns the value of *option* from section *section* converted to an integer with variable interpolation.

`c.has_option(section, option)`

Returns `True` if section *section* has an option named *option*.

`c.has_section(section)`

Returns `True` if there is a section named *section*.

`c.items(section [, raw [, vars]])`

Returns a list of (*option*, *value*) pairs from section *section*. *raw* is a Boolean flag that disables the interpolation feature if set to `True`. *vars* is a dictionary of additional values that can be used in `'%'` expansions.

`c.options(section)`

Returns a list of all options in section *section*.

`c.optionxform(option)`

Transforms the option name *option* to the string that's used to refer to the option. By default, this is a lowercase conversion.

`c.read(filenames)`

Reads configuration options from a list of filenames and stores them. *filenames* is either a single string, in which case that is the filename that is read, or a list of filenames. If any of the given filenames can't be found, they are ignored. This is useful if you want to read configuration files from many possible locations, but where such files may or may not be defined. A list of the successfully parsed filenames is returned.

c.readfp(*fp* [, *filename*])

Reads configuration options from a file-like object that has already been opened in *fp*. *filename* specifies the filename associated with *fp* (if any). By default, the filename is taken from *fp*.name or is set to '<???>' if no such attribute is defined.

c.remove_option(*section*, *option*)

Removes *option* from section *section*.

c.remove_section(*section*)

Removes section *section*.

c.sections()

Returns a list of all section names.

c.set(*section*, *option*, **value**)

Sets a configuration option *option* to *value* in section *section*. *value* should be a string.

c.write(*file*)

Writes all of the currently held configuration data to *file*. *file* is a file-like object that has already been opened.

Example

The ConfigParser module is often overlooked, but it is an extremely useful tool for controlling programs that have an extremely complicated user configuration or runtime environment. For example, if you're writing a component that has to run inside of a large framework, a configuration file is often an elegant way to supply runtime parameters. Similarly, a configuration file may be a more elegant approach than having a program read large numbers of command-line options using the optparse module. There are also subtle, but important, differences between using configuration files and simply reading configuration data from a Python source script.

The following few examples illustrate some of the more interesting features of the ConfigParser module. First, consider a sample .ini file:

```
# appconfig.ini
# Configuration file for my mondo application

[output]
LOGFILE=%(LOGDIR)s/app.log
LOGGING=on
LOGDIR=%(BASEDIR)s/logs

[input]
INFILE=%(INDIR)s/initial.dat
INDIR=%(BASEDIR)s/input
```

The following code illustrates how you read a configuration file and supply default values to some of the variables:

```
from configparser import ConfigParser  # Use from ConfigParser in Python 2

# Dictionary of default variable settings
defaults = {
    'basedir' : '/Users/beazley/app'
}

# Create a ConfigParser object and read the .ini file
cfg = ConfigParser(defaults)
cfg.read('appconfig.ini')
```

After you have read a configuration file, you use the `get()` method to retrieve option values. For example:

```
>>> cfg.get('output','logfile')
'/Users/beazley/app/logs/app.log'
>>> cfg.get('input','infile')
'/Users/beazley/app/input/initial.dat'
>>> cfg.getboolean('output','logging')
True
>>>
```

Here, you immediately see some interesting features. First, configuration parameters are case insensitive. Thus, if your program is reading a parameter `'logfile'`, it does not matter if the configuration file uses `'logfile'`, `'LOGFILE'`, or `'LogFile'`. Second, configuration parameters can include variable substitutions such as `'%(BASEDIR)s'` and `'%(LOGDIR)s'` as seen in the file. These substitutions are also case insensitive. Moreover, the definition order of configuration parameters does not matter in these substitutions. For example, in `appconfig.ini`, the `LOGFILE` parameter makes a reference to the `LOGDIR` parameter, which is defined later in the file. Finally, values in configuration files are often interpreted correctly even if they don't exactly match Python syntax or datatypes. For example, the `'on'` value of the `LOGGING` parameter is interpreted as `True` by the `cfg.getboolean()` method.

Configuration files also have the ability to be merged together. For example, suppose the user had their own configuration file with custom settings:

```
; userconfig.ini
;
; Per-user settings

[output]
logging=off

[input]
BASEDIR=/tmp
```

You can merge the contents of this file in with already loaded configuration parameters. For example:

```
>>> cfg.read('userconfig.ini')
['userconfig.ini']
>>> cfg.get('output','logfile')
'/Users/beazley/app/logs/app.log'
>>> cfg.get('output','logging')
'off'
>>> cfg.get('input','infile')
'/tmp/input/initial.dat'
>>>
```

Here, you will notice that the newly loaded configuration selectively replaces the parameters that were already defined. Moreover, if you change one of the configuration parameters that's used in variable substitutions of other configuration parameters, the changes correctly propagate. For example, the new setting of BASEDIR in the input section affects previously defined configuration parameters in that section such as INFILE. This behavior is an important but subtle difference between using a config file and simply defining a set of program parameters in a Python script.

Notes

Two other classes can be used in place of ConfigParser. The class RawConfigParser provides all of the functionality of ConfigParser but doesn't perform any variable interpolation. The SafeConfigParser class provides the same functionality as ConfigParser, but it addresses some subtle problems that arise if configuration values themselves literally include special formatting characters used by the interpolation feature (e.g., '%').

datetime

The datetime module provides a variety of classes for representing and manipulating dates and times. Large parts of this module are simply related to different ways of creating and outputting date and time information. Other major features include mathematical operations such as comparisons and calculations of time deltas. Date manipulation is a complex subject, and readers would be strongly advised to consult Python's online documentation for an introductory background concerning the design of this module.

date **Objects**

A date object represents a simple date consisting of a year, month, and day. The following four functions are used to create dates:

`date(year, month, day)`

Creates a new date object. *year* is an integer in the range datetime.MINYEAR to datetime.MAXYEAR. *month* is an integer in the range 1 to 12, and *day* is an integer in the range 1 to the number of days in the given month. The returned date object is immutable and has the attributes *year*, *month*, and *day* corresponding to the values of the supplied arguments.

`date.today()`

A class method that returns a date object corresponding to the current date.

`date.fromtimestamp(timestamp)`

A class method that returns a date object corresponding to the timestamp *timestamp*. *timestamp* is a value returned by the time.time() function.

`date.fromordinal(ordinal)`

A class method that returns a date object corresponding to an *ordinal* number of days from the minimum allowable date (January 1 of year 1 has ordinal value 1 and January 1, 2006 has ordinal value 732312).

The following class attributes describe the maximum rate and resolution of date instances.

date.min

Class attribute representing the earliest date that can be represented (`datetime.date(1,1,1)`).

date.max

Class attribute representing the latest possible date (`datetime.date(9999,12,31)`).

date.resolution

Smallest resolvable difference between non-equal date objects (`datetime.timedelta(1)`).

An instance, *d*, of date has read-only attributes *d*.year, *d*.month, and *d*.day and additionally provides the following methods:

d.ctime()

Returns a string representing the date in the same format as normally used by the time.ctime() function.

d.isocalendar()

Returns the date as a tuple (*iso_year, iso_week, iso_weekday*), where *iso_week* is in the range 1 to 53 and *iso_weekday* is the range 1 (Monday) to 7 (Sunday). The first *iso_week* is the first week of the year that contains a Thursday. The range of values for the three tuple components are determined by the ISO 8601 standard.

d.isoformat()

Returns an ISO 8601–formatted string of the form '*YYYY-MM-DD*' representing the date.

d.isoweekday()

Returns the day of the week in the range 1 (Monday) to 7 (Sunday).

d.replace([year [, month [, day]]])

Returns a new date object with one or more of the supplied components replaced by a new value. For example, *d*.replace(month=4) returns a new date where the month has been replaced by 4.

d.strftime(format)

Returns a string representing the date formatted according to the same rules as the time.strftime() function. This function only works for dates later than the year 1900. Moreover, format codes for components missing from date objects (such as hours, minutes, and so on) should not be used.

d.timetuple()

Returns a time.struct_time object suitable for use by functions in the time module. Values related to the time of day (hours, minutes, seconds) will be set to 0.

d.toordinal()

Converts *d* to an ordinal value. January 1 of year 1 has ordinal value 1.

d.weekday()

Returns the day of the week in the range 0 (Monday) to 6 (Sunday).

time **Objects**

time objects are used to represent a time in hours, minutes, seconds, and microseconds. Times are created using the following class constructor:

time(*hour* [, *minute* [, *second* [, *microsecond* [, *tzinfo*]]]])

Creates a time object representing a time where 0 <= *hour* < 24, 0 <= *minute* < 60, 0 <= *second* < 60, and 0 <= *microsecond* < 1000000. *tzinfo* provides time zone information and is an instance of the tzinfo class described later in this section. The returned time object has the attributes hour, minute, second, microsecond, and tzinfo, which hold the corresponding values supplied as arguments.

The following class attributes of time describe the range of allowed values and resolution of time instances:

time.min

Class attribute representing the minimum representable time (datetime.time(0,0)).

time.max

Class attribute representing the maximum representable time (datetime.time(23,59, 59, 999999)).

time.resolution

Smallest resolvable difference between non-equal time objects (datetime.timedelta(0,0,1)).

An instance, *t*, of a time object has attributes *t*.hour, *t*.minute, *t*.second, *t*.microsecond, and *t*.tzinfo in addition to the following methods:

t.dst()

Returns the value of *t*.tzinfo.dst(None). The returned object is a timedelta object. If no time zone is set, None is returned.

t.isoformat()

Returns a string representing the time as 'HH:MM:SS.mmmmmm'. If the microseconds are 0, that part of the string is omitted. If time zone information has been supplied, the time may have an offset added to it (for example, 'HH:MM:SS.mmmmmm+HH:MM').

t.replace([*hour* [, *minute* [, *second* [, *microsecond* [, *tzinfo*]]]]])

Returns a new time object, where one or more components have been replaced by the supplied values. For example, *t*.replace(second=30) changes the seconds field to 30 and returns a new time object. The arguments have the same meaning as those supplied to the time() function shown earlier.

t.strftime(*format*)

Returns a string formatted according to the same rules as the time.strftime() function in the time module. Because date information is unavailable, only the formatting codes for time-related information should be used.

`t.tzname()`

Returns the value of `t.tzinfo.tzname()`. If no time zone is set, None is returned.

`t.utcoffset()`

Returns the value of `t.tzinfo.utcoffset(None)`. The returned object is a `timedelta` object. If no time zone has been set, None is returned.

datetime **objects**

datetime objects are used to represent dates and times together. There are many possible ways to create a datetime instance:

`datetime(year, month, day [, hour [, minute [, second [, microsecond [, tzinfo]]]]])`

Creates a new datetime object that combines all the features of date and time objects. The arguments have the same meaning as arguments provided to date() and time().

`datetime.combine(date, time)`

A class method that creates a datetime object by combining the contents of a date object, date, and a time object, time.

`datetime.fromordinal(ordinal)`

A class method that creates a datetime object given an ordinal day (integer number of days since datetime.min). The time components are all set to 0, and tzinfo is set to None.

`datetime.fromtimestamp(timestamp [, tz])`

A class method that creates a datetime object from a timestamp returned by the time.time() function. tz provides optional time zone information and is a tzinfo instance.

`datetime.now([tz])`

A class method that creates a datetime object from the current local date and time. tz provides optional time zone information and is an instance of tzinfo.

`datetime.strptime(datestring, format)`

A class method that creates a datetime object by parsing the date string in datestring according to the date format in format. The parsing is performed using the strptime() function in the time module.

`datetime.utcfromtimestamp(timestamp)`

A class method that creates a datetime object from a timestamp typically returned by time.gmtime().

`datetime.utcnow()`

A class method that creates a datetime object from the current UTC date and time.

The following class attributes describe the range of allowed dates and resolution:

datetime.min

Earliest representable date and time (`datetime.datetime(1,1,1,0,0)`).

datetime.max

Latest representable date and time (`datetime.
datetime(9999,12,31,23,59,59,999999)`).

datetime.resolution

Smallest resolvable difference between non-equal `datetime` objects
(`datetime.timedelta(0,0,1)`).

An instance, `d`, of a `datetime` object has the same methods as `date` and `time`
objects combined. In additional, the following methods are available:

d.astimezone(tz)

Returns a new `datetime` object but in a different time zone, `tz`. The members of the
new object will be adjusted to represent the same UTC time but in the time zone `tz`.

d.date()

Returns a `date` object with the same date.

d.replace([year [, month [, day [, hour [, minute [, second [, microsecond [, tzinfo]]]]]]])

Returns a new `datetime` object with one or more of the listed parameters replaced by
new values. Use keyword arguments to replace an individual value.

d.time()

Returns a `time` object with the same time. The resulting `time` object has no time zone
information set.

d.timetz()

Returns a `time` object with the same time and time zone information.

d.utctimetuple()

Returns a `time.struct_time` object containing date and time information normalized
to UTC time.

timedelta **objects**

`timedelta` objects represent the difference between two dates or times. These objects
are normally created as the result of computing a difference between two `datetime`
instances using the `-` operator. However, they can be manually constructed using the
following class:

timedelta([days [, seconds [, microseconds [, milliseconds [, minutes [, hours [, weeks]]]]]]])

Creates a `timedelta` object that represents the difference between two dates and times.
The only significant parameters are `days`, `seconds`, and `microseconds`, which are used
internally to represent a difference. The other parameters, if supplied, are converted into
days, seconds, and microseconds. The attributes `days`, `seconds`, and `microseconds` of
the returned `timedelta` object contain these values.

The following class attributes describe the maximum range and resolution of `timedelta` instances:

`timedelta.min`

The most negative `timedelta` object that can be represented (`timedelta(-999999999)`)

`timedelta.max`

The most positive `timedelta` object that can be represented (`timedelta(days=999999999, hours=23, minutes=59, seconds=59, microseconds=999999)`).

`timedelta.resolution`

A `timedelta` object representing the smallest resolvable difference between non-equal `timedelta` objects (`timedelta(microseconds=1)`).

Mathematical Operations Involving Dates

A significant feature of the `datetime` module is that it supports mathematical operations involving dates. Both `date` and `datetime` objects support the following operations:

Operation	Description
`td = date1 - date2`	Returns a `timedelta` object
`date2 = date1 + td`	Adds a `timedelta` to a `date`
`date2 = date1 - td`	Subtracts a `timedelta` from a `date`
`date1 < date2`	Date comparison
`date1 <= date2`	
`date1 == date2`	
`date1 != date2`	
`date1 > date2`	
`date1 >= date2`	

When comparing dates, you must use care when time zone information has been supplied. If a date includes `tzinfo` information, that date can only be compared with other dates that include `tzinfo`; otherwise, a `TypeError` is generated. When two dates in different time zones are compared, they are first adjusted to UTC before being compared.

`timedelta` objects also support a variety of mathematical operations:

Operation	Description
`td3 = td2 + td1`	Adds two time deltas
`td3 = td2 - td1`	Subtracts two time deltas
`td2 = td1 * i`	Multiplication by an integer
`td2 = i * td2`	
`td2 = td1 // i`	Floor division by an integer, i
`td2 = -td1`	Unary subtraction, addition
`td2 = +td1`	
`abs(td)`	Absolute value

Operation	Description
td1 < td2	Comparison
td1 <= td2	
td1 == td2	
td1 != td2	
td1 > td2	
td1 >= td2	

Here are some examples:

```
>>> today = datetime.datetime.now()
>>> today.ctime()
'Thu Oct 20 11:10:10 2005'
>>> oneday = datetime.timedelta(days=1)
>>> tomorrow = today + oneday
>>> tomorrow.ctime()
'Fri Oct 21 11:10:10 2005'
>>>
```

In addition to these operations, all date, datetime, time, and timedelta objects are immutable. This means that they can be used as dictionary keys, placed in sets, and used in a variety of other operations.

tzinfo Objects

Many of the methods in the datetime module manipulate special tzinfo objects that represent information about a time zone. tzinfo is merely a base class. Individual time zones are created by inheriting from tzinfo and implementing the following methods:

tz.dst(dt)

Returns a timedelta object representing daylight savings time adjustments, if applicable. Returns None if no information is known about DST. The argument dt is either a datetime object or None.

tz.fromutc(dt)

Converts a datetime object, dt, from UTC time to the local time zone and returns a new datetime object. This method is called by the astimezone() method on datetime objects. A default implementation is already provided by tzinfo, so it's usually not necessary to redefine this method.

tz.tzname(dt)

Returns a string with the name of the time zone (for example, "US/Central"). dt is either a datetime object or None.

tz.utcoffset(dt)

Returns a timedelta object representing the offset of local time from UTC in minutes east of UTC. The offset incorporates all elements that make up the local time, including daylight savings time, if applicable. The argument dt is either a datetime object or None.

The following example shows a basic prototype of how one would define a time zone:

```
# Variables that must be defined
# TZOFFSET   - Timezone offset in hours from UTC. For
#               example, US/CST is -6 hours
# DSTNAME    - Name of timezone when DST is in effect
# STDNAME    - Name of timezone when DST not in effect

class SomeZone(datetime.tzinfo):
        def utcoffset(self,dt):
                return datetime.timedelta(hours=TZOFFSET) + self.dst(dt)
        def dst(self,dt):
                        # is_dst() is a function you must implement to see
                # whether DST is in effect according to local timezone rules.
                if is_dst(dt):
                        return datetime.timedelta(hours=1)
                else:
                        return datetime.timedelta(0)
        def tzname(self,dt):
                if is_dst(dt):
                        return DSTNAME
                else:
                        return STDNAME
```

A number of examples of defining time zones can also be found in the online documentation for datetime.

Date and Time Parsing

A common question that arises with date handling is how to parse different kinds of time and date strings into an appropriate datetime object. The only parsing function that is really provided by the datetime module is datetime.strptime(). However, in order to use this, you need to specify the precise date format using various combinations of format codes (see time.strptime()). For example, to parse the date string s="Aug 23, 2008", you would have to use d = datetime.datetime.strptime(s, "%b %d, %Y").

For "fuzzy" date parsing that automatically understands a number of common date formats, you must turn to third-party modules. Go to the Python Package Index (http://pypi.python.org) and do a search for "datetime" to find a wide variety of utility modules that expand the feature set of the datetime module.

> **See also:**
>
> time (**p. 405**)

errno

The errno module defines symbolic names for the integer error codes returned by various operating system calls, especially those found in the os and socket modules. These codes are typically found in the errno attribute of an OSError or IOError exception. The os.strerror() function can be used to translate an error code into a string error message. The following dictionary can also be used to translate an integer error code into its symbolic name:

`errorcode`

This dictionary maps `errno` integers to symbolic names (such as `'EPERM'`).

POSIX Error Codes

The following table shows the POSIX symbolic names for common system error codes. The error codes listed here are supported on almost every version of UNIX, Macintosh OS-X, and Windows. Different UNIX systems may provide additional error codes that are less common and not listed here. If such errors occur, you can consult the `errorcode` dictionary to find the appropriate symbolic name to use in your program.

Error Code	Description
E2BIG	Arg list too long.
EACCES	Permission denied.
EADDRINUSE	Address already in use.
EADDRNOTAVAIL	Cannot assign requested address.
EAFNOSUPPORT	Address family not supported by protocol.
EAGAIN	Try again.
EALREADY	Operation already in progress.
EBADF	Bad file number.
EBUSY	Device or resource busy.
ECHILD	No child processes.
ECONNABORTED	Software caused connection abort.
ECONNREFUSED	Connection refused.
ECONNRESET	Connection reset by peer.
EDEADLK	Resource deadlock would occur.
EDEADLOCK	File-locking deadlock error.
EDESTADDRREQ	Destination address required.
EDOM	Math argument out of domain of function.
EDQUOT	Quota exceeded.
EEXIST	File exists.
EFAULT	Bad address.
EFBIG	File too large.
EHOSTDOWN	Host is down.
EHOSTUNREACH	No route to host.
EILSEQ	Illegal byte sequence.
EINPROGRESS	Operation now in progress.
EINTR	Interrupted system call.
EINVAL	Invalid argument.
EIO	I/O error.
EISCONN	Transport endpoint is already connected.
EISDIR	Is a directory.
ELOOP	Too many symbolic links encountered.
EMFILE	Too many open files.
EMLINK	Too many links.

Error Code	Description
EMSGSIZE	Message too long.
ENETDOWN	Network is down.
ENETRESET	Network dropped connection due to reset.
ENETUNREACH	Network is unreachable.
ENFILE	File table overflow.
ENOBUFS	No buffer space available.
ENODEV	No such device.
ENOENT	No such file or directory.
ENOEXEC	Exec format error.
ENOLCK	No record locks available.
ENOMEM	Out of memory.
ENOPROTOOPT	Protocol not available.
ENOSPC	No space left on device.
ENOSYS	Function not implemented.
ENOTCONN	Transport endpoint is not connected.
ENOTDIR	Not a directory.
ENOTEMPTY	Directory not empty.
ENOTSOCK	Socket operation on non-socket.
ENOTTY	Not a terminal.
ENXIO	No such device or address.
EOPNOTSUPP	Operation not supported on transport endpoint.
EPERM	Operation not permitted.
EPFNOSUPPORT	Protocol family not supported.
EPIPE	Broken pipe.
EPROTONOSUPPORT	Protocol not supported.
EPROTOTYPE	Protocol wrong type for socket.
ERANGE	Math result not representable.
EREMOTE	Object is remote.
EROFS	Read-only file system.
ESHUTDOWN	Cannot send after transport endpoint shutdown.
ESOCKTNOSUPPORT	Socket type not supported.
ESPIPE	Illegal seek.
ESRCH	No such process.
ESTALE	Stale NFS file handle.
ETIMEDOUT	Connection timed out.
ETOOMANYREFS	Too many references: Cannot splice.
EUSERS	Too many users.
EWOULDBLOCK	Operation would block.
EXDEV	Cross-device link.

Windows Error Codes

The error codes in the following table are only available on Windows.

Error Code	Description
WSAEACCES	Permission denied.
WSAEADDRINUSE	Address already in use.
WSAEADDRNOTAVAIL	Cannot assign requested address.
WSAEAFNOSUPPORT	Address family not supported by protocol family.
WSAEALREADY	Operation already in progress.
WSAEBADF	Invalid file handle.
WSAECONNABORTED	Software caused connection abort.
WSAECONNREFUSED	Connection refused.
WSAECONNRESET	Connection reset by peer.
WSAEDESTADDRREQ	Destination address required.
WSAEDISCON	Remote shutdown.
WSAEDQUOT	Disk quota exceeded.
WSAEFAULT	Bad address.
WSAEHOSTDOWN	Host is down.
WSAEHOSTUNREACH	No route to host.
WSAEINPROGRESS	Operation now in progress.
WSAEINTR	Interrupted system call.
WSAEINVAL	Invalid argument.
WSAEISCONN	Socket already connected.
WSAELOOP	Cannot translate name.
WSAEMFILE	Too many open files.
WSAEMSGSIZE	Message too long.
WSAENAMETOOLONG	Name too long.
WSAENETDOWN	Network is down.
WSAENETRESET	Network dropped connection on reset.
WSAENETUNREACH	Network is unreachable.
WSAENOBUFS	No buffer space is available.
WSAENOPROTOOPT	Bad protocol option.
WSAENOTCONN	Socket is not connected.
WSAENOTEMPTY	Cannot remove non-empty directory.
WSAENOTSOCK	Socket operation on non-socket.
WSAEOPNOTSUPP	Operation not supported.
WSAEPFNOSUPPORT	Protocol family not supported.
WSAEPROCLIM	Too many processes.
WSAEPROTONOSUPPORT	Protocol not supported.
WSAEPROTOTYPE	Protocol wrong type for socket.
WSAEREMOTE	Item not available locally.
WSAESHUTDOWN	Cannot send after socket shutdown.
WSAESOCKTNOSUPPORT	Socket type not supported.
WSAESTALE	File handle no longer available.
WSAETIMEDOUT	Connection timed out.

Error Code	Description
WSAETOOMANYREFS	Too many references to a kernel object.
WSAEUSERS	Quota exceeded.
WSAEWOULDBLOCK	Resource temporarily unavailable.
WSANOTINITIALISED	Successful WSA startup not performed.
WSASYSNOTREADY	Network subsystem not available.
WSAVERNOTSUPPORTED	Winsock.dll version out of range.

fcntl

The fcntl module performs file and I/O control on UNIX file descriptors. File descriptors can be obtained using the fileno() method of a file or socket object.

fcntl(*fd*, *cmd* [, *arg*])

Performs a command, *cmd*, on an open file descriptor, *fd*. *cmd* is an integer command code. *arg* is an optional argument that's either an integer or a string. If *arg* is passed as an integer, the return value of this function is an integer. If *arg* is a string, it's interpreted as a binary data structure, and the return value of the call is the contents of the buffer converted back into a string object. In this case, the supplied argument and return value should be less than 1,024 bytes to avoid possible data corruption. The following commands are available:

Command	Description
F_DUPFD	Duplicates a file descriptor. *arg* is the lowest number that the new file descriptor can assume. Similar to the os.dup() system call.
F_SETFD	Sets the close-on-exec flag to *arg* (0 or 1). If set, the file is closed on an exec() system call.
F_GETFD	Returns the close-on-exec flag.
F_SETFL	Sets status flags to *arg*, which is the bitwise OR of the following:
	O_NDELAY—Nonblocking I/O (System V)
	O_APPEND—Append mode (System V)
	O_SYNC—Synchronous write (System V)
	FNDELAY—Nonblocking I/O (BSD)
	FAPPEND—Append mode (BSD)
	FASYNC—Sends SIGIO signal to process group when I/O is possible (BSD)
F_GETFL	Gets status flags as set by F_SETFL.
F_GETOWN	Gets process ID or process group ID set to receive SIGIO and SIGURG signals (BSD).
F_SETOWN	Sets process ID or process group ID to receive SIGIO and SIGURG signals (BSD).
F_GETLK	Returns flock structure used in file-locking operations.
F_SETLK	Locks a file, returning -1 if the file is already locked.
F_SETLKW	Locks a file but waits if the lock cannot be acquired.

An IOError exception is raised if the fcntl() function fails. The F_GETLK and F_SETLK commands are supported through the lockf() function.

ioctl(fd, op, arg [, mutate_flag])

This function is like the fcntl() function, except that the operations supplied in op are generally defined in the library module termios. The extra mutate_flag controls the behavior of this function when a mutable buffer object is passed as an argument. Further details about this can be found in the online documentation. Because the primary use of ioctl() is to interact with device-drivers and other low-level components of the operating system, its use depends highly on the underlying platform. It should not be used in code that aims to be portable.

flock(fd, op)

Performs a lock operation, op, on the file descriptor fd. op is the bitwise OR of the following constants, which are found in fnctl:

Item	Description
LOCK_EX	Exclusive lock. All further attempts to acquire the lock will block until the lock is released.
LOCK_NB	Non-blocking mode. Returns immediately with an IOError if the lock is already in use.
LOCK_SH	Shared lock. Blocks any attempts to acquire an exclusive lock (LOCK_EX), but shared locks can still be acquired.
LOCK_UN	Unlock. Releases any previous held lock.

In nonblocking mode, an IOError exception is raised if the lock cannot be acquired. On some systems, the process of opening and locking a file can be performed in a single operation by adding special flags to the os.open() operation. Consult the os module for more details.

lockf(fd, op [, len [, start [, whence]]])

Performs record or range locking on part of a file. op is the same as for the flock() function. len is the number of bytes to lock. start is the starting position of the lock relative to the value of whence. whence is 0 for the beginning of the file, 1 for the current position, and 2 for the end of the file.

Example

```
import fcntl

# Open a file
f = open("foo","w")

# Set the close-on-exec bit for a file object f
fcntl.fcntl(f.fileno(), fcntl.F_SETFD, 1)

# Lock a file (blocking)
fcntl.flock(f.fileno(), fcntl.LOCK_EX)
```

```
# Lock the first 8192 bytes of a file (non-blocking)
try:
    fcntl.lockf(f.fileno(), fcntl.LOCK_EX | fcntl.LOCK_NB, 8192, 0, 0)
except IOError as e:
    print "Unable to acquire lock %s" % e)
```

Notes

- The set of available fcntl() commands and options is system-dependent. The fcntl module may contain more than 100 constants on some platforms.
- Although locking operations defined in other modules often make use of the context-manager protocol, this is not the case for file locking. If you acquire a file lock, make sure your code is written to properly release the lock.
- Many of the functions in this module can also be applied to the file descriptors of sockets.

io

The io module implements classes for various forms of I/O as well as the built-in open() function that is used in Python 3. The module is also available for use in Python 2.6.

The central problem addressed by the io module is the seamless handling of different forms of basic I/O. For example, working with text is slightly different than working with binary data because of issues related to newlines and character encodings. To handle these differences, the module is built as a series of layers, each of which adds more functionality to the last.

Base I/O Interface

The io module defines a basic I/O programming interface that all file-like objects implement. This interface is defined by a base class IOBase. An instance f of IOBase supports these basic operations:

Attribute	Description
f.closed	Flag indicating whether or not the file is closed.
f.close()	Closes the file.
f.fileno()	Returns the integer file descriptor.
f.flush()	Flushes the I/O buffers (if any).
f.isatty()	Returns True if f is a terminal.
f.readable()	Returns True if f was opened for reading.
f.readline([limit])	Reads one line from the stream. limit is the maximum number of bytes to read.
f.readlines([limit])	Reads all lines from f and return as a list. limit, if provided, is the maximum number of bytes that can be read before stopping. The actual number of bytes read will be slightly greater to accommodate the last line, which is kept intact.

Attribute	Description
f.seek(*offset*, [*whence*])	Moves the file pointer to a new position relative to the location specified in *whence*. *offset* is the number of bytes. *whence* is 0 for the start of the file, 1 for the current position, and 2 for the end of the file.
f.seekable()	Returns True if *f* is seekable.
f.tell()	Returns the current value of the file pointer.
f.truncate([*size*])	Truncates the file size so that it is at most *size* bytes. If *size* isn't given, it truncates the file to 0 bytes.
f.writable()	Returns True if *f* was opened for writing.
f.writelines(*lines*)	Writes a sequence of lines to *f*. Line endings are not added so they must already be part of each line.

Raw I/O

The lowest level of the I/O system is related to direct I/O involving raw bytes. The core object for this is FileIO, which provides a fairly direct interface to low-level system calls such as read() and write().

FileIO(*name* [, *mode* [, *closefd*]])

A class for performing raw low-level I/O on a file or system file descriptor. *name* is either a filename or an integer file descriptor such as that returned by the os.open() function or the fileno() method of other file objects. *mode* is one of 'r' (the default); 'w'; or 'a' for reading, writing, or appending. A '+' can be added to the mode for update mode in which both reading and writing is supported. *closefd* is a flag that determines if the close() method actually closes the underlying file. By default, this is True, but it can be set False if you're using FileIO to put a wrapper around a file that was already opened elsewhere. If a filename was given, the resulting file object is opened directly using the operating system's open() call. There is no internal buffering, and all data is processed as raw byte strings. An instance *f* of FileIO has all of the basic I/O operations described earlier plus the following attributes and methods:

Attribute	Description
f.closefd	Flag that determines if the underlying file descriptor will be closed on f.close() (read-only).
f.mode	File mode used when opening (read-only).
f.name	filename (read-only).
f.read([*size*])	Reads at most *size* bytes using a single system call. If *size* is omitted, as much data as possible is returned using f.readall(). This operation may returns fewer bytes than requested so you must use len() to check. None is returned if no data is available in non-blocking mode.
f.readall()	Reads as much data as is available and returns as a single byte string. An empty string is returned on EOF. In non-blocking mode, only as much data as is immediately available is returned.
f.write(*bytes*)	Writes a byte string or byte-array to *f* using a single system call. The number of bytes actually written is returned—which may be less than the number supplied in *bytes*.

It is important to emphasize that FileIO objects are extremely low-level, providing a rather thin layer over operating system calls such as read() and write(). Specifically, users of this object will need to diligently check return codes as there is no guarantee that the f.read() or f.write() operations will read or write all of the requested data. The fcntl module can be used to change low-level aspects of files such as file locking, blocking behavior, and so forth.

FileIO objects should not be used for line-oriented data such as text. Although methods such as f.readline() and f.readlines() are defined, these come from the IOBase base class where they are both implemented entirely in Python and work by issuing f.read() operations for a single byte at a time. Needless to say, the resulting performance is horrible. For example, using f.readline() on a FileIO object f is more than 750 times slower than using f.readline() on a standard file object created by the open() function in Python 2.6.

Buffered Binary I/O

The buffered I/O layer contains a collection of file objects that read and write raw binary data, but with in-memory buffering. As input, these objects all require a file object that implements raw I/O such as the FileIO object in the previous section. All of the classes in this section inherit from BufferedIOBase.

BufferedReader(raw [, buffer_size])

A class for buffered binary reading on a raw file specified in raw. buffer_size specifies the buffer size to use in bytes. If omitted, the value of DEFAULT_BUFFER_SIZE is used (8,192 bytes as of this writing). An instance f of BufferedReader supports all of the operations provided on IOBase in addition to these operations:

Method	Description
f.peek([n])	Returns at most n bytes of data from the I/O buffer without moving the file pointer. If n is omitted, a single byte is returned. If necessary, a read operation will be issued to fill the buffer if it is currently empty. This operation never returns more bytes than the current buffer size, so the result may be smaller than the requested number of bytes in n.
f.read([n])	Reads n bytes and returns as a byte string. If n is omitted, all available data (up to EOF) is read and returned. If the underlying file is non-blocking, any available data is read and returned. If a non-blocking file is read and no data is available, a BlockingIOError exception is raised.
f.read1([n])	Reads up to n bytes and returns as a byte string using a single system call. If any data is already loaded in the buffer, it is simply returned. Otherwise, a single read() is made on the raw file to return data. Unlike f.read(), this operation may return less data than requested even if the underlying file is not at EOF.
f.readinto(b)	Reads len(b) bytes of data from the file into an existing bytearray object b. The actual number of bytes read is returned. If the underlying file is in non-blocking mode, a BlockingIOError exception is raised if no data is available.

`BufferedWriter(raw [, buffer_size [, max_buffer_size]])`

A class for buffered binary writing on a raw file specified in `raw`. `buffer_size` specifies the number of bytes that can be saved in the buffer before data is flushed to the underlying I/O stream. The default value is `DEFAULT_BUFFER_SIZE`. `max_buffer_size` specifies the maximum buffer size to use for storing output data that is being written to a non-blocking stream and defaults to twice the value of `buffer_size`. This value is larger to allow for continued writing while the previous buffer contents are written to the I/O stream by the operating system. An instance `f` of `BufferedWriter` supports the following operations:

Method	Description
`f.flush()`	Writes all bytes stored in the buffer to the underlying I/O stream. Raises a `BlockingIOError` exception if the file is in non-blocking mode and the operation would block (e.g., if the stream can't accept any new data at the moment).
`f.write(bytes)`	Writes the bytes in `bytes` to the I/O stream and returns the number of bytes actually written. If the underlying stream is non-blocking, a `BlockingIOError` exception is raised if write operation would block.

`BufferedRWPair(reader, writer [, buffer_size [, max_buffer_size]])`

A class for buffered binary reading and writing on a pair of raw I/O streams. `reader` is a raw file that supports reading, and `writing` is a raw file that supports writing. These files may be different, which may be useful for certain kinds of communication involving pipes and sockets. The buffer size parameters have the same meaning as for `BufferedWriter`. An instance `f` of `BufferedRWPair` supports all of the operations for `BufferedReader` and `BufferedWriter`.

`BufferedRandom(raw [, buffer_size [, max_buffer_size]])`

A class for buffered binary reading and writing on a raw I/O stream that supports random access (e.g., seeking). `raw` must be a raw file that supports both read, write, and seek operations. The buffer size parameters have the same meaning as for `BufferedWriter`. An instance `f` of `BufferedRandom` supports all of the operations for `BufferedReader` and `BufferedWriter`.

`BytesIO([bytes])`

An in-memory file that implements the functionality of a buffered I/O stream. `bytes` is a byte string that specifies the initial contents of the file. An instance `b` of `BytesIO` supports all of the operations of `BufferedReader` and `BufferedWriter` objects. In addition, a method `b.getvalue()` can be used to return the current contents of the file as a byte string.

As with `FileIO` objects, all the file objects in this section should not be used with line-oriented data such as text. Although it's not quite as bad due to buffering, the resulting performance is still quite poor (e.g., more than 50 times slower than reading lines with files created using the Python 2.6 built-in `open()` function). Also, because of internal buffering, you need to take care to manage `flush()` operations when writing. For example, if you use `f.seek()` to move the file pointer to a new location, you should first use `f.flush()` to flush any previously written data (if any).

Also, be aware that the buffer size parameters only specify a limit at which writes occur and do not necessarily set a limit on internal resource use. For example, when you do a `f.write(data)` on a buffered file `f`, all of the bytes in `data` are first copied into the internal buffers. If `data` represents a very large byte array, this copying will substantially increase the memory use of your program. Thus, it is better to write large amounts of data in reasonably sized chunks, not all at once with a single `write()` operation. It should be noted that because the `io` module is relatively new, this behavior might be different in future versions.

Text I/O

The text I/O layer is used to process line-oriented character data. The classes defined in this section build upon buffered I/O streams and add line-oriented processing as well as Unicode character encoding and decoding. All of the classes here inherit from `TextIOBase`.

`TextIOWrapper(buffered [, encoding [, errors [, newline [, line_buffering]]]])`

A class for a buffered text stream. `buffered` is a buffered I/O as described in the previous section. `encoding` is a string such as `'ascii'` or `'utf-8'` that specifies the text encoding. `errors` specifies the Unicode error-handling policy and is `'strict'` by default (see Chapter 9, "Input and Output," for a description). `newline` is the character sequence representing a newline and may be `None`, `''`, `'\n'`, `'\r'`, or `'\r\n'`. If `None` is given, then universal newline mode is enabled in which any of the other line endings are translated into `'\n'` when reading and `os.linesep` is used as the newline on output. If `newline` is one of the other values, then all `'\n'` characters are translated into the specified newline on output. `line_buffering` is a flag that controls whether or not a `flush()` operation is performed when any write operation contains the newline character. By default, this is `False`. An instance `f` of `TextIOWrapper` supports all of the operations defined on `IOBase` as well as the following:

Method	Description
`f.encoding`	The name of the text encoding being used.
`f.errors`	Encoding and decoding error handling policy.
`f.line_buffering`	Flag that determines line buffering behavior.
`f.newlines`	None, a string, or a tuple giving all of the different forms of newlines translated.
`f.read([n])`	Reads at most n characters from the underlying stream and returns as a string. If n is omitted, then this reads all available data to the end of file. Returns the empty string at EOF. The returned strings are decoded according to the encoding setting in `f.encoding`.
`f.readline([limit])`	Reads a single line of text and returns as a string. Returns an empty string at EOF. `limit` is the maximum number of bytes to read.
`f.write(s)`	Writes string s to the underlying stream using the text encoding in `f.encoding`.

`StringIO([initial [, encoding [, errors [, newline]]]])`

An in-memory file object with the same behavior as a `TextIOWrapper`. `initial` is a string that specifies the initial contents of the file. The other parameters have the same meaning as with TextIOWrapper. An instance *s* of StringIO supports all of the usual file operations, in addition to a method *s*.getvalue() that returns the current contents of the memory buffer.

The open() Function

The io module defines the following open() function, which is the same as the built-in open() function in Python 3.

open(*file* [, *mode* [, *buffering* [, *encoding* [, *errors* [, *newline* [, *closefd*]]]]]])

Opens *file* and returns an appropriate I/O object. *file* is either a string specifying the name of a file or an integer file descriptor for an I/O stream that has already been opened. The result of this function is one of the I/O classes defined in the io module depending on the settings of *mode* and *buffering*. If *mode* is any of the text modes such as 'r', 'w', 'a', or 'U', then an instance of TextIOWrapper is returned. If *mode* is a binary mode such as 'rb' or 'wb', then the result depends on the setting of *buffering*. If *buffering* is 0, then an instance of FileIO is returned for performing raw unbuffered I/O. If *buffering* is any other value, then an instance of BufferReader, BufferedWriter, or BufferedRandom is returned depending on the file mode. The *encoding*, *errors*, and *errors* parameters are only applicable to files opened in text mode and passed to the TextIOWrapper constructor. The *closefd* is only applicable if *file* is an integer descriptor and is passed to the FileIO constructor.

Abstract Base Classes

The io module defines the following abstract base classes that can be used for type checking and defining new I/O classes:

Abstract Class	Description
IOBase	Base class for all I/O classes.
RawIOBase	Base class for objects that support raw binary I/O. Inherits from IOBase.
BufferedIOBase	Base class for objects that support buffered binary I/O. Inherits from IOBase.
TextIOBase	Base class for objects that support text streams. Inherits from IOBase.

It is rare for most programmers to work with these classes directly. You should refer to the online documentation for details concerning their use and definition.

> **Note**
>
> The io module is a new addition to Python, first appearing in Python 3 and backported to Python 2.6. As of this writing, the module is immature and has extremely poor run-time performance—especially for any application that involves heavy amounts of text I/O. If you are using Python 2, you will be better served by the built-in open() function than using the I/O classes defined in the io module. If you are using Python 3, there seems to be no other alternative. Although performance improvements are likely in future releases, this layered approach to I/O coupled with Unicode decoding is unlikely to match the raw I/O performance found in the C standard library, which is the basis for I/O in Python 2.

logging

The `logging` module provides a flexible facility for applications to log events, errors, warnings, and debugging information. This information can be collected, filtered, written to files, sent to the system log, and even sent over the network to remote machines. This section covers the essential details of using this module for most common cases.

Logging Levels

The main focus of the `logging` module concerns the issuing and handling of log messages. Each message consists of some text along with an associated level that indicates its severity. Levels have both a symbolic name and numerical value as follows:

Level	Value	Description
CRITICAL	50	Critical errors/messages
ERROR	40	Errors
WARNING	30	Warning messages
INFO	20	Informative messages
DEBUG	10	Debugging
NOTSET	0	No level set

These different levels are the basis for various functions and methods throughout the `logging` module. For example, there are methods to issue log messages at each level as well as filters that work by blocking messages that don't meet a certain threshold value.

Basic Configuration

Before using any other functions in the `logging` module, you should first perform some basic configuration of a special object known as the *root logger*. The root logger is responsible for managing the default behavior of log messages including the logging level, output destination, message format, and other basic details. The following function is used for configuration:

`basicConfig([**kwargs])`

Performs basic configuration of the root logger. This function should be called before any other logging calls are made. The function accepts a number of keyword arguments:

Keyword Argument	Description
filename	Appends log messages to a file with the given filename.
filemode	Specifies the mode used to open the file. By default, mode `'a'` (append) is used.
format	Format string used to produce log messages.
datefmt	Format string used to output dates and times.
level	Sets the level of the root logger. All log messages with a level equal to or above this level will be processed. Lower-level messages will be silently ignored.
stream	Provides an open file to which log messages are sent. The default stream is `sys.stderr`. This parameter may not be used simultaneously with the `filename` parameter.

Most of these parameters are self-explanatory. The *format* argument is used to specify the format of log messages along with optional contextual information such as filenames, levels, line numbers, and so forth. *datefmt* is a date format string compatible with the `time.strftime()` function. If omitted, the date format is set to the ISO8601 format.

The following expansions are recognized in *format*:

Format	Description
`%(name)s`	Name of the logger.
`%(levelno)s`	Numeric logging level.
`%(levelname)s`	Text name of the logging level.
`%(pathname)s`	Pathname of the source file where the logging call was executed.
`%(filename)s`	filename of the source file where the logging call was executed.
`%(funcName)s`	Function name in which the logging call was made.
`%(module)s`	Module name where the logging call executed.
`%(lineno)d`	Line number where the logging call executed.
`%(created)f`	Time when the logging call executed. The value is a number as returned by `time.time()`.
`%(asctime)s`	ASCII-formatted date and time when the logging call was executed.
`%(msecs)s`	Millisecond portion of the time when the logging call executed.
`%(thread)d`	Thread ID.
`%(threadName)s`	Thread name.
`%(process)d`	Process ID.
`%(message)s`	The logged message (supplied by user).

Here is an example that illustrates a single configuration where log messages with a level of INFO or higher are appended to a file:

```
import logging
logging.basicConfig(
    filename = "app.log",
    format   = "%(levelname)-10s %(asctime)s %(message)s",
    level    = logging.INFO
)
```

With this configuration, a CRITICAL log message of 'Hello World' will appear as follows in the log file 'app.log'.

```
CRITICAL   2005-10-25 20:46:57,126 Hello World
```

Logger **Objects**

In order to issue log messages, you have to obtain a Logger object. This section describes the process of creating, configuring, and using these objects.

Creating a Logger

To create a new Logger object, you use the following function:

`getLogger([logname])`

Returns a Logger instance associated with the name *logname*. If no such object exists, a new Logger instance is created and returned. *logname* is a string that specifies a name or series of names separated by periods (for example `'app'` or `'app.net'`). If you omit `logname`, you will get the `Logger` object associated with the root logger.

The creation of `Logger` instances is different than what you find in most other library modules. When you create a `Logger`, you always give it a name which is passed to `getLogger()` as the `logname` parameter. Internally, `getLogger()` keeps a cache of the `Logger` instances along with their associated names. If another part of the program requests a logger with the same name, the previously created instance is returned. This arrangement greatly simplifies the handling of log messages in large applications because you don't have to figure out how to pass `Logger` instances around between different program modules. Instead, in each module where you want logging, you just use `getLogger()` to get a reference to the appropriate `Logger` object.

Picking Names

For reasons that will become clear later, you should always pick meaningful names when using `getLogger()`. For example, if your application is called `'app'`, then you should minimally use `getLogger('app')` at the top of every program module that makes up the application. For example:

```
import logging
log = logging.getLogger('app')
```

You might also consider adding the module name to the logger such as `getLogger('app.net')` or `getLogger('app.user')` in order to more clearly indicate the source of log messages. This can be done using statements such as this:

```
import logging
log = logging.getLogger('app.'+__name__)
```

Adding the module name makes it easier to selectively turn off or reconfigure the logging for specific program modules as will be described later.

Issuing Log Messages

If `log` is an instance of a `Logger` object (created using the `getLogger()` function in the previous section), the following methods are used to issue log messages at the different logging levels:

Logging Level	Method
CRITICAL	`log.critical(fmt [, *args [, exc_info [, extra]]])`
ERROR	`log.error(fmt [, *args [, exc_info [, extra]]])`
WARNING	`log.warning(fmt [, *args [, exc_info [, extra]]])`
INFO	`log.info(fmt [, *args [, exc_info [, extra]]])`
DEBUG	`log.debug(fmt [, *args [, exc_info [, extra]]])`

The `fmt` argument is a format string that specifies the format of the log message. Any remaining arguments in `args` serve as arguments for format specifiers in the format string. The string formatting operator % is used to form the resulting message from these arguments. If multiple arguments are provided, they are placed into a tuple for formatting. If a single argument is provided, it is placed directly after the % when formatting.

Thus, if you pass a single dictionary as an argument, the format string can include dictionary key names. Here are a few examples that illustrate how this works:

```
log = logging.getLogger("app")
# A log message using positional formatting
log.critical("Can't connect to %s at port %d", host, port)

# A log message using dictionary formatting
parms = {
    'host' : 'www.python.org',
    'port' : 80
}
log.critical("Can't connect to %(host)s at port %(port)d", parms)
```

The keyword argument *exc_info*, if set to True, adds exception information from sys.exc_info() to the log message. If *exc_info* is set to an exception tuple such as that returned by sys.exc_info(), then that information is used. The *extra* keyword argument is a dictionary that supplies additional values for use in log message format strings (described later). Both *exc_info* and *extra* must be specified as keyword arguments.

When issuing log messages, you should avoid code that carries out string formatting at the time the message is issued (that is, formatting a message and then passing the result into the logging module). For example,

```
log.critical("Can't connect to %s at port %d" % (host, port))
```

In this example, the string formatting operation always occurs *before* the call to log.critical() because the arguments to a function or method have to be fully evaluated. However, in the example at the top of the page, the parameters used for string formatting operation are merely passed to the logging module and used only if the log message is actually going to be handled. This is a very subtle distinction, but because many applications choose to filter log messages or only emit logs during debugging, the first approach performs less work and runs faster when logging is disabled.

In addition to the methods shown, there are a few additional methods for issuing log messages on a Logger instance *log*.

log.exception(*fmt* [, **args*])

Issues a message at the ERROR level but adds exception information from the current exception being handled. This can only be used inside except blocks.

log.log(*level*, fmt [, **args* [, *exc_info* [, *extra*]]])

Issues a logging message at the level specified by *level*. This can be used if the logging level is determined by a variable or if you want to have additional logging levels not covered by the five basic levels.

log.findCaller()

Returns a tuple (*filename*, *lineno*, *funcname*) corresponding to the caller's source filename, line number, and function name. This information is sometimes useful when issuing log messages—for example, if you want to add information about the location of the logging call to a message.

Filtering Log Messages

Each `Logger` object *log* has an internal level and filtering mechanism that determines which log messages get handled. The following two methods are used to perform simple filtering based on the numeric level of log messages:

`log.setLevel(level)`

Sets the level of *log*. Only logging messages with a level greater than or equal to *level* will be handled. All other messages are simply ignored. By default, the level is `logging.NOTSET` which processes all log messages.

`log.isEnabledFor(level)`

Returns `True` if a logging message at level *level* would be processed.

Logging messages can also be filtered based on information associated with the message itself—for example, the filename, the line number, and other details. The following methods are used for this:

`log.addFilter(filt)`

Adds a filter object, *filt*, to the logger.

`log.removeFilter(filt)`

Removes a filter object, *filt*, from the logger.

In both methods, *filt* is an instance of a `Filter` object.

`Filter(logname)`

Creates a filter that only allows log messages from *logname* or its children to pass through. For example, if *logname* is `'app'`, then messages from loggers such as `'app'`, `'app.net'`, or `'app.user'` will pass, but messages from a logger such as `'spam'` will not.

Custom filters can be created by subclassing `Filter` and implementing the method `filter(record)` that receives as input a record containing information about a logging message. As output, `True` or `False` is returned depending on whether or not the message should be handled. The *record* object passed to this method typically has the following attributes:

Attribute	Description
record.name	Logger name
record.levelname	Level name
record.levelno	Level number
record.pathname	Pathname of the module
record.filename	Base filename
record.module	Module name
record.exc_info	Exception information
record.lineno	Line number where log message was issued
record.funcName	Function name where log message was issued
record.created	Time at which issued
record.thread	Thread identifier
record.threadName	Thread name
record.process	PID of currently executing process

The following example illustrates how you create a custom filter:

```
class FilterFunc(logging.Filter):
    def __init__(self,name):
        self.funcName = name
    def filter(self, record):
        if record.funcName == self.funcName: return False
        else: return True

log.addFilter(FilterFunc('foo'))    # Ignore all messages originating from foo()
log.addFilter(FilterFunc('bar'))    # Ignore all messages originating from bar()
```

Message Propagation and Hierarchical Loggers

In advanced logging applications, Logger objects can be organized into a hierarchy. This is done by giving a logger object a name such as 'app.net.client'. Here, there are actually three different Logger objects called 'app', 'app.net', and 'app.net.client'. When a message is issued on any of the loggers and it successfully passes that logger's filter, it propagates to and is handled by all of the parents. For example, a message successfully issued on 'app.net.client' also propagates to 'app.net', 'app' and the root logger.

The following attributes and methods of a Logger object *log* control this propagation.

log.propagate

A Boolean flag that indicates whether or not messages propagate to the parent logger. By default, this is set to True.

log.getEffectiveLevel()

Returns the effective level of the logger. If a level has been set using setLevel(), that level is returned. If no level has been explicitly set (the level is logging.NOTSET in this case), this function returns the effective level of the parent logger instead. If none of the parent loggers have a level set, the effective level of the root logger will be returned.

The primary purpose of hierarchical logging is to be able to more easily filter log messages originating from different parts of a large application. For example, if you wanted to shut down log messages from the 'app.net.client' part of an application, you might add configuration code such as the following:

```
import logging
logging.getLogger('app.net.client').propagate = False
```

Or, in this code, we're ignoring all but the most severe messages from a program module:

```
import logging
logging.getLogger('app.net.client').setLevel(logging.CRITICAL)
```

A subtle aspect of hierarchical loggers is that the decision to handle a log message is made entirely by the level and filters on the Logger object on which the message was issued, not by the filters on any of the parents. Thus, if a message passes the first set of filters, it is propagated to *and handled* by all the parent loggers regardless of their own filter and level settings—even if these filters would have rejected the message. At first glance, the behavior is counterintuitive and might even seem like a bug. However, setting the level of a child logger to a value that is lower than its parent is one way to override the settings on the parent, achieving a kind of level promotion. Here is an example:

```
import logging

# The top-level logger 'app'.
log = logging.getLogger('app')
log.setLevel(logging.CRITICAL)          # Only accept CRITICAL level messages.

# A child logger 'app.net'
net_log = logging.getLogger('app.net')
net_log.setLevel(logging.ERROR)         # Accept ERROR messages on 'app.net'.
                                        # These messages will now be handled by the
                                        # 'app' logger even though its level is
                                        # CRITICAL.
```

When using hierarchical loggers, you only have to configure the logging objects where you want to change the filtering or propagation behavior. Because messages naturally propagate to the root logger, it will ultimately be responsible for producing the output and any configuration that you made using `basicConfig()` will apply.

Message Handling

Normally, messages are handled by the root logger. However, any `Logger` object can have special handlers added to it that receive and process log messages. This is done using these methods of a `Logger` instance *log*.

`log.addHandler(handler)`

Adds a `Handler` object to the logger.

`log.removeHandler(handler)`

Removes the `Handler` object *handler* from the logger.

    The `logging` module has a variety of pre-built handlers for writing log messages to files, streams, system logs, and so forth. These are described in further detail in the next section. However, the following example shows how loggers and handlers are hooked together using these methods.

```
import logging
import sys

# Create a top-level logger called 'app'
app_log = logging.getLogger("app")
app_log.setLevel(logging.INFO)
app_log.propagate = False

# Add some message handlers to the 'app' log
app_log.addHandler(logging.FileHandler('app.log'))
app_log.addHandler(logging.StreamHandler(sys.stderr))

# Issue some messages.  These go to app.log and sys.stderr
app_log.critical("Creeping death detected!")
app_log.info("FYI")
```

When you add your own handlers to process messages, it is often your intent to override the behavior of the root logger. This is why message propagation is disabled in the previous example (i.e., the `'app'` logger is simply going to handle all of the messages).

Handler Objects

The `logging` module provides a collection of pre-built handlers that can process log messages in various in ways. These handlers are added to `Logger` objects using their `addHandler()` method. In addition, each handler can be configured with its own filtering and levels.

Built-In Handlers

The following handler objects are built-in. Some of these handlers are defined in a sub-module `logging.handlers`, which must be imported specifically if necessary.

handlers.DatagramHandler(*host,port*)

Sends log messages to a UDP server located on the given *host* and *port*. Log messages are encoded by taking the dictionary of the corresponding `LogRecord` object and encoding it using the `pickle` module. The transmitted network message consists of a 4-byte network order (big-endian) length followed by the pickled record data. To reconstruct the message, the receiver must strip the length header, read the entire message, unpickle the contents, and call `logging.makeLogRecord()`. Because UDP is unreliable, network errors may result in lost log messages.

FileHandler(*filename* [, *mode* [, *encoding* [, *delay*]]])

Writes log messages to the file *filename*. *mode* is the file mode to use when opening the file and defaults to `'a'`. *encoding* is the file encoding. *delay* is a Boolean flag that, if set `True`, defers the opening of the log file until the first log message is issued. By default, it is `False`.

handlers.HTTPHandler(*host, url* [, *method*])

Uploads log messages to an HTTP server using HTTP `GET` or `POST` methods. *host* specifies the host machine, *url* is the URL to use, and *method* is either `'GET'` (the default) or `'POST'`. The log message is encoded by taking the dictionary of the corresponding `LogRecord` object and encoding it as a set of URL query-string variables using the `urllib.urlencode()` function.

handlers.MemoryHandler(*capacity* [, *flushLevel* [, *target*]])

This handler is used to collect log messages in memory and to flush them to another handler, *target*, periodically. *capacity* is the size of the memory buffer in bytes. *flushLevel* is a numeric logging level that forces a memory flush should a logging message of that level or higher appear. The default value is `ERROR`. *target* is another `Handler` object that receives the messages. If *target* is omitted, you will need to set a target using the `setTarget()` method of the resulting handler object in order for this handler to do anything.

handlers.NTEventLogHandler(*appname* [, *dllname* [, *logtype*]])

Sends messages to the event log on Windows NT, Windows 2000, or Windows XP. *appname* is the name of the application name to use in the event log. *dllname* is a full path name to a `.DLL` or `.EXE` file that provides message definitions to hold in the log. If omitted, dllname is set to `'win32service.pyd'`. *logtype* is either `'Application'`, `'System'`, or `'Security'`. The default value is `'Application'`. This handler is only available if Win32 extensions for Python have been installed.

handlers.RotatingFileHandler(*filename* **[,** *mode* **[,** *maxBytes* **[,** *backupCount* **[,**
encoding **[,** *delay***]]]]])**

Writes log messages to the file *filename*. However, if the file exceeds the size specified
by *maxBytes*, the file is rotated to *filename*.1 and a new log file, *filename*, is
opened. *backupCount* specifies the maximum number of backup files to create. By
default, the value of *backupCount* is 0. However, when specified, backup files are rotated through the sequence *filename*.1, *filename*.2, ... ,*filename*.*N*, where
filename.1 is always the most recent backup and *filename*.*N* is always the oldest
backup. *mode* specifies the file mode to use when opening the log file. The default
mode is 'a'. If *maxBytes* is 0 (the default), the log file is never rolled over and is
allowed to grow indefinitely. *encoding* and *delay* have the same meaning as with
FileHandler.

handlers.SMTPHandler(*mailhost, fromaddr, toaddrs, subject* **[,** *credentials***])**

Sends log messages to a remote host using email. *mailhost* is the address of an SMTP
server that can receive the message. The address can be a simple host name specified as a
string or a tuple (*host, port*). *fromaddr* is the from address, *toaddrs* is the destination address, and *subject* is the subject to use in the message. *credentials* is a tuple
(*username, password*) with the username and password.

handlers.SocketHandler(*host, port***)**

Sends log messages to a remote host using a TCP socket connection. *host* and *port*
specify the destination. Messages are sent in the same format as described for
DatagramHandler. Unlike DatagramHandler, this handler reliably delivers log messages.

StreamHandler([*fileobj***])**

Writes log messages to an already open file-like object, *fileobj*. If no argument is provided, messages are written to sys.stderr.

handlers.SysLogHandler([*address* **[,** *facility***]])**

Sends log messages to a UNIX system logging daemon. *address* specifies the destination as a (*host, port*) tuple. If omitted, a destination of ('localhost', 514) is
used. *facility* is an integer facility code and is set to SysLogHandler.LOG_USER by
default. A full list of facility codes can be found in the definition of SysLogHandler.

handlers.TimedRotatingFileHandler(*filename* **[,** *when* **[,** *interval* **[,** *backupCount* **[,**
encoding **[,** *delay* **[,** *utc***]]]]]])**

The same as RotatingFileHandler, but the rotation of files is controlled by time
instead of file size. *interval* is a number, and *when* is a string that specifies units.
Possible values for *when* are 'S' (seconds), 'M' (minutes), 'H' (hours), 'D' (days), 'W'
(weeks), and 'midnight' (roll over at midnight). For example, setting *interval* to 3
and *when* to 'D' rolls the log every three days. *backupCount* specifies the maximum
number of backup files to keep. *utc* is a Boolean flag that determines whether or not to
use local time (the default) or UTC time.

handlers.WatchedFileHandler(*filename* **[,** *mode* **[,** *encoding* **[,** *delay***]]])**

The same as FileHandler, but the inode and device of the opened log file is moni-
tored. If it changes since the last log message was issued, the file is closed and reopened

again using the same filename. These changes might occur if a log file has been deleted or moved as a result of a log rotation operation carried out externally to the running program. This handler only works on UNIX systems.

Handler Configuration

Each `Handler` object `h` can be configured with its own level and filtering. The following methods are used to do this:

h.setLevel(level)

Sets the threshold of messages to be handled. `level` is a numeric code such as ERROR or CRITICAL.

h.addFilter(filt)

Adds a `Filter` object, `filt`, to the handler. See the `addFilter()` method of `Logger` objects for more information.

h.removeFilter(filt)

Removes a `Filter` object, `filt`, from the handler.

It is important to stress that levels and filters can be set on handlers independently from any settings used on the `Logger` objects to which handlers are attached. Here is an example that illustrates this:

```
import logging
import sys

# Create a handler that prints CRITICAL level messages to stderr
crit_hand = logging.StreamHandler(sys.stderr)
crit_hand.setLevel(logging.CRITICAL)

# Create a top-level logger called 'app'
app_log = logging.getLogger("app")
app_log.setLevel(logging.INFO)
app_log.addHandler(logging.FileHandler('app.log'))
app_log.addHandler(crit_handler)
```

In this example, there is a single logger called 'app' with a level of INFO. Two handlers are attached to it, but one of the handlers (`crit_handler`) has its own level setting of CRITICAL. Although this handler will receive log messages with a level of INFO or higher, it selectively discards those that are not CRITICAL.

Handler Cleanup

The following methods are used on handlers to perform cleanup.

h.flush()

Flushes all logging output.

h.close()

Closes the handler.

Message Formatting

By default, `Handler` objects emit log messages exactly as they are formatted in logging calls. However, sometimes you want to add additional contextual information to the messages such as timestamps, filenames, line numbers, and so forth. This section describes how this extra information can be automatically added to log messages.

Formatter Objects

To change the log message format, you must first create a `Formatter` object:

```
Formatter([fmt [, datefmt]])
```

Creates a new `Formatter` object. `fmt` provides a format string for messages. Within `fmt`, you can place various expansions as previously described for the `basicConfig()` function. `datefmt` is a date format string compatible with the `time.strftime()` function. If omitted, the date format is set to the ISO8601 format.

To take effect, `Formatter` objects must be attached to handler objects. This is done using the `h.setFormatter()` method of a `Handler` instance `h`.

```
h.setFormatter(format)
```

Sets the message formatter object used to create log messages on the `Handler` instance `h`. `format` must be an instance of `Formatter`.

Here is an example that illustrates how to customize the log message format on a handler:

```
import logging
import sys

# Set the message format
format = logging.Formatter("%(levelname)-10s %(asctime)s %(message)s")

# Create a handler that prints CRITICAL level messages to stderr
crit_hand = logging.StreamHandler(sys.stderr)
crit_hand.setLevel(logging.CRITICAL)
crit_hand.setFormatter(format)
```

In this example, a custom `Formatter` is set on the `crit_hand` handler. If a logging message such as `"Creeping death detected."` is processed by this handler, the following log message is produced:

```
CRITICAL   2005-10-25 20:46:57,126 Creeping death detected.
```

Adding Extra Context to Messages

In certain applications, it is useful to add additional context information to log messages. This extra information can be provided in one of two ways. First, all of the basic logging operations (e.g., `log.critical()`, `log.warning()`, etc.) have a keyword parameter `extra` that is used to supply a dictionary of additional fields for use in message format strings. These fields are merged in with the context data previously described for `Formatter` objects. Here is an example:

```
import logging, socket
logging.basicConfig(
    format = "%(hostname)s %(levelname)-10s %(asctime)s %(message)s"
)
# Some extra context
netinfo = {
    'hostname' : socket.gethostname(),
    'ip'       : socket.gethostbyname(socket.gethostname())
}
log = logging.getLogger('app')

# Issue a log message with the extra context data
```

```
log.critical("Could not connect to server", extra=netinfo)
```

The downside of this approach is that you have to make sure every logging operation includes the extra information or else the program will crash. An alternative approach is to use the `LogAdapter` class as a wrapper for an existing logger.

LogAdapter(*log* [, *extra*])

Creates a wrapper around a `Logger` object *log*. *extra* is a dictionary of extra context information to be supplied to message formatters. An instance of `LogAdapter` has the same interface as a `Logger` object. However, operations that issue log messages will automatically add the extra information supplied in *extra*.

Here is an example of using a `LogAdapter` object:

```
import logging, socket
logging.basicConfig(
    format = "%(hostname)s %(levelname)-10s %(asctime)s %(message)s"
)
# Some extra context
netinfo = {
    'hostname' : socket.gethostname(),
    'ip'       : socket.gethostbyname(socket.gethostname())
}

# Create a logger
log = logging.LogAdapter(logging.getLogger("app"), netinfo)

# Issue a log message. Extra context data is supplied by the LogAdapter
log.critical("Could not connect to server")
```

Miscellaneous Utility Functions

The following functions in `logging` control a few other aspects of logging:

disable(*level*)

Globally disables all logging messages below the level specified in *level*. This can be used to turn off logging on a applicationwide basis—for instance, if you want to temporarily disable or reduce the amount of logging output.

addLevelName(*level*, *levelName*)

Creates an entirely new logging level and name. *level* is a number and *levelName* is a string. This can be used to change the names of the built-in levels or to add more levels than are supported by default.

getLevelName(*level*)

Returns the name of the level corresponding to the numeric value *level*.

shutdown()

Shuts down all logging objects, flushing output if necessary.

Logging Configuration

Setting an application to use the `logging` module typically involves the following basic steps:

1. Use `getLogger()` to create various `Logger` objects. Set parameters such as the

level, as appropriate.

2. Create `Handler` objects by instantiating one of the various types of handlers (`FileHandler`, `StreamHandler`, `SocketHandler`, and so on) and set an appropriate level.

3. Create message `Formatter` objects and attach them to the `Handler` objects using the `setFormatter()` method.

4. Attach the `Handler` objects to the `Logger` objects using the `addHandler()` method.

Because the configuration of each step can be somewhat involved, your best bet is to put all the logging configuration into a single well-documented location. For example, you might create a file `applogconfig.py` that is imported by the main program of your application:

```
# applogconfig.py
import logging
import sys

# Set the message format
format = logging.Formatter("%(levelname)-10s %(asctime)s %(message)s")

# Create a handler that prints CRITICAL level messages to stderr
crit_hand = logging.StreamHandler(sys.stderr)
crit_hand.setLevel(logging.CRITICAL)
crit_hand.setFormatter(format)

# Create a handler that prints messages to a file
applog_hand = logging.FileHandler('app.log')
applog_hand.setFormatter(format)

# Create a top-level logger called 'app'
app_log = logging.getLogger("app")
app_log.setLevel(logging.INFO)
app_log.addHandler(applog_hand)
app_log.addHandler(crit_hand)

# Change the level on the 'app.net' logger
logging.getLogger("app.net").setLevel(logging.ERROR)
```

If changes need to be made to any part of the logging configuration, having everything in one location makes things easier to maintain. Keep in mind that this special file only needs to be imported once and in only one location in the program. In other parts of the code where you want to issue log messages, you simply include code like this:

```
import logging
app_log = logging.getLogger("app")
...
app_log.critical("An error occurred")
```

The `logging.config` Submodule

As an alternative to hard-coding the logging configuration in Python code, it is also possible to configure the logging module through the use of an INI-format configuration file. To do this, use the following functions found in `logging.config`.

fileConfig(*filename* [, *defaults* [, *disable_existing_loggers*]])

Reads the logging configuration from the configuration file *filename*. *defaults* is a dictionary of default configuration parameters for use in the config file. The specified filename is read using the `ConfigParser` module. *disable_existing_loggers* is a Boolean flag that specifies whether or not any existing loggers are disabled when new configuration data is read. By default, this is `True`.

The online documentation for the `logging` module goes into some detail on the expected format of configuration files. However, experienced programmers can probably extrapolate from the following example, which is a configuration file version of `applogconfig.py` shown in the previous section.

```
; applogconfig.ini
;
; Configuration file for setting up logging

; The following sections provide names for Logger, Handler, and Formatter
; objects that will be configured later in the file.

[loggers]
keys=root,app,app_net

[handlers]
keys=crit,applog

[formatters]
keys=format

[logger_root]
level=NOTSET
handlers=

[logger_app]
level=INFO
propagate=0
qualname=app
handlers=crit,applog

[logger_app_net]
level=ERROR
propagate=1
qualname=app.net
handlers=

[handler_crit]
class=StreamHandler
level=CRITICAL
formatter=format
args=(sys.stderr,)

[handler_applog]
class=FileHandler
level=NOTSET
formatter=format
args=('app.log',)

[formatter_format]
format=%(levelname)-10s %(asctime)s %(message)s
datefmt=
```

To read this configuration file and set up logging, you would use this code:

```
import logging.config
```

```
logging.config.fileConfig('applogconfig.ini')
```

As before, modules that want to issue log messages do not need to worry about the details of loading the logging configuration. They merely import the `logging` module and get a reference to the appropriate `Logger` object. For example:

```
import logging
app_log = logging.getLogger("app")
...
app_log.critical("An error occurred")
```

Performance Considerations

Adding logging to an application can severely degrade its performance if you aren't careful. However, there are some techniques that can be used to reduce the overhead.

First, Python's optimized mode (-O) removes all code that is conditionally executed using statements such as if `__debug__`: *statements*. If the sole purpose of logging is debugging, you could conditionally execute all of the logging calls and have the calls removed in optimized mode.

A second technique would be to use a Null object in place of a `Logger` object when logging is to be completely disabled. This is different than using `None`. Instead, you want to use an instance of an object that silently swallows all operations that get performed on it. For example:

```
class Null(object):
    def __init__(self, *args, **kwargs): pass
    def __call__(self, *args, **kwargs): return self
    def __getattribute__(self, name): return self
    def __setattr__(self, name, value): pass
    def __delattr__(self,name): pass

log = Null()
log.critical("An error occurred.")      # Does nothing
```

Depending on your cleverness, logging can also be managed through the use of decorators and metaclasses. Because these features of Python operate at the time that functions, methods, and classes are defined, they can be used to selectively add or remove logging features from parts of a program in a way that does not impact performance when logging is disabled. Please refer to Chapter 6, "Functions and Functional Programming," and Chapter 7, "Classes and Object-Oriented Programming," for further details.

Notes

- The `logging` module provides a large number of customization options not discussed here. Readers should consult online documentation for further details.

- It is safe to use the `logging` module with programs that use threads. In particular, it is not necessary to add locking operations around code that is issuing log messages.

mmap

The `mmap` module provides support for a memory-mapped file object. This object behaves both like a file and a byte string and can be used in most places where an ordinary file or byte string is expected. Furthermore, the contents of a memory-mapped file are mutable. This means that modifications can be made using index-assignment and slice-assignment operators. Unless a private mapping of the file has been made, such changes directly alter the contents of the underlying file.

A memory-mapping file is created by the mmap() function, which is slightly different on UNIX and Windows.

`mmap(fileno, length [, flags, [prot [,access [, offset]]]])`

(UNIX). Returns an mmap object that maps *length* bytes from the file with an integer file descriptor, *fileno*. If *fileno* is -1, anonymous memory is mapped. *flags* specifies the nature of the mapping and is one of the following:

Flag	Meaning
MAP_PRIVATE	Creates a private copy-on-write mapping. Changes to the object will be private to this process.
MAP_SHARED	Shares the mapping with all other processes mapping the same areas of the file. Changes to the object will affect all mappings.

The default *flags* setting is MAP_SHARED. *prot* specifies the memory protections of the object and is the bitwise OR of the following:

Setting	Meaning
PROT_READ	Data can be read from the object.
PROT_WRITE	Modifications can be made to the object.
PROT_EXEC	The object can contain executable instructions.

The default value of *prot* is PROT_READ | PROT_WRITE. The modes specified in *prot* must match the access permissions used to open the underlying file descriptor *fileno*. In most cases, this means that the file should be opened in read/write mode (for example, os.open(*name*, os.O_RDWR)).

The optional *access* parameter may be used as an alternative to *flags* and *prot*. If given, it has one of the following values:

Access	Meaning
ACCESS_READ	Read-only access.
ACCESS_WRITE	Read/write access with write-through. Modifications affect the underlying file.
ACCESS_COPY	Read/write access with copy-on-write. Modifications affect memory but do not change the underlying file.

When *access* is supplied, it is typically given as a keyword argument—for example, mmap(*fileno*, *length*, access=ACCESS_READ). It is an error to supply values for both *access* and *flags*. The *offset* parameter specifies the number of bytes from the start of the file and defaults to 0. It must be a multiple of mmap.ALLOCATIONGRANULARITY.

`mmap(fileno, length[, tagname [,access [, offset]]])`

(Windows) Returns an mmap object that maps *length* bytes from the file specified by the integer file descriptor *fileno*. Use a *fileno* of -1 for anonymous memory. If *length* is larger than the current size of the file, the file is extended to *length* bytes. If *length* is 0, the current length of the file is used as the length as long as the file is non-empty (otherwise, an exception will be raised). *tagname* is an optional string that can be used to name the mapping. If *tagname* refers to an existing mapping, that mapping is opened. Otherwise, a new mapping is created. If *tagname* is None, an unnamed mapping is created. *access* is an optional parameter that specifies the access mode. It takes the same values for *access* as described for the UNIX version of mmap() shown earlier. By default, *access* is ACCESS_WRITE. *offset* is the number of bytes from the beginning of the file and defaults to 0. It must be a multiple of mmap.ALLOCATIONGRANULARITY.

A memory-mapped file object, *m*, supports the following methods.

m.close()

Closes the file. Subsequent operations will result in an exception.

m.find(*string*[, *start*])

Returns the index of the first occurrence of *string*. *start* specifies an optional starting position. Returns -1 if no match is found.

m.flush([*offset*, *size*])

Flushes modifications of the in-memory copy back to the file system. *offset* and *size* specify an optional range of bytes to flush. Otherwise, the entire mapping is flushed.

m.move(*dst*, *src*, *count*)

Copies *count* bytes starting at index *src* to the destination index *dst*. This copy is performed using the C memmove() function, which is guaranteed to work correctly when the source and destination regions happen to overlap.

m.read(*n*)

Reads up to *n* bytes from the current file position and returns the data as a string.

m.read_byte()

Reads a single byte from the current file position and returns as a string of length 1.

m.readline()

Returns a line of input starting at the current file position.

m.resize(*newsize*)

Resizes the memory-mapped object to contain *newsize* bytes.

m.seek(*pos*[, *whence*])

Sets the file position to a new value. *pos* and *whence* have the same meaning as for the seek() method on file objects.

m.size()

Returns the length of the file. This value may be larger than the size of the memory-mapped region.

m.tell()

Returns the value of the file pointer.

m.write(*string*)

Writes a string of bytes to the file at the current file pointer.

m.write_byte(*byte*)

Writes a single byte into memory at the current file pointer.

Notes

- Although UNIX and Windows supply slightly different mmap() functions, this module can be used in a portable manner by relying on the optional access parameter that is common to both functions. For example, mmap(*fileno, length*, access=ACCESS_WRITE) will work on both UNIX and Windows.

- Certain memory mapping may only work with a length that's a multiple of the system page size, which is contained in the constant mmap.PAGESIZE.

- On UNIX SVR4 systems, anonymous mapped memory can be obtained by calling mmap() on the file /dev/zero, opened with appropriate permissions.

- On UNIX BSD systems, anonymous mapped memory can be obtained by calling mmap() with a negative file descriptor and the flag mmap.MAP_ANON.

msvcrt

The msvcrt module provides access to a number of useful functions in the Microsoft Visual C runtime library. This module is available only on Windows.

getch()

Reads a keypress and returns the resulting character. This call blocks if a keypress is not available. If the pressed key was a special function key, the call returns '\000' or '\xe0' and the next call returns the keycode. This function doesn't echo characters to the console, nor can the function be used to read Ctrl+C.

getwch()

The same as getch() except that a Unicode character is returned.

getche()

Like getch() except that characters are echoed (if printable).

getwche()

The same as getche() except that a Unicode character is returned.

get_osfhandle(*fd*)

Returns the file handle for file descriptor *fd*. Raises IOError if *fd* is not recognized.

heapmin()

Forces the internal Python memory manager to return unused blocks to the operating system. This works only on Windows NT and raises IOError on failure.

`kbhit()`

Returns True if a keypress is waiting to be read.

`locking(fd, mode, nbytes)`

Locks part of a file, given a file descriptor from the C runtime. *nbytes* is the number of bytes to lock relative to the current file pointer. *mode* is one of the following integers:

Setting	Description
0	Unlocks the file region (LK_UNLCK)
1	Locks the file region (LK_LOCK)
2	Locks the file region; nonblocking (LK_NBLCK)
3	Locks for writing (LK_RLCK)
4	Locks for writing; nonblocking (LK_NBRLCK)

Attempts to acquire a lock that takes more than approximately 10 seconds results in an IOError exception.

`open_osfhandle(handle, flags)`

Creates a C runtime file descriptor from the file handle *handle*. *flags* is the bitwise OR of os.O_APPEND, os.O_RDONLY, and os.O_TEXT. Returns an integer file descriptor that can be used as a parameter to os.fdopen() to create a file object.

`putch(char)`

Prints the character *char* to the console without buffering.

`putwch(char)`

The same as putch() except that *char* is a Unicode character.

`setmode(fd, flags)`

Sets the line-end translation mode for file descriptor *fd*. *flags* is os.O_TEXT for text mode and os.O_BINARY for binary mode.

`ungetch(char)`

Causes the character *char* to be "pushed back" into the console buffer. It will be the next character read by getch() or getche().

`ungetwch(char)`

The same as ungetch() except that *char* is a Unicode character.

> **Note**
>
> A wide variety of Win32 extensions are available that provide access to the Microsoft Foundation Classes, COM components, graphical user interfaces, and so forth. These topics are far beyond the scope of this book, but detailed information about many of these topics is available in *Python Programming on Win32* by Mark Hammond and Andy Robinson (O'Reilly & Associates, 2000). Also, http://www.python.org maintains an extensive list of contributed modules for use under Windows.

See Also:
winreg **(p. 408)**

optparse

The optparse module provides high-level support for processing UNIX-style command-line options supplied in sys.argv. A simple example of using the module is found in Chapter 9. Use of optparse primarily focuses on the OptionParser class.

OptionParser([**args])

Creates a new command option parser and returns an OptionParser instance. A variety of optional keyword arguments can be supplied to control configuration. These keyword arguments are described in the following list:

Keyword Argument	Description
add_help_option	Specifies whether or not a special help option (--help and -h) is supported. By default, this is set to True.
conflict_handler	Specifies the handling of conflicting command-line options. May be set to either 'error' (the default value) or 'resolve'. In 'error' mode, an optparse.OptionConflictError exception will be raised if conflicting option strings are added to the parser. In 'resolve' mode, conflicts are resolved so that options added later take priority. However, earlier options may still be available if they were added under multiple names and no conflicts exist for at least one of the names.
description	A string that provides a description of the program for display during help. This string will automatically be reformatted to fit the screen when displayed.
formatter	Instance of an optparse.HelpFormatter class used to format text when printing help. May be either optparse.IndentedHelpFormatter (the default) or optparse.TitledHelpFormatter.
option_class	The Python class that's used to hold information about each command-line option. The default class is optparse.Option.
option_list	A list of options used to populate the parser. By default, this list is empty, and options are added using the add_option() method instead. If supplied, this list contains objects of type Option.
prog	The program name used to replace '%prog' in help text.
usage	The usage string that's printed when the --help option is used or incorrect options are passed. The default value is the string '%prog [options]', where the '%prog' keyword gets replaced with either the value of os.path.basename (sys.argv[0]) or the value of the prog keyword argument (if supplied). The value optparse.SUPPRESS_USAGE can be given to suppress the usage message entirely.
version	Version string that's printed when the -version option is supplied. By default, version is None and no --version option is added. When this string is supplied, -version is automatically added. The special keyword '%prog' is replaced by the program name.

Unless you really need to customize option processing in some way, an `OptionParser` will usually be created with no arguments. For example:

```
p = optparse.OptionParser()
```

An instance, *p*, of `OptionParser` supports the following methods:

p.add_option(*name1*, ..., *nameN* [, **parms*])

Adds a new option to *p*. The arguments *name1*, *name2*, and so on are all of the various names for the option. For example, you might include short and long option names such as `'-f'` and `'--file'`. Following the option names, an optional set of keyword arguments is supplied that specifies how the option will be processed when parsed. These keyword arguments are described in the following list:

Keyword Argument	Description
action	Action to perform when the option is parsed. Acceptable values are as follows:
	`'store'`—Option has an argument that is read and stored. This is the default if no action is specified explicitly.
	`'store_const'`—The option takes no arguments, but when the option is encountered, a constant value specified with the `const` keyword argument is stored.
	`'store_true'`—Like `'store_const'` but stores a Boolean `True` when the option is parsed.
	`'store_false'`—Like `'store_true'` but stores `False` instead.
	`'append'`—Option has an argument that is appended to a list when parsed. This is used if the same command-line option is used to specify multiple values.
	`'count'`—Option takes no arguments, but a counter value is stored. The counter value is increased by one each time the argument is encountered.
	`'callback'`—Invokes a callback function specified with the `callback` keyword argument when the option is encountered.
	`'help'`—Prints a help message when the option is parsed. This is only needed if you want help to be displayed via a different option than the standard `-h` or `--help` option.
	`'version'`—Prints the version number supplied to `OptionParser()`, if any. Only used if you want to display version information using an option other than the standard `-v` or `--version` option.
callback	Specifies a callback function to be invoked when the option is encountered. This callback function is a Python callable object that is invoked as `callback(option, opt_str, value, parser, *args, **kwargs)`. The `option` argument is an instance of `optparse.Option`, `opt_str` is the option string supplied on the command line that triggered the callback, `value` is the value of the option (if any), `parser` is the instance of `OptionParser` that's running, `args` are positional arguments supplied using the `callback_args` keyword argument, and `kwargs` are keyword arguments supplied using the `callback_kwargs` keyword argument.

Keyword Argument	Description
callback_args	Optional positional arguments supplied to a callback function specified with the callback argument.
callback_kwargs	Optional keyword arguments supplied to a callback function specified with the callback argument.
choices	A list of strings that specifies all possible option values. Used when an option only has a limited set of values (for example, ['small', 'medium', 'large']).
const	The constant value that's stored with the 'store_const' action.
default	Sets the default value of the option if not supplied. By default, the default value is None.
dest	Sets the name of the attribute used to store option values during parsing. Normally the name is derived from the option name itself.
help	Help text for this particular option. If this is not supplied, the option will be listed in help without a description. The value optparse.SUPPRESS_HELP can be used to hide an option. The special keyword '%default' is replaced by the option default value in the help string.
metavar	Specifies the name of an option argument that's used when printing help text.
nargs	Specifies the number of option arguments for actions that expect arguments. The default value is 1. If a number greater than 1 is used, option arguments will be collected into a tuple that is then used whenever arguments are handled.
type	Specifies the type of an option. Valid types are 'string' (the default), 'int', 'long', 'choice', 'float', and 'complex'.

p.disable_interspersed_args()

Disallows the mixing of simple options with positional arguments. For example, if '-x' and '-y' are options that take no parameters, the options must appear before any arguments (for example, 'prog -x -y arg1 arg2 arg3').

p.enable_interspersed_args()

Allows the mixing of options with positional arguments. For example, if '-x' and '-y' are simple options that take no parameters, they may be mixed with the arguments, such as in 'prog -x arg1 arg2 -y arg3'. This is the default behavior.

p.parse_args([arglist])

Parses command-line options and returns a tuple (options, args) where options is an object containing the values of all the options and args is a list of all the remaining positional arguments left over. The options object stores all the option data in attributes with names that match the option name. For example, the option '--output' would have its value stored in options.output. If the option does not appear, the value will be None. The name of the attribute can be set using the dest keyword argument to add_option(), described previously. By default, arguments are taken from sys.argv[1:]. However, a different source of arguments can be supplied as an optional argument, arglist.

p.set_defaults(*dest=value, ... dest=value*)

Sets the default values of particular option destinations. You simply supply keyword arguments that specify the destinations you wish to set. The name of the keyword arguments should match the names specified using the dest parameter in add_option(), described earlier.

p.set_usage(*usage*)

Changes the usage string displayed in text produced by the --help option.

Example

```
# foo.py
import optparse
p = optparse.OptionParser()

# A simple option, with no arguments
p.add_option("-t", action="store_true", dest="tracing")

# An option that accepts a string argument
p.add_option("-o", "--outfile", action="store", type="string", dest="outfile")

# An option requires an integer argument
p.add_option("-d", "--debuglevel", action="store", type="int", dest="debug")

# An option with a few choices
p.add_option("--speed", action="store", type="choice", dest="speed",
             choices=["slow","fast","ludicrous"])

# An option taking multiple arguments
p.add_option("--coord", action="store", type="int", dest="coord", nargs=2)

# A set of options that control a common destination
p.add_option("--novice", action="store_const", const="novice", dest="mode")
p.add_option("--guru", action="store_const", const="guru", dest="mode")

# Set default values for the various option destinations
p.set_defaults(tracing=False,
               debug=0,
               speed="fast",
               coord=(0,0),
               mode="novice")

# Parse the arguments
opt, args = p.parse_args()

# Print option values
print "tracing    :", opt.tracing
print "outfile    :", opt.outfile
print "debug      :", opt.debug
print "speed      :", opt.speed
print "coord      :", opt.coord
print "mode       :", opt.mode

# Print remaining arguments
print "args       :", args
```

Here is a short interactive UNIX session that shows how the previous code works:

```
% python foo.py -h
usage: foo.py [options]

options:
  -h, --help            show this help message and exit
  -t
  -o OUTFILE, --outfile=OUTFILE
  -d DEBUG, --debuglevel=DEBUG
  --speed=SPEED
  --coord=COORD
  --novice
  --guru

% python foo.py -t -o outfile.dat -d 3 --coord 3 4 --speed=ludicrous blah
tracing    : True
outfile    : outfile.dat
debug      : 3
speed      : ludicrous
coord      : (3, 4)
mode       : novice
args       : ['blah']

% python foo.py --speed=insane
usage: foo.py [options]

foo.py:error:option --speed:invalid choice:'insane'
(choose from 'slow', 'fast', 'ludicrous')
```

Notes

- When specifying option names, use a single dash to specify a short name such as `'-x'` and a double-dash to specify a long name such as `'--exclude'`. An OptionError exception will be raised if you attempt to define an option that is a mix of the two styles, such as `'-exclude'`.

- Python also includes a module getopt that provides support for command-line parsing in a style similar to a C library of the same name. For all practical purposes, there is no benefit to using that module over optparse (which is much higher level and requires far less coding).

- The optparse module contains a considerable number of advanced features related to customization and specialized handling of certain kinds of command-line options. However, none of these features are required for the most common types of command-line option parsing. Readers should consult the online library documentation for more details and additional examples.

os

The os module provides a portable interface to common operating-system services. It does this by searching for an OS-dependent built-in module such as nt or posix and exporting the functions and data as found there. Unless otherwise noted, functions are available on Windows and UNIX. UNIX systems include both Linux and Mac OS X.

The following general-purpose variables are defined:

environ

A mapping object representing the current environment variables. Changes to the mapping are reflected in the current environment. If the `putenv()` function is also available, then changes are also reflected in subprocesses.

linesep

The string used to separate lines on the current platform. May be a single character such as `'\n'` for POSIX or multiple characters such as `'\r\n'` for Windows.

name

The name of the OS-dependent module imported: `'posix'`, `'nt'`, `'dos'`, `'mac'`, `'ce'`, `'java'`, `'os2'`, or `'riscos'`.

path

The OS-dependent standard module for pathname operations. This module can also be loaded using `import os.path`.

Process Environment

The following functions are used to access and modify various parameters related to the environment in which a process runs. Process, group, process group, and session IDs are integers unless otherwise noted.

chdir(_path_)

Changes the current working directory to _path_.

chroot(_path_)

Changes the root directory of the current process (UNIX).

ctermid()

Returns a string with the filename of the control terminal for the process (UNIX).

fchdir(_fd_)

Changes the current working directory. _fd_ is a file descriptor to an opened directory (UNIX).

getcwd()

Returns a string with the current working directory.

getcwdu()

Returns a Unicode string with the current working directory.

getegid()

Returns the effective group ID (UNIX).

geteuid()

Returns the effective user ID (UNIX).

`getgid()`

Returns the real group ID of the process (UNIX).

`getgroups()`

Returns a list of integer group IDs to which the process owner belongs (UNIX).

`getlogin()`

Returns the user name associated with the effective user ID (UNIX).

`getpgid(pid)`

Returns the process group ID of the process with process ID *pid*. If *pid* is 0, the process group of the calling process is returned (UNIX).

`getpgrp()`

Returns the ID of the current process group. Process groups are typically used in conjunction with job control. The process group is not necessarily the same as the group ID of the process (UNIX).

`getpid()`

Returns the real process ID of the current process (UNIX and Windows).

`getppid()`

Returns the process ID of the parent process (UNIX).

`getsid(pid)`

Returns the process session identifier of process *pid*. If *pid* is 0, the identifier of the current process is returned (UNIX).

`getuid()`

Returns the real user ID of the current process (UNIX).

`putenv(varname, value)`

Sets environment variable *varname* to *value*. Changes affect subprocesses started with `os.system()`, `popen()`, `fork()`, and `execv()`. Assignments to items in `os.environ` automatically call `putenv()`. However, calls to `putenv()` don't update `os.environ` (UNIX and Windows).

`setegid(egid)`

Sets the effective group ID (UNIX).

`seteuid(euid)`

Sets the effective user ID (UNIX).

`setgid(gid)`

Sets the group ID of the current process (UNIX).

`setgroups(groups)`

Sets the group access list of the current process. *groups* is a sequence of integers specifying group identifiers. Can only be called by root (UNIX).

`setpgrp()`

Creates a new process group by calling the system call `setpgrp()` or `setpgrp(0, 0)`, depending on which version is implemented (if any). Returns the ID of the new process group (UNIX).

`setpgid(pid, pgrp)`

Assigns process `pid` to process group `pgrp`. If `pid` is equal to `pgrp`, the process becomes a new process group leader. If `pid` is not equal to `pgrp`, the process joins an existing group. If `pid` is 0, the process ID of the calling process is used. If `pgrp` is 0, the process specified by `pid` becomes a process group leader (UNIX).

`setreuid(ruid, euid)`

Sets the real and effective user ID of the calling process (UNIX).

`setregid(rgid, egid)`

Sets the real and effective group ID of the calling process (UNIX).

`setsid()`

Creates a new session and returns the newly created session ID. Sessions are typically associated with terminal devices and the job control of processes that are started within them (UNIX).

`setuid(uid)`

Sets the real user ID of the current process. This function is privileged and often can be performed only by processes running as root (UNIX).

`strerror(code)`

Returns the error message corresponding to the integer error `code` (UNIX and Windows). The `errno` module defines symbolic names for these error codes.

`umask(mask)`

Sets the current numeric umask and returns the previous umask. The umask is used to clear permissions bits on files that are created by the process (UNIX and Windows).

`uname()`

Returns a tuple of strings (`sysname`, `nodename`, `release`, `version`, `machine`) identifying the system type (UNIX).

`unsetenv(name)`

Unsets the environment variable `name`.

File Creation and File Descriptors

The following functions provide a low-level interface for manipulating files and pipes. In these functions, files are manipulated in terms of an integer file descriptor, `fd`. The file descriptor can be extracted from a file object by invoking its `fileno()` method.

`close(fd)`

Closes the file descriptor `fd` previously returned by `open()` or `pipe()`.

`closerange(low, high)`

Closes all file descriptors `fd` in the range `low <= fd < high`. Errors are ignored.

`dup(fd)`

Duplicates file descriptor `fd`. Returns a new file descriptor that's the lowest-numbered unused file descriptor for the process. The new and old file descriptors can be used interchangeably. Furthermore, they share state, such as the current file pointer and locks (UNIX and Windows).

`dup2(oldfd, newfd)`

Duplicates file descriptor `oldfd` to `newfd`. If `newfd` already corresponds to a valid file descriptor, it's closed first (UNIX and Windows).

`fchmod(fd, mode)`

Changes the mode of the file associated with `fd` to `mode`. See the description of `os.open()` for a description of `mode` (UNIX).

`fchown(fd, uid, gid)`

Changes the owner and group ID of the file associated with `fd` to `uid` and `gid`. Use a valid of -1 for `uid` or `gid` to keep the value unchanged (UNIX).

`fdatasync(fd)`

Forces all cached data written to `fd` to be flushed to disk (UNIX).

`fdopen(fd [, mode [, bufsize]])`

Creates an open file object connected to file descriptor `fd`. The `mode` and `bufsize` arguments have the same meaning as in the built-in `open()` function. `mode` should be a string such as `'r'`, `'w'`, or `'a'`. On Python 3, this function accepts any additional parameters that work with the built-in `open()` function such as specifications for the encoding and line ending. However, if portability with Python 2 is a concern, you should only use the `mode` and `bufsize` arguments described here.

`fpathconf(fd, name)`

Returns configurable pathname variables associated with the open file with descriptor `fd`. `name` is a string that specifies the name of the value to retrieve. The values are usually taken from parameters contained in system header files such as `<limits.h>` and `<unistd.h>`. POSIX defines the following constants for `name`:

Constant	Description
`"PC_ASYNC_IO"`	Indicates whether asynchronous I/O can be performed on `fd`.
`"PC_CHOWN_RESTRICTED"`	Indicates whether the `chown()` function can be used. If `fd` refers to a directory, this applies to all files in the directory.
`"PC_FILESIZEBITS"`	Maximum size of a file.
`"PC_LINK_MAX"`	Maximum value of the file's link count.
`"PC_MAX_CANON"`	Maximum length of a formatted input line. `fd` refers to a terminal.
`"PC_MAX_INPUT"`	Maximum length of an input line. `fd` refers to a terminal.

Constant	Description
`"PC_NAME_MAX"`	Maximum length of a filename in a directory.
`"PC_NO_TRUNC"`	Indicates whether an attempt to create a file with a name longer than `PC_NAME_MAX` for a directory will fail with an `ENAMETOOLONG` error.
`"PC_PATH_MAX"`	Maximum length of a relative path name when the directory `fd` is the current working directory.
`"PC_PIPE_BUF"`	Size of the pipe buffer when `fd` refers to a pipe or FIFO.
`"PC_PRIO_IO"`	Indicates whether priority I/O can be performed on `fd`.
`"PC_SYNC_IO"`	Indicates whether synchronous I/O can be performed on `fd`.
`"PC_VDISABLE"`	Indicates whether `fd` allows special-character processing to be disabled. `fd` must refer to a terminal.

Not all names are available on all platforms, and some systems may define additional configuration parameters. However, a list of the names known to the operating system can be found in the dictionary `os.pathconf_names`. If a known configuration name is not included in `os.pathconf_names`, its integer value can also be passed as *name*. Even if a name is recognized by Python, this function may still raise an `OSError` if the host operating system doesn't recognize the parameter or associate it with the file `fd`. This function is only available on some versions of UNIX.

fstat(fd)

Returns the status for file descriptor `fd`. Returns the same values as the `os.stat()` function (UNIX and Windows).

fstatvfs(fd)

Returns information about the file system containing the file associated with file descriptor `fd`. Returns the same values as the `os.statvfs()` function (UNIX).

fsync(fd)

Forces any unwritten data on `fd` to be written to disk. Note that if you are using an object with buffered I/O (for example, a Python `file` object), you should first flush the data before calling `fsync()`. Available on UNIX and Windows.

ftruncate(fd, length)

Truncates the file corresponding to file descriptor `fd` so that it's at most `length` bytes in size (UNIX).

isatty(fd)

Returns `True` if `fd` is associated with a TTY-like device such as a terminal (UNIX).

lseek(fd, pos, how)

Sets the current position of file descriptor `fd` to position *pos*. Values of *how* are as follows: `SEEK_SET` sets the position relative to the beginning of the file, `SEEK_CUR` sets it relative to the current position, and `SEEK_END` sets it relative to the end of the file. In older Python code, it is common to see these constants replaced with their numeric values of 0, 1, or 2, respectively.

`open(file [, flags [, mode]])`

Opens the file *file*. *flags* is the bitwise OR of the following constant values:

Value	Description
O_RDONLY	Open the file for reading.
O_WRONLY	Open the file for writing.
O_RDWR	Open for reading and writing (updates).
O_APPEND	Append bytes to the end of the file.
O_CREAT	Create the file if it doesn't exist.
O_NONBLOCK	Don't block on open, read, or write (UNIX).
O_NDELAY	Same as O_NONBLOCK (UNIX).
O_DSYNC	Synchronous writes (UNIX).
O_NOCTTY	When opening a device, don't set controlling terminal (UNIX).
O_TRUNC	If the file exists, truncates to zero length.
O_RSYNC	Synchronous reads (UNIX).
O_SYNC	Synchronous writes (UNIX).
O_EXCL	Error if O_CREAT and the file already exists.
O_EXLOCK	Set an exclusive lock on the file.
O_SHLOCK	Set a shared lock on the file.
O_ASYNC	Enables asynchronous input mode in which a SIGIO signal is generated with input is available.
O_DIRECT	Use direct I/O mode where reads and writes go directly to the disk instead of the operating system read/write caches.
O_DIRECTORY	Raises an error if the file is not a directory.
O_NOFOLLOW	Don't follow symbolic links.
O_NOATIME	Don't update the last access time of the file.
O_TEXT	Text mode (Windows).
O_BINARY	Binary mode (Windows).
O_NOINHERIT	File not inherited by child processes (Windows).
O_SHORT_LIVED	Hint to system that the file is used for short-term storage (Windows).
O_TEMPORARY	Delete file when closed (Windows).
O_RANDOM	Hint to system that file will be used for random access (Windows).
O_SEQUENTIAL	Hint to system that file will be accessed sequentially (Windows).

Synchronous I/O modes (O_SYNC, O_DSYNC, O_RSYNC) force I/O operations to block until they've been completed at the hardware level (for example, a write will block until the bytes have been physically written to disk). The *mode* parameter contains the file permissions represented as the bitwise OR of the following octal values (which are defined as constants in the stat module as indicated):

Mode	Meaning
0100	User has execute permission (stat.S_IXUSR).
0200	User has write permission (stat.S_IWUSR).
0400	User has read permission (stat.S_IRUSR).
0700	User has read/write/exec permission (stat.S_IRWXU).

Mode	Meaning
0010	Group has execute permission (stat.S_IXGRP).
0020	Group has write permission (stat.S_IWGRP).
0040	Group has read permission (stat.S_IRGRP).
0070	Group has read/write/exec permission (stat.S_IRWXG).
0001	Others have execute permission (stat.S_IXOTH).
0002	Others have write permission (stat.S_IWOTH).
0004	Others have read permission (stat.S_IROTH).
0007	Others have read/write/exec permission (stat.S_IRWXO).
4000	Set UID mode (stat.S_ISUID).
2000	Set GID mode (stat.S_ISGID).
1000	Set the sticky bit (stat.S_ISVTX).

The default mode of a file is (0777 & ~umask), where the umask setting is used to remove selected permissions. For example, a umask of 0022 removes the write permission for groups and others. The umask can be changed using the os.umask() function. The umask setting has no effect on Windows.

openpty()

Opens a psuedo-terminal and returns a pair of file descriptors (master, slave) for the PTY and TTY. Available on some versions of UNIX.

pipe()

Creates a pipe that can be used to establish unidirectional communication with another process. Returns a pair of file descriptors (r, w) usable for reading and writing, respectively. This function is usually called prior to executing a fork() function. After the fork(), the sending process closes the read end of the pipe and the receiving process closes the write end of the pipe. At this point, the pipe is activated and data can be sent from one process to another using read() and write() functions (UNIX).

read(fd, n)

Reads at most n bytes from file descriptor fd. Returns a byte string containing the bytes read.

tcgetpgrp(fd)

Returns the process group associated with the control terminal given by fd (UNIX).

tcsetpgrp(fd, pg)

Sets the process group associated with the control terminal given by fd (UNIX).

ttyname(fd)

Returns a string that specifies the terminal device associated with file descriptor fd. If fd is not associated with a terminal device, an OSError exception is raised (UNIX).

write(fd, str)

Writes the byte string str to file descriptor fd. Returns the number of bytes actually written.

Files and Directories

The following functions and variables are used to manipulate files and directories on the file system. To handle variances in filenaming schemes, the following variables contain information about the construction of path names:

Variable	Description
altsep	An alternative character used by the OS to separate pathname components, or None if only one separator character exists. This is set to '/' on DOS and Windows systems, where sep is a backslash.
curdir	The string used to refer to the current working directory: '.' for UNIX and Windows and ':' for the Macintosh.
devnull	The path of the null device (for example, /dev/null).
extsep	Character that separates the base filename from its type (for example, the '.' in 'foo.txt').
pardir	The string used to refer to the parent directory: '..' for UNIX and Windows and '::' for the Macintosh.
pathsep	The character used to separate search path components (as contained in the $PATH environment variable): ':' for UNIX and ';' for DOS and Windows.
sep	The character used to separate pathname components: '/' for UNIX and Windows and ':' for the Macintosh.

The following functions are used to manipulate files:

access(*path*, *accessmode*)

Checks read/write/execute permissions for this process to access the file *path*. *accessmode* is R_OK, W_OK, X_OK, or F_OK for read, write, execute, or existence, respectively. Returns 1 if access is granted, 0 if not.

chflags(*path*, *flags*)

Changes the file flags on *path*. *flags* is the bitwise-or of the constants listed next. Flags starting with UF_ can be set by any user, whereas SF_ flags can only be changed by the superuser (UNIX).

Flag	Meaning
stat.UF_NODUMP	Do not dump the file.
stat.UF_IMMUTABLE	The file is read-only.
stat.UF_APPEND	The file only supports append operations.
stat.UF_OPAQUE	The directory is opaque.
stat.UF_NOUNLINK	The file may not be deleted or renamed.
stat.SF_ARCHIVED	The file can be archived.
stat.SF_IMMUTABLE	The file is read-only.
stat.SF_APPEND	The file only supports append operations.
stat.SF_NOUNLINK	The file may not be deleted or renamed.
stat.SF_SNAPSHOT	The file is a snapshot file.

chmod(`path`, `mode`)

Changes the mode of `path`. `mode` has the same values as described for the `open()` function (UNIX and Windows).

chown(`path`, `uid`, `gid`)

Changes the owner and group ID of `path` to the numeric `uid` and `gid`. Setting `uid` or `gid` to -1 causes that parameter to remain unmodified (UNIX).

lchflags(`path`, `flags`)

The same as `chflags()`, but doesn't follow symbolic links (UNIX).

lchmod(`path`, `mode`)

The same as `chmod()` except that if `path` is a symbolic link, it modifies the link itself, not the file the link refers to.

lchown(`path`, `uid`, `gid`)

The same as `chown()` but doesn't follow symbolic links (UNIX).

link(`src`, `dst`)

Creates a hard link named `dst` that points to `src` (UNIX).

listdir(`path`)

Returns a list containing the names of the entries in the directory `path`. The list is returned in arbitrary order and doesn't include the special entries of '`.`' and '`..`'. If `path` is Unicode, the resulting list will only contain Unicode strings. Be aware that if any filenames in the directory can't be properly encoded into Unicode, they are silently skipped. If `path` is given as a byte string, then all filenames are returned as a list of byte strings.

lstat(`path`)

Like `stat()` but doesn't follow symbolic links (UNIX).

makedev(`major`, `minor`)

Creates a raw device number given major and minor device numbers (UNIX).

major(`devicenum`)

Returns the major device number from a raw device number `devicenum` created by `makedev()`.

minor(`devicenum`)

Returns the minor device number from a raw device number `devicenum` created by `makedev()`.

makedirs(`path` [, `mode`])

Recursive directory-creation function. Like `mkdir()` but makes all the intermediate-level directories needed to contain the leaf directory. Raises an `OSError` exception if the leaf directory already exists or cannot be created.

`mkdir(path [, mode])`

Creates a directory named `path` with numeric mode `mode`. The default mode is `0777`. On non-UNIX systems, the mode setting may have no effect or be ignored.

`mkfifo(path [, mode])`

Creates a FIFO (a named pipe) named `path` with numeric mode `mode`. The default mode is `0666` (UNIX).

`mknod(path [, mode, device])`

Creates a device-special file. `path` is the name of the file, `mode` specifies the permissions and type of file, and `device` is the raw device number created using `os.makedev()`. The `mode` parameter accepts the same parameters as `open()` when setting the file's access permissions. In addition, the flags `stat.S_IFREG`, `stat.S_IFCHR`, `stat.S_IFBLK`, and `stat.S_IFIFO` are added to `mode` to indicate a file type (UNIX).

`pathconf(path, name)`

Returns configurable system parameters related to the path name `path`. `name` is a string that specifies the name of the parameter and is the same as described for the `fpathconf()` function (UNIX).

`readlink(path)`

Returns a string representing the path to which a symbolic link, `path`, points (UNIX).

`remove(path)`

Removes the file `path`. This is identical to the `unlink()` function.

`removedirs(path)`

Recursive directory-removal function. Works like `rmdir()` except that, if the leaf directory is successfully removed, directories corresponding to the rightmost path segments will be pruned away until either the whole path is consumed or an error is raised (which is ignored because it generally means that a parent directory isn't empty). Raises an `OSError` exception if the leaf directory could not be removed successfully.

`rename(src, dst)`

Renames the file or directory `src` to `dst`.

`renames(old, new)`

Recursive directory-renaming or file-renaming function. Works like `rename()` except it first attempts to create any intermediate directories needed to make the new path name. After the rename, directories corresponding to the rightmost path segments of the old name will be pruned away using `removedirs()`.

`rmdir(path)`

Removes the directory `path`.

`stat(path)`

Performs a `stat()` system call on the given `path` to extract information about a file. The return value is an object whose attributes contain file information. Common attributes include:

Attribute	Description
st_mode	Inode protection mode
st_ino	Inode number
st_dev	Device the inode resides on
st_nlink	Number of links to the inode
st_uid	User ID of the owner
st_gid	Group ID of the owner
st_size	File size in bytes
st_atime	Time of last access
st_mtime	Time of last modification
st_ctime	Time of last status change

However, additional attributes may be available depending on the system. The object returned by stat() also looks like a 10-tuple containing the parameters (st_mode, st_ino, st_dev, st_nlink, st_uid, st_gid, st_size, st_atime, st_mtime, st_ctime). This latter form is provided for backward compatibility. The stat module defines constants that are used to extract fields from this tuple.

stat_float_times([newvalue])

Returns True if the times returned by stat() are floating-point numbers instead of integers. The behavior can be changed by supplying a Boolean value for newvalue.

statvfs(path)

Performs a statvfs() system call on the given path to get information about the file system. The return value is an object whose attributes describe the file system. Common attributes include:

Attribute	Description
f_bsize	Preferred system block size
f_frsize	Fundamental file system block size
f_blocks	Total number of blocks in the file system
f_bfree	Total number of free blocks
f_bavail	Free blocks available to a non-superuser
f_files	Total number of file inodes
f_ffree	Total number of free file inodes
f_favail	Free nodes available to a non-superuser
f_flag	Flags (system-dependent)
f_namemax	Maximum filename length

The returned object also behaves like a tuple containing these attributes in the order listed. The standard module statvfs defines constants that can be used to extract information from the returned statvfs data (UNIX).

symlink(src, dst)

Creates a symbolic link named dst that points to src.

`unlink(path)`

Removes the file *path*. Same as `remove()`.

`utime(path, (atime, mtime))`

Sets the access and modified time of the file to the given values. (The second argument is a tuple of two items.) The time arguments are specified in terms of the numbers returned by the `time.time()` function.

`walk(top [, topdown [, onerror [,followlinks]]])`

Creates a generator object that walks through a directory tree. *top* specifies the top of the directory, and *topdown* is a Boolean that indicates whether to traverse directories in a top-down (the default) or bottom-up order. The returned generator produces tuples (*dirpath*, *dirnames*, *filenames*) where *dirpath* is a string containing the path to the directory, *dirnames* is a list of all subdirectories in *dirpath*, and *filenames* is a list of the files in *dirpath*, not including directories. The *onerror* parameter is a function accepting a single argument. If any errors occur during processing, this function will be called with an instance of `os.error`. The default behavior is to ignore errors. If a directory is walked in a top-down manner, modifications to *dirnames* will affect the walking process. For example, if directories are removed from *dirnames*, those directories will be skipped. By default, symbolic links are not followed unless the *followlinks* argument is set to `True`.

Process Management

The following functions and variables are used to create, destroy, and manage processes:

`abort()`

Generates a `SIGABRT` signal that's sent to the calling process. Unless the signal is caught with a signal handler, the default is for the process to terminate with an error.

`defpath`

This variable contains the default search path used by the `exec*p*()` functions if the environment doesn't have a `'PATH'` variable.

`execl(path, arg0, arg1, ...)`

Equivalent to `execv(path, (arg0, arg1, ...))`.

`execle(path, arg0, arg1, ..., env)`

Equivalent to `execve(path, (arg0, arg1, ...), env)`.

`execlp(path, arg0, arg1, ...)`

Equivalent to `execvp(path, (arg0, arg1, ...))`.

`execv(path, args)`

Executes the program *path* with the argument list *args*, replacing the current process (that is, the Python interpreter). The argument list may be a tuple or list of strings.

execve(*path*, *args*, *env*)

Executes a new program like execv() but additionally accepts a dictionary, *env*, that defines the environment in which the program runs. *env* must be a dictionary mapping strings to strings.

execvp(*path*, *args*)

Like execv(*path*, *args*) but duplicates the shell's actions in searching for an executable file in a list of directories. The directory list is obtained from environ['PATH'].

execvpe(*path*, *args*, *env*)

Like execvp() but with an additional environment variable as in the execve() function.

_exit(*n*)

Exits immediately to the system with status *n*, without performing any cleanup actions. This is typically only done in child processes created by fork(). This is also different than calling sys.exit(), which performs a graceful shutdown of the interpreter. The exit code *n* is application-dependent, but a value of 0 usually indicates success, whereas a nonzero value indicates an error of some kind. Depending on the system, a number of standard exit code values may be defined:

Value	Description
EX_OK	No errors.
EX_USAGE	Incorrect command usage.
EX_DATAERR	Incorrect input data.
EX_NOINPUT	Missing input.
EX_NOUSER	User doesn't exist.
EX_NOHOST	Host doesn't exist.
EX_NOTFOUND	Not found.
EX_UNAVAILABLE	Service unavailable.
EX_SOFTWARE	Internal software error.
EX_OSERR	Operating system error.
EX_OSFILE	File system error.
EX_CANTCREAT	Can't create output.
EX_IOERR	I/O error.
EX_TEMPFAIL	Temporary failure.
EX_PROTOCOL	Protocol error.
EX_NOPERM	Insufficient permissions.
EX_CONFIG	Configuration error.

fork()

Creates a child process. Returns 0 in the newly created child process and the child's process ID in the original process. The child process is a clone of the original process and shares many resources such as open files (UNIX).

`forkpty()`

Creates a child process using a new pseudo-terminal as the child's controlling terminal. Returns a pair (`pid`, `fd`), in which `pid` is 0 in the child and `fd` is a file descriptor of the master end of the pseudo-terminal. This function is available only in certain versions of UNIX.

`kill(pid, sig)`

Sends the process `pid` the signal `sig`. A list of signal names can be found in the `signal` module (UNIX).

`killpg(pgid, sig)`

Sends the process group `pgid` the signal `sig`. A list of signal names can be found in the `signal` module (UNIX).

`nice(increment)`

Adds an increment to the scheduling priority (the "niceness") of the process. Returns the new niceness. Typically, users can only decrease the priority of a process because increasing the priority requires root access. The effect of changing the priority is system-dependent, but decreasing the priority is commonly done to make a process run in the background in a way such that it doesn't noticeably impact the performance of other processes (UNIX).

`plock(op)`

Locks program segments into memory, preventing them from being swapped. The value of `op` is an integer that determines which segments are locked. The value of `op` is platform-specific but is typically one of UNLOCK, PROCLOCK, TXTLOCK, or DATLOCK. These constants are not defined by Python but might be found in the `<sys/lock.h>` header file. This function is not available on all platforms and often can be performed only by a process with an effective user ID of 0 (root) (UNIX).

`popen(command [, mode [, bufsize]])`

Opens a pipe to or from a command. The return value is an open file object connected to the pipe, which can be read or written depending on whether `mode` is `'r'` (the default) or `'w'`. `bufsize` has the same meaning as in the built-in `open()` function. The exit status of the command is returned by the `close()` method of the returned file object, except that when the exit status is zero, `None` is returned.

`spawnv(mode, path, args)`

Executes the program `path` in a new process, passing the arguments specified in `args` as command-line parameters. `args` can be a list or a tuple. The first element of `args` should be the name of the program. `mode` is one of the following constants:

Constant	Description
P_WAIT	Executes the program and waits for it to terminate. Returns the program's exit code.
P_NOWAIT	Executes the program and returns the process handle.
P_NOWAITO	Same as P_NOWAIT.

Constant	Description
P_OVERLAY	Executes the program and destroys the calling process (same as the `exec` functions).
P_DETACH	Executes the program and detaches from it. The calling program continues to run but cannot wait for the spawned process.

`spawnv()` is available on Windows and some versions of UNIX.

spawnve(mode, path, args, env)

Executes the program *path* in a new process, passing the arguments specified in *args* as command-line parameters and the contents of the mapping *env* as the environment. *args* can be a list or a tuple. *mode* has the same meaning as described for `spawnv()`.

spawnl(mode, path, arg1, ..., argn)

The same as `spawnv()` except that all the arguments are supplied as extra parameters.

spawnle(mode, path, arg1, ... , argn, env)

The same as `spawnve()` except that the arguments are supplied as parameters. The last parameter is a mapping containing the environment variables.

spawnlp(mode, file, arg1, ... , argn)

The same as `spawnl()` but looks for *file* using the settings of the PATH environment variable (UNIX).

spawnlpe(mode, file, arg1, ... , argn, env)

The same as `spawnle()` but looks for *file* using the settings of the PATH environment variable (UNIX).

spawnvp(mode, file, args)

The same as `spawnv()` but looks for *file* using the settings of the PATH environment variable (UNIX).

spawnvpe(mode, file, args, env)

The same as `spawnve()` but looks for *file* using the settings of the PATH environment variable (UNIX).

startfile(path [, operation])

Launches the application associated with the file *path*. This performs the same action as would occur if you double-clicked the file in Windows Explorer. The function returns as soon as the application is launched. Furthermore, there is no way to wait for completion or to obtain exit codes from the application. *path* is a relative to the current directory. *operation* is an optional string that specifies the action to perform when opening *path*. By default, it is set to 'open', but it may be set to 'print', 'edit', 'explore', or 'find' (the exact list depends on the type of *path* (Windows)).

system(command)

Executes *command* (a string) in a subshell. On UNIX, the return value is the exit status of the process as returned by `wait()`. On Windows, the exit code is always 0. The subprocess module provides considerably more power and is the preferred way to launch subprocesses.

`times()`

Returns a 5-tuple of floating-point numbers indicating accumulated times in seconds. On UNIX, the tuple contains the user time, system time, children's user time, children's system time, and elapsed real time in that order. On Windows, the tuple contains the user time, system time, and zeros for the other three values.

`wait([pid])`

Waits for completion of a child process and returns a tuple containing its process ID and exit status. The exit status is a 16-bit number whose low byte is the signal number that killed the process and whose high byte is the exit status (if the signal number is zero). The high bit of the low byte is set if a core file was produced. *pid*, if given, specifies the process to wait for. If it's omitted, `wait()` returns when any child process exits (UNIX).

`waitpid(pid, options)`

Waits for a change in the state of a child process given by process ID *pid* and returns a tuple containing its process ID and exit status indication, encoded as for `wait()`. *options* should be 0 for normal operation or `WNOHANG` to avoid hanging if no child process status is available immediately. This function can also be used to gather information about child processes that have only stopped executing for some reason. Setting *options* to `WCONTINUED` gathers information from a child when it resumes operation after being stopped via job control. Setting *options* to `WUNTRACED` gathers information from a child that has been stopped, but from which no status information has been reported yet.

`wait3([options])`

The same as `waitpid()` except that the function waits for a change in any child process. Returns a 3-tuple (*pid, status, rusage*), where *pid* is the child process ID, *status* is the exit status code, and *rusage* contains resource usage information as returned by `resource.getrusage()`. The *options* parameter has the same meaning as for `waitpid()`.

`wait4(pid, options)`

The same as `waitpid()` except that the return result is the same tuple as returned by `wait3()`.

The following functions take a process status code as returned by `waitpid()`, `wait3()`, or `wait4()` and are used to examine the state of the process (UNIX).

`WCOREDUMP(status)`

Returns `True` if the process dumped core.

`WIFEXITED(status)`

Returns `True` if the process exited using the `exit()` system call.

`WEXITSTATUS(status)`

If `WIFEXITED(status)` is true, the integer parameter to the `exit()` system call is returned. Otherwise, the return value is meaningless.

`WIFCONTINUED(status)`

Returns `True` if the process has resumed from a job-control stop.

`WIFSIGNALED(status)`

Returns `True` if the process exited due to a signal.

`WIFSTOPPED(status)`

Returns `True` if the process has been stopped.

`WSTOPSIG(status)`

Returns the signal that caused the process to stop.

`WTERMSIG(status)`

Returns the signal that caused the process to exit.

System Configuration

The following functions are used to obtain system configuration information:

`confstr(name)`

Returns a string-valued system configuration variable. *name* is a string specifying the name of the variable. The acceptable names are platform-specific, but a dictionary of known names for the host system is found in `os.confstr_names`. If a configuration value for a specified name is not defined, the empty string is returned. If *name* is unknown, `ValueError` is raised. An `OSError` may also be raised if the host system doesn't support the configuration name. The parameters returned by this function mostly pertain to the build environment on the host machine and include paths of system utilities, compiler options for various program configurations (for example, 32-bit, 64-bit, and large-file support), and linker options (UNIX).

`getloadavg()`

Returns a 3-tuple containing the average number of items in the system run-queue over the last 1, 5, and 15 minutes (UNIX).

`sysconf(name)`

Returns an integer-valued system-configuration variable. *name* is a string specifying the name of the variable. The names defined on the host system can be found in the dictionary `os.sysconf_names`. Returns -1 if the configuration name is known but the value is not defined. Otherwise, a `ValueError` or `OSError` may be raised. Some systems may define more than 100 different system parameters. However, the following list details the parameters defined by POSIX.1 that should be available on most UNIX systems:

Parameter	Description
`"SC_ARG_MAX"`	Maximum length of the arguments that can be used with `exec()`.
`"SC_CHILD_MAX"`	Maximum number of processes per user ID.
`"SC_CLK_TCK"`	Number of clock ticks per second.
`"SC_NGROUPS_MAX"`	Maximum number of simultaneous supplementary group IDs.
`"SC_STREAM_MAX"`	Maximum number of streams a process can open at one time.

Parameter	Description
`"SC_TZNAME_MAX"`	Maximum number of bytes in a time zone name.
`"SC_OPEN_MAX"`	Maximum number of files a process can open at one time.
`"SC_JOB_CONTROL"`	System supports job control.
`"SC_SAVED_IDS"`	Indicates whether each process has a saved set-user-ID and a saved set-group-ID.

`urandom(n)`

Returns a string containing *n* random bytes generated by the system (for example, `/dev/urandom` on UNIX). The returned bytes are suitable for cryptography.

Exceptions

The os module defines a single exception to indicate errors.

`error`

Exception raised when a function returns a system–related error. This is the same as the built-in exception `OSError`. The exception carries two values: `errno` and `strerr`. The first contains the integer error value as described for the `errno` module. The latter contains a string error message. For exceptions involving the file system, the exception also contains a third attribute, `filename`, which is the filename passed to the function.

os.path

The `os.path` module is used to manipulate pathnames in a portable manner. It's imported by the os module.

`abspath(path)`

Returns an absolute version of the path name *path*, taking the current working directory into account. For example, `abspath('../Python/foo')` might return `'/home/beazley/Python/foo'`.

`basename(path)`

Returns the base name of path name *path*. For example, `basename('/usr/local/python')` returns `'python'`.

`commonprefix(list)`

Returns the longest string that's a prefix of all strings in *list*. If *list* is empty, the empty string is returned.

`dirname(path)`

Returns the directory name of path name *path*. For example, `dirname('/usr/local/python')` returns `'/usr/local'`.

`exists(path)`

Returns `True` if *path* refers to an existing path. Returns `False` if *path* refers to a broken symbolic link.

expanduser(*path*)

Replaces path names of the form `'~user'` with a user's home directory. If the expansion fails or *path* does not begin with `'~'`, the path is returned unmodified.

expandvars(*path*)

Expands environment variables of the form `'$name'` or `'${name}'` in *path*. Malformed or nonexistent variable names are left unchanged.

getatime(*path*)

Returns the time of last access as the number of seconds since the epoch (see the `time` module). The return value may be a floating-point number if `os.stat_float_times()` returns `True`.

getctime(*path*)

Returns the time of last modification on UNIX and the time of creation on Windows. The time is returned as the number of seconds since the epoch (see the `time` module). The return value may be a floating-point number in certain cases (see `getatime()`).

getmtime(*path*)

Returns the time of last modification as the number of seconds since the epoch (see the `time` module). The return value may be a floating-point number in certain cases (see `getatime()`).

getsize(*path*)

Returns the file size in bytes.

isabs(*path*)

Returns `True` if *path* is an absolute path name (begins with a slash).

isfile(*path*)

Returns `True` if *path* is a regular file. This function follows symbolic links, so both `islink()` and `isfile()` can be true for the same path.

isdir(*path*)

Returns `True` if *path* is a directory. Follows symbolic links.

islink(*path*)

Returns `True` if *path* refers to a symbolic link. Returns `False` if symbolic links are unsupported.

ismount(*path*)

Returns `True` if *path* is a mount point.

join(*path1* [, *path2* [, ...]])

Intelligently joins one or more path components into a pathname. For example, `join('home', 'beazley', 'Python')` returns `'home/beazley/Python'`.

lexists(*path*)

Returns `True` if *path* exists. Returns `True` for all symbolic links, even if the link is broken.

`normcase(path)`

Normalizes the case of a path name. On non-case-sensitive file systems, this converts `path` to lowercase. On Windows, forward slashes are also converted to backslashes.

`normpath(path)`

Normalizes a path name. This collapses redundant separators and up-level references so that `'A//B'`, `'A/./B'`, and `'A/foo/../B'` all become `'A/B'`. On Windows, forward slashes are converted to backslashes.

`realpath(path)`

Returns the real path of `path`, eliminating symbolic links if any (UNIX).

`relpath(path [, start])`

Returns a relative path to `path` from the current working directory. `start` can be supplied to specify a different starting directory.

`samefile(path1, path2)`

Returns `True` if `path1` and `path2` refer to the same file or directory (UNIX).

`sameopenfile(fp1, fp2)`

Returns `True` if the open file objects `fp1` and `fp2` refer to the same file (UNIX).

`samestat(stat1, stat2)`

Returns `True` if the stat tuples `stat1` and `stat2` as returned by `fstat()`, `lstat()`, or `stat()` refer to the same file (UNIX).

`split(path)`

Splits `path` into a pair `(head, tail)`, where `tail` is the last pathname component and `head` is everything leading up to that. For example, `'/home/user/foo'` gets split into `('/home/user', 'foo')`. This tuple is the same as would be returned by `(dirname(), basename())`.

`splitdrive(path)`

Splits `path` into a pair `(drive, filename)` where `drive` is either a drive specification or the empty string. `drive` is always the empty string on machines without drive specifications.

`splitext(path)`

Splits a path name into a base filename and suffix. For example, `splitext('foo.txt')` returns `('foo', '.txt')`.

`splitunc(path)`

Splits a path name into a pair `(unc, rest)` where `unc` is a UNC (Universal Naming Convention) mount point and `rest` the remainder of the path (Windows).

`supports_unicode_filenames`

Variable set to `True` if the file system allows Unicode filenames.

> **Note**
>
> On Windows, some care is required when working with filenames that include a drive let-
> ter (for example, `'C:spam.txt'`). In most cases, filenames are interpreted as being
> relative to the current working directory. For example, if the current directory is
> `'C:\Foo\'`, then the file `'C:spam.txt'` is interpreted as the file
> `'C:\Foo\C:spam.txt'`, not the file `'C:\spam.txt'`.

> **See Also:**
>
> `fnmatch` (**p. 316**), `glob` (**p. 317**), `os` (**p. 378**).

signal

The `signal` module is used to write signal handlers in Python. Signals usually correspond to asynchronous events that are sent to a program due to the expiration of a
timer, arrival of incoming data, or some action performed by a user. The signal interface
emulates that of UNIX, although parts of the module are supported on other platforms.

`alarm(time)`

If `time` is nonzero, a `SIGALRM` signal is scheduled to be sent to the program in `time`
seconds. Any previously scheduled alarm is canceled. If `time` is zero, no alarm is scheduled and any previously set alarm is canceled. Returns the number of seconds remaining before any previously scheduled alarm or zero if no alarm was scheduled (UNIX).

`getsignal(signalnum)`

Returns the signal handler for signal `signalnum`. The returned object is a callable
Python object. The function may also return `SIG_IGN` for an ignored signal, `SIG_DFL`
for the default signal handler, or `None` if the signal handler was not installed from the
Python interpreter.

`getitimer(which)`

Returns the current value of an internal timer identified by `which`.

`pause()`

Goes to sleep until the next signal is received (UNIX).

`set_wakeup_fd(fd)`

Sets a file descriptor `fd` on which a `'\0'` byte will be written when a signal is received.
This, in turn, can be used to handle signals in programs that are polling file descriptors
using functions such as those found in the `select` module. The file described by `fd`
must be opened in non-blocking mode for this to work.

`setitimer(which, seconds [, interval])`

Sets an internal timer to generate a signal after `seconds` seconds and repeatedly there-
after every `interval` seconds. Both of these parameters are specified as floating-point
numbers. The `which` parameter is one of `ITIMER_REAL`, `ITIMER_VIRTUAL`, or
`ITIMER_PROF`. The choice of `which` determines what signal is generated after the timer
has expired. `SIGALRM` is generated for `ITIMER_REAL`, `SIGVTALRM` is generated for

ITIMER_VIRTUAL, and SIGPROF is generated for ITIMER_PROF. Set *seconds* to 0 to clear a timer. Returns a tuple (*seconds, interval*) with the previous settings of the timer.

siginterrupt(*signalnum, flag*)

Sets the system call restart behavior for a given signal number. If *flag* is False, system calls interrupted by signal *signalnum* will be automatically restarted. If set True, the system call will be interrupted. An interrupted system call will typically result in an OSError or IOError exception where the associated error number is set to errno.EINTR or errno.EAGAIN.

signal(*signalnum, handler*)

Sets a signal handler for signal *signalnum* to the function *handler*. *handler* must be a callable Python object taking two arguments: the signal number and frame object. SIG_IGN or SIG_DFL can also be given to ignore a signal or use the default signal handler, respectively. The return value is the previous signal handler, SIG_IGN, or SIG_DFL. When threads are enabled, this function can only be called from the main thread. Otherwise, a ValueError exception is raised.

Individual signals are identified using symbolic constants of the form SIG*. These names correspond to integer values that are machine-specific. Typical values are as follows:

Signal Name	Description
SIGABRT	Abnormal termination
SIGALRM	Alarm
SIGBUS	Bus error
SIGCHLD	Change in child status
SIGCLD	Change in child status
SIGCONT	Continue
SIGFPE	Floating-point error
SIGHUP	Hang up
SIGILL	Illegal instruction
SIGINT	Terminal interrupt character
SIGIO	Asynchronous I/O
SIGIOT	Hardware fault
SIGKILL	Terminate
SIGPIPE	Write to pipe, no readers
SIGPOLL	Pollable event
SIGPROF	Profiling alarm
SIGPWR	Power failure
SIGQUIT	Terminal quit character
SIGSEGV	Segmentation fault
SIGSTOP	Stop
SIGTERM	Termination
SIGTRAP	Hardware fault
SIGTSTP	Terminal stop character
SIGTTIN	Control TTY

Signal Name	Description
SIGTTOU	Control TTY
SIGURG	Urgent condition
SIGUSR1	User defined
SIGUSR2	User defined
SIGVTALRM	Virtual time alarm
SIGWINCH	Window size change
SIGXCPU	CPU limit exceeded
SIGXFSZ	File size limit exceeded

In addition, the module defines the following variables:

Variable	Description
SIG_DFL	Signal handler that invokes the default signal handler
SIG_IGN	Signal handler that ignores a signal
NSIG	One more than the highest signal number

Example

The following example illustrates a timeout on establishing a network connection (the socket module already provides a timeout option so this example is merely meant to illustrate the basic concept of using the signal module).

```
import signal, socket
def handler(signum, frame):
    print 'Timeout!'
    raise IOError, 'Host not responding.'
sock = socket.socket(socket.AF_INET, socket.SOCK_STREAM)
signal.signal(signal.SIGALRM, handler)
signal.alarm(5)                            # 5-second alarm
sock.connect('www.python.org', 80)   # Connect
signal.alarm(0)                            # Clear alarm
```

Notes

- Signal handlers remain installed until explicitly reset, with the exception of SIGCHLD (whose behavior is implementation-specific).
- It's not possible to temporarily disable signals.
- Signals are only handled between the atomic instructions of the Python interpreter. The delivery of a signal can be delayed by long-running calculations written in C (as might be performed in an extension module).
- If a signal occurs during an I/O operation, the I/O operation may fail with an exception. In this case, the errno value is set to errno.EINTR to indicate an interrupted system call.
- Certain signals such as SIGSEGV cannot be handled from Python.
- Python installs a small number of signal handlers by default. SIGPIPE is ignored, SIGINT is translated into a KeyboardInterrupt exception, and SIGTERM is caught in order to perform cleanup and invoke sys.exitfunc.

- Extreme care is needed if signals and threads are used in the same program. Currently, only the main thread of execution can set new signal handlers or receive signals.
- Signal handling on Windows is of only limited functionality. The number of supported signals is extremely limited on this platform.

subprocess

The subprocess module contains functions and objects that generalize the task of creating new processes, controlling input and output streams, and handling return codes. The module centralizes functionality contained in a variety of other modules such as os, popen2, and commands.

Popen(*args*, ***parms*)

Executes a new command as a subprocess and returns a Popen object representing the new process. The command is specified in *args* as either a string, such as 'ls -l', or as a list of strings, such as ['ls', '-l']. *parms* represents a collection of keyword arguments that can be set to control various properties of the subprocess. The following keyword parameters are understood:

Keyword	Description
bufsize	Specifies the buffering behavior, where 0 is unbuffered, 1 is line-buffered, a negative value uses the system default, and other positive values specify the approximate buffer size. The default value is 0.
close_fds	If True, all file descriptors except 0, 1, and 2 are closed prior to execution of the child process. The default value is False.
creation_flags	Specifies process-creation flags on Windows. The only flag currently available is CREATE_NEW_CONSOLE. The default value is 0.
cwd	The directory in which the command will execute. The current directory of the child process is changed to cwd prior to execution. The default value is None, which uses the current directory of the parent process.
env	Dictionary of environment variables for the new process. The default value is None, which uses the environment variables of the parent process.
executable	Specifies the name of the executable program to use. This is rarely needed because the program name is already included in *args*. If shell has been given, this parameter specifies the name of the shell to use. The default value is None.
preexec_fn	Specifies a function that will be called in the child process just before the command is executed. The function should take no arguments.
shell	If True, the command is executed using the UNIX shell like the os.system() function. The default shell is /bin/sh, but this can be changed by also setting executable. The default value of shell is None.

Keyword	Description
startupinfo	Provides startup flags used when creating processes on Windows. The default value is None. Possible values include STARTF_USESHOWWINDOW and STARTF_USESTDHANDLERS.
stderr	File object representing the file to use for stderr in the child process. May be a file object created via open(), an integer file descriptor, or the special value PIPE, which indicates that a new pipe should be created. The default value is None.
stdin	File object representing the file to use for stdin in the child process. May be set to the same values as stderr. The default value is None.
stdout	File object representing the file to use for stdout in the child process. May be set to the same values as stderr. The default value is None.
universal_newlines	If True, the files representing stdin, stdout, and stderr are opened in text mode with universal newline mode enabled. See the open() function for a full description.

call(args, **parms)

This function is exactly the same as Popen(), except that it simply executes the command and returns its status code instead (that is, it does not return a Popen object). This function is useful if you just want to execute a command but are not concerned with capturing its output or controlling it in other ways. The parameters have the same meaning as with Popen().

check_call(args, **parms)

The same as call() except that if the exit code is non-zero, the CalledProcessError exception is raised. This exception has the exit code stored in its returncode attribute.

The Popen object p returned by Popen() has a variety of methods and attributes that can be used for interacting with the subprocess.

p.communicate([input])

Communicates with the child process by sending the data supplied in input to the standard input of the process. Once data is sent, the method waits for the process to terminate while collecting output received on standard output and standard error. Returns a tuple (stdout, stderr) where stdout and stderr are strings. If no data is sent to the child process, input is set to None (the default).

p.kill()

Kills the subprocess by sending it a SIGKILL signal on UNIX or calling the p.terminate() method on Windows.

p.poll()

Checks to see if p has terminated. If so, the return code of the subprocess is returned. Otherwise, None is returned.

p.send_signal(signal)

Sends a signal to the subprocess. signal is a signal number as defined in the signal module. On Windows, the only supported signal is SIGTERM.

`p.terminate()`

Terminates the subprocess by sending it a SIGTERM signal on UNIX or calling the
Win32 API TerminateProcess function on Windows.

`p.wait()`

Waits for *p* to terminate and returns the return code.

`p.pid`

Process ID of the child process.

`p.returncode`

Numeric return code of the process. If None, the process has not terminated yet. If negative, it indicates the process was terminated by a signal (UNIX).

`p.stdin, p.stdout, p.stderr`

These three attributes are set to open file objects whenever the corresponding I/O
stream is opened as a pipe (for example, setting the *stdout* argument in Popen() to
PIPE). These file objects are provided so that the pipe can be connected to other subprocesses. These attributes are set to None if pipes are not in use.

Examples

```
# Execute a basic system command.  Like os.system()
ret = subprocess.call("ls -l", shell=True)

# Silently execute a basic system command
ret = subprocess.call("rm -f *.java",shell=True,
                       stdout=open("/dev/null"))

# Execute a system command, but capture the output
p = subprocess.Popen("ls -l", shell=True, stdout=subprocess.PIPE)
out = p.stdout.read()

# Execute a command, but send input and receive output
p = subprocess.Popen("wc", shell=True, stdin=subprocess.PIPE,
                      stdout=subprocess.PIPE, stderr=subprocess.PIPE)
out, err = p.communicate(s)     # Send string s to the process

# Create two subprocesses and link them together via a pipe
p1 = subprocess.Popen("ls -l", shell=True, stdout=subprocess.PIPE)
p2 = subprocess.Popen("wc",shell=True, stdin=p1.stdout,
                      stdout=subprocess.PIPE)
out = p2.stdout.read()
```

Notes

- As a general rule, it is better to supply the command line as a list of
  strings instead of a single string with a shell command (for example,
  ['wc','filename'] instead of 'wc filename'). On many systems, it is common for filenames to include funny characters and spaces (for example, the
  "Documents and Settings" folder on Windows). If you stick to supplying command arguments as a list, everything will work normally. If you try to form a
  shell command, you will have to take additional steps to make sure special characters and spaces are properly escaped.

- On Windows, pipes are opened in binary file mode. Thus, if you are reading text output from a subprocess, line endings will include the extra carriage return character ('\r\n' instead of '\n'). If this is a concern, supply the universal_newlines option to Popen().

- The subprocess module can not be used to control processes that expect to be running in a terminal or TTY. The most common example is any program that expects a user to enter a password (such as ssh, ftp, svn, and so on). To control these programs, look for third-party modules based on the popular "Expect" UNIX utility.

time

The time module provides various time-related functions. In Python, time is measured as the number of seconds since the epoch. The *epoch* is the beginning of time (the point at which time = 0 seconds). The epoch is January 1, 1970, on UNIX and can be determined by calling time.gmtime(0) on other systems.

The following variables are defined:

accept2dyear

A Boolean value that indicates whether two-digit years are accepted. Normally this is True, but it's set to False if the environment variable $PYTHONY2K is set to a non-empty string. The value can be changed manually as well.

altzone

The time zone used during daylight saving time (DST), if applicable.

daylight

Is set to a nonzero value if a DST time zone has been defined.

timezone

The local (non-DST) time zone.

tzname

A tuple containing the name of the local time zone and the name of the local daylight saving time zone (if defined).

The following functions can be used:

asctime([tuple])

Converts a tuple representing a time as returned by gmtime() or localtime() to a string of the form 'Mon Jul 12 14:45:23 1999'. If no arguments are supplied, the current time is used.

clock()

Returns the current CPU time in seconds as a floating-point number.

ctime([secs])

Converts a time expressed in seconds since the epoch to a string representing local time. ctime(secs) is the same as asctime(localtime(secs)). If secs is omitted or None, the current time is used.

gmtime([*secs*])

Converts a time expressed in seconds since the epoch to a time in UTC Coordinated Universal Time (a.k.a. Greenwich Mean Time). This function returns a struct_time object with the following attributes:

Attribute	Value
tm_year	A four-digit value such as 1998
tm_mon	1-12
tm_mday	1-31
tm_hour	0-23
tm_min	0-59
tm_sec	0-61
tm_wday	0-6 (0=Monday)
tm_yday	1-366
tm_isdst	-1, 0, 1

The tm_isdst attribute is 1 if DST is in effect, 0 if not, and -1 if no information is available. If *secs* is omitted or None, the current time is used. For backward compatibility, the returned struct_time object also behaves like a 9-tuple containing the preceding attribute values in the same order as listed.

localtime([*secs*])

Returns a struct_time object as with gmtime(), but corresponding to the local time zone. If *secs* is omitted or None, the current time is used.

mktime(*tuple*)

This function takes a struct_time object or tuple representing a time in the local time zone (in the same format as returned by localtime()) and returns a floating-point number representing the number of seconds since the epoch. An OverflowError exception is raised if the input value is not a valid time.

sleep(*secs*)

Puts the calling thread to sleep for *secs* seconds. *secs* is a floating-point number.

strftime(*format* [, *tm*])

Converts a struct_time object *tm* representing a time as returned by gmtime() or localtime() to a string (for backwards compatibility, *tm* may also be a tuple representing a time value). *format* is a format string in which the following format codes can be embedded:

Directive	Meaning
%a	Locale's abbreviated weekday name
%A	Locale's full weekday name
%b	Locale's abbreviated month name
%B	Locale's full month name
%c	Locale's appropriate date and time representation
%d	Day of the month as a decimal number [01-31]
%H	Hour (24-hour clock) as a decimal number [00-23]

Directive	Meaning
%I	Hour (12-hour clock) as a decimal number [01-12]
%j	Day of the year as a decimal number [001-366]
%m	Month as a decimal number [01-12]
%M	Minute as a decimal number [00-59]
%p	Locale's equivalent of either AM or PM
%S	Seconds as a decimal number [00-61]
%U	Week number of the year [00-53] (Sunday as first day)
%w	Weekday as a decimal number [0-6] (0 = Sunday)
%W	Week number of the year (Monday as first day)
%x	Locale's appropriate date representation
%X	Locale's appropriate time representation
%y	Year without century as a decimal number [00-99]
%Y	Year with century as a decimal number
%Z	Time zone name (or by no characters if no time zone exists)
%%	The % character

The format codes can include a width and precision in the same manner as used with the % operator on strings. ValueError is raised if any of the tuple fields are out of range. If *tuple* is omitted, the time tuple corresponding to the current time is used.

strptime(*string* [, *format*])

Parses a string representing a time and returns a struct_time object as returned by localtime() or gmtime(). The *format* parameter uses the same specifiers as used by strftime() and defaults to '%a %b %d %H:%M:%S %Y'. This is the same format as produced by the ctime() function. If the string cannot be parsed, a ValueError exception is raised.

time()

Returns the current time as the number of seconds since the epoch in UTC (Coordinated Universal Time).

tzset()

Resets the time zone setting based on the value of the TZ environment variable on UNIX. For example:

```
os.environ['TZ'] = 'US/Mountain'
time.tzset()

os.environ['TZ'] = "CST+06CDT,M4.1.0,M10.5.0"
time.tzset()
```

Notes

- When two-digit years are accepted, they're converted to four-digit years according to the POSIX X/Open standard, where the values 69-99 are mapped to 1969-1999 and the values 0-68 are mapped to 2000-2068.

- The accuracy of the time functions is often much less than what might be suggested by the units in which time is represented. For example, the operating system might only update the time 50–100 times a second.

See Also:

datetime (**p. 336**)

winreg

The winreg module (_winreg in Python 2) provides a low-level interface to the Windows registry. The registry is a large hierarchical tree in which each node is called a *key*. The children of a particular key are known as *subkeys* and may contain additional subkeys or values. For example, the setting of the Python sys.path variable is typically contained in the registry as follows:

\HKEY_LOCAL_MACHINE\Software\Python\PythonCore\2.6\PythonPath

In this case, Software is a subkey of HKEY_LOCAL_MACHINE, Python is a subkey of Software, and so forth. The value of the PythonPath key contains the actual path setting.

Keys are accessed through open and close operations. Open keys are represented by special handles (which are wrappers around the integer handle identifiers normally used by Windows).

CloseKey(*key*)

Closes a previously opened registry key with handle *key*.

ConnectRegistry(*computer_name*, *key*)

Returns a handle to a predefined registry key on another computer. *computer_name* is the name of the remote machine as a string of the *computername*. If *computer_name* is None, the local registry is used. *key* is a predefined handle such as HKEY_CURRENT_USER or HKEY_USERS. Raises EnvironmentError on failure. The following list shows all HKEY_* values defined in the _winreg module:

- HKEY_CLASSES_ROOT
- HKEY_CURRENT_CONFIG
- HKEY_CURRENT_USER
- HKEY_DYN_DATA
- HKEY_LOCAL_MACHINE
- HKEY_PERFORMANCE_DATA
- HKEY_USERS

CreateKey(*key*, *sub_key*)

Creates or opens a key and returns a handle. *key* is a previously opened key or a predefined key defined by the HKEY_* constants. *sub_key* is the name of the key that will be opened or created. If *key* is a predefined key, *sub_key* may be None, in which case *key* is returned.

DeleteKey(*key, sub_key*)

Deletes *sub_key*. *key* is an open key or one of the predefined HKEY_* constants. *sub_key* is a string that identifies the key to delete. *sub_key* must not have any sub-keys; otherwise, EnvironmentError is raised.

DeleteValue(*key, value*)

Deletes a named value from a registry key. *key* is an open key or one of the predefined HKEY_* constants. *value* is a string containing the name of the value to remove.

EnumKey(*key, index*)

Returns the name of a subkey by index. *key* is an open key or one of the predefined HKEY_* constants. *index* is an integer that specifies the key to retrieve. If *index* is out of range, an EnvironmentError is raised.

EnumValue(*key, index*)

Returns a value of an open key. *key* is an open key or a predefined HKEY_* constant. *index* is an integer specifying the value to retrieve. The function returns a tuple (*name, data, type*) in which *name* is the value name, *data* is an object holding the value data, and *type* is an integer that specifies the type of the value data. The following type codes are currently defined:

Code	Description
REG_BINARY	Binary data
REG_DWORD	32-bit number
REG_DWORD_LITTLE_ENDIAN	32-bit little-endian number
REG_DWORD_BIG_ENDIAN	32-bit number in big-endian format
REG_EXPAND_SZ	Null-terminated string with unexpanded references to environment variables
REG_LINK	Unicode symbolic link
REG_MULTI_SZ	Sequence of null-terminated strings
REG_NONE	No defined value type
REG_RESOURCE_LIST	Device driver resource list
REG_SZ	Null-terminated string

ExpandEnvironmentStrings(*s*)

Expands environment strings of the form %*name*% in Unicode string *s*.

FlushKey(*key*)

Writes the attributes of *key* to the registry, forcing changes to disk. This function should only be called if an application requires absolute certainty that registry data is stored on disk. It does not return until data is written. It is not necessary to use this function under normal circumstances.

RegLoadKey(*key, sub_key, filename*)

Creates a subkey and stores registration information from a file into it. *key* is an open key or a predefined HKEY_* constant. *sub_key* is a string identifying the subkey to load. *filename* is the name of the file from which to load data. The contents of this file must be created with the SaveKey() function, and the calling process must have SE_RESTORE_ PRIVILEGE for this to work. If *key* was returned by ConnectRegistry(), *filename* should be a path that's relative to the remote computer.

OpenKey(*key*, *sub_key*[, *res* [, *sam*]])

Opens a key. *key* is an open key or an HKEY_* constant. *sub_key* is a string identifying the subkey to open. *res* is a reserved integer that must be zero (the default). *sam* is an integer defining the security access mask for the key. The default is KEY_READ. Here are the other possible values for *sam*:

- KEY_ALL_ACCESS
- KEY_CREATE_LINK
- KEY_CREATE_SUB_KEY
- KEY_ENUMERATE_SUB_KEYS
- KEY_EXECUTE
- KEY_NOTIFY
- KEY_QUERY_VALUE
- KEY_READ
- KEY_SET_VALUE
- KEY_WRITE

OpenKeyEx()

Same as OpenKey().

QueryInfoKey(*key*)

Returns information about a key as a tuple (*num_subkeys*, *num_values*, *last_modified*) in which *num_subkeys* is the number of subkeys, *num_values* is the number of values, and *last_modified* is a long integer containing the time of last modification. Time is measured from January 1, 1601, in units of 100 nanoseconds.

QueryValue(*key*, *sub_key*)

Returns the unnamed value for a key as a string. *key* is an open key or an HKEY_* constant. *sub_key* is the name of the subkey to use, if any. If omitted, the function returns the value associated with *key* instead. This function returns the data for the first value with a null name. However, the type is returned (use QueryValueEx instead).

QueryValueEx(*key*, *value_name*)

Returns a tuple (*value*, *type*) containing the data value and type for a key. *key* is an open key or HKEY_* constant. *value_name* is the name of the value to return. The returned type is one of the integer codes as described for the EnumValue() function.

SaveKey(*key*, *filename*)

Saves *key* and all its subkeys to a file. *key* is an open key or a predefined HKEY_* constant. *filename* must not already exist and should not include a filename extension. Furthermore, the caller must have backup privileges for the operation to succeed.

`SetValue(`*`key,`* *`sub_key,`* *`type,`* *`value`*`)`

Sets the value of a key. *key* is an open key or `HKEY_*` constant. *sub_key* is the name of the subkey with which to associate the value. *type* is an integer type code, currently limited to `REG_SZ`. *value* is a string containing the value data. If *sub_key* does not exist, it is created. *key* must have been opened with `KEY_SET_VALUE` access for this function to succeed.

`SetValueEx(`*`key,`* *`value_name,`* *`reserved,`* *`type,`* *`value`*`)`

Sets the value field of a key. *key* is an open key or an `HKEY_*` constant. *value_name* is the name of the value. *type* is an integer type code as described for the `EnumValue()` function. *value* is a string containing the new value. When the values of numeric types (for example, `REG_DWORD`) are being set, *value* is still a string containing the raw data. This string can be created using the `struct` module. *reserved* is currently ignored and can be set to anything (the value is not used).

Notes

- Functions that return a Windows HKEY object return a special registry handle object described by the class `PyHKEY`. This object can be converted into a Windows handle value using `int()`. This object can also be used with the context-management protocol to automatically close the underlying handle—for example:

```
with winreg.OpenKey(winreg.HKEY_LOCAL_MACHINE, "spam") as key:
    statements
```

Threads and Concurrency

This chapter describes library modules and programming strategies for writing concurrent programs in Python. Topics include threads, message passing, multiprocessing, and coroutines. Before covering specific library modules, some basic concepts are first described.

Basic Concepts

A running program is called a *process*. Each process has its own system state, which includes memory, lists of open files, a program counter that keeps track of the instruction being executed, and a call stack used to hold the local variables of functions. Normally, a process executes statements one after the other in a single sequence of control flow, which is sometimes called the *main thread* of the process. At any given time, the program is only doing one thing.

A program can create new processes using library functions such as those found in the os or subprocess modules (e.g., os.fork(), subprocess.Popen(), etc.). However, these processes, known as *subprocesses*, run as completely independent entities—each with their own private system state and main thread of execution. Because a subprocess is independent, it executes concurrently with the original process. That is, the process that created the subprocess can go on to work on other things while the subprocess carries out its own work behind the scenes.

Although processes are isolated, they can communicate with each other—something known as *interprocess communication (IPC)*. One of the most common forms of IPC is based on *message passing*. A *message* is simply a buffer of raw bytes. Primitive operations such as send() and recv() are then used to transmit or receive messages through an I/O channel such as a pipe or network socket. Another somewhat less common IPC mechanism relies upon memory-mapped regions (see the mmap module). With memory mapping, processes can create shared regions of memory. Modifications to these regions are then visible in all processes that happen to be viewing them.

Multiple processes can be used by an application if it wants to work on multiple tasks at the same time—with each process responsible for part of the processing. However, another approach for subdividing work into tasks is to use threads. A *thread* is similar to a process in that it has its own control flow and execution stack. However, a thread runs inside the process that created it, sharing all of the data and system resources. Threads are useful when an application wants to perform tasks concurrently, but there is a potentially large amount of system state that needs to be shared by the tasks.

When multiple processes or threads are used, the host operating system is responsible for scheduling their work. This is done by giving each process (or thread) a small time slice and rapidly cycling between all of the active tasks—giving each a portion of the available CPU cycles. For example, if your system had 10 active processes running, the operating system would allocate approximately 1/10th of its CPU time to each process and cycle between processes in rapid succession. On systems with more than one CPU core, the operating system can schedule processes so that each CPU is kept busy, executing processes in parallel.

Writing programs that take advantage of concurrent execution is something that is intrinsically complicated. A major source of complexity concerns synchronization and access to shared data. In particular, attempts to update a data structure by multiple tasks at approximately the same time can lead to a corrupted and inconsistent program state (a problem formally known as a *race condition*). To fix these problems, concurrent programs must identify critical sections of code and protect them using mutual-exclusion locks and other similar synchronization primitives. For example, if different threads were trying to write data to the same file at the same time, you might use a mutual exclusion lock to synchronize their operation so that once one of the threads starts writing, the other threads have to wait until it has finished before they are allowed to start writing. The code for this scenario typically looks like this:

```
write_lock = Lock()
...
# Critical section where writing occurs
write_lock.acquire()
f.write("Here's some data.\n")
f.write("Here's more data.\n")
...
write_lock.release()
```

There's a joke attributed to Jason Whittington that goes like this: "Why did the multi-threaded chicken cross the road? to To other side. get the". This joke typifies the kinds of problems that arise with task synchronization and concurrent programming. If you're scratching your head saying, "I don't get it," then it might be wise to do a bit more reading before diving into the rest of this chapter.

Concurrent Programming and Python

Python supports both message passing and thread-based concurrent programming on most systems. Although most programmers tend to be familiar with the thread interface, Python threads are actually rather restricted. Although minimally thread-safe, the Python interpreter uses an internal global interpreter lock (the GIL) that only allows a single Python thread to execute at any given moment. This restricts Python programs to run on a single processor regardless of how many CPU cores might be available on the system. Although the GIL is often a heated source of debate in the Python community, it is unlikely to be removed at any time in the foreseeable future.

The presence of the GIL has a direct impact on how many Python programmers address concurrent programming problems. If an application is mostly I/O bound, it is generally fine to use threads because extra processors aren't going to do much to help a program that spends most of its time waiting for events. For applications that involve heavy amounts of CPU processing, using threads to subdivide work doesn't provide any benefit and will make the program run slower (often *much* slower than you would guess). For this, you'll want to rely on subprocesses and message passing.

Even when threads are used, many programmers find their scaling properties to be rather mysterious. For example, a threaded network server that works fine with 100 threads may have horrible performance if it's scaled up to 10,000 threads. As a general rule, you really don't want to be writing programs with 10,000 threads because each thread requires its own system resources and the overhead associated with thread context switching, locking, and other matters starts to become significant (not to mention the fact that all threads are constrained to run on a single CPU). To deal with this, it is somewhat common to see such applications restructured as asynchronous event-handling systems. For example, a central event loop might monitor all of the I/O sources using the `select` module and dispatch asynchronous events to a large collection of I/O handlers. This is the basis for library modules such as `asyncore` as well as popular third-party modules such as Twisted (http://twistedmatrix/com).

Looking forward, message passing is a concept that you should probably embrace for any kind of concurrent programming in Python. Even when working with threads, an often-recommended approach is to structure your application as a collection of independent threads that exchange data through message queues. This particular approach tends to be less error-prone because it greatly reduces the need to use locks and other synchronization primitives. Message passing also naturally extends into networking and distributed systems. For example, if part of a program starts out as a thread to which you send messages, that component can later be migrated to a separate process or onto a different machine by sending the messages over a network connection. The message passing abstraction is also tied to advanced Python features such as coroutines. For example, a *coroutine* is a function that can receive and process messages that are sent to it. So, by embracing message passing, you will find that you can write programs that have a great deal of flexibility.

The remainder of this chapter looks at different library modules for supporting concurrent programming. At the end, more detailed information on common programming idioms is provided.

multiprocessing

The `multiprocessing` module provides support for launching tasks in a subprocess, communicating and sharing data, and performing various forms of synchronization. The programming interface is meant to mimic the programming interface for threads in the `threading` module. However, unlike threads, it is important to emphasize that processes do not have any shared state. Thus, if a process modifies data, that change is local only to that process.

The features of the `multiprocessing` module are vast, making it one of the larger and most advanced built-in libraries. Covering every detail of the module is impossible here, but the essential parts of it along with examples will be given. Experienced programmers should be able to take the examples and expand them to larger problems.

Processes

All of the features of the `multiprocessing` module are focused on processes. They are described by the following class.

`Process([group [, target [, name [, args [, kwargs]]]]])`

A class that represents a task running in a subprocess. The arguments in the constructor should always be specified using keyword arguments. `target` is a callable object that will execute when the process starts, `args` is a tuple of positional arguments passed to `target`, and `kwargs` is a dictionary of keyword arguments passed to `target`. If `args` and `kwargs` are omitted, `target` is called with no arguments. `name` is a string that gives a descriptive name to the process. `group` is unused and is always set to `None`. Its presence here is simply to make the construction of a `Process` mimic the creation of a thread in the `threading` module.

An instance *p* of `Process` has the following methods:

`p.is_alive()`

Returns `True` if *p* is still running.

`p.join([timeout])`

Waits for process *p* to terminate. `timeout` specifies an optional timeout period. A process can be joined as many times as you wish, but it is an error for a process to try and join itself.

`p.run()`

The method that runs when the process starts. By default, this invokes `target` that was passed to the `Process` constructor. As an alternative, a process can be defined by inheriting from `Process` and reimplementing `run()`.

`p.start()`

Starts the process. This launches the subprocess that represents the process and invokes `p.run()` in that subprocess.

`p.terminate()`

Forcefully terminates the process. If this is invoked, the process *p* is terminated immediately without performing any kind of cleanup actions. If the process *p* created subprocesses of its own, those processes will turn into zombies. Some care is required when using this method. If *p* holds a lock or is involved with interprocess communication, terminating it might cause a deadlock or corrupted I/O.

A `Process` instance *p* also has the following data attributes:

`p.authkey`

The process' authentication key. Unless explicitly set, this is a 32-character string generated by `os.urandom()`. The purpose of this key is to provide security for low-level interprocess communication involving network connections. Such connections only work if both ends have the same authentication key.

`p.daemon`

A Boolean flag that indicates whether or not the process is daemonic. A *daemonic* process is automatically terminated when the Python process that created it terminates. In addition, a daemonic process is prohibited from creating new processes on its own. The value of *p*.daemon must be set before a process is started using `p.start()`.

p.exitcode

The integer exit code of the process. If the process is still running, this is None. If the value is negative, a value of –N means the process was terminated by signal N.

p.name

The name of the process.

p.pid

The integer process ID of the process.

Here is an example that shows how to create and launch a function (or other callable) as a separate process:

```python
import multiprocessing
import time

def clock(interval):
    while True:
        print("The time is %s" % time.ctime())
        time.sleep(interval)

if __name__ == '__main__':
    p = multiprocessing.Process(target=clock, args=(15,))
    p.start()
```

Here is an example that shows how to define this process as a class that inherits from Process:

```python
import multiprocessing
import time

class ClockProcess(multiprocessing.Process):
    def __init__(self,interval):
        multiprocessing.Process.__init__(self)
        self.interval = interval
    def run(self):
        while True:
            print("The time is %s" % time.ctime())
            time.sleep(self.interval)

if __name__ == '__main__':
    p = ClockProcess(15)
    p.start()
```

In both examples, the time should be printed by the subprocess every 15 seconds. It is important to emphasize that for cross-platform portability, new processes should only be created by the main program as shown. Although this is optional on UNIX, it is required on Windows. It should also be noted that on Windows, you will probably need to run the preceding examples in the command shell (cmd.exe) instead of a Python IDE, such as IDLE.

Interprocess Communication

Two primary forms of interprocess communication are supported by the multiprocessing module: pipes and queues. Both methods are implemented using message passing. However, the queue interface is meant to mimic the use of queues commonly used with thread programs.

`Queue([maxsize])`

Creates a shared process queue. *maxsize* is the maximum number of items allowed in the queue. If omitted, there is no size limit. The underlying queue is implemented using pipes and locks. In addition, a support thread is launched in order to feed queued data into the underlying pipe.

An instance *q* of `Queue` has the following methods:

`q.cancel_join_thread()`

Don't automatically join the background thread on process exit. This prevents the `join_thread()` method from blocking.

`q.close()`

Closes the queue, preventing any more data from being added to it. When this is called, the background thread will continue to write any queued data not yet written but will shut down as soon as this is complete. This method is called automatically if *q* is garbage-collected. Closing a queue does not generate any kind of end-of-data signal or exception in queue consumers. For example, if a consumer is blocking on a `get()` operation, closing the queue in the producer does not cause the `get()` to return with an error.

`q.empty()`

Returns `True` if *q* is empty at the time of the call. If other processes or threads are being used to add queue items, be aware that the result is not reliable (e.g., new items could have been added to the queue in between the time that the result is returned and used).

`q.full()`

Returns `True` if *q* is full. The result is also not reliable due to threads (see *q*.`empty()`).

`q.get([block [, timeout]])`

Returns an item from *q*. If *q* is empty, blocks until a queue item becomes available. *block* controls the blocking behavior and is `True` by default. If set to `False`, a `Queue.Empty` exception (defined in the `Queue` library module) is raised if the queue is empty. *timeout* is an optional timeout to use in blocking mode. If no items become available in the specified time interval, a `Queue.Empty` exception is raised.

`q.get_nowait()`

The same as *q*.`get(False)`.

`q.join_thread()`

Joins the queue's background thread. This is used to wait for all queue items to be consumed after *q*.`close()` has been called. This method gets called by default in all processes that are not the original creator of *q*. This behavior can be disabled by called *q*.`cancel_join_thread()`.

`q.put(item [, block [, timeout]])`

Puts *item* onto the queue. If the queue is full, block until space becomes available. *block* controls the blocking behavior and is `True` by default. If set to `False`, a `Queue.Full` exception (defined in the `Queue` library module) is raised if the queue is full. *timeout* specifies how long to wait for space to become available in blocking mode. A `Queue.Full` exception is raised on timeout.

q.put_nowait(*item*)

The same as q.put(*item*, False).

q.qsize()

Returns the approximate number of items currently in the queue. The result of this function is not reliable because items may have been added or removed from the queue in between the time the result is returned and later used in a program. On some systems, this method may raise an NotImplementedError.

JoinableQueue([*maxsize*])

Creates a joinable shared process queue. This is just like a Queue except that the queue allows a consumer of items to notify the producer that the items have been successfully been processed. The notification process is implemented using a shared semaphore and condition variable.

An instance q of JoinableQueue has the same methods as Queue, but it has the following additional methods:

q.task_done()

Used by a consumer to signal that an enqueued item returned by q.get() has been processed. A ValueError exception is raised if this is called more times than have been removed from the queue.

q.join()

Used by a producer to block until all items placed in a queue have been processed. This blocks until q.task_done() is called for every item placed into the queue.

The following example shows how you set up a process that runs forever, consuming and processing items on a queue. The producer feeds items into the queue and waits for them to be processed.

```
import multiprocessing

def consumer(input_q):
    while True:
        item = input_q.get()
        # Process item
        print(item)          # Replace with useful work
        # Signal task completion
        input_q.task_done()

def producer(sequence, output_q):
    for item in sequence:
        # Put the item on the queue
        output_q.put(item)

# Set up
if __name__ == '__main__':
    q = multiprocessing.JoinableQueue()
    # Launch the consumer process
    cons_p = multiprocessing.Process(target=consumer,args=(q,))
    cons_p.daemon=True
    cons_p.start()

    # Produce items.  sequence represents a sequence of items to
    # be sent to the consumer.  In practice, this could be the output
```

```
# of a generator or produced in some other manner.
sequence = [1,2,3,4]
producer(sequence, q)

# Wait for all items to be processed
q.join()
```

In this example, the consumer process is set to daemonic because it runs forever and we want it to terminate when the main program finishes (if you forget this, the program will hang). A JoinableQueue is being used so that the producer actually knows when all of the items put in the queue have been successfully processed. The join() operation ensures this; if you forget this step, the consumer will be terminated before it has had time to complete all of its work.

If desired, multiple processes can put and get items from the same queue. For example, if you wanted to have a pool of consumer processes, you could just write code like this:

```
if __name__ == '__main__':
    q = multiprocessing.JoinableQueue()
    # Launch some consumer processes
    cons_p1 = multiprocessing.Process(target=consumer,args=(q,))
    cons_p1.daemon=True
    cons_p1.start()

    cons_p2 = multiprocessing.Process(target=consumer,args=(q,))
    cons_p2.daemon=True
    cons_p2.start()

    # Produce items.  sequence represents a sequence of items to
    # be sent to the consumer.  In practice, this could be the output
    # of a generator or produced in some other manner.
    sequence = [1,2,3,4]
    producer(sequence, q)

    # Wait for all items to be processed
    q.join()
```

When writing code such as this, be aware that every item placed into the queue is pickled and sent to the process over a pipe or socket connection. As a general rule, it is better to send fewer large objects than many small objects.

In certain applications, a producer may want to signal consumers that no more items will be produced and that they should shut down. To do this, you should write code that uses a *sentinel*—a special value that indicates completion. Here is an example that illustrates this concept using None as a sentinel:

```
import multiprocessing

def consumer(input_q):
    while True:
        item = input_q.get()
        if item is None:
            break
        # Process item
        print(item)          # Replace with useful work
    # Shutdown
    print("Consumer done")

def producer(sequence, output_q):
    for item in sequence:
```

```
        # Put the item on the queue
        output_q.put(item)

if __name__ == '__main__':
    q = multiprocessing.Queue()
    # Launch the consumer process
    cons_p = multiprocessing.Process(target=consumer,args=(q,))
    cons_p.start()

    # Produce items
    sequence = [1,2,3,4]
    producer(sequence, q)

    # Signal completion by putting the sentinel on the queue
    q.put(None)
    # Wait for the consumer process to shutdown
    cons_p.join()
```

If you are using sentinels as shown in this example, be aware that you will need to put a sentinel on the queue for every single consumer. For example, if there were three consumer processes consuming items on the queue, the producer needs to put three sentinels on the queue to get all of the consumers to shut down.

As an alternative to using queues, a pipe can be used to perform message passing between processes.

Pipe([duplex])

Creates a pipe between processes and returns a tuple (*conn1*, *conn2*) where *conn1* and *conn2* are Connection objects representing the ends of the pipe. By default, the pipe is bidirectional. If *duplex* is set False, then *conn1* can only be used for receiving and *conn2* can only be used for sending. Pipe() must be called prior to creating and launching any Process objects that use the pipe.

An instance *c* of a Connection object returned by Pipe() has the following methods and attributes:

c.close()

Closes the connection. Called automatically if *c* is garbage collected.

c.fileno()

Returns the integer file descriptor used by the connection.

c.poll([timeout])

Returns True if data is available on the connection. *timeout* specifies the maximum amount of time to wait. If omitted, the method returns immediately with a result. If *timeout* is set to None, then the operation will wait indefinitely for data to arrive.

c.recv()

Receives an object sent by *c*.send(). Raises EOFError if the other end of the connection has been closed and there is no more data.

c.recv_bytes([maxlength])

Receives a complete byte message sent by *c*.send_bytes(). *maxlength* specifies the maximum number of bytes to receive. If an incoming message exceeds this, an IOError is raised and no further reads can be made on the connection. Raises EOFError if the other end of the connection has been closed and there is no more data.

`c.recv_bytes_into(buffer [, offset])`

Receives a complete byte message and stores it in the object *buffer*, which supports the writable buffer interface (e.g., a bytearray object or similar). *offset* specifies the byte offset into the buffer where to place the message. Returns the number of bytes received. Raises `BufferTooShort` if the length of the message exceeds available buffer space.

`c.send(obj)`

Sends an object through the connection. *obj* is any object that is compatible with pickle.

`c.send_bytes(buffer [, offset [, size]])`

Sends a buffer of byte data through the connection. *buffer* is any object that supports the buffer interface, *offset* is the byte offset into the buffer, and *size* is the number of bytes to send. The resulting data is sent as a single message to be received using a single call to `c.recv_bytes()`.

Pipes can be used in a similar manner as queues. Here is an example that shows the previous producer-consumer problem implemented using pipes:

```python
import multiprocessing
# Consume items on a pipe.
def consumer(pipe):
    output_p, input_p = pipe
    input_p.close()        # Close the input end of the pipe
    while True:
        try:
            item = output_p.recv()
        except EOFError:
            break
        # Process item
        print(item)          # Replace with useful work
    # Shutdown
    print("Consumer done")

# Produce items and put on a queue.  sequence is an
# iterable representing items to be processed.
def producer(sequence, input_p):
    for item in sequence:
        # Put the item on the queue
        input_p.send(item)

if __name__ == '__main__':
    (output_p, input_p) = multiprocessing.Pipe()
    # Launch the consumer process
    cons_p = multiprocessing.Process(target=consumer,args=((output_p, input_p),))
    cons_p.start()

    # Close the output pipe in the producer
    output_p.close()

    # Produce items
    sequence = [1,2,3,4]
    producer(sequence, input_p)

    # Signal completion by closing the input pipe
    input_p.close()

    # Wait for the consumer process to shutdown
    cons_p.join()
```

Great attention should be given to proper management of the pipe endpoints. If one of the ends of the pipe is not used in either the producer or consumer, it should be closed. This explains, for instance, why the output end of the pipe is closed in the producer and the input end of the pipe is closed in the consumer. If you forget one of these steps, the program may hang on the recv() operation in the consumer. Pipes are reference counted by the operating system and have to be closed in all processes to produce the EOFError exception. Thus, closing the pipe in the producer doesn't have any effect unless the consumer also closes the same end of the pipe.

Pipes can be used for bidirectional communication. This can be used to write programs that interact with a process using a request/response model typically associated with client/server computing or remote procedure call. Here is an example:

```python
import multiprocessing
# A server process
def adder(pipe):
    server_p, client_p = pipe
    client_p.close()
    while True:
        try:
            x,y = server_p.recv()
        except EOFError:
            break
        result = x + y
        server_p.send(result)
    # Shutdown
    print("Server done")

if __name__ == '__main__':
    (server_p, client_p) = multiprocessing.Pipe()
    # Launch the server process
    adder_p = multiprocessing.Process(target=adder,args=((server_p, client_p),))
    adder_p.start()

    # Close the server pipe in the client
    server_p.close()

    # Make some requests on the server
    client_p.send((3,4))
    print(client_p.recv())

    client_p.send(('Hello','World'))
    print(client_p.recv())

    # Done. Close the pipe
    client_p.close()

    # Wait for the consumer process to shutdown
    adder_p.join()
```

In this example, the adder() function runs as a server waiting for messages to arrive on its end of the pipe. When received, it performs some processing and sends the result back on the pipe. Keep in mind that send() and recv() use the pickle module to serialize objects. In the example, the server receives a tuple (x, y) as input and returns the result $x + y$. For more advanced applications that use remote procedure call, however, you should use a process pool as described next.

Process Pools

The following class allows you to create a pool of processes to which various kind of data processing tasks can be submitted. The functionality provided by a pool is somewhat similar to that provided by list comprehensions and functional programming operations such as map-reduce.

`Pool([numprocess [,initializer [, initargs]]])`

Creates a pool of worker processes. *numprocess* is the number of processes to create. If omitted, the value of cpu_count() is used. *initializer* is a callable object that will be executed in each worker process upon startup. *initargs* is a tuple of arguments to pass to *initializer*. By default, *initializer* is None.

An instance *p* of Pool supports the following operations:

`p.apply(func [, args [, kwargs]])`

Executes *func(*args, **kwargs)* in one of the pool workers and returns the result. It is important to emphasize this does not execute *func* in parallel in all pool workers. If you want *func* to execute concurrently with different arguments, you either have to call *p*.apply() from different threads or use *p*.apply_async().

`p.apply_async(func [, args [, kwargs [, callback]]])`

Executes *func(*args, **kwargs)* in one of the pool workers and returns the result asynchronously. The result of this method is an instance of AsyncResult which can be used to obtain the final result at a later time. *callback* is a callable object that accepts a single input argument. When the result of *func* becomes available, it is immediately passed to *callback*. *callback* should not perform any blocking operations or else it will block the reception of results in other asynchronous operations.

`p.close()`

Closes the process pool, preventing any further operations. If any operations are still pending, they will be completed before the worker processes terminate.

`p.join()`

Waits for all worker processes to exit. This can only be called after close() or terminate().

`p.imap(func, iterable [, chunksize])`

A version of map() that returns an iterator instead of a list of results.

`p.imap_unordered(func, iterable [, chunksize])`

The same as imap() except that the results are returned in an arbitrary order based on when they are received from the worker processes.

`p.map(func, iterable [, chunksize])`

Applies the callable object *func* to all of the items in *iterable* and returns the result as a list. The operation is carried out in parallel by splitting *iterable* into chunks and farming out the work to the worker processes. *chunksize* specifies the number of items in each chunk. For large amounts of data, increasing the *chunksize* will improve performance.

p.map_async(*func, iterable* [, *chunksize* [, *callback*]])

The same as map() except that the result is returned asynchronously. The return value is an instance of AsyncResult that can be used to later obtain the result. *callback* is a callable object accepting a single argument. If supplied, *callback* is called with the result when it becomes available.

p.terminate()

Immediately terminates all of the worker processes without performing any cleanup or finishing any pending work. If *p* is garbage-collected, this is called.

The methods apply_async() and map_async() return an AsyncResult instance as a result. An instance *a* of AsyncResult has the following methods:

a.get([*timeout*])

Returns the result, waiting for it to arrive if necessary. *timeout* is an optional timeout. If the result does not arrive in the given time, a multiprocessing.TimeoutError exception is raised. If an exception was raised in the remote operation, it is reraised when this method is called.

a.ready()

Returns True if the call has completed.

a.sucessful()

Returns True if the call completed without any exceptions. An AssertionError is raised if this method is called prior to the result being ready.

a.wait([*timeout*])

Waits for the result to become available. *timeout* is an optional timeout.

The following example illustrates the use of a process pool to build a dictionary mapping filenames to SHA512 digest values for an entire directory of files:

```
import os
import multiprocessing
import hashlib

# Some parameters you can tweak
BUFSIZE = 8192          # Read buffer size
POOLSIZE = 2            # Number of workers

def compute_digest(filename):
    try:
        f = open(filename,"rb")
    except IOError:
        return None
    digest = hashlib.sha512()
    while True:
        chunk = f.read(BUFSIZE)
        if not chunk: break
        digest.update(chunk)
    f.close()
    return filename, digest.digest()

def build_digest_map(topdir):
    digest_pool = multiprocessing.Pool(POOLSIZE)
```

```
    allfiles = (os.path.join(path,name)
                  for path, dirs, files in os.walk(topdir)
                      for name in files)

    digest_map = dict(digest_pool.imap_unordered(compute_digest,allfiles,20))
    digest_pool.close()
    return digest_map
# Try it out.  Change the directory name as desired.
if __name__ == '__main__':
    digest_map = build_digest_map("/Users/beazley/Software/Python-3.0")
    print(len(digest_map))
```

In the example, a sequence of pathnames for all files in a directory tree is specified using a generator expression. This sequence is then chopped up and farmed out to a process pool using the imap_unordered() function. Each pool worker computes a SHA512 digest value for its files using the compute_digest() function. The results are sent back to the master and collected into a Python dictionary. Although it's by no means a scientific result, this example gives a 75 percent speedup over a single-process solution when run on the author's dual-core Macbook.

Keep in mind that it only makes sense to use a process pool if the pool workers perform enough work to justify the extra communication overhead. As a general rule, it would not make sense to use a pool for simple calculations such as just adding two numbers together.

Shared Data and Synchronization

Normally, processes are completely isolated from each other with the only means of communication being queues or pipes. However, two objects can be used to represent shared data. Underneath the covers, these objects use shared memory (via mmap) to make access possible in multiple processes.

Value(*typecode, arg1, ... argN, lock*)

Creates a ctypes object in shared memory. *typecode* is either a string containing a type code as used by the array module (e.g., 'i', 'd', etc.) or a type object from the ctypes module (e.g., ctypes.c_int, ctypes.c_double, etc.). All extra positional arguments *arg1*, *arg2*, ... *argN* are passed to the constructor for the given type. *lock* is a keyword-only argument that if set to True (the default), a new lock is created to protect access to the value. If you pass in an existing lock such as a Lock or RLock instance, then that lock is used for synchronization. If *v* is an instance of a shared value created by Value, then the underlying value is accessed used *v*.value. For example, reading *v*.value will get the value and assigning *v*.value will change the value.

RawValue(*typecode, arg1, ..., argN*)

The same as Value except that there is no locking.

Array(*typecode, initializer, lock*)

Creates a ctypes array in shared memory. *typecode* describes the contents of the array and has the same meaning as described for Value(). *initializer* is either an integer that sets the initial size of the array or a sequence of items whose values and size are used to initialize the array. *lock* is a keyword-only argument with the same meaning as described for Value(). If *a* is an instance of a shared array created by Array, then you access its contents using the standard Python indexing, slicing, and iteration operations, each of which are synchronized by the lock. For byte strings, a will also have an a.value attribute to access the entire array as a single string.

RawArray(*typecode, initializer*)

The same as Array except that there is no locking. If you are writing programs that must manipulate a large number of array items all at once, the performance will be significantly better if you use this datatype along with a separate lock for synchronization (if needed).

In addition to shared values created using Value() and Array(), the multiprocessing module provides shared versions of the following synchronization primitives:

Primitive	Description
Lock	Mutual exclusion lock
RLock	Reentrant mutual exclusion lock (can be acquired multiple times by the same process without blocking)
Semaphore	Semaphore
BoundedSemaphore	Bounded semaphore
Event	Event
Condition	Condition variable

The behavior of these objects mimics the synchronization primitives defined in the threading module with identical names. Please refer to the threading documentation for further details.

It should be noted that with multiprocessing, it is not normally necessary to worry about low-level synchronization with locks, semaphores, or similar constructs to the same degree as with threads. In part, send() and receive() operations on pipes and put() and get() operations on queues already provide synchronization. However, shared values and locks can have uses in certain specialized settings. Here is an example that sends a Python list of floats to another process using a shared array instead of a pipe:

```python
import multiprocessing

class FloatChannel(object):
    def __init__(self, maxsize):
        self.buffer     = multiprocessing.RawArray('d',maxsize)
        self.buffer_len = multiprocessing.Value('i')
        self.empty      = multiprocessing.Semaphore(1)
        self.full       = multiprocessing.Semaphore(0)
    def send(self,values):
        self.empty.acquire()                   # Only proceed if buffer empty
        nitems = len(values)
        self.buffer_len = nitems               # Set the buffer size
        self.buffer[:nitems] = values          # Copy values into the buffer
        self.full.release()                    # Signal that buffer is full
    def recv(self):
        self.full.acquire()                    # Only proceed if buffer full
        values = self.buffer[:self.buffer_len.value]   # Copy values
        self.empty.release()                   # Signal that buffer is empty
        return values
```

```
# Performance test.  Receive a bunch of messages
def consume_test(count, ch):
    for i in xrange(count):
        values = ch.recv()

# Performance test. Send a bunch of messages
def produce_test(count, values, ch):
    for i in xrange(count):
        ch.send(values)

if __name__ == '__main__':
    ch = FloatChannel(100000)
    p = multiprocessing.Process(target=consume_test,
                                args=(1000,ch))
    p.start()
    values = [float(x) for x in xrange(100000)]
    produce_test(1000, values, ch)
    print("Done")
    p.join()
```

Further study of this example is left to the reader. However, in a performance test on the author's machine, sending a large list of floats through the FloatChannel is about 80 percent faster than sending the list through a Pipe (which has to pickle and unpickle all of the values).

Managed Objects

Unlike threads, processes do not support shared objects. Although you can create shared values and arrays as shown in the previous section, this doesn't work for more advanced Python objects such as dictionaries, lists, or instances of user-defined classes. The multiprocessing module does, however, provide a way to work with shared objects if they run under the control of a so-called *manager*. A *manager* is a separate subprocess where the real objects exist and which operates as a server. Other processes access the shared objects through the use of proxies that operate as clients of the manager server.

The most straightforward way to work with simple managed objects is to use the Manager() function.

Manager()

Creates a running manager server in a separate process. Returns an instance of type SyncManager which is defined in the multiprocessing.managers submodule.

An instance m of SyncManager as returned by Manager() has a series of methods for creating shared objects and returning a proxy which can be used to access them. Normally, you would create a manager and use these methods to create shared objects *before* launching any new processes. The following methods are defined:

m.Array(*typecode*, *sequence*)

Creates a shared Array instance on the server and returns a proxy to it. See the "Shared Data and Synchronization" section for a description of the arguments.

m.BoundedSemaphore([*value*])

Creates a shared threading.BoundedSemaphore instance on the server and returns a proxy to it.

`m.Condition([lock])`

Creates a shared `threading.Condition` instance on the server and returns a proxy to it. `lock` is a proxy instance created by `m.Lock()` or `m.Rlock()`.

`m.dict([args])`

Creates a shared `dict` instance on the server and returns a proxy to it. The arguments to this method are the same as for the built-in `dict()` function.

`m.Event()`

Creates a shared `threading.Event` instance on the server and returns a proxy to it.

`m.list([sequence])`

Creates a shared `list` instance on the server and returns a proxy to it. The arguments to this method are the same as for the built-in `list()` function.

`m.Lock()`

Creates a shared `threading.Lock` instance on the server and returns a proxy to it.

`m.Namespace()`

Creates a shared namespace object on the server and returns a proxy to it. A *namespace* is an object that is somewhat similar to a Python module. For example, if *n* is a namespace proxy, you can assign and read attributes using (.) such as *n.name* = *value* or *value* = *n.name*. However, the choice of *name* is significant. If *name* starts with a letter, then that value is part of the shared object held by the manager and is accessible in all other processes. If *name* starts with an underscore, it is only part of the proxy object and is not shared.

`m.Queue()`

Creates a shared `Queue.Queue` object on the server and returns a proxy to it.

`m.RLock()`

Creates a shared `threading.Rlock` object on the server and returns a proxy to it.

`m.Semaphore([value])`

Creates a shared `threading.Semaphore` object on the server and returns a proxy to it.

`m.Value(typecode, value)`

Creates a shared `Value` object on the server and returns a proxy to it. See the "Shared Data and Synchronization" section for a description of the arguments.

The following example shows how you would use a manager in order to create a dictionary shared between processes.

```
import multiprocessing
import time

# print out d whenever the passed event gets set
def watch(d, evt):
    while True:
        evt.wait()
        print(d)
        evt.clear()
```

```
if __name__ == '__main__':
    m   = multiprocessing.Manager()
    d   = m.dict()            # Create a shared dict
    evt = m.Event()           # Create a shared Event

    # Launch a process that watches the dictionary
    p = multiprocessing.Process(target=watch,args=(d,evt))
    p.daemon=True
    p.start()

    # Update the dictionary and notify the watcher
    d['foo'] = 42
    evt.set()
    time.sleep(5)

    # Update the dictionary and notify the watcher
    d['bar'] = 37
    evt.set()
    time.sleep(5)

    # Terminate the process and manager
    p.terminate()
    m.shutdown()
```

If you run this example, the watch() function prints out the value of d every time the passed event gets set. In the main program, a shared dictionary and event are created and manipulated in the main process. When you run this, you will see the child process printing data.

If you want to have shared objects of other types such as instances of user-defined classes, you have to create your custom manager object. To do this, you create a class that inherits from BaseManager, which is defined in the multiprocessing.managers submodule.

managers.BaseManager([address [, authkey]])

Base class used to create custom manager servers for user-defined objects. address is an optional tuple (hostname, port) that specifies a network address for the server. If omitted, the operating system will simply assign an address corresponding to some free port number. authkey is a string that is used to authenticate clients connecting to the server. If omitted, the value of current_process().authkey is used.

If mgrclass is a class that inherits from BaseManager, the following class method is used to create methods for returning proxies to shared objects.

mgrclass.register(typeid [, callable [, proxytype [, exposed [, method_to_typeid [, create_method]]]]])

Registers a new data type with the manager class. typeid is a string that is used to name a particular kind of shared object. This string should be a valid Python identifier. callable is a callable object that creates or returns the instance to be shared. proxytype is a class that provides the implementation of the proxy objects to be used in clients. Normally, these classes are generated by default so this is normally set to None. exposed is a sequence of method names on the shared object that will be exposed to proxy objects. If omitted, the value of proxytype._exposed_ is used and if that is undefined, then all public methods (all callable methods that don't start with an underscore (_) are used). method_to_typeid is a mapping from method names to type IDS that is used to specify which methods should return their results using proxy objects. If a method is not found in this mapping, the return value is copied and returned. If *method_to_typeid* is None, the value of *proxytype._method_to_typeid_* is used if it is defined. *create_method* is a Boolean flag that specifies whether a method with the name *typeid* should be created in *mgrclass*. By default, this is True.

An instance m of a manager derived from BaseManager must be manually started to operate. The following attributes and methods are related to this:

m.address

A tuple (*hostname, port*) that has the address being used by the manager server.

m.connect()

Connects to a remote manager object, the address of which was given to the BaseManager constructor.

m.serve_forever()

Runs the manager server in the current process.

m.shutdown()

Shuts down a manager server launched by the m.start() method.

m.start()

Starts a separate subprocess and starts the manager server in that process.

The following example shows how to create a manager for a user-defined class:

```
import multiprocessing
from multiprocessing.managers import BaseManager

class A(object):
    def __init__(self,value):
        self.x = value
    def __repr__(self):
        return "A(%s)" % self.x
    def getX(self):
        return self.x
    def setX(self,value):
        self.x = value
    def __iadd__(self,value):
        self.x += value
        return self

class MyManager(BaseManager): pass
MyManager.register("A",A)

if __name__ == '__main__':
    m = MyManager()
    m.start()
    # Create a managed object
    a = m.A(37)
    ...
```

In this example, the last statement creates an instance of A that lives on the manager server. The variable a in the previous code is only a proxy for this instance. The behavior of this proxy is similar to (but not completely identical to) *referent*, the object on the server. First, you will find that data attributes and properties cannot be accessed. Instead, you have to use access functions:

```
>>> a.x
Traceback (most recent call last):
  File "<stdin>", line 1, in <module>
AttributeError: 'AutoProxy[A]' object has no attribute 'x'
>>> a.getX()
37
>>> a.setX(42)
>>>
```

With proxies, the repr() function returns a string representing the proxy, whereas str() returns the output of __repr__() on the referent. For example:

```
>>> a
<AutoProxy[A] object, typeid 'A' at 0xcef230>
>>> print(a)
A(37)
>>>
```

Special methods and any method starting with an underscore (_) are not accessible on proxies. For example, if you tried to invoke a.__iadd__(), it doesn't work:

```
>>> a += 37
Traceback (most recent call last):
  File "<stdin>", line 1, in <module>
TypeError: unsupported operand type(s) for +=: 'AutoProxy[A]' and 'int'
>>> a.__iadd__(37)
Traceback (most recent call last):
  File "<stdin>", line 1, in <module>
AttributeError: 'AutoProxy[A]' object has no attribute '__iadd__'
>>>
```

In more advanced applications, it is possible to customize proxies to more carefully control access. This is done by defining a class that inherits from BaseProxy, which is defined in multiprocessing.managers. The following code shows how you could make a custom proxy to the A class in the previous example that properly exposes the __iadd__() method and which uses a property to expose the x attribute:

```
from multiprocessing.managers import BaseProxy

class AProxy(BaseProxy):
    # A list of all methods exposed on the referent
    _exposed_ = ['__iadd__','getX','setX']
    # Implement the public interface of the proxy
    def __iadd__(self,value):
        self._callmethod('__iadd__',(value,))
        return self
    @property
    def x(self):
        return self._callmethod('getX',())
    @x.setter
    def x(self,value):
        self._callmethod('setX',(value,))

class MyManager(BaseManager): pass
MyManager.register("A", A, proxytype=AProxy)
```

An instance *proxy* of a class derived from BaseProxy has the following methods:

proxy._callmethod(*name* [, *args* [, *kwargs*]])

Calls the method *name* on the proxy's referent object. *name* is a string with the method name, *args* is a tuple containing positional arguments, and *kwargs* is a dictionary of keyword arguments. The method *name* must be explicitly exposed. Normally this is done by including the name in the _exposed_ class attribute of the proxy class.

proxy._getvalue()

Returns a copy of the referent in the caller. If this call is made in a different process, the referent object is pickled, sent to the caller, and is unpickled. An exception is raised if the referent can't be pickled.

Connections

Programs that use the multiprocessing module can perform message passing with other processes running on the same machine or with processes located on remote systems. This can be useful if you want to take a program written to work on a single system and expand it work on a computing cluster. The multiprocessing.connection submodule has functions and classes for this purpose:

connections.Client(*address* [, *family* [, *authenticate* [, *authkey*]]])

Connects to another process which must already be listening at address *address*. *address* is a tuple (*hostname* , *port*) representing a network address, a file name representing a UNIX domain socket, or a string of the form r'*servername*\pipe*pipename*' representing a Windows named pipe on a remote system *servername* (use a *servername* of '.' for the local machine). *family* is a string representing the addess format and is typically one of 'AF_INET', 'AF_UNIX', or 'AF_PIPE'. If omitted, the family is inferred from the format of *address*. *authentication* is a Boolean flag that specifies whether digest authentication is to be used. *authkey* is a string containing the authentication key. If omitted, then the value of current_process().authkey is used. The return value from this function is a Connection object, which was previously described in the pipes section of "Interprocess Communication."

connections.Listener([*address* [, *family* [, *backlog* [, *authenticate* [, *authkey*]]]]])

A class that implements a server for listening for and handling connections made by the Client() function. The *address*, *family*, *authenticate*, and *authkey* arguments have the same meaning as for Client(). *backlog* is an integer corresponding to the value passed to the listen() method of sockets if the *address* parameter specifies a network connection. By default, *backlog* is 1. If *address* is omitted, then a default address is chosen. If both *address* and *family* are omitted, then the fastest available communications scheme on the local system is chosen.

An instance *s* of Listener supports the following methods and attributes:

s.accept()

Accepts a new connection and returns a Connection object. Raises AuthenticationError if authentication fails.

s.address

The address that the listener is using.

```
s.close()
```

Closes the pipe or socket being used by the listener.

```
s.last_accepted
```

The address of the last client that was accepted.

Here is an example of a server program that listens for clients and implements a simple remote operation (adding):

```
from multiprocessing.connection import Listener

serv = Listener(('',15000),authkey='12345')
while True:
    conn = serv.accept()
    while True:
        try:
            x,y = conn.recv()
        except EOFError:
            break
        result = x + y
        conn.send(result)
    conn.close()
```

Here is a simple client program that connects to this server and sends some messages:

```
from multiprocessing.connection import Client
conn = Client(('localhost',15000), authkey="12345")

conn.send((3,4))
r = conn.recv()
print(r)            # Prints '7'

conn.send(("Hello","World"))
r = conn.recv()
print(r)            # Prints 'HelloWorld'

conn.close()
```

Miscellaneous Utility Functions

The following utility functions are also defined:

```
active_children()
```

Returns a list of Process objects for all active child processes.

```
cpu_count()
```

Returns the number of CPUs on the system if it can be determined.

```
current_process()
```

Returns the Process object for the current process.

```
freeze_support()
```

A function that should be included as the first statement of the main program in an application that will be "frozen" using various packaging tools such as py2exe. This is needed to prevent runtime errors associated with launching subprocesses in a frozen application.

`get_logger()`

Returns the logging object associated with the multiprocessing module, creating it if it doesn't already exist. The returned logger does not propagate messages to the root logger, has a level of `logging.NOTSET`, and prints all logging messages to standard error.

`set_executable(executable)`

Sets the name of the Python executable used to execute subprocesses. This is only defined on Windows.

General Advice on Multiprocessing

The `multiprocessing` module is one of the most advanced and powerful modules in the Python library. Here are some general tips for keeping your head from exploding:

- Carefully read the online documentation before building a large application. Although this section has covered the essential basics, the official documentation covers some of the more sneaky issues that can arise.

- Make sure that all data passed between processes is compatible with pickle.

- Avoid shared data and learn to love message passing and queues. With message passing, you don't have to worry so much about synchronization, locking, and other issues. It also tends to provide better scaling as the number of processes increases.

- Don't use global variables inside functions that are meant to run in separate processes. It is better to explicitly pass parameters instead.

- Try not to mix threads and multiprocessing together in the same program unless you're vastly trying to improve your job security (or to have it reduced depending on who is doing the code review).

- Pay very careful attention to how processes get shut down. As a general rule, you will want to explicitly close processes and have a well-defined termination scheme in place as opposed to just relying on garbage collection or having to forcefully terminate children using the `terminate()` operation.

- The use of managers and proxies is closely related to a variety of concepts in distributed computing (e.g., distributed objects). A good distributed computing book might be a useful reference.

- The `multiprocessing` module originated from a third-party library known as `pyprocessing`. Searching for usage tips and information on this library may be a useful resource.

- Although this module works on Windows, you should carefully read the official documentation for a variety of subtle details. For example, to launch a new process on Windows, the multiprocessing module implements its own clone of the UNIX `fork()` operation, in which process state is copied to the child process over a pipe. As a general rule, this module is much more tuned to UNIX systems.

- Above all else, try to keep things as simple as possible.

threading

The threading module provides a Thread class and a variety of synchronization primitives for writing multithreaded programs.

Thread **Objects**

The Thread class is used to represent a separate thread of control. A new thread can be created as follows:

```
Thread(group=None, target=None, name=None, args=(), kwargs={})
```

This creates a new Thread instance. group is None and is reserved for future extensions. target is a callable object invoked by the run() method when the thread starts. By default, it's None, meaning that nothing is called. name is the thread name. By default, a unique name of the form "Thread-N" is created. args is a tuple of arguments passed to the target function. kwargs is a dictionary of keyword arguments passed to target.

A Thread instance t supports the following methods and attributes:

t.start()

Starts the thread by invoking the run() method in a separate thread of control. This method can be invoked only once.

t.run()

This method is called when the thread starts. By default, it calls the target function passed in the constructor. This method can also be redefined in subclasses of Thread.

t.join([timeout])

Waits until the thread terminates or a timeout occurs. timeout is a floating-point number specifying a timeout in seconds. A thread cannot join itself, and it's an error to join a thread before it has been started.

t.is_alive()

Returns True if the thread is alive and False otherwise. A thread is alive from the moment the start() method returns until its run() method terminates. t.isAlive() is an alias for this method in older code.

t.name

The thread name. This is a string that is used for identification only and which can be changed to a more meaningful value if desired (which may simplify debugging). In older code, t.getName() and t.setName(name) are used to manipulate the thread name.

t.ident

An integer thread identifier. If the thread has not yet started, the value is None.

t.daemon

The thread's Boolean daemonic flag. This must be set prior to calling start() and the initial value is inherited from daemonic status of the creating thread. The entire Python program exits when no active non-daemon threads are left. All programs have a main thread that represents the initial thread of control and which is not daemonic. In older code, `t.setDaemon(flag)` and `t.isDaemon()` are used to manipulate this value.

Here is an example that shows how to create and launch a function (or other callable) as a thread:

```
import threading
import time

def clock(interval):
    while True:
        print("The time is %s" % time.ctime())
        time.sleep(interval)

t = threading.Thread(target=clock, args=(15,))
t.daemon = True
t.start()
```

Here is an example that shows how to define the same thread as a class:

```
import threading
import time

class ClockThread(threading.Thread):
    def __init__(self,interval):
        threading.Thread.__init__(self)
        self.daemon = True
        self.interval = interval
    def run(self):
        while True:
            print("The time is %s" % time.ctime())
            time.sleep(self.interval)

t = ClockProcess(15)
t.start()
```

If you define a thread as a class and define your own __init__() method, it is critically important to call the base class constructor `Thread.__init__()` as shown. If you forget this, you will get a nasty error. Other than `run()`, it is an error to override any of the other methods already defined for a thread.

The setting of the daemon attribute in these examples is a common feature of threads that will run forever in the background. Normally, Python waits for all threads to terminate before the interpreter exits. However, for nonterminating background tasks, this behavior is often undesirable. Setting the daemon flag makes the interpreter quit immediately after the main program exits. In this case, the daemonic threads are simply destroyed.

Timer Objects

A `Timer` object is used to execute a function at some later time.

`Timer(interval, func [, args [, kwargs]])`

Creates a timer object that runs the function *func* after *interval* seconds have elapsed. *args* and *kwargs* provide the arguments and keyword arguments passed to *func*. The timer does not start until the `start()` method is called.

A `Timer` object, `t,` has the following methods:

`t.start()`

Starts the timer. The function *func* supplied to `Timer()` will be executed after the specified timer interval.

`t.cancel()`

Cancels the timer if the function has not executed yet.

Lock **Objects**

A *primitive lock* (or *mutual exclusion lock*) is a synchronization primitive that's in either a "locked" or "unlocked" state. Two methods, `acquire()` and `release()`, are used to change the state of the lock. If the state is locked, attempts to acquire the lock are blocked until the lock is released. If more than one thread is waiting to acquire the lock, only one is allowed to proceed when the lock is released. The order in which waiting threads proceed is undefined.

A new `Lock` instance is created using the following constructor:

`Lock()`

Creates a new `Lock` object that's initially unlocked.

A `Lock` instance, `lock`, supports the following methods:

`lock.acquire([blocking ])`

Acquires the lock, blocking until the lock is released if necessary. If blocking is supplied and set to `False`, the function returns immediately with a value of `False` if the lock could not be acquired or `True` if locking was successful.

`lock.release()`

Releases a lock. It's an error to call this method when the lock is in an unlocked state or from a different thread than the one that originally called `acquire()`.

RLock

A *reentrant lock* is a synchronization primitive that's similar to a `Lock` object, but it can be acquired multiple times by the same thread. This allows the thread owning the lock to perform nested `acquire()` and `release()` operations. In this case, only the outermost `release()` operation resets the lock to its unlocked state.

A new `RLock` object is created using the following constructor:

`RLock()`

Creates a new reentrant lock object. An `RLock` object, `rlock`, supports the following methods:

`rlock.acquire([blocking ])`

Acquires the lock, blocking until the lock is released if necessary. If no thread owns the lock, it's locked and the recursion level is set to `1`. If this thread already owns the lock, the recursion level of the lock is increased by one and the function returns immediately.

`rlock.release()`

Releases a lock by decrementing its recursion level. If the recursion level is zero after the decrement, the lock is reset to the unlocked state. Otherwise, the lock remains locked. This function should only be called by the thread that currently owns the lock.

Semaphore and Bounded Semaphore

A *semaphore* is a synchronization primitive based on a counter that's decremented by each `acquire()` call and incremented by each `release()` call. If the counter ever reaches zero, the `acquire()` method blocks until some other thread calls `release()`.

`Semaphore([value])`

Creates a new semaphore. `value` is the initial value for the counter. If omitted, the counter is set to a value of 1.

A `Semaphore` instance, `s`, supports the following methods:

`s.acquire([blocking])`

Acquires the semaphore. If the internal counter is larger than zero on entry, this method decrements it by 1 and returns immediately. If it's zero, this method blocks until another thread calls `release()`. The blocking argument has the same behavior as described for `Lock` and `RLock` objects.

`s.release()`

Releases a semaphore by incrementing the internal counter by 1. If the counter is zero and another thread is waiting, that thread is awakened. If multiple threads are waiting, only one will be returned from its `acquire()` call. The order in which threads are released is not deterministic.

`BoundedSemaphore([value])`

Creates a new semaphore. `value` is the initial value for the counter. If `value` is omitted, the counter is set to a value of 1. A `BoundedSemaphore` works exactly like a `Semaphore` except the number of `release()` operations cannot exceed the number of `acquire()` operations.

A subtle difference between a semaphore and a mutex lock is that a semaphore can be used for signaling. For example, the `acquire()` and `release()` methods can be called from different threads to communicate between producer and consumer threads.

```python
produced = threading.Semaphore(0)
consumed = threading.Semaphore(1)

def producer():
    while True:
        consumed.acquire()
        produce_item()
        produced.release()

def consumer():
    while True:
        produced.acquire()
        item = get_item()
        consumed.release()
```

The kind of signaling shown in this example is often instead carried out using condition variables, which will be described shortly.

Events

Events are used to communicate between threads. One thread signals an "event," and one or more other threads wait for it. An Event instance manages an internal flag that can be set to true with the set() method and reset to false with the clear() method. The wait() method blocks until the flag is true.

Event()

Creates a new Event instance with the internal flag set to false. An Event instance, e, supports the following methods:

e.is_set()

Returns true only if the internal flag is true. This method is called isSet() in older code.

e.set()

Sets the internal flag to true. All threads waiting for it to become true are awakened.

e.clear()

Resets the internal flag to false.

e.wait([*timeout*])

Blocks until the internal flag is true. If the internal flag is true on entry, this method returns immediately. Otherwise, it blocks until another thread calls set() to set the flag to true or until the optional timeout occurs. *timeout* is a floating-point number specifying a timeout period in seconds.

Although Event objects can be used to signal other threads, they should not be used to implement the kind of notification that is typical in producer/consumer problems. For example, you should avoid code like this:

```
evt = Event()

def producer():
    while True:
        # produce item
        ...
        evt.signal()

def consumer():
    while True:
        # Wait for an item
        evt.wait()
        # Consume the item
        ...
        # Clear the event and wait again
        evt.clear()
```

This code does not work reliably because the producer might produce a new item in between the evt.wait() and evt.clear() operations. However, by clearing the event, this new item won't be seen by the consumer until the producer creates a new item. In the best case, the program will experience a minor hiccup where the processing of an item is inexplicably delayed. In the worst case, the whole program will hang due to the loss of an event signal. For these types of problems, you are better off using condition variables.

Condition Variables

A *condition variable* is a synchronization primitive, built on top of another lock that's used when a thread is interested in a particular change of state or event occurring. A typical use is a producer-consumer problem where one thread is producing data to be consumed by another thread. A new Condition instance is created using the following constructor:

`Condition([lock])`

Creates a new condition variable. `lock` is an optional Lock or RLock instance. If not supplied, a new RLock instance is created for use with the condition variable.

A condition variable, `cv`, supports the following methods:

`cv.acquire(*args)`

Acquires the underlying lock. This method calls the corresponding acquire(*args) method on the underlying lock and returns the result.

`cv.release()`

Releases the underlying lock. This method calls the corresponding release() method on the underlying lock.

`cv.wait([timeout])`

Waits until notified or until a timeout occurs. This method is called after the calling thread has already acquired the lock. When called, the underlying lock is released, and the thread goes to sleep until it's awakened by a notify() or notifyAll() call performed on the condition variable by another thread. Once awakened, the thread reacquires the lock and the method returns. timeout is a floating-point number in seconds. If this time expires, the thread is awakened, the lock reacquired, and control returned.

`cv.notify([n])`

Wakes up one or more threads waiting on this condition variable. This method is called only after the calling thread has acquired the lock, and it does nothing if no threads are waiting. n specifies the number of threads to awaken and defaults to 1. Awakened threads don't return from the wait() call until they can reacquire the lock.

`cv.notify_all()`

Wakes up all threads waiting on this condition. This method is called notifyAll() in older code.

Here is an example that provides a template of using condition variables:

```
cv = threading.Condition()
def producer():
    while True:
        cv.acquire()
        produce_item()
        cv.notify()
        cv.release()
```

```
def consumer():
    while True:
        cv.acquire()
        while not item_is_available():
            cv.wait()     # Wait for an item to show up
        cv.release()
        consume_item()
```

A subtle aspect of using condition variables is that if there are multiple threads waiting on the same condition, the `notify()` operation may awaken one or more of them (this behavior often depends on the underlying operating system). Because of this, there is always a possibility that a thread will awaken only to find that the condition of interest no longer holds. This explains, for instance, why a `while` loop is used in the `consumer()` function. If the thread awakens, but the produced item is already gone, it just goes back to waiting for the next signal.

Working with Locks

Great care must be taken when working with any of the locking primitives such as `Lock`, `RLock`, or `Semaphore`. Mismanagement of locks is a frequent source of deadlock or race conditions. Code that relies on a lock should always make sure locks get properly released even when exceptions occur. Typical code looks like this:

```
try:
    lock.acquire()
    # critical section
    statements
    ...
finally:
    lock.release()
```

Alternatively, all of the locks also support the context management protocol which is a little cleaner:

```
with lock:
    # critical section
    statements
    ...
```

In this last example, the lock is automatically acquired by the `with` statement and released when control flow leaves the context.

Also, as a general rule you should avoid writing code where more than one lock is acquired at any given time. For example:

```
with lock_A:
    # critical section
    statements
    ...
    with lock_B:
        # critical section on B
        statements
    ...
```

This is usually a good way to have your application mysteriously deadlock. Although there are strategies for avoiding this (for example, hierarchical locking), you're often better off writing code that avoids this altogether.

Thread Termination and Suspension

Threads do not have any methods for forceful termination or suspension. This omission is by design and due to the intrinsic complexity of writing threaded programs. For example, if a thread has acquired a lock, forcefully terminating or suspending it before it is able to release the lock may cause the entire application to deadlock. Moreover, it is generally not possible to simply "release all locks" on termination either because complicated thread synchronization often involves locking and unlocking operations that must be carried out in a very precise sequence to work.

If you want to support termination or suspension, you need to build these features yourself. Typically, it's done by making a thread run in a loop that periodically checks its status to see if it should terminate. For example:

```
class StoppableThread(threading.Thread):
    def __init__(self):
        threading.Thread.__init__()
        self._terminate    = False
        self._suspend_lock = threading.Lock()
    def terminate(self):
        self._terminate = True
    def suspend(self):
        self._suspend_lock.acquire()
    def resume(self):
        self._suspend_lock.release()
    def run(self):
        while True:
            if self._terminate:
                break
            self._suspend_lock.acquire()
            self._suspend_lock.release()
            statements
            ...
```

Keep in mind that to make this approach work reliability, the thread should take great care not to perform any kind of blocking I/O operation. For example, if the thread blocks waiting for data to arrive, it won't terminate until it wakes up from that operation. Because of this, you would probably want to make the implementation use timeouts, non-blocking I/O, and other advanced features to make sure that that the termination check executes every so often.

Utility Functions

The following utility functions are available:

`active_count()`

Returns the number of currently active `Thread` objects.

`current_thread()`

Returns the `Thread` object corresponding to the caller's thread of control.

`enumerate()`

Returns a list of all currently active `Thread` objects.

`local()`

Returns a `local` object that allows for the storage of thread-local data. This object is guaranteed to be unique in each thread.

`setprofile(func)`

Sets a profile function that will be used for all threads created. `func` is passed to `sys.setprofile()` before each thread starts running.

`settrace(func)`

Sets a tracing function that will be used for all threads created. `func` is passed to `sys.settrace()` before each thread starts running.

`stack_size([size])`

Returns the stack size used when creating new threads. If an optional integer `size` is given, it sets the stack size to be used for creating new threads. `size` can be a value that is 32768 (32KB) or greater and a multiple of 4096 (4KB) for maximum portability. A `ThreadError` exception is raised if this operation isn't supported on the system.

The Global Interpreter Lock

The Python interpreter is protected by a lock that only allows one thread to execute at a time even if there are multiple processors available. This severely limits the usefulness of threads in compute-intensive programs—in fact, the use of threads will often make CPU-bound programs run significantly worse than would be the case if they just sequentially carried out the same work. Thus, threads should really only be reserved for programs that are primarily concerned with I/O such as network servers. For more compute-intensive tasks, consider using C extension modules or the `multiprocessing` module instead. C extensions have the option of releasing the interpreter lock and running in parallel, provided that they don't interact with the interpreter when the lock is released. The `multiprocessing` module farms work out to independent subprocesses that aren't restricted by the lock.

Programming with Threads

Although it is possible to write very traditional multithreaded programs in Python using various combinations of locks and synchronization primitives, there is one style of programming that is recommended over all others—and that's to try and organize multithreaded programs as a collection of independent tasks that communicate through message queues. This is described in the next section (the `queue` module) along with an example.

queue, Queue

The `queue` module (named `Queue` in Python 2) implements various multiproducer, multiconsumer queues that can be used to safely exchange information between multiple threads of execution.

The `queue` module defines three different queue classes:

`Queue([maxsize])`

Creates a FIFO (first-in first-out) queue. `maxsize` is the maximum number of items that can be placed in the queue. If `maxsize` omitted or 0, the queue size is infinite.

`LifoQueue([maxsize])`

Creates a LIFO (last-in, first-out) queue (also known as a *stack*).

`PriorityQueue([maxsize])`

Creates a priority queue in which items are ordered from lowest to highest priority. When working with this queue, items should be tuples of the form (`priority, data`) where `priority` is a number.

An instance q of any of the queue classes has the following methods:

`q.qsize()`

Returns the approximate size of the queue. Because other threads may be updating the queue, this number is not entirely reliable.

`q.empty()`

Returns `True` if the queue is empty and returns `False` otherwise.

`q.full()`

Returns `True` if the queue is full and returns `False` otherwise.

`q.put(item [, block [, timeout]])`

Puts `item` into the queue. If optional argument `block` is `True` (the default), the caller blocks until a free slot is available. Otherwise (`block` is `False`), the `Full` exception is raised if the queue is full. `timeout` supplies an optional timeout value in seconds. If a timeout occurs, the `Full` exception is raised.

`q.put_nowait(item)`

Equivalent to q.put(`item, False`).

`q.get([block [, timeout]])`

Removes and returns an item from the queue. If optional argument `block` is `True` (the default), the caller blocks until an item is available. Otherwise (`block` is `False`), the `Empty` exception is raised if the queue is empty. `timeout` supplies an optional timeout value in seconds. If a timeout occurs, the `Empty` exception is raised.

`q.get_nowait()`

Equivalent to get(0).

`q.task_done()`

Used by consumers of queued data to indicate that processing of an item has been finished. If this is used, it should be called once for every item removed from the queue.

`q.join()`

Blocks until all items on the queue have been removed and processed. This will only return once q.task_done() has been called for every item placed on the queue.

Queue Example with Threads

Multithreaded programs are often simplified with the use of queues. For example, instead of relying upon shared state that must be protected by locks, threads can be linked together using shared queues. In this model, worker threads typically operate as consumers of data. Here is an example that illustrates the concept:

```
import threading
from queue import Queue  # Use from Queue on Python 2

class WorkerThread(threading.Thread):
    def __init__(self,*args,**kwargs):
        threading.Thread.__init__(self,*args,**kwargs)
        self.input_queue = Queue()
    def send(self,item):
        self.input_queue.put(item)
    def close(self):
        self.input_queue.put(None)
        self.input_queue.join()
    def run(self):
        while True:
            item = self.input_queue.get()
            if item is None:
                break
            # Process the item (replace with useful work)
            print(item)
            self.input_queue.task_done()
        # Done.  Indicate that sentinel was received and return
        self.input_queue.task_done()
        return

# Example use
w = WorkerThread()
w.start()
w.send("hello")      # Send items to the worker (via queue)
w.send("world")
w.close()
```

The design of this class has been chosen very carefully. First, you will notice that the programming API is a subset of the Connection objects that get created by pipes in the multiprocessing module. This allows for future expansion. For example, workers could later be migrated into a separate process without breaking the code that sends them data.

Second, the programming interface allows for thread termination. The close() method places a sentinel onto the queue which, in turn, causes the thread to shut down when processed.

Finally, the programming API is also almost identical to a coroutine. If the work to be performed doesn't involve any blocking operations, you could reimplement the run() method as a coroutine and dispense with threads altogether. This latter approach might run faster because there would no longer be any overhead due to thread context switching.

Coroutines and Microthreading

In certain kinds of applications, it is possible to implement cooperative user-space multithreading using a task scheduler and a collection of generators or coroutines. This is sometimes called *microthreading,* although the terminology varies—sometimes this is described in the context of *tasklets, green threads, greenlets,* etc. A common use of this technique is in programs that need to manage a large collection of open files or sockets. For example, a network server that wants to simultaneously manage 1,000 client connections. Instead of creating 1,000 threads to do that, asynchronous I/O or polling (using the select module) is used in conjunction with a task scheduler that processes I/O events.

The underlying concept that drives this programming technique is the fact that the yield statement in a generator or coroutine function suspends the execution of the function until it is later resumed with a next() or send() operation. This makes it possible to cooperatively multitask between a set of generator functions using a scheduler loop. Here is an example that illustrates the idea:

```
def foo():
    for n in xrange(5):
        print("I'm foo %d" % n)
        yield

def bar():
    for n in xrange(10):
        print("I'm bar %d" % n)
        yield

def spam():
    for n in xrange(7):
        print("I'm spam %d" % n)
        yield

# Create and populate a task queue
from collections import deque
taskqueue = deque()
taskqueue.append(foo())        # Add some tasks (generators)
taskqueue.append(bar())
taskqueue.append(spam())

# Run all of the tasks
while taskqueue:
    # Get the next task
    task = taskqueue.pop()
    try:
        # Run it to the next yield and enqueue
        next(task)
        taskqueue.appendleft(task)
    except StopIteration:
        # Task is done
        pass
```

It is uncommon for a program to define a series of CPU-bound coroutines and schedule them as shown. Instead, you are more likely to see this technique used with I/O bound tasks, polling, or event handling. An advanced example showing this technique is found in the select module section of Chapter 21, "Network Programming and Sockets."

## 21

Network Programming and Sockets

This chapter describes the modules used to implement low-level network servers and clients. Python provides extensive network support, ranging from programming directly with sockets to working with high-level application protocols such as HTTP. To begin, a very brief (and admittedly terse) introduction to network programming is presented. Readers are advised to consult a book such as *UNIX Network Programming, Volume 1: Networking APIs: Sockets and XTI* by W. Richard Stevens (Prentice Hall, 1997, ISBN 0-13-490012-X) for many of the advanced details. Chapter 22, "Internet Application Programming," describes modules related to application-level protocols.

Network Programming Basics

Python's network programming modules primarily support two Internet protocols: TCP and UDP. The *TCP protocol* is a reliable connection-oriented protocol used to establish a two-way communications stream between machines. *UDP* is a lower-level packet-based protocol (connectionless) in which machines send and receive discrete packets of information without formally establishing a connection. Unlike TCP, UDP communication is unreliable and thus inherently more complicated to manage in applications that require reliable communications. Consequently, most Internet applications utilize TCP connections.

Both network protocols are handled through a programming abstraction known as a socket. A *socket* is an object similar to a file that allows a program to accept incoming connections, make outgoing connections, and send and receive data. Before two machines can communicate, both must create a socket object.

The machine receiving the connection (the server) must bind its socket object to a known port number. A *port* is a 16-bit number in the range 0–65535 that's managed by the operating system and used by clients to uniquely identify servers. Ports 0–1023 are reserved by the system and used by common network protocols. The following table shows the port assignments for a couple of common protocols (a more complete list can be found at http://www.iana.org/assignments/port-numbers):

Service	Port Number
FTP-Data	20
FTP-Control	21
SSH	22
Telnet	23
SMTP (Mail)	25
HTTP (WWW)	80
POP3	110
IMAP	143
HTTPS (Secure WWW)	443

The process of establishing a TCP connection involves a precise sequence of steps on both the server and client, as shown in Figure 21.1.

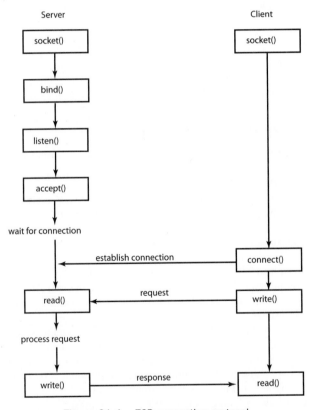

Figure 21.1   TCP connection protocol.

For TCP servers, the socket object used to receive connections is not the same socket used to perform subsequent communication with the client. In particular, the accept() system call returns a new socket object that's actually used for the connection. This allows a server to manage connections from a large number of clients simultaneously.

UDP communication is performed in a similar manner, except that clients and servers don't establish a "connection" with each other, as shown in Figure 21.2.

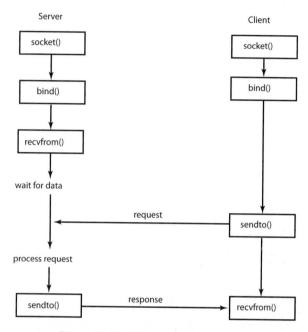

Figure 21.2   UDP connection protocol.

The following example illustrates the TCP protocol with a client and server written using the socket module. In this case, the server simply returns the current time to the client as a string.

```
# Time server program
from socket import *
import time

s = socket(AF_INET, SOCK_STREAM)   # Create a TCP socket
s.bind(('',8888))                   # Bind to port 8888
s.listen(5)                         # Listen, but allow no more than
                                    # 5 pending connections.
while True:
    client,addr = s.accept()        # Get a connection
    print("Got a connection from %s" % str(addr))
    timestr = time.ctime(time.time()) + "\r\n"
    client.send(timestr.encode('ascii'))
    client.close()
```

Here's the client program:

```
# Time client program
from socket import *
s = socket(AF_INET,SOCK_STREAM)     # Create a TCP socket
s.connect(('localhost', 8888))      # Connect to the server
tm = s.recv(1024)                   # Receive no more than 1024 bytes
s.close()
print("The time is %s" % tm.decode('ascii'))
```

An example of establishing a UDP connection appears in the socket module section later in this chapter.

It is common for network protocols to exchange data in the form of text. However, great attention needs to be given to text encoding. In Python 3, all strings are Unicode. Therefore, if any kind of text string is to be sent across the network, it needs to be encoded. This is why the server is using the encode('ascii') method on the data it transmits. Likewise, when a client receives network data, that data is first received as raw unencoded bytes. If you print it out or try to process it as text, you're unlikely to get what you expected. Instead, you need to decode it first. This is why the client code is using decode('ascii') on the result.

The remainder of this chapter describes modules that are related to socket programming. Chapter 22 describes higher-level modules that provide support for various Internet applications such as email and the Web.

asynchat

The asynchat module simplifies the implementation of applications that implement asynchronous networking using the asyncore module. It does this by wrapping the low-level I/O functionality of asyncore with a higher-level programming interface that is designed for network protocols based on simple request/response mechanisms (for example, HTTP).

To use this module, you must define a class that inherits from async_chat. Within this class, you must define two methods: collect_incoming_data() and found_terminator(). The first method is invoked whenever data is received on the network connection. Typically, it would simply take the data and store it someplace. The found_terminator() method is called when the end of a request has been detected. For example, in HTTP, requests are terminated by a blank line.

For data output, async_chat maintains a producer FIFO queue. If you need to output data, it is simply added to this queue. Then, whenever writes are possible on the network connection, data is transparently taken from this queue.

async_chat([sock])

Base class used to define new handlers. async_chat inherits from asyncore.dispatcher and provides the same methods. sock is a socket object that's used for communication.

An instance, a, of async_chat has the following methods in addition to those already provided by the asyncore.dispatcher base class:

a.close_when_done()

Signals an end-of-file on the outgoing data stream by pushing None onto the producer FIFO queue. When this is reached by the writer, the channel will be closed.

a.collect_incoming_data(data)

Called whenever data is received on the channel. data is the received data and is typically stored for later processing. This method must be implemented by the user.

a.discard_buffers()

Discards all data held in input/output buffers and the producer FIFO queue.

`a.found_terminator()`

Called when the termination condition set by `set_terminator()` holds. This method must be implemented by the user. Typically, it would process data previously collected by the `collect_incoming_data()` method.

`a.get_terminator()`

Returns the terminator for the channel.

`a.push(data)`

Pushes data onto the channel's outgoing producer FIFO queue. `data` is a string containing the data to be sent.

`a.push_with_producer(producer)`

Pushes a producer object, `producer`, onto the producer FIFO queue. `producer` may be any object that has a simple method, `more()`. The `more()` method should produce a string each time it is invoked. An empty string is returned to signal the end of data. Internally, the `async_chat` class repeatedly calls `more()` to obtain data to write on the outgoing channel. More than one producer object can be pushed onto the FIFO by calling `push_with_producer()` repeatedly.

`s.set_terminator(term)`

Sets the termination condition on the channel. `term` may either be a string, an integer, or None. If `term` is a string, the method `found_terminator()` is called whenever that string appears in the input stream. If `term` is an integer, it specifies a byte count. After many bytes have been read, `found_terminator()` will be called. If `term` is None, data is collected forever.

The module defines one class that can produce data for the `a.push_with_producer()` method.

`simple_producer(data [, buffer_size])`

Creates a simple producer object that produces chunks from a byte string `data`. `buffer_size` specifies the chunk size and is 512 by default.

The asynchat module is always used in conjunction with the asyncore module. For instance, asyncore is used to set up the high-level server, which accepts incoming connections. asynchat is then used to implement handlers for each connection. The following example shows how this works by implementing a minimalistic web server that handles GET requests. The example omits a lot of error checking and details but should be enough to get you started. Readers should compare this example to the example in the asyncore module, which is covered next.

```
# An asynchronous HTTP server using asynchat
import asynchat, asyncore, socket
import os
import mimetypes
try:
    from http.client import responses        # Python 3
except ImportError:
    from httplib import responses            # Python 2
```

```python
# This class plugs into the asyncore module and merely handles accept events
class async_http(asyncore.dispatcher):
    def __init__(self,port):
        asyncore.dispatcher.__init__(self)
        self.create_socket(socket.AF_INET,socket.SOCK_STREAM)
        self.setsockopt(socket.SOL_SOCKET, socket.SO_REUSEADDR, 1)
        self.bind(('',port))
        self.listen(5)

    def handle_accept(self):
        client,addr = self.accept()
        return async_http_handler(client)

# Class that handles asynchronous HTTP requests.
class async_http_handler(asynchat.async_chat):
    def __init__(self,conn=None):
        asynchat.async_chat.__init__(self,conn)
        self.data = []
        self.got_header = False
        self.set_terminator(b"\r\n\r\n")

    # Get incoming data and append to data buffer
    def collect_incoming_data(self,data):
        if not self.got_header:
            self.data.append(data)

    # Got a terminator (the blank line)
    def found_terminator(self):
        self.got_header = True
        header_data     = b"".join(self.data)
        # Decode header data (binary) into text for further processing
        header_text     = header_data.decode('latin-1')
        header_lines    = header_text.splitlines()
        request         = header_lines[0].split()
        op              = request[0]
        url             = request[1][1:]
        self.process_request(op,url)

    # Push text onto the outgoing stream, but encode it first
    def push_text(self,text):
        self.push(text.encode('latin-1'))

    # Process the request
    def process_request(self, op, url):
        if op == "GET":
            if not os.path.exists(url):
                self.send_error(404,"File %s not found\r\n")
            else:
                type, encoding = mimetypes.guess_type(url)
                size = os.path.getsize(url)
                self.push_text("HTTP/1.0 200 OK\r\n")
                self.push_text("Content-length: %s\r\n" % size)
                self.push_text("Content-type: %s\r\n" % type)
                self.push_text("\r\n")
                self.push_with_producer(file_producer(url))
        else:
            self.send_error(501,"%s method not implemented" % op)
        self.close_when_done()
```

```
      # Error handling
      def send_error(self,code,message):
          self.push_text("HTTP/1.0 %s %s\r\n" % (code, responses[code]))
          self.push_text("Content-type: text/plain\r\n")
          self.push_text("\r\n")
          self.push_text(message)
class file_producer(object):
    def __init__(self,filename,buffer_size=512):
        self.f = open(filename,"rb")
        self.buffer_size = buffer_size
    def more(self):
        data = self.f.read(self.buffer_size)
        if not data:
            self.f.close()
        return data

a = async_http(8080)
asyncore.loop()
```

To test this example, you will need to supply a URL corresponding to a file in the same directory as where you are running the server.

asyncore

The asyncore module is used to build network applications in which network activity is handled asynchronously as a series of events dispatched by an event loop, built using the select() system call. Such an approach is useful in network programs that want to provide concurrency, but without the use of threads or processes. This method can also provide high performance for short transactions. All the functionality of this module is provided by the dispatcher class, which is a thin wrapper around an ordinary socket object.

dispatcher([*sock*])

Base class defining an event-driven nonblocking socket object. *sock* is an existing socket object. If omitted, a socket must be created using the create_socket() method (described shortly). Once it's created, network events are handled by special handler methods. In addition, all open dispatcher objects are saved in an internal list that's used by a number of polling functions.

The following methods of the dispatcher class are called to handle network events. They should be defined in classes derived from dispatcher.

d.handle_accept()

Called on listening sockets when a new connection arrives.

d.handle_close()

Called when the socket is closed.

d.handle_connect()

Called when a connection is made.

d.handle_error()

Called when an uncaught Python exception occurs.

d.handle_expt()

Called when out-of-band data for a socket is received.

d.handle_read()

Called when new data is available to be read from a socket.

d.handle_write()

Called when an attempt to write data is made.

d.readable()

This function is used by the select() loop to see whether the object is willing to read data. Returns True if so, False if not. This method is called to see if the handle_read() method should be called with new data.

d.writable()

Called by the select() loop to see if the object wants to write data. Returns True if so, False otherwise. This method is always called to see whether the handle_write() method should be called to produce output.

In addition to the preceding methods, the following methods are used to perform low-level socket operations. They're similar to those available on a socket object.

d.accept()

Accepts a connection. Returns a pair (client, addr) where client is a socket object used to send and receive data on the connection and addr is the address of the client.

d.bind(address)

Binds the socket to address. address is typically a tuple (host, port), but this depends the address family being used.

d.close()

Closes the socket.

d.connect(address)

Makes a connection. address is a tuple (host, port).

d.create_socket(family, type)

Creates a new socket. Arguments are the same as for socket.socket().

d.listen([backlog])

Listens for incoming connections. backlog is an integer that is passed to the underlying socket.listen() function.

d.recv(size)

Receives at most size bytes. An empty string indicates the client has closed the channel.

d.send(data)

Sends data. data is a byte string.

The following function is used to start the event loop and process events:

```
loop([timeout [, use_poll [, map [, count]]]])
```

Polls for events indefinitely. The `select()` function is used for polling unless the `use_poll` parameter is `True`, in which case `poll()` is used instead. `timeout` is the timeout period and is set to 30 seconds by default. `map` is a dictionary containing all the channels to monitor. `count` specifies how many polling operations to perform before returning. If `count` is `None` (the default), `loop()` polls forever until all channels are closed. If `count` is 1, the function will execute a single poll for events and return.

Example

The following example implements a minimalistic web server using `asyncore`. It implements two classes—`asynhttp` for accepting connections and `asynclient` for processing client requests. This should be compared with the example in the `asynchat` module. The main difference is that this example is somewhat lower-level—requiring us to worry about breaking the input stream into lines, buffering excess data, and identifying the blank line that terminates the request header.

```python
# An asynchronous HTTP server
import asyncore, socket
import os
import mimetypes
import collections
try:
    from http.client import responses      # Python 3
except ImportError:
    from httplib import responses          # Python 2

# This class merely handles accept events
class async_http(asyncore.dispatcher):
    def __init__(self,port):
        asyncore.dispatcher.__init__(self)
        self.create_socket(socket.AF_INET,socket.SOCK_STREAM)
        self.setsockopt(socket.SOL_SOCKET, socket.SO_REUSEADDR, 1)
        self.bind(('',port))
        self.listen(5)

    def handle_accept(self):
        client,addr = self.accept()
        return async_http_handler(client)

# Handle clients
class async_http_handler(asyncore.dispatcher):
    def __init__(self, sock = None):
        asyncore.dispatcher.__init__(self,sock)
        self.got_request    = False                  # Read HTTP request?
        self.request_data   = b""
        self.write_queue    = collections.deque()
        self.responding     = False

    # Only readable if request header not read
    def readable(self):
        return not self.got_request
```

```python
# Read incoming request data
def handle_read(self):
    chunk = self.recv(8192)
    self.request_data += chunk
    if b'\r\n\r\n' in self.request_data:
        self.handle_request()

# Handle an incoming request
def handle_request(self):
    self.got_request = True
    header_data  = self.request_data[:self.request_data.find(b'\r\n\r\n')]
    header_text  = header_data.decode('latin-1')
    header_lines = header_text.splitlines()
    request      = header_lines[0].split()
    op       = request[0]
    url      = request[1][1:]
    self.process_request(op,url)

# Process the request
def process_request(self,op,url):
    self.responding = True
    if op == "GET":
        if not os.path.exists(url):
            self.send_error(404,"File %s not found\r\n" % url)
        else:
            type, encoding = mimetypes.guess_type(url)
            size = os.path.getsize(url)
            self.push_text('HTTP/1.0 200 OK\r\n')
            self.push_text('Content-length: %d\r\n' % size)
            self.push_text('Content-type: %s\r\n' % type)
            self.push_text('\r\n')
            self.push(open(url,"rb").read())
    else:
        self.send_error(501,"%s method not implemented" % self.op)

# Error handling
def send_error(self,code,message):
    self.push_text('HTTP/1.0 %s %s\r\n' % (code, responses[code]))
    self.push_text('Content-type: text/plain\r\n')
    self.push_text('\r\n')
    self.push_text(message)

# Add binary data to the output queue
def push(self,data):
    self.write_queue.append(data)

# Add text data to the output queue
def push_text(self,text):
    self.push(text.encode('latin-1'))

# Only writable if a response is ready
def writable(self):
    return self.responding and self.write_queue

# Write response data
def handle_write(self):
    chunk = self.write_queue.popleft()
    bytes_sent = self.send(chunk)
    if bytes_sent != len(chunk):
        self.write_queue.appendleft(chunk[bytes_sent:])
    if not self.write_queue:
        self.close()
```

```
# Create the server
a = async_http(8080)
# Poll forever
asyncore.loop()
```

> **See Also:**
> socket (**p. 469**), select (**p. 459**), http (**p. 500**), SocketServer (**p. 489**)

select

The select module provides access to the select() and poll() system calls. select() is typically used to implement polling or to multiplex processing across multiple input/output streams without using threads or subprocesses. On UNIX, it works for files, sockets, pipes, and most other file types. On Windows, it only works for sockets.

select(*iwtd, owtd, ewtd* [, *timeout*])

Queries the input, output, and exceptional status of a group of file descriptors. The first three arguments are lists containing either integer file descriptors or objects with a method, fileno(), that can be used to return a file descriptor. The *iwtd* parameter specifies objects waiting for input, *owtd* specifies objects waiting for output, and *ewtd* specifies objects waiting for an exceptional condition. Each list may be empty. *timeout* is a floating-point number specifying a timeout period in seconds. If *timeout* is omitted, the function waits until at least one file descriptor is ready. If it's 0, the function merely performs a poll and returns immediately. The return value is a tuple of lists containing the objects that are ready. These are subsets of the first three arguments. If none of the objects is ready before the timeout occurs, three empty lists are returned. If an error occurs, a select.error exception raised. Its value is the same as that returned by IOError and OSError.

poll()

Creates a polling object that utilizes the poll() system call. This is only available on systems that support poll().

A polling object, *p*, returned by poll() supports the following methods:

p.register(*fd* [, *eventmask*])

Registers a new file descriptor, *fd*. *fd* is either an integer file descriptor or an object that provides the fileno() method from which the descriptor can be obtained. *eventmask* is the bitwise OR of the following flags, which indicate events of interest:

Constant	Description
POLLIN	Data is available for reading.
POLLPRI	Urgent data is available for reading.
POLLOUT	Ready for writing.
POLLERR	Error condition.

Constant	Description
POLLHUP	Hang up.
POLLNVAL	Invalid request.

If *eventmask* is omitted, the POLLIN, POLLPRI, and POLLOUT events are checked.

p.unregister(*fd*)

Removes the file descriptor *fd* from the polling object. Raises KeyError if the file is not registered.

p.poll([*timeout*])

Polls for events on all the registered file descriptors. *timeout* is an optional timeout specified in milliseconds. Returns a list of tuples (*fd*, *event*), where *fd* is a file descriptor and *event* is a bitmask indicating events. The fields of this bitmask correspond to the constants POLLIN, POLLOUT, and so on. For example, to check for the POLLIN event, simply test the value using *event* & POLLIN. If an empty list is returned, it means a timeout occurred and no events occurred.

Advanced Module Features

The select() and poll() functions are the most generally portable functions defined by this module. On Linux systems, the select module also provides an interface to the edge and level trigger polling (epoll) interface which can offer significantly better performance. On BSD systems, access to kernel queue and event objects is provided. These programming interfaces are described in the online documentation for select at http://docs.python.org/library/select.

Advanced Asynchronous I/O Example

The select module is sometimes used to implement servers based on tasklets or coroutines—a technique that can be used to provide concurrent execution without threads or processes. The following advanced example illustrates this concept by implementing an I/O-based task scheduler for coroutines. Be forewarned—this is the most advanced example in the book and it will require some study for it to make sense. You might also want to consult my PyCON'09 tutorial "A Curious Course on Coroutines and Concurrency" (http://www.dabeaz.com/coroutines) for additional reference material.

```
import select
import types
import collections
```

```python
# Object that represents a running task
class Task(object):
    def __init__(self,target):
        self.target  = target     # A coroutine
        self.sendval = None       # Value to send when resuming
        self.stack   = []         # Call stack
    def run(self):
        try:
            result = self.target.send(self.sendval)
            if isinstance(result,SystemCall):
                return result
            if isinstance(result,types.GeneratorType):
                self.stack.append(self.target)
                self.sendval = None
                self.target = result
            else:
                if not self.stack: return
                self.sendval = result
                self.target = self.stack.pop()
        except StopIteration:
            if not self.stack: raise
            self.sendval = None
            self.target = self.stack.pop()

# Object that represents a "system call"
class SystemCall(object):
    def handle(self,sched,task):
        pass

# Scheduler object
class Scheduler(object):
    def __init__(self):
        self.task_queue     = collections.deque()
        self.read_waiting   = {}
        self.write_waiting  = {}
        self.numtasks       = 0

    # Create a new task out of a coroutine
    def new(self,target):
        newtask = Task(target)
        self.schedule(newtask)
        self.numtasks += 1

    # Put a task on the task queue
    def schedule(self,task):
        self.task_queue.append(task)

    # Have a task wait for data on a file descriptor
    def readwait(self,task,fd):
        self.read_waiting[fd] = task
```

```
# Have a task wait for writing on a file descriptor
def writewait(self,task,fd):
    self.write_waiting[fd] = task

# Main scheduler loop
def mainloop(self,count=-1,timeout=None):
    while self.numtasks:
        # Check for I/O events to handle
        if self.read_waiting or self.write_waiting:
            wait = 0 if self.task_queue else timeout
            r,w,e = select.select(self.read_waiting, self.write_waiting, [],
                                  wait)
            for fileno in r:
                self.schedule(self.read_waiting.pop(fileno))
            for fileno in w:
                self.schedule(self.write_waiting.pop(fileno))

        # Run all of the tasks on the queue that are ready to run
        while self.task_queue:
            task = self.task_queue.popleft()
            try:
                result = task.run()
                if isinstance(result,SystemCall):
                    result.handle(self,task)
                else:
                    self.schedule(task)
            except StopIteration:
                self.numtasks -= 1

        # If no tasks can run, we decide if we wait or return
        else:
            if count > 0: count -= 1
            if count == 0:
                return

# Implementation of different system calls
class ReadWait(SystemCall):
    def __init__(self,f):
        self.f = f
    def handle(self,sched,task):
        fileno = self.f.fileno()
        sched.readwait(task,fileno)

class WriteWait(SystemCall):
    def __init__(self,f):
        self.f = f
    def handle(self,sched,task):
        fileno = self.f.fileno()
        sched.writewait(task,fileno)

class NewTask(SystemCall):
    def __init__(self,target):
        self.target = target
    def handle(self,sched,task):
        sched.new(self.target)
        sched.schedule(task)
```

The code in this example implements a very tiny "operating system." Here are some details concerning its operation:

- All work is carried out by coroutine functions. Recall that a coroutine uses the yield statement like a generator except that instead of iterating on it, you send it values using a send(value) method.

- The `Task` class represents a running task and is just a thin layer on top of a coroutine. A `Task` object *task* has only one operation, *task*.`run()`. This resumes the task and runs it until it hits the next `yield` statement, at which point the task suspends. When running a task, the *task*.`sendval` attribute contains the value that is to be sent into the task's corresponding `yield` expression. Tasks run until they encounter the next `yield` statement. The value produced by this `yield` controls what happens next in the task:
  - If the value is another coroutine (`type.GeneratorType`), it means that the task wants to temporarily transfer control to that coroutine. The `stack` attribute of `Task` objects represents a call-stack of coroutines that is built up when this happens. The next time the task runs, control will be transferred into this new coroutine.
  - If the value is a `SystemCall` instance, it means that the task wants the scheduler to do something on its behalf (such as launch a new task, wait for I/O, and so on). The purpose of this object is described shortly.
  - If the value is any other value, one of two things happens. If the currently executing coroutine was running as a subroutine, it is popped from the task call stack and the value saved so that it can be sent to the caller. The caller will receive this value the next time the task executes. If the coroutine is the only executing coroutine, the return value is simply discarded.
  - The handling of `StopIteration` is to deal with coroutines that have terminated. When this happens, control is returned to the previous coroutine (if there was one) or the exception is propagated to the scheduler so that it knows that the task terminated.
- The `SystemCall` class represents a system call in the scheduler. When a running task wants the scheduler to carry out an operation on its behalf, it yields a `SystemCall` instance. This object is called a "system call" because it mimics the behavior of how programs request the services of a real multitasking operating system such as UNIX or Windows. In particular, if a program wants the services of the operating system, it yields control and provides some information back to the system so that it knows what to do. In this respect, yielding a `SystemCall` is similar to executing a kind of system "trap."
- The `Scheduler` class represents a collection of `Task` objects that are being managed. At its core, the scheduler is built around a task queue (the `task_queue` attribute) that keeps track of tasks that are ready to run. There are four basic operations concerning the task queue. `new()` takes a new coroutine, wraps it with a `Task` object, and places it on the work queue. `schedule()` takes an existing `Task` and puts it back on the work queue. `mainloop()` runs the scheduler in a loop, processing tasks one by one until there are no more tasks. The `readwait()` and `writewait()` methods put a `Task` object into temporary staging areas where it will wait for I/O events. In this case, the `Task` isn't running, but it's not dead either—it's just sitting around biding its time.
- The `mainloop()` method is the heart of the scheduler. This method first checks to see if any tasks are waiting for I/O events. If so, it arranges a call to `select()` in order to poll for I/O activity. If there are any events of interest, the associated tasks are placed back onto the task queue so that they can run. Next, the `mainloop()` method pops tasks off of the task queue and calls their `run()`

method. If any task exits (StopIteration), it is discarded. If a task merely yields, it is just placed back onto the task queue so that it can run again. This continues until there are either no more tasks or all tasks are blocked, waiting for more I/O events. As an option, the mainloop() function accepts a count parameter that can be used to make it return after a specified number of I/O polling operations. This might be useful if the scheduler is to be integrated into another event loop.

- Perhaps the most subtle aspect of the scheduler is the handling of SystemCall instances in the mainloop() method. If a task yields a SystemCall instance, the scheduler invokes its handle() method, passing in the associated Scheduler and Task objects as parameters. The purpose of a system call is to carry out some kind of internal operation concerning tasks or the scheduler itself. The ReadWait(), WriteWait(), and NewTask() classes are examples of system calls that suspend a task for I/O or create a new task. For example, ReadWait() takes a task and invokes the readwait() method on the scheduler. The scheduler then takes the task and places it into an appropriate holding area. Again, there is a critical decoupling of objects going on here. Tasks yield SystemCall objects to request service, but do not directly interact with the scheduler. SystemCall objects, in turn, can perform operations on tasks and schedulers but are not tied to any specific scheduler or task implementation. So, in theory, you could write a completely different scheduler implementation (maybe using threads) that could just be plugged into this whole framework and it would still work.

Here is an example of a simple network time server implemented using this I/O task scheduler. It will illuminate many of the concepts described in the previous list:

```
from socket import socket, AF_INET, SOCK_STREAM
def time_server(address):
    import time
    s = socket(AF_INET,SOCK_STREAM)
    s.bind(address)
    s.listen(5)
    while True:
        yield ReadWait(s)
        conn,addr = s.accept()
        print("Connection from %s" % str(addr))
        yield WriteWait(conn)
        resp = time.ctime() + "\r\n"
        conn.send(resp.encode('latin-1'))
        conn.close()

sched = Scheduler()
sched.new(time_server(('',10000)))    # Server on port 10000
sched.new(time_server(('',11000)))    # Server on port 11000
sched.run()
```

In this example, two different servers are running concurrently—each listening on a different port number (use telnet to connect and test). The yield ReadWait() and yield WriteWait() statements cause the coroutine running each server to suspend until I/O is possible on the associated socket. When these statements return, the code immediately proceeds with an I/O operation such as accept() or send().

The use of `ReadWait` and `WriteWait` might look rather low-level. Fortunately, our design allows these operations to be hidden behind library functions and methods—provided that they are also coroutines. Consider the following object that wraps a socket object and mimics its interface:

```python
class CoSocket(object):
    def __init__(self,sock):
        self.sock = sock
    def close(self):
        yield self.sock.close()
    def bind(self,addr):
        yield self.sock.bind(addr)
    def listen(self,backlog):
        yield self.sock.listen(backlog)
    def connect(self,addr):
        yield WriteWait(self.sock)
        yield self.sock.connect(addr)
    def accept(self):
        yield ReadWait(self.sock)
        conn, addr = self.sock.accept()
        yield CoSocket(conn), addr
    def send(self,data):
        while data:
            evt = yield WriteWait(self.sock)
            nsent = self.sock.send(data)
            data = data[nsent:]
    def recv(self,maxsize):
        yield ReadWait(self.sock)
        yield self.sock.recv(maxsize)
```

Here is a reimplementation of the time server using the `CoSocket` class:

```python
from socket import socket, AF_INET, SOCK_STREAM
def time_server(address):
    import time
    s = CoSocket(socket(AF_INET,SOCK_STREAM))
    yield s.bind(address)
    yield s.listen(5)
    while True:
        conn,addr = yield s.accept()
        print(conn)
        print("Connection from %s" % str(addr))
        resp = time.ctime()+"\r\n"
        yield conn.send(resp.encode('latin-1'))
        yield conn.close()

sched = Scheduler()
sched.new(time_server(('',10000)))    # Server on port 10000
sched.new(time_server(('',11000)))    # Server on port 11000
sched.run()
```

In this example, the programming interface of a `CoSocket` object looks a lot like a normal socket. The only difference is that every operation must be prefaced with `yield` (since every method is defined as a coroutine). At first, it looks crazy so you might ask what does all of this madness buy you? If you run the above server, you will find that it is able to run concurrently without using threads or subprocesses. Not only that, it has "normal" looking control flow as long as you ignore all of the `yield` keywords.

Here is an asynchronous web server that concurrently handles multiple client connections, but which does not use callback functions, threads, or processes. This should be
compared to examples in the asynchat and asyncore modules.

```python
import os
import mimetypes
try:
    from http.client import responses    # Python 3
except ImportError:
    from httplib import responses                # Python 2
from socket import *

def http_server(address):
    s = CoSocket(socket(AF_INET,SOCK_STREAM))
    yield s.bind(address)
    yield s.listen(50)

    while True:
        conn,addr = yield s.accept()
        yield NewTask(http_request(conn,addr))
        del conn, addr

def http_request(conn,addr):
    request = b""
    while True:
        data = yield conn.recv(8192)
        request += data
        if b'\r\n\r\n' in request: break

    header_data   = request[:request.find(b'\r\n\r\n')]
    header_text   = header_data.decode('latin-1')
    header_lines  = header_text.splitlines()
    method, url, proto = header_lines[0].split()
    if method == 'GET':
        if os.path.exists(url[1:]):
            yield serve_file(conn,url[1:])
        else:
            yield error_response(conn,404,"File %s not found" % url)
    else:
        yield error_response(conn,501,"%s method not implemented" % method)
    yield conn.close()

def serve_file(conn,filename):
    content,encoding = mimetypes.guess_type(filename)
    yield conn.send(b"HTTP/1.0 200 OK\r\n")
    yield conn.send(("Content-type: %s\r\n" % content).encode('latin-1'))
    yield conn.send(("Content-length: %d\r\n" %
                       os.path.getsize(filename)).encode('latin-1'))
    yield conn.send(b"\r\n")
    f = open(filename,"rb")
    while True:
        data = f.read(8192)
        if not data: break
        yield conn.send(data)

def error_response(conn,code,message):
    yield conn.send(("HTTP/1.0 %d %s\r\n" %
                       (code, responses[code])).encode('latin-1'))
    yield conn.send(b"Content-type: text/plain\r\n")
    yield conn.send(b"\r\n")
    yield conn.send(message.encode('latin-1'))
```

```
sched = Scheduler()
sched.new(http_server(('',8080)))
sched.mainloop()
```

Careful study of this example will yield tremendous insight into coroutines and concurrent programming techniques used by some very advanced third-party modules. However, excessive usage of these techniques might get you fired after your next code review.

When to Consider Asynchronous Networking

Use of asynchronous I/O (asyncore and asynchat), polling, and coroutines as shown in previous examples remains one of the most mysterious aspects of Python development. Yet, these techniques are used more often than you might think. An often-cited reason for using asynchronous I/O is to minimize the perceived overhead of programming with a large number of threads, especially when managing a large number of clients and in light of restrictions related to the global interpreter lock (refer to Chapter 20, "Threads and Concurrency").

Historically, the asyncore module was one of the first library modules to support asynchronous I/O. The asynchat module followed some time later with the aim of simplifying much of the coding. However, both of these modules take the approach of processing I/O as events. For example, when an I/O event occurs, a callback function is triggered. The callback then reacts in response to the I/O event and carries out some processing. If you build a large application in this style, you will find that event handling infects almost every part of the application (e.g., I/O events trigger callbacks, which trigger more callbacks, which trigger other callbacks, ad nauseum). One of the more popular networking packages, Twisted (http://twistedmatrix.com), takes this approach and significantly builds upon it.

Coroutines are more modern but less commonly understood and used since they were only first introduced in Python 2.5. An important feature of coroutines is that you can write programs that look more like threaded programs in their overall control flow. For instance, the web server in the example does not use any callback functions and looks almost identical to what you would write if you were using threads—you just have to become comfortable with the use of the yield statement. Stackless Python (http://www.stackless.com) takes this idea even further.

As a general rule, you probably should resist the urge to use asynchronous I/O techniques for most network applications. For instance, if you need to write a server that constantly transmits data over hundreds or even thousands of simultaneous network connections, threads will tend to have superior performance. This is because the performance of select() degrades significantly as the number of connections it must monitor increases. On Linux, this penalty can be reduced using special functions such as epoll(), but this limits the portability of your code. Perhaps the main benefit of asynchronous I/O is in applications where networking needs to be integrated with other event loops (e.g., GUIs) or in applications where networking is added into code that also performs a significant amount of CPU processing. In these cases, the use of asynchronous networking may result in quicker response time.

Just to illustrate, consider the following program that carries out the task described in the song "10 million bottles of beer on the wall":

```
bottles = 10000000

def drink_beer():
    remaining = 12.0
    while remaining > 0.0:
        remaining -= 0.1

def drink_bottles():
    global bottles
    while bottles > 0:
        drink_beer()
        bottles -= 1
```

Now, suppose you wanted to add a remote monitoring capability to this code that allows clients to connect and see how many bottles are remaining. One approach is to launch a server in its own thread and have it run alongside the main application like this:

```
def server(port):
    s = socket.socket(socket.AF_INET,socket.SOCK_STREAM)
    s.bind(('',port))
    s.listen(5)
    while True:
        client,addr = s.accept()
        client.send(("%d bottles\r\n" % bottles).encode('latin-1'))
        client.close()
# Launch the monitor server
thr = threading.Thread(target=server,args=(10000,))
thr.daemon=True
thr.start()
drink_bottles()
```

The other approach is to write a server based on I/O polling and embed a polling operation directly into the main computation loop. Here is an example that uses the coroutine scheduler developed earlier:

```
def drink_bottles():
    global bottles
    while bottles > 0:
        drink_beer()
        bottles -= 1
        scheduler.mainloop(count=1,timeout=0)  # Poll for connections

# An asynchronous server based on coroutines.
def server(port):
    s = CoSocket(socket.socket(socket.AF_INET,socket.SOCK_STREAM))
    yield s.bind(('',port))
    yield s.listen(5)
    while True:
        client,addr = yield s.accept()
        yield client.send(("%d bottles\r\n" % bottles).encode('latin-1'))
        yield client.close()

scheduler = Scheduler()
scheduler.new(server(10000))
drink_bottles()
```

If you write a separate program that periodically connects to the bottles of beer program and measures the response time required to receive a status message, the results are surprising. On the author's machine (a dual-core 2 GHZ MacBook), the average response time (measured over 1,000 requests) for the coroutine-based server is about 1ms versus 5ms for threads. This difference is explained by the fact that the coroutine-based code is able to respond as soon as it detects a connection whereas the threaded server doesn't get to run until it is scheduled by the operating system. In the presence of a CPU-bound thread and the Python global interpreter lock, the server may be delayed until the CPU-bound thread exceeds its allotted time slice. On many systems, the time slice is about 10ms so the above rough measurement of thread response time is exactly the average time you might expect to wait for a CPU-bound task to be preempted by the operating system.

The downside to polling is that it introduces significant overhead if it occurs too often. For instance, even though the response time is lower in this example, the program instrumented with polling takes more than 50% longer to run to completion. If you change the code to only poll after every six-pack of beer, the response time increases slightly to 1.2ms whereas the run time of the program is only 3% greater than the program without any polling. Unfortunately, there is often no clear-cut way to know how often to poll other than to make measurements of your application.

Even though this improved response time might look like a win, there are still horrible problems associated with trying to implement your own concurrency. For example, tasks need to be especially careful when performing any kind of blocking operation. In the web server example, there is a fragment of code that opens and reads data from a file. When this operation occurs, the entire program will be frozen—potentially for a long period of time if the file access involves a disk seek. The only way to fix this would be to additionally implement asynchronous file access and add it as a feature to the scheduler. For more complicated operations such as performing a database query, figuring out how to carry out the work in an asynchronous manner becomes rather complex. One way to do it would be to carry out the work in a separate thread and to communicate the results back to the task scheduler when available—something that could be carried out with careful use of message queues. On some systems, there are low-level system calls for asynchronous I/O (such as the aio_* family of functions on UNIX). As of this writing, the Python library provides no access to those functions, although you can probably find bindings through third-party modules. In the author's experience, using such functionality is a lot trickier than it looks and is not really worth the added complexity that gets introduced into your program—you're often better off letting the thread library deal with such matters.

socket

The socket module provides access to the standard BSD socket interface. Although it's based on UNIX, this module is available on all platforms. The socket interface is designed to be generic and is capable of supporting a wide variety of networking protocols (Internet, TIPC, Bluetooth, and so on). However, the most common protocol is the Internet Protocol (IP), which includes both TCP and UDP. Python supports both IPv4 and IPv6, although IPv4 is far more common.

It should be noted that this module is relatively low-level, providing direct access to the network functions provided by the operating system. If you are writing a network application, it may be easier to use the modules described in Chapter 22 or the SocketServer module described at the end of this chapter.

Address Families

Some of the socket functions require the specification of an *address family*. The family specifies the network protocol being used. The following constants are defined for this purpose:

Constant	Description
AF_BLUETOOTH	Bluetooth protocol
AF_INET	IPv4 protocols (TCP, UDP)
AF_INET6	IPv6 protocols (TCP, UDP)
AF_NETLINK	Netlink Interprocess Communication
AF_PACKET	Link-level packets
AF_TIPC	Transparent Inter-Process Communication protocol
AF_UNIX	UNIX domain protocols

Of these, AF_INET and AF_INET6 are the most commonly used because they represent standard Internet connections. AF_BLUETOOTH is only available on systems that support it (typically embedded systems). AF_NETLINK, AF_PACKET, and AF_TIPC are only supported on Linux. AF_NETLINK is used for fast interprocess communication between user applications and the Linux kernel. AF_PACKET is used for working directly at the data-link layer (e.g., raw ethernet packets). AF_TIPC is a protocol used for high-performance IPC on Linux clusters (http://tipc.sourceforge.net/).

Socket Types

Some socket functions also require the specification of a socket type. The socket type specifies the type of communications (streams or packets) to be used within a given protocol family. The following constants are used for this purpose:

Constant	Description
SOCK_STREAM	A reliable connection-oriented byte stream (TCP)
SOCK_DGRAM	Datagrams (UDP)
SOCK_RAW	Raw socket
SOCK_RDM	Reliable datagrams
SOCK_SEQPACKET	Sequenced connection-mode transfer of records

The most common socket types are SOCK_STREAM and SOCK_DGRAM because they correspond to TCP and UDP in the Internet Protocol suite. SOCK_RDM is a reliable form of UDP that guarantees the delivery of a datagram but doesn't preserve ordering (datagrams might be received in a different order than sent). SOCK_SEQPACKET is used to send packets through a stream-oriented connection in a manner that preserves their order and packet boundaries. Neither SOCK_RDM or SOCK_SEQPACKET are widely supported, so it's best not to use them if you care about portability. SOCK_RAW is used to provide low-level access to the raw protocol and is used if you want to carry out special-purpose operations such as sending control messages (e.g., ICMP messages). Use of SOCK_RAW is usually restricted to programs running with superuser or administrator access.

Not every socket type is supported by every protocol family. For example, if you're using AF_PACKET to sniff ethernet packets on Linux, you can't establish a stream-oriented connection using SOCK_STREAM. Instead, you have to use SOCK_DGRAM or SOCK_RAW. For AF_NETLINK sockets, SOCK_RAW is the only supported type.

Addressing

In order to perform any communication on a socket, you have to specify a destination address. The form of the address depends on the address family of the socket.

AF_INET (IPv4)

For Internet applications using IPv4, addresses are specified as a tuple (host, port). Here are two examples:

```
('www.python.org', 80)
('66.113.130.182', 25)
```

If host is the empty string, it has the same meaning as INADDR_ANY, which means any address. This is typically used by servers when creating sockets that any client can connect to. If host is set to '<broadcast>', it has the same meaning as the INADDR_BROADCAST constant in the socket API.

Be aware that when host names such as 'www.python.org' are used, Python uses DNS to resolve the host name into an IP address. Depending on how DNS has been configured, you may get a different IP address each time. Use a raw IP address such as '66.113.130.182' to avoid this behavior, if needed.

AF_INET6 (IPv6)

For IPv6, addresses are specified as a 4-tuple (host, port, flowinfo, scopeid). With IPv6, the host and port components work in the same way as IPv4, except that the numerical form of an IPv6 host address is typically specified by a string of eight colon-separated hexadecimal numbers, such as 'FEDC:BA98:7654:3210:FEDC:BA98:7654:3210' or '080A::4:1' (in this case, the double colon fills in a range of address components with 0s).

The flowinfo parameter is a 32-bit number consisting of a 24-bit flow label (the low 24 bits), a 4-bit priority (the next 4 bits), and four reserved bits (the high 4 bits). A flow label is typically only used when a sender wants to enable special handling by routers. Otherwise, flowinfo is set to 0.

The scopeid parameter is a 32-bit number that's only needed when working with link-local and site-local addresses. A link-local address always starts with the prefix 'FE80:...' and is used between machines on the same LAN (routers will not forward link-local packets). In this case, scopeid an interface index that identifies a specific network interface on the host. This information can be viewed using a command such as 'ifconfig' on UNIX or 'ipv6 if' on Windows. A site-local address always starts with the prefix 'FEC0:...' and is used between machines within the same site (for example, all machines on a given subnet). In this case, scopeid is a site-identifier number.

If no data is given for flowinfo or scopeid, an IPv6 address can be given as the tuple (host, port), as with IPv4.

AF_UNIX

For UNIX domain sockets, the address is a string containing a path name—for example,
'/tmp/myserver'.

AF_PACKET

For the Linux packet protocol, the address is a tuple (*device*, *protonum* [, *pkttype*
[, *hatype* [, *addr*]]]) where *device* is a string specifying the device name such as
"eth0" and *protonum* is an integer specifying the ethernet protocol number as defined
in the <linux/if_ether.h> header file (e.g., 0x0800 for an IP packet). *packet_type* is
an integer specifying the packet type and is one of the following constants:

Constant	Description
PACKET_HOST	Packet address to the local host.
PACKET_BROADCAST	Physical layer broadcast packet.
PACKET_MULTICAST	Physical layer multicast.
PACKET_OTHERHOST	Packet destined for a different host, but caught by a device driver in promiscuous mode.
PACKET_OUTGOING	Packet originating on the machine, but which has looped back to a packet socket.

hatype is an integer specifying the hardware address type as used in the ARP protocol
and defined in the <linux/if_arp.h> header file. *addr* is a byte string containing a
hardware address, the structure of which depends on the value of *hatype*. For ethernet,
addr will be a 6-byte string holding the hardware address.

AF_NETLINK

For the Linux Netlink protocol, the address is a tuple (*pid*, *groups*) where *pid* and
groups are both unsigned integers. *pid* is the unicast address of the socket and is usually
the same as the process ID of the process that created the socket or 0 for the kernel.
groups is a bit mask used to specify multicast groups to join. Refer to the Netlink documentation for more information.

AF_BLUETOOTH

Bluetooth addresses depend on the protocol being used. For L2CAP, the address is a
tuple (*addr*, *psm*) where *addr* is a string such as '01:23:45:67:89:ab' and *psm* is
an unsigned integer. For RFCOMM, the address is a tuple (*addr*, *channel*) where
addr is an address string and *channel* is an integer. For HCI, the address is a 1-tuple
(*deviceno*,) where *deviceno* is an integer device number. For SCO, the address is a
string *host*.

  The constant BDADDR_ANY represents any address and is a string '00:00:00:00:00:00'.
The constant BDADDR_LOCAL is a string '00:00:00:ff:ff:ff'.

AF_TIPC

For TIPC sockets, the address is a tuple (*addr_type*, *v1*, *v2*, *v3* [, *scope*]) where
all fields are unsigned integers. *addr_type* is one of the following values, which also
determines the values of *v1*, *v2*, and *v3*:

Address Type	Description
TIPC_ADDR_NAMESEQ	$v1$ is the server type, $v2$ is the port identifier, and $v3$ is 0.
TIPC_ADDR_NAME	$v1$ is the server type, $v2$ is the lower port number, and $v3$ is the upper port number.
TIPC_ADDR_ID	$v1$ is the node, $v2$ is the reference, and $v3$ is 0.

The optional *scope* field is one of TIPC_ZONE_SCOPE, TIPC_CLUSTER_SCOPE, or TIPC_NODE_SCOPE.

Functions

The socket module defines the following functions:

create_connection(*address* [, *timeout*])

Establishes a SOCK_STREAM connection to *address* and returns an already connected socket object. *address* is tuple of the form (*host, port*), and *timeout* specifies an optional timeout. This function works by first calling getaddrinfo() and then trying to connect to each of the tuples that gets returned.

fromfd(*fd, family, socktype* [, *proto*])

Creates a socket object from an integer file descriptor, *fd*. The address family, socket type, and protocol number are the same as for socket(). The file descriptor must refer to a previously created socket. It returns an instance of SocketType.

getaddrinfo(*host, port* [,*family* [, *socktype* [, *proto* [, *flags*]]]])

Given *host* and *port* information about a host, this function returns a list of tuples containing information needed to open up a socket connection. *host* is a string containing a host name or numerical IP address. *port* is a number or a string representing a service name (for example, "http", "ftp", "smtp"). Each returned tuple consists of five elements (*family, socktype, proto, canonname, sockaddr*). The *family*, *socktype*, and *proto* items have the same values as would be passed to the socket() function. *canonname* is a string representing the canonical name of the host. *sockaddr* is a tuple containing a socket address as described in the earlier section on Internet addresses. Here's an example:

```
>>> getaddrinfo("www.python.org",80)
[(2,2,17,'',('194.109.137.226',80)), (2,1,6,'',('194.109.137.226'),80))]
```

In this example, getaddrinfo() has returned information about two possible socket connections. The first one (*proto*=17) is a UDP connection, and the second one (*proto*=6) is a TCP connection. The additional parameters to getaddrinfo() can be used to narrow the selection. For instance, this example returns information about establishing an IPv4 TCP connection:

```
>>> getaddrinfo("www.python.org",80,AF_INET,SOCK_STREAM)
[(2,1,6,'',('194.109.137.226',80))]
```

The special constant AF_UNSPEC can be used for the address family to look for any kind of connection. For example, this code gets information about any TCP-like connection and may return information for either IPv4 or IPv6:

```
>>> getaddrinfo("www.python.org","http", AF_UNSPEC, SOCK_STREAM)
[(2,1,6,'',('194.109.137.226',80))]
```

getaddrinfo() is intended for a very generic purpose and is applicable to all supported network protocols (IPv4, IPv6, and so on). Use it if you are concerned about compatibility and supporting future protocols, especially if you intend to support IPv6.

getdefaulttimeout()

Returns the default socket timeout in seconds. A value of None indicates that no timeout has been set.

getfqdn([name])

Returns the fully qualified domain name of *name*. If *name* is omitted, the local machine is assumed. For example, getfqdn("foo") might return "foo.quasievil.org".

gethostbyname(*hostname*)

Translates a host name such as 'www.python.org' to an IPv4 address. The IP address is returned as a string, such as '132.151.1.90'. It does not support IPv6.

gethostbyname_ex(*hostname*)

Translates a host name to an IPv4 address but returns a tuple (*hostname*, *aliaslist*, *ipaddrlist*) in which *hostname* is the primary host name, *aliaslist* is a list of alternative host names for the same address, and *ipaddrlist* is a list of IPv4 addresses for the same interface on the same host. For example, gethostbyname_ex('www.python.org') returns something like ('fang.python.org', ['www.python.org'], ['194.109.137.226']). This function does not support IPv6.

gethostname()

Returns the host name of the local machine.

gethostbyaddr(*ip_address*)

Returns the same information as gethostbyname_ex(), given an IP address such as '132.151.1.90'. If *ip_address* is an IPv6 address such as 'FEDC:BA98:7654:3210:FEDC:BA98:7654:3210', information regarding IPv6 will be returned.

getnameinfo(*address*, *flags*)

Given a socket address, *address*, this function translates the address into a 2-tuple (*host*, *port*), depending on the value of *flags*. The *address* parameter is a tuple specifying an address—for example, ('www.python.org',80). *flags* is the bitwise OR of the following constants:

Constant	Description
NI_NOFQDN	Don't use fully qualified name for local hosts.
NI_NUMERICHOST	Returns the address in numeric form.
NI_NAMEREQD	Requires a host name. Returns an error if *address* has no DNS entry.
NI_NUMERICSERV	The returned *port* is returned as a string containing a port number.
NI_DGRAM	Specifies that the service being looked up is a datagram service (UDP) instead of TCP (the default).

The main purpose of this function is to get additional information about an address. Here's an example:

```
>>> getnameinfo(('194.109.137.226',80),0)
('fang.python.org', 'http')
>>> getnameinfo(('194.109.137.226',80),NI_NUMERICSERV)
('fang.python.org','80')
```

getprotobyname(*protocolname*)

Translates an Internet protocol name (such as 'icmp') to a protocol number (such as the value of IPPROTO_ICMP) that can be passed to the third argument of the socket() function. Raises socket.error if the protocol name isn't recognized. Normally, this is only used with raw sockets.

getservbyname(*servicename* [, *protocolname*])

Translates an Internet service name and protocol name to a port number for that service. For example, getservbyname('ftp', 'tcp') returns 21. The protocol name, if supplied, should be 'tcp' or 'udp'. Raises socket.error if *servicename* doesn't match any known service.

getservbyport(*port* [, *protocolname*])

This is the opposite of getservbyname(). Given a numeric port number, *port*, this function returns a string giving the service name, if any. For example, getservbyport(21, 'tcp') returns 'ftp'. The protocol name, if supplied, should be 'tcp' or 'udp'. Raises socket.error if no service name is available for *port*.

has_ipv6

Boolean constant that is True if IPv6 support is available.

htonl(*x*)

Converts 32-bit integers from host to network byte order (big-endian).

htons(*x*)

Converts 16-bit integers from host to network byte order (big-endian).

inet_aton(*ip_string*)

Converts an IPv4 address provided as a string (for example, '135.128.11.209') to a 32-bit packed binary format for use as the raw-encoding of the address. The returned value is a four-character string containing the binary encoding. This may be useful if passing the address to C or if the address must be packed into a data structure passed to other programs. Does not support IPv6.

inet_ntoa(`packedip`)

Converts a binary-packaged IPv4 address into a string that uses the standard dotted representation (for example, '135.128.11.209'). `packedip` is a four-character string containing the raw 32-bit encoding of an IP address. The function may be useful if an address has been received from C or is being unpacked from a data structure. It does not support IPv6.

inet_ntop(`address_family, packed_ip`)

Converts a packed binary string `packed_ip` representing an IP network address into a string such as '123.45.67.89'. `address_family` is the address family and is usually AF_INET or AF_INET6. This can be used to obtain a network address string from a buffer of raw bytes (for instance, from the contents of a low-level network packet).

inet_pton(`address_family, ip_string`)

Converts an IP address such as '123.45.67.89' into a packed byte string. `address_family` is the address family and is usually AF_INET or AF_INET6. This can be used if you're trying to encode a network address into a raw binary data packet.

ntohl(`x`)

Converts 32-bit integers from network (big-endian) to host byte order.

ntohs(`x`)

Converts 16-bit integers from network (big-endian) to host byte order.

setdefaulttimeout(`timeout`)

Sets the default timeout for newly created socket objects. `timeout` is a floating-point number specified in seconds. A value of None may be supplied to indicate no timeout (this is the default).

socket(`family, type` [, `proto`])

Creates a new socket using the given address family, socket type, and protocol number. `family` is the address family and `type` is the socket type as discussed in the first part of this section. To open a TCP connection, use socket(AF_INET, SOCK_STREAM). To open a UDP connection, use socket(AF_INET, SOCK_DGRAM). The function returns an instance of SocketType (described shortly).

The protocol number is usually omitted (and defaults to 0). This is typically only used with raw sockets (SOCK_RAW) and is set to a constant that depends on the address family being used. The following list shows all of the protocol numbers that Python may define for AF_INET and AF_INET6, depending on their availability on the host system:

Constant	Description
IPPROTO_AH	IPv6 authentication header
IPPROTO_BIP	Banyan VINES
IPPROTO_DSTOPTS	IPv6 destination options
IPPROTO_EGP	Exterior gateway protocol

Constant	Description
IPPROTO_EON	ISO CNLP (Connectionless Network Protocol)
IPPROTO_ESP	IPv6 encapsulating security payload
IPPROTO_FRAGMENT	IPv6 fragmentation header
IPPROTO_GGP	Gateway to Gateway Protocol (RFC823)
IPPROTO_GRE	Generic Routing Encapsulation (RFC1701)
IPPROTO_HELLO	Fuzzball HELLO protocol
IPPROTO_HOPOPTS	IPv6 hop-by-hop options
IPPROTO_ICMP	IPv4 ICMP
IPPROTO_ICMPV6	IPv6 ICMP
IPPROTO_IDP	XNS IDP
IPPROTO_IGMP	Group management protocol
IPPROTO_IP	IPv4
IPPROTO_IPCOMP	IP Payload compression protocol
IPPROTO_IPIP	IP inside IP
IPPROTO_IPV4	IPv4 header
IPPROTO_IPV6	IPv6 header
IPPROTO_MOBILE	IP Mobility
IPPROTO_ND	Netdisk protocol
IPPROTO_NONE	IPv6 no next header
IPPROTO_PIM	Protocol Independent Multicast
IPPROTO_PUP	Xerox PARC Universal Packet (PUP)
IPPROTO_RAW	Raw IP packet
IPPROTO_ROUTING	IPv6 routing header
IPPROTO_RSVP	Resource reservation
IPPROTO_TCP	TCP
IPPROTO_TP	OSI Transport Protocol (TP-4)
IPPROTO_UDP	UDP
IPPROTO_VRRP	Virtual Router Redundancy Protocol
IPPROTO_XTP	eXpress Transfer Protocol

The following protocol numbers are used with AF_BLUETOOTH:

Constant	Description
BTPROTO_L2CAP	Logical Link Control and Adaption Protocol
BTPROTO_HCI	Host/Controller Interface
BTPROTO_RFCOMM	Cable replacement protocol
BTPROTO_SCO	Synchronous Connection Oriented Link

`socketpair([family [, type [, proto ]]])`

Creates a pair of connected socket objects using the given *family*, *type*, and *proto* options, which have the same meaning as for the socket() function. This function only applies to UNIX domain sockets (*family*=AF_UNIX). *type* may be either SOCK_DGRAM or SOCK_STREAM. If *type* is SOCK_STREAM, an object known as a *stream pipe* is created. *proto* is usually 0 (the default). The primary use of this function would be to set up interprocess communication between processes created by os.fork(). For example, the parent process would call socketpair() to create a pair of sockets and call os.fork(). The parent and child processes would then communicate with each other using these sockets.

Sockets are represented by an instance of type SocketType. The following methods are available on a socket, s:

s.accept()

Accepts a connection and returns a pair (*conn*, *address*), where *conn* is a new socket object that can be used to send and receive data on the connection and *address* is the address of the socket on the other end of the connection.

s.bind(*address*)

Binds the socket to an address. The format of *address* depends on the address family. In most cases, it's a tuple of the form (*hostname*, *port*). For IP addresses, the empty string represents INADDR_ANY and the string '<broadcast>' represents INADDR_BROADCAST. The INADDR_ANY host name (the empty string) is used to indicate that the server allows connections on any Internet interface on the system. This is often used when a server is multihomed. The INADDR_BROADCAST host name ('<broadcast>') is used when a socket is being used to send a broadcast message.

s.close()

Closes the socket. Sockets are also closed when they're garbage-collected.

s.connect(*address*)

Connects to a remote socket at *address*. The format of *address* depends on the address family, but it's normally a tuple (*hostname*, *port*). It raises socket.error if an error occurs. If you're connecting to a server on the same computer, you can use the name 'localhost' as *hostname*.

s.connect_ex(*address*)

Like connect(*address*), but returns 0 on success or the value of errno on failure.

s.fileno()

Returns the socket's file descriptor.

s.getpeername()

Returns the remote address to which the socket is connected. Usually the return value is a tuple (*ipaddr*, *port*), but this depends on the address family being used. This is not supported on all systems.

s.getsockname()

Returns the socket's own address. Usually this is a tuple (*ipaddr*, *port*).

s.getsockopt(*level*, *optname* [, *buflen*])

Returns the value of a socket option. *level* defines the level of the option and is SOL_SOCKET for socket-level options or a protocol number such as IPPROTO_IP for protocol-related options. *optname* selects a specific option. If *buflen* is omitted, an integer option is assumed and its integer value is returned. If *buflen* is given, it specifies the maximum length of the buffer used to receive the option. This buffer is returned as a byte string, where it's up to the caller to decode its contents using the struct module or other means.

The following tables list the socket options defined by Python. Most of these options are considered part of the Advanced Sockets API and control low-level details of the network. You will need to consult other documentation to find more detailed descriptions. When type names are listed in the value column, that name is same as the standard C data structure associated with the value and used in the standard socket programming interface. Not all options are available on all machines.

The following are commonly used option names for level SOL_SOCKET:

Option Name	Value	Description
SO_ACCEPTCONN	0, 1	Determines whether or not the socket is accepting connections.
SO_BROADCAST	0, 1	Allows sending of broadcast datagrams.
SO_DEBUG	0, 1	Determines whether or not debugging information is being recorded.
SO_DONTROUTE	0, 1	Bypasses routing table lookups.
SO_ERROR	int	Gets error status.
SO_EXCLUSIVEADDRUSE	0,1	Prevents other sockets from being forcibly bound to the same address and port. This disables the SO_REUSEADDR option.
SO_KEEPALIVE	0, 1	Periodically probes the other end of the connection and terminates if it's half-open.
SO_LINGER	linger	Lingers on close() if the send buffer contains data. linger is a packed binary string containing two 32-bit integers (onoff, seconds).
SO_OOBINLINE	0, 1	Places out-of-band data into the input queue.
SO_RCVBUF	int	Size of receive buffer (in bytes).
SO_RCVLOWAT	int	Number of bytes read before select() returns the socket as readable.
SO_RCVTIMEO	timeval	Timeout on receive calls in seconds. timeval is a packed binary string containing two 32-bit unsigned integers (seconds, microseconds).
SO_REUSEADDR	0, 1	Allows local address reuse.
SO_REUSEPORT	0, 1	Allows multiple processes to bind to the same address as long as this socket option is set in all processes.
SO_SNDBUF	int	Size of send buffer (in bytes).
SO_SNDLOWAT	int	Number of bytes available in send buffer before select() returns the socket as writable.
SO_SNDTIMEO	timeval	Timeout on send calls in seconds. See SO_RCVTIMEO for a description of timeval.
SO_TYPE	int	Gets socket type.
SO_USELOOPBACK	0, 1	Routing socket gets copy of what it sends.

The following options are available for level IPPROTO_IP:

Option Name	Value	Description
IP_ADD_MEMBERSHIP	ip_mreg	Join a multicast group (set only). ip_mreg is a packed binary string containing two 32-bit IP addresses (multiaddr, localaddr), where multiaddr is the multicast address and localaddr is the IP of the local interface being used.
IP_DROP_MEMBERSHIP	ip_mreg	Leave a multicast group (set only). ip_mreg is described above.
IP_HDRINCL	int	IP header included with data.
IP_MAX_MEMBERSHIPS	int	Maximum number of multicast groups.
IP_MULTICAST_IF	in_addr	Outgoing interface. in_addr is a packed binary string containing a 32-bit IP address.
IP_MULTICAST_LOOP	0,1	Loopback.
IP_MULTICAST_TTL	uint8	Time to live. uint8 is a packed binary string containing a 1-byte unsigned char.
IP_OPTIONS	ipopts	IP header options. ipopts is a packed binary string of no more than 44 bytes. The contents of this string are described in RFC 791.
IP_RECVDSTADDR	0,1	Receive IP destination address with datagram.
IP_RECVOPTS	0,1	Receive all IP options with datagram.
IP_RECVRETOPTS	0,1	Receive IP options with response.
IP_RETOPTS	0,1	Same as IP_RECVOPTS, leaves the options unprocessed with no timestamp or route record options filled in.
IP_TOS	int	Type of service.
IP_TTL	int	Time to live.

The following options are available for level IPPROTO_IPV6:

Option Name	Value	Description
IPV6_CHECKSUM	0,1	Have system compute checksum.
IPV6_DONTFRAG	0,1	Don't fragment packets if they exceed the MTU size.
IPV6_DSTOPTS	ip6_dest	Destination options. ip6_dest is a packed binary string of the form (next, len, options) where next is an 8-bit integer giving the option type of the next header; len is an 8-bit integer specifying the length of the header in units of 8 bytes, not including the first 8 bytes; and options is the encoded options.
IPV6_HOPLIMIT	int	Hop limit.
IPV6_HOPOPTS	ip6_hbh	Hop-by-hop options. ip6_hbh has the same encoding as ip6_dest.

Option Name	Value	Description
IPV6_JOIN_GROUP	ip6_mreq	Join multicast group. ip6_mreq is a packed binary string containing (multiaddr, index) where multiaddr is a 128-bit IPv6 multicast address and index is a 32-bit unsigned integer interface index for the local interface.
IPV6_LEAVE_GROUP	ip6_mreq	Leave multicast group.
IPV6_MULTICAST_HOPS	int	Hop-limit for multicast packets.
IPV6_MULTICAST_IF	int	Interface index for outgoing multicast packets.
IPV6_MULTICAST_LOOP	0,1	Deliver outgoing multicast packets back to local application.
IPV6_NEXTHOP	sockaddr_in6	Set the next hop address for outgoing packets. sockaddr_in6 is a packed binary string containing the C sockaddr_in6 structure as typically defined in <netinet/in.h>.
IPV6_PKTINFO	ip6_pktinfo	Packet information structure. ip6_pktinfo is a packed binary string containing (addr, index) where addr is a 128-bit IPv6 address and index is a 32-bit unsigned integer with the interface index.
IPV6_RECVDSTOPTS	0,1	Receive destination options.
IPV6_RECVHOPLIMIT	0,1	Receive the hop limit.
IPV6_RECVHOPOPTS	0,1	Receive hop-by-hop options.
IPV6_RECVPKTINFO	0,1	Receive packet information.
IPV6_RECVRTHDR	0,1	Receive routing header.
IPV6_RECVTCLASS	0,1	Receive the traffic class.
IPV6_RTHDR	ip6_rthdr	Routing header. ip6_rthdr is a packed binary string containing (next, len, type, segleft, data) where next, len, type, and segleft are all 8-bit unsigned integers and data is routing data. See RFC 2460.
IPV6_RTHDRDSTOPTS	ip6_dest	Destination options header before the routing options header.
IPV6_RECVPATHMTU	0,1	Enable the receipt of IPV6_PATHMTU ancillary data items.
IPV6_TCLASS	int	Traffic class.
IPV6_UNICAST_HOPS	int	Hop limit for unicast packets.
IPV6_USE_MIN_MTU	-1,0,1	Path MTU discovery. 1 disables it for all desinations. -1 disables it only for multicast destinations.
IPV6_V6ONLY	0,1	Only connect to other IPV6 nodes.

The following options are available for level SOL_TCP:

Option Name	Value	Description
TCP_CORK	0,1	Don't send out partial frames if set.
TCP_DEFER_ACCEPT	0,1	Awake listener only when data arrives on socket.
TCP_INFO	tcp_info	Returns a structure containing information about the socket. tcp_info is implementation specific.
TCP_KEEPCNT	int	Maximum number of keepalive probes TCP should send before dropping a connection.
TCP_KEEPIDLE	int	Time in seconds the connection should be idle before TCP starts sending keepalive probes if the TCP_KEEPALIVE option has been set.
TCP_KEEPINTVL	int	Time in seconds between keepalive probes.
TCP_LINGER2	int	Lifetime of orphaned FIN_WAIT2 state sockets.
TCP_MAXSEG	int	Maximum segment size for outgoing TCP packets.
TCP_NODELAY	0,1	If set, disables the Nagle algorithm.
TCP_QUICKACK	0,1	If set, ACKs are sent immediately. Disables the TCP delayed ACK algorithm.
TCP_SYNCNT	int	Number of SYN retransmits before aborting a connection request.
TCP_WINDOW_CLAMP	int	Sets an upper bound on the advertised TCP window size.

s.gettimeout()

Returns the current timeout value if any. Returns a floating-point number in seconds or None if no timeout is set.

s.ioctl(control, option)

Provides limited access to the WSAIoctl interface on Windows. The only supported value for control is SIO_RCVALL which is used to capture all received IP packets on the network. This requires Administrator access. The following values can be used for options:

Option	Description
RCVALL_OFF	Prevent the socket from receiving all IPv4 or IPv6 packets.
RCVALL_ON	Enable promiscuous mode, allowing the socket to receive all IPv4 or IPv6 packets on the network. The type of packet received depends on the socket address family. This does not capture packets associated with other network protocols such as ARP.
RCVALL_IPLEVEL	Receive all IP packets received on the network, but do not enable promiscuous mode. This will capture all IP packets directed at the host for any configured IP address.

s.listen(*backlog*)

Starts listening for incoming connections. *backlog* specifies the maximum number of pending connections the operating system should queue before connections are refused. The value should be at least 1, with 5 being sufficient for most applications.

s.makefile([*mode* [, *bufsize*]])

Creates a file object associated with the socket. *mode* and *bufsize* have the same meaning as with the built-in open() function. The file object uses a duplicated version of the socket file descriptor, created using os.dup(), so the file object and socket object can be closed or garbage-collected independently. The socket *s* should not have a time-out and should not be configured in nonblocking mode.

s.recv(*bufsize* [, *flags*])

Receives data from the socket. The data is returned as a string. The maximum amount of data to be received is specified by *bufsize*. *flags* provides additional information about the message and is usually omitted (in which case it defaults to zero). If used, it's usually set to one of the following constants (system-dependent):

Constant	Description
MSG_DONTROUTE	Bypasses routing table lookup (sends only).
MSG_DONTWAIT	Non-blocking operation.
MSG_EOR	Indicates that the message is last in a record. Usually only used when sending data on SOCK_SEQPACKET sockets.
MSG_PEEK	Looks at data but doesn't discard (receives only).
MSG_OOB	Receives/sends out-of-band data.
MSG_WAITALL	Doesn't return until the requested number of bytes have been read (receives only).

s.recv_into(*buffer* [, *nbytes* [, *flags*]])

The same as recv() except that data is written into a an object *buffer* supporting the buffer interface. *nbytes* is the maximum number of bytes to receive. If omitted, the maximum size is taken from the buffer size. *flags* has the same meaning as for recv().

s.recvfrom(*bufsize* [, *flags*])

Like the recv() method except that the return value is a pair (*data*, *address*) in which *data* is a string containing the data received and *address* is the address of the socket sending the data. The optional *flags* argument has the same meaning as for recv(). This function is primarily used in conjunction with the UDP protocol.

s.recvfrom_info(*buffer* [, *nbytes* [, *flags*]])

The same as recvfrom() but the received data is stored in the buffer object *buffer*. *nbytes* specifies the maximum number of bytes of receive. If omitted, the maximum size is taken from the size of *buffer*. *flags* has the same meaning as for recv().

`s.send(`*`string`* `[,` *`flags`*`])`

Sends data in *string* to a connected socket. The optional *flags* argument has the same meaning as for recv(), described earlier. Returns the number of bytes sent, which may be fewer than the number of bytes in *string*. Raises an exception if an error occurs.

`s.sendall(`*`string`* `[,` *`flags`*`])`

Sends data in *string* to a connected socket, except that an attempt is made to send all of the data before returning. Returns None on success; raises an exception on failure. *flags* has the same meaning as for send().

`s.sendto(`*`string`* `[,` *`flags`*`],` *`address`*`)`

Sends data to the socket. *flags* has the same meaning as for recv(). *address* is a tuple of the form (*host, port*), which specifies the remote address. The socket should not already be connected. Returns the number of bytes sent. This function is primarily used in conjunction with the UDP protocol.

`s.setblocking(`*`flag`*`)`

If *flag* is zero, the socket is set to nonblocking mode. Otherwise, the socket is set to blocking mode (the default). In nonblocking mode, if a recv() call doesn't find any data or if a send() call cannot immediately send the data, the socket.error exception is raised. In blocking mode, these calls block until they can proceed.

`s.setsockopt(`*`level, optname, value`*`)`

Sets the value of the given socket option. *level* and *optname* have the same meaning as for getsockopt(). The value can be an integer or a string representing the contents of a buffer. In the latter case, it's up to the caller to ensure that the string contains the proper data. See getsockopt() for socket option names, values, and descriptions.

`s.settimeout(`*`timeout`*`)`

Sets a timeout on socket operations. *timeout* is a floating-point number in seconds. A value of None means no timeout. If a timeout occurs, a socket.timeout exception is raised. As a general rule, timeouts should be set as soon as a socket is created because they can be applied to operations involved in establishing a connection (such as connect()).

`s.shutdown(`*`how`*`)`

Shuts down one or both halves of the connection. If *how* is 0, further receives are disallowed. If *how* is 1, further sends are disallowed. If *how* is 2, further sends and receives are disallowed.

In addition to these methods, a socket instance *s* also has the following read-only properties which correspond to the arguments passed to the socket() function.

Property	Description
s.family	The socket address family (e.g., AF_INET)
s.proto	The socket protocol
s.type	The socket type (e.g., SOCK_STREAM)

Exceptions

The following exceptions are defined by the socket module.

error

This exception is raised for socket- or address-related errors. It returns a pair (*errno*, *mesg*) with the error returned by the underlying system call. Inherits from IOError.

herror

Error raised for address-related errors. Returns a tuple (*herrno*, *hmesg*) containing an error number and error message. Inherits from error.

gaierror

Error raised for address-related errors in the getaddrinfo() and getnameinfo() functions. The error value is a tuple (*errno*, *mesg*), where *errno* is an error number and *mesg* is a string containing a message. *errno* is set to one of the following constants defined in the socket module:

Constant	Description
EAI_ADDRFAMILY	Address family not supported.
EAI_AGAIN	Temporary failure in name resolution.
EAI_BADFLAGS	Invalid flags.
EAI_BADHINTS	Bad hints.
EAI_FAIL	Nonrecoverable failure in name resolution.
EAI_FAMILY	Address family not supported by host.
EAI_MEMORY	Memory allocation failure.
EAI_NODATA	No address associated with node name.
EAI_NONAME	No node name or service name provided.
EAI_PROTOCOL	Protocol not supported.
EAI_SERVICE	Service name not supported for socket type.
EAI_SOCKTYPE	Socket type not supported.
EAI_SYSTEM	System error.

timeout

Exception raised when a socket operation times out. This only occurs if a timeout has been set using the setdefaulttimeout() function or settimeout() method of a socket object. Exception value is a string, 'timeout'. Inherits from error.

Example

A simple example of a TCP connection is shown in the introduction to this chapter. The following example illustrates a simple UDP echo server:

```
# UDP message server
# Receive small packets from anywhere and print them out
import socket
s = socket.socket(socket.AF_INET, socket.SOCK_DGRAM)
s.bind(("",10000))
while True:
    data, address = s.recvfrom(256)
    print("Received a connection from %s" % str(address))
    s.sendto(b"echo:" + data, address)
```

Here a client that sends messages to the previous server:

```
# UDP message client
import socket
s = socket.socket(socket.AF_INET, socket.SOCK_DGRAM)
s.sendto(b"Hello World", ("", 10000))
resp, addr = s.recvfrom(256)
print(resp)
s.sendto(b"Spam", ("", 10000))
resp, addr = s.recvfrom(256)
print(resp)
s.close()
```

Notes

- Not all constants and socket options are available on all platforms. If portability is your goal, you should only rely upon options that are documented in major sources such as the W. Richard Stevens *UNIX Network Programming* book cited at the beginning of this section.

- Notable omissions from the `socket` module are `recvmsg()` and `sendmsg()` system calls, commonly used to work with ancillary data and advanced network options related to packet headers, routing, and other details. For this functionality, you must install a third-party module such as PyXAPI (http://pypi.python.org/pypi/PyXAPI).

- There is a subtle difference between nonblocking socket operations and operations involving a timeout. When a socket function is used in nonblocking mode, it will return immediately with an error if the operation would have blocked. When a timeout is set, a function returns an error only if the operation doesn't complete within a specified timeout.

ssl

The `ssl` module is used to wrap socket objects with the Secure Sockets Layer (SSL), which provides data encryption and peer authentication. Python uses the OpenSSL library (http://www.openssl.org) to implement this module. A full discussion concerning the theory and operation of SSL is beyond the scope of what can be covered here. So, just the essential elements of using this module are covered here with the assumption that you know what you're doing when it comes to SSL configuration, keys, certificates, and other related matters:

wrap_socket(*sock* [, **opts*])

Wraps an existing socket *sock* (created by the `socket` module) with SSL support and returns an instance of `SSLSocket`. This function should be used before subsequent `connect()` or `accept()` operations are made. *opts* represents a number of keyword arguments that are used to specify additional configuration data.

Keyword Argument	Description
server_side	A Boolean flag that indicates whether or not the socket is operating as a server (True) or a client (False). By default, this is False.
keyfile	The key file used to identify the local side of the connection. This should be a PEM-format file and usually only included if the file specified with the certfile doesn't include the key.
certfile	The certificate file used to identify the local side of the connection. This should be a PEM-format file.
cert_reqs	Specifies whether a certificate is required from the other side of the connection and whether or not it will be validated. A value of CERT_NONE means that certificates are ignored, CERT_OPTIONAL means that certificates are not required but will be validated if given, and CERT_REQUIRED means that certificates are required and will be validated. If certificates are going to be validated, the ca_certs parameter must also be given.
ca_certs	Filename of the file holding certificate authority certificates used for validation.
ssl_version	SSL protocol version to use. Possible values are PROTOCOL_TLSv1, PROTOCOL_SSLv2, PROTOCOL_SSLv23, or PROTOCOL_SSLv3. The default protocol is PROTOCOL_SSLv3.
do_handshake_on_connect	Boolean flag that specifies whether or not the SSL handshake is performed automatically on connect. By default, this is True.
suppress_ragged_eofs	Specifies how read() handles an unexpected EOF on the connection. If True (the default), a normal EOF is signaled. If False, an exception is raised.

An instance *s* of SSLSocket inherits from socket.socket and additionally supports the following operations:

s.cipher()

Returns a tuple (*name*, *version*, *secretbits*) where *name* is the cipher name being used, *version* is the SSL protocol, and *secretbits* is the number of secret bits being used.

s.do_handshake()

Performs the SSL handshake. Normally this is done automatically unless the do_handshake_on_connect option was set to False in the wrap_socket() function. If the underlying socket *s* is nonblocking, an SSLError exception will be raised if the operation couldn't be completed. The e.args[0] attribute of an SSLError exception *e* will have the value SSL_ERROR_WANT_READ or SSL_ERROR_WANT_WRITE depending on the operation that needs to be performed. To continue the handshake process once reading or writing can continue, simply call *s*.do_handshake() again.

`s.getpeercert([binary_form])`

Returns the certificate from the other end of the connection, if any. If there is no certificate None is returned. If there was a certificate but it wasn't validated, an empty dictionary is returned. If a validated certificate is received, a dictionary with the keys 'subject' and 'notAfter' is returned. If `binary_form` is set True, the certificate is returned as a DER-encoded byte sequence.

`s.read([nbytes])`

Reads up to `nbytes` of data and returns it. If `nbytes` is omitted, up to 1,024 bytes are returned.

`s.write(data)`

Writes the byte string `data`. Returns the number of bytes written.

`s.unwrap()`

Shuts down the SSL connection and returns the underlying socket object on which further unencrypted communication can be carried out.

The following utility functions are also defined by the module:

`cert_time_to_seconds(timestring)`

Converts a string `timestring` from the format used in certificates to a floating-point number as compatible with the `time.time()` function.

`DER_cert_to_PEM_cert(derbytes)`

Given a byte string `derbytes` containing a DER-encoded certificate, returns a PEM-encoded string version of the certificate.

`PEM_cert_to_DER_cert(pemstring)`

Given a string `pemstring` containing a PEM-encoded string version of a certificate, returns a DER-encoded byte string version of the certificate.

`get_server_certificate(addr [, ssl_version [, ca_certs]])`

Retrieves the certificate of an SSL server and returns it as a PEM-encoded string. `addr` is an address of the form (`hostname`, `port`). `ssl_version` is the SSL version number, and `ca_certs` is the name of a file containing certificate authority certificates as described for the `wrap_socket()` function.

`RAND_status()`

Returns True or False if the SSL layer thinks that the pseudorandom number generator has been seeded with enough randomness.

`RAND_egd(path)`

Reads 256 bytes of randomness from an entropy-gathering daemon and adds it to the pseudorandom number generator. `path` is the name of a UNIX-domain socket for the daemon.

`RAND_add(bytes, entropy)`

Adds the bytes in byte string `bytes` into the pseudorandom number generator. `entropy` is a nonnegative floating-point number giving the lower bound on the entropy.

Examples

The following example shows how to use this module to open an SSL–client connection:

```
import socket, ssl

s = socket.socket(socket.AF_INET, socket.SOCK_STREAM)
ssl_s = ssl.wrap_socket(s)
ssl_s.connect(('gmail.google.com',443))
print(ssl_s.cipher())
# Send a request
ssl_s.write(b"GET / HTTP/1.0\r\n\r\n")
# Get the response
while True:
    data = ssl_s.read()
    if not data: break
    print(data)
ssl_s.close()
```

Here is an example of an SSL-secured time server:

```
import socket, ssl, time

s = socket.socket(socket.AF_INET, socket.SOCK_STREAM)
s.setsockopt(socket.SOL_SOCKET, socket.SO_REUSEADDR,1)
s.bind(('',12345))
s.listen(5)

while True:
    client, addr = s.accept()        # Get a connection
    print "Connection from", addr
    client_ssl = ssl.wrap_socket(client,
                                 server_side=True,
                                 certfile="timecert.pem")

    client_ssl.sendall(b"HTTP/1.0 200 OK\r\n")
    client_ssl.sendall(b"Connection: Close\r\n")
    client_ssl.sendall(b"Content-type: text/plain\r\n\r\n")
    resp = time.ctime() + "\r\n"
    client_ssl.sendall(resp.encode('latin-1'))
    client_ssl.close()
    client.close()
```

In order to run this server, you will need to have a signed server certificate in the file `timecert.pem`. For the purposes of testing, you can create one using this UNIX command:

```
% openssl req -new -x509 -days 30 -nodes -out timecert.pem -keyout timecert.pem
```

To test this server, try connecting with a browser using a URL such as `'https://localhost:1234'`. If it works, the browser will issue a warning message about you using a self-signed certificate. If you agree, you should see the output of the server.

SocketServer

This module is called `socketserver` in Python 3. The `SocketServer` module provides classes that simplify the implementation of TCP, UDP, and UNIX domain socket servers.

Handlers

To use the module, you define a handler class that inherits from the base class
`BaseRequestHandler`. An instance *h* of `BaseRequestHandler` implements one or
more of the following methods:

h.finish()

Called to perform cleanup actions after the `handle()` method has completed. By
default, it does nothing. It's not called if either the `setup()` or `handle()` method generates an exception.

h.handle()

This method is called to perform the actual work of a request. It's called with no arguments, but several instance variables contain useful values. `h.request` contains the
request, `h.client_address` contains the client address, and `h.server` contains an
instance of the server that called the handler. For stream services such as TCP, the
`h.request` attribute is a socket object. For datagram services, it's a byte string containing the received data.

h.setup()

This method is called before the `handle()` method to perform initialization actions. By
default, it does nothing. If you wanted a server to implement further connection setup
such as establishing a SSL connection, you could implement it here.

Here is an example of a handler class that implements a simple time server that
operates with streams or datagrams:

```
try:
    from socketserver import BaseRequestHandler   # Python 3
except ImportError:
    from SocketServer import BaseRequestHandler   # Python 2
import socket
import time

class TimeServer(BaseRequestHandler):
    def handle(self):
        resp = time.ctime() + "\r\n"
        if isinstance(self.request,socket.socket):
            # A stream-oriented connection
            self.request.sendall(resp.encode('latin-1'))
        else:
            # A datagram-oriented connection
            self.server.socket.sendto(resp.encode('latin-1'),self.client_address)
```

If you know that a handler is only going to operate on stream-oriented connections
such as TCP, have it inherit from `StreamRequestHandler` instead of
`BaseRequestHandler`. This class sets two attributes: *h*.`wfile` is a file-like object that
writes data to the client, and *h*.`rfile` is a file-like object that reads data from the
client. Here is an example:

```
try:
    from socketserver import StreamRequestHandler   # Python 3
except ImportError:
    from SocketServer import StreamRequestHandler   # Python 2
import time
```

```
class TimeServer(StreamRequestHandler):
    def handle(self):
        resp = time.ctime() + "\r\n"
        self.wfile.write(resp.encode('latin-1'))
```

If you are writing a handler that only operates with packets and always sends a response back to the sender, have it inherit from `DatagramRequestHandler` instead of `BaseRequestHandler`. It provides the same file-like interface as `StreamRequestHandler`. For example:

```
try:
    from socketserver import DatagramRequestHandler  # Python 3
except ImportError:
    from SocketServer import DatagramRequestHandler  # Python 2
import time

class TimeServer(DatagramRequestHandler):
    def handle(self):
        resp = time.ctime() + "\r\n"
        self.wfile.write(resp.encode('latin-1')
```

In this case, all of the data written to `self.wfile` is collected into a single packet that is returned after the `handle()` method returns.

Servers

To use a handler, it has to be plugged into a server object. There are four basic server classes defined:

TCPServer(*address, handler*)

A server supporting the TCP protocol using IPv4. *address* is a tuple of the form (*host, port*). *handler* is an instance of a subclass of the `BaseRequestHandler` class described later.

UDPServer(*address, handler*)

A server supporting the Internet UDP protocol using IPv4. *address* and *handler* are the same as for `TCPServer()`.

UnixStreamServer(*address, handler*)

A server implementing a stream-oriented protocol using UNIX domain sockets. Inherits from `TCPServer`.

UnixDatagramServer(*address, handler*)

A server implementing a datagram protocol using UNIX domain sockets. This inherits from `UDPServer`.

Instances of all four server classes have the following basic methods:

s.fileno()

Returns the integer file descriptor for the server socket. The presence of this method makes it legal to use server instances with polling operations such as the `select()` function.

s.serve_forever()

Handles an infinite number of requests.

s.shutdown()

Stops the serve_forever() loop.

The following attributes give some basic information about the configuration of a running server:

s.RequestHandlerClass

The user-provided request handler class that was passed to the server constructor.

s.server_address

The address on which the server is listening, such as the tuple ('127.0.0.1', 80).

s.socket

The socket object being used for incoming requests.

Here is an example of running the TimeHandler as a TCP server:

```
from SocketServer import TCPServer

serv = TCPServer(('',10000,TimeHandler)
serv.serve_forever()
```

Here is an example of running the handler as a UDP server:

```
from SocketServer import UDPServer

serv = UDPServer(('',10000,TimeHandler)
serv.serve_forever()
```

A key aspect of the SocketServer module is that handlers are decoupled from servers. That is, once you have written a handler, you can plug it into many different kinds of servers without having to change its implementation.

Defining Customized Servers

Servers often need special configuration to account for different network address families, timeouts, concurrency, and other features. This customization is carried out by inheriting from one of the four basic servers described in the previous section. The following class attributes can be defined to customize basic settings of the underlying network socket:

Server.address_family

The address family used by the server socket. The default value is socket.AF_INET. Use socket.AF_INET6 if you want to use IPv6.

Server.allow_reuse_address

A Boolean flag that indicates whether or not a socket should reuse an address. This is useful when you want to immediately restart a server on the same port after a program has terminated (otherwise, you have to wait a few minutes). The default value is False.

Server.request_queue_size

The size of the request queue that's passed to the socket's listen() method. The default value is 5.

Server.`socket_type`

The socket type used by the server, such as `socket.SOCK_STREAM` or `socket.SOCK_DGRAM`.

Server.`timeout`

Timeout period in seconds that the server waits for a new request. On timeout, the server calls the `handle_timeout()` method (described below) and goes back to waiting. This timeout is *not* used to set a socket timeout. However, if a socket timeout has been set, its value is used instead of this value.

Here is an example of how to create a server that allows the port number to be reused:

```
from SocketServer import TCPServer

class TimeServer(TCPServer):
    allow_reuse_address = True

serv = TimeServer(('',10000,TimeHandler)
serv.serve_forever()
```

If desired, the following methods are most useful to extend in classes that inherit from one of the servers. If you define any of these methods in your own server, make sure you call the same method in the superclass.

Server.`activate()`

Method that carries out the `listen()` operation on the server. The server socket is referenced as `self.socket`.

Server.`bind()`

Method that carries out the `bind()` operation on the server.

Server.`handle_error(`*request, client_address*`)`

Method that handles uncaught exceptions that occur in handling. To get information about the last exception, use `sys.exc_info()` or functions in the `traceback` module.

Server.`handle_timeout()`

Method that is called when the server timeout occurs. By redefining this method and adjusting the timeout setting, you can integrate other processing into the server event loop.

Server.`verify_request(`*request, client_address*`)`

Method that is called to verify the connection before any further processing. By redefining this method, you can implement a firewall or perform other kinds of a validation.

Finally, additional server features are available through the use of mixin classes. This is how concurrency via threads or processing forking is added. The following classes are defined for this purpose:

`ForkingMixIn`

A mixin class that adds UNIX process forking to a server, allowing it to serve multiple clients. The class variable `max_children` controls the maximum number of child processes, and the timeout variable determines how much time elapses between attempts to collect zombie processes. An instance variable active_children keeps track of how many active processes are running.

ThreadingMixIn

A mixin class that modifies a server so that it can serve multiple clients with threads. There is no limit placed on the number of threads that can be created. By default, threads are non-daemonic unless the class variable daemon_threads is set to True.

To add these features to a server, you use multiple inheritance where the mixin class is listed first. For example, here is a forking time server:

```
from SocketServer import TCPServer, ForkingMixIn

class TimeServer(ForkingMixIn, TCPServer):
    allow_reuse_address = True
    max_children = 10

serv = TimeServer(('',10000,TimeHandler)
serv.serve_forever()
```

Since concurrent servers are relatively common, the SocketServer predefines the following server classes for this purpose.

- ForkingUDPServer(*address*, *handler*)
- ForkingTCPServer(*address*, *handler*)
- ThreadingUDPServer(*address*, *handler*)
- ThreadingTCPServer(*address*, *handler*)

These classes are actually just defined in terms of the mixins and server classes. For example, here is the definition of ForkingTCPServer:

```
class ForkingTCPServer(ForkingMixIn, TCPServer): pass
```

Customization of Application Servers

Other library modules often use the SocketServer class to implement servers for application-level protocols such as HTTP and XML-RPC. Those servers can also be customized via inheritance and extending the methods defined for basic server operation. For example, here is a forking XML-RPC server that only accepts connections originating on the loopback interface:

```
try:
    from xmlrpc.server import SimpleXMLRPCServer      # Python 3
    from socketserver import ForkingMixIn
except ImportError:                                   # Python 2
    from SimpleXMLRPCServer import SimpleXMLRPCServer
    from SocketServer import ForkingMixIn

class MyXMLRPCServer(ForkingMixIn,SimpleXMLRPCServer):
    def verify_request(self, request, client_address):
        host, port = client_address
        if host != '127.0.0.1':
            return False
        return SimpleXMLRPCServer.verify_request(self,request,client_address)
```

```
# Sample use
def add(x,y):
    return x+y
server = MyXMLRPCServer(("",45000))
server.register_function(add)
server.serve_forever()
```

To test this, you will need to use the xmlrpclib module. Run the previous server and then start a separate Python process:

```
>>> import xmlrpclib
>>> s = xmlrpclib.ServerProxy("http://localhost:45000")
>>> s.add(3,4)
7
>>>
```

To test the rejection of connections, try the same code, but from a different machine on the network. For this, you will need to replace "localhost" with the hostname of the machine that's running the server.

## 22

Internet Application Programming

This chapter describes modules related to Internet application protocols including HTTP, XML-RPC, FTP, and SMTP. Web programming topics such as CGI scripting are covered in Chapter 23, "Web Programming." Modules related to dealing with common Internet-related data formats are covered in Chapter 24, "Internet Data Handling and Encoding."

The organization of network-related library modules is one area where there are significant differences between Python 2 and 3. In the interest of looking forward, this chapter assumes the Python 3 library organization because it is more logical. However, the functionality provided by the library modules is virtually identical between Python versions as of this writing. When applicable, Python 2 module names are noted in each section.

ftplib

The `ftplib` module implements the client side of the FTP protocol. It's rarely necessary to use this module directly because the `urllib` package provides a higher-level interface. However, this module may still be useful if you want to have more control over the low-level details of an FTP connection. In order to use this module, it may be helpful to know some of the details of the FTP protocol which is described in Internet RFC 959.

A single class is defined for establishing an FTP connection:

`FTP([host [, user [, passwd [, acct [, timeout]]]]])`

Creates an object representing an FTP connection. *host* is a string specifying a host name. *user*, *passwd*, and *acct* optionally specify a username, password, and account. If no arguments are given, the `connect()` and `login()` methods must be called explicitly to initiate the actual connection. If *host* is given, `connect()` is automatically invoked. If *user*, *passwd*, and *acct* are given, `login()` is invoked. *timeout* is a timeout period in seconds.

An instance *f* of `FTP` has the following methods:

`f.abort()`

Attempts to abort a file transfer that is in progress. This may or may not work depending on the remote server.

`f.close()`

Closes the FTP connection. After this has been invoked, no further operations can be performed on the FTP object `f`.

`f.connect(host [, port [, timeout]])`

Opens an FTP connection to a given host and port. `host` is a string specifying the host name. `port` is the integer port number of the FTP server and defaults to port 21. `timeout` is the timeout period in seconds. It is not necessary to call this if a host name was already given to `FTP()`.

`f.cwd(pathname)`

Changes the current working directory on the server to `pathname`.

`f.delete(filename)`

Removes the file `filename` from the server.

`f.dir([dirname [, ... [, callback]]])`

Generates a directory listing as produced by the `'LIST'` command. `dirname` optionally supplies the name of a directory to list. In addition, if any additional arguments are supplied, they are simply passed as additional arguments to `'LIST'`. If the last argument `callback` is a function, it is used as a callback function to process the returned directory listing data. This callback function works in the same way as the callback used by the `retrlines()` method. By default, this method prints the directory list to `sys.stdout`.

`f.login([user, [passwd [, acct]]])`

Logs in to the server using the specified username, password, and account. `user` is a string giving the username and defaults to `'anonymous'`. `passwd` is a string containing the password and defaults to the empty string `''`. `acct` is a string and defaults to the empty string. It is not necessary to call this method if this information was already given to `FTP()`.

`f.mkd(pathname)`

Creates a new directory on the server.

`f.ntransfercmd(command [, rest])`

The same as `transfercmd()` except that a tuple (`sock, size`) is returned where `sock` is a socket object corresponding to the data connection and `size` is the expected size of the data in bytes, or `None` if the size could not be determined.

`f.pwd()`

Returns a string containing the current working directory on the server.

`f.quit()`

Closes the FTP connection by sending the `'QUIT'` command to the server.

`f.rename(oldname, newname)`

Renames a file on the server.

f.retrbinary(*command, callback* [, *blocksize* [, *rest*]])

Returns the results of executing a command on the server using binary transfer mode. *command* is a string that specifies the appropriate file retrieval command and is almost always 'RETR *filename*'. *callback* is a callback function that is invoked each time a block of data is received. This callback function is invoked with a single argument which is the received data in the form of a string. *blocksize* is the maximum block size to use and defaults to 8192 bytes. *rest* is an optional offset into the file. If supplied, this specifies the position in the file where you want to start the transfer. However, this is not supported by all FTP servers so this may result in an error_reply exception.

f.retrlines(*command* [, *callback*])

Returns the results of executing a command on the server using text transfer mode. *command* is a string that specifies the command and is usually something like 'RETR *filename*'. *callback* is a callback function that is invoked each time a line of data is received. This callback function is called with a single argument which is a string containing the received data. If *callback* is omitted, the returned data is printed to sys.stdout.

f.rmd(*pathname*)

Removes a directory from the server.

f.sendcmd(*command*)

Sends a simple command to the server and returns the server response. *command* is a string containing the command. This method should only be used for commands that don't involve the transfer of data.

f.set_pasv(*pasv*)

Sets passive mode. *pasv* is a Boolean flag that turns passive mode on if True or off if False. By default, passive mode is on.

f.size(*filename*)

Returns the size of *filename* in bytes. Returns None if the size can't be determined for some reason.

f.storbinary(*command, file* [, *blocksize*])

Executes a command on the server and transmits data using binary transfer mode. *command* is a string that specifies the low-level command. It is almost always set to 'STOR *filename*', where *filename* is the name of a file you want to place on the server. *file* is an open file-object from which data will be read using file.read(*blocksize*) and transferred to the server. *blocksize* is the blocksize to use in the transfer. By default, it is 8192 bytes.

f.storlines(*command, file*)

Executes a command on the server and transfers data using text transfer mode. *command* is a string which specifies the low-level command. It is usually 'STOR *filename*'. *file* is an open file-object from which data will be read using file.readline() and sent to the server.

f.transfercmd(*command* [, *rest*])

Initiates a transfer over the FTP data connection. If active mode is being used, this sends a 'PORT' or 'EPRT' command and accepts the resulting connection from the server. If passive mode is being used, this sends a 'EPSV' or 'PASV' command followed by a connection to the server. In either case, once the data connection has been established, the FTP command in *command* is then issued. This function returns a socket object corresponding to the open data connection. The optional *rest* parameter specifies a starting byte offset into files requested on the server. However, this is not supported on all servers and could result in an error_reply exception.

Example

The following example shows how to use this module to upload a file to a FTP server:

```
host     = "ftp.foo.com"
username = "dave"
password = "1235"
filename = "somefile.dat"

import ftplib
ftp_serv = ftplib.FTP(host,username,password)
# Open the file you want to send
f = open(filename,"rb")
# Send it to the FTP server
resp = ftp_serv.storbinary("STOR "+filename, f)
# Close the connection
ftp_serv.close
```

To fetch documents from an FTP server, use the urllib package. For example:

```
try:
    from urllib.request import urlopen    # Python 3
except ImportError:
    from urllib2 import urlopen           # Python 2

u = urlopen("ftp://username:password@somehostname/somefile")
contents = u.read()
```

http **Package**

The http package consists of modules for writing HTTP clients and servers as well as support for state management (cookies). The Hypertext Transfer Protocol (HTTP) is a simple text-based protocol that works as follows:

1. A client makes a connection to an HTTP server and sends a request header of the following form:

```
GET /document.html HTTP/1.0
Connection: Keep-Alive
User-Agent: Mozilla/4.61 [en] (X11; U; SunOS 5.6 sun4u)
Host: rustler.cs.uchicago.edu:8000
Accept: image/gif, image/x-xbitmap, image/jpeg, image/pjpeg, image/png, */*
Accept-Encoding: gzip
Accept-Language: en
Accept-Charset: iso-8859-1,*,utf-8

Optional data
...
```

The first line defines the request type, document (the selector), and protocol version. Following the request line is a series of header lines containing various information about the client, such as passwords, cookies, cache preferences, and client software. Following the header lines, a single blank line indicates the end of the header lines. After the header, data may appear in the event that the request is sending information from a form or uploading a file. Each of the lines in the header should be terminated by a carriage return and a newline (`'\r\n'`).

2. The server sends a response of the following form:

```
HTTP/1.0  200  OK
Content-type: text/html
Content-length:  72883 bytes
...
Header: data

Data
...
```

The first line of the server response indicates the HTTP protocol version, a success code, and a return message. Following the response line is a series of header fields that contain information about the type of the returned document, the document size, web server software, cookies, and so forth. The header is terminated by a single blank line followed by the raw data of the requested document.

The following request methods are the most common:

Method	Description
GET	Get a document.
POST	Post data to a form.
HEAD	Return header information only.
PUT	Upload data to the server.

The response codes detailed in Table 22.1 are most commonly returned by servers. The Symbolic Constant column is the name of a predefined variable in `http.client` that holds the integer response code value and which can be used in code to improve readability.

Table 22.1   **Response Codes Commonly Returned by Servers**

Code	Description	Symbolic Constant
Success Codes (2xx)		
200	OK	OK
201	Created	CREATED
202	Accepted	ACCEPTED
204	No content	NO_CONTENT
Redirection (3xx)		
300	Multiple choices	MULTIPLE_CHOICES
301	Moved permanently	MOVED_PERMANENTLY
302	Moved temporarily	MOVED_TEMPORARILY
303	Not modified	NOT_MODIFIED

Table 22.1　**Continued**

Code	Description	Symbolic Constant
Client Error (4xx)		
400	Bad request	BAD_REQUEST
401	Unauthorized	UNAUTHORIZED
403	Forbidden	FORBIDDEN
404	Not found	NOT_FOUND
Server Error (5xx)		
500	Internal server error	INTERNAL_SERVER_ERROR
501	Not implemented	NOT_IMPLEMENTED
502	Bad gateway	BAD_GATEWAY
503	Service unavailable	SERVICE_UNAVAILABLE

The headers that appear in both requests and responses are encoded in a format widely known as RFC-822. Then general form of each header is *Headername: data*, although further details can be found in the RFC. It is almost never necessary to parse these headers as Python usually does it for you when applicable.

http.client (httplib)

The http.client module provides low-level support for the client side of HTTP. In Python 2, this module is called httplib. Use functions in the urllib package instead. The module supports both HTTP/1.0 and HTTP/1.1 and additionally allows connections via SSL if Python is built with OpenSSL support. Normally, you do not use this package directly; instead, you should consider using the urllib package. However, because HTTP is such an important protocol, you may encounter situations where you need to work with the low-level details in a way that urllib cannot easily address—for example, if you wanted to send requests with commands other than GET or POST. For more details about HTTP, consult RFC 2616 (HTTP/1.1) and RFC 1945 (HTTP/1.0).

The following classes can be used to establish an HTTP connection with a server:

HTTPConnection(*host* [,*port*])

Creates an HTTP connection. *host* is the host name, and *port* is the remote port number. The default port is 80. Returns an HTTPConnection instance.

HTTPSConnection(*host* [, *port* [, key_file=*kfile* [, cert_file=*cfile*]]])

Creates an HTTP connection but uses a secure socket. The default port is 443. key_file and cert_file are optional keyword arguments that specify client PEM-formatted private-key and certificate chain files, should they be needed for client authentication. However, no validation of server certificates is performed. Returns an HTTPSConnection instance.

An instance, *h*, of HTTPConnection or HTTPSConnection supports the following methods:

h.connect()

Initializes the connection to the host and port given to HTTPConnection() or HTTPSConnection(). Other methods call this automatically if a connection hasn't been made yet.

h.close()

Closes the connection.

h.send(*bytes*)

Sends a byte string, *bytes*, to the server. Direct use of this function is discouraged because it may break the underlying response/request protocol. It's most commonly used to send data to the server after h.endheaders() has been called.

h.putrequest(*method, selector* [, *skip_host* [, *skip_accept_encoding*]])

Sends a request to the server. *method* is the HTTP method, such as 'GET' or 'POST'. *selector* specifies the object to be returned, such as '/index.html'. The *skip_host* and *skip_accept_encoding* parameters are flags that disable the sending of Host: and Accept-Encoding: headers in the HTTP request. By default, both of these arguments are False. Because the HTTP/1.1 protocol allows multiple requests to be sent over a single connection, a CannotSendRequest exception may be raised if the connection is in a state that prohibits new requests from being issued.

h.putheader(*header, value, ...*)

Sends an RFC-822–style header to the server. It sends a line to the server, consisting of the header, a colon and a space, and the value. Additional arguments are encoded as continuation lines in the header. Raises a CannotSendHeader exception if *h* is not in a state that allows headers to be sent.

h.endheaders()

Sends a blank line to the server, indicating the end of the header lines.

h.request(*method, url* [, *body* [, *headers*]])

Sends a complete HTTP request to the server. *method* and *url* have the same meaning as for h.putrequest(). *body* is an optional string containing data to upload to the server after the request has been sent. If *body* is supplied, the Context-length: header will automatically be set to an appropriate value. *headers* is a dictionary containing *header:value* pairs to be given to the h.putheader() method.

h.getresponse()

Gets a response from the server and returns an HTTPResponse instance that can be used to read data. Raises a ResponseNotReady exception if *h* is not in a state where a response would be received.

An HTTPResponse instance, *r*, as returned by the getresponse() method, supports the following methods:

`r.read([size])`

Reads up to *size* bytes from the server. If *size* is omitted, all the data for this request is returned.

`r.getheader(name [,default])`

Gets a response header. *name* is the name of the header. *default* is the default value to return if the header is not found.

`r.getheaders()`

Returns a list of (*header*, *value*) tuples.

An HTTPResponse instance *r* also has the following attributes:

`r.version`

HTTP version used by the server.

`r.status`

HTTP status code returned by the server.

`r.reason`

HTTP error message returned by the server.

`r.length`

Number of bytes left in the response.

Exceptions

The following exceptions may be raised in the course of handling HTTP connections:

Exception	Description
HTTPException	Base class of all HTTP-related errors.
NotConnected	Request was made but not connected.
InvalidURL	Bad URL or port number given.
UnknownProtocol	Unknown HTTP protocol number.
UnknownTransferEncoding	Unknown transfer encoding.
UnimplementedFileMode	Unimplemented file mode.
IncompleteRead	Incomplete data received.
BadStatusLine	Unknown status code received.

The following exceptions are related to the state of HTTP/1.1 connections. Because HTTP/1.1 allows multiple requests/responses to be sent over a single connection, extra rules are imposed as to when requests can be sent and responses received. Performing operations in the wrong order will generate an exception.

Exception	Description
ImproperConnectionState	Base class of all HTTP-connection state errors.
CannotSendRequest	Can't send a request.
CannotSendHeader	Can't send headers.
ResponseNotReady	Can't read a response.

Example

The following example shows how the HTTPConnection class can be used to perform a memory-efficient file upload to a server using a POST request—something that is not easily accomplished within the urllib framework.

```python
import os
try:
    from httplib import HTTPConnection      # Python 2
except ImportError:
    from http.client import HTTPConnection  # Python 3

BOUNDARY = "$Python-Essential-Reference$"
CRLF     = '\r\n'

def upload(addr, url, formfields, filefields):
    # Create the sections for form fields
    formsections = []
    for name in formfields:
        section = [
            '--'+BOUNDARY,
            'Content-disposition: form-data; name="%s"' % name,
            '',
            formfields[name]
            ]
        formsections.append(CRLF.join(section)+CRLF)

    # Collect information about all of the files to be uploaded
    fileinfo = [(os.path.getsize(filename), formname, filename)
                    for formname, filename in filefields.items()]

    # Create the HTTP headers for each file
    filebytes = 0
    fileheaders = []
    for filesize, formname,filename in fileinfo:
        headers = [
            '--'+BOUNDARY,
            'Content-Disposition: form-data; name="%s"; filename="%s"' % \
                        (formname, filename),
            'Content-length: %d' % filesize,
            ''
            ]
        fileheaders.append(CRLF.join(headers)+CRLF)
        filebytes += filesize

    # Closing marker
    closing = "--"+BOUNDARY+"--\r\n"

    # Determine the entire length of the request
    content_size = (sum(len(f) for f in  formsections) +
                    sum(len(f) for f in  fileheaders) +
                    filebytes+len(closing))

    # Upload it
    conn = HTTPConnection(*addr)
    conn.putrequest("POST",url)
    conn.putheader("Content-type", 'multipart/form-data; boundary=%s' % BOUNDARY)
    conn.putheader("Content-length", str(content_size))
    conn.endheaders()
```

```
    # Send all form sections
    for s in formsections:
        conn.send(s.encode('latin-1'))

    # Send all files
    for head,filename in zip(fileheaders,filefields.values()):
        conn.send(head.encode('latin-1'))
        f = open(filename,"rb")
        while True:
            chunk = f.read(16384)
            if not chunk: break
            conn.send(chunk)
        f.close()
    conn.send(closing.encode('latin-1'))
    r = conn.getresponse()
    responsedata = r.read()
    conn.close()
    return responsedata

# Sample: Upload some files.  The form fields 'name', 'email'
# 'file_1','file_2', and so forth are what the remote server
# is expecting (obviously this will vary).
server      = ('localhost', 8080)
url         = '/cgi-bin/upload.py'
formfields = {
    'name' : 'Dave',
    'email' : 'dave@dabeaz.com'
}
filefields = {
    'file_1' : 'IMG_1008.JPG',
    'file_2' : 'IMG_1757.JPG'
}
resp = upload(server, url,formfields,filefields)
print(resp)
```

http.server (BaseHTTPServer, CGIHTTPServer, SimpleHTTPServer)

The http.server module provides various classes for implementing HTTP servers. In Python 2, the contents of this module are split across three library modules: BaseHTTPServer, CGIHTTPServer, and SimpleHTTPServer.

HTTPServer

The following class implements a basic HTTP server. In Python 2, it is located in the BaseHTTPServer module.

HTTPServer(*server_address*, *request_handler*)

Creates a new HTTPServer object. *server_address* is a tuple of the form (*host*, *port*) on which the server will listen. *request_handler* is a handler class derived from BaseHTTPRequestHandler, which is described later.

HTTPServer inherits directly from TCPServer defined in the socketserver module. Thus, if you want to customize the operation of the HTTP server in any way, you inherit from HTTPServer and extend it. Here is how you would define a multithreaded HTTP server that only accepts connections from a specific subnet:

```
try:
    from http.server import HTTPServer       # Python 3
    from socketserver import ThreadingMixIn
except ImportError:
    from BaseHTTPServer import HTTPServer     # Python 2
    from SocketServer import ThreadingMixIn

class MyHTTPServer(ThreadingMixIn,HTTPServer):
    def __init__(self,addr,handler,subnet):
        HTTPServer.__init__(self,addr,handler)
        self.subnet = subnet
    def verify_request(self, request, client_address):
        host, port = client_address
        if not host.startswith(subnet):
            return False
        return HTTPServer.verify_request(self,request,client_address)

# Example of how the server runs
serv = MyHTTPServer(('',8080), SomeHandler, '192.168.69.')
serv.serve_forever()
```

The HTTPServer class only deals with the low-level HTTP protocol. To get the server to actually do anything, you have to supply a handler class. There are two built-in handlers and a base class that can be used for defining your own custom handling. These are described next.

SimpleHTTPRequestHandler **and** CGIHTTPRequestHandler

Two prebuilt web server handler classes can be used if you want to quickly set up a simple stand-alone web server. These classes operate independently of any third-party web server such as Apache.

CGIHTTPRequestHandler(*request, client_address, server*)

Serves files from the current directory and all its subdirectories. In addition, the handler will run a file as a CGI script if it's located in a special CGI directory (defined by the cgi_directories class variable which is set to ['/cgi-bin', '/htbin'] by default). The handler supports GET, HEAD, and POST methods. However, it does not support HTTP redirects (HTTP code 302), which limits its use to only more simple CGI applications. For security purposes, CGI scripts are executed with a UID of nobody. In Python 2, this class is defined in the CGIHTTPServer module.

SimpleHTTPRequestHandler(*request, client_address, server*)

Serves files from the current directory and all its subdirectories. The class provides support for HEAD and GET requests, respectively. All IOError exceptions result in a "404 File not found" error. Attempts to access a directory result in a "403 Directory listing not supported" error. In Python 2, this class is defined in the SimpleHTTPServer module.

Both of these handlers define the following class variables that can be changed via inheritance if desired:

handler.server_version

Server version string returned to clients. By default, this is set to a string such as 'SimpleHTTP/0.6'.

`handler.extensions_map`

A dictionary mapping suffixes to MIME types. Unrecognized file types are considered to be of type `'application/octet-stream'`.

Here is an example of using these handler classes to run a stand-alone web server capable of running CGI scripts:

```
try:
    from http.server import HTTPServer, CGIHTTPRequestHandler  # Python 3
except ImportError:
    from BaseHTTPServer import HTTPServer                       # Python 2
    from CGIHTTPServer import CGIHTTPRequestHandler
import os

# Change to the document root
os.chdir("/home/httpd/html")
# Start the CGIHTTP server on port 8080
serv = HTTPServer(("",8080),CGIHTTPRequestHandler)
serv.serve_forever()
```

BaseHTTPRequestHandler

The `BaseHTTPRequestHandler` class is a base class that's used if you want to define your own custom HTTP server handling. The prebuilt handlers such as `SimpleHTTPRequestHandler` and `CGIHTTPRequestHandler` inherit from this. In Python 2, this class is defined in the `BaseHTTPServer` module.

`BaseHTTPRequestHandler(request, client_address, server)`

Base handler class used to handle HTTP requests. When a connection is received, the request and HTTP headers are parsed. An attempt is then made to execute a method of the form do_*REQUEST* based on the request type. For example, a `'GET'` method invokes do_GET() and a `'POST'` method invokes do_POST. By default, this class does nothing, so these methods are expected to be defined in subclasses.

The following class variables are defined for `BaseHTTPRequestHandler` and can be redefined in subclasses.

`BaseHTTPRequestHandler.server_version`

Specifies the server software version string that the server reports to clients—for example, `'ServerName/1.2'`.

`BaseHTTPRequestHandler.sys_version`

Python system version, such as `'Python/2.6'`.

`BaseHTTPRequestHandler.error_message_format`

Format string used to build error messages sent to the client. The format string is applied to a dictionary containing the attributes code, message, and explain. For example:

```
'''<head>
<title>Error response</title>
</head>
<body>
<h1>Error response</h1>
<p>Error code %(code)d.
<p>Message: %(message)s.
<p>Error code explanation: %(code)s = %(explain)s.
</body>'''
```

BaseHTTPRequestHandler.protocol_version

HTTP protocol version used in responses. The default is 'HTTP/1.0'.

BaseHTTPRequestHandler.responses

Mapping of integer HTTP error codes to two-element tuples (*message*, *explain*) that describe the problem. For example, the integer code 404 is mapped to ("Not Found", "Nothing matches the given URI"). The integer code and strings in this mapping are use when creating error messages as defined in the error_message_format attribute shown previously.

When created to handle a connection, an instance, *b*, of BaseHTTPRequestHandler has the following attributes:

Attribute	Description
b.client_address	Client address as a tuple (host, port).
b.command	Request type, such as 'GET', 'POST', 'HEAD', and so on.
b.path	The request path such as '/index.html'.
b.request_version	HTTP version string from the request, such as 'HTTP/1.0'.
b.headers	HTTP headers stored in a mapping object. To test for or extract the contents of a header, use dictionary operations such as *headername* in *b*.headers or *headerval* = *b*.headers[*headername*].
b.rfile	Input stream for reading optional input data. This is used when a client is uploading data (for example, during a POST request).
b.wfile	Output stream for writing a response back to the client.

The following methods are commonly used or redefined in subclasses:

b.send_error(*code* [, *message*])

Sends a response for an unsuccessful request. *code* is the numeric HTTP response code. *message* is an optional error message. log_error() is called to record the error. This method creates a complete error response using the error_message_format class variable, sends it to the client, and closes the connection. No further operations should be performed after calling this.

b.send_response(*code* [, *message*])

Sends a response for a successful request. The HTTP response line is sent, followed by Server and Date headers. *code* is an HTTP response code, and *message* is an optional message. log_request() is called to record the request.

b.send_header(*keyword*, *value*)

Writes a MIME header entry to the output stream. *keyword* is the header keyword, and *value* is its value. This should only be called after send_response().

b.end_headers()

Sends a blank line to signal the end of the MIME headers.

b.`log_request([code [, size]])`

Logs a successful request. *code* is the HTTP code, and *size* is the size of the response in bytes (if available). By default, `log_message()` is called for logging.

b.`log_error(format, ...)`

Logs an error message. By default, `log_message()` is called for logging.

b.`log_message(format, ...)`

Logs an arbitrary message to `sys.stderr`. *format* is a format string applied to any additional arguments passed. The client address and current time are prefixed to every message.

Here is an example of creating a custom HTTP server that runs in a separate thread and lets you monitor the contents of a dictionary, interpreting the request path as a key.

```
try:
    from http.server import BaseHTTPRequestHandler, HTTPServer      # Py 3
except ImportError:
    from BaseHTTPServer import BaseHTTPRequestHandler, HTTPServer    # Py 2

class DictRequestHandler(BaseHTTPRequestHandler):
    def __init__(self,thedict,*args,**kwargs):
        self.thedict = thedict
        BaseHTTPRequestHandler.__init__(self,*args,**kwargs)

    def do_GET(self):
        key = self.path[1:]         # Strip the leading '/'
        if not key in self.thedict:
            self.send_error(404, "No such key")
        else:
            self.send_response(200)
            self.send_header('content-type','text/plain')
            self.end_headers()
            resp  = "Key   : %s\n" % key
            resp += "Value: %s\n" % self.thedict[key]
            self.wfile.write(resp.encode('latin-1'))

# Example use
d = {
    'name' : 'Dave',
    'values' : [1,2,3,4,5],
    'email' : 'dave@dabeaz.com'
}
from functools import partial
serv = HTTPServer(("",9000), partial(DictRequestHandler,d))

import threading
d_mon = threading.Thread(target=serv.serve_forever)
d_mon.start()
```

To test this example, run the server and then enter a URL such as http://localhost:9000/name or http://localhost:9000/values into a browser. If it works, you'll see the contents of the dictionary being displayed.

This example also shows a technique for how to get servers to instantiate handler classes with extra parameters. Normally, servers create handlers using a predefined set of arguments that are passed to `__init__()`. If you want to add additional parameters, use the `functools.partial()` function as shown. This creates a callable object that includes your extra parameter but preserves the calling signature expected by the server.

http.cookies (Cookie)

The http.cookies module provides server-side support for working with HTTP cookies. In Python 2, the module is called Cookie.

Cookies are used to provide state management in servers that implement sessions, user logins, and related features. To drop a cookie on a user's browser, an HTTP server typically adds an HTTP header similar to the following to an HTTP response:

```
Set-Cookie: session=8273612; expires=Sun, 18-Feb-2001 15:00:00 GMT; \
            path=/; domain=foo.bar.com
```

Alternatively, a cookie can be set by embedding JavaScript in the <head> section of an HTML document:

```
<SCRIPT LANGUAGE="JavaScript">
document.cookie = "session=8273612; expires=Sun, 18-Feb-2001 15:00:00 GMT; \
    Feb 17; Path=/; Domain=foo.bar.com;"
</SCRIPT>
```

The http.cookies module simplifies the task of generating cookie values by providing a special dictionary-like object which stores and manages collections of cookie values known as *morsels*. Each morsel has a name, a value, and a set of optional attributes containing metadata to be supplied to the browser {expires, path, comment, domain, max-age, secure, version, httponly}. The name is usually a simple identifier such as "name" and must not be the same as one of the metadata names such as "expires" or "path". The value is usually a short string. To create a cookie, simply create a cookie object like this:

```
c = SimpleCookie()
```

Next, cookie values (morsels) can be set using ordinary dictionary assignment:

```
c["session"] = 8273612
c["user"] = "beazley"
```

Additional attributes of a specific morsel are set as follows:

```
c["session"]["path"] = "/"
c["session"]["domain"] = "foo.bar.com"
c["session"]["expires"] = "18-Feb-2001 15:00:00 GMT"
```

To create output representing the cookie data as a set of HTTP headers, use the c.output() method. For example:

```
print(c.output())
# Produces two lines of output
# Set-Cookie: session=8273612; expires=...; path=/; domain=...
# Set-Cookie: user=beazley
```

When a browser sends a cookie back to an HTTP server, it is encoded as a string of *key=value* pairs, such as "session=8273612; user=beazley". Optional attributes such as expires, path, and domain are not returned. The cookie string can usually be found in the HTTP_COOKIE environment variable, which can be read by CGI applications. To recover cookie values, use code similar to the following:

```
c = SimpleCookie(os.environ["HTTP_COOKIE"])
session = c["session"].value
user    = c["user"].value
```

The following documentation describes the SimpleCookie object in more detail.

`SimpleCookie([input])`

Defines a cookie object in which cookie values are stored as simple strings.

A cookie instance, `c`, provides the following methods:

`c.output([attrs [,header [,sep]]])`

Generates a string suitable for use in setting cookie values in HTTP headers. `attrs` is an optional list of the optional attributes to include (`"expires"`, `"path"`, `"domain"`, and so on). By default, all cookie attributes are included. `header` is the HTTP header to use (`'Set-Cookie:'` by default). `sep` is the character used to join the headers together and is a newline by default.

`c.js_output([attrs])`

Generates a string containing JavaScript code that will set the cookie if executed on a browser supporting JavaScript. `attrs` is an optional list of the attributes to include.

`c.load(rawdata)`

Loads the cookie `c` with data found in `rawdata`. If `rawdata` is a string, it's assumed to be in the same format as the `HTTP_COOKIE` environment variable in a CGI program. If `rawdata` is a dictionary, each `key-value` pair is interpreted by setting `c[key]=value`.

Internally, the `key/value` pairs used to store a cookie value are instances of a `Morsel` class. An instance, `m`, of `Morsel` behaves like a dictionary and allows the optional `"expires"`, `"path"`, `"comment"`, `"domain"`, `"max-age"`, `"secure"`, `"version"`, and `"httponly"` keys to be set. In addition, the morsel `m` has the following methods and attributes:

`m.value`

A string containing the raw value of the cookie.

`m.coded_value`

A string containing the encoded value of the cookie that would be sent to or received from the browser.

`m.key`

The cookie name.

`m.set(key,value,coded_value)`

Sets the values of `m.key`, `m.value`, and `m.coded_value` shown previously.

`m.isReservedKey(k)`

Tests whether `k` is a reserved keyword, such as `"expires"`, `"path"`, `"domain"`, and so on.

`m.output([attrs [,header]])`

Produces the HTTP header string for this morsel. `attrs` is an optional list of the additional attributes to include (`"expires"`, `"path"`, and so on). `header` is the header string to use (`'Set-Cookie:'` by default).

`m.js_output([attrs])`

Outputs JavaScript code that sets the cookie when executed.

m.OutputString([*attrs*])

Returns the cookie string without any HTTP headers or JavaScript code.

Exceptions

If an error occurs during the parsing or generation of cookie values, a `CookieError` exception is raised.

http.cookiejar (cookielib)

The `http.cookiejar` module provides client-side support for storing and managing HTTP cookies. In Python 2, the module is called `cookielib`.

The primary role of this module is to provide objects in which HTTP cookies can be stored so that they can be used in conjunction with the `urllib` package, which is used to access documents on the Internet. For instance, the `http.cookiejar` module can be used to capture cookies and to retransmit them on subsequent connection requests. It can also be used to work with files containing cookie data such as files created by various browsers.

The following objects are defined by the module:

`CookieJar()`

An object that manages HTTP cookie values, storing cookies received as a result of HTTP requests, and adding cookies to outgoing HTTP requests. Cookies are stored entirely in memory and lost when the `CookieJar` instance is garbage-collected.

`FileCookieJar(filename [, delayload ])`

Creates a `FileCookieJar` instance that retrieves and stores cookie information to a file. `filename` is the name of the file. `delayload`, if `True`, enables lazy access to the file. That is, the file won't be read or stored except by demand.

`MozillaCookieJar(filename [, delayload ])`

Creates a `FileCookieJar` instance that is compatible with the Mozilla `cookies.txt` file.

`LWPCookieJar(filename [, delayload ])`

Creates a `FileCookieJar` instance that is compatible with the libwww-perl `Set-Cookie3` file format.

It is somewhat rare to work with the methods and attributes of these objects directly. If you need to know their low-level programming interface, consult the online documentation. Instead, it is more common to simply instantiate one of the cookie jar objects and plug it into something else that wants to work with cookies. An example of this is shown in the `urllib.request` section of this chapter.

smtplib

The `smtplib` module provides a low-level SMTP client interface that can be used to send mail using the SMTP protocol described in RFC 821 and RFC 1869. This module contains a number of low-level functions and methods that are described in detail in the online documentation. However, the following covers the most useful parts of this module:

`SMTP([host [, port]])`

Creates an object representing a connection to an SMTP server. If *host* is given, it specifies the name of the SMTP server. *port* is an optional port number. The default port is 25. If *host* is supplied, the `connect()` method is called automatically. Otherwise, you will need to manually call `connect()` on the returned object to establish the connection.

An instance *s* of `SMTP` has the following methods:

`s.connect([host [, port]])`

Connects to the SMTP server on *host*. If *host* is omitted, a connection is made to the local host (`'127.0.0.1'`). *port* is an optional port number that defaults to 25 if omitted. It is not necessary to call `connect()` if a host name was given to `SMTP()`.

`s.login(user, password)`

Logs into the server if authentication is required. *user* is a username, and *password* is a password.

`s.quit()`

Terminates the session by sending a `'QUIT'` command to the server.

`s.sendmail(fromaddr, toaddrs, message)`

Sends a mail message to the server. *fromaddr* is a string containing the email address of the sender. *toaddrs* is a list of strings containing the email addresses of recipients. *message* is a string containing a completely formatted RFC-822 compliant message. The `email` package is commonly used to create such messages. It is important to note that although *message* can be given as a text string, it should only contain valid ASCII characters with values in the range 0 to 127. Otherwise, you will get an encoding error. If you need to send a message in a different encoding such as UTF-8, encode it into a byte string first and supply the byte string as *message*.

Example

The following example shows how the module can be used to send a message:

```
import smtplib
fromaddr = "someone@some.com"
toaddrs = ["recipient@other.com"]
msg = "From: %s\r\nTo: %s\r\n\r\n" % (fromaddr, ",".join(toaddrs))
msg += """
Refinance your mortgage to buy stocks and Viagra!
"""

server = smtplib.SMTP('localhost')
server.sendmail(fromaddr, toaddrs, msg)
server.quit()
```

`urllib` Package

The `urllib` package provides a high-level interface for writing clients that need to interact with HTTP servers, FTP servers, and local files. Typical applications include scraping data from web pages, automation, proxies, web crawlers, and so forth. This is one of the most highly configurable library modules, so every last detail is not presented here. Instead, the most common uses of the package are described.

In Python 2, the urllib functionality is spread across several different library modules including urllib, urllib2, urlparse, and robotparser. In Python 3, all of this functionality has been consolidated and reorganized under the urllib package.

urllib.request (urllib2)

The urllib.request module provides functions and classes to open and fetch data from URLs. In Python 2, this functionality is found in a module urllib2.

The most common use of this module is to fetch data from web servers using HTTP. For example, this code shows the easiest way to simply fetch a web page:

```
try:
    from urllib.request import urlopen     # Python 3
except ImportError:
    from urllib2 import urlopen            # Python 2

u = urlopen("http://docs.python.org/3.0/library/urllib.request.html")
data = u.read()
```

Of course, many complexities arise when interacting with servers in the real world. For example, you might have to worry about proxy servers, authentication, cookies, user agents, and other matters. All of these are supported, but the code is more complicated (keep reading).

urlopen() and Requests

The most straightforward way to make a request is to use the urlopen() function.

```
urlopen(url [, data [, timeout]])
```

Opens the URL *url* and returns a file-like object that can be used to read the returned data. *url* may either be a string containing a URL or an instance of the Request class, described shortly. *data* is a URL-encoded string containing form data to be uploaded to the server. When supplied, the HTTP 'POST' method is used instead of 'GET' (the default). Data is generally created using a function such as urllib.parse.urlencode(). *timeout* is an optional timeout in seconds for all blocking operations used internally.

The file-like object u returned by urlopen() supports the following methods:

Method	Description
u.read([*nbytes*])	Reads *nbytes* of data as a byte string.
u.readline()	Reads a single line of text as a byte string.
u.readlines()	Reads all input lines and returns a list.
u.fileno()	Returns the integer file descriptor.
u.close()	Closes the connection.
u.info()	Returns a mapping object with meta-information associated with the URL. For HTTP, the HTTP headers included with the server response are returned. For FTP, the headers include 'content-length'. For local files, the headers include a date, 'content-length', and 'content-type' field.
u.getcode()	Returns the HTTP response code as an integer—for example, 200 for success or 404 for file not found.
u.geturl()	Returns the real URL of the returned data, taking into account any redirection that may have occurred.

It is important to emphasize that the file-like object u operates in binary mode. If you need to process the response data as text, you will need to decode it using the codecs module or some other means.

If an error occurs during download, an URLError exception is raised. This includes errors related to the HTTP protocol itself such as forbidden access or requests for authentication. For these kinds of errors, a server typically returns content that gives more descriptive information. To get this content, the exception instance itself operates as a file-like object that can be read. For example:

```
try:
    u = urlopen("http://www.python.org/perl.html")
    resp = u.read()
except HTTPError as e:
    resp = e.read()
```

A very common error that arises with urlopen() is accessing web pages through a proxy server. For example, if your organization routes all web traffic through a proxy, requests may fail. If the proxy server doesn't require any kind of authentication, you may be able to fix this by merely setting the HTTP_PROXY environment variable in the os.environ dictionary. For example, os.environ['HTTP_PROXY'] = 'http://example.com:12345'.

For simple requests, the url parameter to urlopen() is a string such as 'http://www.python.org'. If you need to do anything more complicated such as make modifications to HTTP request headers, create a Request instance and use that as the url parameter.

Request(url [, data [, headers [, origin_req_host [, unverifiable]]]])

Creates a new Request instance. url specifies the URL (for example, 'http://www.foo.bar/spam.html'). data is URL-encoded data to be uploaded to the server in HTTP requests. When this is supplied, it changes the HTTP request type from 'GET' to 'POST'. headers is a dictionary containing key-value mappings representing the contents of the HTTP headers. origin_req_host is set to the request-host of the transaction—typically it's the host name from which the request is originating. unverifiable is set to True if the request is for an unverifiable URL. An *unverifiable* URL is informally defined as a URL not directly entered by the user—for instance, a URL embedded within a page that loads an image. The default value of unverifiable is False.

An instance r of Request has the following methods:

r.add_data(data)

Adds data to a request. If the request is an HTTP request, the method is changed to 'POST'. data is URL-encoded data as described for Request(). This does not append data to any previously set data; it simply replaces the old data with data.

r.add_header(key, val)

Adds header information to the request. key is the header name, and val is the header value. Both arguments are strings.

r.add_unredirected_header(*key*, *val*)

Adds header information to a request that will not be added to redirected requests. *key* and *val* have the same meaning as for add_header().

r.get_data()

Returns the request data (if any).

r.get_full_url()

Returns the full URL of a request.

r.get_host()

Returns the host to which the request will be sent.

r.get_method()

Returns the HTTP method, which is either 'GET' or 'POST'.

r.get_origin_req_host()

Returns the request-host of the originating transaction.

r.get_selector()

Returns the selector part of the URL (for example, '/index.html').

r.get_type()

Returns the URL type (for example, 'http').

r.has_data()

Returns True if data is part of the request.

r.is_unverifiable()

Returns True if the request is unverifiable.

r.has_header(*header*)

Returns True if the request has header *header*.

r.set_proxy(*host*, *type*)

Prepares the request for connecting to a proxy server. This replaces the original host with *host* and the original type of the request with *type*. The selector part of the URL is set to the original URL.

Here is an example that uses a Request object to change the 'User-Agent' header used by urlopen(). You might use this if you wanted a server to think you were making a connection from Internet Explorer, Firefox, or some other browser.

```
headers = {
  'User-Agent':
      'Mozilla/4.0 (compatible; MSIE 7.0; Windows NT 5.1; .NET CLR 2.0.50727)'
}

r = Request("http://somedomain.com/",headers=headers)
u = urlopen(r)
```

Custom Openers

The basic `urlopen()` function does not provide support for authentication, cookies, or other advanced features of HTTP. To add support, you must create your own custom opener object using the `build_opener()` function:

`build_opener([handler1 [, handler2, ... ]])`

Builds a custom opener object for opening URLs. The arguments `handler1`, `handler2`, and so on are all instances of special handler objects. The purpose of these handlers is to add various capabilities to the resulting opener object. The following lists all the available handler objects:

Handler	Description
CacheFTPHandler	FTP handler with persistent FTP connections
FileHandler	Opens local files
FTPHandler	Opens URLs via FTP
HTTPBasicAuthHandler	Basic HTTP authentication handling
HTTPCookieProcessor	Processing of HTTP cookies
HTTPDefaultErrorHandler	Handles HTTP errors by raising an HTTPError exception
HTTPDigestAuthHandler	HTTP digest authentication handling
HTTPHandler	Opens URLs via HTTP
HTTPRedirectHandler	Handles HTTP redirects
HTTPSHandler	Opens URLs via secure HTTP
ProxyHandler	Redirects requests through a proxy
ProxyBasicAuthHandler	Basic proxy authentication
ProxyDigestAuthHandler	Digest proxy authentication
UnknownHandler	Handler that deals with all unknown URLs

By default, an opener is always created with the handlers `ProxyHandler`, `UnknownHandler`, `HTTPHandler`, `HTTPSHandler`, `HTTPDefaultErrorHandler`, `HTTPRedirectHandler`, `FTPHandler`, `FileHandler`, and `HTTPErrorProcessor`. These handlers provide a basic level of functionality. Extra handlers supplied as arguments are added to this list. However, if any of the extra handlers are of the same type as the defaults, they take precedence. For example, if you added an instance of `HTTPHandler` or some class that derived from `HTTPHandler`, it would be used instead of the default.

The object returned by `build_opener()` has a method, `open(url [, data [, timeout]])`, that is used to open URLs according to all the rules provided by the various handlers. The arguments to `open()` are the same as what are passed to the `urlopen()` function.

`install_opener(opener)`

Installs a different opener object for use as the global URL opener used by `urlopen()`. `opener` is usually an opener object created by `build_opener()`.

The next few sections show how to create custom openers for some of the more common scenarios that arise when using `urlib.request` module.

Password Authentication

To handle requests involving password authentication, you create an opener with some combination of HTTPBasicAuthHandler, HTTPDigestAuthHandler, ProxyBasicAuthHandler, or ProxyDigestAuthHandler handlers added to it. Each of these handlers has the following method which can be used to set password:

h.add_password(*realm*, *uri*, *user*, *passwd*)

Adds user and password information for a given realm and URI. All parameters are strings. *uri* can optionally be a sequence of URIs, in which case the user and password information is applied to all the URIs in the sequence. The *realm* is a name or description associated with the authentication. Its value depends on the remote server. However, it's usually a common name associated with a collection of related web pages. *uri* is a base URL associated with the authentication. Typical values for *realm* and *uri* might be something like ('Administrator', 'http://www.somesite.com'). *user* and *password* specify a username and password, respectively.

Here is an example of how to set up an opener with basic authentication:

```
auth = HTTPBasicAuthHandler()
auth.add_password("Administrator","http://www.secretlair.com","drevil","12345")

# Create opener with authentication added
opener = build_opener(auth)

# Open URL
u = opener.open("http://www.secretlair.com/evilplan.html")
```

HTTP Cookies

To manage HTTP cookies, create an opener object with an HTTPCookieProcessor handler added to it. For example:

```
cookiehand = HTTPCookieProcessor()
opener = build_opener(cookiehand)
u = opener.open("http://www.example.com/")
```

By default, the HTTPCookieProcessor uses the CookieJar object found in the http.cookiejar module. Different types of cookie processing can be supported by supplying a different CookieJar object as an argument to HTTPCookieProcessor. For example:

```
cookiehand = HTTPCookieProcessor(
            http.cookiejar.MozillaCookieJar("cookies.txt")
            )
opener = build_opener(cookiehand)
u = opener.open("http://www.example.com/")
```

Proxies

If requests need to be redirected through a proxy, create an instance of ProxyHandler.

ProxyHandler([*proxies*])

Creates a proxy handler that routes requests through a proxy. The argument *proxies* is a dictionary that maps protocol names (for example, 'http', 'ftp', and so on) to the URLs of the corresponding proxy server.

The following example shows how to use this:

```
proxy = ProxyHandler({'http': 'http://someproxy.com:8080/'}
auth  = HTTPBasicAuthHandler()
auth.add_password("realm","host", "username", "password")
opener = build_opener(proxy, auth)

u = opener.open("http://www.example.com/doc.html")
```

urllib.response

This is an internal module that implements the file-like objects returned by functions in the urllib.request module. There is no public API.

urllib.parse

The urllib.parse module is used to manipulate URL strings such as "http://www.python.org".

URL Parsing (urlparse Module in Python 2)

The general form of a URL is "scheme://netloc/path;parameters?query#fragment". In addition, the netloc part of a URL may include a port number such as "hostname:port" or user authentication information such as "user:pass@hostname". The following function is used to parse a URL:

```
urlparse(urlstring [, default_scheme [, allow_fragments]])
```

Parses the URL in urlstring and returns a ParseResult instance. default_scheme specifies the scheme ("http", "ftp", and so on) to be used if none is present in the URL. If allow_fragments is zero, fragment identifiers are not allowed. A ParseResult instance r is a named tuple the form (scheme, netloc, path, parameters, query, fragment). However, the following read-only attributes are also defined:

Attribute	Description
r.scheme	URL scheme specifier (for example, 'http')
r.netloc	Netloc specifier (for example, 'www.python.org')
r.path	Hierarchical path (for example, '/index.html')
r.params	Parameters for the last path element
r.query	Query string (for example, 'name=Dave&id=42')
r.fragment	Fragment identifier without the leading '#'
r.username	Username component if the netloc specifier is of the form 'username:password@hostname'
r.password	Password component from the netloc specifier
r.hostname	Host name component from the netloc specifier
r.port	Port number from the netloc specifier if it is of the form 'hostname:port'

A ParseResult instance can be turned back into a URL string using r.geturl().

urlunparse(*parts*)

Constructs a URL string from a tuple-representation of a URL as returned by urlparse(). *parts* must be a tuple or iterable with six components.

urlsplit(*url* [, *default_scheme* [, *allow_fragments*]])

The same as urlparse() except that the *parameters* portion of a URL is left unmodified in the path. This allows for parsing of URLs where parameters might be attached to individual path components such as 'scheme://netloc/path1;param1/path2;param2/path3?query#fragment'. The result is an instance of SplitResult, which is a named tuple containing (*scheme*, *netloc*, *path*, *query*, *fragment*). The following read-only attributes are also defined:

Attribute	Description
r.scheme	URL scheme specifier (for example, 'http')
r.netloc	Netloc specifier (for example, 'www.python.org')
r.path	Hierarchical path (for example, '/index.html')
r.query	Query string (for example, 'name=Dave&id=42')
r.fragment	Fragment identifier without the leading '#'
r.username	Username component if the netloc specifier is of the form 'username:password@hostname'
r.password	Password component from the netloc specifier
r.hostname	Host name component from the netloc specifier
r.port	Port number from the netloc specifier if it is of the form 'hostname:port'

A SplitResult instance can be turned back into a URL string using *r*.geturl().

urlunsplit(*parts*)

Constructs a URL from the tuple-representation created by urlsplit(). *parts* is a tuple or iterable with the five URL components.

urldefrag(*url*)

Returns a tuple (*newurl*, *fragment*) where *newurl* is *url* stripped of fragments and *fragment* is a string containing the fragment part (if any). If there are no fragments in *url*, then *newurl* is the same as *url* and *fragment* is an empty string.

urljoin(*base*, *url* [, *allow_fragments*])

Constructs an absolute URL by combining a base URL, *base*, with a relative URL. *url*. *allow_fragments* has the same meaning as for urlparse(). If the last component of the base URL is not a directory, it's stripped.

parse_qs(*qs* [, *keep_blank_values* [, *strict_parsing*]])

Parses a URL-encoded (MIME type application/x-www-form-urlencoded) query string *qs* and returns a dictionary where the keys are the query variable names and the values are lists of values defined for each name. *keep_blank_values* is a Boolean flag that controls how blank values are handled. If `True`, they are included in the dictionary with a value set to the empty string. If `False` (the default), they are discarded. `strict_parsing` is a Boolean flag that if `True`, turns parsing errors into a `ValueError` exception. By default, errors are silently ignored.

`parse_qsl(qs [, keep_blank_values [, strict_parsing]])`

The same as `parse_qs()` except that the result is a list of pairs `(name, value)` where `name` is the name of a query variable and `value` is the value.

URL Encoding (`urllib` **Module in Python 2**)

The following functions are used to encode and decode data that make up URLs.

`quote(string [, safe [, encoding [, errors]]])`

Replaces special characters in `string` with escape sequences suitable for including in a URL. Letters, digits, and the underscore (_), comma (,), period (.), and hyphen (-) characters are unchanged. All other characters are converted into escape sequences of the form `'%xx'`. `safe` provides a string of additional characters that should not be quoted and is `'/'` by default. `encoding` specifies the encoding to use for non-ASCII characters. By default, it is `'utf-8'`. `errors` specifies what to do when encoding errors are encountered and is `'strict'` by default. The `encoding` and `errors` parameters are only available in Python 3.

`quote_plus(string [, safe [, encoding [, errors]]])`

Calls `quote()` and additionally replaces all spaces with plus signs. `string` and `safe` are the same as in `quote()`. `encoding` and `errors` are the same as with `quote()`.

`quote_from_bytes(bytes [, safe])`

The same as `quote()` but accepts a byte-string and performs no encoding. The return result is a text string. Python 3 only.

`unquote(string [, encoding [, errors]])`

Replaces escape sequences of the form `'%xx'` with their single-character equivalent. `encoding` and `errors` specify the encoding and error handling for decoding data in `'%xx'` escapes. The default encoding is `'utf-8'`, and the default `errors` policy is `'replace'`. `encoding` and `errors` are Python 3 only.

`unquote_plus(string [, encoding [, errors]])`

Like `unquote()` but also replaces plus signs with spaces.

`unquote_to_bytes(string)`

The same as `unquote()` but performs no decoding and returns a byte string.

`urlencode(query [, doseq])`

Converts query values in `query` to a URL-encoded string suitable for inclusion as the `query` parameter of a URL or for uploading as part of a POST request. `query` is either a dictionary or a sequence of `(key, value)` pairs. The resulting string is a series of `'key=value'` pairs separated by `'&'` characters, where both `key` and `value` are quoted using `quote_plus()`. The `doseq` parameter is a Boolean flag that should be set to `True` if any `value` in `query` is a sequence, representing multiple values for the same key. In this case, a separate `'key=v'` string is created for each `v` in `value`.

Examples

The following examples show how to turn a dictionary of query variables into a URL suitable for use in an HTTP GET request and how you can parse a URL:

```
try:
    from urllib.parse import urlparse, urlencode, parse_qsl  # Python 3
except ImportError:
    from urlparse import urlparse, parse_qsl                 # Python 2
    from urllib import urlencode

# Example of creating a URL with properly encoded query varibles
form_fields = {
    'name'  : 'Dave',
    'email' : 'dave@dabeaz.com',
    'uid'   : '12345'
}
form_data = urlencode(form_fields)
url = "http://www.somehost.com/cgi-bin/view.py?"+form_data

# Example of parsing a URL into components
r = urlparse(url)
print(r.scheme)       # 'http'
print(r.netloc)       # 'www.somehost.com'
print(r.path)         # '/cgi-bin/view.py'
print(r.params)       # ''
print(r.query)        # 'uid=12345&name=Dave&email=dave%40dabeaz.com'
print(r.fragment)     # ''

# Extract query data
parsed_fields = dict(parse_qsl(r.query))
assert form_fields == parsed_fields
```

urllib.error

The urllib.error module defines exceptions used by the urllib package.

ContentTooShort

Raised when the amount of downloaded data is less than the expected amount (as defined by the 'Content-Length' header). Defined in the urllib module in Python 2.

HTTPError

Raised to indicate problems with the HTTP protocol. This error may be used to signal events such as authentication required. This exception can also be used as a file object to read the data returned by the server that's associated with the error. This is a subclass of URLError. It is defined in the urllib2 module in Python 2.

URLError

Error raised by handlers when a problem is detected. This is a subclass of IOError. The reason attribute of the exception instance has more information about the problem. This is defined in the urllib2 module in Python 2.

urllib.robotparser (robotparser)

The urllib.robotparser module (robotparser in Python 2) is used to fetch and parse the contents of 'robots.txt' files used to instruct web crawlers. Consult the online documentation for further usage information.

Notes

- Advanced users of the `urllib` package can customize its behavior in almost every way imaginable. This includes creating new kinds of openers, handlers, requests, protocols, etc. This topic is beyond the scope of what can be covered here, but the online documentation has some further details.

- Users of Python 2 should take note that the `urllib.urlopen()` function, which is in widespread use, is officially deprecated in Python 2.6 and eliminated in Python 3. Instead of using `urllib.urlopen()`, you should use `urllib2.urlopen()`, which provides the same functionality as `urllib.request.urlopen()` described here.

`xmlrpc` **Package**

The `xmlrpc` package contains modules for implement XML-RPC servers and clients. *XML-RPC* is a remote procedure call mechanism that uses XML for data encoding and HTTP as a transport mechanism. The underlying protocol is not specific to Python so programs using these modules can potentially interact with programs written in other languages. More information about XML-RPC can be obtained at http://www.xmlrpc.com.

`xmlrpc.client` (`xmlrpclib`)

The `xmlrpc.client` module is used to write XML-RPC clients. In Python 2, this module is called `xmlrpclib`. To operate as a client, you create an instance of `ServerProxy`:

```
ServerProxy(uri [, transport [, encoding [, verbose [, allow_none [, use_datetime]]]]])
```

`uri` is the location of the remote XML-RPC server—for example, `"http://www.foo.com/RPC2"`. If necessary, basic authentication information can be added to the URI using the format `"http://user:pass@host:port/path"`, where `user:pass` is the username and password. This information is base-64 encoded and put in an `'Authorization:'` header on transport. If Python is configured with OpenSSL support, HTTPS can also be used. `transport` specifies a factory function for creating an internal transport object used for low-level communication. This argument is only used if XML-RPC is being used over some kind of connection other than HTTP or HTTPS. It is almost never necessary to supply this argument in normal use (consult the online documentation for details). `encoding` specifies the encoding, which is UTF-8 by default. `verbose` displays some debugging information if `True`. `allow_none`, if `True`, allows the value `None` to be sent to remote servers. By default, this is disabled because it's not universally supported. `use_datetime` is a Boolean flag that if set to `True`, uses the `datetime` module to represent dates and times. By default, this is `False`.

An instance, `s`, of `ServerProxy` transparently exposes all the methods on the remote server. The methods are accessed as attributes of `s`. For example, this code gets the current time from a remote server providing that service:

```
>>> s = ServerProxy("http://www.xmlrpc.com/RPC2")
>>> s.currentTime.getCurrentTime()
<DateTime u'20051102T20:08:24' at 2c77d8>
>>>
```

For the most part, RPC calls work just like ordinary Python functions. However, only a limited number of argument types and return values are supported by the XML-RPC protocol:

XML-RPC Type	Python Equivalent
boolean	`True` and `False`
integer	int
float	float
string	string or unicode (must only contain characters valid in XML)
array	Any sequence containing valid XML-RPC types
structure	Dictionary containing string keys and values of valid types
dates	Date and time (`xmlrpc.client.DateTime`)
binary	Binary data (`xmlrpc.client.Binary`)

When dates are received, they are stored in an `xmlrpc.client.DateTime` instance *d*. The *d*.value attribute contains the date as an ISO 8601 time/date string. To convert it into a time tuple compatible with the `time` module, use *d*.`timetuple()`. When binary data is received, it is stored in an `xmlrpc.client.Binary` instance *b*. The *b*.data attribute contains the data as a byte string. Be aware that strings are assumed to be Unicode and that you will have to worry about using proper encodings. Sending raw Python 2 byte strings will work if they contain ASCII but will break otherwise. To deal with this, convert to a Unicode string first.

If you make an RPC call with arguments involving invalid types, you may get a `TypeError` or an `xmlrpclib.Fault` exception.

If the remote XML-RPC server supports introspection, the following methods may be available:

s.`system.listMethods()`

Returns a list of strings listing all the methods provided by the XML-RPC server.

s.`methodSignatures(name)`

Given the name of a method, *name*, returns a list of possible calling signatures for the method. Each signature is a list of types in the form of a comma-separated string (for example, `'string, int, int'`), where the first item is the return type and the remaining items are argument types. Multiple signatures may be returned due to over-loading. In XML-RPC servers implemented in Python, signatures are typically empty because functions and methods are dynamically typed.

s.`methodHelp(name)`

Given the name of a method, *name*, returns a documentation string describing the use of that method. Documentation strings may contain HTML markup. An empty string is returned if no documentation is available.

The following utility functions are available in the `xmlrpclib` module:

`boolean(value)`

Creates an XML-RPC Boolean object from *value*. This function predates the existence of the Python Boolean type, so you may see it used in older code.

Binary(*data*)

Creates an XML-RPC object containing binary data. *data* is a string containing the raw data. Returns a Binary instance. The returned Binary instance is transparently encoded/decoded using base 64 during transmission. To extract binary from Binary instance *b*, use *b*.data.

DateTime(*daytime*)

Creates an XML-RPC object containing a date. *daytime* is either an ISO 8601 format date string, a time tuple or struct as returned by time.localtime(), or a datetime instance from the datetime module.

dumps(*params* [, *methodname* [, *methodresponse* [, *encoding* [, *allow_none*]]]])

Converts *params* into an XML-RPC request or response, where *params* is either a tuple of arguments or an instance of the Fault exception. *methodname* is the name of the method as a string. *methodresponse* is a Boolean flag. If True, then the result is an XML-RPC response. In this case, only one value can be supplied in *params*. *encoding* specifies the text encoding in the generated XML and defaults to UTF-8. *allow_none* is a flag that specifies whether or not None is supported as a parameter type. None is not explicitly mentioned by the XML-RPC specification, but many servers support it. By default, *allow_none* is False.

loads(*data*)

Converts *data* containing an XML-RPC request or response into a tuple (*params*, *methodname*) where *params* is a tuple of parameters and *methodname* is a string containing the method name. If the request represents a fault condition instead of an actual value, then the Fault exception is raised.

MultiCall(*server*)

Creates a MultiCall object that allows multiple XML-RPC requests to be packaged together and sent as a single request. This can be a useful performance optimization if many different RPC requests need to be made on the same server. *server* is an instance of ServerProxy, representing a connection to a remote server. The returned MultiCall object is used in exactly the same way as ServerProxy. However, instead of immediately executing the remote methods, the method calls as queued until the MultiCall object is called as a function. Once this occurs, the RPC requests are transmitted. The return value of this operation is a generator that yields the return result of each RPC operation in sequence. Note that MultiCall() only works if the remote server provides a system.multicall() method.

Here is an example that illustrates the use of MultiCall:

```
multi = MultiCall(server)
multi.foo(4,6,7)                # Remote method foo
multi.bar("hello world")        # Remote method bar
multi.spam()                    # Remote method spam
# Now, actually send the XML-RPC request and get return results
foo_result, bar_result, spam_result = multi()
```

Exceptions

The following exceptions are defined in `xmlrpc.client`:

`Fault`

Indicates an XML-RPC fault. The `faultCode` attribute contains a string with the fault type. The `faultString` attribute contains a descriptive message related to the fault.

`ProtocolError`

Indicates a problem with the underlying networking—for example, a bad URL or a connection problem of some kind. The `url` attribute contains the URI that triggered the error. The `errcode` attribute contains an error code. The `errmsg` attribute contains a descriptive string. The `headers` attribute contains all the HTTP headers of the request that triggered the error.

`xmlrpc.server` (`SimpleXMLRPCServer`, `DocXMLRPCServer`)

The `xmlrpc.server` module contains classes for implementing different variants of XML-RPC servers. In Python 2, this functionality is found in two separate modules: `SimpleXMLRPCServer` and `DocXMLRPCServer`.

`SimpleXMLRPCServer(addr [, requestHandler [, logRequests]])`

Creates an XML-RPC server listening on the socket address *addr* (for example, (`'localhost'`,`8080`)). *requestHandler* is factory function that creates handler request objects when connections are received. By default, it is set to `SimpleXMLRPCRequestHandler`, which is currently the only available handler. *logRequests* is a Boolean flag that indicates whether or not to log incoming requests. The default value is `True`.

`DocXMLRPCServer(addr [, requestHandler [, logRequest]])`

Creates a documenting XML-RPC that additionally responds to HTTP GET requests (normally sent by a browser). If received, the server generates documentation from the documentation strings found in all of the registered methods and objects. The arguments have the same meaning as for `SimpleXMLRPCServer`.

An instance, *s*, of `SimpleXMLRPCServer` or `DocXMLRPCServer` has the following methods:

`s.register_function(func [, name])`

Registers a new function, *func*, with the XML-RPC server. *name* is an optional name to use for the function. If *name* is supplied, it's the name clients will use to access the function. This name may contain characters that are not part of valid Python identifiers, including periods (.). If *name* is not supplied, then the actual function name of *func* is used instead.

`s.register_instance(instance [, allow_dotted_names])`

Registers an object that's used to resolve method names not registered with the `register_function()` method. If the instance *instance* defines the method `_dispatch(self, methodname, params)`, it is called to process requests. *methodname* is the name of the method, and *params* is a tuple containing arguments. The return value of `_dispatch()` is returned to clients. If no `_dispatch()` method is defined, the instance is checked to see if the method name matches the names of any methods defined for `instance`. If so, the method is called directly. The `allow_dotted_names` parameter is a flag that indicates whether a hierarchical search should be performed when checking for method names. For example, if a request for method `'foo.bar.spam'` is received, this determines whether or not a search for `instance.foo.bar.spam` is made. By default, this is `False`. It should not be set to `True` unless the client has been verified. Otherwise, it opens up a security hole that can allow intruders to execute arbitrary Python code. Note that, at most, only one instance can be registered at a time.

s.register_introspection_functions()

Adds XML-RPC introspection functions `system.listMethods()`, `system.methodHelp()`, and `system.methodSignature()` to the XML-RPC server. `system.methodHelp()` returns the documentation string for a method (if any). The `system.methodSignature()` function simply returns a message indicating that the operation is unsupported (because Python is dynamically typed, type information is available).

s.register_multicall_functions()

Adds XML-RPC multicall function support by adding the `system.multicall()` function to the server.

An instance of `DocXMLRPCServer` additionally provides these methods:

s.set_server_title(*server_title*)

Sets the title of the server in HTML documentation. The string is placed in the HTML `<title>` tag.

s.set_server_name(*server_name*)

Sets the name of the server in HTML documentation. The string appears at the top of the page in an `<h1>` tag.

s.set_server_documentation(*server_documentation*)

Adds a descriptive paragraph to the generated HTML output. This string is added right after the server name, but before a description of the XML-RPC functions.

Although it is common for an XML-RPC server to operate as a stand-alone process, it can also run inside a CGI script. The following classes are used for this:

CGIXMLRPCRequestHandler([*allow_none* [, *encoding*]])

A CGI Request handler that operates in the same manner as `SimpleXMLRPCServer`. The arguments have the same meaning as described for `SimpleXMLRPCServer`.

DocCGIXMLRPCRequestHandler()

A CGI Request handler that operates in the same manner as `DocXMLRPCServer`. Please note that as of this writing, the calling arguments are different than `CGIXMLRPCRequestHandler()`. This might be a Python bug so you should consult the online documentation in future releases.

An instance, `c`, of either CGI handler has the same methods as a normal XML-RPC server for registering functions and instances. However, they additionally define the following method:

c.handle_request([*request_text*])

Processes an XML-RPC request. By default, the request is read from standard input. If *request_text* is supplied, it contains the request data in the form received by an HTTP POST request.

Examples

Here is a very simple example of writing a standalone server. It adds a single function, add. In addition, it adds the entire contents of the math module as an instance, exposing all the functions it contains.

```
try:
    from xmlrpc.server import SimpleXMLRPCServer      # Python 3
except ImportError:
    from SimpleXMLRPCServer import SimpleXMLRPCServer # Python 2
import math

def add(x,y):
    "Adds two numbers"
    return x+y

s = SimpleXMLRPCServer(('',8080))
s.register_function(add)
s.register_instance(math)
s.register_introspection_functions()
s.serve_forever()
```

Here is the same functionality implemented as CGI-script:

```
try:
    from xmlrpc.server import CGIXMLRPCRequestHandler      # Python 3
except ImportError:
    from SimpleXMLRPCServer import CGIXMLRPCRequestHandler # Python 2
import math

def add(x,y):
    "Adds two numbers"
    return x+y

s = CGIXMLRPCRequestHandler()
s.register_function(add)
s.register_instance(math)
s.register_introspection_functions()
s.handle_request()
```

To access XML-RPC functions from other Python programs, use the xmlrpc.client or xmlrpclib module. Here is a short interactive session that shows how it works:

```
>>> from xmlrpc.client import ServerProxy
>>> s = ServerProxy("http://localhost:8080")
>>> s.add(3,5)
8
>>> s.system.listMethods()
['acos', 'add', 'asin', 'atan', 'atan2', 'ceil', 'cos', 'cosh', 'degrees', 'exp',
'fabs', 'floor', 'fmod', 'frexp', 'hypot', 'ldexp', 'log', 'log10', 'modf',
'pow', 'radians', 'sin', 'sinh', 'sqrt', 'system.listMethods',
'system.methodHelp', 'system.methodSignature', 'tan', 'tanh']
>>> s.tan(4.5)
4.637332054551847
>>>
```

Advanced Server Customization

The XML-RPC server modules are easy to use for basic kinds of distributed computing. For example, XML-RPC could be used as a protocol for high-level control of
other systems on the network, provided they were all running a suitable XML-RPC
server. More interesting objects can also be passed between systems if you additionally
use the `pickle` module.

One concern with XML-RPC is that of security. By default, an XML-RPC server
runs as an open service on the network, so anyone who knows the address and port of
the server can connect to it (unless it's shielded by a firewall). In addition, XML-RPC
servers place no limit on the amount of data that can be sent in a request. An attacker
could potentially crash the server by sending an HTTP POST request with a payload so
large as to exhaust memory.

If you want to address any of these issues, you will need to customize the XML-
RPC server classes or request handlers. All of the server classes inherit from TCPServer
in the socketserver module. Thus, the servers can be customized in the same manner
as other socket server classes (for example, adding threading, forking, or validating client
addresses). A validation wrapper can be placed around the request handlers by inheriting
from SimpleXMLRPCRequestHandler or DocXMLRPCRequestHandler and extending
the do_POST() method. Here is an example that limits the size of incoming requests:

```
try:
    from xmlrpc.server import (SimpleXMLRPCServer,
                               SimpleXMLRPCRequestHandler)
except ImportError:
    from SimpleXMLRPCServer import (SimpleXMLRPCServer,
                                    SimpleXMLRPCRequestHandler)
class MaxSizeXMLRPCHandler(SimpleXMLRPCRequestHandler):
    MAXSIZE = 1024*1024   # 1MB
    def do_POST(self):
        size = int(self.headers.get('content-length',0))
        if size >= self.MAXSIZE:
            self.send_error(400,"Bad request")
        else:
            SimpleXMLRPCRequestHandler.do_POST(self)

s = SimpleXMLRPCServer(('',8080),MaxSizeXMLRPCHandler)
```

If you wanted to add any kind of HTTP-based authentication, it could also be implemented in a similar manner.

## 23

Web Programming

Python is widely used when building websites and serves several different roles in this capacity. First, Python scripts are often a useful way to simply generate a set of static HTML pages to be delivered by a web server. For example, a script can be used to take raw content and decorate it with additional features that you typically see on a website (navigation bars, sidebars, advertisements, stylesheets, etc.). This is mainly just a matter of file handling and text processing—topics that have been covered in other sections of the book.

Second, Python scripts are used to generate dynamic content. For example, a website might operate using a standard webserver such as Apache but would use Python scripts to dynamically handle certain kinds of requests. This use of Python is primarily associated with form processing. For example, an HTML page might include a form like this:

```
<FORM ACTION='/cgi-bin/subscribe.py' METHOD='GET'>
Your name : <INPUT type='Text' name='name' size='30'>
Your email address: <INPUT type='Text' name='email' size='30'>
<INPUT type='Submit' name='submit-button' value='Subscribe'>
</FORM>
```

Within the form, the ACTION attribute names a Python script 'subscribe.py' that will execute on the server when the form is submitted.

Another common scenario involving dynamic content generation is with AJAX (Asynchronous Javascript and XML). With AJAX, JavaScript event handlers are associated with certain HTML elements on a page. For example, when the mouse hovers over a specific document element, a JavaScript function might execute and send an HTTP request to the webserver that gets processed (possibly by a Python script). When the associated response is received, another JavaScript function executes to process the response data and displays the result. There are many ways in which results might be returned. For example, a server might return data as plaintext, XML, JSON, or any number of other formats. Here is an example HTML document that illustrates one way to implement a hover popup where moving the mouse over selected elements causes a popup window to appear.

```
<html>
  <head>
    <title>ACME Officials Quiet After Corruption Probe</title>
    <style type="text/css">
      .popup { border-bottom:1px dashed green; }
      .popup:hover { background-color: #c0c0ff; }
    </style>
  </head>
  <body>
```

```
    <span id="popupbox"
        style="visibility:hidden; position:absolute; background-color:
#ffffff;">
      <span id="popupcontent"></span>
    </span>
    <script>
        /* Get a reference to the popup box element */
        var popup = document.getElementById("popupbox");
        var popupcontent = document.getElementById("popupcontent");

        /* Get pop-up data from the server and display when received */
        function ShowPopup(hoveritem,name) {
            var request = new XMLHttpRequest();
            request.open("GET","cgi-bin/popupdata.py?name="+name, true);
            request.onreadystatechange = function() {
                var done = 4, ok = 200;
                if (request.readyState == done && request.status == ok) {
                    if (request.responseText) {
                        popupcontent.innerHTML = request.responseText;
                        popup.style.left = hoveritem.offsetLeft+10;
                        popup.style.top  = hoveritem.offsetTop+20;
                        popup.style.visibility = "Visible";
                    }
                }
            };
            request.send();
        }

        /* Hide the popup box */
        function HidePopup() {
            popup.style.visibility = "Hidden";
        }
    </script>

    <h3>ACME Officials Quiet After Corruption Probe</h3>
    <p>
    Today, shares of ACME corporation
    (<span class="popup" onMouseOver="ShowPopup(this,'ACME');"
           onMouseOut="HidePopup();">ACME</span>)
    plummetted by more than 75% after federal investigators revealed that
    the board of directors is the target of a corruption probe involving
    the Governor, state lottery officials, and the archbishop.
    </p>

  </body>
</html>
```

In this example, the JavaScript function ShowPopup() initiates a request to a Python
script popupdata.py on the server. The result of this script is just a fragment of
HTML, which is then displayed in a popup window. Figure 23.1 shows what this might
look like in the browser.

Finally, the entire website might run under the control of Python within the context
of a framework written in Python. It has been humorously noted that Python has
"more web programming frameworks than language keywords." The topic of web
frameworks is far beyond the scope of this book, but http://wiki.python.org/
moin/WebFrameworks is a good starting point for finding more information.

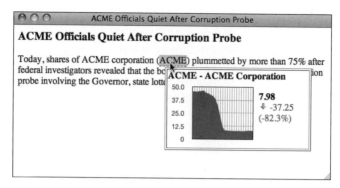

Figure 23.1   Possible browser display where the background text is just an ordinary HTML document and the pop-up window is dynamically generated by the popupdata.py script.

The rest of this chapter describes built-in modules related to the low-level interface by which Python interfaces with webservers and frameworks. Topics include CGI scripting, a technique used to access Python from third-party web servers and WSGI, a middleware layer used for writing components that integrate with Python's various web frameworks.

cgi

The cgi module is used to implement *CGI scripts*, which are programs typically executed by a webserver when it wants to process user input from a form or generate dynamic content of some kind.

When a request corresponding to a CGI script is submitted, the webserver executes the CGI program as a subprocess. CGI programs receive input from two sources: sys.stdin and environment variables set by the server. The following list details common environment variables set by webservers:

Variable	Description
AUTH_TYPE	Authentication method
CONTENT_LENGTH	Length of data passed in sys.stdin
CONTENT_TYPE	Type of query data
DOCUMENT_ROOT	Document root directory
GATEWAY_INTERFACE	CGI revision string
HTTP_ACCEPT	MIME types accepted by the client
HTTP_COOKIE	Netscape persistent cookie value
HTTP_FROM	Email address of client (often disabled)
HTTP_REFERER	Referring URL
HTTP_USER_AGENT	Client browser
PATH_INFO	Extra path information passed
PATH_TRANSLATED	Translated version of PATH_INFO
QUERY_STRING	Query string
REMOTE_ADDR	Remote IP address of the client
REMOTE_HOST	Remote host name of the client

Variable	Description
REMOTE_IDENT	User making the request
REMOTE_USER	Authenticated username
REQUEST_METHOD	Method ('GET' or 'POST')
SCRIPT_NAME	Name of the program
SERVER_NAME	Server host name
SERVER_PORT	Server port number
SERVER_PROTOCOL	Server protocol
SERVER_SOFTWARE	Name and version of the server software

As output, a CGI program writes to standard output sys.stdout. The gory details of CGI programming can be found in a book such as *CGI Programming with Perl*, 2nd Edition, by Shishir Gundavaram (O'Reilly & Associates, 2000). For our purposes, there are really only two things to know. First, the contents of an HTML form are passed to a CGI program in a sequence of text known as a *query string*. In Python, the contents of the query string are accessed using the FieldStorage class. For example:

```
import cgi
form = cgi.FieldStorage()
name = form.getvalue('name')      # Get 'name' field from a form
email = form.getvalue('email')    # Get 'email' field from a form
```

Second, the output of a CGI program consists of two parts: an HTTP header and the raw data (which is typically HTML). A blank line always separates these two components. A simple HTTP header looks like this:

```
print 'Content-type: text/html\r'    # HTML Output
print '\r'                           # Blank line (required!)
```

The rest of the output is the raw output. For example:

```
print '<TITLE>My CGI Script</TITLE>'
print '<H1>Hello World!</H1>'
print 'You are %s (%s)' % (name, email)
```

It is standard practice that HTTP headers are terminated using the Windows line-ending convention of '\r\n'. That is why the '\r' appears in the example. If you need to signal an error, include a special 'Status:' header in the output. For example:

```
print 'Status: 401 Forbidden\r'     # HTTP Error code
print 'Content-type: text/plain\r'
print '\r'                          # Blank line (required)
print 'You're not worthy of accessing this page!'
```

If you need to redirect the client to a different page, create output like this:

```
print 'Status: 302 Moved\r'
print 'Location: http://www.foo.com/orderconfirm.html\r'
print '\r'
```

Most of the work in the cgi module is performed by creating an instance of the FieldStorage class.

FieldStorage([input [, headers [, outerboundary [, environ [, keep_blank_values [, strict_parsing]]]]]])

Read the contents of a form by reading and parsing the query string passed in an environment variable or standard input. *input* specifies a file-like object from which form data will be read in a POST request. By default, sys.stdin is used. *headers* and *outerboundary* are used internally and should not be given. *environ* is a dictionary from which CGI environment variables are read. *keep_blank_values* is a Boolean flag that controls whether blank values are retained or not. By default, it is False. *strict_parsing* is a Boolean flag that causes an exception to be raised if there is any kind of parsing problem. By default, it is False.

A FieldStorage instance *form* works similarly to a dictionary. For example, *f* = *form[key]* will extract an entry for a given parameter *key*. An instance *f* extracted in this manner is either another instance of FieldStorage or an instance of MiniFieldStorage. The following attributes are defined on *f*:

Attribute	Description
f.name	The field name, if specified
f.filename	Client-side filename used in uploads
f.value	Value as a string
f.file	File-like object from which data can be read
f.type	Content type
f.type_options	Dictionary of options specified on the content-type line of the HTTP request
f.disposition	The 'content-disposition' field; None if not specified
f.disposition_options	Dictionary of disposition options
f.headers	A dictionary-like object containing all the HTTP header contents

Values from a form can be extracted using the following methods:

form.getvalue(*fieldname* [, *default*])

Returns the value of a given field with the name *fieldname*. If a field is defined twice, this function will return a list of all values defined. If *default* is supplied, it specifies the value to return if the field is not present. One caution with this method is that if the same form field name is included twice in the request, the returned value will be a list containing both values. To simplify programming, you can use *form.getfirst()*, which simply returns the first value found.

form.getfirst(*fieldname* [, *default*])

Returns the first value defined for a field with the name *fieldname*. If *default* is supplied, it specifies the value to return if the field is not present.

form.getlist(*fieldname*)

Returns a list of all values defined for *fieldname*. It always returns a list, even if only one value is defined, and returns an empty list if no values exist.

In addition, the cgi module defines a class, MiniFieldStorage, that contains only the attribute's name and value. This class is used to represent individual fields of a form passed in the query string, whereas FieldStorage is used to contain multiple fields and multipart data.

Instances of FieldStorage are accessed like a Python dictionary, where the keys are the field names on the form. When accessed in this manner, the objects returned are themselves an instance of FieldStorage for multipart data (content type is 'multipart/form-data') or file uploads, an instance of MiniFieldStorage for simple fields (content type is 'application/x-www-form-urlencoded'), or a list of such instances in cases where a form contains multiple fields with the same name. For example:

```
form = cgi.FieldStorage()
if "name" not in form:
    error("Name is missing")
    return
name = form['name'].value      # Get 'name' field from a form
email = form['email'].value    # Get 'email' field from a form
```

If a field represents an uploaded file, accessing the value attribute reads the entire file into memory as a byte string. Because this may consume a large amount of memory on the server, it may be preferable to read uploaded data in smaller pieces by reading from the file attribute directly. For instance, the following example reads uploaded data line by line:

```
fileitem = form['userfile']
if fileitem.file:
    # It's an uploaded file; count lines
    linecount = 0
    while True:
        line = fileitem.file.readline()
        if not line: break
        linecount = linecount + 1
```

The following utility functions are often used in CGI scripts:

escape(s [, quote])

Converts the characters '&', '<', and '>' in string s to HTML-safe sequences such as '&', '<', and '>'. If the optional flag quote is true, the double-quote character (") is also translated to '"'.

parse_header(string)

Parses the data supplied after an HTTP header field such as 'content-type'. The data is split into a primary value and a dictionary of secondary parameters that are returned in a tuple. For example, the command

```
parse_header('text/html; a=hello; b="world"')
```

returns this result:

```
('text/html', {'a':'hello', 'b':'world'}).
```

parse_multipart(fp,pdict)

Parses input of type 'multipart/form-data' as is commonly used with file uploads. fp is the input file, and pdict is a dictionary containing parameters of the content-type header. It returns a dictionary mapping field names to lists of values. This function doesn't work with nested multipart data. The FieldStorage class should be used instead.

```
print_directory()
```

Formats the name of the current working directory in HTML and prints it out. The resulting output will be sent back to the browser, which can be useful for debugging.

```
print_environ()
```

Creates a list of all environment variables formatted in HTML and is used for debugging.

```
print_environ_usage()
```

Prints a more selected list of useful environment variables in HTML and is used for debugging.

```
print_form(form)
```

Formats the data supplied on a form in HTML. *form* must be an instance of FieldStorage. Used for debugging.

```
test()
```

Writes a minimal HTTP header and prints all the information provided to the script in HTML format. Primarily used for debugging to make sure your CGI environment is set up correctly.

CGI Programming Advice

In the current age of web frameworks, CGI scripting seems to have fallen out of fashion. However, if you are going to use it, there are a couple of programming tips that can simplify your life.

First, don't write CGI scripts where you are using a huge number of print statements to produce hard-coded HTML output. The resulting program will be a horrible tangled mess of Python and HTML that is not only impossible to read, but also impossible to maintain. A better approach is to rely on templates. Minimally, the string.Template object can be used for this. Here is an example that outlines the concept:

```
import cgi
from string import Template

def error(message):
    temp = Template(open("errormsg.html").read())
    print 'Content-type: text/html\r'
    print '\r'
    print temp.substitute({'message' : message})

form = cgi.FieldStorage()
name  = form.getfirst('name')
email = form.getfirst('email')
if not name:
    error("name not specified")
    raise SystemExit
elif not email:
    error("email not specified")
    raise SystemExit

# Do various processing
confirmation = subscribe(name, email)
```

```
# Print the output page
values = {
    'name' : name,
    'email' : email,
    'confirmation' : confirmation,
    # Add other values here...
}
temp = Template(open("success.html").read())
print temp.substitute(values)
```

In this example, the files `'error.html'` and `'success.html'` are HTML pages that have all of the output but include $variable$ substitutions corresponding to dynamically generated values used in the CGI script. For example, the `'success.html'` file might look like this:

```
<HTML>
    <HEAD>
       <TITLE>Success</TITLE>
    </HEAD>
    <BODY>
    Welcome $name.  You have successfully subscribed to our
    newsletter.  Your confirmation code is $confirmation.
    </BODY>
</HTML>
```

The `temp.substitute()` operation in the script is simply filling in the variables in this file. An obvious benefit of this approach is that if you want to change the appearance of the output, you just modify the template files, not the CGI script. There are many third-party template engines available for Python—maybe in even greater numbers than web frameworks. These take the templating concept and build upon it in substantial ways. See http://wiki.python.org/moin/Templating more details.

Second, if you need to save data from a CGI script, try to use a database. Although it is easy enough to write data directly to files, webservers operate concurrently, and unless you've taken steps to properly lock and synchronize resources, it is possible that files will get corrupted. Database servers and their associated Python interface usually don't have this problem. So if you need to save data, try to use a module such as sqlite3 or a third-party module for something like MySQL.

Finally, if you find yourself writing dozens of CGI scripts and code that has to deal with low-level details of HTTP such as cookies, authentication, encoding, and so forth, you may want to consider a web framework instead. The whole point of using a framework is so that you don't have to worry about those details—well, at least not as much. So, don't reinvent the wheel.

Notes

- The process of installing a CGI program varies widely according to the type of webserver being used. Typically programs are placed in a special cgi-bin directory. A server may also require additional configuration. You should consult the documentation for the server or the server's administrator for more details.

- On UNIX, Python CGI programs may require appropriate execute permissions to be set and a line such as the following to appear as the first line of the program:

```
#!/usr/bin/env python
import cgi
...
```

- To simplify debugging, import the cgitb module—for example, import cgitb; cgitb.enable(). This modifies exception handling so that errors are displayed in the web browser.

- If you invoke an external program—for example, via the os.system() or os.popen() function—be careful not to pass arbitrary strings received from the client to the shell. This is a well-known security hole that hackers can use to execute arbitrary shell commands on the server (because the command passed to these functions is first interpreted by the UNIX shell as opposed to being executed directly). In particular, never pass any part of a URL or form data to a shell command unless it has first been thoroughly checked by making sure that the string contains only alphanumeric characters, dashes, underscores, and periods.

- On UNIX, don't give a CGI program setuid mode. This is a security liability and not supported on all machines.

- Don't use 'from cgi import *' with this module. The cgi module defines a wide variety of names and symbols that you probably don't want in your namespace.

cgitb

This module provides an alternative exception handler that displays a detailed report whenever an uncaught exception occurs. The report contains source code, values of parameters, and local variables. Originally, this module was developed to help debug CGI scripts, but it can be used in any application.

enable([display [, logdir [, context [, format]]]])

Enables special exception handling. display is a flag that determines whether any information is displayed when an error occurs. The default value is 1. logdir specifies a directory in which error reports will be written to files instead of printed to standard output. When logdir is given, each error report is written to a unique file created by the tempfile.mkstemp() function. context is an integer specifying the number of lines of source code to display around lines upon which the exception occurred. format is a string that specifies the output format. A format of 'html' specifies HTML (the default). Any other value results in plain-text format.

handle([info])

Handles an exception using the default settings of the enable() function. info is a tuple (exctype, excvalue, tb) where exctype is an exception type, excvalue is an exception value, and tb is a traceback object. This tuple is normally obtained using sys.exc_info(). If info is omitted, the current exception is used.

> **Note**
> To enable special exception handling in CGI scripts, include the line `import cgitb;`
> `enable()` at the beginning of the script.

wsgiref

WSGI (Python Web Server Gateway Interface) is a standardized interface between web-servers and web applications that is designed to promote portability of applications across different webservers and frameworks. An official description of the standard is found in PEP 333 (http://www.python.org/dev/peps/pep-0333). More information about the standard and its use can also be found at http://www.wsgi.org. The `wsgiref` package is a reference implementation that can be used for testing, validation, and simple deployments.

The WSGI Specification

With WSGI, a web application is implemented as a function or callable object `webapp(environ, start_response)` that accepts two arguments. `environ` is a dictionary of environment settings that is minimally required to have the following values which have the same meaning and names as is used in CGI scripting:

environ Variables	Description
CONTENT_LENGTH	Length of data passed
CONTENT_TYPE	Type of query data
HTTP_ACCEPT	MIME types accepted by the client
HTTP_COOKIE	Netscape persistent cookie value
HTTP_REFERER	Referring URL
HTTP_USER_AGENT	Client browser
PATH_INFO	Extra path information passed
QUERY_STRING	Query string
REQUEST_METHOD	Method ('GET' or 'POST')
SCRIPT_NAME	Name of the program
SERVER_NAME	Server host name
SERVER_PORT	Server port number
SERVER_PROTOCOL	Server protocol

In addition, the `environ` dictionary is required to contain the following WSGI-specific values:

environ Variables	Description
wsgi.version	Tuple representing the WSGI version (e.g., (1,0) for WSGI 1.0).
wsgi.url_scheme	String representing the scheme component of the URL. For example, 'http' or 'https'.
wsgi.input	A file-like object representing the input stream. Additional data such as form data or uploads are read from this.
wsgi.errors	A file-like object opened in text mode for writing error output.

`environ` Variables	Description
`wsgi.multithread`	A Boolean flag that's `True` if the application can be executed concurrently by another thread in the same process.
`wsgi.multiprocess`	A Boolean flag that's `True` if the application can be executed concurrently by another process.
`wsgi.run_once`	A Boolean flag that's `True` if the application will only be executed once during the lifetime of the executing process.

The `start_response` parameter is a callable object of the form `start_response(status, headers)` that is used by the application to start a response. `status` is a string such as `'200 OK'` or `'404 Not Found'`. `headers` is a list of tuples, each of the form (`name, value`) corresponding to a HTTP header to be included in the response—for example, (`'Content-type'`, `'text/html'`).

The data or body of a response is returned by the web application function as an iterable object that produces a sequence of byte strings or text strings that only contain characters which can be encoded as a single byte (e.g., compatible with the ISO-8859-1 or Latin-1 character set). Examples include a list of byte strings or a generator function producing byte strings. If an application needs to do any kind of character encoding such as UTF-8, it must do this itself.

Here is an example of a simple WSGI application that reads form fields and produces some output, similar to what was shown in the `cgi` module section:

```python
import cgi
def subscribe_app(environ, start_response):
    fields = cgi.FieldStorage(environ['wsgi.input'],
                              environ=environ)

    name = fields.getvalue("name")
    email = fields.getvalue("email")

    # Various processing

    status = "200 OK"
    headers = [('Content-type','text/plain')]
    start_response(status, headers)

    response = [
        'Hi %s. Thank you for subscribing.' % name,
        'You should expect a response soon.'
        ]
    return (line.encode('utf-8') for line in response)
```

There are a few critical details in this example. First, WSGI application components are not tied to specific framework, webserver, or set of library modules. In the example, we're only using one library module, `cgi`, simply because it has some convenience functions for parsing query variables. The example shows how the `start_response()` function is used to initiate a response and supply headers. The response itself is constructed as a list of strings. The final statement in this application is a generator expression that turns all strings into byte strings. If you're using Python 3, this is a critical step—all WSGI applications are expected to return encoded bytes, not unencoded Unicode data.

To deploy a WSGI application, it has to be registered with the web programming framework you happen to be using. For this, you'll have to read the manual.

wsgiref **Package**

The wsgiref package provides a reference implementation of the WSGI standard that allows applications to be tested in stand-alone servers or executed as normal CGI scripts.

wsgiref.simple_server

The wsgiref.simple_server module implements a simple stand-alone HTTP server that runs a single WSGI application. There are just two functions of interest:

make_server(*host*, *port*, *app*)

Creates an HTTP server that accepts connections on the given host name *host* and port number *port*. *app* is a function or callable object that implements a WSGI application. To run the server, use *s*.serve_forever() where *s* is an instance of the server that is returned.

demo_app(*environ*, *start_response*)

A complete WSGI application that returns a page with a "Hello World" message on it. This can be used as the *app* argument to make_server() to verify that the server is working correctly.

Here is an example of running a simple WSGI server:

```
def my_app(environ, start_response):
    # Some application
    start_response("200 OK",[('Content-type','text/plain')])
    return ['Hello World']

if __name__ == '__main__':
    from wsgiref.simple_server import make_server
    serv = make_server('',8080, my_app)
    serv.serve_forever()
```

wsgiref.handlers

The wsgiref.handlers module contains handler objects for setting up a WSGI execution environment so that applications can run within another webserver (e.g., CGI scripting under Apache). There are few different objects.

CGIHandler()

Creates a WSGI handler object that runs inside a standard CGI environment. This handler collects information from the standard environment variables and I/O streams as described in the cgi library module.

BaseCGIHandler(*stdin*, *stdout*, *stderr*, *environ* [, *multithread* [, *multiprocess*]])

Creates a WSGI handler that operates within a CGI environment, but where the standard I/O streams and environment variables might be set up in a different way. *stdin*, *stdout*, and *stderr* specify file-like objects for the standard I/O streams. *environ* is a dictionary of environment variables that is expected to already contain the standard CGI environment variables. *multithread* and *multiprocess* are Boolean flags that are used to set the wsgi.multithread and wsgi.multiprocess environment variables. By default, *multithread* is True and *multiprocess* is False.

SimpleHandler(*stdin, stdout, stderr, environ* [, *multithread* [, *multiprocess*]])

Creates a WSGI handler that is similar to BaseCGIHandler, but which gives the underlying application direct access to *stdin*, *stdout*, *stderr*, and *environ*. This is slightly
different than BaseCGIHandler that provides extra logic to process certain features correctly (e.g., in BaseCGIHandler, response codes are translated into Status: headers).

All of these handlers have a method run(*app*) that is used to run a WSGI application within the handler. Here is an example of a WSGI application running as a traditional CGI script:

```
#!/usr/bin/env python
def my_app(environ, start_response):
    # Some application
    start_response("200 OK",[('Content-type','text/plain')])
    return ['Hello World']

from wgiref.handlers import CGIHandler
hand = CGIHandler()
hand.run(my_app)
```

wsgiref.validate

The wsgiref.validate module has a function that wraps a WSGI application with a
validation wrapper to ensure that both it and the server are operating according to the
standard.

validator(*app*)

Creates a new WSGI application that wraps the WSGI application *app*. The new application transparently works in the same way as *app* except that extensive error-checking
is added to make sure the application and the server are following the WSGI standard.
Any violation results in an AssertionError exception.

Here is an example of using the validator:

```
def my_app(environ, start_response):
    # Some application
    start_response("200 OK",[('Content-type','text/plain')])
    return ['Hello World']

if __name__ == '__main__':
    from wsgiref.simple_server import make_server
    from wsgiref.validate import validator
    serv = make_server('',8080, validator(my_app))
    serv.serve_forever()
```

> **Note**
>
> The material in this section is primarily aimed at users of WSGI who want to create
> application objects. If, on the other hand, you are implementing yet another web frame-
> work for Python, you should consult PEP 333 for official details on precisely what is
> needed to make your framework support WSGI. If you are using a third-party web frame-
> work, you will need to consult the framework documentation for details concerning its
> support for WSGI objects. Given that WSGI is an officially blessed specification with a
> reference implementation in the standard library, it is increasingly common for frame-
> works to provide some level of support for it.

webbrowser

The `webbrowser` module provides utility functions for opening documents in a web browser in a platform-independent manner. The main use of this module is in development and testing situations. For example, if you wrote a script that generated HTML output, you could use the functions in this module to automatically direct your system's browser to view the results.

open(url [, new [, autoraise]])

Displays `url` with the default browser on the system. If `new` is 0, the URL is opened in the same window as a running browser, if possible. If `new` is 1, a new browser window is created. If `new` is 2, the URL is opened within a new tab within the browser. If `autoraise` is `True`, the browser window is raised.

open_new(url)

Displays `url` in a new window of the default browser. The same as `open(url, 1)`.

open_new_tab(url)

Displays `url` in a new tab of the default browser. The same as `open(url, 2)`.

get([name])

Returns a controller object for manipulating a browser. `name` is the name of the browser type and is typically a string such as `'netscape'`, `'mozilla'`, `'kfm'`, `'grail'`, `'windows-default'`, `'internet-config'`, or `'command-line'`. The returned controller object has methods `open()` and `open_new()` that accept the same arguments and perform the same operation as the two previous functions. If `name` is omitted, a controller object for the default browser is returned.

register(name, constructor[, controller])

Registers a new browser type for use with the `get()` function. `name` is the name of the browser. `constructor` is called without arguments to create a controller object for opening pages in the browser. `controller` is a controller instance to use instead. If supplied, `constructor` is ignored and may be `None`.

A controller instance, `c`, returned by the `get()` function has the following methods:

c.open(url[, new])

Same as the `open()` function.

c.open_new(url)

Same as the `open_new()` function.

## 24

Internet Data Handling and Encoding

This chapter describes modules related to processing common Internet data formats and encodings such as base 64, HTML, XML, and JSON.

base64

The `base64` module is used to encode and decode binary data into text using base 64, base 32, or base 16 encoding. Base 64 is commonly used to embed binary data in mail attachments and with parts of the HTTP protocol. Official details can be found in RFC-3548 and RFC-1421.

Base 64 encoding works by grouping the data to be encoded into groups of 24 bits (3 bytes). Each 24-bit group is then subdivided into four 6-bit components. Each 6-bit value is then represented by a printable ASCII character from the following alphabet:

Value	Encoding
0–25	ABCDEFGHIJKLMNOPQRSTUVWXYZ
26–51	abcdefghijklmnopqrstuvwxyz
52–61	0123456789
62	+
63	/
pad	=

If the number of bytes in the input stream is not a multiple of 3 (24 bits), the data is padded to form a complete 24-bit group. The extra padding is then indicated by special '=' characters that appear at the end of the encoding. For example, if you encode a 16-byte character sequence, there are five 3-byte groups with 1 byte left over. The remaining byte is padded to form a 3-byte group. This group then produces two characters from the base 64 alphabet (the first 12 bits, which include 8 bits of real data), followed by the sequence '==', representing the bits of extra padding. A valid base 64 encoding will only have zero, one (=), or two (==) padding characters at the end of the encoding.

Base 32 encoding works by grouping binary data into groups of 40 bits (5 bytes). Each 40-bit group is subdivided into eight 5-bit components. Each 5-bit value is then encoded using the following alphabet:

Value	Encoding
0–25	ABCDEFGHIJKLMNOPQRSTUVWXYZ
26–31	2–7

As with base 64, if the end of the input stream does not form a 40-bit group, it is padded to 40 bits and the '=' character is used to represent the extra padding in the output. At most, there will be six padding characters ('======'), which occurs if the final group only includes 1 byte of data.

Base 16 encoding is the standard hexadecimal encoding of data. Each 4-bit group is represented by the digits '0'–'9' and the letters 'A'–'F'. There is no extra padding or pad characters for base 16 encoding.

b64encode(s [, altchars])

Encodes a byte string s using base 64 encoding. altchars, if given, is a two-character string that specifies alternative characters to use for '+' and '/' characters that normally appear in base 64 output. This is useful if base 64 encoding is being used with filenames or URLs.

b64decode(s [, altchars])

Decodes string s, which is encoded as base 64 and returns a byte string with the decoded data. altchars, if given, is a two-character string that specifies the alternative characters for '+' and '/' that normally appear in base 64–encoded data. TypeError is raised if the input s contains extraneous characters or is incorrectly padded.

standard_b64encode(s)

Encodes a byte string s using the standard base 64 encoding.

standard_b64decode(s)

Decodes string s using standard base 64 encoding.

urlsafe_b64encode(s)

Encodes a byte string s using base 64 but uses the characters '-' and '_' instead of '+' and '/', respectively. The same as b64encode(s, '-_').

urlsafe_b64decode(s)

Decodes string s encoded with a URL-safe base 64 encoding.

b32encode(s)

Encodes a byte string s using base 32 encoding.

b32decode(s [, casefold [, map01]])

Decodes string s using base 32 encoding. If casefold is True, both uppercase and lowercase letters are accepted. Otherwise, only uppercase letters may appear (the default). map01, if present, specifies which letter the digit 1 maps to (for example, the letter 'I' or the letter 'L'). If this argument is given, the digit '0' is also mapped to the letter 'O'. A `TypeError` is raised if the input string contains extraneous characters or is incorrectly padded.

b16encode(s)

Encodes a byte string s using base 16 (hex) encoding.

b16decode(s [,casefold])

Decodes string s using base 16 (hex) encoding. If `casefold` is `True`, letters may be uppercase or lowercase. Otherwise, hexadecimal letters 'A'—'F' must be uppercase (the default). Raises `TypeError` if the input string contains extraneous characters or is malformed in any way.

The following functions are part of an older base 64 module interface that you may see used in existing Python code:

decode(input, output)

Decodes base 64—encoded data. `input` is a filename or a file object open for reading. `output` is a filename or a file object open for writing in binary mode.

decodestring(s)

Decodes a base 64—encoded string, s. Returns a string containing the decoded binary data.

encode(input, output)

Encodes data using base 64. `input` is a filename or a file object open for reading in binary mode. `output` is a filename or a file object open for writing.

encodestring(s)

Encodes a byte string, s, using base 64.

binascii

The `binascii` module contains low-level functions for converting data between binary and a variety of ASCII encodings, such as base 64, BinHex, and UUencoding.

a2b_uu(s)

Converts a line of uuencoded text s to binary and returns a byte string. Lines normally contain 45 (binary) bytes, except for the last line that may be less. Line data may be followed by whitespace.

b2a_uu(data)

Converts a string of binary data to a line of uuencoded ASCII characters. The length of `data` should not be more than 45 bytes. Otherwise, the `Error` exception is raised.

a2b_base64(string)

Converts a string of base 64—encoded text to binary and returns a byte string.

b2a_base64(data)

Converts a string of binary data to a line of base 64—encoded ASCII characters. The length of `data` should not be more than 57 bytes if the resulting output is to be transmitted through email (otherwise it might get truncated).

a2b_hex(*string*)

Converts a string of hexadecimal digits to binary data. This function is also called as unhexlify(*string*).

b2a_hex(*data*)

Converts a string of binary data to a hexadecimal encoding. This function is also called as hexlify(*data*).

a2b_hqx(*string*)

Converts a string of BinHex 4–encoded data to binary without performing RLE (Run-Length Encoding) decompression.

rledecode_hqx(*data*)

Performs an RLE decompression of the binary data in *data*. Returns the decompressed data unless the data input is incomplete, in which case the Incomplete exception is raised.

rlecode_hqx(*data*)

Performs a BinHex 4 RLE compression of *data*.

b2a_hqx(*data*)

Converts the binary data to a string of BinHex 4–encoded ASCII characters. *data* should already be RLE-coded. Also, unless *data* is the last data fragment, the length of *data* should be divisible by 3.

crc_hqx(*data*, *crc*)

Computes the BinHex 4 CRC checksum of the byte string *data*. *crc* is a starting value of the checksum.

crc32(*data* [, *crc*])

Computes the CRC-32 checksum of the byte string *data*. *crc* is an optional initial CRC value. If omitted, *crc* defaults to 0.

CSV

The csv module is used to read and write files consisting of comma-separated values (CSV). A CSV file consists of rows of text, each row consisting of values separated by a delimiter character, typically a comma (,) or a tab. Here's an example:

```
Blues,Elwood,"1060 W Addison","Chicago, IL 60613","B263-1655-2187",116,56
```

Variants of this format commonly occur when working with databases and spreadsheets. For instance, a database might export tables in CSV format, allowing the tables to be read by other programs. Subtle complexities arise when fields contain the delimiter character. For instance, in the preceding example, one of the fields contains a comma and must be placed in quotes. This is why using basic string operations such as split(',') are often not enough to work with such files.

```
reader(csvfile [, dialect [, **fmtparams]])
```

Returns a reader object that produces the values for each line of input of the input file `csvfile`. `csvfile` is any iterable object that produces a complete line of text on each iteration. The returned reader object is an iterator that produces a list of strings on each iteration. The `dialect` parameter is either a string containing the name of a dialect or a `Dialect` object. The purpose of the `dialect` parameter is to account for differences between different CSV encodings. The only built-in dialects supported by this module are `'excel'` (which is the default value) and `'excel-tab'`, but others can be defined by the user as described later in this section. `fmtparams` is a set of keyword arguments that customize various aspects of the dialect. The following keyword arguments can be given:

Keyword Argument	Description
delimiter	Character used to separate fields (the default is `','`).
doublequote	Boolean flag that determines how the quote character (quotechar) is handled when it appears in a field. If `True`, the character is simply doubled. If `False`, an escape character (escapechar) is used as a prefix. The default is `True`.
escapechar	Character used as an escape character when the delimiter appears in a field and `quoting` is `QUOTE_NONE`. The default value is `None`.
lineterminator	Line termination sequence (`'\r\n'` is the default).
quotechar	Character used to quote fields that contain the delimiter (`'"'` is the default).
skipinitialspace	If `True`, whitespace immediately following the delimiter is ignored (`False` is the default).

```
writer(csvfile [, dialect [, **fmtparam]])
```

Returns a writer object that can be used to create a CSV file. `csvfile` is any file-like object that supports a `write()` method. `dialect` has the same meaning as for `reader()` and is used to handle differences between various CSV encodings. `fmtparams` has the same meaning as for readers. However, one additional keyword argument is available:

Keyword Argument	Description
quoting	Controls the quoting behavior of output data. It's set to one of `QUOTE_ALL` (quotes all fields), `QUOTE_MINIMAL` (only quote fields that contain the delimiter or start with the quote character), `QUOTE_NONNUMERIC` (quote all nonnumeric fields), or `QUOTE_NONE` (never quote fields). The default value is `QUOTE_MINIMAL`.

A writer instance, *w*, supports the following methods:

```
w.writerow(row)
```

Writes a single row of data to the file. `row` must be a sequence of strings or numbers.

`w.writerows(`*rows*`)`

Writes multiple rows of data. *rows* must be a sequence of rows as passed to the `writerow()` method.

`DictReader(`*csvfile* `[,` *fieldnames* `[,` *restkey* `[,` *restval* `[,` *dialect* `[,`
➥`**`*fmtparams*`]]]]])`

Returns a reader object that operates like the ordinary reader but returns dictionary objects instead of lists of strings when reading the file. *fieldnames* provides a list of field names used as keys in the returned dictionary. If omitted, the dictionary key names are taken from the first row of the input file. *restkey* provides the name of a dictionary key that's used to store excess data—for instance, if a row has more data fields than field names. *restval* is a default value that's used as the value for fields that are missing from the input—for instance, if a row does not have enough fields. The default value of *restkey* and *restval* is None. *dialect* and *fmtparams* have the same meaning as for `reader()`.

`DictWriter(`*csvfile*`,` *fieldnames* `[,` *restval* `[,` *extrasaction* `[,` *dialect* `[,`
➥`**`*fmtparams*`]]]])`

Returns a writer object that operates like the ordinary writer but writes dictionaries into output rows. *fieldnames* specifies the order and names of attributes that will be written to the file. *restval* is the value that's written if the dictionary being written is missing one of the field names in *fieldnames*. *extrasaction* is a string that specifies what to do if a dictionary being written has keys not listed in *fieldnames*. The default value of *extrasaction* is `'raise'`, which raises a ValueError exception. A value of `'ignore'` may be used, in which case extra values in the dictionary are ignored. *dialect* and *fmtparams* have the same meaning as with `writer()`.

A DictWriter instance, *w*, supports the following methods:

`w.writerow(`*row*`)`

Writes a single row of data to the file. *row* must be a dictionary that maps field names to values.

`w.writerows(`*rows*`)`

Writes multiple rows of data. *rows* must be a sequence of rows as passed to the `writerow()` method.

`Sniffer()`

Creates a Sniffer object that is used to try and automatically detect the format of a CSV file.

A Sniffer instance, *s*, has the following methods:

`s.sniff(`*sample* `[,` *delimiters*`])`

Looks at data in *sample* and returns an appropriate Dialect object representing the data format. *sample* is a portion of a CSV file containing at least one row of data. *delimiters*, if supplied, is a string containing possible field delimiter characters.

`s.has_header(`*sample*`)`

Looks at the CSV data in *sample* and returns True if the first row looks like a collection of column headers.

Dialects

Many of the functions and methods in the csv module involve a special dialect parameter. The purpose of this parameter is to accommodate different formatting conventions
of CSV files (for which there is no official "standard" format)—for example, differences
between comma-separated values and tab-delimited values, quoting conventions, and so
forth.

Dialects are defined by inheriting from the class Dialect and defining the same set
of attributes as the formatting parameters given to the reader() and writer() functions (delimiter, doublequote, escapechar, lineterminator, quotechar,
quoting, skipinitialspace).

The following utility functions are used to manage dialects:

register_dialect(*name, dialect*)

Registers a new Dialect object, *dialect*, under the name *name*.

unregister_dislect(*name*)

Removes the Dialect object with name *name*.

get_dialect(*name*)

Returns the Dialect object with name *name*.

list_dialects()

Returns a list of all registered dialect names. Currently, there are only two built-in
dialects: 'excel' and 'excel-tab'.

Example

```
import csv
# Read a basic CSV file
f = open("scmods.csv","r")
for r in csv.reader(f):
    lastname, firstname, street, city, zip = r
    print("{0} {1} {2} {3} {4}".format(*r))

# Using a DictReader instead
f = open("address.csv")
r = csv.DictReader(f,['lastname','firstname','street','city','zip'])
for a in r:
    print("{firstname} {lastname} {street} {city} {zip}".format(**a))

# Write a basic CSV file
data = [
  ['Blues','Elwood','1060 W Addison','Chicago','IL','60613' ],
  ['McGurn','Jack','4802 N Broadway','Chicago','IL','60640' ],
]
f = open("address.csv","w")
w = csv.writer(f)
w.writerows(data)
f.close()
```

email **Package**

The email package provides a wide variety of functions and objects for representing, parsing and manipulating email messages encoded according to the MIME standard.

Covering every detail of the email package is not practical here, nor would it be of interest to most readers. Thus, the rest of this section focuses on two common practical problems—parsing email messages in order to extract useful information and creating email messages so that they can be sent using the smtplib module.

Parsing Email

At the top level, the email module provides two functions for parsing messages:

message_from_file(f)

Parses an email message read from the file-like object f which must be opened in text mode. The input message should be a complete MIME-encoded email message including all headers, text, and attachments. Returns a Message instance.

message_from_string(str)

Parses an email message by reading an email message from the text string str. Returns a Message instance.

A Message instance m returned by the previous functions emulates a dictionary and supports the following operations for looking up message data:

Operation	Description
m[name]	Returns the value of header name.
m.keys()	Returns a list of all message header names.
m.values()	Returns a list of message header values.
m.items()	Returns a list of tuples containing message header names and values.
m.get(name [,def])	Returns a header value for header name. def specifies a default value to return if not found.
len(m)	Returns the number of message headers.
str(m)	Turns the message into a string. The same as the as_string() method.
name in m	Returns True if name is the name of a header in the message.

In addition to these operators, m has the following methods that can be used to extract information:

m.get_all(name [, default])

Returns a list of all values for a header with name name. Returns default if no such header exists.

m.get_boundary([default])

Returns the boundary parameter found within the 'Content-type' header of a message. Typically the boundary is a string such as '================0995017162=='' that's used to separate the different subparts of a message. Returns default if no boundary parameter could be found.

`m.get_charset()`

Returns the character set associated with the message payload (for instance, `'iso-8859-1'`).

`m.get_charsets([default])`

Returns a list of all character sets that appear in the message. For multipart messages, the list will represent the character set of each subpart. The character set of each part is taken from `'Content-type'` headers that appear in the message. If no character set is specified or the content-type header is missing, the character set for that part is set to the value of *default* (which is None by default).

`m.get_content_charset([default])`

Returns the character set from the first `'Content-type'` header in the message. If the header is not found or no character set is specified, *default* is returned.

`m.get_content_maintype()`

Returns the main content type (for example, `'text'` or `'multipart'`).

`m.get_content_subtype()`

Returns the subcontent type (for example, `'plain'` or `'mixed'`).

`m.get_content_type()`

Returns a string containing the message content type (for example, `'multipart/mixed'` or `'text/plain'`).

`m.get_default_type()`

Returns the default content type (for example, `'text/plain'` for simple messages).

`m.get_filename([default])`

Returns the `filename` parameter from a `'Content-Disposition'` header, if any. Returns *default* if the header is missing or does not have a `filename` parameter.

`m.get_param(param [, default [, header [, unquote]]])`

Email headers often have parameters attached to them such as the `'charset'` and `'format'` parts of the header `'Content-Type: text/plain; charset="utf-8"; format=flowed'`. This method returns the value of a specific header parameter. *param* is a parameter name, *default* is a default value to return if the parameter is not found, *header* is the name of the header, and *unquote* specifies whether or not to unquote the parameter. If no value is given for *header*, parameters are taken from the `'Content-type'` header. The default value of *unquote* is True. The return value is either a string or a 3-tuple (*charset, language, value*) in the event the parameter was encoded according to RFC-2231 conventions. In this case, *charset* is a string such as `'iso-8859-1'`, *language* is a string containing a language code such as `'en'`, and *value* is the parameter value.

`m.get_params([default [, header [, unquote]]])`

Returns all parameters for *header* as a list. *default* specifies the value to return if the header isn't found. If *header* is omitted, the `'Content-type'` header is used. *unquote* is a flag that specifies whether or not to unquote values (True by default). The contents of the returned list are tuples (*name*, *value*) where *name* is the parameter name and *value* is the value as returned by the get_param() method.

m.get_payload([i [, decode]])

Returns the payload of a message. If the message is a simple message, a *byte string* containing the message body is returned. If the message is a multipart message, a list containing all the subparts is returned. For multipart messages, *i* specifies an optional index in this list. If supplied, only that message component will be returned. If *decode* is True, the payload is decoded according to the setting of any 'Content-Transfer-Encoding' header that might be present (for example, 'quoted-printable', 'base64', and so on). To decode the payload of a simple non-multipart message, set *i* to None and *decode* to True or specify *decode* using a keyword argument. It should be emphasized that the payload is returned as a byte string containing the raw content. If the payload represents text encoded in UTF-8 or some other encoding, you will need to use the decode() method on the result to convert it.

m.get_unixfrom()

Returns the UNIX-style 'From ...' line, if any.

m.is_multipart()

Returns True if *m* is a multipart message.

m.walk()

Creates a generator that iterates over all the subparts of a message, each of which is also represented by a Message instance. The iteration is a depth-first traversal of the message. Typically, this function could be used to process all the components of a multipart message.

Finally, Message instances have a few attributes that are related to low-level parsing process.

m.preamble

Any text that appears in a multipart message between the blank line that signals the end of the headers and the first occurrence of the multipart boundary string that marks the first subpart of the message.

m.epilogue

Any text in the message that appears after the last multipart boundary string and the end of the message.

m.defects

A list of all message defects found when parsing the message. Consult the online documentation for the email.errors module for further details.

The following example illustrates how the Message class is used while parsing an email message. The following code reads an email message, prints a short summary of useful headers, prints the plain text portions of the message, and saves any attachments.

```
import email
import sys

f = open(sys.argv[1],"r")          # Open message file
m = email.message_from_file(f)     # Parse message
```

```
# Print short summary of sender/recipient
print("From    : %s" % m["from"])
print("To      : %s" % m["to"])
print("Subject : %s" % m["subject"])
print("")

if not m.is_multipart():
    # Simple message. Just print the payload
    payload = m.get_payload(decode=True)
    charset = m.get_content_charset('iso-8859-1')
    print(payload.decode(charset))
else:
    # Multipart message.   Walk over all subparts and
    #      1. Print text/plain fragments
    #      2. Save any attachments
    for s in m.walk():
        filename = s.get_filename()
        if filename:
            print("Saving attachment: %s" % filename)
            data = s.get_payload(decode=True)
            open(filename,"wb").write(data)
        else:
            if s.get_content_type() == 'text/plain':
                payload = s.get_payload(decode=True)
                charset = s.get_content_charset('iso-8859-1')
                print(payload.decode(charset))
```

In this example, it is important to emphasize that operations that extract the payload of a message always return byte strings. If the payload represents text, you also need to decode it according to some character set. The m.get_content_charset() and payload.decode() operations in the example are carrying out this conversion.

Composing Email

To compose an email message, you can either create an empty instance of a Message object, which is defined in the email.message module, or you can use a Message object that was created by parsing an email message (see the previous section).

Message()

Creates a new message that is initially empty.

An instance m of Message supports the following methods for populating a message with content, headers, and other information.

m.add_header(name, value, **params)

Adds a new message header. name is the name of the header, value is the value of the header, and params is a set of keyword arguments that supply additional optional parameters. For example, add_header('Foo','Bar',spam='major') adds the header line 'Foo: Bar; spam="major"' to the message.

m.as_string([unixfrom])

Converts the entire message to a string. unixfrom is a Boolean flag. If this is set to True, a UNIX-style 'From ...' line appears as the first line. By default, unixfrom is False.

m.attach(payload)

Adds an attachment to a multipart message. *payload* must be another Message object (for example, email.mime.text.MIMEText). Internally, *payload* is appended to a list that keeps track of the different parts of the message. If the message is not a multipart message, use set_payload() to set the body of a message to a simple string.

m.del_param(param [, header [, requote]])

Deletes the parameter *param* from header *header*. For example, if a message has the header 'Foo: Bar; spam="major"', del_param('spam','Foo') would delete the 'spam="major"' portion of the header. If *requote* is True (the default), all remaining values are quoted when the header is rewritten. If *header* is omitted, the operation is applied to the 'Content-type' header.

m.replace_header(name, value)

Replaces the value of the first occurrence of the header *name* with value *value*. Raises KeyError if the header is not found.

m.set_boundary(boundary)

Sets the boundary parameter of a message to the string *boundary*. This string gets added as the boundary parameter to the 'Content-type' header in the message. Raises HeaderParseError if the message has no content-type header.

m.set_charset(charset)

Sets the default character set used by a message. *charset* may be a string such as 'iso-8859-1' or 'euc-jp'. Setting a character set normally adds a parameter to the 'Content-type' header of a message (for example, 'Content-type: text/html; charset="iso-8859-1"').

m.set_default_type(ctype)

Sets the default message content type to *ctype*. *ctype* is a string containing a MIME type such as 'text/plain' or 'message/rfc822'. This type is not stored in the 'Content-type' header of the message.

m.set_param(param, value [, header [, requote [, charset [, language]]]])

Sets the value of a header parameter. *param* is the parameter name, and *value* is the parameter value. *header* specifies the name of the header and defaults to 'Content-type'. *requote* specifies whether or not to requote all the values in the header after adding the parameter. By default, this is True. *charset* and *language* specify optional character set and language information. If these are supplied, the parameter is encoded according to RFC-2231. This produces parameter text such as param*="'iso-8859-1'en-us'some%20value".

m.set_payload(payload [, charset])

Sets the entire message payload to *payload*. For simple messages, *payload* can be a byte string containing the message body. For multipart messages, *payload* is a list of Message objects. *charset* optionally specifies the character set that was used to encode the text (see set_charset).

m.set_type(*type* [, *header* [, *requote*]])

Sets the type used in the 'Content-type' header. *type* is a string specifying the type, such as 'text/plain' or 'multipart/mixed'. *header* specifies an alternative header other than the default 'Content-type' header. *requote* quotes the value of any parameters already attached to the header. By default, this is True.

m.set_unixfrom(*unixfrom*)

Sets the text of the UNIX-style 'From ...' line. *unixfrom* is a string containing the complete text including the 'From' text. This text is only output if the *unixfrom* parameter of m.as_string() is set to True.

Rather than creating raw Message objects and building them up from scratch each time, there are a collection of prebuilt message objects corresponding to different types of content. These message objects are especially useful for creating multipart MIME messages. For instance, you would create a new message and attach different parts using the attach() method of Message. Each of these objects is defined in a different submodule, which is noted in each description.

MIMEApplication(*data* [, *subtype* [, *encoder* [, **params*]]])

Defined in email.mime.application. Creates a message containing application data. *data* is a byte string containing the raw data. *subtype* specifies the data subtype and is 'octet-stream' by default. *encoder* is an optional encoding function from the email.encoders subpackage. By default, data is encoded as base 64. *params* represents optional keyword arguments and values that will be added to the 'Content-type' header of the message.

MIMEAudio(*data* [, *subtype* [, *encoder* [, **params*]]])

Defined in email.mime.audio. Creates a message containing audio data. *data* is a byte string containing the raw binary audio data. *subtype* specifies the type of the data and is a string such as 'mpeg' or 'wav'. If no subtype is provided, the audio type will be guessed by looking at the data using the sndhdr module. *encoder* and *params* have the same meaning as for MIMEApplication.

MIMEImage(*data* [, *subtype* [, *encoder* [, **params*]]])

Defined in email.mime.image. Creates a message containing image data. *data* is a byte string containing the raw image data. *subtype* specifies the image type and is a string such as 'jpg' or 'png'. If no *subtype* is provided, the type will be guessed using a function in the imghdr module. *encoder* and *params* have the same meaning as for MIMEApplication.

MIMEMessage(*msg* [, *subtype*])

Defined in email.mime.message. Creates a new non-multipart MIME message. *msg* is a message object containing the initial payload of the message. *subtype* is the type of the message and defaults to 'rfc822'.

MIMEMultipart([*subtype* [, *boundary* [, *subparts* [, **params*]]]])

Defined in email.mime.multipart. Creates a new MIME multipart message. *subtype* specifies the optional subtype to be added to the 'Content-type: multipart/*subtype*' header. By default, *subtype* is 'mixed'. *boundary* is a string that specifies the boundary separator used to make each message subpart. If set to None

or omitted, a suitable boundary is determined automatically. *subparts* is a sequence of
Message objects that make up the contents of the message. *params* represents optional
keyword arguments and values that are added to the 'Content-type' header of the
message. Once a multipart message has been created, additional subparts can be added
using the Message.attach() method.

MIMEText(*data* [, *subtype* [, *charset*]])

Defined in email.mime.text. Creates a message containing textual data. *data* is a
string containing the message payload. *subtype* specifies the text type and is a string
such as 'plain' (the default) or 'html'. *charset* is the character set, which defaults
to 'us-ascii'. The message may be encoded depending on the contents of the message.

The following example shows how to compose and send an email message using the
classes in this section:

```
import smtplib
from email.mime.text import MIMEText
from email.mime.multipart import MIMEMultipart
from email.mime.audio import MIMEAudio

sender  = "jon@nogodiggydie.net"
receiver= "dave@dabeaz.com"
subject = "Faders up!"
body    = "I never should have moved out of Texas. -J.\n"
audio   = "TexasFuneral.mp3"

m = MIMEMultipart()
m["to"]       = receiver
m["from"]     = sender
m["subject"] = subject

m.attach(MIMEText(body))
apart = MIMEAudio(open(audio,"rb").read(),"mpeg")
apart.add_header("Content-Disposition","attachment",filename=audio)
m.attach(apart)

# Send the email message
s = smtplib.SMTP()
s.connect()
s.sendmail(sender, [receiver],m.as_string())
s.close()
```

Notes

- A number of advanced customization and configuration options have not been
  discussed. Readers should consult the online documentation for advanced uses of
  this module.

- The email package has gone through at least four different versions, where the
  underlying programming interface has been changed (i.e., submodules renamed,
  classes moved to different locations, etc.). This section has documented version
  4.0 of the interface that is used in both Python 2.6 and Python 3.0. If you are
  working with legacy code, the basic concepts still apply, but you may have to
  adjust the locations of classes and submodules.

hashlib

The hashlib module implements a variety of secure hash and message digest algorithms such as MD5 and SHA1. To compute a hash value, you start by calling one of the following functions, the name of which is the same as represented algorithm:

Function	Description
md5()	MD5 hash (128 bits)
sha1()	SHA1 hash (160 bits)
sha224()	SHA224 hash (224 bits)
sha256()	SHA256 hash (256 bits)
sha384()	SHA384 hash (384 bits)
sha512()	SHA512 hash (512 bits)

An instance d of the digest object returned by any of these functions has the following interface:

Method or Attribute	Description
d.update(data)	Updates the hash with new data. data must be a byte string. Repeated calls are the same as a single call with concatenated data.
d.digest()	Returns the value of the digest as a raw byte string.
d.hexdigest()	Returns a text string with the value of the digest encoded as a series of hex digits.
d.copy()	Returns a copy of the digest. The copy preserves the internal state of the original digest.
d.digest_size	Size of the resulting hash in bytes.
d.block_size	Internal block size of the hash algorithm in bytes.

An alternative construction interface is also provided by the module:

new(hashname)

Creates a new digest object. hashname is a string such as 'md5' or 'sha256' specifying the name of the hashing algorithm to use. The name of the hash can minimally be any of the previous hashing algorithms or a hashing algorithm exposed by the OpenSSL library (which depends on the installation).

hmac

The hmac module provides support for HMAC (Keyed-Hashing for Message Authentication), which is described in RFC-2104. HMAC is a mechanism used for message authentication that is built upon cryptographic hashing functions such as MD5 and SHA-1.

new(key [, msg [, digest]])

Creates a new HMAC object. Here, key is a byte string containing the starting key for the hash, msg contains initial data to process, and digest is the digest constructor that should be used for cryptographic hashing. By default, digest is hashlib.md5.

Normally, the initial key value is determined at random using a cryptographically strong random number generator.

An HMAC object, *h*, has the following methods:

h.update(*msg*)

Adds the string *msg* to the HMAC object.

h.digest()

Returns the digest of all data processed so far and returns a byte string containing the digest value. The length of the string depends on the underlying hashing function. For MD5, it is 16 characters; for SHA-1, it is 20 characters.

h.hexdigest()

Returns the digest as a string of hexadecimal digits.

h.copy()

Makes a copy of the HMAC object.

Example

The primary use of the hmac module is in applications that need to authenticate the sender of a message. To do this, the *key* parameter to new() is a byte string representing a secret key known by both the sender and receiver of a message. When sending a message, the sender will create a new HMAC object with the given key, update the object with message data to be sent, and then send the message data along with the resulting HMAC digest value to the receiver. The receiver can verify the message by computing its own HMAC digest value (using the same key and message data) and comparing the result to the digest value received. Here is an example:

```
import hmac
secret_key = b"peekaboo"        # Byte string only known to me.  Typically
                                # you would want to use a string of random bytes
                                # computed using os.urandom() or similar.


data = b"Hello World"           # The message to send

# Send the message somewhere.  out represents a socket or some
# other I/O channel on which we are sending data.
h = hmac.new(secret_key)
h.update(data)
out.send(data)                  # Send the data
out.send(h.digest())            # Send the digest


# Receive the message
# in represents a socket or some other I/O channel
# out which we are receiving data.
h = hmac.new(secret_key)
data = in.receive()             # Get the message data
h.update(data)
digest = in.receive()           # Get the digest sent by the sender
if digest != h.digest():
    raise AuthenticationError('Message not authenticated')
```

HTMLParser

In Python 3, this module is called `html.parser`. The `HTMLParser` module defines a class `HTMLParser` that can be used to parse HTML and XHTML documents. To use this module, you define your own class that inherits from `HTMLParser` and redefines methods as appropriate.

`HTMLParser()`

This is a base class that is used to create HTML parsers. It is initialized without any arguments.

An instance *h* of `HTMLParser` has the following methods:

`h.close()`

Closes the parser and forces the processing of any remaining unparsed data. This method is called after all HTML data has been fed to the parser.

`h.feed(data)`

Supplies new data to the parser. This data will be immediately parsed. However, if the data is incomplete (for example, it ends with an incomplete HTML element), the incomplete portion will be buffered and parsed the next time `feed()` is called with more data.

`h.getpos()`

Returns the current line number and character offset into that line as a tuple (`line`, `offset`).

`h.get_starttag_text()`

Returns the text corresponding to the most recently opened start tag.

`h.handle_charref(name)`

This handler method is called whenever a character reference such as `'&#ref;'` is encountered. *name* is a string containing the name of the reference. For example, when parsing `'&#229;'`, *name* will be set to `'229'`.

`h.handle_comment(data)`

This handler method is called whenever a comment is encountered. *data* is a string containing the text of the comment. For example, when parsing the comment `'<!--comment-->'`, *data* will contain the text `'comment'`.

`h.handle_data(data)`

This handler is called to process data that appears between tags. *data* is a string containing text.

`h.handle_decl(decl)`

This handler is called to process declarations such as `'<!DOCTYPE HTML ...>'`. *decl* is a string containing the text of the declaration not including the leading `'<!'` and trailing `'>'`.

h.handle_endtag(*tag*)

This handler is called whenever end tags are encountered. *tag* is the name of the tag converted to lowercase. For example, if the end tag is '</BODY>', *tag* is the string 'body'.

h.handle_entityref(*name*)

This handler is called to handle entity references such as '&*name*;'. *name* is a string containing the name of the reference. For example, if parsing '<', *name* will be set to 'lt'.

h.handle_pi(*data*)

This handler is called to handle processing instructions such as '<?*processing instruction*>'. *data* is a string containing the text of the processing instruction not including the leading '<?' or trailing '>'. When called on XHTML-style instructions of the form '<?...?>', the last '?' will be included in *data*.

h.handle_startendtag(*tag*, *attrs*)

This handler processes XHTML-style empty tags such as '<*tag* name="*value*"... />'. *tag* is a string containing the name of the tag. *attrs* contains attribute information and is a list of tuples of the form (*name*, *value*) where *name* is the attribute name converted to lowercase and *value* is the attribute value. When extracting values, quotes and character entities are replaced. For example, if parsing '<a href="http://www.foo.com"/>', *tag* is 'a' and *attrs* is [('href','http://www.foo.com')]. If not defined in derived classes, the default implementation of this method simply calls handle_starttag() and handle_endtag().

h.handle_starttag(*tag*, *attrs*)

This handler processes start tags such as '<*tag* name="*value*" ...>'. *tag* and *attrs* have the same meaning as described for handle_startendtag().

h.reset()

Resets the parser, discarding any unprocessed data.

The following exception is provided:

HTMLParserError

Exception raised as a result of parsing errors. The exception has three attributes. The msg attribute contains a message describing the error, the lineno attribute is the line number where the parsing error occurred, and the offset attribute is the character offset into the line.

Example

The following example fetches an HTML document using the urllib package and prints all links that have been specified with '<a href="...">' declarations:

```
# printlinks.py
try:
    from HTMLParser import HTMLParser
    from urllib2 import urlopen
except ImportError:
    from html.parser import HTMLParser
```

```
    from urllib.request import urlopen
import sys

class PrintLinks(HTMLParser):
    def handle_starttag(self,tag,attrs):
        if tag == 'a':
            for name,value in attrs:
                if name == 'href':  print(value)
p    = PrintLinks()
u    = urlopen(sys.argv[1])
data = u.read()
charset = u.info().getparam('charset')        # Python 2
#charset = u.info().get_content_charset()     # Python 3
p.feed(data.decode(charset))
p.close()
```

In the example, it must be noted that any HTML fetched using urllib is returned as a byte string. To properly parse it, it must be decoded into text according to the document character set encoding. The example shows how to obtain this in Python 2 and Python 3.

> **Note**
>
> The parsing capabilities of HTMLParser tend to be rather limited. In fact, with very complicated and/or malformed HTML, the parser can break. Users also find this module to be lower-level than is useful. If you are writing programs that must scrape data from HTML pages, consider the Beautiful Soup package (http://pypi.python.org/pypi/BeautifulSoup).

json

The json module is used to serialize and unserialize objects represented using JavaScript Object Notation (JSON). More information about JSON is available at http://json.org, but the format is really just a subset of JavaScript syntax. Incidentally, it's almost the same as Python syntax for representing lists and dictionaries. For example, a JSON array is written as [value1, value2, ...], and a JSON object is written as {name:value, name:value, ... }.

The following list shows how JSON values and Python values are mapped. The Python types listed in parentheses are accepted when encoding but are not returned when decoding (instead, the first listed type is returned).

JSON Type	Python Type
object	dict
array	list (tuple)
string	unicode (str, bytes)
number	int, float
true	True
false	False
null	None

For string data, you should assume the use of Unicode. If byte strings are encountered during encoding, they will be decoded into a Unicode string using `'utf-8'` by default (although this can be controlled). JSON strings are always returned as Unicode when decoding.

The following functions are used to encode/decode JSON documents:

`dump(obj, f, **opts)`

Serializes `obj` to a file-like object `f`. `opts` represents a collection of keyword arguments that can be specified to control the serialization process:

Keyword Argument	Description
skipkeys	Boolean flag that controls what to do when dictionary keys (not the values) are not a basic type such as a string or number. If True, the keys are skipped. If False (the default), a TypeError is raised.
ensure_ascii	Boolean flag that determines whether or not Unicode strings can be written to the file `f`. By default, this is False. Only set this to True if `f` is a file that correctly handles Unicode, such as a file created by the codecs module or opened with a specific encoding set.
check_circular	Boolean flag that determines whether circular references are checked for containers. By default, this is True. If set to False and a circular reference is encountered, an OverflowError exception is raised.
allow_nan	Boolean flag that determines whether out-of-range floating-point values are serialized (e.g., NaN, inf, -inf). By default this is True.
cls	A subclass of JSONEncoder to use. You would specify this if you created your own custom encoder by inheriting from JSONEncoder. If there are any additional keyword arguments given to dump(), they are passed as arguments to the constructor of this class.
indent	A non-negative integer that sets the amount indentation to use when printing array and object members. Setting this results in a kind of pretty-printing. By default, it is None, which causes the result to be in the most compact representation.
separators	A tuple of the form (`item_separator, dict_separator`) where `item_separator` is a string containing the separator used between array items and `dict_separator` is a string containing the separator used between dictionary keys and values. By default, the value is (`', ', ': '`).
encoding	Encoding to use for Unicode strings—`'utf-8'` by default.
default	A function used to serialize objects that are not any of the basic supported types. It should either return a value that can be serialized (i.e., a string) or raise TypeError. By default, a TypeError is raised for unsupported types.

`dumps(obj, **opts)`

The same as `dump()` except that a string containing the result is returned.

```
load(f, **opts)
```

Deserializes a JSON object on the file-like object *f* and returns it. *opts* represents a set of keyword arguments that can be specified to control the decoding process and are described next. Be aware that this function calls `f.read()` to consume the entire contents of *f*. Because of this, it should not be used on any kind of streaming file such as a socket where JSON data might be received as part of a larger or ongoing data stream.

Keyword Argument	Description
encoding	Encoding used to interpret any of the string values that are decoded. By default, this is `'utf-8'`.
strict	Boolean flag that determines whether or not literal (unescaped) newlines are allowed to appear in JSON strings. By default, this is `True`, which means that an exception is generated for such strings.
cls	A subclass of `JSONDecoder` to use for decoding. Only specified if you've created a custom decoder by inheriting from `JSONDecoder`. Any extra keyword arguments to `load()` are supplied to the class constructor.
object_hook	A function that's called with the result of every JSON object that is decoded. By default, this is the built-in `dict()` function.
parse_float	A function that's called to decode JSON floating-point values. By default, this is the built-in `float()` function.
parse_int	A function that's called to decode JSON integer values. By default, this is the built-in `int()` function.
parse_constant	A function that's called to decode JSON constants such as `'NaN'`, `'true'`, `'false'`, etc.

```
loads(s, **opts)
```

The same as `load()` except that an object is deserialized from the string *s*.

Although these functions share the same names as functions from the `pickle` and `marshal` modules and they serialize data, they are not used in the same way. Specifically, you should not use `dump()` to write more than one JSON-encoded object to the same file. Similarly, `load()` cannot be used to read more than one JSON-encoded object from the same file (if the input file has more than one object in it, you'll get an error). JSON-encoded objects should be treated in the same manner as HTML or XML. For example, you usually don't take two completely separate XML documents and just concatenate them together in the same file.

If you want to customize the encoding or decoding process, inherit from these base classes:

```
JSONDecoder(**opts)
```

A class that decodes JSON data. *opts* represents a set of keyword arguments that are identical to those used by the `load()` function. An instance *d* of `JSONDecoder` has the following two methods:

```
d.decode(s)
```

Returns the Python representation of the JSON object in *s*. *s* is a string.

d.raw_decode(*s*)

Returns a tuple (*pyobj*, *index*) where *pyobj* is the Python representation of a JSON object in *s* and *index* is the position in *s* where the JSON object ended. This can be used if you are trying to parse an object out of an input stream where there is extra data at the end.

JSONEncoder(***opts*)

A class that encodes a Python object into JSON. *opts* represents a set of keyword arguments that are identical to those used by the dump() function. An instance *e* of JSONEncoder has the following methods:

e.default(*obj*)

Method called when a Python object *obj* can't be encoded according to any of the normal encoding rules. The method should return a result which is one of the types that can be encoded (for example, a string, list, or dictionary).

e.encode(*obj*)

Method that's called to create a JSON representation of Python object *obj*.

e.iterencode(*obj*)

Creates an iterator that produces the strings making up the JSON representation of Python object *obj* as they are computed. The process of creating a JSON string is highly recursive in nature. For instance, it involves iterating over the keys of a dictionary and traversing down into other dictionaries and lists found along the way. If you use this method, you can process the output in a piecemeal manner as opposed to having everything collected into a huge in-memory string.

If you define subclasses that inherit from JSONDecoder or JSONEncoder, you need to exercise caution if your class also defines __init__(). To deal with all of the keyword arguments, here is how you should define it:

```
class MyJSONDecoder(JSONDecoder):
    def __init__(self, **kwargs):
            # Get my own arguments
            foo = kwargs.pop('foo',None)
            bar = kwargs.pop('bar',None)
            # Initialize the parent with everything left over
            JSONDecoder.__init__(self,**kwargs)
```

mimetypes

The mimetypes module is used to guess the MIME type associated with a file, based on its filename extension. It also converts MIME types to their standard filename extensions. MIME types consist of a type/subtype pair—for example 'text/html', 'image/png', or 'audio/mpeg'.

guess_type(*filename* [, *strict*])

Guesses the MIME type of a file based on its filename or URL. Returns a tuple (*type*, *encoding*) in which *type* is a string of the form "*type/subtype*" and *encoding* is the program used to encode the data for transfer (for example, compress or gzip). Returns (None, None) if the type cannot be guessed. If *strict* is True (the default), then only official MIME types registered with IANA are recognized (see http://www.iana.org/assignments/media-types). Otherwise, some common, but unofficial MIME types are also recognized.

guess_extension(*type* [, *strict*])

Guesses the standard file extension for a file based on its MIME type. Returns a string with the filename extension including the leading dot (.). Returns None for unknown types. If *strict* is True (the default), then only official MIME types are recognized.

guess_all_extensions(*type* [, *strict*])

The same as guess_extension() but returns a list of all possible filename extensions.

init([*files*])

Initializes the module. *files* is a sequence of filenames that are read to extract type information. These files contain lines that map a MIME type to a list of acceptable file suffixes such as the following:

```
image/jpeg:   jpe jpeg jpg
text/html:    htm html
...
```

read_mime_types(*filename*)

Loads type mapping from a given filename. Returns a dictionary mapping filename extensions to MIME type strings. Returns None if *filename* doesn't exist or cannot be read.

add_type(*type, ext* [, *strict*])

Adds a new MIME type to the mapping. *type* is a MIME type such as 'text/plain', *ext* is a filename extension such as '.txt', and *strict* is a Boolean indicating whether the type is an officially registered MIME type. By default, *strict* is True.

quopri

The quopri module performs quoted-printable transport encoding and decoding of byte strings. This format is used primarily to encode 8-bit text files that are mostly readable as ASCII but which may contain a small number of non-printing or special characters (for example, control characters or non-ASCII characters in the range 128-255). The following rules describe how the quoted-printable encoding works:

- Any printable non-whitespace ASCII character, with the exception of '=', is represented as is.

- The '=' character is used as an escape character. When followed by two hexadecimal digits, it represents a character with that value (for example, '=0C'). The equals sign is represented by '=3D'. If '=' appears at the end of a line, it denotes a soft line break. This only occurs if a long line of input text must be split into multiple output lines.

- Spaces and tabs are left as is but may not appear at the end of line.

It is fairly common to see this format used when documents make use of special characters in the extended ASCII character set. For example, if a document contained the
text "Copyright © 2009", this might be represented by the Python byte string
b'Copyright \xa9 2009'. The quoted-printed version of the string is b'Copyright
=A9 2009' where the special character '\xa9' has been replaced by the escape
sequence '=A9'.

decode(*input*, *output* [, *header*])

Decodes bytes into quopri format. *input* and *output* are file objects opened in binary
mode. If *header* is True, then the underscore (_) will be interpreted as a space.
Otherwise, it is left alone. This is used when decoding MIME headers that have been
encoded. By default, *header* is False.

decodestring(*s* [, *header*])

Decodes a string *s*. *s* may be a Unicode or byte string, but the result is always a byte
string. *header* has the same meaning as with decode().

encode(*input*, *output*, *quotetabs* [, *header*])

Encodes bytes into quopri format. *input* and *output* are file objects opened in binary
mode. *quotetabs*, if set to True, forces tab characters to be quoted in addition to the
normal quoting rules. Otherwise, tabs are left as is. By default, *quotetabs* is False.
header has the same meaning as for decode().

encodestring(*s* [, *quotetabs* [, *header*]])

Encodes byte string *s*. The result is also a byte string. *quotetabs* and *header* have the
same meaning as with encode().

> **Notes**
>
> The quoted-printable data encoding predates Unicode and is only applicable to 8-bit
> data. Even though it is most commonly applied to text, it really only applies to ASCII and
> extended ASCII characters represented as single bytes. When you use this module,
> make sure all files are in binary mode and that you are working with byte strings.

xml **Package**

Python includes a variety of modules for processing XML data. The topic of XML processing is large, and covering every detail is beyond the scope of this book. This section
assumes the reader is already familiar with some basic XML concepts. A book such as
Inside XML by Steve Holzner (New Riders) or *XML in a Nutshell* by Elliotte Harold
and W. Scott Means (O'Reilly and Associates) will be useful in explaining basic XML
concepts. Several books discuss XML processing with Python including *Python & XML*
by Christopher Jones (O'Reilly and Associates) and *XML Processing with Python* by Sean
McGrath (Prentice Hall).

Python provides two kinds of XML support. First, there is basic support for two
industry-standard approaches to XML parsing—SAX and DOM. SAX (Simple API for
XML) is based on event handling where an XML document is read sequentially and as
XML elements are encountered, handler functions get triggered to perform processing.
DOM (Document Object Model) builds a tree structure representing an entire XML

document. Once the tree has been built, DOM provides an interface for traversing the tree and extracting data. Neither the SAX nor DOM APIs originate with Python. Instead, Python simply copies the standard programming interface that was developed for Java and JavaScript.

Although you can certainly process XML using the SAX and DOM interfaces, the most convenient programming interface in the standard library is the ElementTree interface. This is a Python-specific approach to XML parsing that takes full advantage of Python language features and which most users find to be significantly easier and faster than SAX or DOM. The rest of this section covers all three XML parsing approaches, but the ElementTree approach is given the most detail.

Readers are advised that the coverage here is really only focused on basic parsing of XML data. Python also includes XML modules related to implementing new kinds of parsers, building XML documents from scratch, and so forth. In addition, a variety of third-party extensions extend Python's capabilities with additional XML features such as support for XSLT and XPATH. Links to further information can be found at http://wiki.python.org/moin/PythonXml.

XML Example Document

The following example illustrates a typical XML document, in this case a description of a recipe.

```
<?xml version="1.0" encoding="iso-8859-1"?>
<recipe>
    <title>
    Famous Guacamole
    </title>
    <description>
    A southwest favorite!
    </description>
    <ingredients>
        <item num="4"> Large avocados, chopped </item>
        <item num="1"> Tomato, chopped </item>
        <item num="1/2" units="C"> White onion, chopped </item>
        <item num="2" units="tbl"> Fresh squeezed lemon juice </item>
        <item num="1"> Jalapeno pepper, diced </item>
        <item num="1" units="tbl"> Fresh cilantro, minced </item>
        <item num="1" units="tbl"> Garlic, minced </item>
        <item num="3" units="tsp"> Salt </item>
        <item num="12" units="bottles"> Ice-cold beer </item>
    </ingredients>
    <directions>
    Combine all ingredients and hand whisk to desired consistency.
    Serve and enjoy with ice-cold beers.
    </directions>
</recipe>
```

The document consists of *elements* that start and end with tags such as `<title>...</title>`. Elements are typically nested and organized into a hierarchy—for example, the `<item>` elements that appear under `<ingredients>`. Within each document, a single element is the document root. In the example, this is the `<receipe>` element. Elements optionally have attributes as shown for the item elements `<item num="4">Large avocados, chopped</item>`.

Working with XML documents typically involves all of these basic features. For example, you may want to extract text and attributes from specific element types. To locate elements, you have to navigate through the document hierarchy starting at the root element.

xml.dom.minidom

The `xml.dom.minicom` module provides basic support for parsing an XML document and storing it in memory as a tree structure according to the conventions of DOM. There are two parsing functions:

parse(`file` [, `parser`])

Parses the contents of `file` and returns a node representing the top of the document tree. `file` is a filename or an already-open file object. `parser` is an optional SAX2-compatible parser object that will be used to construct the tree. If omitted, a default parser will be used.

parseString(`string` [, `parser`])

The same as `parse()`, except that the input data is supplied in a string instead of a file.

Nodes

The document tree returned by the parsing functions consists of a collection of nodes linked together. Each node n has the following attributes which can be used to extract information and navigate through the tree structure:

Node Attribute	Description
n.attributes	Mapping object that holds attribute values (if any).
n.childNodes	A list of all child nodes of n.
n.firstChild	The first child of node n.
n.lastChild	The last child of node n.
n.localName	Local tag name of an element. If a colon appears in the tag (for example, '<foo:bar ...>'), then this only contains the part after the colon.
n.namespaceURI	Namespace associated with n, if any.
n.nextSibling	The node that appears after n in the tree and has the same parent. Is None if n is the last sibling.
n.nodeName	The name of the node. The meaning depends on the node type.
n.nodeType	Integer describing the node type. It is set to one of the following values which are class variables of the Node class: ATTRIBUTE_NODE, CDATA_SECTION_NODE, COMMENT_NODE, DOCUMENT_FRAGMENT_NODE, DOCUMENT_NODE, DOCUMENT_TYPE_NODE, ELEMENT_NODE, ENTITY_NODE, ENTITY_REFERENCE_NODE, NOTATION_NODE, PROCESSING_INSTRUCTION_NODE, or TEXT_NODE.
n.nodeValue	The value of the node. The meaning depends on the node type.
n.parentNode	A reference to the parent node.
n.prefix	Part of a tag name that appears before a colon. For example, the element '<foo:bar ...>' would have a prefix of 'foo'.
n.previousSibling	The node that appears before n in the tree and has the same parent.

In addition to these attributes, all nodes have the following methods. Typically, these are used to manipulate the tree structure.

`n.appendChild(child)`

Adds a new child node, `child`, to `n`. The new child is added at the end of any other children.

`n.cloneNode(deep)`

Makes a copy of the node `n`. If `deep` is `True`, all child nodes are also cloned.

`n.hasAttributes()`

Returns `True` if the node has any attributes.

`n.hasChildNodes()`

Returns `True` if the node has any children.

`n.insertBefore(newchild, ichild)`

Inserts a new child, `newchild`, before another child, `ichild`. `ichild` must already be a child of `n`.

`n.isSameNode(other)`

Returns `True` if the node `other` refers to the same DOM node as `n`.

`n.normalize()`

Joins adjacent text nodes into a single text node.

`n.removeChild(child)`

Removes child `child` from `n`.

`n.replaceChild(newchild,oldchild)`

Replaces the child `oldchild` with `newchild`. `oldchild` must already be a child of `n`.

Although there are many different types of nodes that might appear in a tree, it is most common to work with `Document`, `Element`, and `Text` nodes. Each is briefly described next.

Document **Nodes**

A `Document` node `d` appears at the top of the entire document tree and represents the entire document as a whole. It has the following methods and attributes:

`d.documentElement`

Contains the root element of the entire document.

`d.getElementsByTagName(tagname)`

Searches all child nodes and returns a list of elements with a given tag name `tagname`.

`d.getElementsByTagNameNS(namespaceuri, localname)`

Searches all child nodes and returns a list of elements with a given namespace URI and local name. The returned list is an object of type `NodeList`.

Element **Nodes**

An `Element` node `e` represents a single XML element such as `'<foo>...</foo>'`. To get the text from an element, you need to look for `Text` nodes as children. The following attributes and methods are defined to get other information:

`e.tagName`

The tag name of the element. For example, if the element is defined by `'<foo ...>'`, the tag name is `'foo'`.

`e.getElementsByTagName(tagname)`

Returns a list of all children with a given tag name.

`e.getElementsByTagNameNS(namespaceuri, localname)`

Returns a list of all children with a given tag name in a namespace. `namespaceuri` and `localname` are strings that specify the namespace and tag name. If a namespace has been declared using a declaration such as `'<foo xmlns:foo="http://www.spam.com/foo">'`, `namespaceuri` is set to `'http://www.spam.com/foo'`. If searching for a subsequent element `'<foo:bar>'`, `localname` is set to `'bar'`. The returned object is of type `NodeList`.

`e.hasAttribute(name)`

Returns `True` if an element has an attribute with name `name`.

`e.hasAttributeNS(namespaceuri, localname)`

Returns `True` if an element has an attribute named by `namespaceuri` and `localname`. The arguments have the same meaning as described for `getElementsByTagNameNS()`.

`e.getAttribute(name)`

Returns the value of attribute `name`. The return value is a string. If the attribute doesn't exist, an empty string is returned.

`e.getAttributeNS(namespaceuri, localname)`

Returns the value of the attributed named by `namespaceuri` and `localname`. The return value is a string. An empty string is returned if the attribute does not exist. The arguments are the same as described for `getElementsByTagNameNS()`.

Text **Nodes**

`Text` nodes are used to represent text data. Text data is stored in the `t.data` attribute of a `Text` object `t`. The text associated with a given document element is always stored in `Text` nodes that are children of the element.

Utility Functions

The following utility methods are defined on nodes. These are not part of the DOM standard, but are provided by Python for general convenience and for debugging.

`n.toprettyxml([indent [, newl]])`

Creates a nicely formatted string containing the XML represented by node `n` and its children. `indent` specifies an indentation string and defaults to a tab (`'\t'`). `newl` specifies the newline character and defaults to `'\n'`.

***n*.toxml([*encoding*])**

Creates a string containing the XML represented by node *n* and its children. *encoding* specifies the encoding (for example, 'utf-8'). If no encoding is given, none is specified in the output text.

***n*.writexml(*writer* [, *indent* [, *addindent* [, *newl*]]])**

Writes XML to *writer*. *writer* can be any object that provides a write() method that is compatible with the file interface. *indent* specifies the indentation of *n*. It is a string that is prepended to the start of node *n* in the output. *addindent* is a string that specifies the incremental indentation to apply to child nodes of *n*. *newl* specifies the newline character.

DOM Example

The following example shows how to use the xml.dom.minidom module to parse and extract information from an XML file:

```
from xml.dom import minidom
doc = minidom.parse("recipe.xml")

ingredients = doc.getElementsByTagName("ingredients")[0]
items       = ingredients.getElementsByTagName("item")

for item in items:
    num      = item.getAttribute("num")
    units    = item.getAttribute("units")
    text     = item.firstChild.data.strip()
    quantity = "%s %s" % (num,units)
    print("%-10s %s" % (quantity,text))
```

> **Note**
>
> The xml.dom.minidom module has many more features for changing the parse tree and working with different kinds of XML node types. More information can be found in the online documentation.

xml.etree.ElementTree

The xml.etree.ElementTree module defines a flexible container object ElementTree for storing and manipulating hierarchical data. Although this object is commonly used in conjunction with XML processing, it is actually quite general-purpose—serving a role that's a cross between a list and dictionary.

ElementTree **objects**

The following class is used to define a new ElementTree object and represents the top level of a hierarchy.

ElementTree([*element* [, *file*]])

Creates a new ElementTree object. *element* is an instance representing the root node of the tree. This instance supports the element interface described next. *file* is either a filename or a file-like object from which XML data will be read to populate the tree.

An instance *tree* of `ElementTree` has the following methods:

`tree._setroot(element)`

Sets the root element to *element*.

`tree.find(path)`

Finds and returns the first top-level element in the tree whose type matches the given path. *path* is a string that describes the element type and its location relative to other elements. The following list describes the path syntax:

Path	Description
`'tag'`	Matches only top-level elements with the given tag—for example, `<tag>...</tag>`. Does not match elements defined at lower levels. A element of type *tag* embedded inside another element such as `<foo><tag>...</tag></foo>` is not matched.
`'parent/tag'`	Matches an element with tag `'tag'` if it's a child of an element with tag `'parent'`. As many path name components can be specified as desired.
`'*'`	Selects all child elements. For example, `'*/tag'` would match all grandchild elements with a tag name of `'tag'`.
`'.'`	Starts the search with the current node.
`'//'`	Selects all subelements on all levels beneath an element. For example, `'.//tag'` matches all elements with tag `'tag'` at all sublevels.

If you are working with a document involving XML namespaces, the *tag* strings in a path should have the form `'{uri}tag'` where *uri* is a string such as `'http://www.w3.org/TR/html4/'`.

`tree.findall(path)`

Finds all top-level elements in the tree that match the given path and returns them in document order as a list or an iterator.

`tree.findtext(path [, default])`

Returns the element text for the first top-level element in the tree matching the given path. *default* is a string to return if no matching element can be found.

`tree.getiterator([tag])`

Creates an iterator that produces all elements in the tree, in section order, whose tag matches *tag*. If *tag* is omitted, then every element in the tree is returned in order.

`tree.getroot()`

Returns the root element for the tree.

`tree.parse(source [, parser])`

Parses external XML data and replaces the root element with the result. *source* is either a filename or file-like object representing XML data. *parser* is an optional instance of `TreeBuilder`, which is described later.

`tree.write(file [, encoding])`

Writes the entire contents of the tree to a file. `file` is either a filename or a file-like object opened for writing. `encoding` is the output encoding to use and defaults to the interpreter default encoding if not specified (`'utf-8'` or `'ascii'` in most cases).

Creating Elements

The types of elements held in an `ElementTree` are represented by instances of varying types that are either created internally by parsing a file or with the following construction functions:

`Comment([text])`

Creates a new comment element. `text` is a string or byte string containing the element text. This element is mapped to XML comments when parsing or writing output.

`Element(tag [, attrib [, **extra]])`

Creates a new element. `tag` is the name of the element name. For example, if you were creating an element `'<foo>....</foo>'`, `tag` would be `'foo'`. `attrib` is a dictionary of element attributes specified as strings or byte strings. Any extra keyword arguments supplied in `extra` are also used to set element attributes.

`fromstring(text)`

Creates an element from a fragment of XML text in `text`—the same as `XML()` described next.

`ProcessingInstruction(target [, text])`

Creates a new element corresponding to a processing instruction. `target` and `text` are both strings or byte strings. When mapped to XML, this element corresponds to `'<?target text?>'`.

`SubElement(parent, tag [, attrib [, **extra]])`

The same as `Element()`, but it automatically adds the new element as a child of the element in `parent`.

`XML(text)`

Creates an element by parsing a fragment of XML code in `text`. For example, if you set `text` to `'<foo>....</foo>'`, this will create a standard element with a tag of `'foo'`.

`XMLID(text)`

The same as `XML(text)` except that `'id'` attributes are collected and used to build a dictionary mapping ID values to elements. Returns a tuple `(elem, idmap)` where `elem` is the new element and `idmap` is the ID mapping dictionary. For example, `XMLID('<foo id="123"><bar id="456">Hello</bar></foo>')` returns `(<Element foo>, {'123': <Element foo>, '456': <Element bar>})`.

The Element Interface

Although the elements stored in an `ElementTree` may have varying types, they all support a common interface. If `elem` is any element, then the following Python operators are defined:

Operator	Description
`elem[n]`	Returns the *n*th child element of `elem`.
`elem[n]` `=` `newelem`	Changes the *n*th child element of `elem` to a different element `newelem`.
`del` `elem[n]`	Deletes the *n*th child element of `elem`.
`len(elem)`	Number of child elements of `elem`.

All elements have the following basic data attributes:

Attribute	Description
`elem.tag`	String identifying the element type. For example, `<foo>...</foo>` has a tag of `'foo'`.
`elem.text`	Data associated with the element. Usually a string containing text between the start and ending tags of an XML element.
`elem.tail`	Additional data stored with the attribute. For XML, this is usually a string containing whitespace found after the element's end tag but before the next tag starts.
`elem.attrib`	Dictionary containing the element attributes.

Elements support the following methods, some of which emulate methods on dictionaries:

`elem.append(subelement)`

Appends the element `subelement` to the list of children.

`elem.clear()`

Clears all of the data in an element including attributes, text, and children.

`elem.find(path)`

Finds the first subelement whose type matches `path`.

`elem.findall(path)`

Finds all subelements whose type matches `path`. Returns a list or an iterable with the matching elements in document order.

`elem.findtext(path [, default])`

Finds the text for the first element whose type patches `path`. `default` is a string giving the value to return if there is no match.

`elem.get(key [, default])`

Gets the value of attribute `key`. `default` is a default value to return if the attribute doesn't exist. If XML namespaces are involved, then `key` will be a string of the form `'{uri}key}'` where `uri` is a string such as `'http://www.w3.org/TR/html4/'`.

elem.getchildren()

Returns all subelements in document order.

elem.getiterator([*tag*])

Returns an iterator that produces all subelements whose type matches *tag*.

elem.insert(*index, subelement*)

Inserts a subelement at position *index* in the list of children.

elem.items()

Returns all element attributes as a list of (*name, value*) pairs.

elem.keys()

Returns a list of all of the attribute names.

elem.remove(*subelement*)

Removes element *subelement* from the list of children.

elem.set(*key, value*)

Sets attribute *key* to value *value*.

Tree Building

An ElementTree object is easy to create from other tree-like structures. The following object is used for this purpose.

TreeBuilder([*element_factory*])

A class that builds an ElementTree structure using a series of start(), end(), and data() calls as would be triggered while parsing a file or traversing another tree structure. *element_factory* is an operation function that is called to create new element instances.

An instance *t* of TreeBuilder has these methods:

t.close()

Closes the tree builder and returns the top-level ElementTree object that has been created.

t.data(*data*)

Adds text data to the current element being processed.

t.end(*tag*)

Closes the current element being processed and returns the final element object.

t.start(*tag, attrs*)

Creates a new element. *tag* is the element name, and *attrs* is a dictionary with the attribute values.

Utility Functions

The following utility functions are defined:

`dump(elem)`

Dumps the element structure of `elem` to `sys.stdout` for debugging. The output is usually XML.

`iselement(elem)`

Checks if `elem` is a valid element object.

`iterparse(source [, events])`

Incrementally parses XML from `source`. `source` is a filename or a file-like object referring to XML data. `events` is a list of event types to produce. Possible event types are `'start'`, `'end'`, `'start-ns'`, and `'end-ns'`. If omitted, only `'end'` events are produced. The value returned by this function is an iterator that produces tuples `(event, elem)` where `event` is a string such as `'start'` or `'end'` and `elem` is the element being processed. For `'start'` events, the element is newly created and initially empty except for attributes. For `'end'` events, the element is fully populated and includes all subelements.

`parse(source)`

Fully parses an XML source into an `ElementTree` object. `source` is a filename or file-like object with XML data.

`tostring(elem)`

Creates an XML string representing `elem` and all of its subelements.

XML Examples

Here is an example of using `ElementTree` to parse the sample recipe file and print an ingredient list. It is similar to the example shown for DOM.

```
from xml.etree.ElementTree import ElementTree

doc = ElementTree(file="recipe.xml")
ingredients = doc.find('ingredients')

for item in ingredients.findall('item'):
    num   = item.get('num')
    units = item.get('units','')
    text  = item.text.strip()
    quantity = "%s %s" % (num, units)
    print("%-10s %s" % (quantity, text))
```

The path syntax of `ElementTree` makes it easier to simplify certain tasks and to take shortcuts as necessary. For example, here is a different version of the previous code that uses the path syntax to simply extract all `<item>...</item>` elements.

```
from xml.etree.ElementTree import ElementTree

doc = ElementTree(file="recipe.xml")
for item in doc.findall(".//item"):
    num   = item.get('num')
    units = item.get('units','')
    text  = item.text.strip()
    quantity = "%s %s" % (num, units)
    print("%-10s %s" % (quantity, text))
```

Consider an XML file `'recipens.xml'` that makes use of namespaces:

```
<?xml version="1.0" encoding="iso-8859-1"?>
<recipe xmlns:r="http://www.dabeaz.com/namespaces/recipe">
    <r:title>
    Famous Guacamole
    </r:title>
    <r:description>
    A southwest favorite!
    </r:description>
    <r:ingredients>
        <r:item num="4"> Large avocados, chopped </r:item>
        ...
    </r:ingredients>
    <r:directions>
    Combine all ingredients and hand whisk to desired consistency.
    Serve and enjoy with ice-cold beers.
    </r:directions>
</recipe>
```

To work with the namespaces, it is usually easiest to use a dictionary that maps the namespace prefix to the associated namespace URI. You then use string formatting operators to fill in the URI as shown here:

```
from xml.etree.ElementTree import ElementTree
doc = ElementTree(file="recipens.xml")
ns = {
    'r' : 'http://www.dabeaz.com/namespaces/recipe'
}
ingredients = doc.find('{%(r)s}ingredients' % ns)
for item in ingredients.findall('{%(r)s}item' % ns):
    num   = item.get('num')
    units = item.get('units','')
    text  = item.text.strip()
    quantity = "%s %s" % (num, units)
    print("%-10s %s" % (quantity, text))
```

For small XML files, it is fine to use the `ElementTree` module to quickly load them into memory so that you can work with them. However, suppose you are working with a huge XML file with a structure such as this:

```
<?xml version="1.0" encoding="utf-8"?>
<music>
    <album>
        <title>A Texas Funeral</title>
        <artist>Jon Wayne</artist>
        ...
    </album>
    <album>
        <title>Metaphysical Graffiti</title>
        <artist>The Dead Milkmen</artist>
        ...
    </album>
    ... continues for 100000 more albums ...
</music>
```

Reading a large XML file into memory tends to consume vast amounts of memory. For example, reading a 10MB XML file may result in an in-memory data structure of more than 100MB. If you're trying to extract information from such files, the easiest way to

do it is to use the `ElementTree.iterparse()` function. Here is an example of iteratively processing `<album>` nodes in the previous file:

```
from xml.etree.ElementTree import iterparse

iparse = iterparse("music.xml", ['start','end'])
# Find the top-level music element
for event, elem in iparse:
    if event == 'start' and elem.tag == 'music':
        musicNode = elem
        break

# Get all albums
albums = (elem for event, elem in iparse
                if event == 'end' and elem.tag == 'album')

for album in albums:
    # Do some kind of processing
    ...
    musicNode.remove(album)              # Throw away the album when done
```

The key to using `iterparse()` effectively is to get rid of data that you're no longer
using. The last statement `musicNode.remove(album)` is throwing away each `<album>`
element after we are done processing it (by removing it from its parent). If you monitor
the memory footprint of the previous program, you will find that it stays low even if
the input file is massive.

Notes

- The `ElementTree` module is by far the easiest and most flexible way of handling
  simple XML documents in Python. However, it does not provide a lot of bells
  and whistles. For example, there is no support for validation, nor does it provide
  any apparent way to handle complex aspects of XML documents such as DTDs.
  For these things, you'll need to install third-party packages. One such package,
  `lxml.etree` (at http://codespeak.net/lxml/), provides an ElementTree API to
  the popular libxml2 and libxslt libraries and provides full support for XPATH,
  XSLT, and other features.

- The `ElementTree` module itself is a third-party package maintained by Fredrik
  Lundh at http://effbot.org/zone/element-index.htm. At this site you can find
  versions that are more modern than what is included in the standard library and
  which offer additional features.

xml.sax

The `xml.sax` module provides support for parsing XML documents using the SAX2
API.

parse(*file, handler* [, *error_handler*])

Parses an XML document, *file*. *file* is either the name of a file or an open file
object. *handler* is a content handler object. *error_handler* is an optional SAX error-
handler object that is described further in the online documentation.

parseString(*string, handler* [, *error_handler*])

The same as `parse()` but parses XML data contained in a string instead.

Handler Objects

To perform any processing, you have to supply a content handler object to the `parse()` or `parseString()` functions. To define a handler, you define a class that inherits from `ContentHandler`. An instance `c` of `ContentHandler` has the following methods, all of which can be overridden in your handler class as needed:

`c.characters(content)`

Called by the parser to supply raw character data. `content` is a string containing the characters.

`c.endDocument()`

Called by the parser when the end of the document is reached.

`c.endElement(name)`

Called when the end of element `name` is reached. For example, if `'</foo>'` is parsed, this method is called with `name` set to `'foo'`.

`c.endElementNS(name, qname)`

Called when the end of an element involving an XML namespace is reached. `name` is a tuple of strings `(uri, localname)` and `qname` is the fully qualified name. Usually `qname` is None unless the SAX `namespace-prefixes` feature has been enabled. For example, if the element is defined as `'<foo:bar xmlns:foo="http://spam.com">'`, then the `name` tuple is `(u'http://spam.com', u'bar')`.

`c.endPrefixMapping(prefix)`

Called when the end of an XML namespace is reached. `prefix` is the name of the namespace.

`c.ignorableWhitespace(whitespace)`

Called when ignorable whitespace is encountered in a document. `whitespace` is a string containing the whitespace.

`c.processingInstruction(target, data)`

Called when an XML processing instruction enclosed in `<?` ... `?>` is encountered. `target` is the type of instruction, and `data` is the instruction data. For example, if the instruction is `'<?xml-stylesheet href="mystyle.css" type="text/css"?>`, `target` is set to `'xml-stylesheet'` and `data` is the remainder of the instruction text `'href="mystyle.css" type="text/css"'`.

`c.setDocumentLocator(locator)`

Called by the parser to supply a locator object that can be used for tracking line numbers, columns, and other information. The primary purpose of this method is simply to store the locator someplace so that you can use it later—for instance, if you needed to print an error message. The locator object supplied in `locator` provides four methods—`getColumnNumber()`, `getLineNumber()`, `getPublicId()`, and `getSystemId()`—that can be used to get location information.

`c.skippedEntity(name)`

Called whenever the parser skips an entity. `name` is the name of the entity that was skipped.

`c.startDocument()`

Called at the start of a document.

`c.startElement(name, attrs)`

Called whenever a new XML element is encountered. *name* is the name of the element, and *attrs* is an object containing attribute information. For example, if the XML element is `'<foo bar="whatever" spam="yes">'`, *name* is set to `'foo'` and *attrs* contains information about the bar and spam attributes. The *attrs* object provides a number of methods for obtaining attribute information:

Method	Description
`attrs.getLength()`	Returns the number of attributes
`attrs.getNames()`	Returns a list of attribute names
`attrs.getType(name)`	Gets the type of attribute *name*
`attrs.getValue(name)`	Gets the value of attribute *name*

`c.startElementNS(name, qname, attrs)`

Called when a new XML element is encountered and XML namespaces are being used. *name* is a tuple (*uri*, *localname*) and *qname* is a fully qualified element name (normally set to None unless the SAX2 namespace-prefixes feature has been enabled). *attrs* is an object containing attribute information. For example, if the XML element is `'<foo:bar xmlns:foo="http://spam.com" blah="whatever">'`, then *name* is (u'http://spam.com', u'bar'), *qname* is None, and *attrs* contains information about the attribute blah. The *attrs* object has the same methods as used in when accessing attributes in the startElement() method shown earlier. In addition, the following additional methods are added to deal with namespaces:

Method	Description
`attrs.getValueByQName(qname)`	Returns value for qualified name.
`attrs.getNameByQName(qname)`	Returns (*namespace*, *localname*) tuple for a name.
`attrs.getQNameByName(name)`	Returns qualified name for *name* specified as a tuple (*namespace*, *localname*).
`attrs.getQNames()`	Returns qualified names of all attributes.

`c.startPrefixMapping(prefix, uri)`

Called at the start of an XML namespace declaration. For example, if an element is defined as `'<foo:bar xmlns:foo="http://spam.com">'`, then *prefix* is set to `'foo'` and *uri* is set to `'http://spam.com'`.

Example

The following example illustrates a SAX-based parser, by printing out the ingredient list from the recipe file shown earlier. This should be compared with the example in the xml.dom.minidom section.

```
from xml.sax import ContentHandler, parse

class RecipeHandler(ContentHandler):
    def startDocument(self):
        self.initem = False
    def startElement(self,name,attrs):
        if name == 'item':
            self.num   = attrs.get('num','1')
            self.units = attrs.get('units','none')
            self.text = []
            self.initem = True
    def endElement(self,name):
        if name == 'item':
            text = "".join(self.text)
            if self.units == 'none': self.units = ""
            unitstr = "%s %s" % (self.num, self.units)
            print("%-10s %s" % (unitstr,text.strip()))
            self.initem = False
    def characters(self,data):
        if self.initem:
            self.text.append(data)

parse("recipe.xml",RecipeHandler())
```

Notes

The xml.sax module has many more features for working with different kinds of XML data and creating custom parsers. For example, there are handler objects that can be defined to parse DTD data and other parts of the document. More information can be found in the online documentation.

xml.sax.saxutils

The xml.sax.saxutils module defines some utility functions and objects that are often used with SAX parsers, but are often generally useful elsewhere.

escape(data [, entities])

Given a string, data, this function replaces certain characters with escape sequences. For example, '<' gets replaced by '<'. entities is an optional dictionary that maps characters to the escape sequences. For example, setting entities to { u'\xf1' : 'ñ' } would replace occurences of ñ with 'ñ'.

unescape(data [, entities])

Unescapes special escape sequences that appear in data. For instance, '<' is replaced by '<'. entities is an optional dictionary mapping entities to unescaped character values. entities is the inverse of the dictionary used with escape()—for example, { 'ñ' : u'\xf1' }.

quoteattr(data [, entities])

Escapes the string data, but performs additional processing that allows the result value to be used as an XML attribute value. The return value can be printed directly as an attribute value—for example, print "<element attr=%s>" % quoteattr(somevalue). entities is a dictionary compatible for use with the escape() function.

XMLGenerator([out [, encoding]])

A ContentHandler object that merely echoes parsed XML data back to the output stream as an XML document. This re-creates the original XML document. out is the output document and defaults to sys.stdout. encoding is the character encoding to use and defaults to 'iso-8859-1'. This can be useful if you're trying to debug your parsing code and use a handler that is known to work.

25

Miscellaneous Library Modules

The modules listed in this section are not covered in detail in this book but are still considered to be part of the standard library. These modules have mostly been omitted from previous chapters because they are either extremely low-level and of limited use, restricted to very specific platforms, obsolete, or so complicated that coverage would require a complete book on the topic. Although these modules are have been omitted from this book, online documentation is available for each module at http://docs.python.org/library/*modname*. An index of all modules is also available at http://docs.python.org/library/modindex.html.

The modules listed here represent a common subset of functionality between Python 2 and Python 3. If you are using a module that is not listed here, chances are it has been officially deprecated. Some modules have changed names in Python 3. The new name is shown in parentheses, if applicable.

Python Services

The following modules provide additional services related to the Python language and execution of the Python interpreter. Many of these modules are related to parsing and compilation of Python source code.

Module	Description
bdb	Access to the debugger framework
code	Interpreter base classes
codeop	Compiles Python code
compileall	Byte-compiles Python files in a directory
copy_reg (copyreg)	Register built-in types for use with the pickle module
dis	Disassembler
distutils	Distribution of Python modules
fpectl	Floating-point exception control
imp	Provides access to the implementation of the import statement
keyword	Tests whether a string is a Python keyword
linecache	Retrieves lines from source files
modulefinder	Finds modules used by a script

Module	Description
parser	Accesses parse trees of Python source code
pickletools	Tools for pickle developers
pkgutil	Package extension utility
pprint	Prettyprinter for objects
pyclbr	Extracts information for class browsers
py_compile	Compiles Python source to bytecode files
repr (reprlib)	Alternate implementation of the repr() function
symbol	Constants used to represent internal nodes of parse trees
tabnanny	Detection of ambiguous indentation
test	Regression testing package
token	Terminal nodes of the parse tree
tokenize	Scanner for Python source code
user	User configuration file parsing
zipimport	Import modules from zip archives

String Processing

The following modules are some older, now obsolete, modules used for string processing.

Module	Description
difflib	Compute deltas between strings
fpformat	Floating-point number formatting
stringprep	Internet string preparation
textwrap	Text wrapping

Operating System Modules

These modules provide additional operating system services. In some cases, the functionality of a module listed here is already incorporated into the functionality of other modules covered in Chapter 19, "Operating System Services."

Module	Description
crypt	Access to the UNIX crypt function
curses	Curses library interface
grp	Access to the group database
pty	Pseudo terminal handling
pipes	Interface to shell pipelines
nis	Interface to Sun's NIS
platform	Access to platform-specific information
pwd	Access to the password database
readline	Access to GNU readline library
rlcompleter	Completion function for GNU readline

Module	Description
resource	Resource usage information
sched	Event scheduler
spwd	Access to the shadow password database
stat	Support for interpreting results of os.stat()
syslog	Interface to UNIX syslog daemon
termios	UNIX TTY control
tty	Terminal control functions

Network

The following modules provide support for lesser-used network protocols:

Module	Description
imaplib	IMAP protocol
nntplib	NNTP protocol
poplib	POP3 protocol
smtpd	SMTP server
telnetlib	Telnet protocol

Internet Data Handling

The following modules provide additional support for Internet data processing not covered in Chapter 24, "Internet Data Handling and Encoding."

Module	Description
binhex	BinHex4 file format support
formatter	Generic output formatting
mailcap	Mailcap file handling
mailbox	Reading various mailbox formats
netrc	Netrc file processing
plistlib	Macintosh plist file processing
uu	UUencode file support
xdrlib	Encode and decode Sun XDR data

Internationalization

The following modules are used for writing internationalized applications:

Module	Description
gettext	Multilingual text handling services
locale	Internationalization functions provided by the system

Multimedia Services

The following modules provide support for handling various kinds of multimedia files:

Module	Description
audioop	Manipulates raw audio data
aifc	Reads and writes AIFF and AIFC files
sunau	Reads and writes Sun AU files
wave	Reads and writes WAV files
chunk	Reads IFF chunked data
colorsys	Conversions between color systems
imghdr	Determines the type of an image
sndhdr	Determines the type of a sound file
ossaudiodev	Access to OSS-compatible audio devices

Miscellaneous

The following modules round out the list and don't really neatly fall into any of the other categories:

Module	Description
cmd	Line-oriented command interpreters
calendar	Calendar-generation functions
shlex	Simple lexical analysis module
Tkinter (tkinter)	Python interface to Tcl/Tk
winsound	Playing sounds on Windows

Extending and Embedding

26

Extending and Embedding Python

One of the most powerful features of Python is its ability to interface with software written in C. There are two common strategies for integrating Python with foreign code. First, foreign functions can be packaged into a Python library module for use with the `import` statement. Such modules are known as *extension modules* because they extend the interpreter with additional functionality not written in Python. This is, by far, the most common form of Python-C integration because it gives Python applications access to high-performance programming libraries. The other form of Python-C integration is *embedding*. This is a process by which Python programs and the interpreter are accessed as a library from C. This latter approach is sometimes used by programmers who want to embed the Python interpreter into an existing C application framework for some reason—usually as some kind of scripting engine.

This chapter covers the absolute basics of the Python-C programming interface. First, the essential parts of the C API used to build extension modules and embed the Python interpreter are covered. This section is not intended to be a tutorial, so readers new to this topic should consult the "Embedding and Extending the Python Interpreter" document available at http://docs.python.org/extending, as well as the "Python/C API Reference Manual" available at http://docs.python.org/c-api. Next, the `ctypes` library module is covered. This is an extremely useful module that allows you to access functions in C libraries without writing any additional C code or using a C compiler.

It should be noted that for advanced extension and embedding applications, most programmers tend to turn to advanced code generators and programming libraries. For example, the SWIG project (http://www.swig.org) is a compiler that creates Python extension modules by parsing the contents of C header files. References to this and other extension building tools can be found at http://wiki.python.org/moin/IntegratingPythonWithOtherLanguages.

Extension Modules

This section outlines the basic process of creating a handwritten C extension module for Python. When you create an extension module, you are building an interface

between Python and existing functionality written in C. For C libraries, you usually
start from a header file such as the following:

```
/* file : example.h */
#include <stdio.h>
#include <string.h>
#include <math.h>

typedef struct Point {
  double x;
  double y;
} Point;

/* Compute the GCD of two integers x and y */
extern int    gcd(int x, int y);

/* Replace och with nch in s and return the number of replacements */
extern int    replace(char *s, char och, char nch);

/* Compute the distance between two points */
extern double distance(Point *a, Point *b);

/* A preprocessor constant */
#define MAGIC 0x31337
```

These function prototypes have some kind of implementation in a separate file. For
example:

```
/* example.c */
#include "example.h"
/* Compute GCD of two positive integers x and y */
int gcd(int x, int y) {
    int g;
    g = y;
    while (x > 0) {
        g = x;
        x = y % x;
        y = g;
    }
    return g;
}

/* Replace a character in a string */
int replace(char *s, char oldch, char newch) {
  int nrep = 0;
  while (s = strchr(s,oldch)) {
    *(s++) = newch;
    nrep++;
  }
  return nrep;
}

/* Distance between two points */
double distance(Point *a, Point *b) {
  double dx,dy;
  dx = a->x - b->x;
  dy = a->y - b->y;
  return sqrt(dx*dx + dy*dy);
}
```

Here is a C main() program that illustrates the use of these functions:

```c
/* main.c */
#include "example.h"
int main() {
  /* Test the gcd() function */
  {
    printf("%d\n", gcd(128,72));
    printf("%d\n", gcd(37,42));
  }
  /* Test the replace() function */
  {
    char s[] = "Skipping along unaware of the unspeakable peril.";
    int  nrep;
    nrep = replace(s,' ','-');
    printf("%d\n", nrep);
    printf("%s\n",s);
  }
  /* Test the distance() function */
  {
    Point a = { 10.0, 15.0 };
    Point b = { 13.0, 11.0 };
    printf("%0.2f\n", distance(&a,&b));
  }
}
```

Here is the output of the previous program:

```
% a.out
8
1
6
Skipping-along-unaware-of-the-unspeakable-peril.
5.00
```

An Extension Module Prototype

Extension modules are built by writing a separate C source file that contains a set of wrapper functions which provide the glue between the Python interpreter and the underlying C code. Here is an example of a basic extension module called _example:

```c
/* pyexample.c */

#include "Python.h"
#include "example.h"

static char py_gcd_doc[] = "Computes the GCD of two integers";
static PyObject *
py_gcd(PyObject *self, PyObject *args) {
  int x,y,r;
  if (!PyArg_ParseTuple(args,"ii:gcd",&x,&y)) {
      return NULL;
  }
  r = gcd(x,y);
  return Py_BuildValue("i",r);
}

static char py_replace_doc[] = "Replaces all characters in a string";
static PyObject *
```

```
py_replace(PyObject *self, PyObject *args, PyObject *kwargs) {
  static char *argnames[] = {"s","och","nch",NULL};
  char      *s,*sdup;
  char      och, nch;
  int       nrep;
  PyObject *result;
  if (!PyArg_ParseTupleAndKeywords(args,kwargs, "scc:replace",
                                   argnames, &s, &och, &nch)) {
      return NULL;
  }
  sdup = (char *) malloc(strlen(s)+1);
  strcpy(sdup,s);
  nrep = replace(sdup,och,nch);
  result = Py_BuildValue("(is)",nrep,sdup);
  free(sdup);
  return result;
}

static char py_distance_doc[] = "Computes the distance between two points";
static PyObject *
py_distance(PyObject *self, PyObject *args) {
  PyErr_SetString(PyExc_NotImplementedError,"distance() not implemented.");
  return NULL;
}

static PyMethodDef _examplemethods[] = {
  {"gcd", py_gcd, METH_VARARGS, py_gcd_doc},
  {"replace", py_replace, METH_VARARGS | METH_KEYWORDS, py_replace_doc},
  {"distance",py_distance,METH_VARARGS, py_distance_doc},
  {NULL, NULL, 0, NULL}
};

#if PY_MAJOR_VERSION < 3
/* Python 2 module initialization */
void init_example(void) {
  PyObject *mod;
  mod = Py_InitModule("_example", _examplemethods);
  PyModule_AddIntMacro(mod,MAGIC);
}
#else
/* Python 3 module initialization */
static struct PyModuleDef _examplemodule = {
   PyModuleDef_HEAD_INIT,
   "_example",   /* name of module */
   NULL,         /* module documentation, may be NULL */
   -1,
   _examplemethods
};
PyMODINIT_FUNC
PyInit__example(void) {
  PyObject *mod;
  mod = PyModule_Create(&_examplemodule);
  PyModule_AddIntMacro(mod, MAGIC);
  return mod;
}
#endif
```

Extension modules always need to include "Python.h". For each C function to be
accessed, a wrapper function is written. These wrapper functions accept either two
arguments (self and args, both of type PyObject *) or three arguments (self, args,

and kwargs, all of type PyObject *). The self parameter is used when the wrapper function is implementing a built-in method to be applied to an instance of some object. In this case, the instance is placed in the self parameter. Otherwise, self is set to NULL. args is a tuple containing the function arguments passed by the interpreter. kwargs is a dictionary containing keyword arguments.

Arguments are converted from Python to C using the PyArg_ParseTuple() or PyArg_ParseTupleAndKeywords() function. Similarly, the Py_BuildValue() function is used to construct an acceptable return value. These functions are described in later sections.

Documentation strings for extension functions should be placed in separate string variables such as py_gcd_doc and py_replace_doc as shown. These variables are referenced during module initialization (described shortly).

Wrapper functions should never, under penalty of certain flaming death, mutate data received by reference from the interpreter. This is why the py_replace() wrapper is making a copy of the received string before passing it to the C function (which modifies it in place). If this step is omitted, the wrapper function may violate Python's string immutability.

If you want to raise an exception, you use the PyExc_SetString() function as shown in the py_distance() wrapper. NULL is returned to signal that an error has occurred.

The method table _examplemethods is used to associate Python names with the C wrapper functions. These are the names used to call the function from the interpreter. The METH_VARARGS flag indicates the calling conventions for a wrapper. In this case, only positional arguments in the form of a tuple are accepted. It can also be set to METH_VARARGS | METH_KEYWORDS to indicate a wrapper function accepting keyword arguments. The method table additionally sets the documentation strings for each wrapper function.

The final part of an extension module performs an initialization procedure that varies between Python 2 and Python 3. In Python 2, the module initialization function init_example is used to initialize the contents of the module. In this case, the Py_InitModule("_example",_examplemethods) function creates a module, _example, and populates it with built-in function objects corresponding to the functions listed in the method table. For Python 3, you have to create an PyModuleDef object _examplemodule that describes the module. You then write a function PyInit__example() that initializes the module as shown. The module initialization function is also the place where you install constants and other parts of a module, if necessary. For example, the PyModule_AddIntMacro() is adding the value of a preprocessor to the module.

It is important to note that naming is critically important for module initialization. If you are creating a module called *modname*, the module initialization function must be called init*modname*() in Python 2 and PyInit_*modname*() in Python 3. If you don't do this, the interpreter won't be able to correctly load your module.

Naming Extension Modules

It is standard practice to name C extension modules with a leading underscore such as '_example'. This convention is followed by the Python standard library itself. For

instance, there are modules named _socket, _thread, _sre, and _fileio corresponding to the C programming components of the socket, threading, re, and io modules. Generally, you do not use these C extension modules directly. Instead, you create a
high-level Python module such as the following:

```
# example.py
from _example import *
# Add additional support code below
...
```

The purpose of this Python wrapper is to supply additional support code for your
module or to provide a higher-level interface. In many cases, it is easier to implement
parts of an extension module in Python instead of C. This design makes it easy to do
this. If you look at many standard library modules, you will find that they have been
implemented as a mix of C and Python in this manner.

Compiling and Packaging Extensions

The preferred mechanism for compiling and packaging an extension module is to use
distutils. To do this, you create a setup.py file that looks like this:

```
# setup.py
from distutils.core import setup, Extension

setup(name="example",
      version="1.0",
      py_modules = ['example.py'],
      ext_modules = [
        Extension("_example",
                  ["pyexample.c","example.c"])
      ]
     )
```

In this file, you need to include the high-level Python file (example.py) and the source
files making up the extension module (pyexample.c, example.c). To build the module
for testing, type the following:

```
% python setup.py build_ext --inplace
```

This will compile the extension code into a shared library and leave it in
the current working directory. The name of this library will be
_examplemodule.so, _examplemodule.pyd, or some similar variant.

If the compilation was successful, using your module is straightforward. For example:

```
% python3.0
Python 3.0 (r30:67503, Dec  4 2008, 09:40:15)
[GCC 4.0.1 (Apple Inc. build 5465)] on darwin
Type "help", "copyright", "credits" or "license" for more information.
>>> import example
>>> example.gcd(78,120)
6
>>> example.replace("Hello World",' ','-')
(1, 'Hello-World')
>>> example.distance()
Traceback (most recent call last):
  File "<stdin>", line 1, in <module>
NotImplementedError: distance() not implemented.
>>>
```

More complicated extension modules may need to supply additional build information, such as include directories, libraries, and preprocessor macros. They can also be included in setup.py, as follows:

```
# setup.py
from distutils.core import setup, Extension

setup(name="example",
      version="1.0",
      py_modules = ['example.py'],
      ext_modules = [
        Extension("_example",
                  ["pyexample.c","example.c"],
                  include_dirs = ["/usr/include/X11","/opt/include"],
                  define_macros = [('DEBUG',1'),
                                   ('MONDO_FLAG',1)],
                  undef_macros = ['HAVE_FOO','HAVE_NOT'],
                  library_dirs= ["/usr/lib/X11", "/opt/lib"],
                  libraries = [ "X11", "Xt", "blah" ])
        ]
      )
```

If you want to install an extension module for general use, you simply type python setup.py install. Further details about this are found in Chapter 8, "Modules, Packages, and Distribution."

In some situations, you may want to build an extension module manually. This almost always requires advanced knowledge of various compiler and linker options. The following is an example on Linux:

```
linux % gcc -c -fpic -I/usr/local/include/python2.6 example.c pyexample.c
linux % gcc -shared example.o pyexample.o -o _examplemodule.so
```

Type Conversion from Python to C

The following functions are used by extension modules to convert arguments passed from Python to C. Their prototypes are defined by including the Python.h header file.

```
int PyArg_ParseTuple(PyObject *args, char *format, ...);
```

Parses a tuple of positional arguments in *args* into a series of C variables. *format* is a format string containing zero or more of the specifier strings from Tables 26.1–26.3, which describe the expected contents of *args*. All the remaining arguments contain the addresses of C variables into which the results will be placed. The order and types of these arguments must match the specifiers used in *format*. Zero is returned if the arguments could not be parsed.

```
int PyArg_ParseTupleAndKeywords(PyObject *args, PyObject *kwargs,
                                char *format, char **kwlist, ...);
```

Parses both a tuple of positional arguments and a dictionary of keyword arguments contained in *kwargs*. *format* has the same meaning as for PyArg_ParseTuple(). The only difference is that *kwlist* is a null-terminated list of strings containing the names of all the arguments. Returns 1 on success, 0 on error.

Table 26.1 lists the format codes that are placed in the *format* argument to convert numbers. The C argument type column lists the C data type that should be passed to the PyArg_Parse*() functions. For numbers, it is always a pointer to a location where the result should be stored.

Table 26.1   **Numeric Conversions and Associated C Data Types for** `PyArg_Parse*`

Format	Python Type	C Argument Type
"b"	Integer	signed char *r
"B"	Integer	unsigned char *r
"h"	Integer	short *r
"H"	Integer	unsigned short *r
"i"	Integer	int *r
"I"	Integer	unsigned int *r
"l"	Integer	long int *r
"k"	Integer	unsigned long *r
"L"	Integer	long long *r
"K"	Integer	unsigned long long *r
"n"	Integer	Py_ssize_t *r
"f"	Float	float *r
"d"	Float	double *r
"D"	Complex	Py_complex *r

When signed integer values are converted, an OverflowError exception is raised if the Python integer is too large to fit into the requested C data type. However, conversions that accept unsigned values (e.g., 'I', 'H', 'K', and so on) do not check for overflow and will silently truncate the value if it exceeds the supported range. For floating-point conversions, a Python int or float may be supplied as input. In this case, integers will be promoted to a float. User-defined classes are accepted as numbers as long as they provide appropriate conversion methods such as __int__() or __float__(). For example, a user-defined class that implements __int__() will be accepted as input for any of the previously shown integer conversions (and __int__() invoked automatically to do the conversion).

Table 26.2 shows the conversions that apply to strings and bytes. Many of the string conversions return both a pointer and length as a result.

Table 26.2   **String Conversions and Associated C Data Types for** `PyArg_Parse*`

Format	Python Type	C Argument Type
"c"	String or byte string of length 1	char *r
"s"	String	char **r
"s#"	String, bytes, or buffer	char **r, int *len
"s*"	String, bytes, or buffer	Py_buffer *r
"z"	String or None	char **r
"z#"	String, bytes, or None	char **r, int *len
"z*"	String, bytes, buffer, or None	Py_buffer *r
"y"	Bytes (null-terminated)	char **r
"y#"	Bytes	char **r, int *len
"y*"	Bytes or buffer	Py_buffer *r
"u"	String (Unicode)	Py_UNICODE **r
"u#"	String (Unicode)	Py_UNICODE **r, int *len
"es"	String	const char *enc, char **r

Table 26.2   **Continued**

Format	Python Type	C Argument Type
"es#"	String or bytes	const char *enc, char **r, int *len
"et"	String or null-terminated bytes	const char *enc, char **r, int *len
"et#"	String or bytes	const char *enc, char **r, int *len
"t#"	Read-only buffer	char **r, int *len
"w"	Read-write buffer	char **r
"w#"	Read-write buffer	char **r, int *len
"w*"	Read-write buffer	Py_buffer *r

String handling presents a special problem for C extensions because the char * datatype is used for many different purposes. For instance, it might refer to text, a single character, or a buffer of raw binary data. There is also the issue of what to do with embedded NULL characters ('\x00') that C uses to signal the end of text strings.

In Table 26.2, the conversion codes of "s", "z", "u", "es", and "et" should be used if you are passing text. For these codes, Python assumes that the input text does not contain any embedded NULLs—if so, a TypeError exception is raised. However, the resulting string in C can be safely assumed to be NULL-terminated. In Python 2, both 8-bit and Unicode strings can be passed, but in Python 3, all conversions except for "et" require the Python str type and do not work with bytes. When Unicode strings are passed to C, they are always encoded using the default Unicode encoding used by the interpreter (usually UTF-8). The one exception is the "u" conversion code that returns a string using Python's internal Unicode representation. This is an array of Py_UNICODE values where Unicode characters are typically represented by the wchar_t type in C.

The "es" and "et" codes allow you to specify an alternative encoding for the text. For these, you supply an encoding name such as 'utf-8' or 'iso-8859-1', and the text will be encoded into a buffer and returned in that format. The "et" code differs from "es" in that if a Python byte-string is given, it is assumed to have already been encoded and is passed through unmodified. One caution with "es" and "et" conversions is that they dynamically allocate memory for the result and require the user to explicitly release it using PyMem_Free(). Thus, code that uses these conversions should look similar to this:

```
PyObject *py_wrapper(PyObject *self, PyObject *args) {
    char *buffer;
    if (!PyArg_ParseTuple(args,"es","utf-8",&buffer)) {
        return NULL;
    }
    /* Do something. */
    ...
    /* Cleanup and return the result */
    PyMem_Free(buffer);
    return result;
}
```

For handling text or binary data, use the `"s#"`, `"z#"`, `"u#"`, `"es#"`, or `"et#"` codes. These conversions work exactly the same as before except that they additionally return a length. Because of this, the restriction on embedded NULL characters is lifted. In addition, these conversions add support for byte strings and any other objects that support something known as the buffer interface. The *buffer interface* is a means by which a Python object can expose a raw binary buffer representing its contents. Typically, you find it on strings, bytes, and arrays (e.g., the arrays created in the `array` module support it). In this case, if an object provides a readable buffer interface, a pointer to the buffer and its size is returned. Finally, if a non-NULL pointer and length are given to the `"es#"` and `"et#"` conversions, it is assumed that these represent a pre-allocated buffer into which the result of the encoding can be placed. In this case, the interpreter does not allocate new memory for the result and you don't have to call `PyMem_Free()`.

The conversion codes of `"s*"` and `"z*"` are similar to `"s#"` and `"z#"` except that they populate a `Py_buffer` structure with information about the received data. More information about this can be found in PEP-3118, but this structure minimally has attributes `char *buf`, `int len`, and `int itemsize` that point to the buffer, the buffer length (in bytes), and the size of items held in the buffer. In addition, the interpreter places a lock on the buffer that prevents it from being changed by other threads as long as it is held by extension code. This allows the extension to work with the buffer contents independently, possibly in a different thread than the interpreter. It is up to the user to call `PyBuffer_Release()` on the buffer after all processing is complete.

The conversion codes of `"t#"`, `"w"`, `"w#"`, and `"w*"` are just like the `"s"` family of codes except that they only accept objects implementing the buffer interface. `"t#"` requires the buffer to be readable. The `"w"` code requires the buffer to be both readable and writable. A Python object supporting a writable buffer is assumed to be mutable. Thus, it is legal for a C extension to overwrite or modify the buffer contents.

The conversion codes of `"y"`, `"y#"`, and `"y*"` are just like the `"s"` family of codes except that they only accept byte strings. Use these to write functions that must only take bytes, not Unicode strings. The `"y"` code only accepts byte strings that do not contain embedded NULL characters.

Table 26.3 lists conversion codes that are used to accept arbitrary Python objects as input and to leave the result as type `PyObject *`. These are sometimes used for C extensions that need to work with Python objects that are more complicated than simple numbers or strings—for example, if you needed a C extension function to accept an instance of a Python class or dictionary.

Table 26.3   **Python Object Conversions and Associated C Data Types for**
`PyArg_Parse*`

Format	Python Type	C Type
`"O"`	Any	`PyObject **r`
`"O!"`	Any	`PyTypeObject *type, PyObject **r`
`"O&"`	Any	`int (*converter)(PyObject *, void *), void *r`
`"S"`	String	`PyObject **r`
`"U"`	Unicode	`PyObject **r`

The "O", "S", and "U" specifiers return raw Python objects of type PyObject *. "S" and "U" restrict this object to be a string or Unicode string, respectively.

The "O!" conversion requires two C arguments: a pointer to a Python type object and a pointer to a PyObject * into which a pointer to the object is placed. A TypeError is raised if the type of the object doesn't match the type object. For example:

```
/* Parse a List Argument */
PyObject *listobj;
PyArg_ParseTuple(args,"O!", &PyList_Type, &listobj);
```

The following list shows the C type names corresponding to some Python container types that might be commonly used with this conversion.

C Name	Python Type
PyList_Type	list
PyDict_Type	dict
PySet_Type	set
PyFrozenSet_Type	frozen_set
PyTuple_Type	tuple
PySlice_Type	slice
PyByteArray_Type	bytearray

The "O&" conversion takes two arguments (*converter*, *addr*) and uses a function to convert a PyObject * to a C data type. *converter* is a pointer to a function with the prototype int *converter*(PyObject *obj, void *addr), where *obj* is the passed Python object and *addr* is the address supplied as the second argument in PyArg_ParseTuple(). *converter*() should return 1 on success, 0 on failure. On error, the converter should also raise an exception. This kind of conversion can be used to map Python objects such as lists or tuples into C data structures. For example, here is a possible implementation of the distance() wrapper from our earlier code:

```
/* Convert a tuple into a Point structure. */
int convert_point(PyObject *obj, void *addr) {
    Point *p = (Point *) addr;
    return PyArg_ParseTuple(obj,"ii", &p->x, &p->y);
}
PyObject *py_distance(PyObject *self, PyObject *args) {
    Point p1, p2;
    double result;
    if (!PyArg_ParseTuple(args, "O&O&",
                          convert_point, &p1, convert_point, &p2)) {
        return NULL;
    }
    result = distance(&p1,&p2);
    return Py_BuildValue("d",result);
}
```

Finally, argument format strings can contain a few additional modifiers related to tuple unpacking, documentation, error messages, and default arguments. The following is a list of these modifiers:

Format String	Description
`"(items)"`	Unpack a tuple of objects. Items consist of format conversions.
`"|"`	Start of optional arguments.
`":"`	End of arguments. The remaining text is the function name.
`";"`	End of arguments. The remaining text is the error message.

The `"(items)"` unpacks values from a Python tuple. This can be a useful way to map tuples into simple C structures. For example, here is another possible implementation of the `py_distance()` wrapper function:

```
PyObject *py_distance(PyObject *self, PyObject *args) {
    Point p1, p2;
    double result;
    if (!PyArg_ParseTuple(args,"(dd)(dd)",
                          &p1.x, &p1.y, &p2.x, &p2.y)) {
        return NULL;
    }
    result = distance(&p1,&p2);
    return Py_BuildValue("d",result);
}
```

The modifier `"|"` specifies that all remaining arguments are optional. This can appear only once in a format specifier and cannot be nested. The modifier `":"` indicates the end of the arguments. Any text that follows is used as the function name in any error messages. The modifier `";"` signals the end of the arguments. Any following text is used as the error message. Note that only one of : and ; should be used. Here are some examples:

```
PyArg_ParseTuple(args,"ii:gcd", &x, &y);
PyArg_ParseTuple(args,"ii; gcd requires 2 integers", &x, &y);

/* Parse with optional arguments */
PyArg_ParseTuple(args,"s|s", &buffer, &delimiter);
```

Type Conversion from C to Python

The following C function is used to convert the values contained in C variables to a Python object:

```
PyObject *Py_BuildValue(char *format, ...)
```

This constructs a Python object from a series of C variables. *format* is a string describing the desired conversion. The remaining arguments are the values of C variables to be converted.

The *format* specifier is similar to that used with the `PyArg_ParseTuple*` functions, as shown in Table 26.4.

Table 26.4   **Format Specifiers for** `Py_BuildValue()`

Format	Python Type	C Type	Description
`""`	None	`void`	Nothing.
`"s"`	String	`char *`	Null-terminated string. If the C string pointer is NULL, None is returned.
`"s#"`	String	`char *, int`	String and length. May contain null bytes. If the C string pointer is NULL, None is returned.
`"y"`	Bytes	`char *`	Same as `"s"` except a byte string is returned.
`"y#"`	Bytes	`char *, int`	Same as `"s#` except a byte string is returned.
`"z"`	String or None	`char *`	Same as `"s"`.
`"z#"`	String or None	`char *, int`	Same as `"s#"`.
`"u"`	Unicode	`Py_UNICODE *`	Null-terminated Unicode string. If the string pointer is NULL, None is returned.
`"u#"`	Unicode	`Py_UNICODE *`	Unicode string and length.
`"U"`	Unicode	`char *`	Converts a null-terminated C string into a Unicode string.
`"U#"`	Unicode	`char *, int`	Converts a C string into Unicode.
`"b"`	Integer	`char`	8-bit integer.
`"B"`	Integer	`unsigned char`	8-bit unsigned integer.
`"h"`	Integer	`short`	Short 16-bit integer.
`"H"`	Integer	`unsigned short`	Unsigned short 16-bit integer.
`"i"`	Integer	`int`	Integer.
`"I"`	Integer	`unsigned int`	Unsigned integer
`"l"`	Integer	`long`	Long integer.
`"L"`	Integer	`unsigned long`	Unsigned long integer.
`"k"`	Integer	`long long`	Long long.
`"K"`	Integer	`unsigned long long`	Unsigned long long.
`"n"`	Integer	`Py_ssize_t`	Python size type.
`"c"`	String	`char`	Single character. Creates a Python string of length 1.
`"f"`	Float	`float`	Single-precision floating point.
`"d"`	Float	`double`	Double-precision floating point.
`"D"`	Complex	`Py_complex`	Complex number.
`"O"`	Any	`PyObject *`	Any Python object. The object is unchanged except for its reference count, which is incremented by 1. If a NULL pointer is given, a NULL pointer is returned. This is useful if an error has been signaled elsewhere and you want it to propagate.

Table 26.4   **Continued**

Format	Python Type	C Type	Description
`"O&"`	Any	`converter, any`	C data processed through a converter function.
`"S"`	String	`PyObject *`	Same as `"O"`.
`"N"`	Any	`PyObject *`	Same as `"O"` except that the reference count is not incremented.
`"(items)"`	Tuple	`vars`	Creates a tuple of items. `items` is a string of format specifiers from this table. `vars` is a list of C variables corresponding to the items in `items`.
`"[items]"`	List	`vars`	Creates a list of items. `items` is a string of format specifiers. `vars` is a list of C variables corresponding to the items in `items`.
`"{items}"`	Dictionary	`vars`	Creates a dictionary of items.

Here are some examples of building different kinds of values:

```
Py_BuildValue("")                         None
Py_BuildValue("i",37)                     37
Py_BuildValue("ids",37,3.4,"hello")       (37, 3.5, "hello")
Py_BuildValue("s#","hello",4)             "hell"
Py_BuildValue("()")                       ()
Py_BuildValue("(i)",37)                   (37,)
Py_BuildValue("[ii]",1,2)                 [1,2]
Py_BuildValue("[i,i]",1,2)                [1,2]
Py_BuildValue("{s:i,s:i}","x",1,"y",2)    {'x':1, 'y':2}
```

For Unicode string conversions involving `char *`, it is assumed that the data consists of a series of bytes encoded using the default Unicode encoding (usually UTF-8). The data will be automatically decoded into a Unicode string when passed to Python. The only exceptions are the `"y"` and `"y#"` conversions that return a raw byte string.

Adding Values to a Module

In the module initialization function of an extension module, it is common to add constants and other support values. The following functions can be used to do this:

```
int PyModule_AddObject(PyObject *module, const char *name, PyObject *value)
```

Adds a new value to a module. `name` is the name of the value, and `value` is a Python object containing the value. You can build this value using `Py_BuildValue()`.

```
int PyModule_AddIntConstant(PyObject *module, const char *name, long value)
```

Adds an integer value to a module.

```
void PyModule_AddStringConstant(PyObject *module, const char *name, const char
*value)
```

Adds a string value to a module. `value` must be a null-terminated string.

```
void PyModule_AddIntMacro(PyObject *module, macro)
```

Adds a macro value to a module as an integer. `macro` must be the name of preprocessor macro.

```
void PyModule_AddStringMacro(PyObject *module, macro)
```

Adds a macro value to a module as a string.

Error Handling

Extension modules indicate errors by returning NULL to the interpreter. Prior to returning NULL, an exception should be set using one of the following functions:

```
void PyErr_NoMemory()
```

Raises a `MemoryError` exception.

```
void PyErr_SetFromErrno(PyObject *exc)
```

Raises an exception. `exc` is an exception object. The value of the exception is taken from the `errno` variable in the C library.

```
void PyErr_SetFromErrnoWithFilename(PyObject *exc, char *filename)
```

Like `PyErr_SetFromErrno()`, but includes the file name in the exception value as well.

```
void PyErr_SetObject(PyObject *exc, PyObject *val)
```

Raises an exception. `exc` is an exception object, and `val` is an object containing the value of the exception.

```
void PyErr_SetString(PyObject *exc, char *msg)
```

Raises an exception. `exc` is an exception object, and `msg` is a message describing what went wrong.

The `exc` argument in these functions can be set to one of the following:

C Name	Python Exception
PyExc_ArithmeticError	ArithmeticError
PyExc_AssertionError	AssertionError
PyExc_AttributeError	AttributeError
PyExc_EnvironmentError	EnvironmentError
PyExc_EOFError	EOFError
PyExc_Exception	Exception
PyExc_FloatingPointError	FloatingPointError
PyExc_ImportError	ImportError
PyExc_IndexError	IndexError
PyExc_IOError	IOError
PyExc_KeyError	KeyError
PyExc_KeyboardInterrupt	KeyboardInterrupt
PyExc_LookupError	LookupError
PyExc_MemoryError	MemoryError
PyExc_NameError	NameError
PyExc_NotImplementedError	NotImplementedError

C Name	Python Exception
PyExc_OSError	OSError
PyExc_OverflowError	OverflowError
PyExc_ReferenceError	ReferenceError
PyExc_RuntimeError	RuntimeError
PyExc_StandardError	StandardError
PyExc_StopIteration	StopIteration
PyExc_SyntaxError	SyntaxError
PyExc_SystemError	SystemError
PyExc_SystemExit	SystemExit
PyExc_TypeError	TypeError
PyExc_UnicodeError	UnicodeError
PyExc_UnicodeEncodeError	UnicodeEncodeError
PyExc_UnicodeDecodeError	UnicodeDecodeError
PyExc_UnicodeTranslateError	UnicodeTranslateError
PyExc_ValueError	ValueError
PyExc_WindowsError	WindowsError
PyExc_ZeroDivisionError	ZeroDivisionError

The following functions are used to query or clear the exception status of the interpreter:

void PyErr_Clear()

Clears any previously raised exceptions.

PyObject *PyErr_Occurred()

Checks to see whether or not an exception has been raised. If so, the current exception value is returned. Otherwise, NULL is returned.

int PyErr_ExceptionMatches(PyObject *exc)

Checks to see if the current exception matches the exception *exc*. Returns 1 if true, 0 otherwise. This function follows the same exception matching rules as in Python code. Therefore, *exc* could be a superclass of the current exception or a tuple of exception classes.

The following prototype shows how to implement a try-except block in C:

```
/* Carry out some operation involving Python objects */
if (PyErr_Occurred()) {
    if (PyErr_ExceptionMatches(PyExc_ValueError)) {
        /* Take some kind of recovery action */
        ...
        PyErr_Clear();
        return result;  /* A valid PyObject * */
    } else {
        return NULL;    /* Propagate the exception to the interpreter */
    }
}
```

Reference Counting

Unlike programs written in Python, C extensions may have to manipulate the reference count of Python objects. This is done using the following macros, all of which are applied to objects of type PyObject *.

Macro	Description
Py_INCREF(obj)	Increments the reference count of obj, which must be non-null.
Py_DECREF(obj)	Decrements the reference count of obj, which must be non-null.
Py_XINCREF(obj)	Increments the reference count of obj, which may be null.
Py_XDECREF(obj)	Decrements the reference count of obj, which may be null.

Manipulating the reference count of Python objects in C is a delicate topic, and readers are strongly advised to consult the "Extending and Embedding the Python Interpreter" document available at http://docs.python.org/extending before proceeding any further. As a general rule, it is not necessary to worry about reference counting in C extension functions except in the following cases:

- If you save a reference to a Python object for later use or in a C structure, you must increase the reference count.

- Similarly, to dispose of an object that was previously saved, decrease its reference count.

- If you are manipulating Python containers (lists, dicts, and so on) from C, you may have to manually manipulate reference counts of the individual items. For example, high-level operations that get or set items in a container typically increase the reference count.

You will know that you have a reference counting problem if your extension code crashes the interpreter (you forgot to increase the reference count) or the interpreter leaks memory as your extension functions are used (you forgot to decrease a reference count).

Threads

A global interpreter lock is used to prevent more than one thread from executing in the interpreter at once. If a function written in an extension module executes for a long time, it will block the execution of other threads until it completes. This is because the lock is held whenever an extension function is invoked. If the extension module is thread-safe, the following macros can be used to release and reacquire the global interpreter lock:

Py_BEGIN_ALLOW_THREADS

Releases the global interpreter lock and allows other threads to run in the interpreter. The C extension must not invoke any functions in the Python C API while the lock is released.

Py_END_ALLOW_THREADS

Reacquires the global interpreter lock. The extension will block until the lock can be acquired successfully in this case.

The following example illustrates the use of these macros:

```
PyObject *py_wrapper(PyObject *self, PyObject *args) {
        ...
        PyArg_ParseTuple(args, ...)
        Py_BEGIN_ALLOW_THREADS
        result = run_long_calculation(args);
        Py_END_ALLOW_THREADS
        ...
        return Py_BuildValue(fmt,result);
}
```

Embedding the Python Interpreter

The Python interpreter can also be embedded into C applications. With embedding, the Python interpreter operates as a programming library where C programs can initialize the interpreter, have the interpreter run scripts and code fragments, load library modules, and manipulate functions and objects implemented in Python.

An Embedding Template

With embedding, your C program is in charge of the interpreter. Here is a simple C program that illustrates the most minimal embedding possible:

```
#include <Python.h>

int main(int argc, char **argv) {
    Py_Initialize();
    PyRun_SimpleString("print('Hello World')");
    Py_Finalize();
    return 0;
}
```

In this example, the interpreter is initialized, a short script is executed as a string, and the interpreter is shut down. Before proceeding any further, it is usually a good idea to get the prior example working first.

Compilation and Linking

To compile an embedded interpreter on UNIX, your code must include the "Python.h" header file and link against the interpreter library such as libpython2.6.a. The header file is typically found in /usr/local/include/python2.6, and the library is typically found in /usr/local/lib/python2.6/config. For Windows, you will need to locate these files in the Python installation directory. Be aware that the interpreter may depend on other libraries you need to include when linking. Unfortunately, this tends to be platform-specific and related to how Python was configured on your machine—you may have to fiddle around for a bit.

Basic Interpreter Operation and Setup

The following functions are used to set up the interpreter and to run scripts:

```
int PyRun_AnyFile(FILE *fp, char *filename)
```

If *fp* is an interactive device such as tty in UNIX, this function calls PyRun_InteractiveLoop(). Otherwise, PyRun_SimpleFile() is called. *filename* is a string that gives a name for the input stream. This name will appear when the inter-preter reports errors. If *filename* is NULL, a default string of "???" is used as the file name.

`int PyRun_SimpleFile(FILE *fp, char *filename)`

Similar to `PyRun_SimpleString()`, except that the program is read from the file *fp*.

`int PyRun_SimpleString(char *command)`

Executes *command* in the `__main__` module of the interpreter. Returns 0 on success, -1 if an exception occurred.

`int PyRun_InteractiveOne(FILE *fp, char *filename)`

Executes a single interactive command.

`int PyRun_InterativeLoop(FILE *fp, char *filename)`

Runs the interpreter in interactive mode.

`void Py_Initialize()`

Initializes the Python interpreter. This function should be called before using any other functions in the C API, with the exception of `Py_SetProgramName()`, `PyEval_InitThreads()`, `PyEval_ReleaseLock()`, and `PyEval_AcquireLock()`.

`int Py_IsInitialized()`

Returns 1 if the interpreter has been initialized, 0 if not.

`void Py_Finalize()`

Cleans up the interpreter by destroying all the sub-interpreters and objects that were created since calling `Py_Initialize()`. Normally, this function frees all the memory allocated by the interpreter. However, circular references and extension modules may introduce memory leaks that cannot be recovered by this function.

`void Py_SetProgramName(char *name)`

Sets the program name that's normally found in the `argv[0]` argument of the `sys` module. This function should only be called before `Py_Initialize()`.

`char *Py_GetPrefix()`

Returns the prefix for installed platform-independent files. This is the same value as found in `sys.prefix`.

`char *Py_GetExecPrefix()`

Returns the `exec-prefix` for installed platform-dependent files. This is the same value as found in `sys.exec_prefix`.

`char *Py_GetProgramFullPath()`

Returns the full path name of the Python executable.

`char *Py_GetPath()`

Returns the default module search path. The path is returned as a string consisting of directory names separated by a platform-dependent delimiters (: on UNIX, ; on DOS/Windows).

```
int PySys_SetArgv(int argc, char **argv)
```

Sets command-line options used to populate the value of sys.argv. This should only be called before Py_Initialize().

Accessing Python from C

Although there are many ways that the interpreter can be accessed from C, four essential tasks are the most common with embedding:

- Importing Python library modules (emulating the import statement)
- Getting references to objects defined in modules
- Calling Python functions, classes, and methods
- Accessing the attributes of objects (data, methods, and so on)

All of these operations can be carried out using these basic operations defined in the Python C API:

```
PyObject *PyImport_ImportModule(const char *modname)
```

Imports a module *modname* and returns a reference to the associated module object.

```
PyObject *PyObject_GetAttrString(PyObject *obj, const char *name)
```

Gets an attribute from an object. This is the same as *obj.name*.

```
int PyObject_SetAttrString(PyObject *obj, const char *name, PyObject *value)
```

Sets an attribute on an object. This is the same as *obj.name* = *value*.

```
PyObject *PyEval_CallObject(PyObject *func, PyObject *args)
```

Calls *func* with arguments *args*. *func* is a Python callable object (function, method, class, and so on). *args* is a tuple of arguments.

```
PyObject *
PyEval_CallObjectWithKeywords(PyObject *func, PyObject *args, PyObject *kwargs)
```

Calls *func* with positional arguments *args* and keyword arguments *kwargs*. *func* is a callable object, *args* is a tuple, and *kwargs* is a dictionary.

The following example illustrates the use of these functions by calling and using various parts of the re module from C. This program prints out all of the lines read from stdin that contain a Python regular expression supplied by the user.

```
#include "Python.h"

int main(int argc, char **argv) {
    PyObject *re;
    PyObject *re_compile;
    PyObject *pat;
    PyObject *pat_search;
    PyObject *args;
    char      buffer[256];

    if (argc != 2) {
        fprintf(stderr,"Usage: %s pattern\n",argv[0]);
        exit(1);
    }

    Py_Initialize();
```

```
    /* import re */
    re   = PyImport_ImportModule("re");

    /* pat = re.compile(pat,flags) */
    re_compile = PyObject_GetAttrString(re,"compile");
    args = Py_BuildValue("(s)", argv[1]);
    pat = PyEval_CallObject(re_compile, args);
    Py_DECREF(args);

    /* pat_search = pat.search  - bound method*/
    pat_search = PyObject_GetAttrString(pat,"search");

    /* Read lines and perform matches */
    while (fgets(buffer,255,stdin)) {
        PyObject *match;
        args = Py_BuildValue("(s)", buffer);

        /* match = pat.search(buffer) */
        match = PyEval_CallObject(pat_search,args);
        Py_DECREF(args);
        if (match != Py_None) {
            printf("%s",buffer);
        }
        Py_XDECREF(match);
    }
    Py_DECREF(pat);
    Py_DECREF(re_compile);
    Py_DECREF(re);
    Py_Finalize();
    return 0;
}
```

In any embedding code, it is critically important to properly manage reference counts. In particular, you will need to decrease the reference count on any objects created from C or returned to C as a result of evaluating functions.

Converting Python Objects to C

A major problem with embedded use of the interpreter is converting the result of a Python function or method call into a suitable C representation. As a general rule, you need to know in advance exactly what kind of data an operation is going to return. Sadly, there is no high-level convenience function like `PyArg_ParseTuple()` for converting a single object value. However, the following lists some low-level conversion functions that will convert a few primitive Python data types into an appropriate C representation as long as you know exactly what kind of Python object you are working with:

Python-to-C Conversion Functions

```
long    PyInt_AsLong(PyObject *)
long    PyLong_AsLong(PyObject *)
double  PyFloat_AsDouble(PyObject *)
char    *PyString_AsString(PyObject *) (Python 2 only)
char    *PyBytes_AsString(PyObject *) (Python 3 only)
```

For any types more complicated than this, you will need to consult the C API documentation (http://docs.python.org/c-api).

ctypes

The `ctypes` module provides Python with access to C functions defined in DLLs and shared libraries. Although you need to know some details about the underlying C library (names, calling arguments, types, and so on), you can use `ctypes` to access C code without having to write C extension wrapper code or compile anything with a C compiler. `ctypes` is a sizable library module with a lot of advanced functionality. Here, we cover the essential parts of it that are needed to get going.

Loading Shared Libraries

The following classes are used to load a C shared library and return an instance representing its contents:

CDLL(name [, mode [, handle [, use_errno [, use_last_error]]]])

A class representing a standard C shared library. `name` is the name of the library such as `'libc.so.6'` or `'msvcrt.dll'`. `mode` provides flags that determine how the library is loaded and are passed to the underlying `dlopen()` function on UNIX. It can be set to the bitwise-or of `RTLD_LOCAL`, `RTLD_GLOBAL`, or `RTLD_DEFAULT` (the default). On Windows, `mode` is ignored. `handle` specifies a handle to an already loaded library (if available). By default, it is `None`. `use_errno` is a Boolean flag that adds an extra layer of safety around the handling of the C errno variable in the loaded library. This layer saves a thread-local copy of errno prior to calling any foreign function and restores the value afterwards. By default, `use_errno` is `False`. `use_last_error` is a Boolean flag that enables a pair of functions `get_last_error()` and `set_last_error()` that can be used to manipulate the system error code. These are more commonly used on Windows. By default, `use_last_error` is `False`.

WinDLL(name [, mode [, handle [, use_errno [, use_last_error]]]])

The same as `CDLL()` except that the functions in the library are assumed to follow the Windows `stdcall` calling conventions (Windows).

The following utility function can be used to locate shared libraries on the system and construct a name suitable for use as the `name` parameter in the previous classes. It is defined in the `ctypes.util` submodule:

find_library(name)

Defined in `ctypes.util`. Returns a path name corresponding to the library `name`. `name` is a library name without any file suffix such as `'libc'`, `'libm'`, and so on The string returned by the function is a full path name such as `'/usr/lib/libc.so.6'`. The behavior of this function is highly system-dependent and depends on the underlying configuration of shared libraries and environment (for example, the setting of `LD_LIBRARY_PATH` and other parameters). Returns `None` if the library can't be located.

Foreign Functions

The shared library instances created by the `CDLL()` class operates as a proxy to the underlying C library. To access library contents, you just use attribute lookup (the operator). For example:

```
>>> import ctypes
>>> libc = ctypes.CDLL("/usr/lib/libc.dylib")
>>> libc.rand()
16807
>>> libc.atoi("12345")
12345
>>>
```

In this example, operations such as libc.rand() and libc.atoi() are directly calling functions in the loaded C library.

ctypes assumes that all functions accept parameters of type int or char * and return results of type int. Thus, even though the previous function calls "worked," calls to other C library functions do not work as expected. For example:

```
>>> libc.atof("34.5")
-1073746168
>>>
```

To address this problem, the type signature and handling of any foreign function *func* can be set by changing the following attributes:

func.argtypes

A tuple of ctypes datatypes (described here) describing the input arguments to *func*.

func.restype

A ctypes datatype describing the return value of *func*. None is used for functions returning void.

func.errcheck

A Python callable object taking three parameters (*result, func, args*) where *result* is the value returned by a foreign function, *func* is a reference to the foreign function itself, and *args* is a tuple of the input arguments. This function is called after a foreign function call and can be used to perform error checking and other actions.

Here is an example of fixing the atof() function interface, as shown in the previous example:

```
>>> libc.atof.restype=ctypes.c_double
>>> libc.atof("34.5")
34.5
>>>
```

The ctypes.d_double is a reference to a predefined datatype. The next section describes these datatypes.

Datatypes

Table 26.5 shows the ctypes datatypes that can be used in the argtypes and restype attributes of foreign functions. The "Python Value" column describes the type of Python data that is accepted for the given data type.

Table 26.5   **ctypes Datatypes**

ctypes Type Name	C Datatype	Python Value
c_bool	bool	True or False
c_bytes	signed char	Small integer
c_char	char	Single character
c_char_p	char *	Null-terminated string or bytes
c_double	double	Floating point
c_longdouble	long double	Floating point
c_float	float	Floating point
c_int	int	Integer
c_int8	signed char	8-bit integer
c_int16	short	16-bit integer
c_int32	int	32-bit integer
c_int64	long long	64-bit integer
c_long	long	Integer
c_longlong	long long	Integer
c_short	short	Integer
c_size_t	size_t	Integer
c_ubyte	unsigned char	Unsigned integer
c_uint	unsigned int	Unsigned integer
c_uint8	unsigned char	8-bit unsigned integer
c_uint16	unsigned short	16-bit unsigned integer
c_uint32	unsigned int	32-bit unsigned integer
c_uint64	unsigned long long	64-bit unsigned integer
c_ulong	unsigned long	Unsigned integer
c_ulonglong	unsigned long long	Unsigned integer
c_ushort	unsigned short	Unsigned integer
c_void_p	void *	Integer
c_wchar	wchar_t	Single Unicode character
c_wchar_p	wchar_t *	Null-terminated Unicode

To create a type representing a C pointer, apply the following function to one of the other types:

POINTER(type)

Defines a type that is a pointer to type *type*. For example, POINTER(c_int) represents the C type int *.

To define a type representing a fixed–size C array, multiply an existing type by the number of array dimensions. For example, c_int*4 represents the C datatype int[4].

To define a type representing a C structure or union, you inherit from one of the base classes Structure or Union. Within each derived class, you define a class variable _fields_ that describes the contents. _fields_ is a list of 2 or 3 tuples of the form (name, ctype) or (name, ctype, width), where *name* is an identifier for the structure field, ctype is a ctype class describing the type, and width is an integer bit-field width. For example, consider the following C structure:

```
struct Point {
    double x, y;
};
```

The ctypes description of this structure is

```
class Point(Structure):
    _fields_ = [ ("x", c_double),
                 ("y", c_double) ]
```

Calling Foreign Functions

To call functions in a library, you simply call the appropriate function with a set of arguments that are compatible with its type signature. For simple datatypes such as c_int, c_double, and so forth, you can just pass compatible Python types as input (integers, floats, and so on). It is also possible to pass instances of c_int, c_double and similar types as input. For arrays, you can just pass a Python sequence of compatible types.

To pass a pointer to a foreign function, you must first create a ctypes instance that represents the value that will be pointed at and then create a pointer object using one of the following functions:

byref(cvalue [, offset])

Represents a lightweight pointer to cvalue. cvalue must be an instance of a ctypes datatype. offset is a byte offset to add to the pointer value. The value returned by the function can only be used in function calls.

pointer(cvalue)

Creates a pointer instance pointing to cvalue. cvalue must be an instance of a ctypes datatype. This creates an instance of the POINTER type described earlier.

Here is an example showing how you would pass a parameter of type double * into a C function:

```
dval = c_double(0.0)          # Create a double instance
r = foo(byref(dval))          # Calls foo(&dval)

p_dval = pointer(dval)        # Creates a pointer variable
r = foo(p_dval)               # Calls foo(p_dval)

# Inspect the value of dval afterwards
print (dval.value)
```

It should be noted that you cannot create pointers to built-in types such as int or float. Passing pointers to such types would violate mutability if the underlying C function changed the value.

The cobj.value attribute of a ctypes instance cobj contains the internal data. For example, the reference to dval.value in the previous code returns the floating-point value stored inside the ctypes c_double instance dval.

To pass a structure to a C function, you must create an instance of the structure or union. To do this, you call a previous defined structure or union type *StructureType* as follows:

```
StructureType(*args, **kwargs)
```

Creates an instance of *StructureType* where *StructureType* is a class derived from Structure or Union. Positional arguments in *args* are used to initialize the structure members in the same order as they are listed in _fields_. Keyword arguments in **kwargs* initialize just the named structure members.

Alternative Type Construction Methods

All instances of ctypes types such as c_int, POINTER, and so forth have some class methods that are used to create instances of ctypes types from memory locations and other objects.

```
ty.from_buffer(source [,offset])
```

Creates an instance of ctypes type *ty* that shares the same memory buffer as *source*. *source* must be any other object that supports the writable buffer interface (e.g., bytearray, array objects in the array module, mmap, and so on). *offset* is the number of bytes from the start of the buffer to use.

```
ty.from_buffer_copy(source [, offset])
```

The same as *ty*.from_buffer() except that a copy of the memory is made and that *source* can be read-only.

```
ty.from_address(address)
```

Creates an instance of ctypes type *ty* from a raw memory address *address* specified as an integer.

```
ty.from_param(obj)
```

Creates an instance of ctypes type *ty* from a Python object *obj*. This only works if the passed object *obj* can be adapted into the appropriate type. For example, a Python integer can be adapted into a c_int instance.

```
ty.in_dll(library, name)
```

Creates an instance of ctypes type *ty* from a symbol in a shared library. *library* is an instance of the loaded library such as the object created by the CDLL class. *name* is the name of a symbol. This method can be used to put a ctypes wrapper around global variables defined in a library.

The following example shows how you might create a reference to a global variable int status defined in a library libexample.so.

```
libexample = ctypes.CDLL("libexample.so")
status = ctypes.c_int.in_dll(libexample,"status")
```

Utility Functions

The following utility functions are defined by `ctypes`:

`addressof(cobj)`

Returns the memory address of `cobj` as an integer. `cobj` must be an instance of a ctypes type.

`alignment(ctype_or_obj)`

Returns the integer alignment requirements of a ctypes type or object. `ctype_or_obj` must be a ctypes type or an instance of a type.

`cast(cobj, ctype)`

Casts a ctypes object `cobj` to a new type given in `ctype`. This only works for pointers, so `cobj` must be a pointer or array and `ctype` must be a pointer type.

`create_string_buffer(init [, size])`

Creates a mutable character buffer as a ctypes array of type `c_char`. `init` is either an integer size or a string representing the initial contents. `size` is an optional parameter that specifies the size to use if `init` is a string. By default, the size is set to be one greater than the number of characters in `init`. Unicode strings are encoded into bytes using the default encoding.

`create_unicode_buffer(init [, size])`

The same as `create_string_buffer()`, except that a ctypes array of type `c_wchar` is created.

`get_errno()`

Returns the current value of the ctypes private copy of `errno`.

`get_last_error()`

Returns the current value of the ctypes private copy of `LastError` on Windows.

`memmove(dst, src, count)`

Copies `count` bytes from `src` to `dst`. `src` and `dst` are either integers representing memory addresses or instances of ctypes types that can be converted to pointers. The same as the C `memmove()` library function.

`memset(dst, c, count)`

Sets `count` bytes of memory starting at `dst` to the byte value `c`. `dst` is either an integer or a ctypes instance. `c` is an integer representing a byte in the range 0–255.

`resize(cobj, size)`

Resizes the internal memory used to represent ctypes object `cobj`. `size` is the new size in bytes.

`set_conversion_mode(encoding, errors)`

Sets the Unicode encoding used when converting from Unicode strings to 8-bit strings. `encoding` is the encoding name such as `'utf-8'`, and `errors` is the error-handling policy such as `'strict'` or `'ignore'`. Returns a tuple (`encoding, errors`) with the previous setting.

```
set_errno(value)
```

Sets the ctypes-private copy of the system *errno* variable. Returns the previous value.

```
set_last_error(value)
```

Sets the Windows `LastError` variable and returns the previous value.

```
sizeof(type_or_cobj)
```

Returns the size of a ctypes type or object in bytes.

```
string_at(address [, size])
```

Returns a byte string representing *size* bytes of memory starting at address *address*. If *size* is omitted, it is assumed that the byte string is NULL-terminated.

```
wstring_at(address [, size])
```

Returns a Unicode string representing *size* wide characters starting at address *address*. If *size* is omitted, the character string is assumed to be NULL-terminated.

Example

The following example illustrates the use of the `ctypes` module by building an interface to the set of C functions used in the very first part of this chapter that covered the details of creating Python extension modules by hand.

```
# example.py

import ctypes
_example = ctypes.CDLL("./libexample.so")

# int gcd(int, int)
gcd = _example.gcd
gcd.argtypes = (ctypes.c_int,
                ctypes.c_int)
gcd.restype = ctypes.c_int


# int replace(char *s, char olcdh, char newch)
_example.replace.argtypes = (ctypes.c_char_p,
                             ctypes.c_char,
                             ctypes.c_char)
_example.replace.restype = ctypes.c_int

def replace(s, oldch, newch):
    sbuffer = ctypes.create_string_buffer(s)
    nrep = _example.replace(sbuffer,oldch,newch)
    return (nrep,sbuffer.value)

# double distance(Point *p1, Point *p2)
class Point(ctypes.Structure):
    _fields_ = [ ("x", ctypes.c_double),
                 ("y", ctypes.c_double) ]

_example.distance.argtypes = (ctypes.POINTER(Point),
                              ctypes.POINTER(Point))
_example.distance.restype = ctypes.c_double

def distance(a,b):
    p1 = Point(*a)
    p2 = Point(*b)
    return _example.distance(byref(p1),byref(p2))
```

As a general note, usage of `ctypes` is always going to involve a Python wrapper layer of varying complexity. For example, it may be the case that you can call a C function directly. However, you may also have to implement a small wrapping layer to account for certain aspects of the underlying C code. In this example, the `replace()` function is taking extra steps to account for the fact that the C library mutates the input buffer. The `distance()` function is performing extra steps to create `Point` instances from tuples and to pass pointers.

> **Note**
>
> The `ctypes` module has a large number of advanced features not covered here. For example, the library can access many different kinds of libraries on Windows, and there is support for callback functions, incomplete types, and other details. The online documentation is filled with many examples so that should be a starting point for further use.

Advanced Extending and Embedding

Creating handwritten extension modules or using `ctypes` is usually straightforward if you are extending Python with simple C code. However, for anything more complex, it can quickly become tedious. For this, you will want to look for a suitable extension building tool. These tools either automate much of the extension building process or provide a programming interface that operates at a much higher level. Links to a variety of such tools can be found at http://wiki.python.org/moin/IntegratingPythonWithOtherLanguages. However, a short example with SWIG (http://www.swig.org) will be shown just to illustrate. In the interest of full disclosure, it should be noted that SWIG was originally created by the author.

With automated tools, you usually just describe the contents of an extension module at a high level. For example, with SWIG, you write a short interface specification that looks like this:

```
/* example.i : Sample Swig specification */
%module example
%{
/* Preamble. Include all required header files here */
#include "example.h"
%}

/* Module contents.  List all C declarations here */
typedef struct Point {
  double x;
  double y;
} Point;
extern int     gcd(int, int);
extern int     replace(char *s, char oldch, char newch);
extern double distance(Point *a, Point *b);
```

Using this specification, SWIG automatically generates everything needed to make a Python extension module. To run SWIG, you just invoke it like a compiler:

```
% swig -python example.i
%
```

As output, it generates a set of `.c` and `.py` files. However, you often don't have to worry much about this. If you are using `distutils` and include a `.i` file in the setup specification, it will run SWIG automatically for you when building an extension. For example, this `setup.py` file automatically runs SWIG on the listed `example.i` file.

```
# setup.py
from distutils.core import setup, Extension
setup(name="example",
      version="1.0",
      py_modules = ['example.py'],
      ext_modules = [
        Extension("_example",
                    ["example.i","example.c"])
      ]
    )
```

It turns out that this `example.i` file and the `setup.py` file are all that are needed to have a working extension module in this example. If you type `python setup.py build_ext --inplace`, you will find that you have a fully working extension in your directory.

Jython and IronPython

Extending and embedding is not restricted to C programs. If you are working with Java, consider the use of Jython (http://www.jython.org), a complete reimplementation of the Python interpreter in Java. With `jython`, you can simply import Java libraries using the `import` statement. For example:

```
bash-3.2$ jython
Jython 2.2.1 on java1.5.0_16
Type "copyright", "credits" or "license" for more information.
>>> from java.lang import System
>>> System.out.println("Hello World")
Hello World
>>>
```

If you are working with the .NET framework on Windows, consider the use of IronPython (http://www.codeplex.com/Wiki/View.aspx?ProjectName=IronPython), a complete reimplementation of the Python interpreter in C#. With IronPython, you can easily access all of the `.NET` libraries from Python in a similar manner. For example:

```
% ipy
IronPython 1.1.2 (1.1.2) on .NET 2.0.50727.42
Copyright (c) Microsoft Corporation. All rights reserved.
>>> import System.Math
>>> dir(System.Math)
['Abs', 'Acos', 'Asin', 'Atan', 'Atan2', 'BigMul', 'Ceiling', 'Cos', 'Cosh', ...]
>>> System.Math.Cos(3)
-0.9899924966
>>>
```

Covering `jython` and `IronPython` in more detail is beyond the scope of this book. However, just keep in mind that they're both Python—the most major differences are in their libraries.

Appendix

Python 3

In December 2008, Python 3.0 was released—a major update to the Python language that breaks backwards compatibility with Python 2 in a number of critical areas. A fairly complete survey of the changes made to Python 3 can be found in the "What's New in Python 3.0" document available at http://docs.python.org/3.0/whatsnew/3.0.html. In some sense, the first 26 chapters of this book can be viewed as the polar opposite of the "What's New" document. That is, all of the material covered so far has focused on features that are *shared* by both Python 2 and Python 3. This includes all of the standard library modules, major language features, and examples. Aside from a few minor naming differences and the fact that `print()` is a function, no unique Python 3 features have been described.

The main focus of this appendix is to describe new features to the Python language that are only available in version 3 as well as some important differences to keep in mind if you are going to migrate existing code. At the end of this appendix, some porting strategies and use of the `2to3` code conversion tool is described.

Who Should Be Using Python 3?

Before going any further, it is important to address the question of who should be using the Python 3.0 release. Within the Python community, it has always been known that the transition to Python 3 would not happen overnight and that the Python 2 branch would continue to be maintained for some time (years) into the future. So, as of this writing, there is no urgent need to drop Python 2 code. I suspect that huge amounts of Python 2 code will continue to be in development when the 5th edition of this book is written years from now.

A major problem facing Python 3.0 concerns the compatibility of third-party libraries. Much of Python's power comes from its large variety of frameworks and libraries. However, unless these libraries are explicitly ported to Python 3, they are almost certain not to work. This problem is amplified by the fact that many libraries depend upon other libraries that depend on yet more libraries. As of this writing (2009), there are major libraries and frameworks for Python that haven't even been ported to Python 2.4, let alone 2.6 or 3.0. So, if you are using Python with the intention of running third-party code, you are better off sticking with Python 2 for now. If you've picked up this book and it's the year 2012, then hopefully the situation will have improved.

Although Python 3 cleans up a lot of minor warts in the language, it is unclear if Python 3 is currently a wise choice for new users just trying to learn the basics. Almost all existing documentation, tutorials, cookbooks, and examples assume Python 2 and use coding conventions that are incompatible. Needless to say, someone is not going to have a positive learning experience if everything appears to be broken. Even the official documentation is not entirely up-to-date with Python 3 coding requirements; while writing this book, the author submitted numerous bug reports concerning documentation errors and omissions.

Finally, even though Python 3.0 is described as the latest and greatest, it suffers from numerous performance and behavioral problems. For example, the I/O system in the initial release exhibits truly horrific and unacceptable runtime performance. The separation of bytes and Unicode is also not without problem. Even some of the built-in library modules are broken due to changes related to I/O and string handling. Obviously these issues will improve with time as more programmers stress-test the release. However, in the opinion of this author, Python 3.0 is really only suitable for experimental use by seasoned Python veterans. If you're looking for stability and production quality code, stick with Python 2 until some of the kinks have had time to be worked out of the Python 3 series.

New Language Features

This section outlines some features of Python 3 that are *not* supported in Python 2.

Source Code Encoding and Identifiers

Python 3 assumes that source code is encoded as UTF-8. In addition, the rules on what characters are legal in an identifier have been relaxed. Specifically, identifiers can contain any valid Unicode character with a code point of U+0080 or greater. For example:

```
π = 3.141592654
r = 4.0
print(2*π*r)
```

Just because you can use such characters in your source code doesn't mean that it's a good idea. Not all editors, terminals, or development tools are equally adept at Unicode handling. Plus, it is extremely annoying to force programmers to type awkward key sequences for characters not visibly present on a standard keyboard (not to mention the fact that it might make some of the gray-bearded hackers in the office tell everyone another amusing APL story). So, it's probably better to reserve the use of Unicode characters for comments and string literals.

Set Literals

A set of items can now be defined by enclosing a collection of values in braces { *items* }. For example:

```
days = { 'Mon', 'Tue', 'Wed', 'Thu', 'Fri', 'Sat', 'Sun' }
```

This syntax is the same as using the set() function:

```
days = set(['Mon', 'Tue', 'Wed', 'Thu', 'Fri', 'Sat', 'Sun'])
```

Set and Dictionary Comprehensions

The syntax { *expr* for *x* in *s* if *conditional*} is a set comprehension. It applies an operation to all of the elements of a set *s* and can be used in a similar manner as list comprehensions. For example:

```
>>> values = { 1, 2, 3, 4 }
>>> squares = {x*x for x in values}
>>> squares
{16, 1, 4, 9}
>>>
```

The syntax { *kexpr*:*vexpr* for *k*,*v* in *s* if *condition* } is a dictionary comprehension. It applies an operation to all of the keys and values in sequence *s* of (*key*, *value*) tuples and returns a dictionary. The keys of the new dictionary are described by an expression *kexpr*, and the values are described by the expression *vexpr*. This can be viewed as a more powerful version of the dict() function.

To illustrate, suppose you had a file of stock prices 'prices.dat' like this:

```
GOOG 509.71
YHOO 28.34
IBM 106.11
MSFT 30.47
AAPL 122.13
```

Here is a program that reads this file into a dictionary mapping stock names to price using a dictionary comprehension:

```
fields = (line.split() for line in open("prices.dat"))
prices = {sym:float(val) for sym,val in fields}
```

Here is an example that converts all of the keys of the prices dictionary to lowercase:

```
d = {sym.lower():price for sym,price in prices.items()}
```

Here is an example that creates a dictionary of prices for stocks over $100.00:

```
d = {sym:price for sym,price in prices.items() if price >= 100.0}
```

Extended Iterable Unpacking

In Python 2, items in an iterable can be unpacked into variables using syntax such as the following:

```
items = [1,2,3,4]
a,b,c,d = items          # Unpack items into variables
```

In order for this unpacking to work, the number of variables and items to be unpacked must exactly match.

In Python 3, you can use a wildcard variable to only unpack some of the items in a sequence, placing any remaining values in a list. For example:

```
a,*rest   = items        # a = 1, rest = [2,3,4]
a,*rest,d = items        # a = 1, rest = [2,3], d = 4
*rest, d  = items        # rest = [1,2,3], d = 4
```

In these examples, the variable prefixed by a * receives all of the extra values and places them in a list. The list may be empty if there are no extra items. One use of this feature is in looping over lists of tuples (or sequences) where the tuples may have differing sizes. For example:

```
points = [ (1,2), (3,4,"red"), (4,5,"blue"), (6,7) ]
for x,y, *opt in points:
    if opt:
        # Additional fields were found
    statements
```

No more than one starred variable can appear in any expansion.

Nonlocal Variables

Inner functions can modify variables in outer functions by using the nonlocal declaration. For example:

```
def countdown(n):
    def decrement():
        nonlocal n
        n -= 1
    while n > 0:
        print("T-minus", n)
        decrement()
```

In Python 2, inner functions can read variables in outer functions but cannot modify them. The nonlocal declaration enables this.

Function Annotations

The arguments and return value of functions can be annotated with arbitrary values. For example:

```
def foo(x:1,y:2) -> 3:
    pass
```

The function attribute __annotations__ is a dictionary mapping argument names to the annotation values. The special 'return' key is mapped to the return value annotation. For example:

```
>>> foo.__annotations__
{'y': 2, 'x': 1, 'return': 3}
>>>
```

The interpreter does not attach any significance to these annotations. In fact, they can be any values whatsoever. However, it is expected that type information will be most useful in the future. For example, you could write this:

```
def foo(x:int, y:int) -> str:
    statements
```

Annotations are not limited to single values. An annotation can be any valid Python expression. For variable positional and keyword arguments, the same syntax applies. For example:

```
def bar(x, *args:"additional", **kwargs:"options"):
    statements
```

Again, it is important to emphasize that Python does not attach any significance to annotations. The intended use is in third-party libraries and frameworks that may want to use them for various applications involving metaprogramming. Examples include, but are not limited to, static analysis tools, documentation, testing, function overloading, marshalling, remote procedure call, IDEs, contracts, etc. Here is an example of a decorator function that enforces assertions on function arguments and return values:

```python
def ensure(func):
    # Extract annotation data
    return_check = func.__annotations__.get('return',None)
    arg_checks   = [(name,func.__annotations__.get(name))
                    for name in func.__code__.co_varnames]

    # Create a wrapper that checks argument values and the return
    # result using the functions specified in annotations

    def assert_call(*args,**kwargs):
        for (name,check),value in zip(arg_checks,args):
            if check: assert check(value), "%s %s" % (name, check.__doc__)
        for name,check in arg_checks[len(args):]:
            if check: assert check(kwargs[name]), "%s %s" % (name, check.__doc__)
        result = func(*args,**kwargs)
        assert return_check(result), "return %s" % return_check.__doc__
        return result

    return assert_call
```

Here is an example of code that uses the previous decorator:

```python
def positive(x):
    "must be positive"
    return x > 0

def negative(x):
    "must be negative"
    return x < 0

@ensure
def foo(a:positive, b:negative) -> positive:
    return a - b
```

Following is some sample output of using the function:

```python
>>> foo(3,-2)
5
>>> foo(-5,2)
Traceback (most recent call last):
  File "<stdin>", line 1, in <module>
  File "meta.py", line 19, in call
    def assert_call(*args,**kwargs):
AssertionError: a must be positive
>>>
```

Keyword-Only Arguments

Functions can specify keyword-only arguments. This is indicated by defining extra parameters after the first starred parameter. For example:

```python
def foo(x, *args, strict=False):
    statements
```

When calling this function, the `strict` parameter can only be specified as a keyword. For example:

```
a = foo(1, strict=True)
```

Any additional positional arguments would just be placed in `args` and not used to set the value of `strict`. If you don't want to accept a variable number of arguments but want keyword-only arguments, use a bare `*` in the parameter list. For example:

```
def foo(x, *, strict=False):
    statements
```

Here is an example of usage:

```
foo(1,True)          # Fails. TypeError: foo() takes 1 positional argument
foo(1,strict=True)   # Ok.
```

Ellipsis as an Expression

The `Ellipsis` object (`...`) can now appear as an expression. This allows it to be placed in containers and assigned to variables. For example:

```
>>> x = ...              # Assignment of Ellipsis
>>> x
Ellipsis
>>> a = [1,2,...]
>>> a
[1, 2, Ellipsis]
>>> ... in a
True
>>> x is ...
True
>>>
```

The interpretation of the ellipsis is still left up to the application that uses it. This feature allows the `...` to be used as an interesting piece of syntax in libraries and frameworks (for example, to indicate a wild-card, continuation, or some similar concept).

Chained Exceptions

Exceptions can now be chained together. Essentially this is a way for the current exception to carry information about the previous exception. The `from` qualifier is used with the `raise` statement to explicitly chain exceptions. For example:

```
try:
    statements
except ValueError as e:
    raise SyntaxError("Couldn't parse configuration") from e
```

When the `SyntaxError` exception is raised, a traceback message such as the following will be generated—showing both exceptions:

```
Traceback (most recent call last):
  File "<stdin>", line 2, in <module>
ValueError: invalid literal for int() with base 10: 'nine'

The above exception was the direct cause of the following exception:
```

```
Traceback (most recent call last):
  File "<stdin>", line 4, in <module>
SyntaxError: Couldn't parse configuration
```

Exception objects have a __cause__ attribute, which is set to the previous exception. Use of the from qualifier with raise sets this attribute.

A more subtle example of exception chaining involves exceptions raised within another exception handler. For example:

```
def error(msg):
    print(m)              # Note: typo is intentional (m undefined)

try:
    statements
except ValueError as e:
    error("Couldn't parse configuration")
```

If you try this in Python 2, you only get an exception related to the NameError in error(). In Python 3, the previous exception being handled is chained with the result. For example, you get this message:

```
Traceback (most recent call last):
  File "<stdin>", line 2, in <module>
ValueError: invalid literal for int() with base 10: 'nine'

During handling of the above exception, another exception occurred:

Traceback (most recent call last):
  File "<stdin>", line 4, in <module>
  File "<stdin>", line 2, in error
NameError: global name 'm' is not defined
```

For implicit chaining, the __context__ attribute of an exception instance e contains a reference to previous exception.

Improved super()

The super() function, used to look up methods in base classes, can be used without any arguments in Python 3. For example:

```
class C(A,B):
    def bar(self):
        return super().bar()       # Call bar() in bases
```

In Python 2, you had to use super(C,self).bar(). The old syntax is still supported but is significantly more clunky.

Advanced Metaclasses

In Python 2, you can define metaclasses that alter the behavior of classes. A subtle facet of the implementation is that the processing carried out by a metaclass only occurs *after* the body of a class has executed. That is, the interpreter executes the entire body of a class and populates a dictionary. Once the dictionary has been populated, the dictionary is passed to the metaclass constructor (after the body of the class has executed).

In Python 3, metaclasses can additionally carry out extra work before the class body executes. This is done by defining a special class method called __prepare__(*cls*, *name*, *bases*, **kwargs*) in the metaclass. This method must return a dictionary as a result. This dictionary is what gets populated as the body of the class definition executes. Here is an example that outlines the basic procedure:

```
class MyMeta(type):
    @classmethod
    def __prepare__(cls,name,bases,**kwargs):
        print("preparing",name,bases,kwargs)
        return {}
    def __new__(cls,name,bases,classdict):
        print("creating",name,bases,classdict)
        return type.__new__(cls,name,bases,classdict)
```

Python 3 uses an alternative syntax for specifying a metaclass. For example, to define a class that uses MyMeta, you use this:

```
class Foo(metaclass=MyMeta):
    print("About to define  methods")
    def __init__(self):
        pass
    def bar(self):
        pass
    print("Done defining methods")
```

If you run the following code, you will see the following output that illustrates the control flow:

```
preparing Foo () {}
About to define methods
Done defining methods
creating Foo () {'__module__': '__main__',
                'bar': <function bar at 0x3845d0>,
                '__init__': <function __init__ at 0x384588>}
```

The additional keyword arguments on the __prepare__() method of the metaclass are passed from keyword arguments used in the bases list of a class statement. For example, the statement class Foo(metaclass=MyMeta,spam=42,blah="Hello") passes the keyword arguments spam and blah to MyMeta.__prepare__(). This convention can be used to pass arbitrary configuration information to a metaclass.

To perform any kind of useful processing with the new __prepare__() method of metaclasses, you generally have the method return a customized dictionary object. For example, if you wanted to perform special processing as a class is defined, you define a class that inherits from dict and reimplements the __setitem__() method to capture assignments to the class dictionary. The following example illustrates this by defining a metaclass that reports errors if any method or class variable is multiply defined.

```
class MultipleDef(dict):
    def __init__(self):
        self.multiple= set()
    def __setitem__(self,name,value):
        if name in self:
            self.multiple.add(name)
        dict.__setitem__(self,name,value)

class MultiMeta(type):
    @classmethod
    def __prepare__(cls,name,bases,**kwargs):
        return MultipleDef()
    def __new__(cls,name,bases,classdict):
        for name in classdict.multiple:
            print(name,"multiply defined")
```

```
    if classdict.multiple:
        raise TypeError("Multiple definitions exist")
    return type.__new__(cls,name,bases,classdict)
```

If you apply this metaclass to another class definition, it will report an error if any method is redefined. For example:

```
class Foo(metaclass=MultiMeta):
    def __init__(self):
        pass
    def __init__(self,x):          # Error. __init__ multiply defined.
        pass
```

Common Pitfalls

If you are migrating from Python 2 to 3, be aware that Python 3 is more than just new syntax and language features. Major parts of the core language and library have been reworked in ways that are sometimes subtle. There are aspects of Python 3 that may seem like bugs to a Python 2 programmer. In other cases, things that used to be "easy" in Python 2 are now forbidden.

This section outlines some of the most major pitfalls that are likely to be encountered by Python 2 programmers making the switch.

Text Versus Bytes

Python 3 makes a very strict distinction between text strings (characters) and binary data (bytes). A literal such as "hello" represents a text string stored as Unicode, whereas b"hello" represents a string of bytes (containing ASCII letters in this case).

Under no circumstances can the str and bytes type be mixed in Python 3. For example, if you try to concatenate strings and bytes together, you will get a TypeError exception. This differs from Python 2 where byte strings would be automatically coerced into Unicode as needed.

To convert a text string s into bytes, you must use s.encode(encoding). For example, s.encode('utf-8') converts s into a UTF-8 encoded byte string. To convert a byte string t back into text, you must use t.decode(encoding). You can view the encode() and decode() methods as a kind of "type cast" between strings and bytes.

Keeping a clean separation between text and bytes is ultimately a good thing—the rules for mixing string types in Python 2 were obscure and difficult to understand at best. However, one consequence of the Python 3 approach is that byte strings are much more restricted in their ability to actually behave like "text." Although there are the standard string methods like split() and replace(), other aspects of byte strings are not the same as in Python 2. For instance, if you print a byte string, you simply get its repr() output with quotes such as b'contents'. Similarly, none of the string formatting operations (%, .format()) work. For example:

```
x = b'Hello World'
print(x)                   # Produces b'Hello World'
print(b"You said '%s'" % x)  # TypeError: % operator not supported
```

The loss of text-like behavior with bytes is a potential pitfall for system programmers. Despite the invasion of Unicode, there are many cases where one actually does want to

work with and manipulate byte-oriented data such as ASCII. You might be inclined to
use the bytes type to avoid all of the overhead and complexity of Unicode. However,
this will actually make everything related to byte-oriented text handling more difficult.
Here is an example that illustrates the potential problems:

```
>>> # Create a response message using strings (Unicode)
>>> status = 200
>>> msg = "OK"
>>> proto = "HTTP/1.0"
>>> response = "%s %d %s" % (proto, status, msg)
>>> print(response)
HTTP/1.0 200 OK

>>> # Create a response message using only bytes (ASCII)
>>> status = 200
>>> msg = b"OK"
>>> proto = b"HTTP/1.0"
>>> response = b"%s %d %s" % (proto, status, msg)
Traceback (most recent call last):
  File "<stdin>", line 1, in <module>
TypeError: unsupported operand type(s) for %: 'bytes' and 'tuple'

>>> response = proto + b" " + str(status) + b" " + msg
Traceback (most recent call last):
  File "<stdin>", line 1, in <module>
TypeError: can't concat bytes to str

>>> bytes(status)
b'\x00\x00\x00\x00\x00\x00\x00\x00\x00\x00....'

>>> bytes(str(status))
Traceback (most recent call last):
  File "<stdin>", line 1, in <module>
TypeError: string argument without an encoding

>>> bytes(str(status),'ascii')
b'200'

>>> response = proto + b" " + bytes(str(status),'ascii') + b" " + msg
>>> print(response)
b'HTTP/1.0 200 OK'

>>> print(response.decode('ascii'))
HTTP/1.0 200 OK
>>>
```

In the example, you can see how Python 3 is strictly enforcing the text/bytes separation. Even operations that seem like they should be simple, such as converting an integer into ASCII characters, are much more complicated with bytes.

The bottom line is that if you're performing any kind of text-based processing or
formatting, you are probably *always* better off using standard text strings. If you need
to obtain a byte-string after the completion of such processing, you can use
s.encode('latin-1') to convert from Unicode.

The text/bytes distinction is somewhat more subtle when working with various
library modules. Some libraries work equally well with text or bytes, while some forbid
bytes altogether. In other cases, the behavior is different depending on what kind of
input is received. For example, the os.listdir(*dirname*) function only returns file-

names that can be successfully decoded as Unicode if *dirname* is a string. If *dirname* is a byte string, then *all* filenames are returned as byte strings.

New I/O System

Python 3 implements an entirely new I/O system, the details of which are described in the io module section of Chapter 19, "Operating System Services." The new I/O system also reflects the strong distinction between text and binary data present with strings.

If you are performing any kind of I/O with text, Python 3 forces you to open files in "text mode" and to supply an optional encoding if you want anything other than the default (usually UTF-8). If you are performing I/O with binary data, you must open files in "binary mode" and use byte strings. A common source of errors is passing output data to a file or I/O stream opened in the wrong mode. For example:

```
>>> f = open("foo.txt","wb")
>>> f.write("Hello World\n")
Traceback (most recent call last):
  File "<stdin>", line 1, in <module>
  File "/tmp/lib/python3.0/io.py", line 1035, in write
    raise TypeError("can't write str to binary stream")
TypeError: can't write str to binary stream
>>>
```

Sockets, pipes, and other kinds of I/O channels should always be assumed to be in binary mode. One potential problem with network code in particular is that many network protocols involve text-based request/response processing (e.g., HTTP, SMTP, FTP, etc.). Given that sockets are binary, this mix of binary I/O and text processing can lead to some of the problems related to mixing text and bytes that were described in the previous section. You'll need to be careful.

print() **and** exec() **Functions**

The print and exec statements from Python 2 are now functions. Use of the print() function compared to its Python 2 counterpart is as follows:

```
print(x,y,z)           # Same as : print x, y, z
print(x,y,z,end=' ')   # Same as : print x, y, z,
print(a,file=f)        # Same as : print >>f, a
```

The fact that print() is a function that means you can replace it with an alternative definition if you want.

exec() is also now a function, but its behavior in Python 3 is subtly different than in Python 2. For example, consider this code:

```
def foo():
    exec("a = 42")
    print(a)
```

In Python 2, calling foo() will print the number '42'. In Python 3, you get a NameError exception with the variable a being undefined. What has happened here is that exec(), as a function, only operates on the dictionaries returned by the globals() and locals() functions. However, the dictionary returned by locals() is actually a *copy* of the local variables. The assignment made in the exec() function is merely modifying this copy of the locals, not the local variables themselves. Here is one workaround:

```
def foo():
    _locals = locals()
    exec("a = 42",globals(),_locals)
    a = _locals['a']        # Extract the set variable
    print(a)
```

As a general rule, don't expect Python 3 to support the same degree of "magic" that was possible using exec(), eval(), and execfile() in Python 2. In fact, execfile() is gone entirely (you can emulate its functionality by passing an open file-like object to exec()).

Use of Iterators and Views

Python 3 makes much greater use of iterators and generators than Python 2. Built-in functions such as zip(), map(), and range() that used to return lists now return iterables. If you need to make a list from the result, use the list() function.

Python 3 takes a slightly different approach to extracting key and value information from a dictionary. In Python 2, you could use methods such as d.keys(), d.values(), or d.items() to obtain lists of keys, values, or key/value pairs, respectively. In Python 3, these methods return so-called *view* objects. For example:

```
>>> s = { 'GOOG': 490.10, 'AAPL': 123.45, 'IBM': 91.10 }
>>> k = s.keys()
>>> k
<dict_keys object at 0x33d950>
>>> v = s.values()
>>> v
<dict_values object at 0x33d960>
>>>
```

These objects support iteration so if you want to view the contents, you can use a for loop. For example:

```
>>> for x in k:
...         print(x)
...
GOOG
AAPL
IBM
>>>
```

View objects are always tied back to the dictionary from which they were created. A subtle aspect of this is that if the underlying dictionary changes, the items produced by the view change as well. For example:

```
>>> s['ACME'] = 5612.25
>>> for x in k:
...         print(x)
...
GOOG
AAPL
IBM
ACME
>>>
```

Should it be necessary to build a list of dictionary keys or values, simply use the list() function—for example, list(s.keys()).

Integers and Integer Division

Python 3 no longer has an `int` type for 32-bit integers and a separate `long` type for long integers. The `int` type now represents an integer of arbitrary precision (the internal details of which are not exposed to the user).

In addition, integer division now always produces a floating-point result. For example, `3/5` is `0.6`, not `0`. The conversion to a float applies even if the result would have been an integer. For example, `8/2` is `4.0`, not `4`.

Comparisons

Python 3 is much more strict about how values are compared. In Python 2, it is the case that any two objects can be compared even if it doesn't make sense. For example:

```
>>> 3 < "Hello"
True
>>>
```

In Python 3, this results in a `TypeError`. For example:

```
>>> 3 < "Hello"
Traceback (most recent call last):
  File "<stdin>", line 1, in <module>
TypeError: unorderable types: int() < str()
>>>
```

This change is minor, but it means that in Python 3, you have to be much more careful about making sure data is of appropriate types. For example, if you use the `sort()` method of a list, all of the items in the list must be compatible with the `<` operator, or you get an error. In Python 2, the operation would be silently carried out anyways with a usually meaningless result.

Iterators and Generators

Python 3 has made a slight change to the iterator protocol. Instead of calling `__iter__()` and the `next()` method to perform iteration, the `next()` method has been renamed to `__next__()`. Most users will be unaffected by this change except if you have written code that manually iterates over an iterable or if you have defined your own custom iterator objects. You will need to make sure you change the name of the `next()` method in your classes. Use the built-in `next()` function to invoke the `next()` or `__next__()` method of an iterator in a portable manner.

File Names, Arguments, and Environment Variables

In Python 3, filenames, command-line arguments in `sys.argv`, and environment variables in `os.environ` may or may not be treated as Unicode depending on local settings. The only problem is that the usage of Unicode within the operating system environment is not entirely universal. For example, on many systems it may be technically possible to specify filenames, command-line options, and environment variables that are just a raw sequence of bytes that don't correspond to a valid Unicode encoding. Although these situations might be rare in practice, it may be of some concern for programming using Python to perform tasks related to systems administration. As previously noted, supplying file and directory names as byte strings will fix many of the problems. For example, `os.listdir(b'/foo')`.

Library Reorganization

Python 3 reorganizes and changes the names of several parts of the standard library, most notably modules related to networking and Internet data formats. In addition, a wide variety of legacy modules have been dropped from the library (e.g., gopherlib, rfc822, and so on).

It is now standard practice to use lowercase names for modules. Several modules such as ConfigParser, Queue, and SocketServer have been renamed to configparser, queue, and socketserver, respectively. You should try to follow similar conventions in your own code.

Packages have been created to reorganize code that was formerly contained in disparate modules—for example, the http package containing all the module used to write HTTP servers, the html package has modules for parsing HTML, the xmlrpc package has modules for XML-RPC, and so forth.

As for deprecated modules, this book has been careful to only document modules that are in current use with Python 2.6 and Python 3.0. If you are working with existing Python 2 code and see it using a module not documented here, there is a good chance that the module has been deprecated in favor of something more modern. Just as an example, Python 3 doesn't have the popen2 module commonly used in Python 2 to launch subprocesses. Instead, you should use the subprocess module.

Absolute Imports

Related to library reorganization, all import statements appearing in submodules of a package use absolute names. This is covered in more detailed in Chapter 8, "Modules, Packages, and Distribution," but suppose you have a package organized like this:

```
foo/
    __init__.py
    spam.py
    bar.py
```

If the file spam.py uses the statement import bar, you get an ImportError exception even though bar.py is located in the same directory. To load this submodule, spam.py either needs to use import foo.bar or a package relative import such as from . import bar.

This differs from Python 2 where import always checks the current directory for a match before moving onto checking other directories in sys.path.

Code Migration and 2to3

Converting code from Python 2 to Python 3 is a delicate topic. Just to be absolutely clear, there are no magic imports, flags, environment variables, or tools that will enable Python 3 to run an arbitrary Python 2 program. However, there are some very specific steps that can be taken to migrate code, each of which is now described.

Porting Code to Python 2.6

It is recommended that anyone porting code to Python 3 first port to Python 2.6. Python 2.6 is not only backwards-compatible with Python 2.5, but it also supports a subset of new features found in Python 3. Examples include advanced string formatting, the new exception syntax, byte literals, I/O library, and abstract base classes. Thus, a

Python 2 program can start to take advantage of useful Python 3 features now even if it is not yet ready to make the full migration.

The other reason to port to Python 2.6 is that Python 2.6 issues warning messages for deprecated features if you run it with the -3 command-line option. For example:

```
bash-3.2$ python -3
Python 2.6 (trunk:66714:66715M, Oct  1 2008, 18:36:04)
[GCC 4.0.1 (Apple Computer, Inc. build 5370)] on darwin
Type "help", "copyright", "credits" or "license" for more information.
>>> a = { }
>>> a.has_key('foo')
__main__:1: DeprecationWarning: dict.has_key() not supported in 3.x; use the in
operator
False
>>
```

Using these warning messages as a guide, you should take great care to make sure that your program runs warning-free on Python 2.6 before moving forward with a Python 3 port.

Providing Test Coverage

Python has useful testing modules including doctest and unittest. Make sure your application has thorough test coverage before attempting a Python 3 port. If your program has not had any tests to this point, now would be a good time to start. You will want to make sure your tests cover as much as possible and that all tests pass without any warning messages when run on Python 2.6.

Using the 2to3 Tool

Python 3 includes a tool called 2to3 that can assist with code migration from Python 2.6 to Python 3. This tool is normally found in the Tools/scripts directory of the Python source distribution and is also installed in the same directory as the python3.0 binary on most systems. It is a command-line tool that would normally run from a UNIX or Windows command shell.

As an example, consider the following program that contains a number of deprecated features.

```
# example.py
import ConfigParser

for i in xrange(10):
    print i, 2*i

def spam(d):
    if not d.has_key("spam"):
        d["spam"] = load_spam()
    return d["spam"]
```

To run 2to3 on this program, type "2to3 example.py". For example:

```
% 2to3 example.py
RefactoringTool: Skipping implicit fixer: buffer
RefactoringTool: Skipping implicit fixer: idioms
RefactoringTool: Skipping implicit fixer: set_literal
RefactoringTool: Skipping implicit fixer: ws_comma
--- example.py (original)
+++ example.py (refactored)
@@ -1,10 +1,10 @@
```

```
 # example.py
-import ConfigParser
+import configparser

-for i in xrange(10):
-    print i, 2*i
+for i in range(10):
+    print(i, 2*i)

 def spam(d):
-    if not d.has_key("spam"):
+    if "spam" not in d:
         d["spam"] = load_spam()
     return d["spam"]
RefactoringTool: Files that need to be modified:
RefactoringTool: example.py
```

As output, 2to3 will identify parts of the program that it considers to be problematic and that might need to be changed. These are shown as context-diffs in the output. Although we have used 2to3 on a single file, if you give it the name of a directory, it recursively looks for all Python files contained in the directory structure and generates a report for everything.

By default, 2to3 does not actually *fix* any of the source code it scans—it merely reports parts of the code that might need to be changed. A challenge faced by 2to3 is that it often only has incomplete information. For example, consider the spam() function in the example code. This function calls a method d.has_key(). For dictionaries, has_key() has been removed in favor of the in operator. 2to3 reports this change, but without more information, it is not clear if spam() is actually manipulating a dictionary or not. It might be the case that d is some other kind of object (a database perhaps) that happens to provide a has_key() method, but where using the in operator would fail. Another problematic area for 2to3 is in the handling of byte strings and Unicode. Given that Python 2 would automatically promote byte strings to Unicode, it is somewhat common to see code that carelessly mixes the two string types together. Unfortunately, 2to3 is unable to sort all of this out. This is one reason why it's important to have good unit test coverage. Of course, all of this depends on the application.

As an option, 2to3 can be instructed to fix selected incompatibilities. First, a list of "fixers" can be obtained by typing 2to3 -l. For example:

```
% 2to3 -l
Available transformations for the -f/--fix option:
apply
basestring
buffer
callable
...
...
xrange
xreadlines
zip
```

Using names from this list, you can see what a selected fix would actually change by simply typing "2to3 -f *fixname filename*". If you want to apply multiple fixes, just specify each one with a separate -f option. If you actually want to apply the fix to a source file, add the -w option as in 2to3 -f *fixname* -w *filename*. Here is an example:

```
% 2to3 -f xrange -w example.py
--- example.py (original)
+++ example.py (refactored)
@@ -1,7 +1,7 @@
 # example.py
 import ConfigParser

-for i in xrange(10):
+for i in range(10):
     print i, 2*i

 def spam(d):
RefactoringTool: Files that were modified:
RefactoringTool: example.py
```

If you look at example.py after this operation, you will find that xrange() has been changed to range() and that no other changes have been made. A backup of the original example.py file is found in example.py.bak.

A counterpart to the -f option is the -x option. If you use 2to3 -x *fixname filename*, it will run all of the fixers except for the ones you listed with the -x option.

Although it is possible to instruct 2to3 to fix everything and to overwrite all of your files, this is probably something best avoided in practice. Keep in mind that code translation is an inexact science and that 2to3 is not always going to do the "right thing." It is always better to approach code migration in a methodical calculated manner as opposed to crossing your fingers and hoping that it all just magically "works."

2to3 has a couple of additional options that may be useful. The -v option enables a verbose mode that prints additional information that might be useful for debugging. The -p option tells 2to3 that you are already using the print statement as a function in your code and that it shouldn't be converted (enabled by the from __future__ import print_statement statement).

A Practical Porting Strategy

Here is a practical strategy for porting Python 2 code to Python 3. Again, it is better to approach migration in a methodical manner as opposed to doing everything at once.

1. Make sure your code has an adequate unit testing suite and that all tests pass under Python 2.

2. Port your code and testing suite to Python 2.6 and make sure that all tests still pass.

3. Turn on the -3 option to Python 2.6. Address all warning messages and make sure your program runs and passes all tests without any warning messages. If you've done this correctly, chances are that your code will still work with Python 2.5 and maybe even earlier releases. You're really just cleaning out some of the cruft that's accumulated in your program.

4. Make a backup of your code (this goes without saying).

5. Port the unit testing suite to Python 3 and make sure that the testing environment itself is working. The individual unit tests themselves will fail (because you haven't yet ported any code). However, a properly written test suite should be able to deal with test failures without having an internal crash of the test software itself.

6. Convert the program itself to Python 3 using 2to3. Run the unit testing suite on the resulting code and fix all of the issues that arise. There are varying strategies for doing this. If you're feeling lucky, you can always tell 2to3 to just fix everything and see what happens. If you're more cautious, you might start by having 2to3 fix the really obvious things (`print`, `except` statements, `xrange()`, library module names, etc.) and then proceed in a more piecemeal manner with the remaining issues.

By the end of this process, your code should pass all unit tests and operate in the same manner as before.

In theory, it is possible to structure code in a way so that it both runs in Python 2.6 and automatically translates to Python 3 without any user intervention. However, this will require very careful adherence to modern Python coding conventions—at the very least you will absolutely need to make sure there are no warnings in Python 2.6. If the automatic translation process requires very specific use of 2to3 (such as running only a selected set of fixers), you should probably write a shell script that automatically carries out the required operations as opposed to requiring users to run 2to3 on their own.

Simultaneous Python 2 and Python 3 Support

A final question concerning Python 3 migration is whether or not it's possible to have a *single* code base that works unmodified on Python 2 and Python 3. Although this is possible in certain cases, the resulting code runs the risk of becoming a contorted mess. For instance, you will have to avoid all `print` statements and make sure all `except` clauses never take any exception values (extracting them from `sys.exc_info()` instead). Other Python features can't be made to work at all. For example, due to syntax differences, there is no possible way to use metaclasses in a way that would be portable between Python 2 and Python 3.

Thus, if you're maintaining code that must work on Python 2 and 3, your best bet is to make sure your code is as clean as possible and runs under Python 2.6, make sure you have a unit testing suite, and try to develop a set of 2to3 fixes to make automatic translation possible.

One case where it might make sense to have a single code base is with unit testing. A test suite that operates without modification on Python 2.6 and Python 3 could be useful in verifying the correct behavior of the application after being translated by 2to3.

Participate

As an open-source project, Python continues to be developed with the contributions of its users. For Python 3, especially, it is critically important to report bugs, performance problems, and other issues. To report a bug, go to http://bugs.python.org. Don't be shy—your feedback makes Python better for everyone.

Index

A

C

class variables, 117

   sharing by all instances, 118

__class__ attribute

   of instances, 50, 131

   of methods, 49

classes, 21

   __del__() method and garbage collection, 221-222

   __init__() method, 118

   __init__() method and inheritance, 120

   __slots__ attribute, 132

   abstract base class, 136, 257

   access control specifiers, lack of, 127

   accessing in modules, 144

   and metaclasses, 138

   as callable, 50

   as namespaces, 117

   attribute binding rules, 118

   class method, 203

   creation of instances, 22, 55, 118

   customizing attribute access, 57-58

   decorators applied to, 102, 141

   defining methods, 21

   descriptor attributes, 58, 126

   difference from C++ or Java, 119

   inheritance, 21, 119

   inheriting from built-in types, 22

   memory management, 128

   mixin, 122

   multiple inheritance, 120-121

   object base class, 119

   old-style, 139

   operating overloading, 54

   optimization of, 195

   optimization of inheritance, 233

   performance of __slots__, 196

   pickling of, 228

   private members, 26

   redefining attribute binding, 132

   scoping rules within, 118

   self parameter of methods, 119

   special methods, 54

   static methods, 22

   super() function in methods, 120

   supporting pickle module, 228

   type of, 47

   uniform access principle, 125

   versus dicts for storing data, 195

@classmethod decorator, 48, 123, 125, 203

ClassType type, old-style classes, 139

cleandoc() function, inspect module, 222

clear() method

   of Element objects, 576

   of Event objects, 440

   of deque objects, 262

   of dicts, 45

   of sets, 46

clear_flags() method, of Context objects, 247

clear_memo() method, of Pickler objects, 228

_clear_type_cache() function, sys module, 233

clearing a dictionary, 45

clearing last exception, 233

Client class, multiprocessing module, 433

client program, 449

   TCP example, 451

   UDP example, 486

client_address attribute

   of BaseHTTPRequestHandler objects, 509

   of BaseRequestHandler objects, 490

clock() function, time module, 191, 405

cloneNode() method, of DOM Node objects, 571

close() function, os module, 381

close() method

   of Connection objects, 297, 421

   of Cursor objects, 298

   of FTP objects, 498

   of HTMLParser objects, 561

   of HTTPConnection objects, 503

   of Handler objects, 364

J

K

L

M

P

Q

R

T

U

X

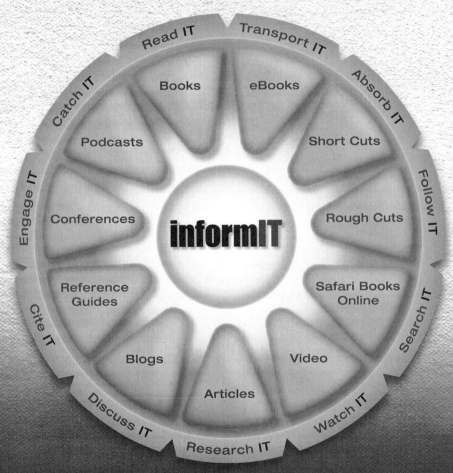